SOUTH-WEST VIRGINIA AND THE VALLEY

HISTORICAL AND BIOGRAPHICAL.

ILLUSTRATED.

A. D. Smith & Co. Staff

HERITAGE BOOKS
2012

HERITAGE BOOKS
AN IMPRINT OF HERITAGE BOOKS, INC.

Books, CDs, and more—Worldwide

For our listing of thousands of titles see our website at
www.HeritageBooks.com

A Facsimile Reprint
Published 2012 by
HERITAGE BOOKS, INC.
Publishing Division
100 Railroad Ave. #104
Westminster, Maryland 21157

Copyright © 1892 A. D. Smith & Co.

Index by Helen Solomon

— Publisher's Notice —
In reprints such as this, it is often not possible to remove blemishes from the original. We feel the contents of this book warrant its reissue despite these blemishes and hope you will agree and read it with pleasure.

International Standard Book Numbers
Paperbound: 978-1-55613-083-0
Clothbound: 978-0-7884-9370-6

PREFACE.

In presenting to the public the first publication of the kind in the State, the publishers feel no small degree of pride. While acknowledging its imperfections, they offer no apology, for experience in compiling, and familiarity with similar works in other States, justify the claim that the product of this their latest effort is the most valuable local historical and biographical work so far brought out.

The essays descriptive of the topography, geology and natural resources of South-west Virginia, and the various historical chapters, are all written by well-known scientists and men of letters, and the facts and figures set forth by them, while in some instances astounding, are correct. Macaulay, the greatest of English historians, has said that the history of a country is best told in a record of the lives of its people, and it is in conformity to this idea that the biographical department of this work has been prepared.

Here will be found, we hope, sketches of none but honorable men, and, while some good and worthy subjects are omitted, the omission is no fault of the publishers. Not having a proper conception of the work, some refused to furnish, upon application, the information necessary to the preparation of sketches, while in a few instances men could not be found, though repeated efforts were made to discover them.

Of one thing, however, we feel satisfied—and the exception, should there be any, will be regretted—and that is, that no unworthy man's life is here held up for imitation.

While the sketches include some men humbler in the walks of life than others, the variety serves more fully to portray to the world the character of a whole people. Here will be found instances of men rising, by individual merit alone, from penury and obscurity to wealth and distinction; of many who, in the pride and strength of young manhood, left the farm and the anvil, the lawyer's office and the counting-room, left every trade and profession, and, at their country's call, went forth valiantly to do or die—men who laid their lives and property upon the altar of their convictions.

Here, also, will be found men whose lives illumine the pages of a nation's history, and whose deeds in war and statesmanship reflect naught but honor upon a noble people—men in whose lives are united the glorious Old South with the unparalleled New.

The work deals with neither politics or religion, and partisan deductions, both from the lives of men and the history of places, have been as much avoided as possible.

Facts only are sought to be presented, and in such form as to enable the readers to shape their own conclusions. And the publishers confidently believe that a perusal of all the pages will give to the thousands of honest seekers after reliable information regarding South-West Virginia and the Valley, and her people, a better insight into the true status of affairs than can be obtained from any other source now accessible.

For much of the historical matter the publishers are under obligations to Mr. Thomas Bruce, author of a valuable work on South-West Virginia and the Shenandoah Valley.

To the gentlemen whose names stand at the heads of the various chapters prepared by them, the publishers return thanks for the faithful and reliable manner in which their work has been performed.

THE PUBLISHERS.

CONTENTS.

CHAPTER I.
PAGE.
EARLY HISTORY AND DEVELOPMENTS 9

CHAPTER II.
THE CITY OF LYNCHBURG: Geographical Position and Environment—Temperature and Healthfulness—Railroad Facilities and Connections—Statistics of Trade and Commerce—Churches and Schools—Water Supply—Land Companies and Street Railways—City Debt, Taxes and Resources............ 21

CHAPTER III.
CITY OF STAUNTON AND AUGUSTA COUNTY: Locations—Limestone Region—Climate—Educational and Religious Advantages—Banking Institutions—The Press—Hotels—Parks—City Government—Taxation—Social Clubs—Railroads—The Bodley Wagon Company........................... 55

CHAPTER IV.
THE CITY OF ROANOKE: Early History—Big Lick—The Shenandoah Railroad—Norfolk and Western Railroad—The Commercial National Bank—The National Exchange Bank—The Citizens Bank—The Traders Loan and Trust Company—The Fidelity Bank—The Roanoke Savings Bank—The State Savings Bank—The Roanoke Loan, Trust and Safe Deposit Company—S. D. Ferguson Bank—Hotels—Manufactures—Real Estate Transactions of 1890—Development Companies—Real Estate—Schools—Churches—Building and Loan Associations—The Press.......................... 93

CHAPTER V.
PAGE.
SALEM, VIRGINIA: Historical Interest—Beginnings—Building Churches—Roanoke College—The War Period—After the War—Recent Growth—Geographical Position—Natural Advantages—A Manufacturing and Commercial Center—The Future of Salem—List of Industries...................... 137

CHAPTER VI.
BUENA VISTA: Population in October, 1889—Population in October, 1891—Colonial Governor, Alexander Spotswood—Iron Ore Resources—Forest and Lumber Material—The Buena Vista Company—Location of the Town—Water-supply—Churches—Schools—Manufactures—Real Estate—Development Companies—Banking Institutions—Railroads 165

CHAPTER VII.
BASIC CITY: A Look at the City—One Way—The City of the Iron Cross—Blue Mountains—Railroad Center—Manufacturers—Conclusive Statements—The Car Works—Match Factory—Cigar Factory—School Furniture Works—Machine Works—Knitting Mill—The Paper Fabrique Company........ 182

CHAPTER VIII.
FRONT ROYAL! Location—Resources—Attractions—Prospects—The Front Royal and Riverton Improvement Company—Railroads—Manufactures—Churches—Schools—Hotels—Press 193

CHAPTER IX.

HALIFAX COUNTY: Population—Location—Climate—Minerals—Railroads—South Boston—Tobacco Business—Stock Company—Manufacturing—South Boston as a Business Center—Halifax Court House—Water-power—Banks 202

CHAPTER X.

BROADWAY: Topographical Features—As it was, and as it is—Advantages of Position—Minerals—Marble, etc—Clay—Timber—Water-power—Broadway Land and Improvement Company 218

CHAPTER XI.

BEDFORD CITY, VIRGINIA: Location—Manufactures—Churches—Schools and Colleges—Banks—Hotels 226

CHAPTER XII.

SHENANDOAH COUNTY: Stock—Manufactures—Minerals—Timber—Churches and Schools—Roads and Railroads—Wood-Stock. 233

CHAPTER XIII.

ROCKBRIDGE COUNTY: The Town of Lexington—Introductory Notes—Locality—Early History—The County Organization—Material Progress—Internal Improvements—Natural Objects of Interest—Topography—Mineral Resources—Ores—Timber—Agricultural Products—Stock Raising—Medicinal Springs—The Civil and Military Record of Her Citizens—Washington and Lee University—The Virginia Military Inftitute—Other Schools—Churches—Local Objects of Interest—Other Towns of the County—Conclusion 244

CHAPTER XIV.

HARRISONBURG: Rockingham, Originally a Part of Augusta County—Population of Harrisonburg—Court-house—Post-office—Manufactures—New Additions to the Town 262

CHAPTER XV.

RADFORD: Location — Railroads — Manufactures—Hotels—Land Companies—Rapid Development 268

CHAPTER XVI.

WYTHEVILLE: Location — Natural Advantages—Mineral Water—Railroads—Hotels—Wythevile as a Resort—Churches—Schools 279

CHAPTER XVII.

WASHINGTON COUNTY AND ABINGDON—Geology—Railroads—The Towns and Villages of Washington County—Abingdon—Bristol—Emory and Henry College—Glade Springs—Saltville—Damascus—Mendota—Meadow View 290

CHAPTER XVIII.

PULASKI: Early History—The First County Courts—Pulaski County—Soil—Climate—Pulaski Land and Improvement Company—Swansea Land Company—Bertha Zinc Works—Pulaski Iron Company—Pulaski Loan and Trust Company—Pulaski National Bank—Lake Springs Land Company—Martin Land Company—Pulaski Development Company—The Gem of the Mountains 302

CHAPTER XIX.

SMYTH COUNTY: Boundaries—Marion, or the Middle Valley—Chilhowee—Athens Tank, Seven-mile Ford, and Groscelosses—St. Clair District, or Valley 313

CONTENTS.

CHAPTER XX.
PAGE.
CHRISTIANSBURG: County Seat of Montgomery County — Location — Churches — Schools — Banks — Hotels ---- 321

CHAPTER XXI.
BLACKSBURG AND THE VIRGINIA AGRICULTURAL AND MECHANICHL COLLEGE ---- 328

CHAPTER XXII.
THE TOWN OF SHENANDOAH: Location — Advantages — Railroads — Manufactures — Development — The Shenandoah Land and Improvement Company ---- 334

CHAPTER XXIII.
LURAY: The Luray Caverns — Population of Luray — Hotels — Churches and Schools — Land Companies ---- 337

CHAPTER XXIV.
CLARKE COUNTY: Berryville, the County Seat — Churches — Schools ---- 342

CHAPTER XXV.
THE NEW RIVER BRANCH OF THE NORFOLK AND WESTERN RAILROAD: The Charter — Capital Stock — Correspondence, etc ---- 345

CHAPTER XXVI.
THE NORFOLK AND WESTERN RAILROAD: The Virginia and Tennessee Railroad Charter — Mineral Resources Along the Line — The Organization — The Cripple Creek Extension — Charter of the Norfolk Terminal Company — The First Shipment of Coal from the Flat Top Region — The Ohio Extension — Passenger Traffic — Freight Traffic — Policy of the Norfolk and Western Railroad Company ---- 362

CHAPTER XXVII.
PAGE.
THE SHENANDOAH VALLEY: Land Grant — Land in Clarke County — The Lands on the South Branch — Early History — The Shenandoah During the War — Mineral Wealth of the Valley ---- 387

CHAPTER XXVIII.
THE SHENANDOAH VALLEY RAILROAD: Relation between the Shenandoah Valley Railroad and the Norfolk and Western — The County Traversed by the Shenandoah Valley Railroad ---- 394

CHAPTER XXIX.
THE COUNTRY EAST OF THE BLUE RIDGE, AND THE EARLY SETTLERS: Governor Spotswood and his Knights of the Golden Horseshoe — Indian War — First Settlers ---- 400

CHAPTER XXX.
THE GREAT VALLEY — SOUTH-WEST VIRGINIA: Geographical Description — Minerals — Mountains — Peaks — Climate — Soil — Cripple-creek-New-river Mineral Region — Iron — The Cost of Producing Iron ---- 417

CHAPTER XXXI.
THE MINERALS OF VIRGINIA: Tide Water — Midland — Piedmont — The Blue Ridge — The Great Valley — Apalachian Virginia — Trans-Apalachian — The Mineral Production of Virginia in 1890 — Limestone — Coal — Buhrstone — Asbestus — Infusorial Earth — Barytes — Ochre — Gypsum — Soapstone — Fibrous Talc — Pyrites — Lead and Zinc — Mica — Granite — Manganese — Precious Stones — Iron Ore ---- 432

CONTENTS.

CHAPTER XXXII.

APALACHIA: The James River—Roanoke River—New River—Notes by Col. R. Harrison—Alleghany County—Alleghany County Minerals at the New Orleans Exposition—Bath County—Bath County Minerals—Bland County—Bland County Minerals—Buchanan County—Craig County—Craig County Minerals—Dickenson County—Giles County—Giles County Minerals—Highland County—Lee County—Lee County Minerals—Russell County—Scott County—Tazewell County—Wise County............ 447

CHAPTER XXXIII.

PIEDMONT VIRGINIA: Albemarle County—Bedford County—Culpeper County—Fauquier County—Franklin County—Greene County—Henry County—Loudoun County—Madison County Minerals—Nelson County—Orange County—Patrick County—Rappahannock County.................. 468

CHAPTER XXXIV.

THE VALLEY COUNTIES SOUTH OF AUGUSTA: Botetort County—Frederick County—Rockingham County—Smyth County—Wythe County................................ 487

SOUTH-WEST VIRGINIA AND THE VALLEY.

CHAPTER I.

EARLY HISTORY AND DEVELOPMENT.

By Prof. C. R. BOYD.

Much has been written from time to time by able historians relative to the early history of the entire State of Virginia — as to the political events, and the wars which have devastated so many fair portions of her domain, once more extensive than any of the original States of "The Union"—but presenting little, however, that shows her real progress of late years.

Virginia is now one of the most important of all the States, not more by reason of the position she occupies on the Atlantic seaboard than by the variety, extent and value of material resources, apparently unmatched by any other area of like extent.

South-western Virginia, bisected by the south-western prolongation of the broad and fertile Shenandoah Valley, if not the most considerable, is one of the chief factors in the elevation of Virginia to a high rank among the superior commonwealths of all sections of the globe.

While many of the facts in the early history of this division of the State may be quite familiar to most of our readers, it may be interesting to recall a few of the salient features of its earlier history.

South-western Virginia and the greater part of the Shenandoah Valley, in the year 1738, was taken out of Orange county and named Augusta.

Botetourt county came next from James river, west; and then, in 1772, Fincastle county was formed of the western portion of Botetourt; and Fincastle county, in 1776, was entirely extinguished by the formation of the three extensive counties of Montgomery, Washington and Kentucky, the last being the present State of Kentucky.

Later than 1776 all Western Virginia still went by the designation of "West Augusta;" and General Washington spoke of the possibility of having to retreat to the mountains of "West Augusta," possibly during the rigors of his encampment at Valley Forge.

During the first revolution South-western Virginia furnished little material for the pen of the historian, except those heroic and successful struggles of pioneers against raids of Indians — as those in Tazewell county, and the severe battle with the Cherokees on Holston river, west of Abingdon, in the latter part of the eighteenth century. To this could well be added the daring and successful exploit of Gen. Wm. Campbell's and Bowen's troops from South-west Virginia, in the battle of Kings Mountain in North Carolina.

Colonel Chiswell, an accomplished British officer, established, about the middle of last century, Fort Chiswell in the present territory of Wythe county. It was by his orders the first work was done in the exploration and discovery of the lead ores at Austinville on New river. So marvelous were the accounts of the richness of these ore deposits and others of the region, as related by Colonel Chiswell to the King's Council at Richmond, that the truth of his statements was questioned by some one present. This so enraged Colonel Chiswell that he drew his sword, attacked and slew his antagonist. In a fit of remorse and chagrin the Colonel then took his own life. All subsequent developments have verified the statements of Colonel Chiswell.

South-western Virginia was then the paradise of the hunter. The last known buffalo in this entire region was killed by a settler who had taken refuge in a block-house near what is now the site of St. Paul on Clinch Valley extension Norfolk and Western Railroad, in Russell county. This occurred on Lick creek, about the year 1795. Capt. John French's company of Giles (then Montgomery) county troops, returning from pursuit of Indians to the Ohio river, killed the last known elk, about the same time, in what is now the county of Logan in West Virginia.

Passing through all the valley counties, from beyond Roanoke county through to Tennessee and Cumberland Gap, is the route of an old buffalo trail, the exact position of which was for many years preserved by the early settlers and their descendants. One of the exact points through which this trail passes is within a few paces south of Wytheville Station on the Norfolk and Western Railroad. This trail is said to have led directly through the extensive salt deposits from which salt is now so largely made at Saltville in Smyth and Washington counties.

During the long period that elapsed between the close of the war of the Revolution and the momentous civil conflict in 1861, there is little to arrest the eye of the reader except interesting biographical matter and those chapters which relate to the conception and final completion of several works of internal improvement. Among these may be mentioned the James River and Kanawha Canal, following James river and thus crossing the great valley of Virginia; the Central Railway (the Chesapeake and Ohio) also crossing the valley, and the Virginia and Tennessee Railroad, now the Norfolk and Western Railroad. The last (the Norfolk and Western), as it now exists, with its double track and several branches, bears but slight resemblance to the Virginia and Tennessee Railroad of 1861. But the labors of those pioneers in railway building, no less than their money, marked out and completed the trunk line of a railway that now traverses a region which is by far the most conspicuous and valuable for the extent and richness of its mineral and agricultural resources, not only in the entire Appalachian system but also on the continent.

Touching this part of the subject, it may be well to remark that, after the war of 1861 the well-directed efforts of such a skillful railway president as General William Mahone, after consolidating a number of lines to Norfolk, could bring the tonnage traffic of this line up to 440,000 tons annually, up to the year 1881. But the combined capital and skill of the Philadelphia syndicate, who, in 1881, purchased this line of railway, and since increased its length of track to quite three times its original length, have raised their tonnage aggregate to nearly, if not quite, five and a half millions of tons.

Since the inauguration of the Norfolk and Western Railroad era, fairly begun in 1862, the history of Southwestern Virginia, in its industrial aspects, owes its significance to the progress of that railway. This progress has been great and unprecedented, and is measured in all the industrial pursuits of life in a ratio proportional with the increase of tonnage handled by the railway, except in the department of agricultural pursuits.

While a powerful faculty of coordination and an incomparable business tact seem to have been displayed by the management of this now splendid railway corporation in directing the successful establishment of mining and manufacturing operations on a large scale, the farming interests in nearly every county complain, with some reason, of a want of fostering care. In fact, it is fair to presume that a desire on the part of the railway officials to secure a large share of western through freight causes them to discriminate in charges against local shippers of the same description of products. Thus, while South-western Virginia, with a variety of soils of remarkable fertility, is capable of becoming one of the largest grain, cattle and sheep producing areas of like size in the world, those industries languish and fall behind, almost exactly in proportion to the difference of treatment evinced by transportation companies as between local producers and shippers from more distant localities. To this condition of things is doubtless due much of the animus of the present agitation by the people against the railway companies. Even those farmers, merchants and manufacturers who sometimes complain of unjust discrimination, have a very just sense of the extraordinary ability displayed by the railway company in building so many permanent monuments to its tact, skill and business enterprise—a progressive spirit, which, united with a rare knowledge of all the resources of the country in detail has completed new railways, mines, manufactories, cities and towns, and has thus increased its own property and that of the public in a far greater ratio than the expense of production.

The Norfolk and Western Railway, at this date, is one of several systems either entering, or seeking to enter, South-west Virginia. The Baltimore and Ohio Railway, now terminating at Lexington, Va., still occasionally threatens to extend its line to the thriving and progressive cities of Salem and Roanoke. The Chesapeake and Ohio Railroad, by its James River line, as well as by its trunk line, crosses "The Valley" twice and has recently built a line from Bessemer to Craig City. The East Tennessee, Virginia and Georgia Railway taps this territory at Bristol. The South Atlantic and Ohio Railroad passes through important agricultural and mineral belts from Bristol to Big Stone Gap. This road gave to Big Stone Gap in Wise county its first impetus as a mining and manufacturing town. The Charleston, Cincinnati and Chicago Railroad has been graded sixty miles across one of the best coal, mineral and agricultural belts in the State. The Louisville and Nashville Railway, excellent in its appointments and connections, with its trunk line and branches reaching all the great marts and rivers of the West and South, enters Virginia at Middlesborough and Cumberland Gap, and the year 1891 signalized its completion to a junction with the Norfolk and Western Railway at the new city of Norton in the county of Wise. Along this line and the Norfolk and Western is pouring in an immense tonnage of western produce on its way to the seaboard at Norfolk for distribution to foreign ports.

This rich territory has invited the incorporation of several other important railways to traverse its marvelous alternations of coal, iron, manganese, lead, zinc, marble and gypsum deposits, interlaced and intertwined with forestal and agricultural lands of the highest value. Notably among these is the Virginia and Kentucky Railroad from Danville to the Kentucky and Ohio systems, traversing the entire Appalachian chain; the Danville and East Tennessee from Danville to Bristol; the Pittsburg Southern from Pittsburg to Glasgow via Lexington, or possibly to Iron Gate, and the possible extension of either the Chesapeake and Ohio or Baltimore and Ohio Railways via

Craig's creek into the coal belt of Clinch river.

The railway from Abingdon, via Damascus, into the North Carolina magnetic iron ore region is nearing completion to Damascus, amidst marvelous resources in iron and manganese ores.

Which way we may ever turn, though, either in looking at the secular history or the material development of South-western Virginia, we come in contact with the Norfolk and Western Railway, now penetrating all her territory. Its influence in directing the destinies of her people is all-powerful! This corporation retains the best talent in all the bars along its lines to represent its interests in the courts, both as permanent and special counsel. From its inception it has invited to the inspection of its marvelous resources the best minds in science and the best skill in practical development. In 1883, when Roanoke was in swaddling clothes, tenderly cared for by its nursing mother the Norfolk and Western Railroad Company, it was visited by the greater part of the membership of the American Institute of Mining Engineers — a body of men to whom is owing, in reality, many of the most important and permanent steps in the development and progress of the entire country. This body, verifying with their own eyes the accounts of the richness and extent of the great coal, iron and other resources of South-western Virginia, gave that impetus to her development which has been so splendidly promoted by the Norfolk and Western Railroad Company.

The accretion of values brought about by this development has almost made up for the losses resulting from the disasters of the war (from 1861 to 1865), and the subsequent unfortunate legislation with reference to the State's indebtedness. This contention among political parties over the adjustment and readjustment of the State debt, carried on so fiercely up to the time of the enactment of the Riddleberger Bill in 1882, affected the interests of South-western Virginia, along with the rest of the State, adversely. But so extensive were the deposits of coal and ores in South-western Virginia; so cheap were the raw materials, and so accessible to fuel of a high grade for their reduction and conversion into merchantable shapes at an exceptionally low cost, that such considerations triumphed over all adverse influences and brought, not only South-western Virginia and the Valley, but all other portions of the State, forward on a tidal wave of progress and development almost without a parallel. So powerful was this impetus, and so beneficent its effects, that even the collapse of entire systems of faulty finance has found South-western Virginia and her institutions of every kind—including her systems of transportation—strong enough to weather successfully the great financial cyclone of the last year, which well-nigh swamped the most stable institutions of the world. And were there now in our midst banking institutions capable of loaning even a small proportion of the present assessed value of property in this region at a low rate of interest, South-western Virginia and the Valley would spring forward with splendid strides in all departments of business in a legitimate field of development and progress, of such proportions that no other age nor country could present a parallel.

As it is now, in this favored region there have sprung into existence since 1882 over forty towns and cities; while many, if not all, the older towns have doubled and, in many instances, trebled their population and industrial enterprises. Roanoke, in 1881, was not in existence; in 1891, this remarkable place has well-nigh 23,000 population; machine-works, turning out locomotives and cars to the value of $2,000,000 annually; furnaces, rolling-mills, steam-generator factories, implement factories, tobacco factories, elegant hotels and institutions of learning. Roanoke is at the junction of the great Ocean line and the great Valley line of railways with the Roanoke Southern Railway, and must continue on a broad highway of rapid progress and improvement.

Salem, seven miles west of Roanoke, has participated so largely in all these advantages that her population and industries have more than trebled in the last two years; the two cities will, ere long, be joined in one great thriving emporium of trade and manufactures. Luray is a great resort on account of its extensive caverns, more marvelous and beautiful, in their natural decoration, than the most cultured artist could paint them. The same may be said of Shendun and the famous Weyer's Cave near by. Milnes is a place where excellent furnaces exist. Cremora, in Augusta County, is the famous location of the largest manganese mines in the United States. Basic City is at the junction of the Shenandoah Valley branch of the Norfolk and Western with the Chesapeake and Ohio Railways and will doubtless become one of the important points in "The Valley" for the manufacture of steel. Staunton, twelve miles west of Basic City, on the Chesapeake and Ohio Railroad, at the junction of the Baltimore and Ohio Railroad with the Chesapeake and Ohio Railroad, holds two of the largest eleemosynary institutions of the State, besides manufactories, elegant female schools and industries of value. Her population will soon reach ten thousand; the increase there in all lines of business being constant, while it is at the same time conservative and permanent.

Lexington—the location of Washington and Lee University and the Virginia Military Institute — the home and the monumental city of the illustrious Southern soldiers Lee and Jackson—pursues a policy of conservatism and rests, with her five thousand population, as the present western termination of the Valley division of the Baltimore and Ohio Railroad and the North River branch of the Chesapeake and Ohio Railroad.

Buena Vista is an entirely new city, in Rockbridge, close to the famous tin ore deposits and the long lines of outcrop of iron and manganese ores in the west flank of the Blue Ridge. Her furnaces, woolen factories, plants and hotels are among the most excellent in Virginia. Natural Bridge has now more than its usual number of attractive features, being a very popular summer resort. Glasgow, at the junction of James and North rivers and the junction of the Shenandoah Valley and Richmond and Alleghany Railways; Buchanan, some miles higher up James river, practically on the two last-named railways, which here form a junction as they come from the south-west and north-west, are assuming importance on account of steel and brass works, foundries and machine-shops.

Fincastle, holding the court-house of Botetourt county, has just formed a junction with the South Virginia branch of the Norfolk and Western Railway at Cloverdale by a short line of railway. This is a beautiful town in the great valley of Virginia, and is at present in a wordy contest with the town of Buchanan with reference to the removal of the court-house to that city.

Bessemer is a new town at Eagle Rock, on James river and on the Richmond and Alleghany branch of the Chesapeake and Ohio Railroad. From this place extends westwardly, through the north section of Botetourt county and the eastern half of Craig county, the new Craig Valley Railroad (branch of the Chesapeake and Ohio Railroad.) This road terminates, for the present, at Craig City (Newcastle), amid a wealth of resources in iron and manganese ores, slate and timber, not exceeded in extent by any other portion of the State. Craig City has a rare situation in the heart of the Alleghanies, with elegant new hotels, deriving their water-supply from pure sources in high mountains, at many hundreds of feet in elevation.

Radford, in Montgomery county, is a creation of the Norfolk and Western Railroad. It lies on New river, at the junction of the New River and Pocahontas branch of the Norfolk and Western Railroad with the trunk line. Radford is rapidly springing forward as a manufacturing centre, being centrally situated as to ores and coal, and having an unlimited water-supply. Radford already has large furnaces, foundries, stove and implement factories, with a population of about five thousand.

Blacksburg, in Montgomery, in a charming valley, is the locus of the Virginia Agricultural and Mechanical College.

Pulaski City, at the junction of the trunk line of the Norfolk and Western with its Cripple creek and North Carolina extension, was among the first new towns to construct iron furnaces and zinc works. Sitting at the mouth, whence flows the immense tonnage of iron ores of the Cripple creek—New river basin—the zinc ores of Wythe county and the gossan iron ores of Carroll, Pulaski City has an assured prosperity of a high order, having now a population of quite 3,000.

Max Meadows, in Wythe county, in a basin of mineral and agricultural wealth, has established within the year a fine furnace, and is also completing a rolling-mill for the manufacture of horse-shoes. These two industries, since the place has equal access to all the ores of Cripple creek, New river and Carroll, and the coke of Pocahontas, render its growth assured.

Wytheville is a beautiful mountain resort, and possesses many other advantages. (See Wytheville chapter).

Ivanhoe, in Wythe county, is on New river, at the junction of the Cripple creek and North Carolina extension of the Norfolk and Western Railroad, at a point where New river breaks through Iron Mountain, the open gateway through which the magnetic ores, gossans, sulphur and copper ores of Carroll, Grayson and North Carolina will seek to meet the iron and manganese ores and the zinc and lead ores of Cripple creek—New river basin. Ivanhoe is two miles west of Austinville (the famous lead and zinc mines and works of the region being located at that point). In reality, Ivanhoe will be one of the greatest of all the new cities of this region, already having valuable furnaces and other factories.

Augsburg and Rural Retreat, near the highest point (2,600 feet alt.) on the trunk line of the Norfolk and Western Railroad, are both places of interest, on account of their proximity to coal and iron as well as their elevation.

Marion, in Smyth county, is the location of the South-western Lunatic Asylum.

Glade Spring, in Washington county, is at the junction of the Saltville branch with the trunk line of the Norfolk and Western Railroad. Besides being the point where the salt and gypsum of Saltville and Robertson's Buena Vista find an outlet, it is also a place of popular summer resort, and has prominent educational institutions.

From Glade Spring it is nine miles by the Saltville branch of the Norfolk and Western Railroad, northwardly, to Robertson's Buena Vista gypsum deposits, and Saltville, where salt has been made on a large scale since the beginning of the second quarter of the century. All this is in the midst of bewitching scenery defying description.

A few miles west of Glade Spring, in Washington, is the old and popular institution of learning, Emory and Henry College. The alumni have filled high places in social, ecclesiastical and political life, some of the finest orators in the Union being among its graduates.

Abingdon, named for the ancient town of that name in England, is a widely noted seat of learning and culture. There are several advanced colleges and seminaries for young ladies and youths. Abingdon contains manufactures of different kinds, and now has a population of 3,000. Among the noted enterprises of her progressive citizens is the railway, now approaching completion, sixteen miles southward to Damascus.

Damascus is the gateway to a great part of the iron and manganese deposits of that region on the Laurel river fork of Holston river, where that stream breaks through the last of a series of great mountain ranges holding vast deposits of the ores mentioned.

Bristol, the city of two States, on the line between Virginia and Tennessee, is at the junction of the Norfolk and Western Railroad, the East Tennessee, Virginia and Georgia, the South Atlantic and Ohio, the Bristol, Elizabethtown and North Carolina, and the Danville and East Tennessee Railways. Bristol now has a new iron furnace of one hundred and twenty-five tons daily capacity, besides cotton, woolen and other factories, and commodious hotels of modern architecture. Its position must soon force Bristol rapidly forward to a very high position among places of commercial importance, now having a population of ten thousand.

The thriving places, Bluefield and Graham, are at the junction of the Clinch Valley and New River and Pocahontas and Ohio divisions of the Norfolk and Western Railroad, one in West Virginia, the other in Virginia. In a short time they will form another city of two States. Bluefield holds the machine-shops of those divisions of the Norfolk and Western Railroad, besides factories. Graham has an excellent new furnace of fine capacity, deriving its ores from that region and its fuel from Pocahontas only a few miles distant.

Pocahontas, of 4,000 inhabitants, is the new mining town now so justly famous for the coke it sends to nearly all manufacturing localities east of the Mississippi river, and its immense tonnage in steam and domestic coals, largely employed on ocean steamers, sending, with other mining places in the flat-top region, over three millions of tons of coal annually over the long lines of the Norfolk and Western Railroad.

Tazewell Court House, on the Clinch Valley Extension, is an old place, now revived under the inspiration of the new line of railway. Its population has largely increased in two or three years, and its enterprises of various kinds have more than trebled. Cedar Bluff and Mouth of Indian, on same branch of railway, in Tazewell county, are places of resort on account of excellent mineral waters, and are important on account of water-powers afforded by Clinch river.

Richlands is a new place, now assuming large proportions on account of its being at the junction of coal mining railways of Big creek with the Clinch Valley Extension, besides holding a fine new rolling-mill and other industries. Richlands is in the beautiful valley of Clinch river, not far from the interesting Paint Lick Mountain, the place where one of the more advanced Indian tribes painted a long message, in well-made characters, on the face of a precipice, in red, which can doubtless be deciphered.

Doran is the next place of promise, three miles below Richlands. These two places being at the junction of coal mine railways with Clinch Valley Extension will continue to grow and finally become one city.

Sword's Creek and Honaker are new towns on the Clinch Valley Railroad, at the mouths of creeks that flow out of the great bituminous coal field. Their growth is constant. The vicinity of both will be utilized for great coal and coke-shipping stations at some day.

Cleveland, also in Russell county, is the central station on the Clinch Valley Railroad, of the county, and is marked by constant but conservative growth.

St. Paul and Minneapolis, twin cities at the junction of the Charleston, Cincinnati and Chicago Railroad with the Clinch Valley Extension, are respectively on the north and south sides of Clinch river in the lower end of Russell county. These are among the promising new towns of the Norfolk and Western system, with the unlimited coal deposits of Lick creek on the north, and massive deposits of iron ores on the south, and a never-failing water-supply flowing between the cities.

Virginia City is a mining town on Russell creek, on the Clinch Valley Extension, in Wise county, Virginia. It is now engaged in shipping coal and coke. It has an unlimited coal field north of it, and the character of the coal is good for all purposes.

Coeburn and Tom's Creek, near Guest's Station, both on Clinch Valley Extension, will all be one large city at a future day. The great coal fields of Wise and Dickenson counties are very accessible by Tom's Creek. The growth of these two places, though so recently established, must be constant.

Tacoma is also a new town on this railway, five miles east of Norton, on Guest's river. It is right on the edge of the great coal field.

Norton, at the junction of the Norfolk and Western's Clinch Valley branch with the Louisville and

Nashville, will doubtless contain the machine-shops of both railways. This city is also at one of the favorable points for an intersection with the Kentucky union line of railway. The great coal seams of Wise county outcrop within the corporate limits of the place, and must soon make the city one of the largest coaling stations on either railway.

Big Stone Gap, near the western end of Wise county, is at the junction of the Louisville and Nashville and South Atlantic and Ohio Railways, on the beautiful Powell's river. Its position at the junction of the Wise county coal field with the great fossil and brown iron ore belt is one the importance of which cannot be overestimated, taken in connection with railway transportation to all points already established. Big Stone Gap now has two large modern furnaces and other manufacturing establishments, a fine hotel and all modern facilities.

Pennington is the station on the Louisville and Nashville where the coal and timber of that vicinity reach the railway, and then on that line there are two or more important new towns in Lee county before you reach Cumberland Gap, the famous place of junction of the three States of Virginia, Tennessee and Kentucky.

It is at this place that the genius of Alexander Aladdin Arthur and his associates have created two cities in the last three years, now numbering ten thousand inhabitants, four iron furnaces, a steel plant, manufacturing establishments without number, a splendid sanitarium and pleasure resort, and splendid hotels. On the Virginia and Tennessee side is Harrowgate, the most elegant resort probably in America; bounded on the north, and separated from it by the great iron ore belt, is Cumberland Gap. Just west of Cumberland Gap is Middlesborough, in the Eastern Kentucky coal field, the widely-famed creation of masterly genius. These places are all practically one, and lie at the junction of the Louisville and Nashville and the Knoxville, Cumberland Gap and Louisville Railways. There is one thing very remarkable about this locality: it is almost exactly in the geographical centre of all the territory of the United States east of the Mississippi river, and the centre of population of the same area approaches the point year by year with rapid strides.

All these cities lately mentioned are on the southern margin of the great interior coal basin of America, of which South-western Virginia holds a large area. Of those places more in the interior, but having close access to important fragments of this great coal belt, Dungannon, on Clinch river, in Scott county, will assume much importance. This place is on Clinch river at the junction of a vast net-work of interior roads with the Charleston, Cincinnati and Chicago Railroad. It is in a belt of country holding large deposits of bituminous coal on its northern margin and unlimited deposits of iron ores beginning just south of the coal belt.

Gate City is a growing place in the extensive marble belt just north of Clinch Mountain, in Scott county, at the junction of the South Atlantic and Ohio and the Charleston, Cincinnati and Chicago Railways.

The southern, or, more properly, the iron, lead, zinc and copper belt of South-west Virginia, presents such new cities and towns as Ivanhoe, Austinville, Foster Falls, Patterson, Outburst and Allisonia, all the creations of the Norfolk and Western Railway.

Further to the south-east, on the eastern margin of this rich territory, are the cities of Lynchburg and Danville, at the intersection of the above-mentioned railway lines with the Richmond and West Point Terminal system. They would require separate chapters to describe their recent unparalleled progress in population and industries.

All the immense progress of Southwestern Virginia and the Valley owes much, if not the greater part, of its progress, outside of the influence exerted by the Norfolk and Western Railroad Company, to an able press, alert and progressive to the utmost degree.

In the fall of the year just passed, 1890, this whole region was visited by an excursion of the British Iron and Steel Institute, at the invitation of the American Institute of Mining Engineers.

Throughout their inspection of the coal and iron fields of South-western Virginia and the Valley from Middlesborough and Cumberland Gap to the great interior, of which Roanoke is the gateway, their endorsement of the extraordinary value and beauty of the entire region was complete. It must be of most extraordinary character, since the Norfolk and Western system, within eight years, has enhanced its property from a value but little over ten millions of dollars to the splendid figures, for all its franchises actually existing, of over nine hundred millions of dollars in the year 1891.

And the concerted movements of well-directed volumes of capital will, in the next ten years, treble this estimate.

CHAPTER II.

THE CITY OF LYNCHBURG.

HISTORICAL.

By C. W. BUTTON.

It were difficult, if not impossible, to invest any of our modern cities with the glamour, the romantic interest that attaches to those venerable with age, whose history and traditions are connected with a remote antiquity. It is not long since the hemisphere in which we dwell was known as "the New World;" and therefore our cities, institutions, laws, manners, all are alike new in comparison with those of Europe, Asia, or even Africa. Nevertheless, we have a history, modern though it be; a history that is impressing itself upon and being studied more and more by the older nations of the earth.

Virginia, though the oldest State in the American Union, has not within her borders any city boasting the antiquity that can be justly ascribed to those that date from a period soon after the Spanish conquest in America, and are still found in a good state of preservation near our Southern frontier, and on both sides of the Gulf of Mexico. In fact, the cavaliers who chiefly settled Virginia did not aim to build cities. So late as the period that immediately preceded her revolt against the government of the mother country, Williamsburg, the seat of government, and the largest and most populous town in the colony, did not contain two thousand souls. Rural life and field sports were the chief joy of her white population in colonial times. Without commerce or manufactures, small need had they of those great centres of trade that constitute the cities of our day.

Alluding to that period in the history of the Old Dominion, Bancroft says: "The eighteenth century was the age of commercial ambition; and Virginia relinquished its commerce to foreign factors. It was the age when nations rushed into debt, when stock-jobbers and bankers competed with land-holders for political power; and Virginia paid its taxes in tobacco, and alone of all the colonies, alone of all the civilized States, resisting the universal tendency of the age, had no debts, no banks, no bills of credit, no paper money." From this it will appear that Virginia had none of the accessories that are essential to the upbuilding of great cities; and her people, loving the independence of patriarchal life, with an alien and inferior race to cultivate their fields, were content to exchange the products of their soil for such articles as they needed from abroad, leaving to "foreign factors" the profits that were to be derived from the carrying trade, and the very limited system of exchanges that then obtained. Such is the picture of Virginia as it was in colonial times.

But the scene has changed since then. The Revolution, with the achievement of independence, and more especially the moulding of the scattered colonies, under the Constitution, into a nation invested with power to levy taxes, coin money, regulate commerce, declare war, and "promote the general welfare" in every way that a supreme government can, revolutionized our colonial habits of restricted exchanges, and gave the first great impulse to the creation of marts of trade, enlarged commerce with foreign nations, and the consequent building of cities on our coast lines to serve as entrepots of commerce both foreign and domestic. Thence followed, as means to an end, the establishment of banks, the use of bills of credit, and the issuing of paper money to facilitate the handling of our increased commerce.

An additional incentive to the upbuilding of cities—centres of capital and trade—has been found in the immense construction of railroads through the interior, that now stretch their briarian arms in every direction to serve as great feeders to the cities of the land, and to distribute therefrom throughout the country the products that are gathered there from all other lands.

A glance at the Virginia of to-day will present a striking contrast with that period in her history described by Bancroft. Not only have seaport cities felt the impulse that has been manifested in their larger growth and greater increment of capital, and those located near interior water-lines experienced, though in smaller degree, the stimulating influence of enlarged commerce, but those great common carriers of the country, railroads, have made it possible to locate interior cities where the natural elements of wealth exist in such profusion as to justify it, and many of these are now developing into great manufacturing centres and distributing points from which the sections supplied with their wares receive them without paying the cost of transporting the crude material out of which they are fabricated to points less favored as manufacturing sites.

We have seen what Virginia was in colonial times: and even after the establishment of the Federal Union it remained, more than anything else, and more than any of the original States, a commonwealth devoted chiefly to agriculture. Notwithstanding her vast and varied resources, her mines of latent wealth of every conceivable kind, comparatively few of these were ever opened and worked, while her blast-furnaces, rolling-foundries, and even agricultural implement manufactories were "few and far between." Nor was it until after the civil war had devastated their fields, denuded many of their forests, and utterly broken up their labor system, that the people of Virginia began to turn their attention seriously to diversified industries, and especially to the importance of an enlarged system of manufactures that would increase the population, wealth, prosperity and importance of the State.

The opening of railroads into new territory was stimulated by the discovery, or previously existing knowledge, of the great natural wealth imbedded in the mountains and valleys of the interior, and these in turn resulted in the location of new towns along the lines thus constructed, which are expected in many cases to be the sites for large and varied manufactures. The older cities, too, feel the influence of this new order of things, and their growth has been stimulated and will continue to be augmented by the increased volume of trade that must naturally come to them from the opening of new avenues to market, and the establishment of way-stations that serve the purpose of collecting agencies, so to speak, along the new highways of trade and travel just opened.

The city of Lynchburg would seem to be the gateway to the magnificent south-western portion of Virginia, and the natural outlet for a large portion of the trade coming from that section and the regions beyond. But respecting the advantages of her geographical position, more and material facts will be submitted in other connections.

It has often been asked why Lynchburg, "The Hill City," so called, was located where it is? To this question the response of Topsy, in "*Uncle Tom's Cabin*," might be appropriate: it "growed so." Doubtless the topographical features of its environment account for the establishment of a ferry at this point by John Lynch, since it was more accessible by the gorge between the Amherst hills just opposite than by any other point within easy reach above or below the town, and the ferry made it not only a thoroughfare for the people of a large portion of the contiguous counties—including Thomas Jefferson's regular migrations between his homes at Monticello, in Albemarle, and Poplar Forest, in Bedford—but developed it into a trading point of considerable importance, which afterwards grew into a city despite its topography. And such has been the history of many other cities in this country that were never expected to expand to such proportions.

Mr. Thomas D. Davis, in his interesting sketch of Lynchburg appended to the Code, published in 1887, says: "There is a tradition that an Indian trail once crossed James river at or near the point chosen for the ferry. For this there is some corroboration in the fact, authenticated by a witness yet living, that there was an Indian settlement and trading station just below Lynchburg, on the flat land between Horse Ford and Winston's Hill, even as late as the beginning of the present century. Indians were reported to be good topographical engineers, but their skill was in a great measure borrowed, and in locating their principal highways they simply followed in the track of the buffalo. The latter in their periodical migrations to the South would naturally, when once east of the Blue Ridge, have sought a passage of James river in the vicinity of Lynch's Ferry, the most southerly point in its course until it reaches Richmond and some miles beyond. In fact, the buffalo's trail can almost be marked out by local geographical names which are still retained in the country tributary to Lynchburg, such as Buffalo Gap, Buffalo River, Buffalo Ridge, &c. It is not improbable, therefore, that the buffalo was one of the factors in the evolution of the busy, bustling city of John Lynch."

Although hilly and irregular in outline, Lynchburg is for that reason exceedingly picturesque and beautiful. It is built up from the shore line of the James, sloping in some portions abruptly from the river, while all of the principal streets running parallel therewith are regular and have excellent grades. For drainage and healthfulness it is unsurpassed. But the city is being extended now beyond the apex of its highest hills to the table-lands and more gently undulating plains that have hitherto constituted its remoter suburbs. The town proper was located in 1786, when the Legislature vested in certain trustees forty-five acres of the lands owned by John Lynch "lying contiguous to Lynch's Ferry in the county of Campbell," and named Lynchburg in honor of the owner of the soil. This John Lynch was the son of an Irish immigrant, though himself "native to the manor born." He drew his first breath near the town he founded, and lies buried in the cemetery near which was located the old Quaker Church, now in ruins, within three or four miles of the city limits. He was a devout member of the Society of Friends; a man of large benevolence, "given to hospitality," and very kindly remembered the poor that were about him. A large holder of slaves until the Society of Friends took action against the institution as being wrong in principle, he then determined to liberate all that he possessed. Mr. Lynch died in 1820, on the lot adjacent to our present court-house, at the advanced age of four-score years.

The town of Lynchburg was first incorporated by act of the General Assembly, passed January 10th, 1805, and in the charter granted by the Legislature May 2d, 1852, the corporate name was changed from "the town of Lynchburg" to the "city of Lynchburg." Thence on until the breaking out of the late civil war its growth was steady and substantial, insomuch that in the decade that immediately preceded that terrible scourge the census returns reported it to be the wealthiest city in the United States, of equal population, save one—New Bedford, Massachusetts. It is not a little remarkable that these two cities achieved wealth and great prosperity in the pursuit mainly of a single industry. Lynchburg's prosperity was based upon her tobacco trade, and that of New Bedford derived from her whaling business. Yet both of these cities have, in late years, been educated up to the idea that general and diversified industries are more in consonance with their true interests and tend to larger growth and more vigorous development.

Lynchburg has always been noted for the industry of its people, the solidity of its enterprises and the stable character of its financial institutions. In those periodical convulsions that have from time to time swept over our country, carrying wreck and ruin to the banking, commercial and manufacturing interests in other industrial centres, it has stood unscathed, an abiding witness of the wise, conservative counsels by which her bankers and leading business men have been guided and controlled. While it is true that much of the previously gathered wealth of the city disappeared with "the Lost Cause"—with which it was so prominently identified — its subsequent rapid recuperation was something wonderful. The emancipation of the very large number of slaves held here, that represented a considerable portion of the inherited and acquired wealth of the white population; the enforced liquidation of every banking institution in the city, occasioned largely by the total loss in value of the paper money of the Confederate government, and the serious depreciation of the issues of the State banks; the upheaval of the old labor system, that for some time afterward arrested production in the fields and deprived our manufacturers of the chief staple, the manipulation of which had brought wealth to this great tobacco mart: these, together with the general impoverishment of the people, as the result of the great war that had been waged on the soil of Virginia for four years, had necessarily a very depressing effect upon the fortunes of Lynchburg, that depended so largely for its prosperity upon a single product of agriculture. But the clouds were lifted at last, and while some of the older citizens, beggared in fortune, were too far advanced in the journey of life to retrieve their individual losses, the younger and more vigorous were stimulated with renewed energy to make the glory of the latter days exceed in material development those of the former. And they are succeeding.

Perhaps the most notable event in the history of Lynchburg was the advance of a Federal army, commanded by General David Hunter, upon the city in June, 1864. When General Grant assumed command of the Federal forces in Virginia he early saw the importance to his adversary, General Lee, of unobstructed communication via Lynchburg with the upper Valley, the South-west and the region immediately south of this city, which made the latter a pivotal point to the Confederates.

Being located upon an interior line of communication with the States to the south and south-west, it served also the purpose of a depot of supplies for the forces set for the defence of Richmond. In this view, it was very important to the invaders to possess and occupy Lynchburg, which, as a base of operations for troops acting in concert with the great force confronting General Lee before Richmond, could have easily cut off his only remaining line of communication with the South—the Richmond and Danville Railroad— left his army without adequate supplies, and thus compelled him to abandon the defence of Richmond.

In General Grant's "general report" of the operations of his army from March, 1864, to May, 1865, he expressed the purpose that he had kept steadily in view: "to hold substantially the ground he then occupied, taking advantage of any favorable circumstances that might present themselves, until the cavalry could be sent to Charlottesville and Gordonsville to effectually break up the railroad connection between Richmond and the Shenandoah Valley and Lynchburg."

In a letter to General Halleck, dated May 25th, 1864, copied from the general report above cited, Grant refers to an expedition that had started under Gen. David Hunter, in the words following: "If Hunter can possibly get to Charlottesville and Lynchburg he should do so, living on the country. The railroads and canal should be destroyed beyond possibility of repairs for weeks. Completing this, he could find his way back to his original base, or from about Gordonsville join this army."

In the general report, Grant refers thus briefly to the issue of that ill-fated expedition of Hunter: "General Hunter immediately took up the offensive, and moving up the Shenandoah Valley met the enemy on the 5th of June at Piedmont, and after a battle of ten hours routed and defeated him, capturing on the field of battle 1,500 men, three pieces of artillery and 300 stand of small arms. On the 8th of the same month he formed a junction with Crook and Averill at Staunton, from which place he moved direct on Lynchburg via Lexington, which place he reached and invested on the 16th day of June. Up to this time he was very successful, and but for the difficulty of taking with him sufficient ordnance stores over so long a march through a hostile country, he would no doubt have captured that (to the enemy) important point. The destruction of the enemy's supplies and manufactories was very great."

With that rare sagacity that characterized General Lee's military operations—whereby he seemed to divine the purposes of his great adversary, and often anticipated the points of attack chosen by General Grant in that famous campaign—he, on the 13th of June, detached General Early with 8,000 infantry and twenty-four pieces of artillery from the Army of Northern Virginia, with instructions to proceed toward Staunton to look after Hunter. Early moved towards Charlottesville, which had been Hunter's objective point, but from which he was deflected by the presence of Breckenridge, who was posted, with 2,500 men, at Rockfish Gap, via Staunton, Lexington, Buchanan, the Peaks of Otter and Liberty.

Upon reaching Charlottesville, to which point his weary troops had marched, Early received intelligence of Hunter's movements in the direction of Lynchburg, and so soon as transportation could be secured moved with a portion of his infantry to meet Hunter, leaving the residue, with all of his artillery, to follow as rapidly as their facilities for transportation would permit. Nor did he reach Lynchburg an hour too soon, for Hunter was even then in the immediate vicinity, and the sound of his artillery was heard in the city only four miles distant, as he pressed back the small cavalry forces of Imboden and McCausland, which could only delay his advance while fighting for time and reinforcements to save the imperiled city. At that time the Confederates had only a small force in the city that Breckenridge brought by a forced march from Rockfish Gap, while its commander was confined to his bed from an injury suffered by the fall of a horse shot under him at Cold Harbor; so that if Hunter, instead of stopping on the way to pillage and burn private property, had pressed forward and reached Lynchburg one day sooner, it would inevitably have fallen into his hands. This opinion was expressed to the writer years afterward by one of his general officers, who had then reached a very high civil position in the government.

General Early, with about half of his infantry, reached Lynchburg on the afternoon of the 17th and proceeded immediately to the outer fortifications distant between one and two miles from the city, leaving the inner line of hastily thrown up earthworks to be manned by the local militia and convalescent soldiers from the hospitals. Early, in his "*Memoir of the Last Year of the War*," says: "My troops, as they arrived, had been ordered in front of the works to bivouac, and I immediately sent orders for them to move out on this road (the Salem turnpike), and two brigades of Ramseur's division arrived just in time to be thrown across the road at a redoubt about two miles from the city, as Imboden's command was driven back by vastly superior numbers. These brigades, with two pieces of artillery in the redoubt, arrested the progress of the enemy, and Ramseur's other brigade, and the part of Gordon's division which had arrived, took position on the same line. The enemy opened a heavy fire of artillery on us, but, as night soon came on, we went into camp on our front."

The next day, the 18th, opened with artillery firing and some heavy skirmishing along the lines, which extended not less than two miles across a hilly and broken country, for the most part unsuited to cavalry warfare between large bodies of such troops. But there was a considerable demonstration of the Federal cavalry in the afternoon, on what is known as the Forest road, from which much was evidently expected. The headquarters of General Hunter were at the house of an old comrade, Maj. George C. Hutten, who had resigned his commission at the beginning of the war, and from him this writer learned, the day after the fight, what disappointment resulted from the failure of this cavalry attack to break the lines of the Confederates.

On top of the highest chimney of his house was posted a signal officer, who observed and reported the progress of that charge. The first information was that "the cavalry were charging splendidly," but not long afterwards the "look-out" reported that they "were giving way"—and that before the opposing forces of Breckenridge's infantry and McCausland's cavalry. Owing to the fact that scarcely more than half of his troops had reached the scene of action, and he was confronted by double the number of his available force, Early acted mainly on the defensive; but his resistance was so spirited and the disposition of his forces so well made that the enemy utterly failed to make any impression upon them, and were beaten back at every point with heavy loss, considering the numbers engaged. General Averill was reported to have said to a member of the family of Major Hutten on the evening of the last day of the fight, that "the battle at Lynchburg would be one of the bloodiest records of the war for the numbers engaged, and the loss had been from 800 to 1,000." But that on the side of the Confederates was surprisingly small, being, as reported at the time, about six killed and ninety-five wounded.

The proportion of killed to wounded on the Confederate side was much below the average. In riding over the field the morning after Hunter retired, the writer counted between forty and fifty of the dead soldiers of the Union that had been left unburied, the most of them in a strip of woods in front of the redoubt before mentioned. From the character of their wounds it was evident that nearly all of these were killed by sharpshooters, who occupied shallow rifle-pits in front of the redoubt. On the left of the Salem turnpike, and near the Quaker church, were five newly made graves, with rude headboards on which were written the names of those laid beneath. These were killed the first day. In the spacious barn of Major Hutten were left 117 severely wounded men, in addition to three that were left among private families on the retreat, and the least seriously wounded that were carried away.

There can be no doubt that Hunter's loss was heavy—perhaps little short of Averill's estimate. Whatever Hunter's force was (though General Early, in his "*Memoir of the Last Year of the War*," says: "From the best information I have received, I am satisfied that Hunter's force exceeded 30,000 men," and Hunter told Hutten that he had 50,000), the Federal commander confidently expected to capture Lynchburg. At the supper-table Friday evening were gathered Hunter, Crook, Averill and Sullivan, and they were in a hilarious mood over the achievements of the first day, saying that "they would dine in Lynchburg the next." But on the evening of the second day the same party, assembled around the same board, evinced by their almost unbroken silence a totally different state of feeling. They had not dined in Lynchburg that day, and were even then, while holding their host a close prisoner in his own house, very quietly preparing for flight.

And thus ended the only military investment of Lynchburg during the great civil war. Had it been captured by Hunter, Richmond would have been evacuated nearly a year sooner than it was.

GEOGRAPHICAL POSITION AND ENVIRONMENT.

Lynchburg is, in respect of population, the fourth city in Virginia; in trade and traffic, as well as capital, the third; and, as an inland city, justly ranks first. It is located nearly in the center of the far-famed piedmont section of the State, concerning which Col. Randolph Harrison, late Commissioner of Agriculture, in his "*Hand Book of Virginia*" published in 1886, says: "For beauty of landscape, variety of scenery, native fertility of soil, water-courses contributing to practical benefit as well as to beauty of scenery, this section is surpassed by few, if any, other sections in the United States." And Dr. Ellzey, of Washington, D. C., formerly Professor of Agriculture in the Agricultural and Mechanical College of Virginia, in an address delivered before the Southern Association, says: "In its physical features, picturesque and lovely to an unusual degree; in climate, temperate and healthful; in the abundance and variety of its productions, unsurpassed; in all that makes life desirable and home what it should be, there is no place in this world which surpasses piedmont Virginia—there are very few which come near it."

Situated upon the south bank of the James river nearly 700 feet above tide-water level, and within twenty miles of the Blue Ridge mountains proper, it occupies a part of what is known as the "subrange," whose ridges and plateaus have a variety of local names, yet all "spurs" and parts of that mighty range of mountains. An intelligent foreigner, the late Edward Pollock, said: "The surroundings of Lynchburg are peculiarly romantic and beautiful. To the south and east, far as the eye can reach, the landscape may be described as irregularly undulating, varied here and there by gently sloping hills and fertile vales and relieved by an occasional remnant of primeval forest. On the north-east the view is bounded by the bluffs, or "Heights" of the neighboring county of Amherst, past whose feet the broad and rapid James, spanned at and near this point by several dams and bridges, hastens with its message of greeting from the mountains to the sea. To the northward, the Blue Ridge mountains rise in gentle grandeur and in varying height, visible in clear weather for seventy-five miles along the range, and culminating at their south-western extremity in the far-famed Peaks of Otter, towering skyward in their matchless stateliness and symmetry."

Lynchburg may be considered the gateway to that magnificent section —South-west Virginia—that is now attracting such well-deserved attention among the capitalists of the Northern States, who are acquiring large pecuniary interests therein. On the most direct line of travel from Boston, New York, Philadelphia, Baltimore and Washington southward, the traveler at this point finds two great lines of railway to the further South, one of which (the Norfolk and Western) will carry him through the heart of South-west Virginia. Likewise, those coming from the North by the various lines of steamers that ply between Norfolk and their respective ports, would reach the South-west via Lynchburg. It is, indeed, the gateway through which they must enter.

Another interesting feature of its environment will be found in the numerous health and pleasure resorts that are all within easy reach of Lynchburg, the larger number by rail. Among these may be mentioned the Bedford Alum, the Blue Ridge, Coyner's, Yellow Sulphur, Rockbridge Alum, White Sulphur, Salt Sulphur, Red Sulphur, Alleghany, Daggers, Buffalo Ridge, The Sweet, The Hot, The Warm, The Healing Springs, The Greenbriar White Sulphur and The Mountain Lake. From Norfolk, the chief seaport in the State and the best on the Atlantic coast, it is distant only 204 miles by rail, from which locality Hygeia Hotel and other popular watering-places by the seaside, can be reached within an hour or less. Also, among the curiosities of nature that are regarded with great interest by tourists, may be noted the Peaks of Otter (within sight, though twenty-five miles away), the Natural Bridge, about the same distance in a different direction, Weyer's Cave and the Luray Caverns, more remote, yet easily accessible from Lynchburg. It would be difficult to find any locality more favored in its surroundings and connections than is the "Hill City."

TEMPERATURE AND HEALTHFULNESS.

The mean temperature of piedmont Virginia, as given by the late Commissioner Randolph, in his *Hand-Book*, is 53.7; winter, 44; summer, 78, and the rain-fall 32 to 44 inches. During the summer months, near the eastern base of the Blue Ridge, it is believed that showers are more frequent than in any other portions of the State. The reasons for this absence of long-continued drought in this favored section are thus given in the language of another: "The prevailing winds of summer come direct from the sea, and its moisture, when driven against the mountain barrier, meets with a colder stratum of air and becomes condensed, thus producing the welcome showers which refresh and invigorate the growing crops, while in less favored sections the ground remains parched and dry." It is very certain that the proximity of the mountains that encircle Lynchburg shield it in a great degree from the furious blasts of winter that work so much destruction in many other sections of our land; while the ozone from those same altitudes that is wafted to her in the gentle and health-laden breezes of summer rarify and temper the air that her people breathe, and exempt them from the stifling or even oppressive heat that is sometimes suffered in the same latitude.

At Lynchburg, the record for 1890, obtained from the United States Signal Office, reveals the following: Mean temperature for the year, 57; highest, 97; lowest, 19; spring, 55.7; summer, 75.7; autumn, 57.7; winter, 38.9. It is very seldom, and at short periods together, that the mercury rises as high as 97 or falls as low as 19°. Equally removed from the extremes of heat and cold in a locality where outdoor work can be done all the year round, the inhabitants of this temperate zone, may realize in experience what Montesquieu says of such a climate: "It is the most powerful of all empires, and gives guaranty alone of future development."

Her natural drainage, the result of her topography and a swiftly flowing river passing by her front; the pure mountain air that her people inhale by day and night; the absence of any local cause for malarial diseases, with the equable climate already described, have jointly contributed to the reputation that Lynchburg enjoys for rare healthfulness. None of those fatal diseases, such as cholera and yellow fever, that are epidemical and often sweep off their thousands of victims from large centres of population, have ever found lodgment here; and a noted physician is quoted as saying that "there never will be a case of cholera within fifty miles of the Peaks of Otter."

The death-rate among the white population for the year 1890, as determined by the Board of Health, was 12.12 in every 1,000. Very few cities in the United States can show as low a bill of mortality in proportion to population. Indeed, the returns of the United States Census Bureau for several decades past do not, with three or four exceptions, give a lower bill of mortality for any city, while in some the death-rate is from two to two and a half times greater than in Lynchburg.

RAILROAD FACILITIES AND CONNECTIONS.

Lynchburg is the greatest railroad centre in Virginia. Three vast lines intersect here, whose united management control 5,502 miles of continuous service, having connections that radiate in every direction from the North Atlantic to the Pacific coast, and reach every prominent point included within this vast area. Two of these lines nearly bisect the State, while the third gives the shortest connection between this common centre and the cities of the Great West. Another that, in its inception, may be regarded as a Lynchburg enterprise, is completed now to Durham, N. C., a distance of 114 miles, and will soon have a direct connection with the port of Wilmington and other seaport cities on the South Atlantic coast. This should be added to the 5,502 miles of trunk-line railway mentioned above as centering here. There is good reason to believe that ere long the West Virginia and Pittsburg Railroad will close up the intervening gaps by tapping the Chesapeake and Ohio at Covington, and thus unite Lynchburg and the great iron city of Western Pennsylvania by the shortest and most direct line practicable.

An examination of any general railroad map will show that Lynchburg is on the great air-line from Boston, New York, Philadelphia, Baltimore and Washington to New Orleans; from Norfolk to Memphis, on the Mississippi; from Norfolk to the Ohio, at Huntington; and from the capital of our country to Charleston and other seaport cities of the South. Taking Norfolk as the base, and the Southern Pacific Railroad as the true—the shortest and best—line, it is on the great highway of nations between Europe and Asia, connecting the Atlantic at Norfolk, and the Pacific at San Diego, and marking that famed line within the 32d parallel—free from the heavy snows that obstruct trade and travel in the higher latitude of the Union and the Northern Pacific Railroads—as the most desirable route between the Eastern and Western nations.

From all this it must appear that, as a receiving and distributing point, Lynchburg possesses exceptional advantages, and should be the centre of large manufacturing industries, and the seat of a great commerce with all sections of the country.

Distant from tide-water, at Richmond, by air-line, ninety-five miles, Lynchburg has no less than four connections with the capital city (a point where sea-going vessels are reached), the shortest being one hundred and twenty miles.

This chapter would not be complete without a statement of the tonnage received during the year 1890 by the railroads tributary to Lynchburg, together with the amount of shipments (all given in pounds) forwarded from here by the same means. The figures were obtained by the Board of Trade from the books of the respective companies, which represent the receipts as amounting to 1,841,174,414 pounds, and the shipments from the city to 820,994,860 pounds. The revenue collected by the railroads at this point on account of freight during the period named was $1,705,930.13. This trade is increasing yearly, as new sections are penetrated by additional lines of railway and avenues to market are thus opened. To indicate its importance as a railroad centre and mart of business, it may be mentioned that forty-eight passenger trains leave Lynchburg every twenty-four hours.

STATISTICS OF TRADE AND COMMERCE.

Before the advent of railroads, Lynchburg, though much smaller than it is now, had a very large wagon trade. But this trade has dwindled greatly, and no record is kept of the commodities brought here by wagons, except at the hay scales, and these only include sheaf-oats, loose hay and fodder brought in from the neighboring farms. Of the former, there was weighed at the public scales during the year 1890, 1,037,585 pounds; of the second, 642,655 pounds, and of corn fodder, 31,380 pounds.

The sales of tobacco at the warehouses in 1890 were 14,445,500 pounds, to which should be added the amount bought in other markets, 5,292,718 pounds, making a total of 19,738,218 pounds, of which there was exported 9,323,600 pounds. Receipts at the Internal Revenue Office show that 4,056,981 pounds of tobacco were manufactured here, 723,413 pounds of which were converted into snuff; the annual tax collected on the manfactures for the year 1890 being $324,458.48.

There were in the city during the year, nine manufactories of plug-tobacco, five of smoking, seven of cigars, two of cigarettes and one of snuff. Including the manufactories of tobacco, there are fifty-odd distinct manufactories located at Lynchburg or in the vicinity, among which may be mentioned a cotton mill, drug and paint mill, iron mills, two shoe manufacturing companies, pulp and paper manufacturing company, spoke works, planing mills, three flour mills, three fertilizer mills, furniture factory, zinc works, plant setter manufacturing company, ice and refrigerating company, machinery works, four wagon works, two agricultural implements, buggies, chewing gum, bark extract, tobacao extract, box factory, sumac factory, candy works, bone fertilizer factory, barytes mills, mattress factory, gas-works, electric light works, etc.

It is not many years since the wholesale trade of the city was inaugurated, and it is now assuming very large proportions. The volume of business during 1890 was $8,954,181, not including leaf tobacco, which amounted to $3,048,406; so that the whole trade might properly be estimated at $12,002,587. It is stated that the purchases of shoes in Boston from the manufacturers, for jobbing purposes at Lynchburg, are greater than those made by any other city in the United States of equal population. *The Shoe and Leather Reporter* of January 8th, 1891, giving the shipments from Boston for the preceding year, shows that Richmond, with its population of 81,338, and *seven* jobbers in this line of goods, purchased 52,283 cases, while Lynchburg, with a population not one-third as large, and only two wholesale houses in this line, purchased in the same city 31,627 cases. No other city in Virginia, and only one other in the South (Atlanta, Ga.), whose purchases amounted to 47,498 cases, shows up as well as Lynchburg in respect to the number of cases purchased, and Atlanta has five houses in this line and is credited with a population of 65,533. This remarkable showing for Lynchburg is not only a compliment to the business energy and enterprise of its wholesale merchants, but indicates to a large extent the character of the country that is tributary to this gate-city for the South-west. The retail business of Lynchburg for 1890, as nearly as could be ascertained by the Board of Trade, is given at $2,000,000.

CHURCHES AND SCHOOLS.

There can be no more conclusive evidence of culture and high civilization than is afforded by the community that builds churches and school-houses—institutions of religion and learning—for the spiritual and moral well-being of their people. Of the former, Lynchburg, with a population in city and suburbs not exceeding 25,000, has twenty-six churches and chapels, being more than one to over 1,000 of population. And some of these are stately temples that would reflect honor upon any community. Nearly all of the best known denominations are thus represented.

There are six large public school-houses owned by the city, and other buildings rented to meet the demand of the school-going population. And these schools, including one for higher education, are among the best of their kind in the country. The number of pupils enrolled in 1890 was, of whites, 1,667; of colored, 1,673; making a total of 3,350. Of the teachers employed there were, white males, 4; white females, 34; and of colored males, 8; females, 16. The amount appropriated for the support of these schools in 1890 was, by the State, $8,774.55, and by the city, $21,656; making an aggregate of $30,430.55 for public schools only. In addition, the Roman Catholic church has a parochial school conducted by Sisters of Charity. The Miller Orphan Asylum for girls, with about eighty-five inmates, employs its teachers in the asylum building; and other private schools, including a boarding-school for young ladies,

are kept up. Plans have lately been matured, the site secured and a large fund raised for the establishment of a great Female College or University, under the auspices of one of the most influential male colleges in Virginia, in a beautiful suburb of Lynchburg. This institution, which is expected to furnish a university education to females, will be open during the year 1892, it is hoped.

WATER-SUPPLY.

The James river, that flows by Lynchburg, affords ample water-power for a number of industrial establishments that now utilize it to propel machinery, and its capacity in this respect could be increased by raising the dam and elevating slightly the banks of the canal. It is also the chief resource of the city for the supply of water required for domestic purposes. The various mineral regions drained by the James for many miles above the city make its water not only palatable but healthful, so that it is regarded as being an excellent beverage. Three large reservoirs for the storage of water for domestic purposes have been erected by the city at a cost of $175,000. They are built of solid masonry and are very sightly and substantial. The upper structure on College Hill is 333 feet above the bank of the river, while the other two on Clay street are at an elevation of 265 feet. The capacity of the three reservoirs is 8,000,000 gallons; the pumping capacity of the four pumps per day 3,000,000 gallons, and the consumption of water 2,000,000 gallons daily. The cost of the pumps was $50,000; of the water-mains $100,000, and of the foundation and houses for the pumping station $25,000. The pressure of water on Main street, where the tallest and most costly buildings are located, is sufficient to force water over the highest four-story houses for the extinguishment of fires. Add to this abundant water-supply the fact that Lynchburg has a most efficient fire department, with fire-alarm stations at convenient intervals all over the city, and it will appear that neither pains nor expense have been spared to provide an ample supply of water for the comfort of the people and the protection of their property against the devouring element of fire.

LAND COMPANIES AND STREET RAILWAYS.

Earnest and well concerted efforts are being made at this time to extend the corporate limits of the city, which, from the original designation of its boundary lines, have been extended seven different times. The Rivermont Company, holding 2,500 acres, has recently erected a magnificent iron bridge from the head of Main street across the deep chasm through which flows Blackwater creek, and connected the beautiful plateau on the other side, known as Daniel's Hill, thus giving more convenient access to and from the old part of the city. Near the western end of this new bridge they propose to erect a large and elegant hotel with the latest improvements in hostelry. This will supply a great want of the city for the better accommodation of the traveling public.

The West Lynchburg Company, owning 955 acres, has been instrumental in locating several large industries, and will have completed, before this announcement reaches the eyes of the public, a spacious hotel on a site that commands a vast and varied landscape of rare loveliness, including the famous Peaks of Otter, towering in solemn grandeur above all surrounding objects. This hotel, having several mineral springs within a hundred yards of it, will prove to be a favorite resort for summer visitors, being connected with the city by electric railway.

The East Lynchburg Land Company owns 321 acres, the South Lynchburg sixty-three acres, and the Park Avenue fifty-seven acres. All of these companies are laboring to develop Lynchburg and make it a centre of great manufactures. The various electric street railway lines in operation, or course of construction, reaching out from the city to the new suburbs embraced in the territory controlled by these land companies respectively, will aggregate fourteen and one-fourth miles. New, spacious, elegant cars, equal in all respects to those used in the larger cities of the

Very Truly Yours
Jno. W. Daniel —

country, are now propelled by electricity through the old city to West Lynchburg, and so soon as the tracks are completed will be in operation through the Rivermont addition.

CITY DEBT, TAXES AND RESOURCES.

The total bonded debt of the city February 1st, 1891, was $1,617,482.43, with a sinking fund of $323,675.11, leaving a net balance of $1,294,167.32 as the bonded debt. No city in the Union is in better credit, or can more readily float its securities.

The real estate within the city limits subject to taxation, as determined by the levy of 1891, aggregates the sum of $8,110,723; the personal property, $2,500,000. Churches and eleemosynary institutions are exempt from taxation; likewise, all new industries located within the city enjoy immunity from taxation for the term of ten years, the object being to encourage the location of manufactories of every kind. And indications encourage the hope that Lynchburg is destined to be one of the greatest manufacturing centres in the South.

HON. JOHN W. DANIEL, United States Senator from Virginia. The father of the distinguished Commodore Stephen Decatur, who was one of the best seamen and most brilliant officers that our Navy ever boasted, was the author of the sentiment, "Our children; they are the property of our country." And so the record of those who have achieved distinction in its service are the heritage and should be the pride of all their countrymen.

The eminent Senator, whose striking features are so well depicted in this volume, having served his people in the field and in the forum, though still in his prime, is one of the most noted men of a Commonwealth that has been singularly prolific of great names crowned with illustrious deeds. As an orator he is justly regarded as being among the first in a State that produced the most remarkable orator of our Revolutionary era, and has since furnished a brilliant array of men highly gifted with the power of speech. Born in Lynchburg September 5th, 1842, of a family, on the paternal side, distinguished for legal lore, his thoughts were naturally turned to the law as his profession, but before he had finished even his literary studies the tocsin of war was sounded, and Virginia called her sons to battle in defence of her soil and for the vindication of those principles of State autonomy for which she had ever contended in the conflict of parties. And young Daniel, before he had completed his nineteenth year, laid aside his text-books and repaired to the field, volunteering as a private in the Wise troop of cavalry organized after the John Brown raid in Lynchburg. He was commissioned by Governor Letcher, May 1st, Second Lieutenant in the Provisional Army of Virginia, and ordered to report to Gen. Jos. E. Johnston at Harper's Ferry, and by him assigned to the command of Colonel Jackson, who was destined to win unfading laurels in the field, and whose pure fame will be perpetuated through the ages to come as the unsurpassed soldier of his day, forever enshrined in the hearts of the people of the South under the *sobriquet* (indicating the heroic firmness of his character), bestowed upon him in the first great battle of the civil war, of "Stonewall" Jackson.

Having acquired some knowledge of tactics at the semi-military college at Lynchburg, Lieutenant Daniel was intrusted with the duty of drilling some of the companies (then raw recruits) of what subsequently constituted the famous "Stonewall Brigade." His first "baptism of fire" was with General Johnston in the affair at Falling Waters, and with his commander made the forced march to Manassas, where Beauregard was waging an unequal contest with the serried hosts of McDowell. In that famous action the young Lieutenant bore himself bravely. He was in the charge made by the Stonewall Brigade upon Sherman's battery. Seeing the standard bearer of the 27th Virginia Infantry (the regiment to which he belonged) shot down, he seized the colors and carried them "full high advanced" to the front. In this engagement he was thrice wounded—by the fragment of a shell in the head, a pistol-ball in the arm, and a minnie ball in the thigh. His services on that day are thus characterized by his superior officer: "Lieutenant Daniel has permission to return home, that he may recover from wounds received in the battle of the 21st of July. His gallant conduct on that day richly entitles him to this furlough."

During his enforced absence from the field his commission in the Provisional Army expired, and Lieutenant Daniel was tendered a commission as First Lieutenant of Artillery in the Army of the Confederate States, coupled with the condition that he should serve in charge of an arsenal in the rear of the army. This offer, which was doubtless tendered with reference to his physical condition, Lieutenant Daniel declined, saying that he "entered the army to fight." Subsequently he was elected Second Lieutenant in Company A, 11th Virginia Infantry, composed of his fellow-townsmen. With them he served in the fight at Dranesville, the siege of Yorktown, and in the battles of Williamsburg and Seven Pines, in which last engagement his horse was killed under him. Immediately after that fight Daniel was promoted to the grade of First Lieutenant and Adjutant of the 11th Virginia Regiment. In this capacity Lieutenant Daniel rendered service in the battles around Richmond, at the second Manassas, and in the fight near Boonsborough, Md., Sept. 14th, 1862. In that engagement he was wounded in the left hand, the bones of which were badly broken, and amputation narrowly averted. When sufficiently recovered he rejoined his regiment and served the succeeding winter at Fredericksburg, and in the next spring was transferred with it to Kingston, N. C. From this point he was strongly recommended by his military associates for promotion, and soon afterwards was made Assistant Adjutant General, with the rank of Major, serving on the staff of Maj. Gen. J. A. Early. In this capacity Major Daniel participated in the battles around Fredericksburg fought in May, 1863, while Jackson was making that wonderful flank movement on "Fighting Joe Hooker's" army at Chancellorsville. In the battle at Winchester, June 20th; in the three days' fight at Gettysburg; in the stand at Rappahannock bridge, Nov. 27th, and in the fight at Mine Run, which occurred soon after, he rendered conspicuous service.

During the spring of 1864, Major Daniel was the recipient of a distinguished mark of approval bestowed by his comrades, a pair of solid silver spurs bearing the following inscription: "Hays' Louisiana Brigade to Maj. J. W. Daniel, February 22d, 1864." He had fairly "won his spurs" in gallant and noble service rendered to his country, and in accepting this tribute of admiration from his fellow-soldiers promised "to part with the token only at the cost of his life." The time came full soon when he who stood continuously "on the perilous edge of battle" and generally in the forefront of danger, was in imminent peril of losing life and spurs together. It was on the 6th day of May, in the fiercely waged battle of the Wilderness, where men shot down and lying for hours between the contending hosts were exposed to the fire of friends and foes alike, as well as to the devouring flames that had been kindled in the woods by the belching fires from heavy artillery. Being the only mounted officer in that vicinity, Major Daniel was rallying a regiment of Pegram's brigade to the charge, when he reeled and fell from his horse, struck by a minnie ball that shattered his leg above the knee. In the ebb and flow of that surging tide of battle he lay for some time within the enemy's lines. But not unmindful of the pledge given to his comrades, he transferred the silver spurs to the breast-pocket of his coat, and with his own hands removed his sash and firmly bound the artery through which his life's blood was ebbing out. This presence of mind doubtless prevented him from being recorded as "Dead on the field of battle!" During the night the Confederates regained the ground they had lost and removed the Major to a field hospital. He had preserved his spurs, and lost nothing but the contents of his haversack, which the enemy looted while he lay on the field in what they regarded as a dying condition.

This last wound was a fearful one,

sufficient to end his active military career. The bone was found so badly shattered above the knee that the surgeons determined to saw off about four inches of it and attempt resection. Later on, a second operation and resection were found necessary to remove decayed bone. For six months he was unable to move himself in bed. The young soldier had fought his last battle, being badly maimed for life. And while he lingered upon a bed of torture the cause for which he struggled so heroically was waning to its end. Higher promotion was sought for him by influential general officers, and his old commander, General Early, longed to have him again in service if his physical condition would permit. But that was not to be.

Like many another soldier of "the Lost Cause," the war being over and the banner of the Southern Cross being furled forever, Major Daniel renewed his allegiance to "the gorgeous ensign of the Republic" and turned his attention wholly to civil pursuits. Taking the law course at the University of Virginia for one year, he closed his connection with that institution as the chosen orator of the Jefferson Society. Very soon thereafter he entered upon the practice of his profession. In 1869 he published his first legal work, entitled "*Daniel on Attachments*," a Virginia treatise, which was warmly endorsed by the professors of the University of Virginia, the Court of Appeals, Judge Sharswood of the Supreme Court of Pennsylvania, and Theophilus Parsons of Massachusetts. His second work was a full treatise on "*The Law of Negotiable Instruments*," which is highly regarded by the profession and has been endorsed by such eminent lawyers as Charles O'Conner, A. G. Thurman, Chief Justice Waite, William M. Evarts, Chancellor Cooper and others.

Major Daniel's first political service was rendered in the House of Delegates of Virginia, to which he was elected in 1869. He was thence, by a vote of the people, transferred to the Senate of Virginia. In 1881 he was nominated as the Democratic candidate for the office of Governor, with the "Readjuster" candidate, William E. Cameron, as his opponent. The question at issue in that contest was not so much one of party politics as of domestic concern, upon which thousands of people voted regardless of party ties and political antecedents. As a consequence, a majority of the voters, including Republicans and Democrats, supported the Democratic "Readjuster," at the same time securing both branches of the Legislature; while the man who stood for the honor and credit of Virginia, believing that the old State could not afford to even squint at the repudiation of any portion of her debt, was overborne. That was a case in which defeat was everyway more honorable than victory.

Serving subsequently as an Elector of President and Vice-President, Major

Daniel was, in 1884, elected Representative from the Sixth District of Virginia to Congress, and before his term expired was chosen by the Legislature of his State successor to Gen. William Mahone in the United States Senate. He had been defeated for the office of Governor by the combination that sent Mahone to the Senate, and retributive justice, apart from his distinguished merit, marked Major Daniel as the man who should succeed the author and promoter of the unsavory alliance, who afterwards carried himself, with all his political wares, into the camp of the enemy. There is every reason to believe that Major Daniel will be his own successor in the great forum whereof he has become one of the most distinguished members.

Very few men of this age have so frequently been called before the public on great occasions to signalize and commemorate by the fervor of eloquence and grace of oratory, characters and events that deserve to be remembered by a grateful posterity. Among these may be mentioned an oration at Kings Mountain, North Carolina, commemorative of the Patriot victory of the Revolution won there; that on the character of Robert E. Lee, delivered on the completion of the recumbent statue of the great soldier, at Lexington; the Washington oration before the two Houses of Congress and other functionaries of the government, celebrating the completion of the Washington Monument at the national metropolis; that delivered before the Legislature of Virginia in memory of Jefferson Davis, and the address before the Virginia Division of the Army of Northern Virginia on "The Campaigns and Battles of Gettysburg." These were all great historic addresses, worthy to be preserved in our text-books as specimens of a fine literary style, while embodying important facts in the history of our country.

Major Daniel is a diligent student of history as well as law, and capable of immense labor. His taste and inclination dispose him to present his thoughts in well-chosen words, believing that whatever is worth saying deserves to be said well, and that the garnishment of rhetoric in nowise detracts from the force of language any more than the adornment of the lichen and the moss impair the solidity of the rock about which they entwine themselves. Gifted with a rich, flexible voice of great compass, and always well modulated and under perfect control in speaking before the public, it is not remarkable that words fall like nectar from his lips. In manner he is graceful and courtly, always deporting himself as becomes the well-bred gentleman; gracious and affable to the humble and lowly, dignified and manly among his peers, and never cringing and supple to such as may happen to be his superiors in rank or fortune.

Such is the man that, for gifts, graces and many other excellencies of character, stands first among the Virginians of the present generation.

DR. WILLIAM H. DULANEY, one of the leading citizens of Lynchburg, Virginia, and a recognized power in the finances of the city, was born in Baltimore, receiving his early education there, and later attended the University of Maryland in which he graduated in the medical department in 1859, and at once began the practice of his profession in Kent county, remaining there until the breaking out of the war, when he enlisted in the Confederate service and was assigned to Lynchburg as acting Assistant Surgeon, where he remained a short time when he was commissioned Assistant Surgeon with General Longstreet in East Tennessee, and was soon advanced to the post of Surgeon of Kershaw's division and served with them through the battle of Cold Harbor and the Wilderness, and together with them and General Gibbs served until the close of the war, when he came to Lynchburg and resumed the practice of his profession. In 1869 he was elected as member of the City Council and has since held this office a number of times. He has also acted in the capacity of President of the Board of Health and Board of Overseers of the Poor. In 1883 he organized the Piedmont Building and Land Fund Association, of which he is now President, and in 1890 assisted in the organization of the Rivermont Development Company, of which he is a member of the Board of Directors, and also on May 1st organized the Rivermont Investment and Construction Company, of which he is President.

He was married in 1864 to Miss Ellen A. Turner, a daughter of George W. Turner, Esq., of this city.

J. E. EDMUNDS, Esq., the eldest son of Paul C. Edmunds, was born in Halifax county, Virginia, in July, 1860. His father, after honorable service in the Virginia Senate for eight years, was elected to the United States Congress from the Sixth District of Virginia, where he is now serving his second term. His mother was Mrs. Phœbe Easley Edmunds, daughter of James A. Easley, Esq., a wealthy and prominent business man of Halifax county.

Mr. Edmunds graduated at the Virginia Military Institute in the class of 1880, and, after teaching at Locust Dale Academy, studied law at the University of Virginia, receiving there the degree of B. L. After completing his studies he located in Lynchburg, Va., where he has ever since been successfully practicing his profession.

Besides being a good lawyer, Mr. Edmunds is a fine business man; is

director in two of the banks of the city, and has the confidence and esteem of all with whom he comes in contact.

HENRY E. McWANE, Esq., the subject of this mention, is a citizen of Lynchburg, and is well known throughout the State of Virginia; is a native of the Old Dominion, his birthplace being at Wytheville, Virginia, and was born January 16th, 1859. The grandfather of Henry E. assisted Silas McCormick to construct the first grain reaper known to the world. Henry spent his early life at Wytheville, attending school in the winter and assisting his father, who was a foundryman, during the vacations, and after he left school he began serving an apprenticeship as an iron moulder in his father's foundry, and at the end of four years assumed the business management of the works and was soon made a partner in the business, and continued as such until 1887, when he came to Lynchburg, and in company with a number of others purchased the Glamorgan Works, taking charge as superintendent of the same, and also taking the general management of it. At the time of the purchase the works were in a demoralized condition, only twenty men being employed in them, but under the new regime they have been greatly enlarged and improved and a force of two hundred and fifty men is now employed. In 1889 Mr. McWane was made President of the company, and remains as such at the present time, discharging the duties of his office to the satisfaction of stockholders and directors. Besides his duties as President of the Glamorgan Works, he is connected with a number of other business enterprises in and about Lynchburg. He was married in 1882 to Miss Blanche Roberts, of Lynchburg, and four children have been born to them, three of whom are living. The family are members of the Christian Church, and active workers in the same.

MAX GUGGENHEIMER, Esq., one of the few men who have been largely interested and instrumental in the building up of Lynchburg, and who is at the present time President of the Lynchburg Cotton Mills, was born in Bavaria, Germany, in 1842. In 1856, when but 14 years old, he came to America, principally to visit relatives living at that time in Lynchburg, but after staying some time he decided to remain, and to complete his education entered the schools of the city, keeping books for a brother in the evenings. He enlisted upon the breaking out of the war, but on account of disability he was honorably discharged in 1862. In 1863, his brother dying, he assumed control of his business and later opened up a wholesale house in shoes and hats, and in 1876, in company with others, began an exclusive wholesale trade in shoes, but eventually directed his entire attention to dry goods and notions, and in the year 1881 erected the building which he now occupies. In 1885 he closed out the largest retail business in the State and then devoted himself exclusively to the wholesale trade. Aside from this, he is a director in the Lynchburg National Bank, and aided in the erection of the Opera-house. In 1879 he was elected a member of the City Council, and largely through him the city was redeemed from its deplorable condition, having been involved in debt almost beyond redemption. He is interested in a large number of enterprises, and it is characteristic that his undertakings are as successful as they are large. He is a prominent member of the Masonic fraternity and his influence is felt there as well as elsewhere for good. Mr. Guggenheimer was married in 1877 to Miss Rosenbaum of Richmond, and one daughter has been born to them. Much of their time is spent in Europe, visiting its prominent places and the homes of their ancestors.

EDMUND SCHAEFER, President of several Lynchburg joint-stock companies, was born in Bremen, Germany, in 1851, where he spent his early life, entering when still young the tobacco trade there, and emigrated to the United States in 1871. He was first located at Baltimore in the employment of a large tobacco firm there, whose interests in Virginia he represented for several years with headquarters at Lynchburg. There he formed a partnership in 1877 with Mr. John Holt, under the firm name of Holt, Schaefer & Co., which firm is still in existence. Mr. Schaefer has since become connected with many other Lynchburg enterprises, notably the Lone Jack Cigarette Company, the Virginia Nail and Iron Works Company, the Lynchburg Ice and Refrigerator Company, and the Washington Zinc Company, in all of which he occupied the place of President. With the management of others he is connected as a director; besides, he is largely interested in valuable coal, iron and timber properties in South-west Virginia.

Mr. Schaefer's first wife was Miss Mary Walker, of Richmond, Va., who died early in 1882. He was since married again to Miss Eugenia C. Martin of Baltimore, Md., and has three sons now living. He and his wife are prominent members of St. Paul's Episcopal Church, and has been for some time one of its vestrymen.

The many duties imposed upon Mr. Schaefer by his various and extensive business interests keep him a thoroughly busy man, and especially does he take an interest in everything tending to enhance the welfare and prosperity of his city.

R. G. H. KEAN, residence, Lynchburg. Mr. Kean was born in Caroline county, Virginia, October, 1828. His early education was at local schools and subsequently at Coleman's (Concord) Academy and the University of Virginia, where he took the degree of M. A. in 1851 and B. L. in 1853.

He settled in Lynchburg and commenced practice as a lawyer in 1853, and with the exception of the four years of the war has followed his profession ever since in that place.

He has never sought public or political office of any kind, nor filled any, save that he has been twice appointed a Visitor of the University of Virginia, serving as Rector of the Board of Visitors from 1872 to 1876.

In April, 1861, he was mustered into the military service as a private in the Lynchburg Home Guard (Company G, 11th Virginia Regiment), and served as an enlisted man in that company until February, 1862, when he was commissioned Captain A. A. G. and assigned to duty with Gen. George W. Randolph. On the appointment of General Randolph as Secretary of War, 1st April, 1862, Mr. Kean was appointed Chief of the Bureau of War, in which capacity he served until the downfall of the Confederacy, resuming the practice of his profession at Lynchburg in 1865.

Mr. Kean has been twice married, first (1854) to Jane N., daughter of Col. T. J. Randolph, at Edgehill, Albemarle county, Virginia; second (1874), to A. N. Prescott of Louisiana, having four children by each marriage. Of his older children one son, L. M. Kean, is a lawyer practicing in Sioux City, Iowa, and another, Dr. Jefferson R. Kean, is Captain Assistant Surgeon in the United States Army.

WILLIAM N. MITCHELL, Esq., at present General Superintendent of the Lynchburg and Durham Railroad, is a native of Virginia, being born in Richmond. He comes of sturdy New England stock, his father being a native of Massachusetts and his mother of New Hampshire. He received his earlier education in Richmond, but eventually graduated from the Military Academy of Connecticut as a civil engineer, but for some years after graduating did not engage in the practice of his profession. In 1880 he connected himself with the Richmond and Alleghany Railroad in the engineering department, remaining with them for one year, when he entered the employ of the Norfolk and Western Railroad and assisted in the construction of the New River division under Major Graham, and on the completion of this work was given charge of the topographic department of the Cripple Creek division. In the early part of 1883 he left the employ of this company, and was engaged for some time with the Kansas City and Gulf Railroad with the general freight office in Kansas City, but left their employ for the Red Line Company as Soliciting Agent. In 1884 he returned to Richmond and served for different companies in positions of importance until in 1888, when he assisted in laying a part of the track of the Lynchburg and Durham Railroad, and on its completion was made Superintendent of Transportation, and in December, 1890, was appointed to the position of General Superintendent, which position he now occupies. Mr. Mitchell was married in 1887 to Miss Mary W. Otey, a daughter of Major Otey, a prominent citizen of Lynchburg.

Surveys, Plans, Specifications and Estimate of Cost for Steam and Street Railways and Structures in Iron and Stone. Topographic Surveys Made and Town Sites Laid Out. Water-works Designed and Built. Expert Examinations and Reports a Specialty.

R. TAYLOR GLEAVES,
Consulting Engineer and Contractor,
811 Main Street,
Lynchburg, Va.

OTEY, WALKER & BOWYER.—The firm of Otey, Walker & Bowyer of Lynchburg, Virginia, is composed of Major Otey, J. Stewart Walker and R. P. Bowyer and is one of the best known firms in the State. Major Otey is a senior member, and is a son of John M. Otey, a man well known in the city by reason of his twenty years of service in the Council and long connection with the old bank of Virginia and as being the father of thirteen children, seven sons of whom served in the Confederate army. Peter John, the youngest, and the subject of this mention, was born in 1840 and received his early education from the resources at command, and later, in 1860, graduated from the Virginia Military Institute, and in 1861 entered the army and served until its close. After the surrender he was employed for a time by the Lynchburg and Danville Railroad Company, but later entered the insurance business, and in 1887 was made cashier of the Lynchburg National Bank. Major Otey was also prevailed upon to accept the Presidency of the Lynchburg and Durham Railroad and now holds that position. Besides this office he holds the position of President of the South Lynchburg Land Company and Vice President of the Rivermont Company. J. Stewart Walker, another member of the firm, first entered business for himself with Adams, Chambers & Co., with whom he remained three years, when he accepted a position with Mr. G. W. Smith, with whom he served for two years, but subsequently accepted a position with the "Lone Jack" Tobacco Company, which he held until his connection in May, 1890, with the present firm. R. P. Bowyer, a third member of the firm, began his career with the Greek Slave Cigarette Company, and served in the capacity of buyer and manager for several leaf tobacco dealers until his connection with Major Otey in May, 1890. Besides the capital invested in their own primary business, these gentlemen are interested as stockholders in all the land companies of the city and have other interests in various places in Southwest Virginia, and have a large amount invested in coal and mineral lands.

F. D. JOHNSON, Esq., one of Lynchburg's most prominent business men, was born at Barboursville, Orange county, Virginia, in 1834, where he spent his early life. When at the age of 15 he was apprenticed to learn the jeweler's trade, which he completely mastered, and as early as 1855 began business for himself in Culpeper. On the outbreak of the war he enlisted in Chew's battery, and served with distinction until the surrender, when he returned to Culpeper and resumed business, where he remained until 1881, when he came to Lynchburg in order that he might from this point carry on a wholesale trade, his previous business being almost exclusively retail. After his removal to this place his business increased to such an extent that he took for a partner his second son, Thomas A. Johnson, who remained for some time in the firm, but eventually removed to Roanoke, Virginia, where he is at present General Secretary of the Roanoke Young Men's Christian Association.

Mr. Johnson was happily united in marriage in 1858, and is the father of four sons, two of whom are at present in the establishment of their father.

Besides the jewelry business which Mr. Johnson has so successfully conducted as to render him a conspicuous figure among the business men of the South, he has found time to turn his attention to other matters of importance, and has, since his residence in Lynchburg, served with credit in some of her principal offices of trust and responsibility. He and his family are members of the First Baptist Church, and are prominent members of the society of Lynchburg.

THE McKAY PLANT-SETTER MANUFACTURING COMPANY of Lynchburg, consisting of W. H. Wrau, President; Henry E. McWane, Vice-President; James E. Tate, Secretary and Treasurer, and J. W. McKay, Daniel Patterson and J. L. Hutton, directors, with a capital stock of $60,000, was organized in October, 1890, for the purpose of manufacturing for the trade a machine doing the work of three men in sowing all kinds of grain and resetting plant life of all kinds. Besides the patents taken out in the United States, they, since their organization, obtained patents in a number of foreign countries, by reason of the enormous demand already created for their at present limited supply. Mr. Tate, the efficient Secretary and Treasurer, holds the same offices in the Lynchburg Shoe Manufacturing Company and of the Commercial Building Association, and is junior partner of the wholesale grocery house of Robinson, Tate & Co.

The stockholders of the McKay enterprise are among the wealthy men of the city and State, and the inventor, Mr. McKay, is a man of enterprise and marked ability. With these important surroundings the Plant-setter cannot fail to win its way into great popularity, although without these favoring circumstances the invention would eventually win its way on its own merits.

WILLIAM H. FORD, Esq.—One of the prominent and most highly respected pioneer business men of Lynchburg was William H. Ford, Esq., who was born in that city in the year 1844. He received but an ordinary education from the schools of the city, and later learned the carpenter trade, which, however, he never followed, but instead began contracting and building, and many of the largest houses and blocks of Lynchburg stand to-day as monuments of his proficiency.

Among the buildings erected under the supervision of Mr. Ford, may be mentioned the Miller Female Orphan Asylum, the Colton and the James River Flouring Mills, at present owned and operated by Mr. John W. Hughes, of whom other mention has been made; also constructed a portion of the Lynchburg and Durham Railroad. In the year 1879 Mr. Ford purchased the Bailey Wagon Works, which business he conducted until his death. He was first married to Mrs. Fannie Mason of this city, who died in 1884, and was again married, in 1885, to Miss Annie Wells, who survives him. By this latter marriage one son was born, William H. Ford, Jr. He took an intense interest in political affairs, but never sought for office of any kind. He made many friends among all classes and conditions of men, and upon his death the city lost a good citizen, a true friend and a loving and indulgent husband and father.

JOHN W. HUGHES, Esq., the present operator of the James River Flouring Mill of Lynchburg, Va., is recognized as one of the prominent business men of the city of Lynchburg, owning large interests in numerous enterprises in and about the city. He at present operates the Wagon Works, and is a member of the firm of Woodson & Hughes, Tobacco Merchants, and of the firm of Hughes & Ford, a prominent contracting firm.

Besides his numerous business interests, Mr. Hughes has found time and inclination to take a prominent and active part in the government of the city, and has held a number of responsible official positions of trust.

THE FIRST NATIONAL BANK. The First National Bank of Lynchburg, is a corporation controlling $1,000,000 of capital stock, and having for its principal representatives John F. Slaughter, Esq., President; J. M. Booker, Esq., Vice President, and Allen W. Talley, Esq., Cashier. The bank was first organized in 1865 by Ambrose Rucker, George Davis, John J. Mean and others. Mr. Rucker served as its first President until 1869, when Mr. Slaughter succeeded him and has since retained the position. Since the organization of the bank it has declared an annual dividend of 10 per cent. besides a special dividend of $100,000, and at the present writing has a surplus of over $80,000. Mr. Slaughter, besides acting as President of this organization, is largely interested in the development of the iron resources of his State and is actively engaged in the production of coal in West Virginia and Kentucky, holding important offices in many of the prominent coal and iron-producing companies of these States..

JACOB H. FRANKLIN, Esq., one of the pioneer grocerymen of Lynchburg, Virginia, was born in Pittsylvania county, Virginia, in 1836. It was while in his native county that Jacob H. received his education, and in 1856 the family removed to Lynchburg, where he entered the employ of the Franklin Brothers as clerk, and in 1859 was made a member of the firm, but on the breaking out of the war he disposed of his interest and enlisted in the 11th Virginia Regiment and remained in the service until the close of the war in 1865. While serving under General Alexander he was made Major—an honor that was deservedly conferred. After his five years of soldier-life he returned to Lynchburg, clerking for two years and then forming a partnership with a brother, which existed until 1870, when he withdrew and went into business with a Mr. Jones, the latter retiring soon. Although the Major has had a number of partners, he has for the past few years conducted the business alone, which since 1882 has been strictly wholesale. He is interested in a large number of enterprises in the city and county, and leads an active and stirring life. A number of large enterprises claim his interest and attention, and his days may be truly described as over-crowded. He was first married, in 1861, to Miss Bennett, a daughter of Colonel Bennett, and by her had seven children. Mrs. Franklin died in 1876, and in 1880 he again married, the second time a Mrs. Neal, by whom he has no family. Mr. Franklin is a Mason, and has always held the esteem of his fellow-brothers and citizens. His business now is one of the largest in the South, aggregating nearly half a million a year.

WILLIAM S. CARROLL, Esq., eldest son of J. W. Carroll, Esq., of Lynchburg, Va., was born in that city, and there received his education, but in early life entered the tobacco trade in the employ of his father, where he remained until 1878, when he began business for himself, manufacturing plug tobacco under the firm name of W. L. Carroll & Co., and continued this for seven years, when he removed to North Carolina, where, in company with others, he resumed the same occupation. Here he remained until 1888, when he returned to Lynchburg and engaged in the manufacture of cigarettes under the firm name of Carroll & Greenstone, but at the end of the second year purchased his partner's interest, and has since conducted the business entirely alone, which has steadily increased until at the present time he employs nearly one hundred operatives in the manufacture of his product, and has the satisfaction of seeing his every effort rewarded by a constantly increasing demand for his goods. Mr. Carroll was also for some time President of the "Lone Jack" Cigarette Company, and is largely interested in the development of the city, and especially is he interested in the development of the mineral resources of that section, and owns a considerable amount of mineral lands.

CHAPTER III.

STAUNTON.

By A. C. GORDON.

Staunton, the metropolis of the Shenandoah Valley, is a city of some 12,000, situated in Augusta county, about midway between the Blue Ridge and the Alleghanies. Campbell, in his *History of Virginia*, states that it was laid off as a town in 1748, and incorporated the year after. Its founder was William Beverly, who, in 1745, conveyed twenty-five acres in the heart of his colonial land grant known as Beverly's Manor to the County Court of Augusta county for the purpose of erecting thereon a court-house, prison, etc. On and about these twenty-five acres grew up the present prosperous and compact little city. At that time Augusta county, of which Staunton is the present county seat, extended indefinitely westward, and its county court sometimes met at what is now Pittsburg, Pennsylvania.

Augusta county has been noted from its earliest settlement for the abundant fertility of the soil and for the sturdy self-reliance and patriotism of its people. It ranks to-day first of all the counties of the State in the value of its farming lands, orchard products, wheat, hay and dairy products, second in amount of cleared land, and fifth in population. Its inhabitants are largely sprung from the descendants of Scotch Covenanters who, after the battle of Bothwell Bridge, emigrated from Scotland to Ulster in the North of Ireland, whence their children and grandchildren, under the lead of the pioneer John Lewis, "who slew the Irish lord," came by way of Pennsylvania to this section. Waddell, in his *Annals of Augusta County*, which is a model local history, says that "the list of prisoners captured at Bothwell Bridge and herded like cattle for months in Greyfriar's Churchyard, Edinburgh, is like a muster-roll of Augusta people." Mingled with this Scotch-Irish strain is a generous complement of Dutch extraction, the Scotch-Irish element predominating in the southern and central portions of the county and the Dutch in the northern. They are a thrifty, industrious, self-reliant population, partaking of all the characteristic qualities which go to constitute good citizenship.

The city of Staunton is situated at

an average altitude of 1,450 feet above sea level, near the middle of an elevated plateau, like Limestone Valley, at this point about twenty-five miles wide, and sloping not far from twenty-five feet to the mile. Its surrounding scenery is unsurpassed for natural beauty and grandeur. Girt about from every point of the compass by mountain ranges etherialized by the glamour of a most pellucid and enchanting atmosphere, in the midst of historic associations of vivid interest, and set down among the most inviting pleasure-resorts to be found in America, Staunton offers many attractions to the tourist.

It is located at the junction of the Chesapeake and Ohio and the Valley Branch of the Baltimore and Ohio Railroads, and is easily accessible from all parts of the country by rail. Twelve miles to the east, along the western base of the Blue Ridge, runs the Norfolk and Western Railroad, soon to be connected with Staunton by a stem-road. It is within six hours' ride of Washington, seven of Baltimore, nine of Philadelphia, eleven of New York, and twelve of Cincinnati.

In the adjoining county of Rockbridge, in a few hours' ride by rail, is the world-famous Natural Bridge. In the same vicinity, and equally accessible, are the Balcony Falls, where James river cuts its way through the stone obstructions of the Blue Ridge mountains. At the base of the same mountains, in Nelson county, bordering Augusta on the east, and at no great distance from the Norfolk and Western Railroad, are the Crabtree Falls, a natural curiosity scarcely less wonderful than the cataract of Niagara itself, though little known, where a stream of clear and sparkling mountain water, from ten to twelve inches in diameter, is precipitated in a sheer cataract for a perpendicular distance of 1,880 feet.

At Iron Gate, sixty-odd miles west of Staunton, is another wonderful break of the head-waters of the James river through a mountain—a perfect arch, as if constructed by the hand of man, outlining itself upon the mountain wall on either side of the river in a series of successive strata several hundred feet high. On the Chesapeake and Ohio Railroad, at a point where it passes the Blue Ridge, twenty miles east of Staunton, lies the valley of Rockfish Gap, a region of no less exquisite natural beauty than the Tyrol.

The limestone region in which Staunton is situated abounds in caves and caverns. The most famous are the wonderful caverns of Luray, at a comparatively short distance by the Norfolk and Western Railroad. Some sixteen miles from Staunton, at the site of the new town of Shendun, and reached by two railroads, or by the more attractive country road through a region of panoramic beauty, are the scarcely less widely-known Grottoes of the Shenandoah, made familiar to the *ante-bellum* readers of

Harper's Magazine by the genius of a Virginia writer, Porte Crayon, as Weyer's Cave and the Cave of the Fountains. Near Mt. Solon, in Augusta county, about fifteen miles from Staunton, are the Cyclopean Towers, gigantic stone cliff pillars of remarkable symmetry and extraordinary geological interest. Many other natural objects of interest lend attractiveness to Staunton by their propinquity, while in many instances are to be found spots even more interesting by reason of their historical or literary associations. On the Staunton and Winchester Turnpike, a little to the north of the city, is the Old Stone Church, the first edifice built for religious worship in the Valley of Virginia of which history gives us account. The original walls and the quaint roof still stand as when, in earlier days, the pioneers gathered within its precincts with their rifles ready at any time for the attack of the Indians, but the inner arrangements of the building have been modernized for the accommodation of the worshipers of later days. Equally near is Tinkling Spring Church, at one time the seat of the ministrations of James Waddell, "the Blind Preacher," so eloquently described by William Wirt in the *British Spy*. The congregations of these two churches have been ministered to at various times by some of the most distinguished divines on the roster of the Presbyterian faith in America, and the history of either church edifice is closely interwoven with that of Presbyterianism in this country.

Near Greenville, twelve miles south of Staunton, is the site of the first academy for the instruction of youth in the Valley of Virginia, that grew from rude beginnings to be a college which gained the fostering care of George Washington, and over which in later days Robert E. Lee presided as its chief executive officer. This is the Washington and Lee University of to-day, which had its origin in the humble log school-house of Augusta county, removed in Washington's time to the classic little town of Lexington. Under the chapel of the University General Lee's body is buried, while over him lies the magnificent recumbent figure of white marble modeled by the Virginia artist Valentine after the fashion of those which rest above the ashes of the Emperor and Empress of Germany at Charlottenburg. In the same town of Lexington, forty miles away by rail, is buried under memorial bronze and granite "Stonewall" Jackson, who, before the war between the States, was a professor in the Virginia Military Institute at this point.

Equally near to Staunton on the east is the University of Virginia, founded by Thomas Jefferson, and overlooked by Monticello, where he lived and was buried.

To the south and west, in more or less immediate contiguity, are many of the most celebrated watering-places and summer resorts of the South, among them the White Sulphur, the Rockbridge Alum, The Warm, The Hot, The Healing, and the old Sweet Springs, all within ready reach of the tourist who makes Staunton his headquarters.

This section abounds in the homes of distinguished men. The residences of Jefferson, Madison and Monroe, three Presidents of the United States; of William C. Rives, Senator and Minister to France; of James Barbour, Governor and Minister to England; of Hugh Nelson, Minister to Spain; of William Wirt, the author of the *British Spy*, and Attorney General of the United States; of James Waddell, "the blind preacher;" of Thomas W. Gilmer, Governor of Virginia; of Merriwether Lewis, the explorer of the great Northwest; of Andrew Stevenson, Minister to England; of Sam Houston, the great Texan soldier and patriot; of Governor McDowell; of John Lewis, "the pioneer;" of Alexander H. H. Stuart, Secretary of the Interior under Fillmore; of "Honest" John Letcher, and of a host of others scarcely less distinguished, were situated in the county of Augusta or the adjoining counties of Albemarle and Rockbridge; while from the border county of Rockingham went westward, in his young manhood, the father of Abraham Lincoln.

Up and down the turnpikes leading into and out of Staunton marched in the days of the Civil War the soldiers of the two contending hosts; and the battle-fields of Cross Keys, of McDowell, of Post Republic, and other scenes of fierce conflict, lie almost in sight of the city.

The climate of this section is as agreeable and healthful as any in the whole country. Its latitude is 38°, 9' north that of Louisville, St. Louis and San Francisco on the west, and Southern Maryland on the east. Its summer temperature is moderated by its elevation, and its winter temperature by the mountain ranges which cut off the winds and storms of the northwest and south-east. It is of this immediate section that Prof. N. S. Shaler says that it possesses a climate " resembling in its range of temperatures those which characterize the most favored regions of the Old World, and it is there, perhaps, that we may look for the preservation of our race's best characteristics."

The commercial locality of Staunton is unsurpassed, lying as it does midway between the Atlantic ocean and the Ohio river, two hundred miles in air-line distance from each, and but one hundred miles direct from tide-water on the James, the Rappahannock and the Potomac rivers. Two great lines of railroad, as has been said, cross each other here at right angles; twelve miles away, through the eastern portion of the county, and soon to be connected with Staunton by a branch line, runs another railroad; a fourth is coming from the North along the eastern base of the Shenandoah mountains; while a fifth road, and perhaps the most important in many respects, is projected from Staunton to Pittsburg through a region of West Virginia unequalled on the American continent for the wealth of its coal and iron deposits and its virgin forests of hard woods.

Its location is no less advantageous from a manufacturing than from a commercial standpoint. With the railroads above mentioned opening up the markets of the world for its manufactured products, they offer it an equally easy access to abundance of raw material. Within its ready reach are the three great coking fields that lie east of the Mississippi—the Connelsville fields of Pennsylvania by the Baltimore and Ohio Railroad, the Pocahontas Flat Top fields of Southwest Virginia by the Norfolk and Western, and the New River fields of West Virginia by the Chesapeake and Ohio.

It is situated in the centre of an iron district where iron-making has been pursued for a hundred years, in a more or less primitive fashion, and where to-day blast furnaces, foundries and steel plants of great proportions and cost are being successfully run.

Speaking of the future of the iron industry of this section, Professor Shaler has recently said:

"The peculiar advantage of the Appalachian district is found in the fact that the ores lie in the neighborhood of excellent coal beds, which, in certain cases, can be used as it comes from the mine, or may be used to serve the needs of the smelter after it has been converted into coke. The average distance of the iron ore from the coal needed to reduce it to a metallic state does not exceed one hundred miles. Enough ore to make a ton of iron can at many points be mined and put into the furnace at a cost of between $1 and $2, while to bring the same amount of raw material from the earth about Lake Superior to the smelting points costs at the present time $8 to $12."

An interesting account of the earlier furnaces in the immediate vicinity of Staunton, a dozen or more in number, is to be found in Peyton's *History of Augusta County.* At the present time some of the most successful coking iron-furnaces in America are in operation in this section along the lines of the Chesapeake and Ohio and the Norfolk and Western Railroads, notable among which are Longdale, Lowmoor, Princess, Victoria, Buena Vista and Milnes. Coal and coking companies engaged in the output of the West Virginia mines do a thriving and lucrative business at their headquarters located at Staunton. The Fire Creek Coal and Coke Company is the pioneer in this region, with a commerce extending from New England to Mexico

At all points of the compass in immediate contiguity to Staunton, and reached in all directions by railroad, lie magnificent iron-ore beds and limestone of the finest quality, all the essentials thus concurring to the manufacture of iron and steel most advantageously and profitably at this point.

In Augusta county and the vicinity of Staunton abound marble, slate, kaolin, fire-clays, glass sand, anthracite coal, ochres and manganese. Marble of great beauty and susceptible of a high degree of polish has been quarried and extensive marble works carried on at Craigsville on the line of the Chesapeake and Ohio, fifteen miles west of Staunton. This marble is pink, purple, gray and black, the black being regarded as especially beautiful, high in quality and valuable. It has met with a large and ready sale in the markets of New York, Cincinnati and Chicago. Kaolin and fire-clay exist in large quantities and have been successfully utilized in the manufacture of pottery and fire-brick. An excellent quality of stone china was made both during and since the war from these clays; and in Pennsylvania this pure white kaolin has been used for weighting paper, for which purpose it was bought by the paper mills at $7 to $15 per ton.

Glass sand, pronounced by Wheeling and Pittsburg experts to be of the very finest character, has been discovered in practically limitless quantities in the vicinity of Staunton, and is now being utilized in the manufacture of glass.

The largest manganese mines in the world, from which two million dollars' worth of ore has been taken, are situated at Crimora, twelve miles east of Staunton on the Norfolk and Western Railroad, and outcroppings of this valuable mineral have been found all along the western foot-hills of the Blue Ridge throughout Augusta county.

Staunton is located upon a number of small hills, and near by are the mountains known as Betsy Bell and Mary Gray, taking their names from a Scotch legend which followed the Covenanters from their native land to the North of Ireland, where it endowed two mountains near the little town of Omagh in County Tyrone, with the same appellations. The city is irregularly laid out, and with its varying slopes, handsome residences, public buildings and beautiful shade-trees, presents a very attractive appearance.

Its educational and religious advantages are of a singularly ample and generous character. It is the seat of the State Institution for the education of the Deaf and Dumb and the Blind, a commodious and imposing structure, equipped and provided for in the most liberal manner by the State government; situated in the midst of extensive grounds, which for natural beauty are unsurpassed anywhere, and attended by the deaf-mutes and blind children from all sections of the commonwealth.

Within two hours' ride by rail are the University of Virginia, at Charlottesville, the Miller Manual Labor School, a technological school admirably equipped and conducted, in Albemarle county; the Washington and Lee University, at Lexington, and the Virginia Military Institute at the same place.

In Staunton itself are located several high-grade colleges for the education of young women, each possessing its own buildings, equipments, grounds and faculty. These colleges, five in number, are the Augusta Female Seminary, the Virginia Female Institute, the Wesleyan Female Institute, the Staunton Female Seminary, and the Roman Catholic School for Young Ladies and Girls. They are among the most thorough and successful institutions of learning in the country, and are each attended by large numbers of students from all sections of the United States.

For boys and young men there is an ably conducted Military Academy at Staunton with an attendance of a hundred and fifty pupils; a successful private classical school, "The Academy," coeval almost with the foundation of the town, and governed by a Board of Trustees chosen from among the most prominent citizens; and a large and flourishing Business College.

In addition to these private schools are the free public schools of Staunton, organized in 1870, contemporaneously with the adoption of the public school system in Virginia, and possessing a reputation for efficiency second to none anywhere. In their inception these public schools were largely aided by the Peabody Educational Fund, whose general agent then was Dr. Barnas Sears, an eminent citizen of Massachusetts, who made his home in Staunton after becoming the agent of this great charity, and spent his latter years in his cottage on what is now known as Sears' Hill, one of the most picturesque spots within the city limits. There are separate public schools for blacks and whites, conducted in handsome buildings belonging to the city.

As the influence of the Scotch Kirk predominated over that of all other religious bodies in colonial Augusta, so up to the present time Presbyterianism has continued to wield a great religious influence in the county and Staunton. There are two large Presbyterian churches in the city, and in its vicinity several others hardly less important. Besides the Presbyterians, the following religious denominations have churches in Staunton: The Methodist Episcopal Church, South, the Protestant Episcopalians, the Baptists, the Lutherans, the Congregation of United Brethren, the Roman Catholics, and the Hebrews. The seating capacity of the churches for whites aggregates 5,000, and the cost of the buildings $200,000. The four colored churches have a seating capacity of over 3,000, with property valued at $70,000. It has been said of Staunton by one of the most eminent divines of the country that "nowhere is there a more generous provision for the ordinances of the gospel."

The history of the Episcopal Church in Staunton goes back to colonial days, as does that of Presbyterianism in the Valley of Virginia. In the old Trinity Church building, in Revolutionary times, the General Assembly of Virginia, which had been driven from Richmond to Charlottesville and from Charlottesville to Staunton by Tarleton, Cornwallis' leader of cavalry, held its meetings, and its walls echoed the voices of Thomas Jefferson, Patrick Henry, Richard Henry Lee and other immortal men of that epoch.

In this connection it is proper to speak of the Young Men's Christian Association of Staunton, a large and influential organization, owning a splendid building in the heart of the city, which is generously equipped with a fine library, gymnasium, ten-pin alley and lecture hall.

The Masons, Pythians, Odd Fellows, Red Men, Good Templars and other similar secret organizations are represented in Staunton, many of them being financially prosperous and owning valuable property, notably the Masons, who possess a fine hall and some of the most desirable business property in the city.

On the eastern suburbs, at the foot of Betsy Bell, one of Staunton's romantically named mountains, is situated the Western Lunatic Asylum of Virginia in the midst of spacious and beautiful grounds. Since its establishment in 1828, the State has expended large sums in making this, which is one of the oldest, one of the best hospitals of its kind in this country. This institution, and that for the Deaf and Dumb and the Blind, which has already been spoken of, circulate in the community from $150,000 to $200,000 per annum.

Staunton has a daily newspaper, the *News*, and three weeklies, the *Spectator*, the *Vindicator* and the *Argus*. In addition are published at this point the *Railway Advertiser* for gratuitous circulation on the trains, and the *Goodson Gazette*, the organ of the deaf-mutes at the Deaf and Dumb and the Blind Institution.

The banking and financial business of Staunton is a good indication of its commercial and manufacturing enterprise and prosperity. There are two National banks, a half-dozen building and loan companies, and a savings bank, all well conducted and prosperous. The combined deposits of the two National banks aggregate a million and a half dollars, and the other institutions mentioned are relatively successfully operated.

Within the past fifteen years Staunton has become a Southern Hartford in the number and success of her insurance companies. The oldest of these companies is the Valley Mutual Life Association, and others, in the order of their foundation, are the Staunton Life, the Interstates and the Equity. These companies have paid out to policy-holders in the last few years several millions of dollars.

The hotels of Staunton are the Virginia, the Kalorama, the Mozart and the Hoover House. A company has recently been organized to build a modern hotel, the Altemonte, at a cost of upwards of one hundred thousand dollars, on a commanding eminence in the eastern part of the city. This hotel when completed will be one of the handsomest and most attractive in the South.

There are a number of boarding-houses in the city with prices to meet the wants of guests, and many find it very agreeable to sojourn here—among others, those of the North in winter and those from the South in summer, while others come to remain longer and avail themselves of the educational advantages here offered for their children.

On the north-western suburbs of the city is Gypsy Hill Park, reached by the street railway, and offering a place of rest and recreation in the summer with its pleasant little Casino, its shady trees and winding walks; while in winter it affords ample opportunity for enjoyment to the pedestrian, the rider and the driver. In this park are a number of splendid springs, the property of the city, which furnish the water consumed by the inhabitants of Staunton. The pump-house stands near the entrance to the park driveway, while on a lofty eminence a short distance away to the south is the reservoir, equal to supplying a city of 30,000 inhabitants, and sending its contents by force of natural gravity into the city with such momentum as to obviate the necessity of fire-engines in throwing the water over the highest houses.

Staunton possesses a well-drilled and disciplined paid fire department, and a system of electric fire-alarms, so that an outbreak of fire in any part of the city is amply guarded against.

Adjoining Gypsy Hill Park the Baldwin District Fair Association, representing twelve or fifteen adjoining counties, owns extensive and beautiful grounds improved with buildings, a race track, boating lake, etc. Its annual autumn exhibition of the products of the Shenandoah Valley and piedmont Virginia attracts large numbers of people from all parts of the State.

The city government of Staunton resembles very nearly the town government of New England, which is regarded by municipal jurisprudents as the most representative local democratic government in the world. A council of twelve citizens, chosen by popular suffrage from the body of the community, legislate for the municipality. They are elected at intervals of two years. The police force is effective and well managed.

In addition to its electric fire alarm system, already mentioned, Staunton has the Thomson-Houston electric arc-light on its streets, and an incandescent light for its residence and business houses. It has five miles and a half of street railway, well paved streets and good sewerage. The Chamber of Commerce, a representative body of business men, meets monthly.

Taxation, in comparison with the rate of other cities, is very light, in view of the advantages afforded by well paved and lighted streets, abundant water-supply, efficient police and thorough fire organization and alarm system.

The city has one of the handsomest opera-houses in the country, the season of which runs from September to April.

By reason of its advantageous location, Staunton was, years ago, selected by the Legislature of the State as one of the three points for the sessions of the Supreme Court of Appeals. The Circuit and County Courts of Augusta county, and the Court of Hustings for Staunton, also meet at regular intervals in the court-house built on the site where Beverley's court-house stood in colonial days.

Conspicuous features of the place are the attractive depots of the Baltimore and Ohio and the Chesapeake and Ohio Railroads, both of which are reached from all parts of the city by street-car. At the latter more passengers are said to embark than at any other point in Virginia located on this great railway system.

A social club, "The Beverley," with a membership of a hundred of the most prominent professional and business men of Staunton and the vicinity, constitutes an attractive feature of life in the city.

During the civil war Staunton was the base of supplies for the Confederate armies in Virginia, second in importance only to Richmond, the capital. Her best energies, both before and after the war, were devoted to a career of commercial activity. Situated in the midst of a magnificent farming and grazing country, she afforded and continues to afford a market for the wheat, corn and other farm products, and for the cattle, horses and sheep of her pastoral back-country. In return, she has for many years been, and still is, the depot of supplies for the farmers and retail merchants of the Shenandoah Valley, and of West Virginia's adjacent counties. While this commercial activity is annually increasing, Staunton has only of late years turned her attention to manufactures, and among her factories and plants can count a tannic extract mill, one of the largest in the world; a large shoe factory; a large furniture factory; a sash, door and blind factory; two large brick works; two marble and granite works; an ice-factory ; a book-bindery; a foundry and machine-shop; a carriage factory; a wagon factory; six cigar factories; a mineral water plant; a mattress factory ; two large steam roller flour and grist-mills; gas-works ; plaster mill ; two fertilizer factories ; a steam corn and feed mill; a patent medicine manu-factory ; a barrel factory, and a can-nery. Within the past year, under the auspices of the Staunton Devel-opment Company, an association of business men organized for the pur-pose of promoting the material pros-perity of the city, there have been located here the following large man-ufacturing plants, in addition to those that have been already enumerated, viz.:

The Bodley Wagon Company, a mammoth enterprise whose buildings and lumber yards cover twenty-four acres of ground, their main building being 840 feet long by 126 feet wide, and two stories high, with a number of outbuildings, and employing 200 operatives ; the Kroder curtain-pole and brass factory, occupying three acres of ground, its main building be-ing three stories high, 50 feet wide by 200 feet long, with several large outbuildings to correspond, and employing 200 mechanics ; the A. J. Sweeny & Sons foundry and machine-shops, occupying five acres of ground and embracing some half-dozen buildings, running from 50 to 200 feet in size, and employing 150 skilled mechanics; the Staunton Wood Mantel Company, whose build-ings occupy half a block, and who employ about 100 high-class work-men ; and the Standard Brick Com-pany, employing fifty-odd hands, with a capacity of 40,000 bricks per day.

The location of these enterprises at Staunton indicate that the manufac-turing business of the town will in a short time, perhaps, exceed its com-mercial business, and there is no reason why this should not be the case. Situated at the crossing of two great systems of railroad, one of which is an east and west overland route reaching practically from the Atlantic to the Pacific Ocean, the other of which is a north-east and south-west route extending practi-cally from Nova Scotia to Mexico; within twelve miles of yet another railroad which traverses the great valley from north-east to south-west, and soon to be directly connected with it ; with two of the greatest dry docks in the world and the finest harbor on the Atlantic coast within 200 miles by rail, at Newport News and Norfolk ; within equally easy reach of several lines of ocean steam-ers ; with mountains of iron east and west and north and south in distances ranging from ten to forty miles ; with a system of labor as good and as cheap and as reliable as anywhere in the world ; with access by three com-peting roads to the coking coal of Connelsville, Pocahontas and New River, with limestone and manganese and kaolin and fire-clays and glass sand and numberless other minerals in easy reach; located in an area of country, which for its wealth of hardwood forest trees, ranging from cedar, walnut and cherry to pine and oak, is inferior to none in America; surrounded by an exceedingly fertile country in the highest state of cultivation; blessed with a healthful and propitious climate; adorned with a surrounding scenery that for natural beauty is unexcelled in the Old World or the New; with every advantage that a cultivated, refined and religious society and an efficient municipal government can afford, Staunton has good right to the *sobriquet* that has been bestowed upon her of "Queen City of the Shenandoah Valley."

M. ERSKINE MILLER.—One of the most conspicuous business men of the Shenandoah Valley is M. Erskine Miller, of Staunton. He was born at Huntsville, Alabama, February 10th, 1843. His father, James Mason Miller, was a native of North Carolina, and his mother was a member of the Erskine family of Virginia. In 1850, when but seven years of age, M. Erskine Miller, accompanied his father to Texas, where he remained until 1861, in which year he enlisted in Company I of the Terry Rangers, in Gen. Albert Sidney Johnston's command. Having served in this company for some months, he was at last forced by ill health to resign. He again enlisted in August, 1862, in Company D, Fourth Texas Regiment, and participated in all the battles around Richmond, being severely wounded in the battle of Gaines' Mill.

At the close of the civil war Mr. Miller returned to Texas and went into business in Gaudaloupe county, where he continued to reside for several years. In 1870 he came to Virginia and married a daughter of Gen. John Echols, of Staunton. In 1871 he disposed of his interests in Texas, and entering business in Staunton built up a large wholesale trade. Mr. Miller was one of the pioneers in opening up the great New River coal region of West Virginia, and has for a number of years been and still is largely and actively identified in the management, as President, director and stockholder, of some of the most important coal and coke companies of that region. He is President and manager of the Staunton Development Company, a great business corporation organized for the material advancement of the city where he resides, and in this capacity has done a great deal towards developing the manufacturing interests of the place. He is also President of the Fire Creek Coal and Coke Company, the New River Coke Company and the Thurmond Coal Company, and is a large stockholder in other important companies in Virginia and West Vir-

ginia. He organized and put into successful operation the First National Bank of Huntington, West Virginia, and is President of the Waynesboro Company, an important corporation doing business at Waynesboro, Augusta county, Virginia.

Mr. Miller, in addition to the many other prominent business positions which he holds, is President of the Inter-States Life Insurance Company of Staunton, and is a large stockholder and director of the National Valley Bank of Staunton.

Though denied the opportunities of a collegiate education, he is thoroughly posted on all current topics of interest, and is a vigorous and effective speaker. His success in business is remarkable and due to his native qualities of energy, industry and clear and accurate judgment. He has never taken part in politics or sought public office.

Mr. ARMISTEAD C. GORDON, author of the historic sketch on Staunton, Virginia, is one of the best-known authors in the State, and many of his productions are read in the homes of thousands of people throughout the South and North. He is a native of Virginia, was born in Albemarle county in 1855, and is the grandson of Gen. William F. Gordon, who represented the Albemarle District in Congress some years, and was a statesman of national reputation.

Our subject received his primary education in a private school at Charlottesville, and completed it at the University of Virginia, where he attended the Summer Law School under Prof. John B. Minor. After completing his education he taught school for five years, and in 1879 removed to Staunton, and the same year was admitted to the Bar, and began the practice of his profession, which he has followed successfully since that time. In 1884 he was elected Mayor of the city, and showed marked ability in the discharge of his duties. At a later period he was President of the Chamber of Commerce, and in 1890 was elected Commonwealth's Attorney and counsel for the city of Staunton, which offices he is now filling. Mr. Gordon has for some time contributed articles to the leading magazines of the country, such as *The Century, Atlantic, Scribner*, and other well-known periodicals. He is an intimate friend of Thomas Nelson Page, and in conjunction with him has published a volume of dialect poems entitled "Befo' De War." Mr. Gordon is original in thought and construction, and his writings are characterized by a quaintness that renders them especially and peculiarly entertaining. Aside from his literary work, he has taken an active part in everything that tended to the advancement of Staunton, and has been active in the organization of improvement and development companies. He is President of the Staunton Savings Bank. As regards his profession, he has kept abreast of the times, and is now one of the foremost lawyers of the Staunton Bar. As a writer of ability, he has been recognized by the best-known publishers of the country. It does not often occur that so comparatively young a man attains the double eminence that Mr. Gordon has achieved as a lawyer and author, and with his best years still ahead of him, there are many bright possibilities within his reach.

MR. J. FRED. EFFINGER, of Staunton, Attorney at Law, was born in Rockingham county in 1846. He received his early education here, and later attended the State University, and also took a course at Washington and Lee University, graduating from the latter in 1871, taking the degree of Bachelor of Law. The same year he was admitted to the Bar of Augusta county, and immediately began practicing at Staunton.

He has large financial interests in West Virginia. Our subject is a man of naturally fine business qualities. His investments are made with tact and rare judgment, and the enterprises in which he is concerned are considered among the best and financially solid ones.

ALLEN C. BRAXTON, Esq., of Staunton, the subject of this sketch, is a member of the law firm of Braxton, Schols & Braxton. He was born in Monroe county, Virginia, in 1862, but spent his early life in King William county, and received his early education in private schools. At an early age he began the study of law in the office of the late Judge James F. Patton of West Virginia. In 1883 he took a course of law in the Virginia State University. He was admitted to the Bar at Staunton the same year and began practice at once, alone; he continued alone until November, 1889, when his brother, Mr. Hugh C. Braxton, entered into partnership with him, forming the firm of Braxton & Braxton, which firm existed until May, 1891, when the brothers dissolved, Hugh C. retiring, and Messrs. Edward Schols and Carter Braxton, a younger brother of Allen, entering the firm, which at present consists of these members under the style of Braxton, Schols & Braxton. Mr. Braxton was the organizer of the Basic City Mining, Manufacturing and Land Company, which resulted in the founding of Basic City. He was President of the Kanawha City Company from July, 1890, to July, 1891, and is attorney for a number of large corporations. He is employed as attorney for the National Valley Bank and the Staunton Life Association; he held the office of Commonwealth's Attorney for the City of Staunton from 1886 to 1890, and at the same time was City Attorney; he also fills a number of other positions and offices of trust and profit. While his life is an unusually busy one, he still finds time for the social amenities, which he enjoys with a zest that work gives to recreation. He is a member of the great trinity of orders, the Masonic, Odd Fellows and Knights of Pythias, and is an enthusiastic worker in all of them. His business is a paying one and he has accumulated a handsome property, which smooths down a good many rugged places in life and makes it look very fair and well worth living.

The *American Wool and Financial Reporter* of Boston, Mass., speaking of the subject of this sketch, says: " Mr. Braxton is one of the brightest, brainiest and most intelligent men I have met in Virginia. He is not only brilliant, but possesses all of the characteristics of a pushing business man from hustling New England."

DR. A. M. HENKEL, a leading physician of Staunton, is a native of New Market, Shenandoah county, Virginia, and was born in 1844.

The Doctor comes of a family of physicians, and, as it were, to the manner born, his father and grandfather having both followed the profession, and were both residents of New Market. He began the study of medicine under the direction of his father, and also engaged in the drug business for a number of years. In 1866 he entered the University of Virginia, taking the medical course, spending two years there, when he attended the University of New York, graduating from there in 1868. He remained in New York some time in hospital practice, when he returned to Virginia and opened an office at Staunton.

Dr. A. M. Henkel is a member of the State Medical Society of Virginia, a member of the National Association of Railway Surgeons, and surgeon for two railroad companies, and is surgeon and physician to a number of institutions.

He was married in 1876 to Mrs. V. M. Moffett, formerly Miss Virginia Moore, a daughter of Samuel Moore, of Shenandoah county, and is the father of one son, S. Godfrey Henkel. The Doctor is a member of the Lutheran Church, and is active in all good works, finding time from his professional duties to make his presence in a community felt as a power and an acquisition. He is a man of refinement and cultivation, and is esteemed by all who know him.

W. P. TAMS, Esq., Cashier of the Augusta National Bank, was born in Rockingham county in the year 1852. His father, William H., was a native of North Carolina, but spent his early life in Pennsylvania, in Philadelphia, graduated at Princeton, New Jersey, and completed his education at the University of Virginia. He died in

Virginia in 1873. W. P. Tams, of whom this sketch pertains, came to Staunton with his mother, and received his early education in the schools of Staunton and the Virginia Military Institute, graduating from the latter in 1873, but remained two years in the Institute as a teacher and lecturer on chemistry. Upon his return to Staunton he entered the Augusta National Bank as clerk, but soon rose to general clerk and was rapidly promoted until in 1880 he was made Cashier, which position he now occupies. Mr. Tams is Treasurer of the Staunton Development Company, and Treasurer of the Rush Coal and Coke Company and is a stockholder in other enterprises, and was at one time President of the Building and Loan Association of Staunton. He has taken quite an active interest in the management and government of the city and has served in the council continuously for six years. In the year 1880 he was united in marriage to Miss Susan L. Frazer, a daughter of the Hon. William Frazer, of Rockingham county.

W. T. McCUE, Esq., is a son of the late Judge J. H. McCue, a native of Augusta county, having been born in Staunton in 1857. He received his education in the schools at home, and at the age of sixteen years began life for himself by establishing a news stand, which he conducted successfully for one year, when he moved to Mississippi on account of ill health, finding employment there and remaining two years. In the summer of 1879 he returned to Staunton and connected himself with Mr. M. Erskin Miller, with whom he remained four years as private secretary and confidential book-keeper, after which he went into the employ of the Valley Mutual Life Association as book-keeper, and afterwards assisted in the organization of the Inter-states Life Association, of which he was made Treasurer and general office man, remaining here until 1890; but during this time he had been interested in the development of the State, and in 1885 assisted in organizing the Augusta Perpetual Building and Loan Company, of which he was director for some time and in 1886 was made Cashier. In February of this present year—1891—with Mr. A. C. Gordon he organized the Staunton Savings Bank, of which he is Vice-President, and also Vice-President and General Manager of the West Iron Gate Land Company, and is associated with a number of other companies as president or manager or director. As a manager of business Mr. McCue is peculiarly successful, as every undertaking with which he has been connected proves him such. He does not greatly interest himself in politics and has never sought or cared for office, though a member of the City

Democratic Committee of Staunton. He is a member of the I. O. O. F. order and the K. of P., and numerous beneficial societies.

Mr. R. W. BURKE, Vice-President of the National Valley Bank, Staunton, Va., was born in the county of Augusta, near this city, in the year 1838, and is a son of Thomas Burke, a highly respected farmer of the same county. R. W. Burke, our subject, received his early schooling in his native place, and at the age of 15 began life as a page in the Virginia State Senate, and served as such until the year 1857, when he was elected door-keeper of the House of Delegates, and later made sergeant-at-arms of this body, holding this position until the close of the war and for some time after. In the fall of 1866 he commenced business as a merchant in Staunton, and continued until 1887, when he retired from business. He was made director in the National Valley Bank in 1871, and in 1877 was made Vice-President. In 1888 he took the active management of the National Valley Bank, of which he had already become one of the largest stockholders. He has always taken an active part in public affairs, and has served the people in the City Council for fourteen years, seven years of which he was President of this body. He is a prominent member of the Democratic party in this State, and was for several years a member of the Executive Committee of the Democratic State Central Committee. Mr. Burke is a member of the Masonic fraternity, and has taken the Commandery degrees, and finds in these orders, as does every conscientious member, much to make his life better and more pleasant in every way. From a business standpoint, his career has been a successful one, and he enjoys the confidence and respect of the community in which he resides. His best and truest interests are centered in the city, and his greatest satisfaction is in its advancement and prosperity.

WAYT & BROTHERS.—The leading drug firm of Staunton, Virginia, is that of Wayt & Brothers, of which J. H. Wayt, the subject of this sketch, is a member. He is a native of the same county of which he is now a resident, and was born in 1845. He spent his early life in his native place, and was educated in the schools of his county. After finishing his education, he entered the drug trade with his brother, Dr. Newton Wayt, and has followed this business continuously ever since. While not neglecting his occupation, he has taken time to interest himself in all that tended towards the advancement of his city and the South-west. In the year 1888, in company with his brother and J. F. Christian, he built the street railway of Roanoke. He is a director in the Augusta Building and Loan Company, and also a director in the Development Company, and president of the Stonewall Investment Company of Clifton Forge, and is financially interested in a number of other leading enterprises in and about Staunton. He is a Mason, and a member of the Staunton Lodge, the oldest lodge in the State, in which he holds the honorable position of E. C. of the Staunton Commandery, and is a member of the I. O. O. F. and K. of P. It is not flattery to say that Mr. Wayt is a man who is more than ordinarily well liked; he has genial, pleasant ways that make him many friends, and he also possesses the rare faculty of keeping them.

MR. B. F. HUGHES, senior member of the firm of Hughes & Beel, druggists of Staunton, was born in Berkley county, West Virginia, in 1854. He made his home in Berkley county until he was sixteen years of age, when he went to Lexington, Virginia, and took the position of clerk in a drug store, remaining here eight years, when, in 1881, he came to Staunton and engaged in business for himself, and later formed the firm of Hughes & Robertson (1886), which existed until 1889 when the present firm was organized. Mr. Hughes was one of the organizers of the West Staunton Land Company, and also a director of the Staunton Savings Bank; director in the West Iron Gate Land Company, and stockholder and director in a number of other important business investments in Staunton and vicinity. He is a member of the Masonic fraternity, having taken the thirty-two degrees of this order, and is also a member of the Odd Fellows' Lodge of Staunton.

WALTER W. ROBERTSON. — The popular Superintendent of the City Public Schools of Staunton, Virginia, Mr. Walter W. Robertson, is a native of Appomattox county, Virginia, and was born in 1856.

His father, Maj. James E. Robertson, now of Bedford county, Virginia, is a highly respected gentleman of decided ability, culture and refinement.

Mr. Robertson is a member of the Methodist church and is a Christian gentleman of the true type, consistent by practice with all his professions, and combines, with an efficient city officer, the qualities of a refined, cultured gentleman.

He is in full possession of vigorous health, and is in the prime of life.

His education, commenced at Union Academy, Appomattox county, Virginia, and completed at Randolph-Macon College, is thorough and scholastic, thus enabling him not only to supervise the work of his teachers, but, at all times when necessary, to assist and direct them in their work.

He has, for the past fourteen years,

taught successfully in every department of our public school system, and is thoroughly familiar with all its workings, having taught in Appomattox and Nelson counties, and for four years as Principal of the Public High School in Harrisonburg, Va.

At each of these places he has been a most untiring and successful worker, and stands to-day in the front rank of his profession as an educator of youth.

For the past five years he has been the efficient Superintendent of the City Public Schools of Staunton, Virginia. During his administration, and owing more to his efficiency than to anything else, the number of pupils and teachers has been largely increased, new and commodious buildings constructed on the most approved plans have been erected, the course of instruction considerably advanced, and many important features of practical knowledge added thereto, until to-day the reputation of the Staunton public schools is second to none in the State.

Mr. Robertson is a gentleman of pleasing address, and possesses wonderful tact in organizing and controlling those with whom he is brought in contact. He was one of the organizers of the Staunton Improvement Company, and also of the West Staunton Land Company, of which he is Secretary and Treasurer.

Socially he is kind and genial, and carries the deep regard and respect of all who know him.

THOMAS S. DOYLE, the subject of this brief paper, has been Principal of the Virginia Institute for the Education of the Deaf and Dumb and the Blind, of Staunton, Virginia, since July 1st, 1880, less the two years between 1882-'84, during which time the Readjuster party had control of the State. Mr. Doyle came to this institution from Natchez, Mississippi, where he had been Superintendent of the Natchez Institute for two years. This was in 1871, and from that date until his election as Principal of the Virginia Institute in 1880 he served as teacher to the blind in this school. He was in the Confederate army four years in the 5th and 33d Regiments of Virginia Infantry (of the Stonewall Brigade), in the latter commanding a company for nearly two years. He was educated in Lexington and in Augusta county, but did not complete an entire course on account of the war. He was born in Greene county, Illinois (but removed to Virginia at the age of five years), and is the son of Robert L. Doyle, a lawyer by profession and a native of Pennsylvania, who came to Rockbridge county, Virginia, about 1822, which county he represented in the Virginia House of Delegates in the session of 1855-'56. He held the position of Lieutenant Colonel of the 62d Virginia Infantry, and was killed in the battle of Piedmont, Virginia, June 5th, 1864. He was a son of John Doyle, a native of Pennsylvania, who was a lawyer by profession, but who was largely interested in the iron industries of Virginia and erected some of the first furnaces worked in the State.

Professor Doyle possesses the rare qualities that constitute a successful teacher of the unfortunate class with whom he kindly casts his life and labor. To the blind he has been eyes, to the deaf he has been a gracious listener, and to the speechless he has been a willing interpreter. As such he is loved by his pupils and valued by the officers of the institution.

DR. BENJAMIN BLACKFORD, Superintendent of the Western Insane Asylum of Staunton, Virginia, was born in the Valley of Virginia. His early life was spent in Lynchburg, and attended the schools of that place, and afterwards entered the Medical Department of the State University, having read medicine prior to this under the preceptorship of his father, who had been a leading physician of the State. Young Blackford left this college, and in 1854 entered the Jefferson Medical College at Philadelphia, graduating from there the next year. After graduating he was selected resident physician to the Blockley Hospital (Philadelphia), filling this position several years, when he returned to Lynchburg and practiced until the breaking out of the war, which he entered as surgeon, and remained in the service until the surrender. He organized and was in charge of several large Confederate hospitals during the war.

After the close of the war the Doctor went to Lynchburg and again began the practice of his profession, acting as medical adviser and examiner to a number of the largest life insurance companies, and was also employed by the city as physician to the Alms-house, and at the same time overseer of the poor at Lynchburg. He is a member of a number of medical societies, and keeps fully abreast with his profession. Mrs. Blackford, his wife, before marriage was a Mrs. Emily Byrd (*nee* Neilson), of Baltimore. Six children have been born to them, all sons, and all living.

In 1889 the Doctor was tendered the position of Superintendent of the Western Insane Asylum, which place he has filled to the satisfaction of all concerned.

MISS M. J. BALDWIN, of Virginia, graduated at Augusta Seminary at Staunton, Virginia, and afterwards availed herself of the advantages afforded by the best schools of Philadelphia, thus eminently fitting and equipping herself for her great life-work. She early exhibited a fondness for teaching and training youthful minds. She conducted very successfully a day school, more for the opportunity it gave her of indulging in her favorite employment than for any pecuniary advantage it could yield. Her fine intellectual attainments, kind, sympathetic nature and pleasant manner of instructing and amusing children, rendered her peculiarly attractive to the young. Her success and aptitude for work of this kind being known by the trustees of Augusta Seminary, she was, in 1862, elected Principal of the school where she had graduated, and Miss Agnes McClung was elected Associate Principal. Success was anticipated from this association, but the advancement and growth of the enterprise far exceeded the expectations of the most sanguine, and the hopes of those most interested. The school opened with eighty scholars, thirty of whom were boarders. It suffered some reverses during the war, but owing to the earnest efforts and indefatigable energy of the Principals, it steadily increased in numbers and in the confidence of the community. Its continued prosperity is rather wonderful, inasmuch as no agents are employed save the influence of the pupils and patrons, and their kind words and efforts in behalf of their *Alma Mater*. At the close of the war the boarding department was enlarged and a handsome chapel erected. In 1880 Miss Agnes McClung, the beloved friend and associate, died. This was the greatest blow the institution has ever sustained, and only those who knew her and saw her in her accustomed place can estimate the loss caused by her death. This was one of the Principal's greatest sorrows; she highly valued her advice and fine judgment. For twelve years Miss Baldwin has had the entire management of the Seminary, a charge and responsibility so great that few would care to assume it. From the time she first engaged in this work she has had but one interest, the prosperity of the institution, and one aim, that it should become a leading school for the higher and liberal education of women. Her ambition has been fully gratified, and it must be a pleasure for her to look upon her work. Her very wonderful success is in a great measure due to this singleness of purpose and her rare executive ability. The increased popularity of the school has compelled her to erect, from time to time, other buildings thoroughly equipped with all the appointments of a first-class institution; they now cover a square. The number of pupils is about 250; 155 of these are boarders. The corps of teachers numbers twenty-five, all specialists and eminent in their several departments. In the selection of her faculty she has shown much wisdom, employing those only who, by their fidelity and efficiency, have made for themselves a reputation. Because of these advantages the school is always full, and many more apply each year than can be accommodated.

Miss Baldwin's fame as an educator is widely known, and is now attracting patronage from the North and

West. There are representatives not only from every Southern State, but from Maryland, Ohio, Pennsylvania, New York, Indiana, Illinois, Missouri, California, and several of the Territories. It offers almost unsurpassed advantages in every department. The instruction given is thorough and the standard for graduation high. Although there are so many pupils, Miss Baldwin manages to give some personal attention to all, thus making each one feel that she is an object of special interest, and in this way she wins their love and confidence. To her many excellent qualities she adds that of an elevated Christian character. She has been for many years an active member of the Presbyterian church. The spiritual welfare of her pupils, has always been a matter of deep solicitude and she feels deeply the responsibility resting upon her of training them for that better and higher life. The religious influence exerted over them has always been a distinguishing feature of the institution. The young ladies have their own prayer-meeting, Missionary and King's Daughters Society.

It is impossible to estimate the powerful influence for good going out from this school from year to year. Many lives are made happier and better by the lessons of piety and love learned here. From among the scholars and teachers many noble women have gone forth to labor in the mission fields of China, Japan and Brazil. Miss Baldwin is liberal in her gifts to all institutions for the spread of the gospel, and her interests are deeply enlisted in every benevolent project. Recognizing the great means of usefulness education is in woman, and the wide-spread influence it enables her to wield, she has educated many and largely assisted others in procuring those advantages entirely beyond their reach.

The institution over which she presides is one in which her community, State and the South may justly feel great pride. For thirty years she has concentrated her time, energy and means upon it, until it now stands a monument to a noble life given up to duty and absorbed in good deeds and thoughts of kindness for others. She is ever busy devising means to promote the greatest good of those entrusted to her care, and how to make them intellectual, refined and useful, and women in the highest sense truly noble. Long may she be spared for usefulness and the continuance of her great work.

Hon. **WILLIAM E. CRAIG,** United States Attorney for the Western District of Virginia, was born in Augusta county in 1851, and is a son of Alexander S. Craig, a highly-respected farmer of this county, who died in the Confederate army.

William E. Craig received his collegiate education in the College of

Roanoke, at Salem, Virginia, and began the study of law in 1872, in the office of Judge J. W. G. Smith, of Staunton, and was admitted to the Bar in 1874 and began practice at once, and has followed his profession continuously, with the exception of two years, from 1883 to 1885, when he was Collector of Revenue. In June, 1889, he was appointed District Attorney, and has continued to fill this place up to the present time. Mr. Craig is a stockholder and director in the Clifton Forge Banking and Construction Company, and stockholder in other large concerns in and around Staunton. Politically, he is known as an ardent Republican, and holds to it as one who has unlimited confidence. He has held the position of Chairman of the County Executive Committee, and is also a member of the State Executive Committee. As a member of the City Council he has done efficient work, the good and welfare of his own town being paramount to all else. His enterprises have been various, but all have tended to the weal of his homeplace and institutions. In the Lodge of I. O. O. F. his genial, social qualities have endeared him to the fraternity in which he finds pleasure, benefit and recreation.

ARISTA HOGE, Esq., present City Treasurer of Staunton, Virginia, and Secretary and Treasurer of the Staunton Perpetual Building and Loan Company, was born in Albemarle county, Virginia, in the year 1847. His father, Peter C. Hoge, was a native of Augusta county, and for many years a leading minister in the Baptist church. Arista Hoge, Esq., of whom we are now writing, spent his early life in Albemarle, and was educated in the schools of that county.

In 1863 he began clerking in a dry-goods store in Scottsville, and afterwards entered the employ of F. M. Young, of Staunton, and remained with him fourteen years. In 1884 he established the Atlas Insurance Agency, with which he is still connected, and in the following year was elected treasurer of the city of Staunton, and has held this office continuously until this time. He assisted in the organization of the Perpetual Building and Loan Company, of which he was elected secretary and treasurer. He is a director in the Augusta National Bank, Staunton Life Association of Virginia, and has financial interests in a number of other enterprises.

Mr. Hoge is a person who is much more felt in business than seen. While he talks but little, he is prolific in execution, and he has been the ready promoter of some of Staunton's best industries.

WILLIAM H. WELLER, Esq., President of the West Staunton Land Company and leading dry goods dealer of Staunton, was born in the city of Richmond in 1843, and is the son of C. R. Weller, Esq., for many years engaged in the hardware, tinware and stove trade of the capital. William H. attended the schools of his native city. When the war broke out he enlisted in the 39th Virginia Battalion of Cavalry, attached to General Lee's headquarters, and served three years, being slightly wounded once and his horse shot from under him at the second battle of Manassas. After the war he came to Augusta county and engaged in farming at Fishersville and remained there one year, when he engaged as clerk in a dry goods house, which position he occupied for six years when the firm of Hilb & Weller was formed, which existed two years. At this time (1875) he married the daughter of A. H. Taylor, Esq., who was then engaged in business here, and at Mr. Taylor's death our subject purchased the stock and has since conducted it alone as W. H. Weller. In the spring of 1890, in company with W. W. Robertson and M. M. Robertson and others, the first Staunton land company was organized, of which he was elected President. He is also Vice-President of the Augusta Perpetual Building and Loan Company, and is President of the Young Men's Building and Loan Association, and is also largely interested in kindred enterprises in Buena Vista and Waynesborough. Of the latter place he is director of the Waynesborough Building and Investment Company, and stockholder and promoter of the West Waynesborough Land Company. Mr. Weller is not deeply absorbed in politics, and only takes an indifferent interest in them. Was formerly a member of the City Council. He finds his religious home in the Presbyterian Church and his social in the Lodge of the Knights of Pythias. His success in business has been extremely gratifying, and, although comparatively young, he has no terrors for the "wolf at the door."

HOGE & HUTCHINSON.—A stand-by among the business houses of Staunton, Virginia, is the house of Hoge & Hutchinson, Wholesale Grocers.

Mr. Henry Hutchinson, a member of this firm, and the subject of this sketch, was born in Monroe county, Virginia, in 1850. The first years of his life were spent in his native county clerking, when, in 1872, he went to Goshen, Rockbridge county, and engaged in a general merchandise business with the firm name of Garrett, Gooch & Co. Mr. Hutchinson remained in this firm until 1882, when he came to Staunton and formed the Co. of the firm of Gooch, Hoge & Co., which existed five years, when he and Mr. Hoge purchased the entire interest, changing the firm name to the present one. The trade of the house is an extensive one, and extends over a large territory. Mr. Hutchinson is also largely interested in a number of other enterprises, prominent among them the Staunton Canning Company and the National Valley Bank, of which he is a director. The first office in the Chamber of Commerce, that of President, fell to him, and other honors and responsibilities abound in his life. Of the churches and their tenets, his preference is for the Presbyterian, of which he is a member. As regards politics, his interest in them has never greatly exceeded the bounds of indifference, holding his opinions firmly, but without argument or ostentation. It is such men who lend character and worth to a place, whose presence is felt for good, and whose absence is a loss hard to be repaired.

MR. FRANK ALEXANDER, member of the firm of Frank Alexander & Co., leading wholesale and retail hardware merchants of Staunton, was born in Augusta county in 1857. In the year 1869 he entered the employ of Mr. H. H. Myers, of Lexington, Virginia, as clerk, and in 1873 came to Staunton, also to clerk with W. M. McIlhany and continued in this until 1878, when, in that year, in company with Mr. H. H. Myers, of Lexington, they purchased a stock of goods of Messrs Woods & Gilkson and started the firm of Alexander & Co., but in the year 1884 Mr. Myers disposed of his interest to Mr. Edward Alexander, the firm name not being changed. Soon after they began operating, the firm went into the wholesale trade, which now extends over a large territory and is yearly extending its limits. Their retail business has also been sustained, and their house is one of the prominent ones in Staunton. Aside from the ordinary business transactions of the firm the Alexanders are extensively interested in enterprises in and about the city, and the public finds in them hearty and willing co-operators in any scheme or plan whose object is to build up and develop the resources of the city or county.

MR. GEORGE C. JORDAN, Vice-President of the Buena Vista Improvement Company, and secretary and manager and chief executive officer in the Inter-state Life Insurance Company, and President of the Southern Investment Company, and largely interested in Buena Vista enterprises, was born in Raleigh, North Carolina, in 1853, and received his education in the schools of Chicago, Illinois, and the College of Notre Dame, South Bend, Indiana.

In 1868 he returned to Raleigh and became the publisher of the *Raleigh Daily News*, doing at the same time State printing. His connection with this paper covered a period of six years, when he engaged in the life insurance business as manager of the Valley Mutual Life Company of Staunton for North and South Carolina, doing one of the largest businesses of this kind in the entire South.

He subsequently withdrew from this company and organized the Inter-state Life Insurance Company of Staunton, of which he is general manager, doing an extensive business in Virginia and in the Carolinas. Mr. Jordan was one of the organizers and chief executive of the Staunton Mutual Amnesty Company, and is the largest stockholder in the Car Company of Basic City, and is one of the owners of the Jordan building. He was married in 1873 to Miss Lola C. Cooke, whose father was the founder of the Institute for the Deaf and Dumb and the Blind of North Carolina.

MAJ. ED. McMAHON, present postmaster of Staunton, Virginia, is a native of Ireland, and was born in Dublin in the year 1821, where he spent his early life. While quite young he began to serve an apprenticeship as stone-cutter and mason, and followed this trade as a journeyman for a number of years, but for three years prior to his coming to America held the position of superintendent to a large contractor. In the year 1847 he came to the United States and found employment in the navy-yard and in the city of Brooklyn, where he remained a year, when he came to Richmond, Virginia, where he stayed until the breaking out of the war, when he was made Chief Quartermaster for South-west Virginia and Tennessee, serving in this capacity until the surrender, being mustered out with the rank of Major. Soon after this the Major came to Staunton, and followed railroad contracting up to the year 1889, when he was appointed postmaster of the city.

Of the many companies in which he is interested for the advancement and development of Staunton and its adjacent cities, the brief space allotted to this sketch would not permit mentioning, but suffice to say that no judicious undertaking whose aim has been to benefit the town or the community but what has received his hearty endorsement and co-operation. In politics he is a thoroughly committed Republican, and is devoted to the tenets of the party and its interests, having faith in its aspirations and its aims. Nearly half a century of his life has been spent in public service, and that he is still retained in it is a compliment that words but half express.

REEVES CATT, Esq., President of the Staunton Improvement Company, is an Englishman by birth, having been born in New Romney, Kent county, England, in 1849. He spent his early life there assisting his father, who was a shepherd, but when quite young began serving an apprenticeship to the butcher's trade, and followed this occupation until he was twenty-one years old, when he came to the United States direct to Staunton, Virginia, and began work at his trade, following it three years as a journeyman, when, in 1873, he began working for himself and followed this business continuously until January, 1891. For a number of years he has been a manufacturer of a fertilizer, which business he still continues. In the early part of 1890 he began making small investments in real estate and was the organizer of the Staunton Improvement Company, of which he was made President, which position he now holds. He is also a director in the West Staunton Land Company, and in the Staunton Steam Roller Mills. He was married in 1879 to Miss Alice V. Blackburn of this city, and one daughter has been born to them. The family are members of the Methodist church and Mr. Catt is superintendent of the Sunday-school in the same society. He has been in every important respect a successful business man, and socially he holds the respect of all who know him.

JUDGE BRISCOE GERARD BALDWIN

was the eldest son of Dr. Cornelius Baldwin, of Winchester, Virginia, and of Mary, a daughter of Col. Gerard Briscoe, of Frederick county, Virginia. Dr. Cornelius was a native of New Jersey, a surgeon in the Revolutionary army, and a member of the Cincinnati Society. Briscoe G. Baldwin was born at Winchester, Virginia, January 4th, 1789. Educated at William and Mary College, he studied law under Judge William Daniel, Sr., who had married his eldest sister, and in 1809 he settled in Staunton and entered upon the practice of his profession, which he continued to pursue with diligence and success until 1842, when he was elected a member of the Supreme Court of Appeals of Virginia, a position which he held until his death, on May 18th, 1852. In 1812 he was married at Spring Farm to Martha Steele, daughter of Chancellor John Brown, of the Staunton District, sister of Judge James E. Brown, of Wythe, and daughter of Frances Peyton. She was a lady of extraordinary intellectual endowments, full of vivacity and wit, and of singularly attractive manners and colloquial powers.

Judge Baldwin devoted himself exclusively to his profession and polite literature. He established, in October, 1831, a law school in Staunton, which he conducted for several years with much success. His lectures, comprising the whole body of common, statute and equity law, still exist in manuscript, and were highly prized by his students. He had no taste for political life, and although qualified for almost any public trust, and one of the most popular men of his day, he never sought to obtain any political office. He represented the county of Augusta, in 1818–'20 and in 1841–'42, in the General Assembly of Virginia. On the first occasion he was elected, during his absence from home, by a spontaneous uprising of the people, who did not wait to ask his consent to serve. In 1841, at the earnest solicitation of the best men of the county, he consented to be voted for as one of their delegates, and was chosen almost by acclamation. Within a few weeks after he took his seat in the Legislature he was elected to fill a place on the Bench of the Court of Appeals of Virginia.

In 1829, Judge Baldwin was chosen by the people of the Senatorial District of which Augusta was then a part, as the colleague of Chapman Johnson, Gen. William McCoy and Samuel McD. Moore, in the memorable convention of 1829-'30.

At the bar Judge Baldwin proved himself to be not only an able lawyer and skillful special pleader, but one of the most eloquent advocates of his day. Half a century ago the Bar of Staunton was one of the ablest in the Commonwealth. The four most distinguished members of it were Chapman Johnson, Daniel Scheffey, John H. Peyton and Briscoe G. Baldwin. In every important civil cause these gentlemen were arrayed — two and two — against each other, and it was an intellectual treat of a high order to witness the forensic contests of these giants in their profession. And it may be added that it was refreshing to observe the high-toned courtesy and absence of everything like personalities which characterized their forensic tilts.

Judge Baldwin possessed high and varied intellectual powers, which had been developed by careful and thorough culture. He was not only a learned lawyer, but an accomplished scholar. In the midst of his professional labors he always found time to keep abreast of the literature of the day. He was familiar with the English classics, and often illustrated his speeches by quotations from Shakespeare, Milton, Pope, and other standard poets.

To great vigor of intellect he united quick and keen perceptions, a rich and poetic imagination and tender sensibilities, which always brought him into close sympathy with the suffering and oppressed. Hence, as an advocate, he was not only a powerful reasoner, but a polished rhetorician and a ready and adroit debater, master of every weapon useful in assault or defence. His great efforts at the bar often displayed wonderful versatility of talent. While he would instruct and convince his audience by his logic, he would often delight them by brilliant sallies of wit, keen *repartee*, pungent sarcasm, scorching denunciation of fraud and injustice, splendid declamation and melting pathos.

But it was during his ten years' service on the bench of the Court of Appeals that Judge Baldwin's talents and learning were most conspicuously displayed.

Shortly after he took his seat on the Bench, he determined that whenever a cause came before the court in which questions were presented in regard to which the law was obscure, or in doubt from conflicting decisions, he would endeavor to sift the matter to the bottom and to educe from the mass of unsatisfactory and often clashing opinions of the courts the true principles which should govern in all such cases. He did not live long enough to carry this beneficent purpose into effect, except to a limited extent. But all who have read his able and lucid opinions, in which he expounded the law on the questions of "Fraud *per se*," "Adverse Possession," "What Decrees are Final," and others to which I need not refer, must admit that the courts, as well as the Bar, are under deep obligations to him for his comprehensive, clear and exhaustive treatment of those subjects. If his life and health had continued ten years longer he would doubtless have erected for himself, by his luminous exposition of intricate questions of law, a monument more durable than marble or bronze.

In all his private relations, as a citizen, a neighbor, a friend, a husband, a father, his character is without spot or blemish, and few men ever lived who were more generally esteemed and beloved, or who died more universally regretted.

He was best known in Augusta county as "General Baldwin," having taken out a company (The Staunton Infantry) in the war of 1812, and having subsequently held a commission as Brigadier of State Militia.

JOHN BROWN BALDWIN was the eldest son of the late Judge Briscoe G. Baldwin, and was born at Spring Farm, near Staunton, on the 11th day of January, 1820. After passing through a course of instruction at several primary schools, he entered the Staunton Academy, where he was prepared for college. At the age of sixteen he entered the University of Virginia, where he prosecuted his studies for three consecutive years.

When his collegiate course closed, he returned to Staunton and studied law for two years under his father, then a lawyer in full practice. At the age of twenty-one he began his professional career as the partner of Hon. A. H. H. Stuart. The partnership continued for nearly three years; he then commenced the practice on his own responsibility. At that time the Bar of Staunton was distinguished for ability and learning, and it required no small amount of talent and industry to insure success in the face of such formidable competition. But he was not dismayed by the difficulties which stood in his way. Conscious of his own powers, he determined to command success, and nobly did he accomplish his purpose.

On the 20th of September, 1842, he intermarried with Susan Madison

Peyton, eldest daughter of the eminent lawyer John Howe Peyton, Esq. It is not the purpose of the writer to intrude into the privacy of domestic life and relate what there occurred; but, having enjoyed the privilege of mingling freely in the scene, he cannot forbear saying that it was one of the utmost felicity. From the time the young couple went to housekeeping in a modest dwelling near the courthouse, until the life of the husband ended in an elegant mansion adorned with all that wealth and taste could provide, their home was a Vale of Tempe, disturbed by no rude wind, and familiar access to it was a source of equisite enjoyment to the guest. The cheerful greeting, the unaffected kindness, the high converse and sparkling wit, can never be forgotten by anyone who ever entered there.

As soon as he attained the age prescribed by the Constitution, he was elected by the people of Augusta a member of the House of Delegates. In the Legislature, although one of the youngest members, he distinguished himself as a debater, and gave ample assurance of future eminence. During the session the question of calling a convention to frame a new Constitution was agitated, and this brought up the issue whether representation in the convention should be upon the "mixed" or the "white basis"—that is, whether persons and property, or persons alone, should be taken into account in adjusting the basis of representation.

Colonel Baldwin took a decided and prominent stand in favor of the former, which was the basis of representation in the Legislature under the existing Constitution, and contended that any departure from it by the General Assembly would be unconstitutional and revolutionary. He firmly maintained his opinions, although he well knew they were unpopular among his constituents. This was his first display of that high moral courage and determination not to sacrifice right to expediency, which marked his whole future career.

Having, as he anticipated, been defeated for the Legislature at the next election, he turned his attention, with renewed energy, to his profession, and never afterwards exhibited a desire to return to public life. When he subsequently held representative trusts in the Convention of 1861, in the Confederate Congress and in the Legislature of 1865–'67, they were not sought by him, but were conferred by the unsolicited suffrages of the people, who had learned to appreciate his talents and moral worth. He acted for several years as Captain of the Staunton Light Infantry, a volunteer military company, and subsequently as Colonel of the 52d Regiment Confederate States army.

In 1859, having already acquired a reputation throughout the State as a leading lawyer, a vacancy occurring on the bench of the Court of Appeals by the death of Judge Samuels, without his agency he was brought before the people by his friends for the position. His successful competitor was Judge William J. Robertson, of Charlottesville, and it may be mentioned as a fact, creditable to both, that the rivalry on that occasion disturbed in no degree the life-long and warm friendship which subsisted between the two candidates.

While not seeking office, Colonel Baldwin was a man of very pronounced political opinions. He was decided in all his convictions, and earnest as well as able and eloquent in maintaining them. He therefore took an active part in the political contests of 1848, 1852, 1856 and 1860. When the question of secession began to agitate the public mind, in 1860, he came forth as one of the most ardent supporters of the Union, and commenced the canvass on the Bell and Everett side in a speech at the club-house in Richmond City. In the great contest of that year he supported, with burning zeal and matchless ability, the Union ticket. His clarion voice rang throughout the State, and he probably contributed more than any other man to turn the scale in Virginia in favor of conciliation and peace between the jarring sections.

Referring to his club-house speech, the Richmond *Whig* of the next day said:

"For over two hours and a half did the able and distinguished speaker hold that vast concourse of persons spellbound by the magic of faultless argument and overpowering eloquence. It was a masterly and extraordinary effort and places Colonel Baldwin in the front rank of the debaters, not only of Virginia, but the entire Union. It was an effort that would have done honor to any deliberative body on earth. Indeed, the delivery of such a speech in the Senate of the United States would have created a profound impression there, and produced a sensation throughout the country. It was a lofty, noble, magnificent effort—a grand and glorious display of high mental power. His unanswerable logic, his wit, his humor, his eloquence—who in all that vast audience but was instructed, elevated, delighted and carried away by his matchless reasoning and the irresistible force of his argument. We are sure that no speech has been delivered here for years which was listened to with more rapt attention and which produced a more powerful and lasting impression upon a Richmond audience. To attempt even a faint outline of Colonel Baldwin's speech on Friday evening would be simply folly on our part, and we therefore forbear."

The State Convention of 1861 being called, Colonel Baldwin was elected one of the three representatives of Augusta county. His earnest appeals there in behalf of the Union and his anxious efforts to avert the civil war are familiar facts. Every reader will recall the transcendent ability which he displayed in his memorable reply to the speeches of two distinguished gentlemen who were regarded as leaders of the secession party. By common consent that speech was pronounced the ablest and most eloquent that was delivered in the convention. The writer happens to know, but not from Colonel Baldwin himself, that years afterwards, while he was sojourning in a distant city, a gentleman, previously unknown to him, sought him out to thank him for the pleasure he had enjoyed in listening to that speech.

It has been stated that Colonel Baldwin finally voted for the ordinance of secession. This is a mistake. He voted against it, and resisted every appeal to change his vote, stating that his negative vote was the true record of his opinions. But after the ordinance had been ratified by the people he signed it as an act of representative duty. During the session of the convention he was delegated by a portion of the Union members as their commissioner to Washington. He proceeded to the city, and after an interview with President Lincoln returned to Richmond greatly disappointed and grieved. At one period of the session, when the fact burst upon him that secession and war were inevitable, he retired with a colleague from the hall to his chamber, and his sturdy frame was convulsed with an emotion which nothing could relieve but a flood of tears. Let it not be supposed that there was any unmanly weakness in this. As well upbraid the Hebrew prophet for weeping over the calamities of his people. It merely betrayed the suffering of a great soul, as with the vision of a "seer," he looked over the field of deadly strife and saw in the background the ruined homesteads and desolated firesides of his native land. The die was cast, however; the path of duty was plain to him; his position was taken, and thenceforth, with brave and cheerful front, he carried himself throughout the war. As he himself expressed it, he felt that it only remained for Virginia to show to the world how gallantly a people could meet the issue they had exhausted every honorable effort to avoid.

After the war began, Colonel Baldwin resigned his seat in the Convention and accepted the office of Inspector General of the Virginia forces, which was tendered to him by Governor Letcher. In that position he rendered signal service to the State. When the troops of Virginia had been organized and turned over to the Confederate States, he was appointed Colonel of the 52d Virginia Regiment of Infantry, raised at Staunton, and went with his command to West Virginia. He continued in active and arduous service at the Alleghany outposts until illness completely prostrated him, and before he had recovered was elected to the Confederate Congress from the Augusta district. The illness referred to was caused by a physical ailment from which he never recovered, which repeatedly subjected him to intense suffering, and finally terminated his life.

While a thorough organizer and disciplinarian, Colonel Baldwin carried into the field the same personal characteristics of courtesy and kindliness to those in subordinate relations which contributed so much to his popularity in civil life. The sturdy yeomen of West Augusta, whom he commanded, recognized in him, too, the high soldierly qualities of a worthy leader. His connection with the regiment was severed with mutual regret. Indeed, we hazard nothing in saying that no officer in the army was more universally admired and respected, alike by superiors and inferiors in rank.

As most of the sessions of the Confederate Congress were secret, the public had no opportunity of hearing or seeing reports of the speeches of its members; but we have the concurrent testimony of all who were present, that Colonel Baldwin was regarded as one of the ablest debaters in that body so distinguished for talent and statesmanship. His speech in opposition to the suspension of the writ of *habeas corpus* has often been described as one of the noblest defences of the principles of liberty ever pronounced in this country.

During the recesses of Congress, Colonel Baldwin acted as Colonel of a regiment of reserves raised in his county, and repeatedly led out his command to repel the enemy.

Upon the surrender of General Lee, when it was manifest that a further continuance of the contest would be fruitless of good, Colonel Baldwin was one of the first to counsel the acceptance of the situation and a restoration of peace to the country. He took an active part in the meeting held in Staunton on the 8th of May, 1865, which had for its objects the preservation of order and the reinstatement of the government. This, it is believed, was the first meeting of the kind ever held in the Southern States, but it was soon followed by similar meetings elsewhere.

In October, 1865, members of the General Assembly under the restored government were elected. Col. Baldwin was absent from home for some weeks and did not return until a few days before the election, but without having announced himself a candidate he was elected a member of the House of Delegates. At the convening of the Legislature in December he was elected Speaker of the House. Almost every page of the journal of that body bears the impress of his talent and patriotism. Nothing was too small and nothing too great to receive his careful consideration. On questions of internal improvement he exhibited wonderful sagacity. He was particularly interested in the Chesapeake and Ohio Railroad and aided materially to secure its completion. The extension of the road to the Ohio river may almost be said to be due to his efforts. As a parliamentarian he had few equals; and in the midst of other employments, he found time to digest the admirable system of rules by which the House of Delegates is still governed. Among the measures originated by him during the session of this Legislature was that establishing the Augusta County Fair. On the floor, as well as in the chair, he added every day to his reputation as a man of practical wisdom, of unsurpassed ability in debate and of unselfish patriotism. His popularity and influence were unrivalled, and there was no office in the gift of the Legislature which he might not have had. Towards the close of the last session he was prominently spoken of for the office of Governor, but as is generally remembered, through the intervention of the Federal Government, the anticipated election was not held.

The great Convention of the people of Virginia met in Richmond in December, 1867, to remonstrate against and organize for the defeat of the "Underwood Constitution," and Colonel Baldwin was one of the most influential members. It was then that he proposed the system of political organization, which, being adopted by the Convention, has been productive of the most beneficial results.

In 1868 a convention of the Conservative party of Virginia was held to nominate candidates for the various State offices filled by popular election. Colonel Baldwin was chosen President of the body, and was importuned to accept the nomination for the office of Governor. For reasons purely patriotic he declined the position; but, notwithstanding his positive refusal, upon counting the votes it was found that he lacked only three of receiving the nomination. Of his speech on this occasion, the Richmond *Enquirer* said: "The eloquent and able address of this gentleman, in declining to allow his name to be used as a candidate for the gubernatorial nomination of the Conservative convention last Friday, was the master speech of the occasion, we think. It is no compliment to Colonel Baldwin to hold him up to the admiration of the people of Virginia, for he has reached the zenith of their confidence and stands before them now almost without a peer, *sans peur et sans reproche;* but no one could hear the able speech in question without perceiving that he was giving another proof of the wisdom of his head and the patriotic love of his heart which have made him almost the idol of the people. Even while he spoke, the charming thought filled the minds of his hearers that such a speech was adding another leaf to the crown of laurels with which his Mother State will some day crown his brow, 'when the King shall claim his own again.'"

He was a member of the National Convention which nominated Seymour and Blair for the Presidency and Vice-Presidency of the United

States, and chairman of the Virginia delegation.

In December, 1868, the House of Representatives at Washington passed a bill requiring the President to cause the "Underwood Constitution" to be submitted as a whole to the people of Virginia, and it was apparent that unless some steps were taken to arrest it the bill would become a law, and thereby the Constitution, with its test-oaths and disfranchisements, be imposed upon our people. At this crisis a few gentlemen of Staunton, perceiving the imminence of the danger, agreed, on consultation, to invite a more general conference in Richmond. About fifty gentlemen accordingly met in that city on the 31st of December, and after due deliberation determined to make an effort to induce Congress to grant the people of Virginia the right to vote separately on the objectionable clauses, so as to eliminate them from the Constitution. A "Committee of Nine," of whom Colonel Baldwin was one, was appointed to go to Washington for the purpose indicated. The mission was successful, and thus the State escaped the threatened evils. In this service Colonel Baldwin displayed marked ability and contributed largely to the success of the scheme. For a time it was misunderstood or misrepresented and opposed by a large portion, if not a majority, of the people. The members of the committee were assailed by invective and ridicule, but they persevered in their effort, and at this day few or none will deny that the measure was one of consummate statesmanship. As remarked by a recent writer in regard to the matter: "A few gentlemen who preferred the welfare of the State to their own popularity organized a movement that saved their fellow-citizens almost in spite of themselves."

Such was the course of John B. Baldwin on all occasions. He never paused to inquire whether a measure were popular or otherwise; he only sought to know whether it was right. Time and again he confronted the popular sentiment, meeting his opponents singly or in crowds and plying them with argument, anecdote and witticism. He has almost literally been known to disperse a mob by a timely joke. He was in no degree a demagogue, yet no man was ever more beloved by all classes of the people, and he never lost his hold upon their affection.

The political services so frequently alluded to were mere episodes in Colonel Baldwin's life. His great efforts were directed to building up the material interests of his State and native county, for which he cherished a filial affection, and to pursue with fidelity his special calling. Distinction as a lawyer was regarded by him as more valuable than any other fame. He never was a grasping money-maker, on the contrary, he was too indifferent to the pecuniary emoluments of his profession.

It is common to speak of Colonel

Baldwin as a self-reliant man, and about most matters he was remarkably so; but there was a class of questions in regard to which he was habitually cautious and distrustful of himself. Wherever his feelings were implicated and action was required, he sought the counsel of friends. His self-confidence never made him supercilious. He never sought to intimidate or overshadow anyone, but the weakest associate or opponent was treated by him with respect, and no inferior in age or intellect came in contact with him without being inspired with a somewhat better opinion of himself. He possessed the art of making such persons feel comfortable in his presence. Hence he was a great favorite with children and servants, the simple and the lowly. He burdened no recipient of his kindness with a sense of gratitude.

For several years Colonel Baldwin was a member of the Board of Visitors of the University of Virginia, and he was ever one of the most devoted and active friends and supporters of that institution.

After an illness of several weeks, his active and useful life was terminated September 30th, 1873. Never before in this community have the sickness and death of anyone caused such interest and sorrow. During his illness our whole population awaited the result with the utmost solicitude; the report of each favorable change in his symptoms was eagerly circulated, and whenever the reverse appeared, sadness was expressed in every countenance; and when, at last, his death was announced, the lamentation was deep and universal. On the occasion of his funeral all business in the town was suspended, the bells of the various churches were tolled, and the whole people rose up to show honor and love to him who had been to each a wise counsellor and sympathizing friend.

[We are mainly indebted for this sketch to the Hon. Joseph A. Waddell.]

CHAPTER IV.

ROANOKE CITY, VIRGINIA.

By JAMES A. PUGH and CHARLES I. STEWART.

The writer who attempts to record the story of the wonderful rise and growth of Roanoke has an inspiring theme. The origin of the forces which have led to the events of the last ten years in this section, and the details of their work, cannot be compressed in the brief space of one chapter.

The history of Roanoke, strictly speaking, dates from February 3, 1882. It was on that date that, by an act of the Legislature of Virginia, the name of Big Lick was thrown aside, and the new town in the valley of the Roanoke river entered upon its new career with a new name.

Prior to this time, the traveler who endured the poor accommodation of the Atlantic, Mississippi and Ohio Railroad, would have seen nothing striking about the sleepy old village of Big Lick to give it a place in his memory, separate from the number of like villages that lined this then bankrupt road.

The Shenandoah Valley Railroad was the forerunner of the great development of the Valley and Southwest Virginia, and its history is inseparably linked with that of Roanoke. It was after a succession of struggles that this road was completed, and the era of progress began. The Shenandoah Valley Railroad Company was chartered February 23d, 1867; the work of construction was begun in 1870. When the great depression of 1873 stopped improvements in every section of the country, the work on the Shenandoah Valley road ceased, but the project was not entirely abandoned. The resources of the region now traversed by it were not forever to be shut off from the outside world, and their development prevented.

In 1878 the line was surveyed from Shepherdstown to Waynesboro, and the work of construction began. On December 15th, 1879, the first construction train ran to the Shenandoah river, a distance of forty-two miles; then track-laying was stopped to build a bridge across that river. The charter was secured for the Maryland division April 4th, 1870, and the line was completed from Shepherdstown to Hagerstown in August, 1880, work having been begun the preceding February. Work was begun at Waynesboro in May, 1880, and rapidly pushed North, until the road coming South was met. The completed road was accepted in March, 1881, and the first schedule train from Hagerstown to Waynesboro, a distance of 144 miles, was run April 18th, 1881. The line had been projected and completed thus far by Philadelphia capital.

What is now the Norfolk and Western road was then the Atlantic, Mississippi and Ohio. Bad management and the depression of the interests of this section had brought the road to bankruptcy. It was advertised for sale, and E. W. Clark, of Philadelphia, who was largely interested in the Shenandoah Valley road went to New York in January, 1881, and saw the advertisement of the sale. He immediately reached the conclusion that the road would make a desirable branch for the new road. At the sale, February 10th, 1881, the road was purchased by Mr. Clark, and immediately re-organized into the Norfolk and Western, Philadelphia and foreign capitalists becoming the members of the new syndicate. It was immediately decided to complete the Shenandoah Valley road from Waynesboro to Big Lick, and work was commenced in June, 1881. The first train ran to Big Lick on June 19th, 1882. With the re-organization of the Norfolk and Western, and the projection of the Southern division of the Shenandoah Valley road, began the activity that has converted the little village of Big Lick with 400 people to the growing city of Roanoke with a population of 25,000.

While it is to succeeding events that the historian of Roanoke must devote most of his attention, yet the early history of Big Lick is not without interest. The land upon which the city is built was originally granted to Thomas Tosh, one of the early settlers of Botetourt county when it included what is now known as Roanoke county. Maps and charts of the original grants are now in possession of the descendants of Mr. Tosh, who are still among the citizens of Roanoke City and Roanoke county.

Upon the completion of the Atlantic, Mississippi and Ohio Road, a few settlers' houses were scattered about the site of Big Lick, and on February 28th, 1874, the little village was incorporated as the town of Big Lick, with John Trout, the father of Hon. H. S. Trout, one of Roanoke's most prominent men, as Mayor. The little town was dependent for its support entirely upon the rich surrounding agricultural region. While this section possesses every resource and every advantage that the agriculturist could desire, yet the little town grew slowly, until the forces of which we have already briefly spoken began their work.

When this brighter day dawned upon this place of destiny there was nothing inviting about the appearance of the easy-going old town. Off from the railroad to the north upon the rolling hills were a few rude buildings. A few wealthy farmers of this section had their residences in and near the town, but there were no stately mansions of surpassing elegance. The streets were of the most primitive character, and the business buildings were constructed for actual necessity rather than for convenience or handsome appearance. While the surrounding scenery is attractive, the immediate site of the city, or what was to be the city, was decidedly uninviting. In fact, what is now the business portion of Roanoke was a marshy swamp, and it is said that one early investor decided not to purchase what is now part of the most valuable business property because of the constant croaking of the frogs in the swamp.

Two streams intersect on Campbell street and these are lined with numerous springs. That portion of the city from the Ponce de Leon Hotel to Woodland Park, embracing the business section, has been thoroughly drained from necessity, and Salem Avenue, the leading business street, has been filled up several feet.

Not long before the completion of the Shenandoah Valley Railroad, Philadelphia capitalists who were interested in this and the Norfolk and Western, with a few of the substantial citizens of Big Lick, organized the Roanoke Land and Improvement Company. This company secured a large part of the site of the present city, and at once began preparations for building the town. That this company did not anticipate the wonderful growth that has marked the history of Roanoke, is evident from the lack of symmetry and system with which the streets were originally laid out. This is the only explanation that Roanoke can make for her present winding and clumsy thoroughfares.

Among the early improvements of the company, additional to the construction of the streets, was the erection of the gas and water-works.

The year 1882 was the initial and eventful year in the history of Roanoke. Besides the naming of the town and the organization of the original land company, the Norfolk and Western road, having practically united with the Shenandoah road, moved its headquarters to this place. The erection of the Roanoke Machine Works, with a capital of $5,000,000, was also commenced. This is one of the largest car and locomotive plants in the South, employing, when working at its full capacity, 1,750 men. It was the first great industry established, and with its completion Roanoke was already a city. Hundreds of mechanics and laborers immediately followed, giving occupation to artisans of the different trades for the construction of homes for the operators. Following these came the merchant and supplier, every new inhabitant becoming imbued with the spirit of progress that pervaded the atmosphere, and uniting with the early citizens in the upbuilding of the growing town.

The young town was early provided with the facilities for conducting the different lines of business.

Big Lick's only banking institution was the old Bank of Virginia, but this was soon liquidated. In 1882, just as the new town was springing into existence, the First National Bank of Roanoke was organized with a capital of $50,000, which was shortly afterwards increased to $100,000. The officers were Hon. H. S. Trout, President; P. L. Terry, Vice-President, and J. W. Shields, Cashier. Messrs. Trout and Terry, original citizens of Big Lick, with a few Philadelphia capitalists who were interested in the beginning of the development of this section, were the first and principal stockholders. These same officers have since controlled the affairs of the bank and made it one of the strongest financial institutions in Virginia.

Closely following this was the organization of the Roanoke Loan, Trust and Safe Deposit Company, in 1883. This institution for conducting a trust and general banking business, was the first institution of its kind in Virginia. It was organized with a capital of $40,000, which has been increased to $250,000. Mr. P. L. Terry has presided over its affairs as President, and has been ably assisted by Mr. S. W. Jamison as Secretary and Treasurer.

Mr. Terry and Mr. Trout, who were the wealthiest and most prominent of the citizens of Big Lick, have been the local leaders in the movement that has built the new city, being prominently connected with every interest and every enterprise that has been inaugurated.

The Commercial National Bank was organized May 9th, 1889, with a capital of $100,000. Mr. J. W. Coon, a wealthy citizen of Roanoke county, has managed its affairs as President, and Mr. J. C. Davenport, for a long time connected with the First National Bank, is its Cashier. This bank is a safe institution, its stockholders being composed of many of the most active and successful business men of the city, who have made their fortunes in Roanoke.

The National Exchange Bank was organized, with a capital of $100,000, May 7th, 1889. Mr. T. T. Fishburne, another of the original citizens of Big Lick, is its President. This bank boasts of the youngest cashier of any bank in the State, in the person of Mr. J. B. Fishburne, who is only 23 years of age. Mr. J. T. Engleby is the Vice-President, and the stockholders and directors embrace many of the city's substantial citizens.

The Citizens Bank was organized May 20th, 1889, under the State laws, with a capital of $40,000, with Mr. J. B. Levy, President. The bank was re-organized early this year into a national bank, with a capital of $100,000. Mr. Levy is still its President, and Mr. H. M. Dickenson, Cashier. Mr. N. Partee, one of the leading builders of the city, is its Vice-President and is closely identified with its management.

The Traders Loan, Trust and Deposit Company commenced business March 1st, 1890, with a capital of $50,000. Mr. A. S. Asberry is President; Mr. J. W. Coon, of the Commercial National Bank, Vice-President, and Mr. E. E. Cole, Secretary and Treasurer. The capital stock is held by a number of young business men of Roanoke, and several outside capitalists are also interested.

The Fidelity Loan and Trust Company is one of the strongest of the younger financial concerns. It began business June 1st, 1890, with a capital of $200,000. Mr. J. T. Engleby, who was among the first new-comers to Roanoke, is its President. Mr. Engleby has made his fortune in Roanoke, and is regarded by all as a safe and conservative business man.

The Roanoke Savings Bank was organized in September, 1890, with a capital of $100,000. Mr. J. D. Smith, a wealthy capitalist, is the principal stockholder and President.

The State Savings Bank is under the management of Mr. Barnes, and was organized at the same time.

Mr. S. D. Ferguson, a young man who has been successful in Roanoke, does an extensive private banking business.

Along with the early growth came all of those institutions that were necessary for the advancement of the business interests and for the convenience and accommodation of the public.

The first first-class hostelry to be constructed was the Hotel Roanoke. This work was undertaken by the Roanoke Land and Improvement Company, and afterwards transferred to the Virginia company. A large tract of land in the centre of the proposed city, lying along the railroad near the Union Depot, was purchased. The first structure was a wooden building that was a credit to the town at that time. From time to time improvements have been made, the grounds have been beautified by a first-class landscape gardener, and a substantial stone wall constructed around the entire grounds.

A magnificent brick and stone structure has taken the place of the old wooden building. The Hotel Roanoke is acknowledged by the traveling public to be one of the most elegant and beautiful hotels in the entire South, and is by many ranked second only to the Hotel Ponce de Leon of Jacksonville, Florida.

Roanoke is well supplied with hostelries. The Ponce de Leon is an elegant six-story brick structure recently opened to the public. The Hotel Felix, the Hotel Continental and Marshall's European Hotel are among the other leading houses of entertainment.

The Ponce de Leon, under the management of Mr. C. G. Smith, is second to Hotel Roanoke only in the lack of the extensive and beautiful grounds that surround that hostelry.

Roanoke was incorporated as a city in 1884. The Hustings Court was inaugurated, with Judge Wm. Gordon Robertson presiding. The different branches of the government of the new city were materially strengthened, and Roanoke entered upon an era of renewed activity. Other industries followed. The Crozer Iron Company, with its twin furnaces, was soon completed. The conservative management of those interested in the enterprises of Roanoke, and the successful effort of the Roanoke Machine Works in securing a large contract for the construction of the rolling stock for a Northern road, helped to tide over the depression of this year. While there were not those strides forward of the two previous years, yet the young city not only held her own, but made some substantial progress. Elegant residences, neat cottages for the mechanic, and substantial business blocks continued to rise up rapidly.

From 1885 to 1890 the record of Roanoke has been one of unbroken progress, steady and rapid, and, in this respect, unparalleled.

Among the industries that have been established during this time are the Rolling Mill, American Bridge Works, Bridgewater Carriage Works, E. H. Stewart's Mattress Factory, the plant of the Roanoke Iron Company; in the West end the Virginia Brewery, two ice-factories, five manufactories of sash, doors and blinds and other building material, two large brick plants, a cold storage plant, a paper-bag factory, an electric light plant, two large planing-mills and other smaller industries.

As already intimated, it is impossible to enter into the details of the growth of this city, but the year 1890 stands out so prominent in the history of Roanoke that it demands special attention. This, of all others, was the great boom year, not only of Roanoke, but of the entire Valley and South-west. It was the golden era of the speculator, and embraces the dates of many of the greatest achievements for the future of Roanoke.

It is usually by the extent of the real estate transactions that booming towns measure their growth. Roanoke disclaims the name of a boom town, and if there are any who persist in calling it by this name, measured by the standard of boomers it will head the list of the boom towns of the country.

The real estate transactions of the year 1890 amounted to $17,000,000 in round numbers, but this is not the only nor the most important period of Roanoke's growth.

One of the principal factors in bringing about the success of these ten years has been the co-operative land companies, and more of these companies were organized in 1890 than in any two previous years of its existence. The entire number of companies organized and chartered during the year 1890 was one hundred and thirty-two, and their aggregate capital is $10,246,300. The objects and purposes of these companies are of sufficient importance to demand more than a passing notice. The majority, and most important of them, have not merely the selfish motives of buying real estate at a low price and selling it at a high one. Of course they are business enterprises, conducted by business men who expect them to pay, but they co-operate for the upbuilding and material good of the city; they construct streets, erect houses provided with all modern improvements, and secure industries that increase the population and business of the city. Many of these companies are organized with at least half of their capital stock set apart for the sole purpose of inducing industries to locate in Roanoke. The Roanoke Development Company is one of the most notable examples, and its organization was one of the great achievments of the year 1890. The capital stock of this company is $1,100,000, held largely by Roanoke capitalists, and outside capitalists who are largely interested in the various enterprises of this city. It has a fund of $600,000 for subscriptions to stock of new enterprises which may be induced to locate, and besides has provided itself with an extensive tract of 1,300 acres lying two miles along Roanoke river, for the purpose of donating sites for desirable industries. This company, though organized in November, 1890, has already demonstrated its value as a factor in the growth and upbuilding of the city. It has secured four industries which will employ about 1,000 operatives, two of these will soon be in operation. It has constructed streets and built three bridges across the Roanoke river, connecting its property with the city.

Among the other events of 1890, was the settlement of Roanoke as the northern terminus of the Roanoke and Southern Railway.

Not long after Roanoke began to reap the benefits of the Shenandoah road, sagacious men, looking over the fertile region between the Roanoke river and the Cape Fear and Yadkin Valley and North-western North Carolina Railroads, realized that a natural railroad route connected the most fertile region of Virginia with the most fertile section of North Carolina, and immediately the movement was set on foot to construct a road from Roanoke to Winston. A company was organized, and after much talk and considerable delay, work on the road was commenced. At Walnut Cove, fourteen miles from Winston, it connected with the Cape Fear and Yadkin Valley, and the first train was put on in June, 1889. The work has slowly progressed, until trains are now run from Winston to Martinsville, a distance of sixty miles, and some of the track has been laid and most of the grading done between Roanoke and Martinsville, a distance of fifty-one miles.

At one time, during the most active real estate speculation in 1890, there was a doubt raised as to whether Roanoke would be the terminus of the road. The price asked for the right-of-way through the city was more than the railroad company was willing to pay. Another obstacle was the favorable inducements offered by Salem. For a time Roanoke was doubtful of securing the prize, but that energy and that enterprise which have been so powerful an influence in every emergency Roanoke has encountered were sufficient for this occasion.

The Roanoke Guarantee and Development Company was organized, and at the annual meeting of the stockholders of the Roanoke and Southern Railway Company held in Roanoke on September 8th, 1890, the Guarantee and Development Company entered into a contract with the railroad company to furnish the right-of-way for a stipulated amount and the road was secured. Soon afterwards the entire line was put under contract, and in a few months Roanoke will have an independent Southern outlet.

Roanoke has been affected by the financial depression that has prevailed since the fall of 1890, as have most other localities. During the previous months the most active, and in some cases reckless, speculation prevailed, and it is remarkable that Roanoke has stood the stringency so well.

Every citizen invested in real estate and the stock of many of the companies that were organized and the various enterprises all that their circumstances would allow, and in many instances men usually considered conservative, by reason of their great confidence in Roanoke, overloaded themselves. Their confidence is entirely justifiable, but the possibility and probability of the events of the financial whirl were not taken into consideration. One who was not a witness to the scenes of that period in Roanoke cannot fully appreciate the situation. Men frequently made neat little fortunes in a few months. Roanoke real estate and the general speculative movement throughout this section was almost the only topic of conversation. Men, and women, too, were excited to such a pitch that they seemed to think of little else, and the stranger who spent a few days here soon found himself in the swim with everybody else.

With the financial stringency and closeness of money in the great money centres of the world following this era of speculation, certainly the most serious results were to be feared, and seemed almost inevitable. Roanoke has weathered the storm for nearly a year, and not a single disastrous failure has resulted. It is true that there has not been the numerous and continual transfers of real estate among the citizens of Roanoke, nor has the amount of capital found investment here since the beginning of the depression as previously, notwithstanding this Roanoke has more than held her own, and made some long strides forward. The year 1891 will result in scarcely less for the real advancement of the city's interest than the previous eventful year of 1890.

An appropriation of $75,000 was secured early in January for the erection of a public building. The freeholders of the city voted $425,000 in bonds for public improvements, including a complete system of sewerage, street improvement, and various public buildings. Hundreds of houses, including many of the best business houses in the city and some of the handsomest residences, have been built this year. The Terry building, now in the course of construction, is one of the most notable. This building will cost $125,000, and be the handsomest office building in Virginia. More industries have been secured this year than in any other one in the history of the city. The buildings for the plants of the Norwich Lock Manufacturing Company, for the manufacture of every description of shelf hardware, are nearing completion. This industry will start at an early day with 300 operatives. The buildings for the Duval Engine Works, which will employ 150 skilled mechanics, are also nearing completion.

The other industries secured, the work on which will soon begin, are the Virginia Blanket Mills, the Monitor Steam Generator Factory, and the enlarged Bridgewater Carriage works. The extensive plants of the Roanoke Iron Company are also nearing completion. The 150-ton blast furnace was in blast last year. The buildings for the bar and plate are completed, and some of the machinery already in place.

The reader has been given a fair idea of Big Lick before enterprise and industry began to develop the wonderful resources of this section. The history of Roanoke has been briefly sketched, but the details of this history still cannot be related, but can be conveyed, in a large measure, by an accurate statement of what Roanoke is to-day.

It is a city of 25,000 people, nestling between the Blue Ridge and Alleghany mountains, at the gateway of the far-famed Valley of Virginia, and in close proximity to the Flat Top coal region and the inexhaustible stores of iron that fill the mountains that surround it.

While it is known as the "Magic City," one who has not been identified with its achievements would, after comparing the city of to-day with Big Lick of ten years ago, believe that it has been touched by a magic wand. There is also a tinge of romance in its name. "Raw-re-noke" is the Indian word for fortune-money, and Roanoke, a more euphonius contraction of this word, is an appropriate name for the city which has filled the purses of many energetic and deserving men.

It is situated at an elevation of 907 feet above the ocean. It is free from the heat of the far South, and is shielded from the winds of the Northern winter by the surrounding mountains. The climate is mild, salubrious and healthful. While it is already indicated that the business part of the city is low, the resident sections are elevated and the high hills command many magnificent views.

No city in the world has a more magnificent water-supply than Roanoke. A lost river finds its way to the light of day, bursting forth in a pure, cold stream at the foot of Mill Mountain, two miles distant. This great spring is the wonder and admiration of every visitor to Roanoke. The water is a mild limestone, and is regarded as a specific for many forms of kidney disease. The supply is sufficient for many cities of Roanoke's population, and the water-works that convey the water to the city were constructed with capacity to supply a population of 50,000.

It is the centre of the Norfolk and Western Railroad system, being the terminus of the Shenandoah Valley, now known as the Washington and Maryland Division of the Norfolk and Western, midway between the termini of the main line, and in close connection with the various branches. It is 150 miles from Bristol, 257 miles from Norfolk, 241 miles from Hagerstown, 296 miles from Washington, 446 miles from New York, and 199 miles from Richmond.

The development of the iron and coal interests adjacent to the city have made iron manufacture the chief industry. It is to the manufacturing interests that Roanoke owes its existence, and it is to extend these interests that the citizens who are working for its continued progress are still devoting their energies.

The industries now in operation employ, in round numbers, 3,000 people, and those in the course of construction will add 1,000 to this number. The annual amount paid to employees of the manufacturing establishments is $5,000,000. With so large an amount of money in constant circulation, Roanoke has been an inviting field for the merchant, and it boasts of many handsome stores in the different lines of trade, and is fast becoming the trading-point of a large section of surrounding country. Its wholesale interests have rapidly increased within the past few years, and with the completion of the Roanoke and Southern Railroad it will offer inducements for wholesale trade second to no place in Virginia. There are already five large wholesale grocery establishments, besides several wholesale houses in other lines.

Roanoke is surrounded by the finest agricultural region in Virginia. The soil is fertile and produces a great variety of farm products. It is especially adapted to the growth of truck, all kinds of vegetables and the cereals. Roanoke county produces more wheat and a higher average yield per acre than any other county in the State, and Roanoke is rapidly growing in importance as a wheat market. Two large roller flouring mills are constantly in operation, turning out 250 barrels of flour per day. A great variety of fruits also thrive in this immediate section, and the canning interest is one of no small importance. Thousands of bushels of apples are shipped annually from this county to Northern markets.

While Roanoke has grown so rapidly that it is impossible for public improvements to keep pace with its rapid growth, it will not be behind in this respect much longer.

The court-house is an elegant two-story brick structure with neat and comfortable offices for the city officials. The jail is to be enlarged at an early date. The fire department is well organized and efficient. The electric fire-alarm has recently been put in place, and modern apparatus provided for the department. One elegant building for the firemen has been erected at a cost of $6,000, and another to cost $10,000 is in course of construction. A public school system was inaugurated soon after Roanoke was incorporated as a town, and while it has been impossible for the necessary school facilities to be provided for the rapidly increasing population, yet the schools are growing in efficiency and extent of accommodations. The city has erected two handsome buildings for white schools and one for colored; two buildings have been rented, and there are now in the city five public schools, one for colored children and four for white, with five colored teachers and twenty-three white teachers. A public high school has also been established recently. The freeholders of the city recently voted $75,000 of bonds for the erection of school buildings, and the improvement of school facilities. This will be expended within a short time.

Among the private schools, the most important are Alleghany Institute for boys and Mrs. Gilmer's school for girls.

Roanoke is a city of church-going people. With the general upbuilding of the business interests that has followed since 1882, the churches have not been neglected. There are now four new organizations of the Southern Methodist church; two of the the Presbyterian church; two of the Missionary Baptist church; two of the Evangelical Lutheran church; two of the Protestant Episcopal church; one of the Christian denomination; one of the Methodist Episcopal church; one of the Roman Catholic church; one of the United Brethren; five colored churches.

The Lutherans are erecting a $60,000 house of worship; the Baptists are building a $25,000 edifice; the Episcopalians are erecting a $40,000 church; the Presbyterians are building a $10,000 church; the Methodists will soon begin the erection of two churches, one to cost $12,000 and one to cost $50,000; the Catholics will, at an early date, build one of the handsomest houses of worship in the city, and also an orphanage.

A fair idea of the growth of Roanoke can be given by a few simple figures. In 1885 the real estate of the city was assessed for taxation at $1,481,632.25; in 1890 it was $6,750,884.

It is not out of place to remark right here, that under the laws of Virginia, real estate is assessed for taxation only once in every five years, therefore the treasury of the city of Roanoke derived no benefit from the great increase in real estate values until after the assessment of 1890, the only yearly increase being the taxable value of the improvements placed upon the property. This, in a measure, accounts for the lack of some of the needed public improvements.

A comparative statement, based on the actual prices at which real estate sold, compared with the assessed value on the tax-books, shows the value of real estate in Roanoke at which it changed hands by the million in 1890, and the prices that are still maintained, to be more than $20,000,000.

The value of personal property, according to assessment, is $1,715,642.

The capital in business on which license is paid is $1,600,000. The amount of deposits in banking institutions is, in round numbers, $2,000,000. The banking capital of the city is more than a million and a quarter dollars.

The capital invested in manufacturing enterprises is $8,125,000. The capital invested in land and improvement companies is, in round numbers, $11,000,000.

Roanoke has eight building and loan associations with a subscribed capital, in round numbers, of $3,000,000.

The business of the banks in 1890 amounted, in round numbers, to $5,000,000.

The population is now composed of people from every State in the Union, and from almost every civilized country in the world, making a unique and cosmopolitan community. Every man in Roanoke has something to do, and usually attends to his own business, and as everybody is comparatively a stranger to everybody else, there is a lack of the meddling into the affairs of others that is sometimes seen in small towns of a more permanent population. The enterprising Yankees who have settled in this Virginia town have lost none of their energy and thrift, and those who have gathered here from all of the more southern climates have caught up the spirit of progress and enterprise.

Roanoke has been well supplied with creditable newspapers from the first of its history. The *Big Lick News*, upon the change of the name of the town, was made the *Saturday's Review*, and the *Roanoke Leader*, with Col. S. S. Brooke, the present Clerk of the Hustings Court, as editor, was the first paper established in the new city. The *Review* finally suspended, and the *Leader* was absorbed by the *Roanoke Times*, which was started by Mr. M. Claytor in the fall of 1886. The *Times* was the first daily paper established here. Mr. Claytor conducted the paper until December 23, 1888, when it was purchased by Messrs. Freedman and Copeland, of Danville, and Mr. A. B. Hammond, the owner of the *Evening Telegram*, an afternoon paper established a few months previously, and was called the *Times-Telegram*, but in a short time the compound name was abandoned. Messrs. C. T. Grandy and J. T. Hall purchased the paper on the 6th of March, 1890, and in August of the same year the Roanoke Times Publishing Company was organized, with Mr. C. T. Grandy as General Manager, and Mr. P. L. Terry, President. The new company immediately took steps to enlarge the new paper. A new outfit complete was purchased, and the Cast Printing Press put in place, and the staff of the paper was re-organized, with Mr. H. J. Browne, late of the *Washington Post*, as editor. The paper was enlarged to an eight-page paper, with an Associated Press service.

In the meantime, the *Roanoke Daily Herald* was established, the first number appearing in January, 1889, James A. Pugh as editor. He is now on the staff of the *Times*.

The *Evening World* was established in January, 1890, the proprietors being Messrs. Dooley, Nicholson and Ackerly.

In May, 1891, Mr. H. J. Browne became the general manager of the *Times*, and Mr. H. D. Lafferty and Mr. D. H. Matson, who were orginally identified with the coal mining interests of this section, as principal proprietors. Mr. Lafferty is the president of the company, and Mr. Matson is the secretary. The *Times* is regarded as the leading newspaper of South-west Virginia.

The consolidation of Vinton, which is two miles east of Roanoke, and Salem, which is six miles west, with this city, was suggested recently by the Roanoke *Times*, and met with favorable response in all three places. These towns now have a combined population of more than 30,000, and are closely connected with each other by the Norfolk and Western Railroad and a system of dummy lines. The entire vacant property between the towns is owned by syndicates, with capital for improving and inducing the location of industries. When consolidated, as it is believed they ultimately will be, our magnificent city will stretch more than ten miles along the lovely valley of the Roanoke river.

The Roanoke Development Company, with its many extensive industries soon to be in operation, will considerably narrow the gap between Roanoke and Salem, and further still is to be the mammoth factory of the Monitor Steam Generator Company, and other industries to be located on the property by the Columbia Land Company. Within a short time an electric road extending through the property of these two companies will more closely unite the two growing cities. Many projected improvements are assured as realities at an early date. The Norfolk and Western Railroad has already begun work on a belt line to extend around the southern boundary of the city and through the new manufacturing section. Plans have been made by the Norfolk and Western engineers and architects for the $100,000 passenger depot soon to be erected. The Gas and Water Company will build a handsome summer hotel with a number of villas on Mill Mountain by the opening of the summer season. The horse-car line will soon be extended and electricity used for motive power.

There is scarcely a doubt that either the Baltimore and Ohio or Chesapeake and Ohio Railroads will seek an entrance to this industrial centre at an early day, and when that day arrives an open-handed and substantial welcome will be extended either; not that Roanoke does not appreciate what the Norfolk and Western has done for her, but that she realizes that she is of sufficient importance in the commercial world to command more railroad facilities. Both the roads mentioned have been looking this way with longing eyes for sometime. The Roanoke and Fincastle road is now in course of construction, most of the grading having been completed between Cloverdale and Fincastle, a distance of eight miles. Cloverdale is about midway between Roanoke and Fincastle. The Roanoke is being built ostensibly by local capital, but it is asserted by those who are in position to know some of the inside facts that the Chesapeake and Ohio is backing the enterprise. With the projected road completed, a connecting link of six miles from Springwood to Fincastle would bring the Chesapeake and Ohio into Roanoke. Whether the Chesapeake and Ohio is interested in the new road or not, it is very evident that it will be very easily controlled when completed.

When the Baltimore and Ohio gets ready to come to Roanoke only forty miles of road will have to be built, from Lexington to this city, more than half of which has already been graded. While there has been no definite deal between the Roanoke and Southern and the Baltimore and Ohio, there are many reasons for believing that it is by means of the Roanoke and Southern that the Baltimore and Ohio hopes ultimately to reach into the South. The facts that

Baltimore capitalists are large stockholders in the Roanoke and Southern, and Baltimore money is now building the road, and recent rumors that the Roanoke and Southern was about to be sold, and the acknowledgment of an official of the road that the Baltimore and Ohio was one of the corporations after the line, are not without significance.

That Roanoke has a great future is acknowledged by everyone who is acquainted with its advantages and its surroundings. Nothing is needed to convince the most doubtful but a trip to Roanoke and a close examination of its institutions and conditions.

Recently the Juniata Valley Press Association of Pennsylvania were the guests of a number of the towns in this section, and part of their time in this State was spent in Roanoke. One of the most prominent of this body, after a most careful study of the situation here, says that Roanoke is destined to be a great city, that it has the material, that it has all the advantages of location, and that it has the people.

While the most sanguine of the early promoters did not hope for such success as has crowned their efforts, yet they now look forward to still greater things than have been revealed by the past.

The resources of this region are so extensive and the prosperity of this city so great, that it has required ten years of constant contact with its development to convince the most hopeful of the early promoters that what has already been achieved is only the beginning of a brighter and still more wonderful career.

Even with the industries that are already established in Roanoke, the population will easily reach 35,000 within a very short time.

From the beginning of the development of this section ten years ago, Roanoke has been the centre of the operations and the favorite of the capitalists who are interested in various enterprises throughout Southwest Virginia and the Valley, and as this development continues the growth of Roanoke is inevitable. Millions of American capital, and many of the wealthiest men of three countries of Europe, are interested in the progress of Roanoke and the success of its every enterprise. Everything that can be done by money, energy and enterprise will be done for the continued growth of this city, and it requires no lengthy argument, aside from the plain statement of the case, to convince the outside man that Roanoke is destined to be one of the greatest industrial and commercial centres of the entire South.

HON. P. L. TERRY.—The President of the Roanoke Land Trust Company is Hon. P. L. Terry, who was born February 2d, 1839, in Campbell county, Virginia, and is a son of Stephen and Lucinda Terry. The

Terrys are among the early and distinguished families of Virginia. Hon. P. L. Terry was educated in Appomattox county, and at the age of thirteen years came to the village of Big Lick and engaged as clerk in a general merchandise store, in which position he remained for about four years, when he went West and located in Texas, where he staid until 1857, when he returned to Roanoke and entered the mercantile business, which occupation he followed until 1861, when he enlisted in Company I, 28th Virginia Regiment, and served during the entire term of the war. His regiment was with Picket's famous brigade, and was in the battle of Gettysburg and all the hard-fought battles of this renowned brigade and regiment. He, however, escaped without a wound, but had the misfortune to be captured with his entire regiment three days before General Lee's surrender. He was held a short time as a prisoner, was paroled and returned home. In the spring of 1866 he again engaged in the wholesale merchandise business at Roanoke, and continued to do an extensive trade until in 1881, when he closed out his stock and in a measure devoted himself to farming, which, during all these years, he had carried on quite extensively, being owner of a valuable farm near the city of Roanoke. In 1882 he organized the Roanoke Loan, Trust and Safe Deposit Company, and was made President of the company, which honorable position he still holds. He is also President of the Home Building and Conveyance Company; Vice-President of the Southern Roanoke Land Company; Vice-President of the Iron Belt Building Association. He was one of the organizers of the Roanoke Gas Company, and served as President of the same until in 1888, at which time the Gas and Water Companies were consolidated, and of which he became a director. In 1857 he married Miss Mary S. Trout, of Roanoke, and four children have been born to them. Mr. Terry is a member of the Lutheran church and President of the Board of Vestrymen. He is active in all church work, and brings to bear upon it a vigorous and capable understanding, to which both church and Sunday-school are indebted for much of their advancement and prosperity.

JAMES S. SIMMONS, Esq., who has long held the front rank among the real estate magnates of the Magic City—Roanoke—is one of the many good men that "My Maryland" has sent to Virginia since as well as during the war, having been born in Frederick county, Maryland, in 1861. After completing his education he entered the employ of the Shenandoah Valley Railroad Company at Hagerstown, and came through on the first train that ever ran over the road to Roanoke, where he located, still in the service of the company.

A year later the real estate firm of J. S. Simmons & Co. sprang into existence, and the history of the enterprises in which it has participated would form a large portion of the history of the city, as a list of the various undertakings would abundantly testify. For instance, he is President of the Central Park Company, North Roanoke Land and Improvement Company, Roanoke Guarantee and Development Company, and is Vice-President of a large number of other companies, and is a thorough cosmopolitan in enterprises. This brief biography does not permit the paying of this gentleman the tribute justly due him for the patriotic and public-spirited course which has endeared him to all the people of the city and so closely identified him with its prosperity.

DR. JOSEPH ADDINGTON GALE was born in Norfolk, Virginia, December 3rd, 1842. His father, Enoch R., was a native of North Carolina, while his mother, J. Louisa (Dryden), was born in the Old Dominion.

Dr. Gale had just finished his academic course when the war between the States began, and he at once entered Col. Frank Huger's Company of Artillery. In 1862 he was appointed Hospital Steward and assigned to duty at Chimborazo Hospital in Richmond, where he remained in charge of the dispensary until the close of the war.

While in Richmond during the war, Dr. Gale had, with the permission of the Surgeon General of the Confederate States army, attended the lectures at the Richmond Medical College, and in the fall of 1865 he matriculated at the Bellevue Hospital Medical College, New York, graduating the following spring. He located at Cave Spring, Virginia, six miles south of what is now Roanoke City, June 14th, 1867, where he remained until August 14th, 1882, when he removed to Roanoke (then a little village known as Big Lick), where he is still actively engaged in the duties of his profession.

In 1870 Dr. Gale married Patty Burwell, daughter of Robert Harvey, Esq., of Roanoke county. She died the following spring. In 1875 he married Eliza, daughter of Capt. S. F. Simmons, of Salem, Virginia, and has two children, Sparrell S. and Lottie D.

Dr. Gale is a member of Trinity Methodist Episcopal Church, South.

Hon. HENRY S. TROUT.—Among the prominent bankers and citizens of Roanoke may be mentioned Hon. Henry S. Trout, President of the First National Bank. He was born October 15th, 1841, in Roanoke county, Virginia.

Henry S. Trout, to whom this sketch is devoted, was educated at Roanoke College, and at the age of nineteen entered the Confederate service as a private in the 28th Virginia Regiment, Picket's Brigade. He was made First Lieutenant, and served in this capacity until the close of the war. He was in all the hard-fought battles of this renowned brigade. At the battle of Gettysburg he was with his company, consisting of thirty-six men, and the little but valiant company, in what is known as Picket's last charge, lost twenty-four of the thirty-six men, being killed or wounded. Lieutenant Trout was twice wounded in his army service—in 1863 at the battle of Seven Pines, and in 1864 at the battle of South Mountain. After the war he returned to Big Lick and engaged in farming, the city of Roanoke now occupying a large portion of his farm. In 1882 he was sent to the Legislature, where he served seven years—three years in the House and four years in the Senate. Perhaps no one has done more to promote the interests of Roanoke than Mr. Trout. He was one of the pioneers and owned large tracts of land, which he laid off in town lots and sold at reasonable prices, and took especial interest in aiding every industry and enterprise which tended to build up the town or develop the resources of this section of the State. In 1882 he organized the First National Bank of Roanoke, and was elected President, which office he still holds. He is also President of the Roanoke Southern Railroad; Vice-President of the Roanoke Trust Company; Vice-President of the Roanoke Land and Improvement Company; Vice-President of the Crystal Springs Land Company, which has a capital of $400,000; member of Roanoke City Council; director of the Roanoke Gas and Water Company; director of the Pocahontas Coal Company; director of the Virginia Development Company, which represents a capital of $5,000,000, besides being stockholder and officially connected with numerous other industries of Roanoke. He is a man of courage and recognized ability, is liberal, kind and considerate to the unfortunate, and much beloved by all who know him. In 1867 he was married to Miss Annie T. Thomas, of Montgomery county, Virginia. He has two daughters and one son.

Mr. Trout has been for many years an active member of the Lutheran church, taking an especial interest in church and Sunday-school work. He is at present Superintendent of the Sunday-school of his own society.

DR. ARTHUR Z. KOINER, one of Virginia's most able physicians, was was born in Augusta county, Virginia, February 26th, 1855. He is the son of Cyrus and Catherine M. Koiner. Dr. Koiner, subject of this sketch, completed an academic course at Roanoke College, where he took the degree of A. M., after which he entered the University of Virginia, where he graduated, taking the degree of M. D. He then entered the University of New York and completed a course, graduating in 1876. From here he went to Germany and took a course in the University of Gottengen. He remained here until 1877, when he went to the Royal Imperial Hospital at Vienna, in which he remained several months. In 1878 he returned to Virginia and began the practice of medicine at Richmond, and in the fall of 1879 was elected to the faculty of the Virginia Medical College of Richmond, to the chair of Materia Medica and Therapeutics. He occupied this chair until the fall of 1880, when, owing to failing health and desirous of rest, he resigned his chair and came to Roanoke, which was at that time only a small village. Here he began the practice of medicine, but in 1889 he returned to Europe and devoted several months to visiting the leading hospitals. Two years prior to this he had, however, taken a course of private instruction in Philadelphia, in the treatment of the eye, ear and throat. His practice is large and remunerative, and he stands pre-eminently at the head of his profession in his own city as elsewhere. He has made a specialty of the eye, ear and throat and general surgery, in which province he is peculiarly successful. He is surgeon for the Norfolk and Western Railroad, also for the Roanoke Machine Works. His is a busy life. He lectures in the Roanoke College, is a member of the American Public Health Association and of the State Medical Society. In 1891 he was a representative to the National Medical Association, which met at Washington. He is President of the Perpetual Loan and Building Association, President of the Standard Investment Company, President of the Virginia, Arsenic, Bromeon and Lithia Spring Company, the combined companies representing nearly $500,000. He is also stockholder and director of a number of other leading industries in Roanoke and vicinity. In 1878 he married Miss Fannie Simmons, daughter of Capt. S. F. Simmons, of Salem, Virginia. In April, 1887, Mrs. Koiner died, and in November, 1889, he married Miss Lizzie Simmons. The Doctor is an active member of the Lutheran church, and has for a number of years been Elder in the church, and is at present superintendent of the building of the new Lutheran church, an elegant structure which is being erected at a cost of $40,000.

J. W. COON, Esq., President of the Commercial National Bank of Roanoke, and Vice-President of the Traders Loan and Trust Company, and Treasurer of the Melrose Land Company, and Secretary and Treasurer of the International Cigarette Company, was born May 22, 1850, near Salem, Virginia, and was reared in Roanoke county. He began business for himself at the age of eighteen, and having accumulated a modest little competency of a quarter of a million, prides himself upon being a self-made man. In 1870 he moved to Kansas, where he became the owner of considerable land, and in 1873 he returned to Virginia and embarked in mercantile business at Salem. He was married in 1875 to Miss Sallie C. Huff, daughter of Hon. Lewis Huff, the first Treasurer of Roanoke county, and is the father of five children. In 1877 he retired to his farm, "Wheatland," and followed an agricultural life until the completion of the Shenandoah Railroad opened up golden opportunities, which he was not slow to appreciate or grasp, thereby amassing a fortune. In 1890 organized the Commercial National Bank and was elected President of said bank, and has filled that position of trust and responsibility to the satisfaction and profit of all concerned. He is the owner of the handsome building in which the bank conducts its business; owns $15,000 stock of the bank, and is a large stockholder in various other interests. He has built several of the finest business houses in the city, which has contributed much to the progress of the City of Roanoke. He is a strong man mentally and financially, and occupies a prominent place in the community in which he is so largely concerned, and in which he has so many friends.

Dr. GEORGE S. LUCK.—When the war broke out, Dr. George S. Luck was arranging to enter Washington College at Lexington, Virginia, to finish his education, which had been elsewhere begun. Instead of entering college, he attended school in his father's neighborhood until the last year of the war, at which time he volunteered in the Confederate service in the 2d Virginia Cavalry (entering the army at seventeen years of age), where he remained in active service until the close of the war. After the close, returning to his home in Bedford county, he engaged in farming, and for two years followed this occupation, after which he engaged in the drug business for a short time. He then returned home and entered the Baptist College at Richmond. After a ten months' session, he again returned home and followed farming until 1869, when he located at Big Lick, now Roanoke, where he read medicine with Dr. James McG. Kent. Reading here a year, he entered Washington College, of Baltimore, from which he graduated in 1873. He then located at Big Springs, Montgomery county, where he practiced for a few months, and then removed to Roanoke, formed a partnership with his preceptor, Dr. J. McG. Kent, and practiced with him four years. At the death of Dr. Kent, he continued the practice alone. The Doctor ranks among the foremost in his profession among the physicians of South-west Virginia, and has built up for himself a fine practice and an enviable name in his profession. He began his professional career in debt, and is now worth nearly $100,000. He is a member of the State Medical Association, in which he has served as vice-president. He is interested in business matters outside of his profession, and is active in all endeavors for the building up and prosperity of his city. He is now about forty-five years of age, being born October 19th, 1846. He married in 1876 Miss Maria L. Moorman, daughter of Capt. R. B. Moorman, of Roanoke. Nine children have been born to them, six living. The Doctor is a member of the Baptist church, a member of the official board, and was at one time Superintendent of the Sunday-school.

TIPTON T. FISHBURNE.—In order that future generations should have a complete knowledge of the lives and characters of those men who, during their lives, were acknowledged leaders in both business and social circles, we have selected for the subject of this mention Tipton T. Fishburne, a native of Virginia, having been born in Franklin county, Virginia, on November 20th, 1849. His ancestors have been natives of the State for more than two hundred years, and while none of them sought public positions or public honors, yet they were all highly respected by the people among whom they resided. His father, Samuel Fishburne, was a highly respected planter of Franklin county, and during his life enjoyed the confidence of his people and was selected by them to fill several offices of trust, the duties of which he discharged in a manner entirely satisfactory to the people.

He was united in marriage to Miss Frances Tinsley, sister of Benjamin T. Tinsley, who at one time was the owner of the land on which the southeast portion of Roanoke is now built. This union was blessed by nine sons, our subject being the sixth. Five of these sons enlisted in the Confederate army on war being declared between the States. Four of them returned home after the surrender of the Confederate army in 1865, but the fifth died while a prisoner of war at Camp Chase. The father's death occurred in 1879, having reached the advanced age of sixty-four years.

Our subject was denied the advantages of a college education, and attended the common schools of the State, generally known as the "Old field schools." Until reaching the age of nineteen years his time was employed at farming. On reaching the above mentioned age he came to Roanoke (then known as Big Lick) and entered the employ of Fergerson & Gamble as clerk in a general merchandise store. The duties of that position he faithfully discharged for five years, when he resigned his position and engaged in merchandising in his native county and continued it for some months. In 1873 he disposed of his stock, returned to Roanoke and engaged in the manufacture of plug and smoking tobaccos. That business he still continues, although in 1891 he abandoned the manufacturing of plug tobacco and devoted his works solely to smoking tobacco. From 1887 to 1891 he was a member of the firm of Fishburne Bros., which did an extensive wholesale grocery business in Roanoke.

In May, 1889, he organized the Exchange National Bank, with a capital stock of $100,000, of which he was elected President. To describe in detail Mr. Fishburne's connections with the various enterprises of Roanoke would perhaps grow tiresome, and we will mention but a few of the more prominent, among which are The Bridgewater Carriage Company of which he is Vice-President, The Diamond Ice Company of which he is a director. He is also a member of the Building and Loan Company.

He was among the first to agitate the question of the building of a city hospital, and it is largely due to his untiring efforts that this much-needed building is now being erected, which, when completed, will stand as a monument to the public-spirited men of Roanoke. The active part Mr. Fishburne took in this enterprise was recognized by the people by choosing him as President.

Mr. Fishburne has never taken any active part in politics, more than to give his hearty support to the cause of temperance and to wage war on the liquor traffic whenever an opportunity presented itself. During his term of service as a member of the City Council his influence on this question was often felt by that body.

While his life has been an unusually active one, yet he has ever found means by which to devote some portion of his time to the interests of his church. He became a member of the M. E. Church when he was quite young, and has ever been an active worker, and has for some years acted as Chairman of the Board of Stewards and Trustees. In May, 1890, he was chosen as a delegate to the General Conference, which met at St. Louis, Missouri, and for many prior years acted as lay delegate.

In 1882 he founded the first Methodist Sunday-school in Roanoke with scholars to the number of thirteen. His labor in behalf of the Sunday-school, both as superintendent and teacher, has been productive of much good, and to-day the combined Methodist schools of that city show a membership of about 1,200 scholars.

He was happily united in marriage in October, 1874, to Miss Callie L. Greer, daughter of Moses Greer, now a resident of the State of Illinois, but formerly of Franklin county, Va.

Mr. Fishburne has, by his own efforts, amassed a large fortune, and proved himself a financier of rare ability. His readiness to aid any enterprise that promised to be for the good of the public, and his many charitable acts, have won for him the love and respect of the people of his chosen home. He is a member of several secret orders—Knights of Honor, Knights of Pythias, and the Masonic fraternity.

Mr. **WILLIAM P. DUPUY,** one of Roanoke's prominent and substantial citizens, was born in Charlotte county in 1845, but when a child removed to Prince Edward county. He entered Hampden-Sydney College, but before the completion of his course he responded to the call "to boot and saddle," and enlisted in the 3d Virginia Cavalry, where he served with marked distinction during the four years struggle. After his return home he engaged in farming and merchandising, both of which pursuits he prosecuted with success and profit for many years. In 1885 he was elected to the Virginia House of Delegates and gave such satisfaction to his constituents by his ability and fidelity that he was re-elected in 1887 and 1889. During the latter year he engaged in the real estate business in Roanoke, and is at present a senior partner in the house of Dupuy & Tallaferro, which occupies a prominent rank in real estate circles. He is President of the Roanoke Exchange, is Secretary and Treasurer of the Transparent Ice Company, Secretary of the Jenette Land Company, Secretary and Treasurer of the Legislative Investment Company, and President of the following companies: The Jefferson Land Company, the Wall Street Investment Company, the Roanoke Drug Company, and is concerned as director in the Roanoke Development Company, and stockholder in the Buena Vista Land Company, the Duvall Engine Company, the Roanoke Iron Company, the Midway Iron Company and the Old Dominion Paper Bag Company. He married, in 1869, Miss Nelia, daughter of Mr. John Booker, of Richmond. They have four children. Mr. Dupuy is an active member of the Presbyterian church. As a man of sterling business qualities, he ranks among the first of his city, and as a pleasant friend and genial companion he is endeared to all who come in contact with him.

Mr. **E. H. STEWART.**—There are few men who have risen more rapidly or occupy a more prominent position in mercantile circles in Virginia than the subject of this mention, Mr. E. H. Stewart. He was born near Spottsylvania Court House, Virginia, in November, 1848. His parents, John A. and Ellen Stewart, were both natives of Virginia, and members of prominent families in their section. His father was by occupation a farmer, which business he followed until his death in 1854. His wife survived him but a few years, her death occurring in 1861. Thus we find our subject, while yet a child, deprived of the assistance of a father's advice and a mother's love. The property of his father's estate, consisting mainly of slaves, having all been swept away by the war between the States, he availed himself of what advantages he had to acquire an education, but realizing the necessity of a more thorough education in order to successfully meet competition in the business world he employed his leisure time in study while clerking in Fredericksburg, and by this means he was able to acquire quite a thorough education, which proved to be of great value to him in after years. He remained with Mr. W. H. Cunningham for some years, but later on connected himself with Messrs. Young & Holmes, then conducting a dry goods business in Fredericksburg. He soon gained the confidence of his new employers by his honesty and close attention to business, and was given charge of a branch store operated by them at Greenbrier White Sulphur Spring, West Virginia. He successfully managed the business for one year, at the end of which time he, in connection with another party, purchased the stock and did an extensive business for eleven years under the firm name of E. H. Stewart & Co. He, in time, enlarged the business and established branch stores at different points throughout the State. Besides his mercantile business he dealt quite largely in lumber, and to some extent in cattle.

In 1882 he disposed of all his interests in West Virginia and spent some time in travel through the Southern States. He returned to Virginia in 1888 and again entered business at Roanoke, retailing furniture and carpets. This he gradually changed into a retail and wholesale business, and later began the manufacture of mattresses, which is rapidly growing. The works at present employ from forty to fifty hands. Besides conducting his extensive business at Roanoke, he also operates a branch store at Bluefield, West Virginia, and is largely interested in a furniture factory at Johnston City, Tennessee.

Mr. Stewart has been untiring in his efforts to advance Roanoke as a business center, and has assisted every enterprise that promised to be for the best interest of the place. He is largely interested in many of the largest and best land and development companies, and is President of the following: Bellemont Land Company, Oak Ridge Land Company, Duval Engine Works Company, Baltimore Investment Company, Mate Creek Coal and Lumber Company, Roanoke Building Company, Crystal Springs Land Company, Highland Terrace Land Company, Piedmont Land and Manufacturing Company, E. H. Stewart Furniture Company, Vice-President of Crystal Springs Street Railway Company and Chester Land and Manufacturing Company of Chester, South Carolina, and stockholder and director in many other

industries of Roanoke. Mr. Stewart's brilliant success in business has made for him a wide circle of acquaintances and many warm personal friends.

He was happily united in marriage in June, 1881, to Miss Ida, eldest daughter of Rev. James H. Lepe, of Frankford, West Virginia. This union has been blessed with one daughter, Nellie V. He is a member of the Baptist church, in which he is a deacon and an active worker.

Mr. Stewart was at one time President of the City Council, which position he resigned because of its interference with his private business. He has never taken any active part in politics nor sought public honors in any way. His life has been wholly devoted to business, and the high position reached by him goes to show that there is nothing impossible to be accomplished when backed by the energy displayed throughout his entire buiness career.

ROBERT H. WOODRUM.—There are few men who can point with greater pride to what they have accomplished in this life than the subject of this sketch, Mr. Robert H. Woodrum. He was born in Fincastle county, Virginia, in May, 1852. His parents, Jordan and Margaret, were natives of that portion of the State now known as West Virginia.

Jordan Woodrum was a farmer by occupation, and also practiced law to some extent. He occupied a high position in the community in which he resided, and held several offices of trust, among them Chief Magistrate of the County Courts. He entered the Confederate army in 1861, and served with distinction during the war. Mr. Woodrum, sr., removed from Fincastle county to Roanoke county when our subject was but two years old, and located at Salem, and it was there that our subject received his youthful training and education. He remained with his father, assisting in the labor of the farm, until reaching his majority. Realizing the necessity of a more thorough education at that time, he entered the Roanoke College, and by the proceeds of his labor during vacations managed to support himself and graduate with honor in 1876. On the completion of his studies in Roanoke College, he began the study of law under D. B. Strouse, of Salem, Va., and in 1877 was admitted to practice. He immediately removed to Texas, and followed his profession there for two years, but was compelled to return to Virginia, the climate not agreeing with him. He returned to his home in Virginia, purchased the old farm from his parents, which he soon disposed of at a handsome profit. This he invested in a steam saw-mill, which he successfully conducted for some years, finding a ready market for his lumber.

As soon as Roanoke began to assume some importance Mr. Woodrum purchased a number of lots, on which he erected houses from lumber sawed at his mill. In 1882 he disposed of the mill, removed to Roanoke and resumed the practice of his profession. He was chosen a member of the committee which, in 1883 and 1884, prepared the charter of Roanoke, and assisted materially in its passage. He had the honor of being Roanoke's first Commonwealth's Attorney, being elected in 1884, and ably discharged the duties of that office for four years.

In July, 1888, he visited South America in the interest of the Bonsack Cigarette Machine Company, where he disposed of the machine and its rights for South America for the sum of $180,000, receiving fifty per cent. of the proceeds and returning home in November of the same year. In the following year he became interested in the Luddington Cigarette Machine, and obtained control of a large amount of foreign territory. He also organized the International Cigarette Company, of which he was elected President.

Mr. Woodrum is largely interested in many large corporations in and about Roanoke, prominent among which are the Ætna Land Company, of which he is President; director of the Commercial National Bank; also a large stockholder and director in the Traders Loan, Trust and Deposit Company, and many other companies.

He was happily married in June, 1877, to Miss Nannie, daughter of Robert Museyear, of Charlottesville, Virginia. This union has been blessed by three sons, as follows: Robert, Jr., Claudien and Clifton.

Mr. Woodrum has never taken any active part in politics or sought public honors. He has ever manifested a liberal spirit towards all that promised to advance Roanoke, and contributed largely of his means.

He and his family are members of the Lutheran church, and occupy a high position in society.

He has erected and now resides in one of the most handsome and attractive homes in South-western Virginia.

JOSEPH T. ENGLEBY, Esq., of Roanoke, President of the Fidelity Loan and Trust Company, was born March 1st, 1856, in Allamakee county, Iowa, and is the son of Thomas and Elizabeth Engleby. The father is of English extraction and the mother a native of this country. Joseph T. Engleby, the subject of this sketch, received his early education in the field schools of Maryland, and while quite young learned the tinning business, which occupation he followed until he was about twenty-two years of age, at which time he engaged in the lumber business in Western Maryland. In 1882 he came to Roanoke and engaged in tinning and plumbing in partnership with his brother, Mr. John Engleby, which partnership continues at this present time. Joseph being of an energetic, pushing turn of mind, soon branched out into wider fields after coming to Roanoke, and in addition to being President of the Fidelity Loan and Trust Company, he is also Vice-President of the Exchange National Bank; President of the Exchange Building and Investment Company, President of the United Investment Company, President of the Roanoke Development and Guarantee Company, Treasurer of the Diamond Ice Company, President of the Cloverdale Iron and Land Company, and a large stockholder in a number of other enterprises of Roanoke. Mr. Engleby is a man of almost unerring business instincts, and it has become proverbial that whatever he takes. hold of or becomes interested in, that undertaking has a fair prospect of being successful. He concentrates his best energies on his work, and he takes no half-hearted convictions into his schemes and undertakings. He was married in June, 1883, to Miss Estella G. Staples, daughter of William Staples, Esq., of Frostburg, Maryland. They have three children—Clara D., William S., and Emma.

Mr. Engleby is a member of the Methodist Episcopal Church, South, in which he is a trustee. He is Assistant Chief of the Roanoke Fire Department, and has served for three years on the Board of the City Council, and during that time, and at the present, is a director of the Roanoke and Southern Railroad.

Col. SAMUEL S. BROOKE received a military education at the Military Institute at Lexington, Virginia, and afterwards entered the University of Virginia, which he left in 1861 and entered the Confederate army as a private in a company of infantry, organized in Stafford county, Virginia, which was afterwards known as Company I, of the 47th Virginia Infantry, Gen. A. P. Hill's division. In the spring of 1862 he was promoted to the office of Captain, in which capacity he served until the close of the war. He was in active service continually and participated in all the battles of Northern Virginia. After the war he located at Fredericksburg, Virginia, and for a short time engaged in the lumber business, but soon returned to his native county of Stafford, where he engaged for a short period in farming, subsequently returning to Fredericksburg and engaging in the practice of law. Being of a literary turn, he drifted into journalism, editing the *Fredericksburg News* and afterwards the *Fredericksburg Star*. In the spring of 1882 he came to Roanoke and established and edited the *Roanoke Leader*, which he successfully conducted until 1886, at which time he was appointed to the office of Clerk of the Courts, to which position he has been twice elected and still holds. He is President of the Magic City Land Company, the Prudential Investment Company, Central Investment Company, and director and stockholder in several other Roanoke industries. Soon after locating in Roanoke, he organized the Roanoke Light Infantry and was the commander of the company, and in the summer of 1890 he was elected Lieutenant Colonel of the 2d Regiment of the Virginia Infantry, which commission he still holds. He was born November, 1844, at Brooke Station, Stafford county, Virginia, and was the son of Samuel S. and Angelina Brooke, both of whom were native Virginians. Colonel Brooke married in April, 1872, Miss Bettie L. Young, daughter of Mr. John J. Young, of Fredericksburg, Virginia. He has five children living. He is a member of the Episcopal church, and a vestryman.

ALEXANDER S. ASBERRY.—It has been said that the history of any country or organization of citizens is not complete without some personal mention of its more prominent members in all trades, professions and callings, and it is in conformity with that idea that we have selected Mr. Alexander S. Asberry to form the subject of this mention.

Mr. Asberry was born at the village of Stewartsville, Bedford county, Virginia, in October, 1852. His parents, Joel and Elizabeth Asberry, were humble though highly-respected people of that county. His father was by occupation a planter, but on war being declared between the States he enlisted in the Confederate army and served with distinction until a short time before his death, in 1864, caused by sickness contracted while in the service. His wife soon followed him, her death occurring the following year—1865.

Our subject was thus left an orphan while yet a mere child, without means of support, the war having swept away the property of his parents and left him, like many others, destitute and dependent solely on his own resources for means of support. He had attended the common schools of the county, more or less, prior to the war, but was denied the advantages of a thorough education. We find him at the age of 13 serving an apprenticeship to the carpenters' trade, which he fully mastered and followed until the fall of 1873, when he entered the employ of J. M. Gambill, of Roanoke (then Big Lick), as clerk in a general merchandise store. He remained with Mr. Gambill one year, when he was offered the position of agent and telegraph operator for the Atlantic, Mississippi and Ohio Railroad at Roanoke. That position he accepted and filled for five years. He resigned it later to engage in the sale of agricultural implements, and was engaged in that business when he was appointed postmaster of Roanoke by President Garfield in 1881. The duties of the office he discharged to the entire satisfaction of the people until his removal by President Cleveland in December, 1885, for political reasons, or, in the President's own language, "offensive partisanship."

In January, 1886, he engaged in the ice trade and conducted a large business, which he afterwards disposed of to the Diamond Ice Company of Roanoke. He then embarked in the real estate business, and his thorough acquaintance with the location and value of property enabled him to soon accumulate a fortune. He was again appointed postmaster in 1889 by President Harrison, and is now discharging his duties eminently satisfactory to the public. The office is about to become a first-class office, which is due largely to the efforts of Mr. Asberry, he having defrayed the expenses of extra clerks himself for some time, until the government could be brought to understand the importance of the office and the necessity for more help. He has ever had the best interest of Roanoke at heart, and it was mainly through his effort that Congress appropriated the $75,000 necessary for the erection of the public building now being built.

Mr. Asberry holds the office of President of the Traders Loan, Trust and Deposit Company, organized in 1890 with a capital stock of $50,000. He assisted in the organization of the Commercial National Bank, of which he is a director. He is also largely interested in various other loan and land companies in Roanoke and elsewhere in the State. His energy and zeal in developing Roanoke has gained for him the esteem of the entire community.

He was happily united in marriage in July, 1879, to Miss Willie, daughter of George F. Rhodes, of Roanoke. That union has been blessed by one son, Joel. He is a member of the Masonic fraternity. He is now building, at a cost of several thousand dollars, one of the most magnificent houses in South-west Virginia.

Judge **WILLIAM S. GOOCH**.— Although yet but a young man, Judge William S. Gooch has earned for himself a prominent and enviable position in the legal fraternity of his State. He was born August 4th, 1858, in Louisa county, Virginia, and was educated at Norwood College and the University of Virginia. His parents were both natives of "the Mother of Presidents" State. The Judge read law under Capt. W. H. Murray, of Louisa, and was admitted to the bar in 1879, and continued active in his practice until he was elected to the office of Judge of the County Court of Louisa in 1885, which honorable and responsible position he occupied until 1890, at which time he resigned and removed to Roanoke, where he resumed the practice of his profession. He is a gentleman of fine scholarly attainments, and the possessor of brilliant social qualities that endear him to all with whom he comes in contact. He was married

WILLIAM E. BIBB.—Senator William E. Bibb, of Roanoke, Virginia, was a graduate of the Law Department of the University of Virginia, in which institution he received his degree in 1870, after which he immediately began the practice of law at the county seat of Louisa county, where he remained in active practice for almost twenty years, during which time he served nearly ten years as Commonwealth Attorney, and in 1885 he was sent to the State Senate, where he served four years. While in the Senate he served on several important committees, and gave marked evidence of ability as a statesman. While located in Louisa county, he served several years as Chairman of the County Democratic Committee, and in other official capacities. He was also assistant counsel for the Chesapeake and Ohio Railroad. In 1889 he located at Roanoke, and, devoting his time and energy to the practice of his profession, has built up a large and handsomely paying business. He is legally trusted with many important cases, and is the attorney for a number of improvement and investment companies of Roanoke and vicinity. He is at present President of the Guarantee Title and Investment Company, and is the author of a book similar to Mayo's Guide, a law book for general use, especially for magistrates and justices of the peace. The subject of our sketch was born March 8th, 1848, in Albemarle county, Virginia. He is the son of William T. and Lucy Farrish Bibb. His father entered the Confederate service and served until the spring of 1864, at which time he, although not seventeen years of age, induced his father to return home, took his place, and served to the end of the war, an example of devotion and patriotism seldom met with.

June 17th, 1886, to Miss Mary Stuart Anderson, daughter of Dr. M. A. Anderson, of Louisa county, Virginia, a brilliant and accomplished lady. They have one child. The Judge is a member of the Christian (or Disciples) church, and is President of the Virginia State Missionary Society of the church, and also a member of the official board of his church at Roanoke. Aside from his law practice, he is interested in various enterprises in different parts of the State, being President of the Old Dominion Investment Company, President of the Vinton and Roanoke Gas and Water Company, President of the Basic City Car Works, Basic City, Virginia; President of the Home Conveyance Company, Clifton Forge, Virginia; President of the Missionary Weekly Publishing Company of Richmond, Virginia. In so brief a sketch the details of so busy a life cannot even be vaguely hinted at, but that the Judge's career is an unusually active one, the most casual reader cannot fail to observe.

Francis B. Kemp

He was married in 1876 to Kate L. Cammack, of Louisa county, Va., a descendant of the old Chew family, of Philadelphia, and a cousin of Addison Cammack, well-known in New York as "The Grizzly Bear" of Wall Street. They have four children, whose names indicate their descent— Janette Herndon, William Chew, John Pendleton and Kathleen Cammack.

Mr. Bibb is a member of the Baptist church, and an active worker in the Sunday-school. He is also an enthusiastic member of the Masonic fraternity, and has passed the chairs of his lodge.

FRANCIS B. KEMP.—There are, perhaps, but few men better known throughout Virginia to real estate men than the subject of this mention, Mr. Francis B. Kemp. Mr. Kemp is a native of New York State, having been born in the city of Brooklyn on January 29th, 1864, but his life has been almost wholly spent in Virginia, his mother's native State. When but eight years old he removed with his parents from New York to Eastern Virginia, and received his early education and training in the schools of this State. He early in life manifested a fondness for business, and at the age of fifteen began clerking for the firm of Smith & Young, then conducting an extensive general merchandise business in Powhattan county, Virginia. He remained with that firm a few months and then connected himself with John H. McRae, of Cumberland county, with whom he remained two years. In 1881 he accepted a position with the Petersburg Railroad Company as clerk under T. H. Bransford, and in the following year, in company with Mr. Bransford, he removed to Roanoke and entered the employ of the Norfolk and Western Railroad and continued with that company until 1888. Being possessed with more than ordinary business foresight, Mr. Kemp foresaw at that time a bright future for Roanoke and determined to avail himself of the opportunity, and in conformity with that idea he resigned his position with the Norfolk and Western Railroad and became a member of the firm of Hanckel, Kemp & Co. Mr. Kemp was given the management of this firm and by energy and close attention to business soon gave the house the reputation of being one of the foremost real estate firms in South-west Virginia. In the year following, September, 1889, he organized the firm of Francis B. Kemp & Co., which to-day ranks among the first houses of the State. Besides conducting an extensive business in Roanoke, they also operate branch offices at Buchanan, Front Royal, Shenandoah, Max Meadows, Virginia, and Winston, North Carolina.

Mr. Kemp has taken an active part in organizing many of the largest corporations in Roanoke, prominent among them are the following: Hyde Park Land Company, Glen Falls Land Company, Pleasant Valley Land Company and the Traders and National Investment Companies, for all of which he formerly acted as agent. He also acts as President of the Buchanan Land and Improvement Company. Mr. Kemp's zeal and energy has gained for him a position in financial and business circles seldom reached by men at his age. He has succeeded in amassing considerable means and making many warm personal friends and admirers. He is a member of the Presbyterian church, and occupies a high position in society.

S. S. FURGUSON, Esq., banker and broker of Roanoke, Virginia, was born April, 1863, in Franklin county, Virginia, and is a son of John C. and Sallie Hatcher Furguson, both parents being natives of Virginia. His father was a farmer by occupation and served as a soldier in the Confederate army during the war between the States. Young Furguson, the subject of this sketch, was educated in Franklin, his native county, and at the age of nineteen years engaged as book-keeper in the Franklin Bank of Rocky Mount, Virginia, where he remained for a short time, and in January, 1882, he came to Roanoke and engaged as book-keeper in the Bank of Virginia, where he remained until 1885, at which time he established himself in the banking and brokerage business at Roanoke, in which he continues at the present time. He is director and stockholder in a number of the industries and land companies of Roanoke and vicinity. Mr. Furguson is a brilliant, pushing, talented young business man, who has secured the confidence of all with whom he comes in contact, either in business or social relations. He was united in marriage February 20th, 1890, to Miss Carrie Franklin, daughter of M. P. Franklin, Esq., of Staunton, Virginia.

CARY A. MOOMAW, Esq., General Manager and head of the Roanoke Vegetable and Canning Company, was born in November, 1854, in Bartoute county, Virginia. He is the son of Benjamin F. and Mary N. Moomaw, both parents being natives of Virginia. His father was an extensive and highly respected farmer. Cary A., the subject of this sketch, was educated in the field schools, and at the age of twenty-one began business in packing and fruit canning on the farm of J. C. Moomaw, of Cloverdale, Virginia, this place being the headquarters and main shipping point. This business was established in 1869, and was the first of the kind in South-west Virginia. It has been very successfully managed, and has grown to immense proportions, employing at the present time about one hundred and fifty hands during the packing season.

This firm have a farm of eighteen hundred acres devoted exclusively to vegetable and fruit growing, and aside from this the company is largely interested in pear culture in Surry county, Virginia, having a pear orchard there of 22,000 bearing trees. Mr. Moomaw has been connected with this enterprise as stockholder for thirteen years, and has been the head of the firm and manager since 1886. He is the owner of valuable property in the city of Roanoke, which place he has made his home since 1888. His business interests are numerous and extensive, and at the present time he is Vice-President of the Fidelity Loan and Trust Company; Vice-President of the Exchange Building and Investment Company; director of the Commercial National Bank; Treasurer of the Pleasant Valley Land Company; Secretary of the Virginia Land Company, and a stockholder in a number of Roanoke's best enterprises. He was married in April, 1889, to Miss Matilda A. Ankney, of Washington county, and one child has been born to them, a daughter, Dorothy A.

G. B. LEVY, Esq., President of the Citizens Bank of Roanoke and President of the Roanoke Construction Company, was educated at the University of Virginia, and in early life connected himself with the Chesapeake and Ohio Railroad, and subsequently engaged in the manufacturing business for a short time. He removed to Roanoke in 1888, and became identified with the Commercial National Bank, of which institution he for some time acted as cashier, displaying an aptness for finance which led to his elevation to the Presidency of the Citizens Bank. The Roanoke Construction Company, of which he is also President, has a paid-up capital and surplus amounting to $120,000, and both of these enterprises show in their liberal but conservative policies evidences of the ability with which they are managed. It is needless to dilate upon the business tact which has manifested itself so decidedly, and it is equally unnecessary to mention among those who know him the courtesy of manner, kindness of heart and openness of hand which have endeared him to all who know him.

Mr. Levy was born at Louisa Court House in 1854, and, notwithstanding his achievements, is yet a comparatively young man.

C. O'LEARY, Esq., was born in Alexandria, Virginia, about thirty-five years ago, and came to Roanoke at the completion of the Shenandoah Valley Railroad. His agreeable manners won for him friends rapidly, and his fine business qualities attracted the attention of the directors of the Roanoke Land Improvement Company, who desired a manager for their immense interests here, and Mr. O'Leary was chosen to that position and filled it to the satisfaction of all for a number of years, and the knowledge he acquired in the real estate business was turned to good account after he left the service of the Improvement Company, and his wealth is now estimated at several hundred thousand dollars and embraces some of the finest property in the city. He is President of the Roanoke Electric Light and Power Company, and Vice-President of the Commercial National Bank, and is connected with several other enterprises as an officer or director. Mr. O'Leary is a strong, a self-made man, and has played a prominent and important part in the development of Roanoke.

WILLIAM H. HORTON was educated at the public school of Nelson county and the High School of Lexington, Virginia. He was born in 1862. After having completed his studies at Lexington in the spring of 1881 he accepted a position as clerk in a general wholesale store owned by J. H. Dever, of Lexington, where he remained one year. He then accepted a position as traveling salesman for a sewing-machine company, which position he filled until the fall of 1886, at which time he came to Roanoke and, with a small capital, began the livery business, having as stock a half-dozen buggies and as many head of horses. He had, however, "come to stay," and with pluck and any amount of energy he soon worked up and established a fine and remunerative trade. At the present time he has forty head of choice horses, is fully equipped with good carriages and his business is second to none in the city or county. In December, 1886, he paid $1,000 for a piece of real estate in Roanoke; and at the end of the year he sold his investment for $6,000. This stroke of good financiering gave this enterprising young man capital which he has judiciously manipulated in the purchase and sale of real estate, and by honesty and integrity has established a fine trade and accumulated a handsome fortune. He is director and stockholder in several of Roanoke's important industries, and takes special interest in aiding permanent enterprises of the city. He married Miss Susie Gray Roberts, daughter of Nathaniel Roberts, of Medicine Lodge, Kansas, in 1890. He is a member of the Baptist church and also of the Masonic order and Mystic Chain.

Mr. JAMES M. GAMBILL, Wholesale Grocer, of Roanoke, Virginia, was born May 12th, 1844, near Portsmouth, Ky. His father, Benjamin Franklin Gambill, was a native of Tennessee, and was a cotton broker and what was known as a "Riverman," having owned stock in several steamboats, devoting much of his time to the command of his boats, and was known as Captain Gambill. He died in 1865.

James M. Gambill, the subject of this sketch, is the only one of the family living. He attended school at Summerville and Decatur, Alabama, and at the age of fifteen entered the Confederate army in the 9th Alabama Infantry as a private. He was wounded at the battle of Williamsburg, Va., May 5th, 1862, and on June 12th his arm was amputated. After recovering, he went to Richmond and took charge of the wounded soldiers which were being sent there for care and treatment. He was employed with the sick during the night, and in the day-time he clerked in the wholesale commission house of William T. Staples & Co., of Richmond, and it was here that he learned the rudiments of the wholesale trade. He remained in Richmond one year, and then located at Big Lick, now Roanoke, and took charge of the Commissary and Quartermaster Departments at Roanoke, his business being to gather supplies for the army. He remained in this position until the close of the war; then farmed one year, the land he farmed being that on which the Roanoke Machine-shops and other industries are now located. He afterwards formed a partnership with Mr. J. M. Ferguson and engaged in the general wholesale business. This firm continued, doing a large business, for fifteen years, and in 1882 Mr. Gambill began the wholesale grocery, milling and grain elevating business, which he is at the present time engaged in. His flouring mill is one of the finest in the State, being equipped with all the best modern milling appliances. His grain elevators have a capacity of seventy-five thousand bushels. His trade extends over South-west Virginia and the State of North Carolina, doing a business of nearly half a million dollars. He is a stockholder and director in the First National Bank, and stockholder and director in several improvement associations of Roanoke. He owns several hundred acres of valuable mineral lands located in Franklin and Patrick counties. In 1864 he married Miss Sarah E., daughter of Abram Childress, of Franklin county, Va. He has three children: Mary J., wife of W. K. Andrews, of Roanoke; Willie T. and Bloomfield K. Mr. Gambill is a member of the Methodist church, and also a member of the church and Sunday-school official boards. He was prominent in the organization of the Roanoke and South-western Railroad, and is still a director and stockholder of the same.

M. T. C. JORDAN, Esq.—Among the most prominent and reliable real estate agents of Roanoke, Virginia, is

M. T. C. Jordan, Esq., who was born at Norfolk, Virginia, March 8th, 1853. The father of our subject was a civil engineer and a man of unusual culture and literary attainments. The mother came of good old Maryland Quaker stock. The father was at one time superintendent of the Navy Yard at Portsmouth, Virginia, and received the appointment of General Superintendent of the Post-office Department at Washington, in which city he died in 1889 at the advanced age of seventy-nine years. Prior to his appointment in the civil service at Washington, he had built and run the first steam saw-mill ever built or run in the State of Maryland. His son, M. T. C. Jordan, the subject of our sketch, attended the public school at Washington, D. C., and afterwards entered the Columbia Business College, where he graduated in 1871. The same year he engaged in the insurance and real estate business at the capital, in which avocation he was especially successful and followed it for the next eight years, when he went to Philadelphia and engaged in the shirt manufacturing business, which occupation he followed for four years, and then entered the commission business in New York City, where he remained until the last of 1887, at which time his attention was called to the rapid growth and brilliant future prospects of South-western Virginia, and at once made up his mind that he would cast his lot in his native State. He accordingly located at Roanoke and began at once making investments in real estate, and in the course of a couple of years had profited handsomely by his investments. He then opened a real estate office, and soon established a large and remunerative business. He is a sagacious, far-seeing man of business, and is full of energy and "push." He is officially connected or is stockholder in several prominent industries of Roanoke, a few of which are below mentioned. He is the organizer and business manager of the Vinton Land and Improvement Company, which has been one of the most successful, and is now one of the most flourishing, companies in South-west Virginia. He is General Manager of the Glade Land Company, Vice-President of the Elliston Land Company, which has a capital stock of one-third of a million dollars. He is General Manager of the Norfolk Investment Company. He is a stockholder in the Roanoke Black Marble Company, the Salem Investment Company, Salem Improvement Company, Vinton Development Company, Old Dominion Paper-bag Company, West Portsmouth Land Company, etc., etc.

It is needless to say that he has great faith in the future of South-west Virginia.

CONWAY C. TALIAFERRO, of the firm of Dupuy & Taliaferro, was born April 11th, 1846, in Culpeper county, Virginia, and is the son of Col. L. H. and Eliza Taliaferro, who were both natives of Virginia. Colonel Taliaferro was a farmer and served as a soldier in the war of 1812. He died at an advanced age in 1879. Conway C. Taliaferro, the subject of this sketch, was educated at Clover Hill Academy and Rappahannock College, leaving the latter place to enter the Confederate service as a private in Company C of the 9th Virginia Regiment of Cavalry. He was subsequently detailed as scout and courier, in which capacity he served during the war. He was wounded twice, and carried the flag of truce at the surrender of Gen. Robert E. Lee's army at Appomattox Court House in April, 1865. After the war he located in Prince Edward county, Virginia, and followed farming and merchandizing until the spring of 1888, at which time he came to Roanoke and formed a partnership which now exists, and engaged in the insurance and real estate business, in which the firm has been peculiarly successful, placing themselves at the front of all similar institutions in the city. Mr. Taliaferro is agent of the Roanoke Land and Improvement Company, which represents a capital of $400,000. He is also stockholder and director of the Transparent Ice Company, the Jefferson Land Company and general manager of the Janett Land Company, besides being a stockholder in several other important industries in South-western Virginia. In 1865 he was married to Miss Nannie Terry, daughter of Mr. B. F. Terry, of Prince Edward county, Virginia. Three children were the result of this union, Lucy P., wife of the Rev. Turner H. Wharton, pastor of the Presbyterian church, Steel Creek, North Carolina; his second child, Lawrence H., was wounded by the premature discharge of a gun while hunting, and died from the effects of the wound, September 6th, 1875. The third and youngest child is named Lizzie. Mr. Taliaferro is a member of the Presbyterian church, and for twenty years prior to his coming to Roanoke was deacon in this society. He is now a communicant of the Presbyterian church of the city in which he resides.

J. R. HOCKADAY, Esq., ex-President of the Roanoke Real Estate Exchange, was born in New Kent county, Virginia, in 1839, and educated under the old log-school system and worked on the farm until he attained the age of eighteen, when he went to Richmond and engaged in carpentering, which he continued until the breaking out of the war, when he returned to his native county and enlisted in the Barnhamsville Greys, afterwards Company B, 53d Virginia Regiment. He was engaged in the seven-days battles around Richmond, receiving a wound in the desperate struggle at Malvern Hill. He also took part in the engagements of second Manassas, Fredericksburg, Harpers' Ferry and Gettysburg. After the last battle he was transferred to the navy and assigned to the iron-clad *Raleigh* on the Cape Fear river, North Carolina. In an engagement off Fort Fisher the *Raleigh* was sunk, but her gallant crew was saved, and the subject of this sketch was assigned to the flagship *Yadkin*, and subsequently detailed to navy-yard duty at Wilmington, North Carolina, where he was taken prisoner February 22d, 1865, and not released until July 2. In January, 1868, he was married to Miss Bettie Thomas Gregery, of Chesterfield county, and by that marriage has nine children living. In January, 1883, he removed to Roanoke and established the Pioneer Real Estate Agency, which still lives and flourishes. Mr. Hockaday is a man of firm will and abundant energy. He is strongly imbued with a sense of Roanoke's wondrous advantages and takes a deep interest in the Real Estate Exchange, and the estimation in which he is held by the members is evidenced by his election to the presidency of that body, a position which he filled to the entire satisfaction of all his associates.

Mr. B. L. GREIDER.—The prominent positions Mr. Greider has held with many of the leading trunk lines of the country, and the active part he has taken in the development of this portion of the State since becoming a resident has gained for him a wide circle of acquaintances.

Mr. Greider was born in Lancaster county, Pennsylvania, in 1860, and continued to reside there until he was 16 years of age, when he entered the employ of the Pennsylvania Railroad Company and was assigned duty on the various lines of that company throughout Pennsylvania and Maryland. He remained with the Pennsylvania Company until 1880, when he connected himself with a railroad contractor of Toronto, Canada, and remained with him for a period of two years.

Mr. Greider resided in Chicago until 1886, and for four years was in the employ of R. B. Hutchinson, better known as "Old Hutch" on the Board of Trade. In 1886 he resigned his position with Mr. Hutchinson and connected himself with the Shenandoah Valley Railroad as agent. It was while serving in this capacity that he became acquainted with the wonderful natural advantages of South-western Virginia and the rapid development of this portion of the State. He remained with the Shenandoah Valley Railroad but one year, and in 1887 entered the real estate business at Roanoke in company with Mr. A. S. Asberry, under the firm name of Asberry, Greider & Co. That firm existed until September, 1888, when Mr. Asberry retired. Mr. Greider continued the business, however, under the firm name of B. L. Greider & Co., and, by energy and close attention to business, made it one of the best-known real estate firms in Virginia. Mr. Greider is considered a thorough business man, and his extensive knowledge of men and business has enabled him to take a prominent part in the management of large corporations of this city. Prominent among them are the Roanoke Marble Company, of which he is President; the Beall Investment Company, the Buchanan Investment Company. He is also Secretary of the Roanoke Racing Association, the Wall Street Investment Company and the Rife Engine Company.

He connected himself by marriage in December, 1886, to one of the first families of Virginia. His wife, Miss Florence Antrim, is the daughter of Col. George Antrim. He and his wife are members of the Church of England.

CEPHES B. MOOMAW, Esq., Attorney at Law at Roanoke, Virginia, of the firm of Moomaw & Woods, was born in October, 1849, in Bartout county, Virginia, and is the son of Joseph and Polly Moomaw, both of whom are natives of the Old Dominion State. The father was a farmer, and highly respected in the community in which he lived. Cephes B. was educated in the old field schools, and when quite a young man began the study of law, and in 1882 he was admitted to the Bar at Roanoke, Virginia.

He practiced alone until 1887, at which date he formed a law partnership with Mr. John W. Woods, with the firm name of Moomaw & Woods, and the firm in an incredibly short period of time established a large and highly remunerative practice. Aside from his law practice, Mr. Moomaw finds time to devote to other interests, and at the present time is Secretary of the Exchange Building and Investment Company, and stockholder in several of the land and improvement companies of Roanoke and vicinity. He is a man of fine business as well as professional abilities, and possesses a way of pushing matters to a successful issue.

He was married in 1873 to Miss Sarah E., daughter of Daniel Mauges, of Bartout county, Virginia, and two children have blessed their union— Edith M. and Hugh M. Mr. Moomaw is a Knight of Pythias, and an industrious member of this thoroughly alive organization.

JAMES A. PUGH was born in Nelson county, Virginia, May 25th, 1849. He received a very limited education in the "old field schools," as they were then called. At thirteen years of age he was acting agent of the Virginia Central (now Chesapeake and Ohio) Railroad at Afton depot, and continued in this position until the war closed, when he accepted a position in the clerk's office of Augusta County Court. Horace Greeley's advice, "Go West, young man," was impressed on his youthful and somewhat romantic mind, and he started for Ohio on foot, taking in the West Virginia battle-fields en route. Altogether, he spent some seven years in the Buckeye State, a part of the time as reporter for several influential papers. Returning to the State of his nativity he engaged in clerical and railroad work for several years, and in 1887 became one of the editors of the *Roanoke Weekly Sun*, a Republican paper started by Charles M. Webber, of Salem. In November, 1889, he accepted the position of city editor of the *Roanoke Daily Times*, owned by M. H. Claytor and edited by Dr. J. W. Davis. The *Times* passed into other hands on January 1st, 1889, and Mr. Pugh determined to start a new daily. With J. T. Hall, now general manager of the Iron Belt, and James F. Beavers, late of the *Pocahontas Headlight*, he issued the first number of the *Daily Herald* on the 15th instant, taking the position of editor-in-chief. On March 1st, 1891, he resigned to accept a place on the staff of the *Times*.

Mr. Pugh organized the Virginia Press Association in Roanoke in 1889, and was honored with the presidency. In 1890 he was re-elected by acclamation. He has brought several press associations from New England and Pennsylvania to Virginia, and in other ways contributed largely to advertising the resources of the Southwest and Valley sections to the world. He is a hard worker, and has established a fine reputation for himself as an all-round newspaper man. He is devoted to Roanoke, his adopted home, and has declined several flattering offers to identify himself with papers elsewhere.

CHAPTER V.

HISTORICAL SKETCH OF SALEM.*

By Prof. F. V. N. PAINTER.

As we stand on Cemetery Hill, a scene of great beauty stretches out before us. Looking westward, we see on the left the rugged hills of the Blue Ridge with Twelve O'clock Knob rising into towering eminence; on the right, the level majestic range of the Catawba Mountain, a part of the Alleghany system, which extends far away to the south-west. Between these picturesque bordering mountains lies the level and fertile Roanoke Valley, with Roanoke river, like a broad belt of silver extending along the base of the Blue Ridge. Half hidden among the green foliage is the older portion of the town of Salem, while on all sides we discover new streets and scattered houses, the result of recent growth and the promise of future prosperity. The deep, cozy valleys and snow-capped summits of Switzerland afford more striking contrasts and sublimer views; but for quiet beauty and sweet attractiveness the Roanoke Valley at Salem may fairly challenge comparison with the most famous regions of the Old or the New World. As we gaze upon its fertility and beauty, we are reminded of the Vale of Siddim, which, in the eyes of Lot, was fair as "the garden of the Lord."

HISTORIC INTEREST.

This fair scene is not without historic interest. Lengthwise through the Valley led the great Indian trail, traversed by the Northern and the Southern Indians on their peaceful or war-like expeditions. When the colonists settled at Jamestown this region was not occupied by any Indian tribe, but was used by all as a common hunting ground. A century and a half ago, when it began to be settled by the hardy pioneers, the Valley became the scene of heroic courage and heart-rending tragedy.

The land on which Salem stands was originally owned by Gen. Andrew Lewis, the hero of Point Pleasant, whose body—still without a monument!—reposes in the town on a hill overlooking the beautiful valley. It was conveyed to him by George III, in a patent dated Sep-

---

* For many facts embodied in this sketch I am indebted to William McCauley, Esq., and Frederick Johnson, Esq., whose efforts to preserve the early history of Salem and Roanoke county deserve general and grateful recognition.

tember 10, 1767, "for divers good causes and considerations, but more especially for and in consideration of the sum of three pounds five shillings of good and lawful money." At the death of General Lewis, the land passed into the possession of his son, Capt. William Lewis.

BEGINNINGS.

The history of Salem does not extend back to a very remote date. The founder of the town was James Simpson, who laid it out in 1802 on land purchased of Captain Lewis a year or two earlier. As compared with recent achievements in town-building in South-western Virginia, the beginning was very modest. There was at first but a single street, and that extended only from what is now Market street to Union street. In 1813 the town was enlarged by extending Main street eastward to Walnut street, now College Avenue, and opening a few cross streets and alleys. But after a dozen years of growth, the houses could be counted on one's fingers, and the population did not exceed a hundred.

It is not commonly known that Salem experienced a brief period of extraordinary business activity (what is now called a "boom") soon after the second war with Great Britain. About the year 1816 the Roanoke Navigation Company was chartered by the Legislature for the purpose of opening Roanoke river for navigation from Weldon, North Carolina, to Salem. At the same time the Lynchburg and Salem turnpike was projected. As the terminus of these two great prospective avenues of trade, Salem became the scene of great commercial enterprise and activity. A number of large houses were built, of which several—the residence of Dr. Dillard and that of the late Dr. Griffin—are still standing. Unfortunately, the Navigation Company, after getting one small barge to Salem, collapsed, and the Lynchburg and Salem turnpike, owing to the failure of the contractor, was not completed. The splendid hopes entertained for a season were not realized.

In 1838 the General Assembly of Virginia created out of parts of Botetourt and Montgomery counties the new county of Roanoke. Salem was selected as the county-seat, and from this time dates the real growth and prosperity of the old town. The first session of the County Court was held on the 24th of May, 1838, at the house of James C. Huff, now the residence of Mr. D. C. Stover, and both the County and Circuit Courts were held there until 1841, when the court-house was completed. Small industries began to spring up, new houses were erected and the population increased. Among the public spirited citizens of this period was Mr. Abraham Hupp, who, after losing one house by fire, speedily built another, and, with flying colors, opened the "Phœnix Tin Establishment," the building now occupied by Messrs. Dame & Francis. He was a leader in every enterprise for the improvement of the town. Another citizen worthy of mention was Mr. George Baughman, who, in 1849, started the *Roanoke Gazette*, a monthly publication costing the modest sum of twenty-five cents a year. It became a valuable medium for the discussion of questions of public interest, and, in connection with its successors, contributed no small share to the improvement of the town. After a career of only a few months, it was succeeded, in 1850, by the *Roanoke Beacon*, a Democratic publication that exerted a wide influence in the county. In 1854 the *Mountain Signal* was established by Mr. William G. Miller in the interest of the Know-Nothings, but after running a year it suspended publication. It was followed by *The Republican*, as a Whig paper, but owing to the death of Mr. Wilson, one of the proprietors, it was soon discontinued. The newspapers of more recent date are the *Salem Register*, the *Roanoke Times*, *The Conservative* and the *Times-Register*, the largest, most influential and best conducted of them all.

The completion of the Virginia and Tennessee Railroad to Salem in 1857 served to stimulate the growth of the town. Its population at different times may be given approximately as follows: In 1844, 200; in 1850, 400; and in 1860, 800.

BUILDING CHURCHES.

To the period we are now considering belongs the building of most of the churches. Their number and architecture reflect credit upon the liberality and piety of the people. To the Methodists, whose missionary activity deserves appreciative recognition, belongs the honor of having built the first church in Salem. It was built in 1813, a small log structure, afterwards weather-boarded and plastered, and stood immediately in the rear of the Fleming block. There was at first no regular pastor or circuit-rider, and the services were conducted by Edward and Samuel Mitchell, local preachers, who enjoyed the confidence of the community. In 1849 the little log church had ceased to meet the wants of the growing congregation, and a larger and better building was erected at a cost of $2,500 on Walnut street, afterwards College street and now College Avenue. It has since been enlarged and improved, and is at present a commodious and comfortable place of worship.

In 1831 a Presbyterian congregation of sixteen members was organized by the Rev. Roswell Tenney, and two years later a church was erected. Subsequently it was used for school purposes, and was long known as the "Academy building." Two years ago it was torn down to make room for the present handsome public school building. In 1852, possibly stimulated in some degree by the activity of the Methodists, the Presbyterians built their present beautiful church on the corner of Main and Market streets.

In 1823 a Baptist church was begun on that part of the cemetery grounds now occupied by the soldiers' graves. For some reason it was never fully completed, and after a long time it was finally blown down by a storm. The present attractive Baptist church on Broad street was built in 1875.

The large Lutheran church on the corner of Main and College streets was built in 1858 at a cost of $6,000. Three of the original members of this congregation, Mr. and Mrs. Peter Shirey and Dr. S. C. Wells, are still worshiping there.

The Episcopal chapel, afterwards remodeled and improved, was built in 1869. Since the war the colored people have erected three substantial and creditable places of worship.

ROANOKE COLLEGE.

Until recently, no other agency contributed so much to the welfare of Salem as Roanoke College. While increasing the volume of business, it has fostered the literary culture of the community. To its influence is due in no small degree the intelligence for which the town has been so long noted.

This institution had its beginning in the Virginia Collegiate Institute, a classical school established by the Rev. C. C. Baughman and the Rev. David F. Bittle at Mount Tabor, in Augusta county. In 1847 the Institute, which had entered upon a prosperous career, was removed to Salem. In 1851 the catalogue showed the number of students to be fifty-five, one-third of whom were preparing for the ministry. In 1853 the Institute, by an act of incorporation, was changed into Roanoke College, and the Rev. David F. Bittle chosen first President. The institution was founded to accomplish three objects: 1. To provide better educational facilities for the Lutheran population of Virginia. 2. To train worthy young men for the gospel ministry. 3. To bring education within the reach of a larger number by reducing as far as possible the cost of living. These principles for many years gave distinctive character to the school, and established it in the confidence and affection of the people.

For twenty-three years the history of the college is inseparably linked with the name of Dr. Bittle. The successful founding of the institution was his life-work. He was peculiarly fitted for the difficult task to which he was called. He had received from nature a strong physical constitution and robust common sense—endowments which, in the task before him, were far more valuable than brilliancy of genius. He was a man of large experience and wide learning. In his bosom beat a great, unselfish heart. His simple and honest manner was the natural expression of a guileless and genial spirit. He was a man of weight, one who inspired confidence, made friends and attracted helpers. In accepting the presidency he was not moved by an idle ambition, but a noble purpose. In the college he saw the means of advancing the church and benefiting society. The buildings, grounds, library, apparatus and cabinets, as we see them to-day, are almost entirely the work of this remarkable man. September 25, 1876, he suddenly expired in the faculty room, dying, as he had lived, at the post of duty.

He was succeeded by the Rev. T. W. Dosh, D. D., who, after one year, resigned. Then followed Prof. J. D. Dreher, Ph. D., the present incumbent. The college, without sectarian bias, inculcates the principles of Christianity. Its ideal is an earnest manhood consecrated to duty and usefulness in the world. The courses of study are thorough and practical, bridging somewhat the chasm that usually divides the higher education from the needs of practical life. It has four large brick buildings, ample and beautiful grounds, a library of 17,000 volumes, a good collection of chemical and physical apparatus, and extensive mineral and geological cabinets. The expense is moderate. It commands a wide patronage—students coming from many States, Indian Territory, Mexico and Japan. Its graduates are found in most of the States of the Union.

THE WAR PERIOD.

The growth of the town was retarded by the civil war, though it did not come within the range of any of the great military campaigns. Its people were loyal to the Confederacy, and furnished their quota of men and supplies to the Southern armies. In 1861 Abraham Hupp organized the Salem Flying Artillery, of which he was elected captain, and of which he retained command till his death, in 1863.

Unlike most of the institutions of its class, Roanoke College did not suspend exercises during the war, but all the students over sixteen years of age were provided with guns and ammunition by the Confederate government, and were required to drill once a week. The College Company, as it was called, was under the command of Capt. George W. Holland, now President of Newberry College in South Carolina, and was subject to call whenever its services were needed to repel invasion.

To the Roanoke Grays, a company raised by Capt. M. P. Deyerle, Salem furnished several men, among them the Rev. R. C. Holland, D. D., now of Charleston, S. C., and the Rev. S. A. Repass, D. D., of Allentown, Pa. This company belonged to Picket's Division, and was in the famous charge on Cemetery Ridge at the battle of Gettysburg. To the Dixie Grays, organized by Capt. A. J. Deyerle, belonged a number of our prominent citizens, among whom we mention William McCauley, J. P. Houtz, M. P. Frantz and the late John M. Evans.

Salem was only twice invaded by Federal troops, once in 1863 by General Averill, and again in 1864 by General Hunter. The town was not given up to pillage, and beyond the uneasiness occasioned by the presence of hostile troops and the burning of several commissary stores, it suffered no material harm.

AFTER THE WAR.

After the war Salem showed a slow but steady growth. The beauty of its location, the salubrity of its climate, the fertility of its soil, and the vicinity of mineral springs, made it a popular summer resort. New hotels, notably the Duval House (now Hotel Lucerne) and the Lake Spring Hotel, were built, and the town thus provided with excellent accommodations for the increasing number of its visitors. From time to time a new manufacturing industry was started, the Hockman Sash, Door and Blind Factory and the Camden Iron Works deserving special mention. Every year new buildings were erected, and under a wise administration of the city government the streets were improved. Within this period Broad street was opened, and became a favorite locality for residences. Its many fine houses make it one of the handsomest thoroughfares in the town. Largely through the enterprise of Mr. F. J. Chapman the town was provided with an excellent system of water-works, which brought pure spring-water within reach of every home.

In 1880 the population had increased to about 1,800, and Salem was widely known as one of the most attractive towns in the Old Dominion. Noted for the refinement, intelligence and morality of its people, it became deservedly popular as a place of residence, and called forth encomiums from admiring visitors. Thus Dr. Washington Gladden wrote in 1882: "The Blue Ridge and the Alleghanies draw close together at Salem, but the valley they include is, with reason, declared to be the fairest and most fertile in all Virginia. * * * * Salem is a handsome town, the neatest and most like New England of any I have seen in Virginia." To the same effect Mr. Charles Dudley Warner wrote in 1883: "Observation leads us to say that it is the abode of a hospitable, industrious and highly moral people. Indeed, I do not know any New England town in which the moral standard of living is higher. In Salem everybody has the habit of going to church, and most of the leading religious denominations are represented. It is a town where the domestic virtues thrive, and there are no scandals."

RECENT GROWTH.

We now come to a story of marvelous growth and prosperity.* It

---

*The reader will elsewhere find biographical sketches of the men—D. B. Strouse, Esq., T. J. Thickel, Capt. S. F. Simmons, J. W. F. Allemong, Col. A. M. Bowman and others—who have been active in promoting the growth of Salem.

began with the organization of the Salem Improvement Company in October, 1889. This company purchased about 900 acres of land adjoining the town, and favorably situated for residences, business houses, and manufacturing purposes. Wide streets and avenues were laid out, and lots placed on the market December 11th, 1889. The sale was successful. Other land companies were soon organized, and all working in harmony and offering great inducements to manufacturers, they located many industrial plants, and gave an extraordinary impetus to the growth of the town.

Since that time the growth of Salem has been more rapid and substantial than that of any other place of its size in Virginia. Although building operations were retarded for lack of material, more than five hundred buildings, many of them handsome residences and costly business houses and factories, have been built. The population has increased from about two thousand to more than four thousand. The business of the post-office and telegraph office has increased 500 per cent. The iron furnace now in blast and the factories in operation and actually secured will employ probably two thousand hands, including females, and insure a large increase of the present population in the near future.

The improvements made in Salem are of a solid and substantial character. It is lighted by electricity.

The new streets have been graded and macadamized on both sides of the river, brick pavements have been laid, the water-works have been extended, and an additional water-supply secured to meet the needs of the large increase in population. A new system of water-works has been put in on the south side of the river, and three handsome iron bridges have been constructed to connect the two parts of the city. College Avenue, seventy-five feet wide, extending from Main street to the new passenger station of the Norfolk and Western Railroad, has been well macadamized. This is destined to become the principal business street of Salem, and as only brick or stone buildings may be erected on it, it is likely to be one of the finest thoroughfares in the State. Among the imposing buildings already erected on this street are the Hotel Salem, a brick edifice of five stories, with more than one hundred rooms, and the Improvement Company's bank and office building, a three-story brick structure trimmed in stone and terra-cotta. A number of handsome brick business houses have already been built on this avenue. At the head of it stands the group of brick buildings of Roanoke College, and at its foot the new stone passenger station of the Norfolk and Western, one of the finest on the line of its road.

GEOGRAPHICAL POSITION.

The natural resources of South-west Virginia are well known. It is destined to become one of the most populous and most wealthy sections of our Union. The work of developing and utilizing this immense mineral wealth is now going forward with extraordinary rapidity. Old towns have been rejuvenated, new towns have sprung up, and furnaces, rolling mills, machine shops, and factories of all kinds have been built with the astonishing rapidity hitherto peculiar to the West.

The natural outlet for the entire region of South-west Virginia is along the Valley belt of counties which extends from north-east to south-west throughout its whole extent. From this central division the other parts of South-west Virginia may be reached, and in considerable measure have been reached, by lateral routes.

A glance at the map will show that Roanoke county, lying between the Alleghany and Blue Ridge mountains, is the natural gate-way to the vast resources farther west. Salem is the favorably-located county-seat, and the great routes of travel and traffic lead, and must continue to lead, by her doors. The geographical position of the town, its present and prospective railway connections, and the immense mineral wealth in the county and in the counties to the north-east and south, as well as to the south-west, mark Salem and its vicinity as a place destined to great industrial and commercial importance. The development of this immediate section is now going forward rapidly. It is confidently believed that this part of the Roanoke Valley will become for the entire State what it already is for South-west Virginia—the leading manufacturing and commercial center. No other point in Roanoke county, or indeed in this great coal and iron region, has greater advantages than Salem.

NATURAL ADVANTAGES.

With respect to natural advantages, Salem may challenge comparison with any other place in the Old Dominion. It is situated in the beautiful and fertile valley of the Roanoke, one thousand one hundred feet above sea level. Its altitude and excellent natural drainage make its healthfulness proverbial. It is free from malaria; it is in the region of mineral springs, several of which are quite near the town. Salem is itself popular as a summer resort for the people of the States farther South, as well as those of Eastern Virginia. "The town of Salem and its surroundings," wrote the late Dr. J. J. Moorman, for forty years resident physician at the famous White Sulphur Springs of West Virginia, "in connection with its elastic and invigorating atmosphere, its abundant supply of pure, living spring-water, brought to the door of every one that desires it; its natural drainage of all superfluous water from the surface of the ground; its freedom from fogs, low and marshy ground, stagnant pools, and all generators of malaria, distinctly point it out as an unusually healthy location, and one most desirable for a life-time residence."

The climate is mild, equable and invigorating. As the summers are exempt from extreme heat, and the winters from extreme cold, the climate is well adapted to people from all parts of our country, and especially to those from New England and the Middle States. No case of sunstroke has occurred here. Tornadoes and cyclones are not known. The average rain-fall is about forty-two inches a year.

The soil of the Roanoke valley is very productive. Large crops of the cereal grains are raised, and vegetables and fruits grow in great profusion. The Roanoke river, which winds about the hills on the southern side of the valley, affords ample water-power. The hills and mountains around Salem are well timbered, and there are also tracts of timbered land in the valley. All the hard woods for wagon-making, and the finer woods for furniture, abound in this part of Virginia.

Iron ores of several varieties and of excellent quality—brown hematite ores, magnetic iron ores, oxides of manganese and ferro-manganese abound in the vicinity of Salem, in other parts of Roanoke county and throughout this section of the State. Limestone of good fluxing quality also abounds at Salem. Pocahontas coal is delivered for manufacturing purposes at a very low price. Pacahontas coke, the best in America for furnace use, can be had in inexhaustible quantities at a price which is fully $1.25 a ton less than it costs many furnaces now using it in the Chattanooga and Northern Alabama districts. Owing to the proximity of all the raw materials, the best quality of foundry iron, mill iron and basic pig can be made at Salem at a large profit, the cost of manfacturing iron here being about four dollars a ton less than in Eastern Pennsylvania. Furnaces in this vicinity are now shipping iron in large quantities to consumers in Pennsylvania and New England.

A MANUFACTURING AND COMMERCIAL CENTER.

Salem is not only the gate-way to to the immense resources of Southwest Virginia, but it has great natural resources immediately around it, and within easy distances in every direction. The various branches and connections of the Norfolk and Western Railroad afford excellent transportation facilities, which will probably be increased by new lines in the near future. Salem is the chartered terminus of the Valley branch of the Baltimore and Ohio Railroad. This branch road, starting at Harper's Ferry, is in operation to Lexington, fifty-four miles north-east of Salem, and fully one-half of the grading has been done between these two points. A dummy railway line of standard gauge, already in operation between

Salem and Roanoke, affords rapid transit between the two cities. A franchise has been obtained for the Salem Electric Street Railway, which will be extended to Roanoke, on the south side of the river. The freight rates to and from Salem are as favorable as from any other point in this section of the State.

The capacity of the Salem Furnace is one hundred and twenty tons a day. A rolling mill now building, will manufacture this pig-iron into cottonties, and such other shapes as may be demanded by the trade or by the manufacturing interests of Salem. Timber is within easy reach. Wool can be obtained in this section, and cotton laid down at Salem at low prices. The climate is adapted to the manufacture of silk goods. The Salem Steam Tannery furnishes leather for the manufacture of shoes, saddles, harness and belting.

Sites for factories are given free, and in many cases liberal subscriptions are made to the capital stock of manufacturing companies. Factories of all kinds are exempt from municipal taxation for ten years. The taxes are low, living is cheap, and labor is abundant. As will be seen from the list of industries appended to this sketch, Salem is a manufacturing center of growing importance.

THE FUTURE OF SALEM.

Salem will continue to grow. This is assured by all the conditions that have brought about its recent remarkable progress. Its natural advantages are unsurpassed. At the head of its business interests are men of energy, experience, sagacity, and integrity. Millions of dollars are invested in its numerous industries and in its land, improvement and development companies, and hundreds of investors, North and South, are interested in its success. The work that has been done may be fairly regarded as only a beginning. The success achieved already in locating plants is the promise and pledge of still greater success in the future. Negotiations are constantly going on to secure additional industries of various kinds. With a people united in their determination to build up their city, and with the strong support and co-operation of the combined capital of the various land companies (more than four million dollars), it will be seen that the largest enterprises are within the reach of Salem, and that such enterprises are actually being located. It is the aim and ambition of the people, not only to build up a prosperous industrial center, but to make Salem a beautiful and attractive place—the "Queen City of the South-west."

LIST OF INDUSTRIES.

The Salem Furnace; capacity, 120 tons of pig-iron a day; furnace will go into blast in August.

The Salem Rolling Mills; site of ten acres secured and buildings in course of erection.

The Holstein Woolen Mills and Clothing Factory; main building and clothing factory completed; in operation.

The Salem Steam Tannery (Leas & McVitty, of Philadelphia); one of the largest tanneries in the South; in operation.

The Edward Corbett Machine-shops for making machinery for roller flouring mills; buildings in course of erection.

The Chadwick Two-wheeler Works (from Olean, New York); extensive buildings in course of erection.

The Salem Wagon Factory; in operation.

The Salem Gas Heater Works; building completed.

Camden Iron Works; castings, iron fronts for buildings, iron fencing, etc.; in operation.

The Electric Light Plant.

The Electric Street Railway; charter secured and company arranging to begin operations.

Salem Folding Chair Factory; has exclusive right to manufacture the Gage Folding Chair for Virginia, North Carolina, Maryland, Delaware and District of Columbia; in operation.

The Conrad Chair and Manufacturing Company; works in operation.

The Mineral Fibre Company; buildings completed.

The Bank of Salem.

The Farmers National Bank of Salem.

The Salem Loan and Trust Company.

The Salem Banking and Investment Company.

The Salem Building and Investment Company.

The *Times-Register* Book and Job Printing Office; publishers of the Salem *Times-Register* and the Roanoke *Collegian*.

The Williams Ink Factory; in operation.

The Salem Carriage Factory; in operation.

N. Hockman's Sash, Door, Blind and Building Establishment; largest and most complete in South-west Virginia; in operation.

The Planing and Building Works of W. G. B. Fitzgerald & Co. (from Danville, Va.); in operation.

Sash, Door, Blind and Building Factory and Lumber Yard of Adams, Clements & Co.; in operation.

The Crystal Ice Company; in operation.

The Gravely Foundry and Machine Works.

Pierpont Brick Works (of North Haven, Connecticut); in operation.

Brick Works of Nininger, Son & Martin; in operation.

Novelty Brick Works of W. H. Shuff & Co.; in operation.

Brick Works of Bethel & Fitzgerald; in operation.

Brick Works of James C. Deyerle; in operation.

Carriage and Wagon Works of Ligon Brothers; in operation.

J. C. Langhorne's Roller Flouring Mills; in operation.

The Salem Roller Fouring Mills; in operation.

Johnson Brothers' Grain Cradle Works; in operation.

The Salem Marble Works; in operation.

J. W. Harveycutter's Tannery; in operation.

Salem Mattress Factory; in operation.

Daniel Scull's Steam Laundry.

Fruit and Vegetable Cannery of Preston, Evans & Co.; in operation.

Fruit Cannery of H. Garst & Son; in operation.

Fruit Cannery of J. A. Garst & Brother; in operation.

The foregoing list includes only those industries which are already in operation, or whose buildings are in course of erection. While works are being built it is not easy to give the exact number of hands that will be employed. It is safe, however, to say that the foregoing list represents a combined force of 2,000 hands.

The chief offices of the following companies are in Salem: The Bonsack Machine Company, capital $1,600,000; the Carper Spark Conductor Company, capital $1,000,000, and the Comas Machine Company, capital $100,000.

The aggregate capital stock of the various land, improvement and development companies of Salem is a little more than $4,000,000, and this financial backing gives a great impetus to the growth of the town and the establishment of manufactories.

Mr. D. B. STRAUSE, of Salem, the subject of this paper, was born July 29th, 1838, in Augusta county, Virginia, on a plantation nine miles from Staunton. He is the son of Peter and Catharine Beard Strause. The father was a native of Pennsylvania, and the mother of Virginia. Peter Strause was a physician and a farmer, doing a farming business in addition to his practice as physician. He died in 1871.

Mr. D. B. Strause was educated at Roanoke College and the Washington and Lee University, graduating from the latter place in 1867. In 1861 he entered the Confederate army as a private, but for the last two years he commanded his company. He was in active service during all the years of the war, and was a brave and valiant soldier. After the war he located at Salem, Virginia, in July, 1867, and engaged in the practice of law, which profession he continued in until 1886, establishing a remunerative and extensive practice, not only in Roanoke and adjacent counties, but in the Superior Court; and during his years of practice he was regarded as one of the most successful attorneys in South-west Virginia. Having become largely interested in important business matters outside of his profession, which required much of his time, he abandoned the practice of law in order to give his entire time to his other pursuits, and it is pleasant to record that he has been as successful in business as he was at the Bar. At the present time he is President of the Bonsack Machine Company, which represents a capital stock of $1,600,000. He is also President and a large stockholder in the Comas Machine Company, the Salem Furnace Company and the Carper Railway Engine Company, and is interested in several of the large and most important enterprises of Roanoke county, having been in sympathy with every enterprise that has had for its object the development of this section of the country.

Mr. Strause was married in June, 1865, to Miss Lucy A. Evans, of Roanoke county, a daughter of Tipton B. Evans, of that county. They have three children—Clarence B., Lillie and Everett. Mr. Strause has been for many years an active and official member of the Lutheran church, and he has taught the Bible Class in the Baptist Sunday-school for more than thirteen years. This may seem strange, that being a Lutheran he should interest himself in the work of the Baptist society, but this merely shows the christian spirit manifested by this gentleman. His services being needed in his sister church, he has thrown down the barrier of sectarianism and shown a willingness to labor in his Master's vineyard, no matter where it may be. Christianity to such men is a living, eternal element, blessed and blessing.

ALPHEUS M. BOWMAN.—The subject of this sketch is a member of the well-known Bowman family of Rockingham county, Virginia, who were among the earliest settlers of Virginia. The old homestead on which Mr. Bowman was born has been in the possession of the Bowmans since the year 1835. Mr. A. M. Bowman was born January 11th, 1847, and is a son of George M. and Sallie Bowman. At the age of sixteen he left school and enlisted in Company H, 12th Virginia Cavalry, better known as Ashby's, serving until 1864, when he was captured during Sheridan's raid through the Valley and taken to Fort Delaware and held prisoner until after General Lee's surrender. Returning home from the war, he resumed his studies for two sessions at the New Market Academy at New Market, Virginia. His father died in 1861, and Mr. Bowman, after finishing his education, returned to the old homestead and farmed until 1869. He then located at Waynesboro, Augusta county, Virginia, and engaged in farming and fine-stock raising, doing much to improve the well-known breed of short-horn cattle.

In 1883 he located at Saltville, Virginia, and in connection with Mr. George W. Palmer organized the Palmer & Bowman Company, Mr. Bowman being the managing director, and made a great success of the business. This company made a specialty of short-horned cattle, owning the largest herd of registered short-horns in the world.

He has also taken a deep interest in agriculture, and was for ten years President of the Baldwin Agricultural Society at Staunton, and for eight years a director of the State Agricultural Society at Richmond.

In December, 1889, he located at Salem, and became actively engaged in the real estate business and the development of Salem; and to his untiring zeal and energy may be attributed, in a reasonable degree, the locating and building of several of Salem's most important industries, being always ready to assist in any work or enterprise which had for its object the good of the town and community. On January 27th, 1890, he organized the Salem Development Company, with an authorized capital of one million dollars, and paid up capital of three hundred and seven thousand dollars, which company was the first in the city of Salem to declare a cash dividend, paying the stockholders fifty per cent., seven months after the company was organized. This company has also located more large industries in Salem than any other company in the city.

Mr. Bowman is also interested in several other industries. He is a director of the Bank of Salem and South Salem Land Company; President of the Salem Real Estate Exchange; President of the Chadwick Two-wheeler Company; Trustee of Roanoke College. He has also taken a prominent part in politics, and is Chairman of the County Executive Committee, a member of the State Executive Committee, and has served as delegate to every Democratic State Convention since 1883. He was Chairman of the Congressional District Committee of the 9th District for six years, and a delegate to the National Democratic Convention which nominated Grover Cleveland in 1880. This interesting fact may be mentioned incidentally in the career of Mr. Bowman: His grandfather voted for every Democratic candidate for President voted for by the people from the foundation of the Government until 1868, when he cast his last vote, and on that day the grandson cast his first vote for the same ticket.

Mr. Bowman was married February 11th, 1869, to Miss Mary E. Killian, only daughter of Rev. Jacob Killian, a well known divine of Augusta county, Virginia. To this union have been born eight children, six of whom survive.

Mr. Bowman has for many years been a member of the Lutheran church, and is an Elder in the Salem Lutheran church, in which he takes great interest, ever ready to lend a helping hand in church work.

Judge WINGFIELD GRIFFIN.—On the 26th day of September, 1846, was born Judge Wingfield Griffin, at Salem, Virginia. He is the son of Dr. J. Hook Griffin, deceased, who was one of the best know and most celebrated physicians in South-western Virginia. Dr. Griffin was a staunch Whig, and a firm believer in the *code duello*. Young Wingfield Griffin responded to the call for volunteers, entering the Confederate service in the 2d Virginia Regiment of Cavalry, in which he served to the end. He was educated at Roanoke College and the Virginia Military Institute. After the close of the war he studied law at the University of Virginia, and after a few years of practice was appointed Judge of the County Court of Roanoke, and was afterwards elected by the people of Roanoke county as Commonwealth's Attorney. After his election Judge Griffin again began the practice of law, and in 1887 he was again elected Judge of the Court of Roanoke, which position he at the present occupies. Aside from his legal pursuits, he takes a deep interest in local affairs and in the progress and advancement of his county and section of the State. He has devoted much time and research in the interest of the mineral resources of Roanoke county, and is the author of many valuable papers which have attracted wide and merited attention. The city of Salem has also come in for a liberal share of his attention, and it possesses no better friend to its welfare than Judge Griffin. He was married in 1878 to Miss Claudine Booker, daughter of James M. Booker, of Lynchburg, Virginia. Two children have been born to him, Eugenia Whyte and Claudine.

Rev. **WILLIAM B. YONCE**, Ph. D., was born in Wythe county, near Wytheville, January 6th, 1827, his ancestors being early settlers of that county. He attended Wittenberg College, Springfield, Ohio, at which institution he graduated with first honor in 1852. During the two succeeding years he taught in the institution and pursued theological studies at the same time. In 1855 he came to Roanoke College and took the position of Principal of the Preparatory Department and assistant in Ancient Languages. He filled this position for three years with entire satisfaction to the Faculty, and in 1857 was called to the Chair of Ancient Languages and Literature, which he has filled since that time with eminent success. During President Bittle's life he also gave instruction at various times in the subjects of Intellectual Philosophy, Psychology, and Logic.

His father, John Peter Yonce, a prominent and influential citizen and well-known agriculturist, died in 1853.

Prof. Dr. Yonce was married in 1856 to E. Victoria Glossbrenner, daughter of the late Bishop J. J. Glossbrenner, of the United Brethren church. Three children were born to them, namely, Prof. G. V. Yonce, who graduated at Roanoke College in the Class of '77, took a two-years post-graduate course of scientific study at Johns Hopkins University, and now occupies the Chair of Natural Science and Higher Mathematics in Lutherville Female Seminary, Lutherville, Maryland; Ivan V. Yonce, of the United States Railway Mail Service between Lynchburg and Bristol; and Rev. C. N. A. Yonce, who graduated at Roanoke College in the Class of '84, and is now pastor of Luther Memorial church at Blacksburg, Virginia, formerly of Scranton, Mississippi.

During his entire connection with the college Rev. Dr. Yonce, the subject of this sketch, has been a minister of the gospel in connection with the Evangelical Lutheran Synod of South-west Virginia. Though never having served as pastor of any special charge, yet he is influential in his church, has held many positions of prominence and importance in his Synod, is a zealous and active worker in his ministerial office, and consecrates his best and noblest efforts to the upbuilding of Christ's cause. He is highly esteemed as a citizen and as a counsellor, and is a friend to all in time of trouble. It is such men who enrich mankind and make the world better for having lived in it.

Col. GEORGE W. HANSBROUGH.—

The subject of this sketch, Colonel Hansbrough, was born August 16th, 1831, in Culpeper county, Virginia, and was a son of A. H. and E. C. Hansbrough, and was educated academically and professionally at the University of Virginia. He located in Taylor county, Virginia, where he practiced his profession, and was Commonwealth's Attorney until the war broke out, when he organized a battalion of six companies of Virginia Infantry (the 9th Va.), but better known as "Hansbrough's Battalion," and was its commandant until it became disorganized by casualties and death; and afterwards, to the end of the war, remained in active service in behalf of the cause of his native South. He was wounded severely on the 13th December, 1861, in the battle of Alleghany Mountain in Highland county, an engagement which, though but slightly mentioned in history, was greatly talked of at the time of its occurrence, and was one of the most fiercely fought of the whole war, and was the one where Gen. Edward Johnson gained his famous *sobriquet* of "Alleghany Johnson." He was also engaged in many other of the battles of the war.

After the close of the war, he moved to his plantation on Roanoke river, two miles west of Salem, where he has ever since resided, but has devoted most of his time to the practice of the law in Roanoke and the adjacent counties. Since 1883 he has been the Reporter of the Supreme Court of Appeals, and has published twelve volumes, without at all dimin-

ishing his large practice in that court or in the courts below.

Colonel Hansbrough has only one child now living, his son Livingston C. Hansbrough, his partner in the practice of the law, about thirty years old, a graduate of Roanoke College in academics and of the University of Virginia in the law. He is also President of the Algoma Coal and Iron Company, and he is thought by all who know him to have a bright future before him. Both are Episcopalians, the younger having been a Vestryman for some years, and both are highly respected for their intellectual and social qualities.

FLAVIUS JOSEPHUS CHAPMAN, Esq., the subject of this article, was born June 29th, 1839, in the county of Roanoke, in one mile of the city of Salem. He is the son of Col. H. H. Chapman, of the Virginia Militia, who died in 1863. Young Flavius attended the county schools twelve months, and at the age of twelve left home and went into the *Beacon* printing office, the first paper in Salem. He served here three years as apprentice, and then at the age of fifteen took charge of his father's hotel in Salem, which business he has been identified with ever since, and at the present time is engaged in. He is the owner of the Hotel Lucerne at Salem, the Lake Spring and Roanoke Red Sulphur Springs, and is also interested in the new Hotel Salem in this place. In 1875 Mr. Chapman became interested in minerals and made exploring expeditions throughout Roanoke and surrounding counties, which were the means of discovering and developing the rich mineral resources so abundantly abounding, but at that time unknown and unrecognized. At one time Mr. Chapman was directly interested in the following mines: the Edith, Rorer, Starkey, Bott, Hopper, Clark Summit, Tipton, Locust Hill, Jackson, Walker, "Gale," Swacker, Jewell, Hall and others, which he has personally located and developed. He has always been deeply and vitally interested in the development and improvement of Salem, and it is largely due to him for its almost unprecedented growth and prosperity. He sought and found capital in which to develop the magnificent resources of the town, and diverted means and influence into the channel of its progress. Mr. Chapman built the Waterworks, the source of supply coming from the springs on his Lake Springs property, of which he gave the right of use to the town. He has been a staunch friend of the laboring classes, and every just cause finds a ready and willing champion in him. He is a man of keen business instincts, which have almost become an intuition. His business transactions all have their reason "for being" a success in every instance. His life might be said to have been a system of good investments, but his success brings no envy, for his prosperity is shared so liberally with all that it seems more like a community's fortunate venture or undertaking than an individual. His married and domestic life has been of the happiest kind. He was married in 1864 to Miss Clementine Persinger, a daughter of James S. Persinger, Esq., of Roanoke county. Eleven children have blessed this union, nine of whom are living, namely, Harry, manager of the Hotel Lucerne; Nannie W., Thomas Clay, Flavius Josephus, Jr., Clementine, Emma, William Watts, Helen and Fred R.

Rev. Dr. **CORNELIUS TYREE** was born in Amherst county, Virginia, September 22d, 1814. He is the son of Jacob Tyree, a farmer of Amherst county, who died at the age of sixty-five years, his mother living to the advanced age of eighty-six. After attending the schools of his native county he went to William and Mary College, and from thence to Columbia College, which college has since conferred upon him the degree of Doctor of Divinity. After leaving Columbia College he became pastor of the Baptist church at Lexington, Virginia, where he remained for five years, leaving there to become pastor of a large congregation at Powhattan, at which place he remained a number of years. In response to a call he went from this place to Bedford City, where he was very popular, his congregation being unwilling to part with him after a pastorate of ten years. In 1883 he came to Salem and took charge of the Baptist church, and by his unceasing work largely increased its membership. He still has charge of this congregation, and is very much loved.

Dr. Tyree has also become widely known by his literary work, which has made for him an enviable reputation. He is the author of a book entitled *The Living Epistle*, which was stolen by an English house, and first published in England, and afterwards reprinted by a New York house under a new title and without its author's name, but which afterwards made the *amende honorable* by issuing a new edition with the reverend author's name affixed and its original title, and paid him a royalty on the sales. Dr. Tyree was also winner of the "Woods" prize for the best essay on the "Glorious Sufficiency of Christ," published by the American Tract Society, competing against some of the most eminent literary men of the country. At present he has in preparation a volume of his sermons, which he hopes to finish during the coming year. Dr. Tyree has also been accorded a just prominence among the evangelists of the State, he being peculiarly successful in this field. The Doctor was first married to Miss Sophia Pullion, of

Spottsylvania county. In 1884 he was again married, to Miss Nannie Abraham, of Powhattan county. One child, a son, has blessed this union, Cornelius, Jr.

Prof. SIMON CARSON WELLS, the subject of this sketch, was born in Frederick county, Virginia, June 14, 1826. His father, Richard Wells, Esq., was of Scotch-Irish extraction, and a well known merchant and farmer of Frederick county. Carson was educated at the Newtown Academy and Preparatory Collegiate Institute near Staunton, and at Penn College, Gettysburg, Pennsylvania. He graduated in 1849, and in the same year accepted the position of teacher of mathematics in the Virginia Collegiate Institute at Salem, occupying this position four years. In the year 1853 the Institute was incorporated as the Roanoke College, and Professor Wells elected to the Chair of Mathematics and Natural Science, and has filled that chair for the long period of thirty-eight years. At the breaking out of the war, he was made engineer of the Salem Light Artillery, and was transferred to the Engineer Corps under General Trimble, and was later commissioned in the Signal Service of the Confederate States, occupying this position until the close of the war, serving in his company as the exigencies of the service required, in the field as scouts, sharp-shooters and supporters of heavy batteries. As soon as the war closed, he resumed his old chair, and in 1876 added Geology, and since that time his chair has been Mathematics, Astronomy and Geology. In 1878 he prepared and read a "History of the Quarto-Centennial of Roanoke College," and also prepared a sketch of Dr. Bittle, a former President of the College. The Professor has been an indefatigable worker in his chosen fields, and has written on many scientific subjects, and delivered lectures on the same. He is well known in the scientific world, and for the past ten years his papers and articles have been widely quoted and discussed. For a number of years, outside of his school duties, he has been engaged in prospecting and developing the mineral resources of the South-west. Since his connection with the college, he has never had a vacation, except the four years of the war, when he was in active service. He was married in 1851 to Miss P. L. Pitzer, a daughter of Madison Pitzer, a well known citizen of Roanoke county. He is the father of four sons, three of whom are living—M. P., in the United States Railway Service; Carson, a prominent railroad contractor, and Russell L., a student at Roanoke College. Luther was drowned in the Grand river, Colorado, and was a prominent contractor in that State.

The Professor in 1870 made the first map of Salem. He is a trustee and elder in the Lutheran church of

Salem, having held both of these positions since the organization of the church in 1850.

Rev. LUTHER A. FOX, D. D.

—It affords a genuine pleasure to write of such men as Rev. Luther A. Fox, D. D., a scholar and author, who is extensively known and valued for his sterling worth, integrity and uprightness of public and private character. Luther Fox was born August 3d, 1843, in Randolph county, North Carolina. His father was a divine; both father and mother were natives of North Carolina. The subject of our sketch graduated at Roanoke College in 1868, and afterwards became pastor of a church at Big Lick, now Roanoke. From here he went to Stroudsburg, Pennsylvania, and from that place to Waynesborough, Virginia, where he remained until he was called to the chair of Philosophy at Roanoke College in 1882, which he fills at this present time. The Professor was married in 1862 to Miss Etta Glossbrenner, of Virginia, but who at the time of their marriage was residing at Baltimore, her father then being Bishop of the United Brethren Church and located in that city. Three children have been born to them, Clarence M., a graduate of Roanoke College, and at the present time studying theology with his father; Allie V. and Horace M. While a minister, Dr. Fox is not a pastor, but preaches frequently upon the invitation of pastors and churches. He is often called to preach special sermons. Much of his leisure time he devotes to literary work, and is well and favorably known in the field of religious literature. He is the author of "History of the Sunday-schools," and "Evidences of Future Life," and is a regular contributor to the *Lutheran Quarterly* and other religious papers and magazines.

ARTHUR BENTON PUGH

was born in Hampshire county, Virginia (now West Virginia), on March 26th, 1854, and is therefore 37 years of age. He worked on his father's farm in early life; was educated in the common schools of the day, and at the University of Virginia; taught in the public schools of his native county two terms; studied law in 1875-'76; was admitted to the Bar in September, 1876; removed at once to Petersburg, Grant county, West Virginia, where he located and entered upon the practice of his profession as an associate of the then well-known legal firm of White, Clayton & Flournoy, which had a large practice in the counties of Hampshire, Hardy and Grant. In the spring of 1877 Colonel White, the senior member of the firm, removed to Wheeling, West Virginia, having been elected Attorney General for the State, and thereupon the partnership was dissolved, and Mr. Pugh practiced alone until January, 1879, when he formed a partnership with Wilbur F. Dyer, Esq., a prominent and leading lawyer of the Grant County Bar. The new firm of Dyer & Pugh had for a number of years a large and lucrative practice in the counties of Grant, Hardy and Pendleton.

In November, 1885, Mr. Pugh was married to Miss Louie Anderson, the only daughter of Mr. David C. Anderson, of Franklin, Pendleton county, West Virginia, and granddaughter of the late Gen. James Boggs, of the same place. Both the father and grandfather of Mrs. Pugh have been prominent and leading citizens of their county and State. Mr. Anderson, who is still living, is regarded as one of the foremost scholars of the present age. Though an invalid for many years, he still takes an active interest in the progress of the times and of the developments in science, literature and the arts. Two children are the result of this marriage—one a boy (Benton Anderson) of four years, and the other a little girl (Mary Louise), now in her second year.

In 1884 Mr. Pugh was the candidate of the Democratic party for the office of Prosecuting Attorney for Grant county (a county largely Republican in politics), and ran considerably ahead of his ticket, being defeated by a small majority.

In July, 1888, he was appointed to and accepted a position in the Law Division of the Interior Department at Washington, D. C., at a salary of $2,000 a year. The duties of the position were exceedingly exacting and the responsibilities great, as compared with the meagre salary. During the period of his service Mr. Pugh prepared legal opinions in many of the most important cases arising under railroad land grants and the General Land Laws of the United States, which came before the Department. Not finding official life at Washington entirely suited to his tastes, and being impressed with the wonderful progress in South-west Virginia, and with the bright prospects for future growth and development, and being anxious to enter again the active practice of his profession, Mr. Pugh, of his own accord and against the expressed wishes of his superiors in office, resigned his position at Washington in November, 1890, and removed to Salem, where the impress of his energy and ability has already been felt in a marked degree, both in his endeavors to advance the interests of his adopted city and in the practice of the law. He has great faith in the future growth of Salem, and is thoroughly imbued with the belief that the city is destined to be one of the principal railroad and manufacturing centers of the Southern country.

A. B. PUGH, ESQ.

In our issue of two weeks since, we noted the fact that A. B. Pugh, Esq., had resigned his position as

Attorney in the Law Division of the Interior Department, at Washington, with a salary of $2,000 per annum. He was appointed to the position in February, 1888. He resigned for the purpose of engaging in the practice of law at Roanoke and Salem, Virginia, where flattering inducements have been offered him. In reply to Mr. Pugh's letter of resignation, the Secretary sends a very complimentary answer, from which we extract the following:

"It gratifies me very much to say that the performance of your very important duties has been most satisfactory. The Assistant Attorney General has frequently spoken to me of your very valuable assistance, and I have had occasion often to recognize it in my review of the work done in his office. You will bear with you to the new field of your duty my entire respect and my best wishes for your success."

Mr. Pugh is deservedly popular in the Interior Department, and is regarded by his associates in the Attorney General's Office as a very able lawyer, and they do not doubt he will win distinction and success at the Bar in his new field of labor. The recent developments at Salem and Roanoke in mineral wealth and enterprise insure a great future for that part of South-west Virginia.

While Mr. Pugh carries with him the best wishes of his late associates and many friends in Washington, the people of Hampshire, the place of his birth and boyhood, will look with pride upon his advancement and prosperity in his newly chosen home.

Mr. Pugh left with his family for Salem on Monday, where he will take up his residence, opening his law office there and in Roanoke, the latter city being connected with the former by a dummy road five miles in length.

DEPARTMENT OF THE INTERIOR,
OFFICE OF ASST. ATTORNEY GEN'L,
Washington, Oct. 22, 1890.

HON. JOHN W. NOBLE,
Secretary of the Interior.

SIR:—I hereby resign the office I now hold in the Law Division of this Department.

Though I have had no intimation that you desired my resignation, I have had the matter of its presentation under serious consideration for several months, owing to the meagre salary of the office as compared with its onerous and responsible duties, and to the further fact, of which I am constantly reminded, that my duty to my family demands more of me than I can reasonably expect to accomplish in official life here.

I have earnestly endeavored to faithfully discharge the duties of the position I now resign, and in taking this step I desire to render grateful acknowledgment for the very considerate treatment I have uniformly received from my superiors in office.

It is my wish that this resignation be accepted to take effect on the fifteenth of November next.

Very respectfully,
A. B. PUGH.

DEPARTMENT OF THE INTERIOR,
Washington, October, 1890.

A. B. PUGH, ESQ.,
Office of the Assistant Attorney General, Interior Department.

SIR:—I have yours of the 23d instant, tendering your resignation of the place you now hold, to take effect November 15th, which is accepted.

It gratifies me very much to say

that the performance of your very important duties has been most satisfactory. The Assistant Attorney General has frequently spoken to me of your very valuable assistance, and I have had occasion often to recognize it in my review of the work done in his office. You will bear with you to the new field of your duty my entire respect, and my best wishes for your success.

   Most respectfully yours,
 (Signed) JOHN W. NOBLE,
        Secretary.

Prof. F. V. N. PAINTER, A. M.—Stroll up the shady walk beneath the graceful trees of the college campus at Salem, Virginia, and you may meet a youthful-looking man, slight of build and rather below the medium height, who will greet you with a pleasing smile and friendly salutation. His hair and beard are light, to match the clear Saxon eyes that beam through the gold-rimmed spectacles with kindly greeting, though at times they can strike down through your own and make you feel that they almost read your thoughts. His face is refined, thoughtful, and full of expression; his dress is plainly neat; his manner courteous and affable. There is something about the man that suggests the student, and if you guess well enough to ask a passing student which one of the professors that is, he will say, "That is Professor Painter, who fills the chair of Modern Languages and Literature in Roanoke College."

He has established his claim to literary recognition chiefly through his "History of Education," published by the Appletons, and a recent work known as "Luther on Education."

Born April 12, 1852, in Hampshire county, Virginia, in ancestry he was peculiarly fortunate. A union of the industry, integrity, and sound judgment for which his paternal German forefathers were noted, with the delicacy of feeling and keenness of intellectual penetration that distinguished his mother's family, the Wilsons, such a union was most favorable for the production of a firm, well-rounded character. To these hereditary advantages, full scope for development was given by natural environments. The inspiring mountain scenery of his boyhood's home in Preston county, West Virginia, fostered in the molding of character a spirit of freedom and of independence; whilst the earnest Christian piety of the early home lent strength, in after years, to resist the manifold temptations of young manhood. A natural love for literature brought intense satisfaction in the eager perusal of whatever books could be found—works of fiction, history, travel, philosophy, and theology. In his childhood, two books of his father's small library were his especial delight—"Rollin's Ancient History," and a work called "Thrilling Adventures," relating to the American pioneers.

After having attended the schools of his native village, where he always held first rank, the young man was at various times salesman in stores, and at intervals devoted about three years to the glove-making business in his father's factory. But the old love for letters caused a refusal of advantageous business offers, and in the fall of 1870 we find him matriculated at Roanoke College. In his studies, methodical and earnest labor brought its reward; for during the last six months of the freshman year an average monthly grade of one hundred clearly foreshadowed the first honor of his class, which was bestowed upon graduation in 1874, together with the gold medal awarded for proficiency in metaphysical studies.

The same year he returned to his home in Aurora, West Virginia, and by the aid of an appropriation from the Peabody Fund established a graded school, introducing methods recommended by the best educational authorities. The school was popular from the start, and attracted a large patronage from a distance. Its success is still a pleasant tradition in the community. In 1875, having declined the nomination for the office of County Superintendent of Schools, he returned to Salem and entered the Lutheran Theological Seminary, graduating after a three-years course. During the last year at the seminary he served as pastor in an adjoining county by an arrangement requiring two days of the week to be spent in the saddle. Notwithstanding the unfavorable circumstances, his church grew in numbers and spirituality.

Having accepted a call in the fall of 1878 to serve his *Alma Mater* as Principal of the Boys' School and instructor in Modern Languages, he assiduously devoted the next several years to educational study, enlarging his attainments, especially in French and German, chiefly by a perusal of classic literature. The college granted a leave of absence during the summer months, and this opportunity was improved by securing the tutorship of native French and German teachers in New York City and Amherst, Massachusetts, succeeded by some months of study at Paris and at Bonn. The immediate literary results of this foreign trip were a pamphlet consisting of a series of letters that gave his observations while abroad, and a sketch of the Lutheran church in France published in the *Lutheran Quarterly*.

Upon returning to his college in the fall of 1882, he was made Professor of Modern Languages, and has since given much time and energy to the development of his department, which is now one of the most efficient in the South. Its chief advantages are an extensive field of study and exceptional thoroughness.

It was during his college course that Professor Painter became convinced of an unfortunate gap existing between the wants of practical life and the arrangement of the average curriculum—a conviction firmly established by subsequent study and experience. In 188_, a few weeks before the famous address of Charles Francis Adams at Harvard, he published a pamphlet entitled *The Modern* versus *the Ancient Languages*, in which he contended that greater prominence should be given French and German in our colleges. The discussion of the language question became general in circles of higher education, and in this discussion Professor Painter took a prominent part. In 1884 he read before the Modern Language Association in New York a paper advocating a "Modern Classical Course" in American colleges, to be co-ordinate with the Ancient Classical Course. The Association formally approved the plan, which, although at the time regarded by some as radical, has since been adopted in many institutions. Two years later he was again invited to address the Association in Baltimore, and great applause was accorded his paper on "Recent Educational Tendencies in their Relation to Language Teaching."

In 1883 the "History of Education" appeared in the *International Educational Series*, edited by Dr. W. T. Harris. This book embodies the result of four years study of the subject, and is pronounced the best popular treatise of its kind in America. Having already passed through a large number of editions, it still retains its popularity.

Another educational work, which appeared the present year, is "Luther on Education," comprising excellent translations of Luther's original writings on the subject, as well as a number of valuable chapters added by the translator. It has been received with great favor.

Professor Painter has in preparation a work on English Literature, written on a new plan, and designed to facilitate the teaching of that difficult branch of study in high schools and colleges. It will probably appear the coming year. In addition to these more serious literary efforts, he is a frequent contributor to periodical literature. A story entitled "Cha_tened and Sanctified," published in *The Independent* in 1887, received high praise. His style is remarkably perspicuous and facile.

He is a warm friend of popular education, having conducted for several years summer institutes in Virginia and West Virginia, for which work he is especially fitted because of wide experience and extensive reading, covering the whole field of educational science. Through his efforts was organized, in 1884, the Virginia Teachers' Reading Association, of which he was elected President for several consecutive years. The Association was a success from the start. With a large membership and an excellent course of study, it exerted no small influence upon the educational progress of the State.

In theology he is tolerant, attaching more importance to fundamental and practical truths than to speculative and polemical questions, and desiring Christian unity and concord. "I would rather be a martyr for love," he says, in the words of Baxter, "than for any other article of the Christian creed." His sermons are highly practical, indicative of careful study and an intimate acquintance with Biblical literature. In preaching his style is simple, easy and earnest, at times becoming quite animated as peculiar beauties of the Sacred Word reveal themselves to his devotional and finely poetic nature.

As was the case with Froebel, he is at home in the class-room, and he makes his pupils feel at home. One cannot help being stimulated to effort by the heartiness and deep interest with which he leads his learners into unexplored realms of knowledge. Possessing, as he does, a perfect candor and the soundest of practical views, his students love to inquire of him about questions of interest that may arise, and the information is imparted so pleasingly, and often with such captivating humor, that to spend an hour in his class-room is a pleasure.

Within a ten-minutes walk of the college buildings is the neat and home-like cottage where, with his family of six, he resides in great enjoyment of his domestic surroundings. "The man that does not make much of home-life," he says, "commits a great mistake." Having discovered the emptiness of popular applause, which is valueless unless based on corresponding merit, he believes that high positions bring with them multiplied cares and responsibilities. With the pleasant companionship of a congenial helpmate and loving children, this friend of ours is content to pursue his quiet, busy life, striving by diligent application and a faithful discharge of duty to make himself the best that God will let him be.

J. A. B. S.

CHAPTER VI.

BUENA VISTA, VIRGINIA.

By I. C. SHIELDS.

Buena Vista, Rockbridge county, Virginia, on the North branch of the James river, was founded May 22d, 1889, by the Buena Vista (land) Company. It is situated on two railroads, the Chesapeake and Ohio (James River Division) and the Norfolk and Western Railroad (formerly the Shenandoah Valley Railroad). It is fifty-four miles from Roanoke, forty miles west of Lynchburg, and eight miles east of Lexington, the junction of the Baltimore and Ohio and Chesapeake and Ohio Railroads, and forty miles south of Basic City and Waynesboro junction of the main line of the Chesapeake and Ohio and Norfolk and Western (S. V.) Railroads.

Population, October, 1889, 300; population, October, 1891, 3,500.

When so many gifted and trained and cultured minds have shaped reading matter of Buena Vista, the location of wonderful natural resources, and among the first placed in practical effort for the development of such opportunities, it is no easy task to come upon the scene in continuation, or indulging the hope of imparting a new interest.

To write of Buena Vista as any occasion worthy of its history requires, will call for much research in the past and a good share of industry to obtain all that can and should be compiled of its new life and wonderful growth.

A Colonial Governor, Alexander Spotswood, was the first in Virginia enterprise and sagacity to commence making iron in the Colony. He displayed his efforts successfully in the tide-water country. The purpose may have been in his mind to achieve new distinction in that important branch of our earliest developments when he became the chief of the party of cavaliers, the first of the white race to cross the mountains which separate the east from the section of Virginia known as the Valley and western part of the State. If so, the brief narrative of the achievements of the party, honored with the designation of "Knights of the Golden Horse Shoe," is silent. Had that been his design, the country at and adjacent to Swift Run Gap of the Blue Ridge mountains would have furnished, by investigation, great supplies of iron ore, the chief resource for the continuance, on a larger scale, of the industry successfully established below the mountains. That locality about the center of the famed Shenandoah Valley was the chosen scene for his exploits, that seemed, however, to occupy no more of his attention than to afford better protection to the inhabitants in the east from Indian excursions, as the hostile race made their forays across the mountains in search of plunder and to annoy the civilization moving westward. These events occurred about 1716, and it was sixty-three years afterwards, 1779, that chronicles the first production of iron in the Valley of Virginia or west of the Blue Ridge mountains. The locality where it was produced is only eight miles north of the town of Buena Vista, and was from ores of the same general leads that distinguish the large boundaries of the Buena Vista mineral properties. From that time forward this section of the State has been foremost in iron production, no less than five, including the splendid iron blast furnace now in operation here, having been built upon the inexhaustible resources of the iron ores of the Buena Vista property.

As in iron ore resources there are also numerous deposits of other valuable minerals on the thirteen thousand acres of the Buena Vista possessions. The rare and best of fire-brick clays are here, like the iron ore, in inexhaustible quantities. There are also ochre and umber, immense beds of marl, limestone and sandstone of pink and variegated colors, all furnishing materials for great development, that in varied kinds and at ready command and in immeasurable quantities, such as are nowhere else to be found in such close association.

Of all these valuable resources some, before the late development commenced, were to be observed by a casual examination, but the most careful and thorough research has been made by the first geologists of the country, and the revealed wealth tried in the crucible of the chemist with results as to all, with practical tests as to some, long since established as of the first order.

The immense forest, comprising from six to eight thousand acres of valuable lumber material, furnishes elements of wealth that are rarely found in one compact body and immediately on two trunk lines of railroad and to become benefited by other railroads planning for communication with Buena Vista.

An examination of the maps of the Norfolk and Western and the Chesapeake and Ohio Railroads will show the connections in all directions converging at Buena Vista, and prepare the reader the better to estimate and form conclusions respecting the prospect for the future, as well as to weigh properly the value and solidity of that leading progress which has been achieved.

The Buena Vista Company was organized under a charter obtained from the Virginia Legislature. The proposition to subscribe for the stock was made in January, 1889. The promoters were authorized to offer the property, thirteen thousand acres of farming, mineral and forest lands, at $207,000. The stock was subscribed for in ten days' time, and the company immediately organized under the charter referred to. There were no promoter's fees or anything of that kind, the stockholders obtaining the property for the amount asked for it at the time by the several proprietors.

The location selected for the town shows for itself—healthy, handsome and romantic—the very place for the growth which has taken place, and to realize all the bright and assured prospects of the future.

The area of the town may be considered unnecessarily large, as the matter is viewed in the light of a commencement, but when it is remembered that the plan adopted at the organization of the company, which secured ownership in lots to stockholders, as well as a prudent foresight that made ample reservation of location for industrial plants, etc., the seeming objection is not valid, and so experience has demonstrated. There are thirty avenues that would aggregate something like twenty-five miles in length, and there are about forty streets, the aggregate length of which would be about the same number of miles, and also for the alleys are fifteen miles or more in length of open space. The lots, in the main, are of a uniform depth of one hundred and twenty-five feet.

The perspective map issued by the Buena Vista Company will at a glance present the progress of the place, and will awaken an interest, as the mind is engaged in a review of the present and past, of more than ordinary importance. The buildings of all descriptions thus defined, it will be found, are only, if anything, under six hundred in number, and that every avenue and every street has been more or less improved as the building progress has taken shape. In relation to the character and style of the buildings, it is not out of place to say that much more than is usual, both in architectural display and durability of construction, have been observed at Buena Vista in the large number of elegant and stylish brick buildings. And it may be safely said that the place, in time of two years growth, is without a superior, if the equal is in existence, and this remark applies as well to the elegant industrial establishments as it does to the superb banking and mercantile houses, to the hotels and residences.

This young town, the location of which was a wheat-field in 1889, has now 3,500 inhabitants.

An electric light plant, equal to the demand of a city of twenty thousand or more inhabitants, is one of the completed enterprises.

The water-supply is drawn from the mountains by gravity. It is pure, cold, freestone water. The reservoirs are up in the mountain gorges and give great power to the flow, thereby making the water-works of Buena Vista complete for protection against fire, as well as in the abundance in meeting the wants of the inhabitants.

The following denominations are organized with congregations and have built or are building elegant houses of worship: Presbyterian, Methodist, Episcopalian, Lutheran, German Baptist or Dunkard, Baptist, and Catholic. The first five have completed their church edifices.

The free school facilities and advantages are thorough, and not an inhabitant, white or colored, entitled to the privileges, but receives the same. There are also high schools of the best grades, conducted by private enterprise.

The town government is constituted in a Mayor, Council, police, etc., and is judiciously and economically progressive.

In the several hotels Buena Vista can make a gratifying exhibit of her energy and the liberality of her people in erecting them. Chief among them is the Hotel Buena Vista that has arisen to take the place of its short-lived predecessor. The mournful scenes of a remarkable instantaneous conflagration will be remembered, but providential happenings may find solace in after-time. So the desolation of that fatal July day, 1890, that carried down the chief pride of Buena Vista to ashes, finds in its first annual round a new association of life, of pleasure and beauty. A splendid and completed edifice that now occupies that commanding site, and there to dispense its larger hospitality and to afford a larger opportunity for the throngs that will visit Buena Vista, imparts new animation, and invites to new resolutions and new determinations all the people of the new destiny of this lovely and picturesque valley town. The Romanesque style of architecture is blended in that structure to the extent of perfect relief, and nothing left off that will impart grace and elegance in adornment to the exterior, or that could be more happily associated with the faultless interior, as it shall in coming time dispense its home and its royal comforts in the entertainment at all times of more than two hundred guests.

Following is an accurate summary of the assets and liabilities of the Buena Vista Company ascertained September 26, 1891:

ASSETS.

Miscellaneous.

Cash on hand	$ 7,912 41
Bills receivable	172,226 67
Due on stock	2,244 00
Lumber bills (about)	8,000 00
" stacked on the yard	5,000 00
Wood cut and ranked	4,000 00
Furniture in hotel	4,000 00
	—$ 203,383 08

Negotiable Securities.

B. V. 1st mortgage bonds	$ 31,500
B. V. paper Manfg. Co., bonds	10,000
B. V. Iron Company's bonds	80,000
	—$ 121,500 00

SOUTH-WEST VIRGINIA AND THE VALLEY.

Real Estate.

Office b'ld'g and grounds	$ 30,000	
Hotel and grounds	125,000	
Value of unsold lots and other town property	852,500	
Value of mineral lands	1,000,000	
		$2,007,500 00

Stocks.

B. V. Iron Company	$ 74,000	
B. V. Paper Manfg. Co.	11,000	
B. V. Saddle and Harness Company	1,250	
Wise Wagon Works	15,000	
B. V. Fire Clay Company	345	
Marr Egg Crate Co.	5,000	
A. K. Rarig Company	50,000	
B. V. Glass Company	25,000	
B. V. Steel Company	75,000	
Equity building Co.	4,000	
North B. V. Company	10,000	
		$ 270,575 00
Total Assets,		$2,602,978 08

LIABILITIES.

Capital stock	$ 782,200 00	
Due on realty (as of Jan. 1st)	51,142 36	
Due on A. K. Rarig Co., stock	1,388 35	
Due on B. V. Steel Co., stock	71,864 70	
Due on B. V. Glass Co., stock	1,832 20	
Due on Marr Egg Crate Co., stock	1,000 00	
Due on North B. V. Co., stock	8,000 00	
Due on notes (bills payable)	36,951 54	
		$ 954,379 15
Surplus		1,648,598 93
		2,602,978 08

The several banking and stock companies and industries established at Buena Vista also deserve special reference. They are as follows:

The Buena Vista Iron Company Furnace	$ 300,000
The Buena Vista Steel Works	300,000
The Buena Vista Fire Clay Works	100,000
The Buena Vista Cassimere and Woolen Mills	70,000
The Buena Vista Saddle and Harness Factory	$ 10,000
The Buena Vista Glass Company	150,000
The Buena Vista Paper and Pulp Mills	100,000
The Buena Vista Steam Tannery	75,000
The Buena Vista Red Brick Works	20,000
The Buena Vista Planing Mills	30,000
The Buena Vista Furniture and Chair Factory	10,000
The Buena Vista Wire Fence Factory	10,000
A. K. Rarig Company, Boiler and Machine Works	300,000
Pennsylvania Investment Company	150,000
Building, Water and Light Company	40,000
Lumber Yard	20,000
Electric Light plant	15,000
Egg Crate Factory	50,000
Advocate Newspaper and Job Printing	5,000
Journal Newspaper and Job Printing	3,000
Bank of Buena Vista	100,000
Buena Vista Improvement Company	80,000
Buena Vista Loan and Trust Company, Bankers	100,000
Lexington Investment Company	30,000
Home Investment Company	50,000
Valley Investment Company	10,000
Southern Investment Company	60,000
Hart's Bottom Loan and Land Company	100,000
Loch Laird Land and Improvement Company	30,000
West Buena Vista Company	20,000
West Enderly Company	50,000
Clarkton Land Company	30,000
Waverly Land Company	50,000
Forest Land Company	100,000
Mont Rose Land Company	100,000
Buena Vista Saw-mills	10,000
Virginia Development and Investment Company	100,000
Virginia Real Estate and Investment Company	100,000
South-west Virginia Real Estate and Improvement Company	100,000
Buena Vista Abstract Title and Land Company	50,000
Wise Wagon Works	25,000
First National Bank	50,000
The Buena Vista Company's assets September 26, 1891	2,509,300
Surplus $2,602,978,08	
	$6,003,601

In addition to the above, several million dollars are invested by individuals in real estate, merchandise, etc.

The manufacturing establishments alone give employment to more than fifteen hundred operatives. Of some of their products special mention may be made.

The splendid Iron Blast Furnace, with all its superior outfit in mining and economic facilities, produces more than one hundred tons of pig-iron every twenty-four hours. Eighty-five per cent. of this product is foundry iron, and fifty per cent of the same is number one foundry iron.

The Fire-brick Works are turning out large quantities of the superior material, and for a variety of purposes for which it is adapted.

The Glass Works, because of their novelty and without a similar industry in the State, attract much attention, and the scenes at the works when the glass-blowers and all the aiding system of progress are in operation makes the establishment a place of much animation and interest.

Remarks of the same purport could be made of the Cassimere Mills, the great Rarig Works, and of other of the manufacturing industries, without trenching upon the bounds of propriety.

The accommodation for passenger and freight traffic by the two railroads is well advanced in the two buildings some time since erected by the Chesapeake and Ohio line, as well as in the passenger station of the Norfolk and Western Railroad. The latter, however, is to be superseded by one of the finest pink-colored stone structures, now in course of erection, of all that are or will be found on the extended route of that great trunk line. It will be complete in every feature, and will cost well on the way to forty thousand dollars, and it can be imagined what it will be in comfort and adornment, as it will stand, occupying 47 feet by 115 feet, in the center of the beautiful block of 235 feet by 400 feet donated for the purpose by the Buena Vista Company. To follow this grand improvement are others in a brick freight depot, a round-house and other buildings for railroad supplies, including a relay of engines, all estimated to call for the expenditure of $100,000, thus showing some of the realizing progress of Buena Vista. This movement on the part of the Norfolk and Western people will increase the population at least 100 men, adding thereby from 500 to 600 to the permanent population of the place.

In his report in 1889, on Buena Vista property, Dr. Ruffner, the celebrated Geologist, says: "I am acquainted with many points in Virginia and elsewhere, and have a right to say that there are few spots presenting so many features to lovers of nature as this. Many short excursions could be made from here to objects rare and interesting—such as Crab Tree Falls, Balcony Falls, Natural Bridge, Clifton Forge, Luray Caverns and Lexington."

To these prospective pleasures, as sketched by Dr. Ruffner, might be added the charms of a lake, similar to the one in Giles county, once known as the "Salt Pond," but since it has become a summer-resort is known as "Mountain Lake." The natural formation in the depressed surface of the earth and the flowing water are all in place for it, and all on the Buena Vista property.

The Buena Vista Company is governed by a president and eight directors, constituting a board. Mr. A. T. Barclay, chosen President at the preliminary organization, has been, at each annual meeting of the stockholders, by their direct vote, continued in that office, and always by a unanimous vote and resolutions of the highest approval of his administration. It may also be remarked that a majority of the original members of the directory are still in office, and, as a body, no similar organization is known in which there has been greater unanimity in council and efficient service.

In all that it has done for the section of country in close association—in all its progress—in all the wide and beneficial influences that have gone forth from it, enuring to the prosperity of the State and the country, Buena Vista ranks with the foremost in good returns for labor and capital expended.

Hon. ALEXANDER T. BARCLAY, the subject of this sketch, and President of the Buena Vista Company, was born in the city of Lexington, Virginia, and is the son of Col. Alexander T. Barclay, a highly respected farmer of that county, and a Colonel of the State troops for many years. He received his education in the schools of the county, and graduated from Washington and Lexington College. At the breaking out of the war he entered the Confederate service, and served through the war. He was First Lieutenant of his company, and was once slightly wounded, and was taken prisoner at Spottsylvania Court House, and was held prisoner fourteen months, being released at the close of the war in 1865. In 1867 he established the Lexington *Gazette*, of which paper he was the able editor for ten years, during which period he held a number of county offices, and assisted also in securing connection with Lexington by the Baltimore and Ohio and the Richmond and Alexander Railroads. Besides these duties, he was a member of the Board of Public Works of Virginia a number of times. After disposing of the *Gazette*, he assisted in the organization of the Lexington Manufacturing Company, and acted as President of the same until 1889, when, in company with B. C. Moomaw and Capt. C. F. Jordan, they organized the Buena Vista Company, of which he is now President. He is also director in a number of local companies and of the Trust and Loan Company. He has never taken any part in politics, not having faith that it is his forte, or to his financial advantage to do so. He is a Trustee of Washington and Lee University.

———

Mr. BENJAMIN C. MOOMAW.—One of the pioneers and founders of the city of Buena Vista, who originated and first proposed the scheme of the Buena Vista Company, is Mr. Benjamin C. Moomaw, who was born near Bonsack's in the year 1852. He received his early schooling in the schools of his native county, and after completing his education he spent sometime traveling in the North. In the year 1875 he came to Rockbridge county and purchased the tract of land there owned by the Glasgow family, consisting of four hundred acres. Here he began farming and continued in this occupation until 1880, when the Shenandoah Valley Railroad and Chesapeake and Ohio Railroad were built through the Valley. He laid out the village of Green Forest, afterwards Buena Vista, and secured the location of a number of manufacturing industries, among them a canning factory, tannery, planing mill and pulp mill. In the fall of 1888, in company with others, he organized the Buena Vista Land Company, of which he was made director, and still serves as such. He is a director in the Paper Manufacturing Company, Vice-President of the First National Bank, director in the Buena Vista Iron and Steel Company, director in the Glass Company, and Vice-President of the Buena Vista Fire Clay Company, and is interested in a number of other important development companies, in which he holds the office of President, Vice-President or director. He gives an undivided attention to his work, and politics and other side issues interest him but indifferently. He believes that what is worth doing at all is worth doing *thoroughly well*, and to this excellent maxim is due the almost phenomenal prosperity of the enterprises with which he is connected. Mr. Moomaw is a member of the German Baptist church, and an elder in the same.

———

Capt. CHARLES F. JORDAN, one of the founders of the Buena Vista Company, was born in Rockbridge county in the year 1838. His father Samuel F. Jordan, Esq., was a native of the same county, and was one of the foremost iron men in this part of the State. Captain Jordan, the subject of this sketch, received his early education in the county, and at the age of seventeen years connected himself with B. J. Jordan & Co., taking charge of the charcoal department of their furnace in Alleghany county. Here he remained two years, and then came to Buena Vista and assumed control of the old Buena Vista Furnace, which he continued until the breaking out of the war, when he enlisted in Company C, 1st Virginia Cavalry, and was soon promoted to the rank of Captain, which he held, commanding his company, until the battle of New Market, in October, 1864, where he was wounded, and was not able to again enter the service. When sufficiently recovered to do so he began farming, which he followed for two years and then took the management of the Victoria Furnace for a short period, but coming to this place, Buena Vista, he took charge of the Iron Ore Mines for some years, and assisted in originating the scheme and organization of the Buena Vista Company. In 1889 he assisted in the organization of the company, of which he is now a director, and a member of the Executive Committee Board. Is a director in the First National Bank of Buena Vista, also the Buena Vista Loan and Trust Company, and President of the Hart's Bottom Loan and Land Company, and the Buena Vista Saddle and Harness Company. He was of great assistance to Dr. Ruffner in getting up his report on the mineral resources of Buena Vista, and was the first to discover that there was fire clay on the Buena Vista property.

In 1864 he was married to Miss Mary E. Hamilton, and has six children, four sons and two daughters. He is a member of the Methodist church, and the superintendent of the Sunday-school. Captain Jordan has had an active and busy life, and makes of his business and activity a continual enjoyment; he is a man of fine social qualities, and in his own line of pursuit possesses a fund of valuable information.

JOHN W. BLACKBURN, Esq.—The well and favorably known President of the First National Bank of Buena Vista, John W. Blackburn, Esq., was born in Cecil county, Maryland, in the year 1848, and came to Shenandoah county, Virginia, with his parents, receiving his schooling in this State, which embraced a course in the University of Virginia, where he took the literary and law course. In 1869 he was admitted to the Bar in Rockingham county, and practiced for some years, when he removed to Independence, Kansas, and remained a year and a half, when he returned home and purchased the home farm, which he conducted for a number of years. In 1885 he was made Steward of the Western Lunatic Asylum at Staunton, Virginia, holding this position four years. In 1890 he came to Buena Vista and assisted in the organization of the West Buena Vista Land Company, of which he was made President, and still holds the position.

Mr. Blackburn soon engaged in a general real estate business under the firm name of Blackburn & Stewart, but the firm name has changed a number of times since. He was one of the organizers of the Buena

Vista Improvement Company, of which he is a director, and took an active part in the organization of the First National Bank, of which he is now President. He was married in 1872 to Miss Frances Harnsberger, of Rockingham county, a daughter of the Hon. Henry B. Harnsberger, who represented the county for many years in the Legislature.

Mr. Blackburn, the subject of this brief sketch, deservedly stands in the front rank as a citizen of push and enterprise. The almost phenomenal growth of the city of Buena Vista is altogether due to the efforts of such men, and it is only of such material that a live town can be built.

Mr. JOHN T. DUNLOP, President of the North-west Buena Vista Building and Improvement Company, was born in Frederick county, Maryland, in 1842, and is the son of Col. Henry Dunlop and Catharine Thomas Dunlop, the mother being sister of ex-Governor Francis Thomas, of Maryland.

Our subject received his schooling in the State, and in 1862 he came to Virginia and enlisted in Company G, 7th Virginia Cavalry, and served until the close of the war, when he was married to Miss Mary G. Glasgow, daughter of Robert Glasgow, who owned the Green Forest tract of land, on which a part of the town of Buena Vista is built. Mr. Dunlop assumed the management of this land for eleven years, and then purchased a tract on the other side of the river and devoted himself to farming until the present time. He has always taken an active part in the development of the place, and the well-being and prosperity of Buena Vista has been as "the apple of his eye."

In the year 1890 he founded the syndicate, consisting of capitalists from Washington, which assumed the name of the Forest Land Company, but was re-organized in March, 1891, under the name of the North-west Buena Vista Building and Improvement Company, of which he was made President. He is a director in the First National Bank, and stockholder in many of the more important companies of the place. He has always taken an active part in politics, and is at the present time Chairman of the Democratic Central Committee.

Mr. Dunlop is an elder in the Presbyterian church, and aside from business finds time to enjoy religious and social privileges. His instincts are those of a thorough man of business, who never puts off doing a thing to-day that will not be as well done to-morrow. To his economy of time and opportunity is due his well-earned financial success.

Hon. HUGH A. WHITE, Mayor of the city of Buena Vista, is a native of Brunswick county, Virginia, and was born in 1864. Our subject received his early education in Hardy county, West Virginia, and graduated from Hampden-Sidney College, Virginia, in 1886, after which he took a course of law in the University of Virginia, and in 1887 he was admitted to the Bar in Farmville, Prince Edward county, but began practice at Martinsburg, West Virginia, with Blackburn Hughes, under the firm name of Hughes & White, which partnership existed until the spring of 1890, when Mr. White came to Buena Vista and took an office alone for the practice of his profession, in which he has been more than ordinarily successful. Besides his law practice he is interested as Treasurer and General Manager of several land and development companies. He has taken an active interest in the government of the city, and was appointed to fill the office of Mayor soon after coming to the place, but finding that there was a doubt as to his eligibility, owing to the fact that he had not sufficient time of residence, he declined to serve, but at the first election held by the town he was elected Mayor, and is now discharging the duties of that office. Mr. White is a man who has a quiet but earnest faith in himself, and believes that when a person attempts to do a right and honorable thing, he can do it if he has the quality to persevere. He is popular as an officer, and equally popular as a friend and fellow-citizen.

Mr. CHARLES H. JORDAN, one of the pioneer real estate men of Buena Vista, was born in the city of Chicago in the year 1863. He is the son of James F. Jordan, of North Carolina, who for some years was in the insurance business. At the time of the fire at Chicago he returned to North Carolina, where our subject received his early education in the Military School of Raleigh and the State University. After leaving the University he engaged in the insurance business at Raleigh, and also traveled through Virginia and Maryland. In January, 1890, he came to Buena Vista, which was then in its infancy, and opened a real estate and insurance office. He took an active part in the organization of the Real Estate Exchange, of which he is a director. He is also a director of the Greenbrier and White Sulphur Springs; director of the Roanoke Iron Belt Building and Loan Association, and sole agent of the Southern Investment Company; is manager of the Buena Vista Improvement Company; sole agent of the Alvarado Park Land Company, and a stockholder in the Loan and Trust Company, the Mutual Annuity Company of Staunton, and many other companies. He has been pre-eminently successful in his financial transactions, and enjoys a large and lucrative business. He has also associated in the insurance business with him L. G. Smith, of Staunton, Virginia. Mr. Jordan is a thorough business man. He has made it his study, and with a good understanding of business principles it is not strange that failure has had no share in his experience.

AMBROSE TIMBERLAKE, Esq., President and General Manager of the Buena Vista Cassimere Mills, is a native of Jefferson county, West Virginia. The schools of the State furnished him his education, and after it was completed he engaged as clerk in a store in Charlestown, where he remained until his father's death which occurred in 1873, when he returned home and was appointed administrator of the estate, and connecting himself with a Mr. Young, run out his father's unexpired lease of the Morgan Mills. In 1875, in partnership with Mr. Young, he purchased the Valley Woolen Mills near Middleton, Virginia, and in 1883 he bought out the interest of Mr. Young and sold a part interest to Mr. Thomas Maslin, changing the firm name to Timberlake & Maslin, which firm existed until 1891, when this plant was moved to Buena Vista and created a stock company, of which the original proprietor was made President and General Manager, and at this present time fills these arduous places to the entire satisfaction of the stockholders, directors and all interested in the finaucial success of the works. Mr. Timberlake is also Vice-President of the Perpetual Building and Loan Association, director of the Buena Vista Branch of the Iron Belt Building and Loan Association; director in the Middletown Land and Improvement Company of Fredrick county, and also director in the Valley Investment Company of Middletown. Mr. Timberlake is a married man and lives in Buena Vista, and his entire social interests are here as well as a greater part of his financial. He is a member of the Presbyterian church and takes a substantial enjoyment in seeing and assisting the city in its improvements and progress.

W. G. McDOWELL, Esq., of Buena Vista, a member of the firm of McDowell & Prichard, and real estate dealer of this place, was born near Lexington, Virginia, in 1850. He was educated at Washington and Lee University, from whence he graduated with the degrees of B. S. and C. E., session of 1871-'72. After completing his engineering course, for several years he was engaged on city work for the town of Lexington as engineer. His next work was as resident engineer on the Atlantic and North-western Railroad, a proposed extension of the Richmond and Alleghany Railroad through West Virginia. For several years he was superintendent of construction of the South-western Lunatic Asylum, built at Marion, Virginia. Also planned and built the water-work for said asylum, and while engaged on the latter work planned the water-works of Marion, Virginia. Was next engaged to plan and build the new barracks at the Virginia Agricultural and Mechanical College, Blacksburg, Virginia, and the Agricultural Experiment Station building at the same place. In the fall of 1888 he returned to Lexington, Virginia, and in the spring of 1889 interested himself, with others, in the develpment of Buena Vista, placing about 1,500 shares of the stock in the city of Roanoke in three days. He was one of the directors and engineer for the Loch Laird Land and Improvement Company, the financial success of which is so well known. He began the real estate business in the fall of 1889, and continued alone until November, 1891, when he admitted to partnership N. B. Prichard, of Petersburg, Virginia, under the firm name of McDowell & Prichard. Mr. McDowell has been particularly successful in business, which has not been a matter of chance, but the secret of it is that he has attended strictly to business and given his undivided attention to whatever he undertakes. He is highly respected in the place, and is a citizen who is held in enviable regard.

CHARLES B. GUYER, Esq., Buena Vista's pioneer real estate agent, was born in Frederick county, Virginia, and spent his early life in his native place. He is the son of the late Dr. J. S. Guyer, of Middletown, Virginia, a physician, who, in his life-time, was prominent in his profession, and well known as a citizen of the lower Shenandoah Valley. In the year 1872 he went to Lexington and engaged as clerk in a store, where he remained until 1877, when he returned to his native county and followed school-teaching for a number of years. He then engaged in business, and followed it up to the latter part of 1888, and early in the year 1889 he went to Buena Vista and purchased stock in the Buena Vista Company, and opened a real estate office, which was the first one opened in the town. In the same year he formed a partnership with Mr. Frank D. Coe, under the firm name of Guyer, Coe & Co. In 1891 J. Marshall McClure was taken into the firm, and the name of the firm was changed to Guyer, McClure & Co. In the year 1890 he organized the Buena Vista Loan and Trust Company, which does a banking business, and of which he is President, and is actively engaged in the management of its affairs. He is also a director in a number of other large companies.

Mr. Guyer is a man of more than ordinarily good executive abilities, and possesses a faculty of management to a rare degree. While greatly absorbed in business, he has still time to make himself a genial and companionable friend and acquaintance.

MR. FRANK B. RICHARDS, General Manager of the Buena Vista Iron Company, is a native of Massachusetts, his birth-place being the city of Boston. He received his education in the schools of "The Hub," graduating from the School of Technology in 1883. After graduating he entered the employ of the Stafford Mining Company of Vermont, as chemist and furnace manager, but in the latter part of 1884 he accepted a position in the School of Technology from which he graduated, which position he held for six months, when he accepted another place as assistant chemist with the Joliet Steel Works of Joilet, Illinois, which position he filled to the entire satisfaction of the company for one year, when he entered the employ of Brier Hill Iron and Coal Company of Youngstown, Ohio, as chemist, and later took charge of their furnaces, remaining with them two years. In 1888 he entered the employ of Messrs. Tod, Stambough & Co., of Cleveland, Ohio, as manager of the sales department, in which position he remained until April, 1890, when he was made General Manager of the Buena Vista Iron Co., to which he has devoted his entire time and attention. Mr. Richards takes into his business a fund of valuable experience and a complete knowledge of the branch of work that he has engaged in.

Messrs. BATGHELOR, RICKS & WINBORNE, the leading law firm of Buena Vista, consists of the following gentlemen: Mr. Oliver D. Batchelor, Mr. William B. Ricks and Mr. Robert W. Winborne. Mr. Batchelor, the founder of the firm, is a native of Nashville, North Carolina, receiving his education in the schools of that State, completing his education by a course in the State University, and graduating in 1888. He was licensed to practice law in North Carolina in the fall of 1889, and in the winter following came to Buena Vista, and, in partnership with Mr. Ricks, formed the firm of Batchelor & Ricks, having been admitted to the Bar here.

Mr. Ricks, the second member of the firm, is also a native of North Carolina, and is likewise an *alumnus* of the State University. He was admitted to the Bar of North Carolina, but practiced there only a short time. He came to Buena Vista and assisted in forming the firm, and was admitted to the Rockbridge County Bar in 1890, and began the practice at once.

Mr. Winborne, the third member of the firm, is a native of Hertford county, North Carolina, and, like his partners, received his education in the schools of the State, graduating at the University in 1881 in a literary course, and in 1883 in law, and was admitted to the Bar the same year. He served as a member of the General

Assembly of North Carolina in 1884–'85, and has served two terms as Solicitor of his county. In 1891 he came to Buena Vista and associated himself with the law firm of Batchelor & Ricks, and the firm name was changed to its present one. The firm is one of the strongest in the city, and has an extensive practice, both local and otherwise, and possesses the full confidence of the public.

On September 18th, 1891, Mr. Ricks withdrew from the firm, and is now taking a course in the Vanderbilt University, preparatory to entering the ministry of the Methodist Episcopal Church, South. The present style of the firm is Winborne & Batchelor.

E. B. VAUGHN, Esq., Cashier of the First National Bank of Buena Vista, received his early education in the schools of Douquille and Lynchburg, graduating from the high school of the latter place in 1876, and entered the Peoples National Bank in the following year as assistant book-keeper, remaining there until 1880, at that time connecting himself with the Lynchburg National Bank, and by his diligence and care was soon made chief book-keeper, and remained in this position until the year 1884, when he left the bank and engaged in the tobacco trade, and founded the firm of Vaughn & Keeffe, which firm existed until 1889, when the factory was destroyed by fire. In May, 1890, he came to Buena Vista, and in partnership with Mr. B. C. Moomaw and the present directors, organized the First National Bank, of which he was made Cashier. He is Vice-President of the Buena Vista Loan and Trust Company, and is a stockholder in a number of other enterprises. He is connected with firm of Vaughn Brothers, of the Vaughn Brothers Real Estate Office. Mr. Vaughn has the confidence of the community as a business man and manager to an unusual degree, a confidence which he has abundantly merited by strict attention to his work and perfect integrity of action.

Mr. JOHN W. CHILDS, one of the leading real estate dealers of Buena Vista, is a native of Lynchburg, Virginia, and the greater part of his early life was spent in that city, holding the position of General Express Agent for the Norfolk and Western Railroad for over twelve years. He then engaged in the export tobacco trade and followed this traffic at Lynchburg for about eight years, when he removed to Asheville, North Carolina, and engaged in the same business there, entering the firm known as Childs, Moomaw & Co., which firm still exists. Mr. Childs came to Buena Vista in 1890 and engaged in the real estate and insurance business, which he now conducts. He is Secretary and Treasurer of the

Building, Light and Water Company, and Vice-President and General Manager of the Equity Building Company; is a member of the Board of Directors of the Lynchburg National Bank of Lynchburg, Virginia, and is directly or indirectly connected with a number of other important interests in the city and county, and finds his time more than fully occupied with the various details of his business. He is a man self-trained in business, and has the benefit of an extensive knowledge to forward his undertakings to successful issue.

PHILLIP S. WISE, Esq., founder of the Wise Wagon Works, was born in Rockingham county in the year 1848, and is the son of Peter and Elizabeth Wise, both natives of Virginia. Our subject, P. S. Wise, was educated in his own county, and remained with his father until he was twenty-one years of age, engaged in farming. He also engaged in the sale of farming implements and fertilizers, and later in the sale of hardware, and for a time occupied the position of traveling salesman for the Empire Drill Company, which work he was obliged to abandon on account of ill health. In 1885 he engaged in the manufacture of wagons at New Market in a small way, but the excellency of his wagons soon gained for them a wide reputation, and the business increasing, in December, 1889, a company was organized, known as the Wise Wagon Works, and in April, 1890, the works were moved to Buena Vista, of which he was made General Manager, Secretary and Treasurer, which latter office he resigned in March, 1891, his duties of office so increasing as to render that necessary. He still holds the position of General Manager.

Mr. Wise's knowledge of the business is only such as can be obtained by experience, all of which has been tested as to its practicability. He is a man of practice rather than theory, invariably indulging in the latter quality after the first, finding this to be the best and least expensive way of proceeding.

He was married in 1871 to Miss Virginia F. Bowman. This union was blessed with one son, who died in 1891. Both himself and family are members of the Lutheran church. He is now an elder in Trinity Lutheran church of Buena Vista.

WILLIAM H. HUNTER & Co.—The Real Estate House of William H. Hunter & Company, of Buena Vista, one of the best known in the city, was founded by W. H. Hunter, Esq., who was born in Augusta, Virginia, in 1864, in which place he spent the early years of his life, following farming as an occupation. In the year 1882 he came to Rockbridge county and engaged in the mercantile business in Green Forest, and followed this until the organization of the Buena Vista Company, of which he was one of the original stockholders. In 1889 he opened a real estate office, which he conducts at the present time. He was one of the organizers of the Buena Vista Land and Building Association, of which he is a director, and is interested in a number of other companies whose aim is the development and upbuilding of the place. He feels and takes a deep interest in anything that tends to the advancement and betterment of his town and its people.

R. F. HILL, Esq., the subject of this sketch, general lumber dealer and manufacturer, of Buena Vista, Virginia, is a native of the Old Dominion, and was born in 1852. Mr. Hill followed farming in the earlier years of his life, and afterwards conducted a saw-mill in Orange county for ten years. In 1890, in company with Mr. Julius Graham and Mr. A. S. Jones, he came to Buena Vista and established the business they are now conducting. The business of the firm is quite extensive, their trade extending over a large section of the State.

Mr. Hill was married in 1881 to Miss Esther Garnett, of Madison county, and six children have been born to them. He and his family are members of the Methodist church, and he is an active member of the Masonic fraternity. He has never taken much part in politics, not having the time or the inclination, but, nevertheless, has served as Chairman of the Democratic Central Committee for six years.

Mr. JULIUS BRAHAM, member of the E. F. Hill Company, is a native of Loudoun county, and was born in the year 1850. He, for some years, conducted a large Spoke Mill at Salem, Virginia, and another large mill in Loudoun county, and also managed a merchant mill. Previous to this he was employed as a traveling salesman for the Popular Engine Company, and made a thorough canvass of the Southern States. He was engaged in the same business in Fairfax county prior to his coming to Buena Vista.

Mr. A. S. Jones, also a member of the same firm, was a farmer in Orange county. In the year 1890 he connected himself with the firm, with which he has been ever since. Mr. Jones was a soldier in the Confederate army, enlisted in 1862 as courier for General Ewell, and afterwards serving with Generals Early and Longstreet, and was a participant in a number of hard engagements. He was a brave and efficient soldier. It is needless to say that the firm of which he is now a member is doing an extensive and growing business.

22

CHAPTER VII.

BASIC CITY, VIRGINIA.

By J. H. LINDSAY.

One *immaterial* joke may be adventured in an article the length of this. Years ago on the green red hills about Batesville, the day of all others in the year was "big muster." The idol of the people of the "deestrict"—attired in blue broadcloth and gold buttons and patent-leather boots and bright spurs and waving plumes, mounted on a gorgeously caparisoned horse, was the "Kurnel." Everybody was imposing, save old Sandy—who never could be "proper" an *entire* day. On one occasion, when the militia had been gotten nicely into line, the order from the Colonel sounded to the spectators about this way: "Simultaneous movement by the right"—when the irrepressible Alex., who had climbed into a dead apple-tree and pulled a live quart after him, shouted: "*Simon Tatum 'll not be here to-day, his mare's back's sore.*" The point about this true story touches, only, life's fitful scenes, and the sad side of the dead past. The young people are in the saddle now, and we old stagers must "ride behind." The new years are being made up of hustlers; albeit, some faces remain elongated.

LOOK AT BASIC CITY.

Because inside a year from its foundation, stupendous marble piles on umbrageous avenues, beautiful parks and playing fountains are not seen galore, pessimism calls all "booms" busts. This is true, though, that if fifteen months ago any one of of Basic's splendid factories had been planted anywhere South, the papers all over the country would have been full of it—"The industrial dawn of the new era." The philosophy of this reflection is, simply, that some people are never satisfied. Now, *this* is true, too, that, in the center of the activities of the busiest people of the best part of the world, Basic City has piled up more foundation stones and brick, and has encompassed within her factory walls more spindles and shuttles and presses and expensive machinery than any other town of which we wot within the first year of its existence.

Born in May, 1890, within her natal year enough great plants have been builded to completion, enough costly enterprises established, enough whistles blown and successfully run industries to make her the biggest infant, years considered, thriving on the bosom of the hard times, I ween.

This nourishing tit-for-tat pap is thrown out for the benefit of some municipalities without chivalry—or foundation, in fact. So conspicuous is the position of Basic City, Virginia, that a child student may locate it. Scan the azured contour of the Blue Ridge, and just where the dip touches nearest the emerald valleys, stick a pin—that is Rockfish Gap. Think of the Appalachian system, and you will remember that nature has furrowed but

ONE WAY

through West Virginia's black sea of coal and hundreds of miles of mountain barriers, and that *its* eastern outlet is—where you may stick another pin and strike the same place—at Basic City. The fertile valleys and the great canyon of the Alleghany Mountains look towards one point. The vine-clad hills and the famous orchards of the piedmont region touch it; the beautiful stretches of the rich districts of East Tennessee and their continuation, the blue-grass fields of South-west Virginia hold their lap hitherward; the two great Southern trunk lines of railway, the Chesapeake and Ohio and the Norfolk and Western, taking the hint, come to the same *conclusion* at this same markedly conspicuous place—

THE CITY OF THE IRON CROSS.

The purpose of this article is to call the attention of the people of the United States to the pregnant certainties and magnificent possibilities, and to the *raison d'etre* of this highland metropole. There are hundreds of thousands of young men in this country looking for a home around which are gathered the most favorable conditions; thousands of others of maturer years, with riper experiences, who, with their slowly gotten honest earnings, are seeking for a safe certainty, where, in spite of life's contingencies, they may risk a venture; and then, too, Colonel Sellers, who, whether there be "millions in it" or not, want to "stop this turmoil, Sir, and settle down." *And*, when we see this country doubling its millions of earnest people as the years rush by, it behooves the wise man to look well about him for a place where he may safely risk his savings, so that when the house is full his seat will have been "taken," and then—why, *let* the band play!

Basic City courts a cross-examination by the astutest. If the reader will observe the map of Virginia, he will remark that this place is situated at about—*at*, to be emphatic—the longitudinal center of Augusta county, the most opulent agricultural district in the central part of the famous Shenandoah Valley; that it is squarely off Chesapeake Bay, the most prominent indentation, with the safest harbors and deepest waters, on the Atlantic coast; west a hundred miles on a line bisecting the States back of and above the insiduous approaches of *chilly* tide-water, east of the range of Dryenfurth's drouth guns, north of the reach of pestilential fevers, south of that six-months-in-the-year frozen line in the

BLUE MOUNTAINS,

in that purified air for which tired lungs panteth as the wounded hart for the water-brook does, where the water is pure as when carried to the clouds in the kisses of sunbeams—"Death's pale flag is not advanced there." Well within, too, the embrace of the mineral belt, within hearing of the sighs of primeval forests, and at the embrasure of the New South's great boom.

Seeing that this young city is in the very heart of the industrial activities of the teeming millions that already crowd the East of the coming West, it may be well to consider her position as a

RAILROAD CENTER.

People thrive and cities grow apace on cheap railroad rates—the result of competition. Observe the situation here, and see whether Chattanooga or Roanoke or any of them may hold headlights 'longside o' us. There is but one place on the face of the earth where a grand trunk line of railroad, reaching in its arm's-length the black bottoms of the West, lying down along the inexhaustible coal-stores of West Virginia, bisecting the Valley of Virginia, where, when the grain grows gold west of the Ridge peaches grow blushes east of it, crosses at

RIGHT ANGLES

in the midst of exhaustless beds of rich iron-ores another grand trunk line, which in its connections stretches to the Pacific, and from Memphis traverses Tennessee's cotton-fields, the blue-grass area of South-west Virginia, *its* splendid coal-fields, the Valley of Virginia, the Cumberland Valley, and so on to New York.

From the vast grain-fields of the Western States the converging tracks of these two great roads—the Chesapeake and Ohio through the coal-walled canyon of New river, and the Norfolk and Western through Cumberland Gap and the pastures of Kentucky—bend for a thousand miles towards this point, where *they cross*, within easy reach of the vineyards and matchless orchards of albemarle, the tobacco belt and the picturesque plains of Eastern Virginia unrolled to the ocean. Besides, from the cotton-fields of the Carolinas, the Mississippi compresses; from the groves of Florida and from the prairies of Texas, commerce may elect as between two or more routes to this place. Indeed, if there is a single considerable point within a material radius to which the benefit of competitive rates may not be had from Basic City, the writer is ignorant of the fact—thus giving her virtually *four roads*. These two routes must remain the great common carriers between the surcharged granaries of the West and the open markets and hungry mouths of all Europe, hauling this immense tonnage for all time through the transverse gates, ajar here only, to the deepest water on the Atlantic coast, at Newport News. The Basic City, West Virginia and Petersburg Railroad, for which a charter has been obtained, will be another potent factor in Basic City's rapid upbuilding, will place her in close touch with Pittsburg and add a connection with the Baltimore and Ohio at a point twelve miles, say, distant.

Nature and man have wrought centuries and spent millions bringing these international highways to this unique vantage ground. No conspiration can work a *budge*.

MANUFACTURERS, remembering that this city is immovably on the "first floor," touching raw materials; that her manufactured products may be shipped "*over night,*" at lowest rates, into the vast agricultural regions of the South Atlantic, the South-west and West, may be pleased to read the evidence of eminent men as to her immediate surroundings and advantages. O. Howard Roger, General Passenger Agent, Shenandoah Valley Railroad, says: "Basic City is located near the very heart of the greatest coal, iron and limestone fields of America."

F. J. Kimball, President of Norfolk and Western Railroad, says: "Basic City is destined to be a great industrial centre."

Congressman Wilson says he "sees in Basic a wonderful future."

M. E. Ingall, President of Big Four System: "It, Basic City, is the handsomest place I ever saw for a city."

E. S. Lotts, in *American Wool, Cotton and Financial Reporter,* writes: "The railroads already built give Basic City advantages over other points in Virginia."

Rev. Moses D. Hoge expected to see it "a great and magnificent city."

John J. Green, Charleston (S. C.) *News and Courier:* "There is not, probably, in the whole country a place young as this which has so many industries actually begun. Basic City, standing 1,400 feet above the sea, is not being built on paper. Its foundations are stone and iron."

Major Pardee, *New Haven Palladium,* says: "The Potsdam or Blue Ridge limonite and hematite ores of this region are of proved richness and purity, and are in quantity sufficient to keep many large furnaces in blast for a long series of years, while close to them are inexhaustible stores of limestone, and within short hauling distance by railroad are great coal measures from which coke can be obtained at a minimum cost," etc.

William E. Christian's brilliant pen, in *The Forum,* closes this argument: "To speak specifically of the ores, it is an indisputable and recognized fact that no other point in Virginia, and possibly in the South, can show greater quantity or better quality of iron ores than are deposited at the western base of the Blue Ridge mountains contiguous to Basic City."

Another or two pertinent pointers in this connection: That we may place iron in Pittsburg at $3 per ton less than Alabama plants, and $10 under the Lake Superior output is the testimony of the best authorities; that the supply of brown hematite ores, assaying 50 per cent. metalic iron, is literally limitless in contiguous areas is scientifically demonstrated. *That's the iron* on the ground now. In 1883 the total coal and coke shipments over the Norfolk and Western was a hundred thousand tons in round numbers; in 1889, the shipments ran materially over *two million* tons. *That's the coal* by *one* route, mention not being made of the vastly greater shipments over the Chesapeake and Ohio. Speaking specifically of minerals, we name some of the more prominent deposits, only: From the Cole Mine shipments of rich ores are being made now, and constantly; the Mine Bank deposit is not only rich but immense; enormous supplies from Black Rock have been drawn for years, and are being drawn and shipped North now via Basic City. The richest manganese mines in the world are but half an hour away, at Crimora.

At the tin mines near Vesuvius is being erected the most extensive plant for the reduction of this metal, outside of Wales, the abundant deposits of kaolin here, look to the establishing of many successful enterprises. The magnificent supply of the best glass-sand, moulding-sand and fire-clay in strata, virtually *suburbe*, is an earnest of various diversified industries, here or their coming answered for. The vast virgin forests hard by will furnish for long years abundant supplies of the cheaper and finer hard woods used in the manufacture of machinery, furniture and wooden-ware, generally. From one station, Afton, four miles distant, thousands of tons of tanbark are transported annually; from the same point shipments of Virginia claret are made at an average wholesale price of 35 cents per gallon. Oh, Basic's O. K., 18k. solid. These overwhelming facts *forces* the most favorable conclusions concerning the bright future of this splendid district. Just here, an extract from that sterling publication, the *Financial Reporter*, is deemed germain: "It, the Shenandoah Valley, is as good as Chester Valley or Pequa Valley, or Lancaster or Bucks counties, in Pennsylvania; just as good as any part of Western New York, and better than any part of New England, for farming, grazing or fruit purposes."

The writer thinks the hotels at this place, by all odds, the most attractive in the State. The Brandon stands easily in the front ranks of the most celebrated hostelries in the South. Its exquisite architectural proportions penciled against the blue tracery of the hills beyond form a picture of surpassing beauty. I saw, the other evening, while a guest here, just rising above that divine line, the top of the Blue Ridge, into the bejewelled dome the silvered face of a full moon, and I have witnessed nothing more ineffably delightful.

Health being wealth, the sanitary surroundings of our new cities is a matter of signal moment. Basic City is situated on the fertile, sandy, porous soil between the mountain foot.hills and South river. The river courses round the western and runs through the eastern limits of the city, catching the clear waters of the mountain brooks, and so inducing perfect drainage.

Lithia, freestone, arsenic, iron and sulphur waters for drinking purposes are found in superabundance. The Lithia Spring, one of the grandest in the country, wells a thousand gallons a minute through white pebbles into safe conduits, whence these waters are forced into a reservoir overlooking The Brandon.

CONCLUSIVE STATEMENTS.

In May, 1890, the Mining, Manufacturing and Land Company of Basic City had been chartered and its chief promoters, the head-center of whom is Judge J. M. Quarles, were on the grounds. On Friday its capital stock of $700,000 was placed on the market, and by Tuesday following the whole had been taken by responsible parties—men who always take conservative views of ventures; stable financiers—men who "put" only when morally certain of a "call." In a few days, then, thus, this city was established on a safe basis. To the subsequent lot sales earnest prospectors came from all over the country—from Roanoke and Richmond, the West, Baltimore and Philadelphia—to become, after thorough investigation, anxious buyers. Reasonable figures were obtained from the beginning, and have been steadily maintained. In a great many instances handsome profits have been realized, and this in spite of the then pending crisis.

E. G.—S. Hackerman paid $375, since sold for $1,500; C. A. Holt paid $350, since sold for $900; A. E. Harnsberger paid $575, since sold for $2,500; I. F. Landes paid $710, since sold for $2,500; W. T. Robertson (Richmond) paid $3,060, since sold for $8,450; and so on through a long list.

The broad, comprehensive policy of these founders has always looked to the bringing hither of numerous industrial enterprises, the result being the immediate

APPENDIX
(With many omissions, because of lack of space).

THE CAR WORKS.

Its buildings are: Office, 22 x 46 feet; foundry, 60x100; machine-shop, 60x100; smith-shop, 40x60; patterns, 36x60; frames, 50x125; and additional shops, 60 x 143; paint-shop, 78x143. Capital, $200,000.

MATCH FACTORY.

Successfully run; capital $50,000; daily output, 250 gross of 2,000.

CIGAR FACTORY.

Page & Co.; successfully operated; "The Iron Cross" and "The Belle Brandon" will make any man smoke, or boy—"smoke."

SCHOOL FURNITURE WORKS.

Manufacturers of patent school desks and furniture; main building, 300x75 feet, the side structures being 60x100, 100x60, 17x84, 25x20 feet, respectively, with numerous out-buildings. One of the biggest and most certainly successful enterprises south of the Potomac, or north of it, for that matter. Their trade reaches over the United States, to Canada, South America, Mexico and Hayti. Capital stock, $150,000.

MACHINE-WORKS.

Main building 300 x 100 feet; in the one wing, 400 feet long, boilers will be made; carriages and other machine fixtures in the main building.

KNITTING FACTORY.

Will give employment to fifty people in the manufacture of hosiery, curtains and other kinds of knit and woven fabrics.

THE PAPER FABRIQUE COMPANY.

One of the most substantial industrial enterprises here, main building 160 x 60 feet, besides numerous annexes. The costly machinery is revolving like a flash, printing more playing cards than can be trumped up in all the republic besides; and card-board and enamel paper, some substantial enough, it looks, to "box" the compass. The enumeration reaching too far for this paper, we compile—hardware and building materials, broom factory, straw brick plant, slaughter-house, bottling and ice works, mattress factory, two banks, opera-house, three hotels, stores, billiards and pool, sash, door and blinds, building and loan associations, the Basic City *Advance*, an ably edited paper, and two minor publications; Normal College, free schools, handsome residences, pretty cottages and— *ad infinitum*.

Seeing such a twelve-month's aggregations as this; the straight broad avenues and streets—the latter, crossing by iron bridges the laughing limpid waters of South river up to romantic overhanging bluffs, the poetic culmination of all that's attractive as a place of residence, the former touching throughout their course corner business lots in the very squares made by the "cross-ties" of great transcontinental railway systems—a man living here, up in a climate untouched by miasma, in the blue breath of the mountain breeze, where every morning brings fresh roses for his children's cheeks and a new spring to *his elastic* step on the green carpets of rich meadows where the seams are purling branches of clear, cool brooks, where health stays smiling, till the architect of the univere calls "time." In such a place, the average man might, it would seem, with a little diligence, be more than reasonably certain of comfortable income, and of building unto himself and his, with a minimum of effort that maximum of life, a very—"Home, Sweet Home."

Judge J. M. QUARLES.

—If men were so many seeds, Judge Quarles might be called of the Basic City variety.

Fortune planted him here a year ago, and Basic City popped out of an old field.

Its growth and spread have been helped by many hands, but the root and stem have been the conception and energy of the present General Manager, Judge Quarles.

He is a young man of forty-three, and sprang from the farm of his ancestors in Caroline county. He led there the active life of a country school-boy until he was eleven years of age, when he came to Augusta county.

During the following six years he went to classical schools in Louisa, Goochland and Augusta counties, when he was entered at the Academy.

After a few years drilling as schoolmaster, he took academic schools at the University of Virginia, which he followed by the law course.

He came to Staunton from the University, went forward as a lawyer into a judgeship.

Impressed with the great promise that enticed so many Virginians to the North-west, he went to Minnesota and continued in the practice of his profession.

The thrilling expansion of such cities as St. Paul and Minneapolis was different from anything that the Judge had ever seen before, and set his eyes in a more fixed way than ever upon the industrial panorama of the whole country.

As picture after picture passed by, Virginia suddenly appeared with a vividness which captured and brightened the eye of Virginians, not only in the North-west but everywhere.

Judge Quarles had learned much in the North-west. He had looked at people build cities. He had seen them completed. City building ceased to have the same aspect as that involved in the long growth of old Southern cities, some of which 150 years old were smaller than the five-year old giants of the mighty West.

On his return to Staunton, while yet practicing his profession his mind was full of the hope that seemed to illumine the hearts of the young men, and his mind had become used to looking at large undertakings.

He came to Basic City—a carefully schooled boy—an accurate young schoolmaster, with University training in language and law—with confidence among the boomers of the North-west.

Judge Quarles has had all his faculties taxed in forwarding the scheme originated by him. He is a man of good judgment, slow to speak but earnest at it, with honesty in look and action. He possesses a keen, intuitive knowledge of men not suspected at first, which gives him advantage in meeting strangers. One of the shyest of men, his plans are bold, and his endurance great in working out the details of these plans by personal supervision.

Judge Quarles is the man for his places and his power and purpose are felt by all.

MARSHALL A. BOOKER, Esq., Secretary and Treasurer of the Basic City Car Manufacturing Company, was born at Hampton, Elizabeth county, Virginia, November 15th, 1851, and is a son of George and Anna Booker. He comes of the old and distinguished Virginia stock, and the farm on which he was born was never known to be deeded to any other name until after the late war. His father was a man of culture and ability, who, at the early age of 21, represented Elizabeth county in the State Legislature.

Mr. M. A. Booker, the subject of this sketch, was educated at Petersburg, Virginia, earning the money by hard work that schooled him. After finishing school he taught for a short time and then farmed for about five years, and in 1877 he engaged in business at Hampton, conducting a successful mercantile trade for several years, when he sold out and traveled for the space of five years for a Baltimore hardware house. In 1886 he located at Staunton, Virginia, and engaged in the hardware business until December, 1890, when he disposed of his stock and accepted the position he now holds of Secretary and Treasurer of the Basic City Car Works Company, which are doubtless the most extensive works of the kind in the State. The company was organized and incorporated under the laws of Virginia in the winter of 1890, with a capital stock of $100,000, ninety-eight per cent. of the stock being owned by natives of the "Old Dominion." The works are being equipped with the best of modern improved machinery, and, with experienced and efficient management, are in condition to turn out work that will compare favorably with any in the United States.

Mr. Booker was married to Miss Mollie Bechtel, of Baltimore, Maryland. He is a member of the Episcopal church, and is esteemed by all who know him as a man of sterling integrity and brilliant business qualifications.

Prof. G. W. HOENSHEL, Principal of the Shenandoah Normal College of Basic City, was born in Westmoreland county, Pennsylvania, December 11th, 1858; he attended public school and worked on the farm until he was eighteen years of age. He first taught school in 1876 and 1877, after which he went to Illinois. Mr.

Hoenshel there taught public schools in the counties of Coles, Douglas and Montgomery. He was educated at Central Normal College at Danville, Indiana; East Illinois College, Danville, Illinois, and by private study. He came to Virginia in the summer of 1883, and organized at Middleton, Virginia, the first independent Normal school in the South. In 1887, he went to Harrisonburg, Virginia, and in 1890 came to Basic City. Professor Hoenshel is very thorough in his methods, is a good disciplinarian, preserves in the highest sense the moral tone of his pupils, and impresses all those under his care with his own scholarship and right living. His college is a large, well-equipped building and one of the cherished institutions of Basic City, and is prospering, with promise of greater things to come.

Dr. R. SUMTER GRIFFITH, the subject of this sketch, was born April, 1861, in Anne Arundel county, Maryland, and is the son of F. L. and Mary E. Griffith, both natives of Maryland. His father is a farmer and a man of recognized ability and culture. He represented his county in the State Legislature for one or two terms with credit to himself and constituents. Dr. Griffith was educated at the public schools of his native county, and in 1877 entered the Maryland Agricultural College, near Washington, D. C., where he remained three years, and after completing his course there he taught school three years, and then entered the College of Physicians and Surgeons at Baltimore, graduating from that institution in 1886. However, prior to entering the Medical College, he had studied and practiced medicine in Maryland for about three years. After graduating, he entered the hospital at Baltimore, and at the same time took a course in the Dental College of the same city. From 1886 to 1888 he had an office at Friendship, Maryland, after which he located at Springfield, West Virginia, where he established a large and lucrative practice, but in May, 1891, he removed to Basic City, where he soon established for himself a splendid and enviable reputation and practice. He was married in 1886 to Miss Annie Webb, a daughter of Mr. William M. Webb, of Calvert county, Maryland. The Doctor is a member of the Methodist Church, South, and is a member of the church official board. He is a Mason and an enthusiastic worker in the Masonic Order. He is a strong advocate of temperance, and was one of the organizers of the Lodge of Good Templars, of Springfield, West Virginia, and of Basic City. In the Basic City organization he is at present Past Chief Templar. The Doctor is a man who is highly esteemed as a man of culture and literary attainments, and his influence for good is felt by all with whom he comes in contact.

JAMES HUBERT LINDSAY was born at Melrose, Fauquier county, Virginia, December 29th, 1862; father, Prof. S. C. Lindsay, an educator well known in Virginia and North Carolina; mother, Miss Annie Morgan, of the Kentucky family of that name.

Educated by his father. Began teaching when fifteen years old, and taught in the Staunton Graded School and schools of Culpeper county. Successful as a teacher; began with four pupils in Culpeper, and closed first session with sixty-five enrolled. Read law and medicine privately, and corresponded for newspapers. Went to Kernersville, North Carolina, in 1882, and purchased the *News*, a paper then losing money for its proprietor; greatly improved it, and made it a paying institution. Established a publishing house, and printed several papers under contract for other towns. Held the office of town treasurer, and was elected Secretary and Treasurer of the North Carolina Press Association in 1884, holding office up to time of leaving State in 1887. He was also postmaster of the town under the Cleveland administration, and a prominent member of Democratic Committee. Left in 1887 to take a position in Deaf, Dumb and Blind Institution at Staunton, which he held until he resigned to re-enter journalism. He has gotten out two special editions of the Basic City *Advance*, of which he is proprietor, of eight pages each, one of 30,000, and an Anniversary Edition of 40,000. He was a delegate from Virginia to the National Educational Association, which met this summer in St. Paul, Minnesota, and is at present a member of the Executive Committee of the same. He has built a fine office here, and has one of the best equipped establishments of the kind in Virginia. He began his paper (the *Advance*) in a little frame building (the only one in town), when Basic City was nothing but a wheat field. He is a man of energy, and has faith in the future growth and prosperity of Basic City.

CHAPTER VIII.

FRONT ROYAL, VIRGINIA.

LOCATION—RESOURCES—ATTRACTIONS—PROSPECTS.

By Dr. STEPHEN HARNSBERGER.

Although the first white settlers entered this portion of the Shenandoah Valley in 1731, Front Royal was not incorporated until 1788. Since it has served as the county seat of Warren county. Riverton, one mile to the north, a component part of the industrial growth of this community, has a history of much more recent date. It has a beautiful location at the confluence of the two branches of the Shenandoah river, and is well known to lovers of sport on account of the excellent bass fishing in the limpid waters of this celebrated stream at that point.

The utility and value of this location may be premised by the following simple, yet comprehensive support of facts: A desire for gain is the proximate cause of all effort towards development, and cheap raw material the mediate cause. Water-power, railroads and similar agencies, are only potent accessorial factors.

Railroads and water-powers are valueless without the crude elements of wealth either directly at hand or easily accessible; but where there exists ready formed a vast supply of raw material, these adjuncts and aids to manufactures and wealth are easily secured, provided there are no natural obstructions to interfere.

Front Royal and Riverton have immense natural resources in the way of iron and manganese ores, copper, lead, clays, ochre, building-stone and a variety of the best hard woods. Furniture men, carriage and wagon manufacturers, can find here the very material they need. The builder is in the midst of abundant building-stone, and the brick made of the clay here cannot be surpassed. The iron and steel manufacturer will not be disappointed; for the ores of this section are said to be almost self-fluxing, and carrying, as they do, such a small per cent. of sulphur and phosphorus, their value is scarcely, if at all, to be excelled in this country. Practical experiments made in the various factories attest that we have all the material elements that conduce to industrial prosperity.

We have also a county that can and should sustain a population at Front Royal of fifty thousand people. In fact, tl   county could easily support a p   lation of much greater numbers.

The great North-west is clamorous for a milder climate, a more healthful region, a country with longer seasons, a more certain rain-fall, and a surer and more profitable cropping section. We possess all that they wish, and have none of the repellant forces that they want to abandon. No country has a more diversified agriculture; no country has a more responsive soil; no country has a greater summer rain-fall; no country has a longer growing season; no country has a more healthful climate; no country gives greater impunity to labor; no country offers greater exercise in the open sunshine; no country has more fresh-water streams; no country has a better timber supply; no country is more centrally located; no country affords better chances for a home, health, riches and happiness. The essentials for a successful agriculture are all here, and abundant earth-resources only await the alarm of the latest improved machinery. It will thus be seen that this county is liberally endowed by nature with all the conditions favorable to manufacture and agriculture. Throughout the entire length of its territory are found the resources of a great commonwealth.

Front Royal and Riverton occupy the gate-way to the upper Eastern Valley and to all East Virginia. The Massanutton Mountain, to their south-west, forms an almost impassable barrier to railroads, and just immediately to their east is the only gap in the Blue Ridge range, from the Potomac to the James, where railroads can find an available crossing. At this point the cost of constructing railroads is merely nominal, while we are informed by a competent engineer who has surveyed every depression in this system of mountains, that elsewhere the lowest estimated cost of construction is $176,000 a mile. This, then, is one of the few points where railroads naturally tend to converge. The Norfolk and Western and Richmond and Danville Railroads intersect here. The Norfolk and Western will most certainly construct a shorter line to Washington City, and it will necessarily be direct from this point. The Cumberland Valley road, with its present terminus at Winchester, only eighteen miles distant to the north, wishes to continue south, and nowhere else can it get a favorable outlet. Roads from the west, which are anxious to reach deep water, have run lines to West Point and other ports, and their engineers have invariably reported in favor of Front Royal as the only place where they can get through the

Blue Ridge. What does all this mean? Why, simply that Front Royal is so located that it has to be a great manufacturing and distributing center. The raw materials are here, the railroads cannot pass anywhere else. We have, then, both the proximate and mediate causes which lead to individual and corporate growth and wealth, and in addition, we possess the focal point for an endless accession to our present supply of good railroads.

Front Royal is only seventy miles from deep water at Alexandria, eighty miles of Washington and one hundred and twenty of Baltimore. Ten years ago Front Royal had seven hundred people, now she has *1,800 and Riverton six hundred. All this increase of population is simply the natural outgrowth of a naturally favored section—a substantial growth in spite of opposing influences. Just look at the place and you will see that the town is new, for the houses are all new. A home-like aspect pervades everywhere. It is a nice place in which to live. The people are educated and refined; they have good public and private schools. The people are religious; they have a number of handsome church edifices. There is probably no region where more elements of good combine to meet the urgent desires of man. The scenery is less grand than in many other regions, but it loses nothing, it is more delicately beautiful. It is a picture which the eye loves to dwell upon, and which memory strives to recall—

"And never a picture rarer
For human eye to see."

Eighteen months ago, successful, broad-minded men, realizing what lavish nature had done for this section, grasped the opportunities offered them, and having commenced right, which means that success is half won, the fact is plain that they are going to build up here one of those strong centers of trade where financial depressions only add momentum to the tractive power of success. Money may be withdrawn from here, but its scarcity cannot suspend business activity.

The Front Royal and Riverton Improvement Company was organized under the laws of Virginia, with a capital stock of $500,000. The stock of this company soon commanded a large premium. The charter was received on June 5th, 1890, and, as incredible as it may seem, it is yet true that the entire stock was taken without sending from home a single subscription paper, appointing any agent or paying a cent for advertisements or commissions. Conspicuous also for its absence is the "promoters' fund," each stockholder being on an exact and equal footing with every other one. These are two points of great interest, and should be borne firmly in mind.

---

* The census report (June, 1890) gave Front Royal 864 inhabitants inside of the corporate limits. By actual count, visiting house after house, our population on August 5th, 1891, was 1,856.

Since the organization of the Improvement Company the following companies have been organized: The West End Land Company, the Lexington and Front Royal Investment Company, the Royal Building Company, the Front Royal Investment Company, the Riverton Building and Loan Company.

Such inducements must carry conviction, for Front Royal and Riverton have, without any effort made to procure them, the largest lime works in the South—capacity, five hundred barrels per day; the Riverton Mills Company, $100,000, in the manufacture of flour; the Warren Manufacturing Company, two large cooper shops, tannery, canning factory, cigar factory, collar factory, harness and saddle factory, wagon works, marble works, Cool Alley Mills, Winsboro Mills, Belmont Vineyards (a magnificent estate of 800 acres), the Warren *Sentinel* paper, two banks and three hotels.

Since the organization of the Improvement Company, streets have been laid out, and some of them graded, paved and curbed; "Hotel Royal," an elegant hotel, has been erected and is now open to visitors; the Blue Ridge Knitting Mills, the Maryland Tack Company of Front Royal, the G. W. Shank Manufacturing Company (saw-mill and handle works), the Riverton Baking Company, Carson & Sons Pressed Brick Works, Hoshour & Fadelay Brick Works, Duey Brick Works, Norfolk and Western Railroad rock crushers, and the Gazette Publishing Company, printers and publishers of the *Gazette*, are in operation; the Leicester Piano Company's building is up; the Tonic Remedy Company are preparing to begin work; work is progressing on the Front Royal Furniture Factory; a contract has been signed for a 100-ton iron furnace by D. W Flickwir, of the Norfolk and Western Railroad; the contract has been let for the city water-works; an electric light plant is being established; a $28,000 bridge is to be built across the north branch of the Shenandoah; a large number of residences and business houses are being erected, and the contractors are urging their work on the Randolph-Macon Academy, a building to cost $80,000. This will be a school of high order and standard. It will be ready for matriculates by September, 1892.

Thus, in this brief sketch, will be seen an aggregation of the advantages possessed by this town and county of the famous Shenandoah Valley.

These essentials for successful agriculture and manufacture, with the elements of social, educational and religious life, added to the moral influence of one of the most charming building sites in the world, afford at Front Royal every factor that lends pleasure and comfort to the reality of life.

The position of Front Royal, the extent, diversity and wealth of its natural resources, its climate and beautiful building locations, its railroad facilities, and its magnificent water-power, furnish to the investor an almost absolute security against loss. Opportunities are offered for profit and a rapid extension of business, which rarely exist in the older communities where every ramification of business is filled to a meagre competitive margin.

Front Royal is one of those focal points of trade where prosperity is based on the intrinsic value of legitimate business. The valleys hereabout are studded with rich agricultural and grazing farms. The mountains contain vast deposits of the richest minerals and abound in immense forests of the most valuable woods for both ornamental and commercial purposes. The shifting speculator is a small item here; the merchant, manufacturer and business resident compose the chief population that is coming in as a permanent factor in the growth and success of the town.

One should neither select a place for his home nor invest before studying carefully and deciding in his own mind between that which has actual merit and that which has none. We are confident that the position we take in regard to Front Royal and Riverton will bear the closest scrutiny from intelligent investors. Locate here, and we feel sure that judgment, energy and economy will overcome every contingency that can possibly arise to delay success.

H. H. DOWNING, Esq., attorney at law and President of the Front Royal and Riverton Improvement Company, was born in April, 1853, in Fauquier county, Virginia. He was educated at the University of Virginia, and graduated in law from that institution in 1876. In the following year he began the practice of law at Front Royal, and in 1878 was elected Commonwealth Attorney, and was re-elected to the same position in 1882. In 1885 he was sent to the State Legislature, and re-elected in 1889. During his service in the House he served on many important committees, among which was the committee appointed to try and devise means to bring about a settlement of the State debt with the English bondholders. He assisted in organizing the Front Royal and Riverton Improvement Company, of which he is President, and it was through his influence that there was no promoter's fund. This company has a capital stock of half a million dollars, every cent of which was placed before the charter was obtained. It has been the policy of Mr. Downing to locate and get into successful operation in Front Royal as many solid industries as possible, and a glance at the improvements and plants under way of construction and in operation will suffice to convince the most skeptical of the wise and progressive policy of Mr. Downing. He has retired from the practice of law in order to devote himself more fully and exclusively to the improvement and development of Front Royal and Riverton. It is superfluous to say that he is deeply interested in education: as a substantial evidence of it, he became a large subscriber to the building of the Randolph-Macon Academy, which is now in the course of erection at Front Royal. He was married in October, 1878, to Miss Nannie T. Byrne, of Fauquier county, Virginia. His home is Front Royal, and he is largely interested in farming and grazing, owning some of the best lands in Warren and Fauquier counties.

Prof. GIBSON E. ROY, the efficient and popular Superintendent of Public Instruction of Warren county, Virginia, was born January 24th, 1840, in Warren county, Virginia. He was educated at the Front Royal Academy, and after graduating he began teaching school in the same town, teaching from 1867 until 1875, at which time he abandoned teaching to accept the position of County Superintendent of Public Instruction of his native county, in which position he has served from the time of his first entering on the office until the present time, excepting four years, from 1881 to 1884, during the Mahone rule in Virginia, when he was removed for partisan purposes, but was immediately reinstated at the close of the Mahone dynasty in 1884. Professor Roy has now forty-six schools under his supervision in the county, with about eighteen hundred enrolled attendance.

In 1879 he was elected Surveyor of Warren county, and has filled the office with entire satisfaction up to the present time. He has also for the past fifteen years held the office of Justice of the Peace, and has served for sixteen consecutive years as Mayor of Front Royal.

Professor Roy's interest in the advancement of education, it is needless to say, is paramount to every other interest, and he has made school-work in the main his life-work, and his best energies and abilities are in this field fully called into activity. His labor has been for the elevation of the masses, both intellectually and morally. For more than thirty-three years he has been an efficient and faithful member of the Methodist Episcopal church, and for thirty years has taught a Bible-class in the Sunday-school. At the present time he is teaching a normal Bible-class, which is a preparatory training for teachers in the Sunday-school. He served as lay delegate to the Methodist Conference which met at Roanoke in March, 1890, and he assisted in drafting and offering in that Conference a minority report on the temperance question, which was adopted by the Conference.

He was married in 1870 to Miss Vienna Spangler, of Warren county, and will doubtless spend the remainder of his days in his native county—

Warren—in some educational work or literary pursuit, as he has one of the finest libraries in the State.

J. L. HAILMAN, Esq., President of the West End Land Company of Front Royal, was born September, 1843, in Augusta county, Virginia. He was educated at Roanoke College, but on April 1st, 1861, he left school and entered the Confederate army, he being at that time seventeen years of age. He was assigned to Lee's Riflemen commanded by General Lilly. His health failing him, his father sent a substitute to take his place in 1862. After regaining his health, in 1863 he entered Company A, 1st Virginia Cavalry, and remained in active service until the close of the war. He was with General Lee's army, but was cut off just before reaching Appomattox Court House and was not with the army when the surrender was made. He never did surrender, but, with the balance of the veterans, after the war was over returned home and went to work manfully to restore lost fortunes and rebuild the dilapidated and war-stricken country. He farmed the old homestead for a few years, and then engaged in the mercantile business at Greenville and Newport, following a general merchandise trade about twelve years. In 1890 he located at Front Royal and purchased a large tract of valuable land adjacent to the town and organized the West End Land Company, and at this present time is grading the streets for the site of a new town on the land. He is also stockholder in a number of the Front Royal industries, and is giving his best abilities to the building up of the city. He was married in 1869 to Miss Elizabeth Shuey, of Swoope, Virginia. He has been a member of the Evangelical Lutheran church since boyhood, and is an affable, christian gentleman.

DR. M. L. GARRISON, a leading physician of Front Royal, was born in 1835 in Warren county, Virginia, and was the son of William B. and Nancy Littleton Garrison. His parents were of English and German extraction. Dr. Garrison received his education at the academic schools of Warren and Winchester counties, and in 1858 entered the Medical College at Philadelphia, Pennsylvania, and entered the Virginia Medical College at Richmond in the winter of 1859, graduating therefrom in March, 1860. He at once began practice at Cedarsville, Warren county, Virginia, and after a year of practice entered the Confederate army as a private in Company E, 7th Virginia Cavalry. He served in the ranks about a year, at which time he was appointed to the position of Assistant Surgeon, in which capacity he served until the close of the war, after which he located in Augusta county, Virginia, and practiced a short time, and then removed to Front Royal, where he has remained in active practice ever since. He has made a success of his chosen profession, and has been a credit to it, and a blessing to the town and county where he has so many years lived and labored in behalf of the sick and afflicted. His practice is an extensive one, and extends over a large tract of territory, requiring him to spend many hours in the saddle when his tired and worn-out body called for rest.

He was married in 1874 to an estimable lady, Miss Catharine Jacobs, of Front Royal, and has one child, a daughter, Nannie L. The Doctor is a member of the Methodist Episcopal church, and the same fervor and enthusiasm that he carries into his practice he exhibits in his religious life. There are no half-way measures with him, and he is never satisfied with doing anything less than his best.

STEPHEN HARNSBERGER, M. D., was born on a farm near Willow Spout, Augusta county, Virginia, July 5th, 1852. His father was Robert S. Harnsberger and his mother was Miss Rebecca A., daughter of Capt. William Ingles, of Knoxville, Tennessee. He spent two years at Emory and Henry College, Virginia, and one year at Bethel Military Academy, near Warrenton, Virginia, where he received a handsome gold medal for the best essay, and another medal for the highest standing in the Natural Sciences. At the end of the first half-session his health was so impaired that he had to abandon his studies, at which time the examination gave him "perfect" on seven studies and nine-tenths on the eighth. Had it not been for this, he would have gotten the Scholarship Gold Medal.

In September, 1875, he entered the College of Physicians and Surgeons, Baltimore. He was blood-poisoned in dissecting, and in January, 1876, had to give up his professional studies. In January, 1877, he matriculated at the Kentucky School of Medicine at Louisville, where he graduated in June of the same year. At this school he came within one vote of carrying off the medal for the best thesis.

In November, 1877, he settled at Barterbrook, Virginia, where he soon established a lucrative practice. Four years later he returned to Baltimore to lectures and hospital practice. After practicing two years longer on his old clientage (or old patients) he again visited the lectures and hospitals of Baltimore, and leaving there went to Louisville and assisted Prof. J. M. Mathews, M. D., a distinguished surgeon of that city. In the meantime he had taken two courses of special study in diseases of the lungs and heart. After leaving Louisville he made a specialty of neuralgia, dyspepsia and kindred troubles, using remedies of his own discovery. His treatment was a success, and his remedies are still in demand.

The strain of professional life was more than his naturally frail physical system could bear, and after repeated serious illnesses he was advised to abandon medicine.

Having operated in Alabama in the interests of industrial enterprises with success, he was solicited to come to Virginia in January, 1890. He induced many manufacturing men to locate in the valley towns. Directly and indirectly he has done more in this way than any one person who has operated on that particular line. His special "write-ups" of industrial towns brought him prominently forward as a writer, and inducements were soon offered him by the Front Royal and Riverton Improvement Company to take editorial charge of a newspaper at Front Royal. He is well known as editor and manager of the Front Royal and Riverton *Gazette*, with a wide circulation and influence. He is also President of the Hagerstown Investment Company, and is connected with other financial enterprises. At the contest for the best essay on any subject, offered by the Basic City *Advance* in June, 1890, he was awarded a magnificent gold medal. He is familiar with industrial development, and posted on paying investments.

CHAPTER IX.

HALIFAX COUNTY.

By J. A. PHILLIPS.

A recent industrial writer, whose name I am unable to give, deserves credit for the following eloquent paragraph in eulogy of Virginia:

"The history of no other State has more to appeal to the imagination and the judgment than that of Virginia—a history romantic, heroic and august. What shapes trod her early stage! No experiences of age dispel the charms of her bright romance. No aspiring historian, panting after the iconoclasm, can destroy these idols of childhood. Smith and Pocahontas will be always real and dear; and the sounds of the names of some of her rivers make melodies in our ears now as they did in young and day-dream days. But if her early history is so dear for the charms it gave our childhood, there are eras in the contemplation of which veneration is the fittest mood. Her soil seems hallowed with the ashes of the best and bravest of our countrymen. She seems an 'eternal camping-ground' for fame; and the spirits of her warriors and statesmen crowd their sacred trysting-place—a numerous and immortal concourse. There reposes all that mortality can claim of one of the most revered of Christian warriors and statesmen—Washington. In the soil of Virginia rests the immortal author of the Declaration of Independence—Thomas Jefferson. There, too, lies Patrick Henry, one of the most kindling and enthralling orators of any time. There is buried Randolph of Roanoke, the fierce and fiery tribune, whose 'splendid conflagration' illumined in his day the most august forum of his country — the United States Senate. But who shall call the long roll of heroes in proper tones?"

It is a matter of regret that the accomplished writer was not engaged in particularizing the beauties and advantages of the various counties of Virginia, for I am sure his tribute to Halifax would have formed a glowing and appropriate peroration to such an inspiring theme.

It may seem peculiar, and, perhaps, unfortunate, to begin this sketch in a paradoxical or hypercritical manner, and yet it must at the outset be remarked that a description of Halifax county does not properly belong to a "History of South-western Virginia," if we view the matter from a geographical standpoint. Halifax is not a part of South-western Virginia, but is one of the counties of that portion of middle Virginia known as the "Southside," although it is often designated by writers and speakers as a part of the piedmont division of Virginia—that magnificent belt of country which, beginning at the Potomac, extends 250 miles to the Dan river on the North Carolina line.

The publishers of this work have, however, displayed acute business judgment, and a just and meritorious consideration for this grand old county, in giving it place in this handsome and valuable history of the boundless resources of the "booming" South-west. And the very fact that such honorable recognition has been accorded to Halifax, solely upon its own merits, speaks most eloquently of the high estimation its broad acres, its splendid people, its thriving towns, its creditable past and its bright and promising future have attained in the public mind.

Halifax county was formed from Lunenburg about 1752. In *ante-bellum* days it was one of the largest slave-holding counties in the State, and her people were noted for their princely estates, lavish hospitality, brilliant culture and refinement, and all those charming attributes of aristocratic intellect and wealth which "filled the measure of those good old days."

But the war came, and another page was turned, and as before the irresistible, pitiless force of a tornado, the property of Halifax was depreciated, the possessions of her people swept away, and where plenty and peace had made a happy land, distress, want and penury disclosed their forbidding and unwelcome features. Through these very adversities, however, far-reaching and dreadful as they were in effect and influence, was manifested the nobility of our people. Baptized with fire, they emerged from its crucial test temporarily weakened, it may be, but in no way impoverished in spirit or broken in determination to still own and develop the great county they received as a heritage from their fathers.

Thus, Halifax, since the war, has been pressing forward under the loyal labors of her worthy sons, and attracting the foreigner and immigrant by her great natural advantages. She has never receded from a step once taken, and in her progress has charged ahead of other sister counties which seemed to possess brighter prospects.

The population of Halifax, according the census of 1890 (which, however, is unsatisfactory), is 34,424, thus placing her sixth in rank of all the counties in the State, even including those containing the large cities. If we omit these cities as separate municipalities, *Halifax stands first in population of all the counties in Virginia.* Her area, in round figures is 519,000 acres—*fifth* in size of all the counties of Virginia. Her density of population is 43 to the square mile, which, if we again except the large cities of Virginia, shows Halifax to stand near the head of the list in this respect.

Halifax lies in the heart of the finest tobacco growing section of the world. Indeed, that remarkable modern product, yellow tobacco, was originated in Halifax, and forms now the chief agricultural staple, the "money crop" of the county, although corn, wheat, rye, oats, clover, hay, etc., are grown in large and paying quantities.

The census of 1890 shows Halifax to be easily second of all the counties in Virginia in the production of tobacco, cultivating 14,997 acres, and raising 5,432,487 pounds of tobacco, valued at $630,000.

The county is remarkably well watered, the Stanton river, a magnificent stream navigated by steamboats, skirting its entire northern and north-western boundaries. The Dan, Banister and Hyco rivers, also large and never-failing streams, penetrate the interior; while numerous large creeks and tributaries of all these rivers intersect the intervening country, rendering it unsurpassed in fertility of soil and general productiveness.

The rich upland loams of Halifax cannot be excelled for wheat and tobacco, while heavy crops of the cultivated grasses are produced. The low-grounds of the rivers, named above bear a State reputation for their enormous yields of corn year after year without rest or fertilizer. These low-grounds are capable, also, of producing large crops of heavy shipping tobacco, but this grade has almost been abandoned in Halifax, owing to the greater value of the golden yellow type.

Halifax also possesses another important advantage, in its labor—that powerful factor in the prosperity of all pursuits. "Strikes" have never occurred here, and labor for farms, manufactures, trades and mechanics can be procured here at reasonable prices. It is sober, reliable, contented and peaceable.

In climate, Halifax county is blessed perhaps more than in any other respect, for health is the first constituent of a happy life. Malaria is comparatively unknown, and no epidemic due to climatic influences has ever been heard of. The climate is essentially one of "means," never reaching the extremes of heat and cold of the South and North. Indeed, the same term can be properly applied to it in comparison even with other portions of Virginia, for here the dreadful blasts of winter sometimes felt in the mountain districts, and the sultry, enervating temperature of the flat country, are equally unknown; and, by a simple obeyance of the laws of Nature, and Nature's God, as long, happy and useful a life can be spent here as was ever allotted to man since ante-deluvian days.

Halifax, although not noted as a mineral county, nor, indeed, making any pretensions to such a distinction, is by no means without large and valuable mineral deposits. Coal, iron, copper, gold, silver, plumbago, manganese and mica are found here, but the county has been so intensely agricultural in its pursuits that these deposits have never been developed, nor has their full extent been ascertained. But this present epoch of manufacturing and mining has turned the eyes of our own people and foreign capitalists to our mineral resources, and large companies have been chartered and are now beginning preliminary work upon coal, iron and copper mines in the county, while others are contemplated.

The people of Halifax to-day maintain their old deserved reputation for a high degree of culture, refinement and education. Whenever able, parents are sure to give their children collegiate training, and the public schools of the county, administered by careful officials, are largely attended, and are spreading the rays of enlightenment and knowledge in the homes of the humblest.

In railroad facilities Halifax is greatly to be envied. The Richmond and Danville traverses the county north and south for about forty miles, the Lynchburg and Durham, completed in 1890, crosses the county east and west about fifty miles, and the Atlantic and Danville, running from Norfolk to Danville, strikes the southern portion of the county, passing through it for a distance of thirty-five miles. These two last mentioned roads have been recently built, and open sections of the county, which, while rich in natural advantages, have heretofore been undeveloped and completely cut off from the outside world by lack of railroad accommodations. These three roads combined furnish a system of railroad facilities surpassed by few counties in Virginia, giving direct access to markets north, south, east and west, and are accomplishing a grand work in the material development and progress of Halifax.

To sum up this necessarily discursive sketch, Halifax county, taken in its entirety, offers unusual attractions and advantages to the homeseeker, the manufacturer, the mechanic, the laborer and the farmer. Within its borders are grown tobacco and all the cereals, all the grasses, all the fruits and all the vegetables that can be raised in a mild, temperate and generous climate. Her broad fields can accommodate and sustain any number of cattle, sheep, horses, oxen and hogs, while river, forest, meadow, valley and dale add their benign and necessary contributions in rich abundance to the prosperity of the farmer. Indeed, nature seems to have been lavish in her formative designs when dealing with Halifax, and if in her wide expanse of territory her natural conditions of advantageous location, mild and temperate climate, picturesque and inviting topography, and responsive, fruitful soil can be improved upon or rendered more valuable and completely satisfactory, this writer, at least, is at a loss to imagine how such an improvement can be accomplished.

SOUTH BOSTON.

It is not surprising that Halifax county, with its large dimensions, population and enormous acreage, with its great agricultural resources and capabilities, should need a town of its own, a local home market for its products, a commercial center and exchange, so to speak, where the producer, the tradesman and the consumer could meet and minister to the wants of each other—and such, in brief, were the real primal causes which gave birth to South Boston. The town was a necessity. It was demanded by the changed condition of things after the war. It was absolutely necessary to the material welfare and commercial growth of the people of Halifax. And not only was South Boston a necessity to Halifax, but also to a much larger area in the bordering counties, both of Virginia and North Carolina, for just here it must be noted that South Boston owes its remarkable growth to its magnificent geographical position—that vital principle in the life of every business center. It is situated on Dan river, at the junction of the Lynchburg and Durham and Richmond and Danville Railroads, in the heart of the now world-famous region, generally described as the "bright tobacco belt" of Virginia and North Carolina, one hundred and nine miles from Richmond, thirty-two miles from Danville, sixty-one miles from Lynchburg, fifty-two miles from Durham, North Carolina, while nine miles south the Lynchburg and Durham crosses the Atlantic and Danville Railroad, thus giving a direct line to the sea with all its great advantages. Washington, Baltimore, Philadelphia and New York are easy of access, and, indeed, through its splendid railroad facilities, it is in quick business touch with the more distant markets of the West and South.

In 1880 South Boston was a mere hamlet of three hundred and eighty population. In the town proper there were very few residences, two or three country stores, and no manufacturing or industrial enterprises of any description. By-and-by a little tobacco was sold, as much for experiment as for any other consideration. Struggling on, however, with a brave and hopeful spirit, the people began to entertain hopes of establishing a prosperous tobacco market. Their efforts met with support and encouragement from the surrounding country, which was quick to perceive and appreciate the great importance of a permanent home market, and slowly, but surely, the town moved forward. It is needless to follow each successive stage of its history. Like all other new towns, it met with rebuffs, and had to combat the open enmity and envy of rivals, as well as indifference and lack of confidence on the part of its own people. The tobacco market succeeded, and South Boston now ranks fifth in the markets of Virginia, selling annually from eight to ten million pounds. Its warehouses are among the largest and handsomest in Virginia, and their sales of leaf tobacco are annually increasing.

Tobacco is manufactured here in large quantities, and South Boston's output of plug and twist is reaching enormous figures every year. In this direction the prediction is confidently made that this town will eventually be one of the chief tobacco manufacturing points in the United States.

While the tobacco business in its various departments has been, and still continues to be, the chief commercial pursuit of South Boston, and the source from whence sprang her thrift and prosperity, yet the town is fast outgrowing this one industry, enormous as it is. Other manufacturing establishments are established here, which add materially to the busy vim and vigor of energetic life.

One of the largest plants in Virginia for manufacturing sash, doors, blinds, mouldings, fine ornamental wood-work, etc., is located here, and although its capacity is great and would be notable in a large city, yet it is unable to accommodate its orders.

A stock company with ample capital has been organized for the manufacture of carriages, buggies, carts, wagons, etc. Its new shops and ware-rooms are nearly completed and before these pages reach the public its work will be on the market. This establishment has been eagerly sought after by other towns, and in any would have been advertised as a "star" attraction. Its output will be from 1,200 to 2,000 vehicles per year, employing 150 to 200 operatives.

A spoke and hub factory is here located and is doing an enormous business, and is not able to accept the orders offered it.

Manufacturing in South Boston has just begun; it is in its infancy; but the success which has attended it so far in all lines makes it apparent that the town will be filled with factories of various descriptions. Certainly no point offers greater inducements to manufacturing enterprises. For the manufacture of furniture, farm implements, spokes, hubs, spool, shuttle, bobbin and mechanical woodware generally does it offer special facilities, surrounded as it is by the best oak, hickory, ash, elm, poplar, beech, birch, persimmon, maple, dogwood and other timbers. Corporations and private firms seeking suitable sites for the manufacture of cotton, wool and shoes, in addition to the lines above mentioned, cannot find a more inviting point than South Boston, for here are offered the facilities and inducements of inexpensive plants, low-priced labor, low taxes and insurance that ought to and will prevail in the speedy inauguration of many manufacturing establishments. It may be of interest to give here a partial enumeration of the enterprises already in operation and fixtures in the town, together with their capital:

Saddle and Harness Factory, in operation ....$	5,000
Edmonson Tobacco Company, in operation	100,000
Edmonson Tobacco Manufacturing Company, in operation	25,000
Boss Tobacco Works, in operation...	50,000
Shepherd & Noblin Tobacco Company, in operation....................	75,000
J. A. Glenn Tobacco Works, in operation	20,000
Evans' Building Material Factory, in operation............................	75,000
Norwood & Evans Tobacco Works, in operation............................	75,000
Easley & Lovelace Tobacco Works, in operation	75,000
Branch Am. Tobacco Co...	25,000,000
Brown & Glenn Tobacco Works in operation	25,000
Barbour Buggy Works, in operation, authorized capital	100,000
Piedmont Manufacturing Co., Spokes, Handles, etc., in operation..	15,000
Planters and Merchants Bank—capital and surplus.....................	120,000
Bank of South Boston—capital and surplus	65,000
Electric Light Plant, in operation ...	8,000
Water-works, in operation............	20,000
Building and Loan Association, in operation	75,000
Two Livery Stables, in operation ...	10,000
Halifax Record, Times and *News* and Job Offices, in operation......	5,000
Brickyards, in operation................	10,000

South Boston was incorporated in 1884, and since that time its taxable values have increased over 100 pr. ct.

The town has bought and owns an electric light plant, the system being complete, furnishing both arc and incandescent lights. Good waterworks have recently been completed, and with a well-equipped fire department the town is amply protected from fire.

As a business center South Boston presents some remarkable characteristics. From the amount of its business transactions, strangers and distant correspondents imagine it to be a town of 5,000 to 10,000 inhabitants, but South Boston has not yet reached those figures. It is frequently remarked, however, that her business is done upon a 7,000 population basis.

The tobacco trade has already been alluded to, but in addition to this a large wholesale business in dry-goods and groceries is done here, and it is certain that in a short time nearly every mercantile line will be represented here by extensive wholesale establishments.

South Boston is the chief depot, both for incoming and outgoing freight and passenger traffic, on the Richmond and Danville Railroad between Richmond and Greensboro, North Carolina, excepting Danville only; and on the Lynchburg and Durham Railroad, for the month of May, 1891, it contributed *one-fifth* of the entire earnings of that road, extending from Lynchburg, Virginia, to Durham, North Carolina—114 miles! It is, indeed, the commercial *entrepot* of this entire section, and the chief distributing point.

To handle the enormous business of the town, of course good banking facilities are necessary, and in this respect, also, South Boston is fortunate. Two banks are in operation here, with a large aggregate capital and surplus.

The town owes only a small debt, and taxes are light. The municipal affairs are carefully managed by officers chosen from the leading business men.

As a place of residence South Boston is surpassed by no town in Southside Virginia. Situated on a gently rolling slope, the drainage is superior, because it is natural and sufficient; and, surrounded by a clear, open country, free from swamps or marshes, the healthfulness of the place is excellent. Its people are cultivated and refined, moral and religious. There are seven churches—four white and three colored. Two of the former have been recently built, and are exceedingly handsome and costly. There is a graded public school, with four teachers, located in a handsome brick building, the property of the town. The South Boston Female Institute is a popular college, where young ladies receive instruction in the higher branches of learning.

South Boston is a town with the certainty of a great future. It will, at no very distant day, be ranked among the cities of Virginia. It actually now presents an appearance and a record and annually transacts a volume of business far ahead of many towns of a larger population. It is fast expanding upon a safe, sure, solid and permanent foundation.

Here, with a refined society, with elevated religious influences, superior scholastic facilities and unsurpassed industrial opportunities and resources; here, in a town built up and established upon honest, legitimate values and business principles, is a home for all who would prosper, and South Boston extends a warm welcome to all who would share in her progress and development.

HALIFAX COURT HOUSE.

This beautiful town is situated on the Lynchburg and Durham Railroad, five miles from South Boston, fifty-six miles from Lynchburg, thirty-seven miles from Danville, one hundred and fourteen miles from Richmond and fifty-seven miles from Durham, North Carolina. It is the county-seat, and is the most centrally located town of Halifax—chosen, doubtless, on account of this consideration in the good old days, when, without railroad accommodations, a journey to the court-house was quite a trip, and, therefore, it was advisable and just to have the county seat at the most convenient point. The post-office name has recently been changed to Houston, in honor of Mr. W. C. Houston, Jr., President of the Lynchburg and Durham Railroad.

Halifax Court House is an old and historic village. In *ante-bellum* days it was an important station on one of the great stage routes from the far South to Washington and the North, and here Calhoun and other noted statesmen and public men have often rested on their long trips to and from the national capital.

This town was also in the bailiwick, so to speak, of Patrick Henry, John Randolph, Judge Marshall, Judge Leigh, Daniel Mar and other great lawyers, statesmen and orators, and their inspiring eloquence has often aroused and swayed enormous crowds gathered on the court green.

Halifax Court House of to-day, however, differs very greatly in appearance, as well as in reality, from what it was in those by-gone days. Then it was a delightful, sleepy, old-fashioned country village, whose inhabitants were somewhat given to horse-racing, chicken fights, political speaking, mint-julips, *et cetera*. Now it is a live, modern town, in which business has taken the place of inactivity, and idleness is a lost art. Then the trade of the place was absorbed by two or three prominent "Majors" and "Colonels," and the stores were few and impressed one with their high gables and small windows. Now "competition is the life of trade," younger men are at the helm, the business houses are numerous, handsome and imposing.

The population of Halifax Court House, according to the census of 1890, is 1,285—showing a large percentage of increase in the last ten years.

This town is one of the most delightful in southern Virginia as a place of residence, and, allied to many natural advantages, it is not surprising that a most prosperous future is predicted for it.

There are already established at Halifax Court House several large manufacturing establishments, among which may be mentioned an extensive planing mill (for the manufacture of sash, doors, blinds and builders' supplies generally), a furniture factory, a tobacco hanger and basket factory (manufacturing an ingenious and very valuable device whereby the curing of tobacco can be accomplished more rapidly, conveniently and with better results than by the old method), and a large fruit and vegetable cannery.

The water-power on Banister river at this point is very superior, and ample for almost any number of manufacturing establishments. It has recently been purchased by a western capitalist with a view to its complete development. It will eventually play an important part in the history of this stirring and energetic town.

The people of Halifax Court House sustain with pardonable pride the old reputation of the place for culture, hospitality and refinement, strangers being charmed with the old-time Virginia welcome extended them, while the residents themselves are never so contented and happy as when at home.

There are two banks at Halifax Court House, each doing a splendid business and possessing the unlimited confidence of the entire surrounding section.

Two new and elegant hotels have recently been completed, and, with the imposing court-house, law buildings, stores, churches, residences, etc., a beautiful and attractive town meets the gaze.

There has been a large amount of building completed here in the last two years, and there is no cessation of this unmistakable indication of a thrifty town.

IN CONCLUSION

it only remains to be said that as a county Halifax is great and grand and inviting, in its past, its present and its future promise. South Boston is rapidly reaching up to her final destiny as the chief inland manufacturing and business center in Virginia, while Halifax Court House is keeping step with the tide of prosperity which is sweeping over the county.

Hon. PAUL CARRINGTON EDMUNDS, Congressman from the Sixth District of Virginia, was born in Halifax county, Virginia, November 1st, 1836. He was educated by a private tutor at home, and was three years at the University of Virginia, and graduated in law at William and Mary College, at Williamsburg, Virginia. He practiced law for nearly two years in Jefferson City, Missouri, but returned to Virginia in 1858, and has been engaged in agriculture on his farm in Halifax county ever since. He was elected to the Senate of Virginia in 1881 and served four years, and was re-elected in 1884. He was a delegate from the Sixth District to the National Democratic Cenvention, at Chicago, in 1884, and was elected to the Fifty-first Congress as a Democrat, receiving 17,559 votes, against 13,822 votes for P. H. McCaul, Republican, and 198 votes for S. J. Hopkins, Independent Democrat and Knight of Labor.

Mr. Edmunds is a ripe scholar, and a man to do honor to his constituency in any situation. He combines the too rare qualities of a perfect gentleman with that of a thorough politician and statesman. While many honors have been conferred upon him, doubtless many more await him, and if the signs of the times are at all to be relied upon, he will, at no distant day, grace the Senate of the United States.

Hon. WILLIAM J. JORDAN, State Senator from Halifax county, and a resident of South Boston, was born in this county in the year 1839. His father was a large planter, and both father and mother were natives of Virginia. He received his early education in the schools of the county. While yet quite young, he began clerking for the firm of J. L. & F. Owen, remaining with them four years. In 1861 he enlisted in Company C, 3d Virginia Cavalry, in which he served four years. He was wounded in the battle of Fort Cannon, and was in all the principal engagements in Virginia, acting as courier for General McLaws for over a year. When the war closed he came to Halifax, Virginia, and entered business with his brother Robert, conducting their business at several points throughout the county, one branch of their business being in South Boston, and started a private bank in 1872, which they conducted until about 1885, when they united with the Planters and Merchants Bank, which was organized in 1884, of which he is now director. Mr. Jordan has also large land interests in the county.

In November, 1884, he was elected to the State Legislature, in which he served two years, and in 1889 he was elected State Senator from this county for four years.

He was married in 1876 to Miss Elizabeth Buster, daughter of James S. Buster, of Charlotte county. He is a member of the Baptist church, and a Mason in good standing.

Mr. Jordan, aside from his interest in politics, is actively engaged in the development of the city and the surrounding country, in which he takes a just and practical pride.

HENRY EASLEY, Esq., the subject of this sketch, Cashier of the Planters and Merchants Bank of South Boston, Halifax county, was born in this county in 1847, and is the son of Dr. Henry Easley, who for many years was a successful physician, but is now dead. Henry Easley, Jr., was educated in the schools of the county; enlisted in 1864 in the Confederate service and served until the close of the war. He was in several battles around Petersburg, and in Lee's retreat, but came out from the engagements unscathed. After the war he engaged in the mercantile business at Brooklyn, Virginia, South Boston and other points in the State, following this occupation until 1885, when, in company with his brother, he formed the firms of J. W. Easley & Co., and Henry Easley & Co. The same year, in company with his brother and a number of other business men, he organized the Planters and Merchants Bank, with a capital of $103,000. Mr. Henry Easley was made cashier, which responsible position he now holds. He is also a partner in the firm of Penick & Easley, engaged in the leaf tobacco business. Politics have never interested him especially, or not sufficiently to call him away from his legitimate occupation. He was married in 1873 to Miss Nannie P. Owen; five children have been born to them, three daughters and two sons. His church is that of the Presbyterian, in which he is a faithful and reliable ruling elder.

J. W. EASLEY, Esq., one of the leading business men of South Boston, was born in Halifax county, in 1849, and is a son of Henry Easley, Esq., also of the same county. J. W. Easley received his education in the oldfield schools, and began clerking at an early age at Halifax Court House. In 1868 he came to South Boston and entered the employ of Jordan, Owen & Co., as a clerk, where he remained for three years in this capacity, when he was taken in as a partner and remained in the firm six years, when he purchased the entire business, which he conducted for five years and then formed a partnership with Henry Easley, W. E. Owen and Thornton S. Easley, under the style of J. W. Easley & Co., which firm existed for a number of years, when he again took charge of the entire business, and later formed a partnership with Mr. R. A. Owens. Besides his connection with this firm, he has conducted a warehouse and has been a heavy dealer in leaf tobacco since 1873. He assisted in the organization of the Piedmont Manufacturing Company, of which he was President for some years. He is also a director in the Barlow Buggy Company, and a director in the Planters and Merchants Bank, of which he was one of the organizers. He also assisted in the starting of the W. D. Barbour Hardware Company, and is at present a member of the firm of Easley & Lovelace Tobacco Company, as well as a director in the Building and Loan Association. In 1884 he was elected a member of the Town Council, and has served as City Treasurer ever since. He has large land interests in the county, which, perhaps, as much as any other one thing, concentrates his interest in that section, and makes him especially anxious for its future prosperity. He was married in 1876 to Miss Sallie I. Owen, who died in 1881, having borne to him a daughter. He was again married, in 1885, to Miss Jennie C. Owen, a cousin of his first wife, and three children have been born to them. He is a deacon in the Presbyterian church, and an enthusiastic member of the Masonic fraternity.

Mr. EDWARD L. EVANS, the subject of this article, was born in Chester county, Pennsylvania, in January, 1857, and in the year 1870 came to Virginia, receiving his education at Farmville and Hampden-Sydney College, from which latter he graduated in 1877. After graduating he became book-keeper for the firm of A. R. Venable, Jr., & Co., of Farmville, and occupied this position until the summer of 1882, when he took the position of book-keeper for C. M. Walker & Co., of the same place, where he remained until the fall of 1883, when he came to South Boston and engaged in the hardware business in company with J. J. Owen under the firm name of Evans & Owen, which firm existed until 1887. In the spring of 1886 he started the South Boston Planing Mill and conducted it in connection with his partner until 1887. In the fall of 1884 he organized the firm of G. T. Norwood & Co., leaf tobacco brokers, of which Mr. Evans is still a member. He assisted in the organization of the Barbour Buggy Company, of which he is Vice-President. He was elected Mayor of the town and served four years in that capacity, filling the office in a highly satisfactory manner. He was married in 1884 to Miss Mildred Blanton, of Farmville, and four children have been born to them. Mr. Evans is a member of the Presbyterian church. He has great faith in the future of his town and his best interests are centered here, a fact that makes good citizens and good neighbors.

Dr. ALEXANDER TRENT CLARKE, the subject of this paper, leading physician of South Boston, Virginia, was born in Charles City county, April 14th, 1843. His father, John J. Clarke, Esq., was a planter. Dr. Alexander T. Clarke received his education at Lynchburg and Williamsburg colleges, and then began the study of medicine under Dr. John J. Roane, of Charles City county, entering the Medical College of Virginia at the age of seventeen years. He did not complete his course, but enlisted in the 3d Virginia Cavalry, in which he served four years. He was wounded in 1864, and was not again in active service during the remainder of the war. In 1868 he resumed his studies and graduated the following year from the Medical College of Virginia. He began practice the same year in Charles City county, and remained there until the fall of 1874, when he came to South Boston and has been here ever since, having established a very extensive as well as lucrative practice. He was married in 1872 to Miss Mattie G. Crocker, who died in 1884. She was the mother of six children, four of whom are now living. The Doctor was again married, in 1886, to Miss Carrie V. Sydnor, and two children have blessed this second union. He is a member of the State Medical Society and also a member of the State Board of Medical Examiners. He is an enthusiastic Odd Fellow and a member of the Methodist church. The Doctor finds time from his arduous practice to devote to general literature, and in this, as well as in his profession, he keeps abreast of the times.

ALEXANDER R. GREEN, County Treasurer of Halifax county, Virginia, was born in this county in 1841. His father, Thomas I. Green, Esq., was also born in the same county, and filled the position of Commonwealth Attorney for forty years. He died in 1871. Alexander R.

Green, the subject of this sketch, was wholly educated in his native county. At the age of twenty he enlisted in the Confederate army in Company A, 53d Virginia, which was a part of Montague's Battalion. As a non-commissioned officer he served four years, and was in all the battles around Richmond. He was also in the battle of Gettysburg, Pennsylvania, where he was wounded in the right lung, but continued on the field and remained in the service until the close of the war. After returning home he engaged as clerk and followed this occupation until 1871, when he was appointed Commissioner in Chancery of the County and Circuit Courts, which position he holds at this present time. In 1874 he was appointed Deputy Treasurer, and in 1879 was elected County Treasurer, which office he also holds at this writing. In 1891 he purchased a third interest in the Halifax Planing Mills Company. He also assisted in the organization of the Halifax Canning Company, of which he is President. He has always taken an active part in politics, and finds in the excitement of the calling a pleasure that is peculiar to itself. He was married in 1871 to Miss Lizzie R. Wauhop, of Tennessee. Four children have been born to them. He is a Mason and a member of St. John's Episcopal church, of which he is a vestryman.

WILLIAM HOLMAN SHEPHERD was born near Fork Union, Fluvanna county, Virginia, November 18th, 1843, where he was reared and educated. A portion of his early manhood was spent in the Confederate army, and after the war, several years in business in the city of Richmond. He located in South Boston in 1871, and for the first year was employed as book-keeper for E. H. Vaughn & Co., who were at that time engaged in the mercantile business. He then associated himself with Capt. R. H. Owen in the warehouse and leaf tobacco business, and in 1875 he associated himself with Maj. H. A. Edmonson. The firm of Edmonson & Shepherd existed for nine years, and during that time were the largest dealers, and did a great deal for the permanent establishment of the South Boston market.

In 1884, the firm of Edmonson & Shepherd was dissolved, and Mr. Shepherd continued to deal very largely in the higher grades, bright wrappers, fillers and cutters, until 1890, when he and Mr. Noblin formed a copartnership under the firm name of the Shepherd & Noblin Tobacco Company.

Mr. Shepherd has been one of our most successful business men.

Mr. Shepherd is one of our foremost and most progressive citizens, having for years, until recently, been an active and useful member of the Town Council. All measures for the growth and development of our town, have had his sympathy and suppport.

WINTHROP G. STEPHENS, Esq.,

a leading citizen of Halifax, was born in New York City. He came to Halifax county in 1877 in company with his father, and in 1888 purchased a tract of land on which the city of Halifax now stands, the tract consisting of 321 acres. He had paid much attention to the breeding of fine stock, especially Jersey cattle, and had been financially very successful in this enterprise.

In the year 1888 he opened a real estate office in Halifax, and has been the immediate means of interesting a large amount of Northern capital to investments in this place. He is President of the Tobacco Hangers Manufacturing Company, which represents a large stock. This business has assumed considerable proportions and is rapidly growing, its goods being sold throughout the Southern and all tobacco-growing States. Mr. Stephens is a thorough business man, devoting his entire time and best abilites to his work. Politics have never interested him, and he finds himself equally as well off, and fully as contented to eschew this unsatisfactory calling. He has been very successful in the sale of farm land, and enjoys a large and growing and profitable trade. He is a man to be relied upon, full of enterprise and energy.

EDGAR H. VAUGHN, Esq.,

the popular County Court Clerk of Halifax county, was born in Amelia county in the year 1845. His parents were both natives of Virginia. His father was a planter and died in 1879. Edgar Vaughn, the subject of this sketch, received his education in his native county, and came to Halifax in 1860, and in the following year enlisted in Company G, 6th Virginia Cavalry and served four years, and was in most of the principal battles of this State. After the close of the war he returned to Halifax and accepted a position as clerk in a store, and soon began business for himself at South Boston under the firm name of Yancey & Vaughn, and later as E. H. Vaughn & Co. He continued in this business until November, 1878, when he was elected Clerk of the County Court, which position he holds at the present time. He was married in December, 1867, to Miss Almyra Prover, of South Boston. They have six children. Mr. Vaughn's first wife died in 1885, and he married Miss J. J. Rogers, of Halifax. He and his wife are members of the Church of England and Presbyterian. He is a Mason, and is also a member of the fraternity of Odd Fellows. As county official Mr. Vaughn is justly popular; he gives his best energies to his work.

WILLIAM D. BARBOUR, Esq., a member of the firm of W. D. Barbour & Co., leading wholesale hardware dealers of South Boston, was born in Pittsylvania county, June 7th, 1856. He received a limited education in the schools of the State, and entered a hardware house at the age of thirteen, as clerk, at Lynchburg, and remained six years in this position, when he accepted an offer as traveling salesman, and filled the place for the period of five years, when, in 1883, he came to South Boston, and, in company with J. W. Easley, under the firm name of W. D. Barbour & Co., entered into the retail hardware business, which they continued in exclusively for a time, when they began jobbing, and to-day the house is doing a very extensive wholesale trade, with patrons throughout the State and adjoining ones. They employ two traveling salesmen and operate a branch house at Oxford, North Carolina, and another at Martinsville, Virginia. In the year 1885 he began the manufacture of buggies in a small way, and in 1890 organized the Bourbon Buggy Company, with a capital stock of $100,000 and a paid-up stock of $40,000. He assisted in the organization of the Piedmont Manufacturing Company, and erected the plant, which was afterwards sold to Mr. James Traves. He has taken more or less interest in politics, and has served the people as a member of the Town Council and Mayor, which office he now holds. He was married in 1882 to Miss Lillian Jackson, of Madison Court House, and one son has been born to them. Mr. Barbour is a communicant of the Methodist church and a member of the Masonic fraternity, the Odd Fellows and the Knights of Pythias.

CHAPTER X.

BROADWAY.

By JOHN F. WINFIELD.

This new and enterprising town is situated in Rockingham county, Virginia, twelve miles north of Harrisonburg, on the Valley branch of the Baltimore and Ohio Railroad, and at the junction of Linvill's creek with the north fork of the Shenandoah river.

TOPOGRAPHICAL FEATURES.

Two elevated plateaus with long, gentle slopes facing towards Linvill's creek as a common center, each bordered by parallel ranges of hills, the hills and their corresponding plateaus terminating northward in planes inclined to the banks of the Shenandoah, and then stretching southward to complete the beautiful Valley of Finvill's creek. The meeting of the waters and their joint passage through a miniature canon, comprehend the most striking topographical features of Broadway and immediate surroundings.

The bordering hills have the general direction of the Appalachian chain, and are covered here and there in alternation with forest trees and farms in a high state of cultivation.

Looking upon them from any point in Broadway, they seem to conceal their intervening fertile valleys, and to rise one above the other with the regularity of terraces, until, on the one hand, the North Mountain, and on the other, the Massanutten affords, respectively, a near and more distant, grand and towering background. Add to the whole scene the glamour of one of the gorgeous sunsets so common in this section, and you have a landscape of surpassing loveliness.

AS IT WAS, AND AS IT IS.

In a few years time, comparatively, it has grown from a country store, a flouring mill, and one or two private dwellings, into a place containing a population of about seven hundred, one large pottery, one planing mill, one creamery, a foundry and machine-shop, one broom-handle factory, two wagon factories, one sash, blind and door factory, one barrel factory, five general stores, two agricultural stores, one jewelry store, one drug store, one hardware store, and just outside of the corporate limits, a tannery, flouring mill and corn and plaster mill.

It has besides, two church buildings, one graded school building, a Masonic and Good Templar's hall, an opera-hall, and two weekly newspapers.

A continuous stream of farm and other products pours into the place. Frequently for many days in succession, seventy-five to one hundred wagons are unloaded at the station or other places of business, and the shipments of grain, lumber, bark, etc., equal, if they do not exceed, that of any other point in the Virginia valley.

ADVANTAGES OF POSITION.

Owing to its elevation—1,200 feet above sea level—and its admirable drainage, it is secure from malarial and other influences likely to occasion endemic diseases.

It is shielded from storms and cold north-west winds by the great North Mountain, which rises to the height of four thousand feet.

Its two streams, falling at the rate of forty feet per mile, and numerous bold crystal springs upon its bordering high lands, while affording abundance of power for manufacturing purposes, could, with comparatively little cost, be made to supply every house from cellar to garret with pure water.

It is necessarily a point on the shortest and most feasible route that can be selected to link by rail the great coal-fields of West Virginia, with tide-water.

This statement is not made at hazard, but upon the authority of that accomplished writer and eminent topographical engineer, Jed. Hotchkiss, Esq. In the September (1880) number of his *Virginias*, in an editorial article on Broadway, the following extract will be found: "An inspection of the geological map of the Virginias (see our June number) reveals the fact that it is less than fifty miles, as the crow flies, from Broadway depot to the famous Cumberland coal-field; and those familiar with the topography well know that there is a perfectly feasible route for a railway that shall have moderate grades and a length of less than one hundred miles hence to that great bed of superior coal, and through a region rich in timber, mineral, cattle and other wealth. In fact, this place is nearer by a feasible route to the great coal-field than any other in the valley."

The crowning advantage, however, which Broadway possesses, is its near proximity to the vast mineral and other resources of Brock's Gap and intervening country.

During the summer of 1880, Prof. John T. Campbell, then occupying the chair of Chemistry and Geology in Washington and Lee University, and distinguished for his scientific attainments, in company with the Rev. R. C. Walker, the writer and others, made a tour on foot over this Brock's Gap region, with the view of noting its topographical and geological features, and particularly the indications of its mineral wealth.

The following fall Professor Campbell published a report of his observations in *The Virginias,* accompanying it with a beautiful map and geological section.

As that report bears an intimate relation to our subject, the following extract from it will be altogether appropriate. After premising with a geographical, topographical and geological sketch, he proceeds to say—

"*Lead and Zinc Ores* have been found in the older limestones. Galena, with a small percentage of silver in it, was mined to some extent many years ago at a point two miles north of Broadway. It has been attracting renewed attention recently. Zinc ore of promising quality, but undetermined as to quantity, is found contiguous to and sometimes mingled with the lead ore.

"*The Iron Ores* of Brock's Gap, both on account of quantity and quality, demand our earnest attention.

"Two of the great iron-bearing formations—the Clinton (No. V) and the Oriskany (No. VII)—are conspicuous in this region, and the ore of No. III is said to have been once worked on Little North Mountain.

"I have carefully traced the ores of No. V shales along the western face of Little North Mountain, and have examined in person and learned from others the character of their outcropping on both faces of Church Mountain. On the former some of the ore is inferior, but some of it is of fine quality. It is from a part of this formation that the Messrs. Pennybacker are reported to have been mining a superior ore when the price of iron compelled them to stop their furnace (the old 'Oakland') in this neighborhood many years ago. They also mined ores on both sides of Church Mountain, where their former manager told me they worked beds ten feet in thickness of ore that by their crude process yielded 40 per cent. of pig-iron. This No. V bed, extending for miles along the mountain, could be readily opened by a proper system of mining. It evidently contains a vast quantity of an ore (the red shale) that has long been famous for the quality of its iron.

"The Oriskany formation (No. VII) is, throughout this region, chiefly a heavy bed of coarse sandstone, but evidently contains some beds of rich ores that have not been developed to any great extent, though the outcroppings along the eastern base of Church Mountain are promising. Like beds will doubtless be found elsewhere in the neighborhood. The ores of this form are generally more or less silicious, while those of No. V are argillaceous. Hence, the two are well adapted for mixing, both together fluxing better than either does separately. The sand of the one and the clay of the other, both combining at the same time with the lime of the flux, make a slag that is readily fused in the furnace.

"*Variegated Marble* is another object of interst here. A quarry has been partially opened on lands belonging to Dr. J. Q. Winfield, of Broadway, that promises to yield encrinal and shell marbles equal in texture and beauty to those so extensively quarried at Craigsville, in Augusta county, Virginia. Both are from the same geological formation (No. VI, Helderberg)—a limestone of a later geological age than those of the great Valley. The same beds of limestone, among which the marble is found, will also yield inexhaustible supplies of limestone for furnace flux, for building-stone and for the manufacture of lime. * * *

"*Clay*, of a very infusible character, has been found in several places, and is worthy of a fair trial for firebricks, tiles, terra-cotta work, etc.

"*Timber*, suitable for various kinds of lumber—oak, pine, tulip, poplar, walnut, ash, maple, etc.—abounds at many points easy of access. There are also large forests adapted to coaling, whenever it becomes desirable to make charcoal-iron.

"*Ample Water-power* for furnaces, mills and other kind of machinery can be secured, either within the mountain region or at Broadway, by utilizing the natural fall of the North Fork of the Shenandoah river and its tributaries. For use in a charcoal furnace the ore, limestone and charcoal can be procured in abundance at points not very remote from a common point on the river, at which a furnace could be conveniently located, and to which all the material consumed could be brought by a descending grade. If coke is wanted for fuel, it seems to me that a point on the Valley Railroad near Broadway would afford a most appropriate location. Furnace sites and water-power are there, limestone is at hand in great abundance, coke can easily be brought from Connellsville, Pennsylvania, or from New River, West Virginia, by rail, while the ores could be brought down from Brock's Gap by a tramway or a narrow-gauge railroad at a very moderate cost beyond that of constructing the track."

Since the publication of Professor Campbell's report, as he anticipated, further discoveries of iron ore have been made in Brock's Gap.

A line, or section, extended from Broadway westward to the distance of ten or eleven miles, it may now be safely asserted, would cross not less than five distinct beds of iron ore, averaging at least fifteen feet in thickness, and such beds could be traced many miles on each side of the line. Add to these numerous seams of carbonate of iron, supposed to exist in alternation with seams of coal, and this region can justly claim to possess more iron ore than can be found in any area of like extent in Virginia. A vast proportion of the ore has been upheaved and thrown into arches or columns, so that mining it would be comparatively easy and inexpensive.

Samples of the ores subjected to analysis, yielded from 40 to 55 per cent. of metallic iron. One sample (an average one) taken from a bed in the Oriskany formation, was estimated by an expert to contain 67 per cent. of metal.

Manganese and rock-salt, too, have recently been discovered in Brock's Gap. The former can be traced for miles on the surface. No effort of consequence has yet been made to develop it, beyond a pit excavated to the depth of five or six feet. At this depth, even, the ore was found to be increasing in quantity and improving in quality. The indications of the existence of a vast body of this valuable mineral are very promising. The rock-salt bed was exposed during the present summer by a washout. The extent and quality of the bed is as yet undetermined. In all probability gypsum will be found in connection with the salt, as it is well known to practical miners and geologists that it is rare to find beds of rock-salt without alternating beds of gypsum.

As everything that pertains to Brock's Gap, for reasons already stated, pertains alike to Broadway, the evidences of the existence of coal in the former may be regarded as one of the possible, if not probable, advantages of the latter.

What are these evidences? In the first place, Brock's Gap is geographically and geologically in line with, and is only about twenty miles from, Briery Branch, where coal has been discovered (according to the report of an expert) in commercial quantities. In the next place, the same black shale, scarcely distinguishable from coal, and which covers the Briery Branch coal, is found in abundance in Brock's Gap. Finally, in the latter can be found coarse, gritty sandstones, indicative of coal, coal conglomerates, and even small seams of coal.

BROADWAY LAND AND IMPROVEMENT COMPANIES—WHAT THEY HAVE DONE, ARE DOING AND PROPOSE TO DO.

Within the past year, two such companies have been organized at Broadway.

One, styled "The Virginia Valley Land and Improvement Company," is at present negotiating for several valuable tracts of land on the west side of the town. It is proposed, among other things in their handsome, illustrated prospectus, to lay out and grade streets and avenues, to build a magnificent hotel, and to establish a number of manufacturing enterprises. This company is in alliance with a railroad organization, formed for the avowed purpose of building a railroad from some point on the West Virginia line, through Brock's Gap to Broadway, thence to Riverton, and finally to tide-water and Washington, D. C.

The other improvement company, known as "The Broadway Land and Improvement Company," owns in fee a large tract of land adjoining the corporation on the east side. This property capitalized at $50,000, has been laid off by a competent engineer into streets, avenues and 370 building lots, exclusive of some grounds "reserved for future disposition by the stockholders."

The larger part, if not all, of the stock of this company, has been placed, and a considerable number of the lots have been sold. An avenue fifty feet wide and half a mile in length, has been graded through the property by the company. Lot owners are building upon and otherwise improving their lots. One completed structure deserves especial notice. It is that of a pottery. The main building is 80 x 35 feet, with three stories. The L is 150 feet long and 35 wide, with one and two stories. The entire structure is heated throughout by steam, and is supplied with engines and all the most improved machinery and appliances for the manufacture of porcelain ware. The *Washington Post* of March 31st, 1891, thus speaks of this enterprise:

"Heretofore the *Post* described the Broadway Pottery Company in a commonplace way, and, in fact, without knowing fully the exact style of goods to be manufactured, and it will no doubt astonish its readers to learn, that in about four hours' ride from your magnificent city there is now established and in running order, one of the most complete potteries for the manufacture of bone china and semi-porcelain goods, with specialties of every description. The company intends to compete with foreign potteries, and are using foreign raw material to secure tint and solidity. They will employ thirty decorators, and will furnish to the dealers in Washington and other cities the lighest tints, to-wit, vellum, egg-shell and all styles of bronzes. All of the most modern machinery used in the best foreign potteries are in place and have been tested and put in operation. They have five kilns, and will be able to ship thirty-six tons of ware per week. The company is composed of Albert Radford, now of Broadway, Virginia, and Messrs Winfield, Legget and John E. Roller, of Harrisonburg, Virginia. Messrs. E. T. and Albert Radford, father and son, learned their trade as designers and modelers in Stoke-on-Trent, Staffordshire, England, and are known as men who excel in their workmanship, and have well-earned reputations, Albert Radford being the prize winner in the class of model and design, in solid, at the Philadelphia exhibition in 1889. The pottery will be under their management. It will certainly be a source of pride to the best families of Washington to use at their dinings, sets of china made in their own country, and so near their homes. There is but one other pottery of this class in the United States, and that has only been in operation three months."

TO THE FRONT.

Its location in the midst of one of the finest agricultural regions in the State, its immense water-power, its picturesque and charming surroundings, its proximity to vast mineral and lumber resources, its position directly on the shortest and most feasible railroad route that can be selected between the great western coal-fields and tide-water, giving assurance that it must become a railroad as well as a trade center, its progress already made and bright prospects ahead, entitles Broadway to step to the front rank of advancing Virginia towns.

Mr. GEORGE S. ALDHIZER.—In the year 1884 the first drug-store was opened at Broadway, Virginia, and the first druggist of the place was Mr. George S. Aldhizer, then a man about twenty-eight years of age, our subject having been born on Independence Day, 1856. His birthplace was New Hope, Augusta county, Virginia, where he lived until the age of fifteen, at which time he went into a mill to learn the miller trade, at which he served about six years, and at the expiration of the six years he went to Staunton to learn photography, in which capacity he served for seven years, at the end of which time he started the present business, and in 1886 went to Richmond, Virginia, and passed an examination before the Virginia Board of Pharmacy.

He has been very succesful in his drug business, and has demonstrated the superior policy of sticking to a good thing.

He has made investments in the Broadway Land and Improvement Company, and in the Virginia Valley Land and Improvement Company of the same place. He is also a partner in the Broadway Machine Company and Blue-grass Creamery.

He takes an active and intelligent interest in educational matters, having served as director of the Broadway Graded School for four years. He has represented his ward in the City Council for three years, in which capacity he distinguished himself for his good judgment and sagacity in the administration of the city government.

He is a member of the Baptist church, and on the Building Committee as Treasurer of the United Brethren church, and also Secretary and Treasurer of the Sunday-school of the same denomination, of which he is an efficient and willing worker, as he also is as teacher of the Bible-class in the Methodist Episcopal Sunday-school, having no church of his own in the city.

P. W. PUGH, Esq.—One of the leading merchants of Broadway, Virginia, and Secretary of the Virginia Land Improvement Company, P. W. Pugh, Esq., is a native of Hardy county, West Virginia, and was born there in the year 1837, in which place he spent his early life. At the breaking out of the war he enlisted in the 25th Virginia Infantry as Sergeant of Company A, and served four years, receiving the rank of Second Lieutenant. At the close of the war he came to Broadway and started a small store, the first one in the place, and has remained in the business ever since in this town, he assisted in the organization of the Virginia Land and Improvement Company in 1890, of which he was made secretary, and he has been a member of the Democratic Central Committee for some years. He is a Mason and a member of the Presbyterian church, in which society he is a deacon. He is interested in school matters, and has a firm belief in the efficacy of educated intellect. He has been clerk of the School-board for over twelve years, in which capacity he has shown efficiency.

CHAPTER XI.

BEDFORD CITY, VIRGINIA.

Bedford City, the county seat of Bedford county, is beautifully situated on the main line of the Norfolk and Western Railroad, nearly midway between Lynchburg and Roanoke, being about twenty-five miles from each. Viewed from any of the eminences by which it is surrounded, the city appears to nestle among the richly wooded hills and beautiful valleys which characterize this region, and render it unique in its attractiveness, being the center of a beautiful and fertile expanse of country.

Bedford City is the seat of an important industrial and commercial interest, conveniently situated with relation to the great tobacco growing region of Virginia, and enjoying favorable transportation facilities which bring all the markets of the United States within easy reach. Bedford City has for many years been a distributing point for the raw material, and also a large producer of the manufactured tobacco of all kinds and qualities. Ever since her foundation the town has been the depot for the tobacco grown within the district tributary to her, from the days when the hogsheads were rolled along the highways to market, down to the time when the introduction of railroads offered the planter a less expensive and more expeditious method of transmitting their produce.

Two commodious warehouses supply the necessary accommodations for this trade, which reaches the handsome aggregate of about three million pounds annually. Bedford City has several large and prosperous tobacco factories, some devoted exclusively to the manufacture of plug and twist tobacco, others to that of smoking tobacco, besides several leaf dealers and commission merchants.

There is also located here a large and finely-equipped woollen mill, two prosperous banking institutions, with ample resources for all requirements of the local trade; two flour and grist mills, a foundry and iron works, a spoke factory and several other industrial establishments; numerous mercantile houses, representing all branches of business, and three weekly papers.

CHURCHES.

The city is handsomely equipped with good churches of various denominations—Episcopal, Methodist Episcopal (South), Presbyterian, Baptist, Catholic, etc.

SCHOOLS.

The free schools of Bedford City and county have received as much attention as have those of any other county in the State, and with flattering results. The credit for the rapid progress and flourishing condition of the county free schools is in a great measure due to the energy and exertion of Mr. N. D. Hawkins, the efficient County Superintendent, whose life and faculties are dedicated to this work. The total school population of the county is—white, 6,933; colored, 5,130; total, 12,063. The number of pupils enrolled during the term, 1886-'87, was—white, 4,575; colored, 2,096; total, 6,671, being 66 per cent. of the white, and 41 per cent of the colored school population. The percentage of attendance in 1886-'87, was—white, 79, and colored 76, as against white, 70 and colored, 71, in 1885-'86. The number of pupils studying the higher branches in 1885-'86, was—white, 93; colored, 10. In 1886-'87, these had increased to white, 210; colored, 27.

There are twelve graded schools in the county, namely, nine for white, and three for colored. One hundred and fifty-four teachers are employed. There are in the county one hundred and twenty-eight school-houses, and the value of the school property is estimated at $38,000. There are nine school districts, under the control of twenty-seven trustees.

Besides the excellent free-school system of the county, Bedford City numbers among its scholastic institutions several of a very high order for boys and girls. Virginia has always been famous for the number and high rank of her schools and colleges, and Bedford City has done her share towards establishing and maintaining this enviable reputation.

The Virginia Business College, an institution for boys and girls, formerly of Staunton, Virginia, was located at Bedford City July 1st, 1890. Prof. B. A. Davis, Jr., is the proprietor. The locating this college here has been beneficial in many respects, the patronage has greatly increased, and the college ranks among the best in the State.

Randolph-Macon Academy, a Methodist school, for boys only, opened July 1st, 1890.

Belmont Seminary, Presbyterian, for girls.

Jeter Institute, Baptist, for girls.

St. John's Seminary, Episcopal, for girls.

HOTELS.

Bedford City has two good hotels, the new hotel near the new depot, opened in the fall of 1891, is one of the finest and most beautiful and handsomely equipped hotels in Virginia, and is a monument to the pluck and energy of the projectors of the edifice.

Mr. THOMAS D. BERRY.—Prominent among the successful and substantial men of Bedford City, Virginia, is Mr. Thomas D. Berry,

President of the Frst National Bank, and head of the firm of Berry Brothers, Tobacco Manufacturers, of Bedford City. He was born December 4th 1859, in Bedford, and is the son of W. W. and Mary A. Berry. He was educated at the public schools of his native county, and at the age of thirteen began to employ his leisure time by working in the tobacco factory in the city. Being of a pushing and energetic disposition, he was subsequently appointed to the position of assistant postmaster, where he remained one year, at which time he accepted the position of bookkeeper in the firm of Smyth & Co., tobacco manufacturers, and one year from that time he was admitted to the firm as partner. In 1881 he bought out the interest of Mr. Smyth and took as his partner his brother Mr. J. M. Berry. The new firm built a new factory, and as their business increased they enlarged this, making additions to its capacity, and at the present writing the firm is doing the largest business in the district, employing about two hundred and fifty hands and manufacturing over one million pounds of tobacco a year.

Mr. Berry is also President of the Prudential Building and Loan Association of Bedford, and Chairman of the Committee of Finance of the Liberty Woollen Mill Manufacturing Company. He has served for eight years on the Board of City Council, and is Chairman of the Finance Committee. He organized the First National Bank of Bedford City in March, 1890, which represented a capital stock of $50,000, which, at this time, with their surplus and profits, aggregates the handsome sum of $87,000. That Mr. Berry excels as a financier, his various undertakings and enterprises abundantly testify. In 1881 he was married to Miss Ida W., daughter of O. P. Bell, of Bedford. Four children have been born to them. Mr. Berry is an official member of the Episcopal church.

ROBERT W. COFFEE, Esq.—One of the most noted inventors of Virginia is Robert W. Coffee, Esq. He was born April 14th, 1843, in Bedford county, Virginia, and is a son of Bannister and Elizabeth Coffee, who were both born and raised in Bedford county. His father was a mechanic of considerable inventive talent.

The subject of this sketch, Robert W. Coffee, was educated in the old-field school of his native county, and at the age of 17 years engaged in the carriage manufacturing business. This trade he pursued for eight years, when he began manufacturing spoke-machines of his own invention, and gradually drifted into the making of spokes and handles, doing quite an extensive business. In 1883 he organized his business into a stock company and moved to Bedford City. While more than ordinarily successful in the manufacturing business, it proved that it was not by this that he was to make his fortune and his reputation; but, having more leisure and better opportunities, his inventive genius came to the front, and many valuable and useful patents were the result. The following is a list of his most important inventions: In 1883, an automatic lathe; in 1885, a patent tobacco-dryer, which came into almost immediate use and was a marked success, being regarded as the best yet invented; in 1889, 1890 and 1891 he issued patents for a machine for stemming leaf tobacco, which has every promise of successful introduction, and will in a great measure revolutionize the tobacco business. A company has already been organized with a capital of $1,000,000 for its manufacture. In 1890 he invented a machine for atomizing water, and one for treating fine-cut tobacco, and one for a heating apparatus to be used in public buildings, which is said to save one-half of the ordinary expense of heating a room. He is also the inventor of a rectal pessary for the radical cure of hemorrhoids, which is pronounced an invention of rare merit. He has many other inventions which space forbids to mention, but the above will suffice to, in a measure, show the character of the man. He was married in 1868 to Miss Sallie Miller, of Bedford county.

Dr. ROBERT G. O'HARA, the subject of this sketch, was born April, 1857, in Gort, County Galway, Ireland. His father was Maj. Charles O'Hara, an officer in The Honourable East India Company Service.

The Doctor was educated at Bath, Wimbledon and Cambridge, England, and in Dublin, Ireland. At the age of seventeen he entered the 4th West York Regiment, and resigned Second Senior Lieutenant after five years' service. The Doctor came to America October, 1879, and resided at Charlemont, Bedford county. In 1885 he graduated from the College of Physicians and Surgeons, Baltimore, and commenced the practice of his profession same year, where he resided. In 1889 he removed to Bedford City, Virginia, where he now resides. He married, in 1876, Miss N. Jolliffe, daughter of Dr. J. Jolliffe, of Shepherds-Bush, London, England, and has five children. The Doctor is a member of the Episcopal church, Fellow of the Virginia Medical Society, and a Knight Templar.

Capt. N. D. HAWKINS, the subject of this sketch, is a prominent real estate agent and Superintendent of the public schools of Bedford county, Virginia. He graduated at the Virginia Military Institute in 1872, as Captain of Company D, at the age of twenty-three years, and was the youngest son of six who served in the Confederate army during the civil war. He afterwards accepted a position as teacher in the public schools, which avocation he followed for a number of years. In 1886 he was elected Superintendent of Bedford county public schools, which responsible position he has most efficiently and satisfactorily filled. Bedford county is justly proud of her schools, and its high grade is in a large measure due to the untiring efforts and superior management of its highest official, who has given his best efforts to the work. There are (at the present writing, in 1891) one hundred and fifty-four schools in the county, all of which are under the superintendency of Captain Hawkins. The New London Academy (a chartered institution) is also under his supervision. Besides being a well qualified educator, he is the owner of one of the finest fruit farms in the State, and is also at the head of the real estate company of Hawkins & Company, Bedford City. In 1874 he was married to Miss Janie Smith of Campbell county, Virginia, and the union has been blessed with seven children. Captain Hawkins is a member of the Methodist Episcopal Church, South, and is a genial Christian gentleman, and his well deserved popularity is due to the fact that he metes justice to all and curries favor with none.

Prof. B. A. DAVIS, son of Beverly A. and Mary P. Davis, was born May 27th, 1862, at Patrick Springs, Virginia. His father was a local minister and farmer, and represented Pittsylvania county two terms in the Legislature. Prof. B. A. Davis, subject of this brief sketch, was sent to the public schools of Danville, Virginia, and then entered a Normal college, graduating in 1887. He then taught at Stuart Academy, Stuart, Virginia, for one year, at the expiration of which time he established the Virginia Business College at Stuart. The reputation of the college soon spread and brought him a large and lucrative patronage, and placed the college second to none in the State as a commercial school, he himself superintending the commercial department. This school was successfully operated for two years, and in July, 1890, he established his school at Bedford City. His success here has been both flattering and phenomenal, and the reputation of the school has extended to all the States of the Union, and notwithstanding the institution is but three years old, it carries with it the largest patronage of any school of the kind in Virginia, being represented by students from a large majority of the States, and, judging the future by the past, it will be only a question of a short time before it will take rank with the first schools of the kind in the nation. Professor Davis is a polished, Christian gentleman, and a member of the Methodist Episcopal Church, South. He possesses brilliant social qualities, and, being early thrown upon his own resources, he is, in the truest sense of the word, a self-made man, and is fully equipped to teach and qualify young men for the various avocations of business life.

Mr. ROBERT S. QUARLES, Clerk of Bedford County, was the son of Samuel H. Quarles, who had filled many public positions, among others was Sheriff of Bedford county. He died in June, 1865. Robert S., the subject of this short biography, was educated in the private schools, and while a mere youth he entered the Confederate service in the navy department, and was appointed midshipman, in which capacity he served until the close of the war. On his return home he was appointed Deputy Clerk of the county, and was subsequently appointed to the clerkship to fill a vacancy. At the following election, in November, 1870, he was elected Clerk of the county, and has been re-elected at every succeeding election, since, and has now held the office for twenty-one years, and so entirely efficient and satisfactory has been his clerkship, and so general his popularity, that at the last election he had no opposition, and was the unanimous choice of the people. He has been elected to the councilmanic board and served as Recorder of it, but owing to failing health he has resigned the recordership. He is Treasurer of the Greenwood Land Company, of Bedford City. He was born September 30th, 1847, and was married April 12th, 1871, to Miss M. Louise Mitchell of Bedford county, daughter of Robert C. Mitchell. Ten children have blessed this union. He is a member of the Episcopal church and a vestryman of the same.

JAMES A. CLARK, Esq.—The subject of this sketch, James A. Clark, Esq., head of the tobacco firm of Clark & Co., attended the public schools of Bedford county, Virginia, and subsequently entered the State Agricultural and Mechanical College of Virginia, graduating in the class of 1879–'80. After graduating he remained at the college one year, having been appointed Commandant of Cadets and instructor in the preparatory department of the college. Efficiently filling this responsible place this length of time, he resigned and engaged as book-keeper for Messrs. Berry Brothers, tobacco manufacturers, of Bedford. He remained with this firm two years, and then took the position of book-keeper for G. W. Smith & Co., of Lynchburg, Virginia. After eight months in this city, he returned to his native place, Bedford, and in June, 1884, formed a partnership with S. A. Berry, and engaged in the jobbing of tobacco, under the firm name of Clark & Co. In 1887 this partnership was dissolved, and in the following year his father, Mr. Isaac N. Clark, was admitted as partner to the firm of Clark & Co., the firm now consisting of the father and James A. Clark, the subject of this sketch. Young Mr. Clark is more than an ordinary successful business man, and is justly regarded as one of the solid and pushing young men of Bedford county. The firm does a large jobbing business, keeping from four to six men on the road, their trade extending throughout the Southern States.

James A. Clark was born September 25th, 1861, in Bedford county, and was married November, 1878, to Miss Lucy Thurman, daughter of Senator John R. Thurman. One child has been born to them. Mr. Clark was a director in the Liberty Savings Bank, which place he resigned in June, 1891, and was one of the organizers, and is now a director of the First National Bank of Bedford. He is also a director in the Perpetual Building and Loan Association of his native city.

CHAPTER XII.

SHENANDOAH COUNTY.

By J. W. GRABILL.

Shenandoah county was formed in 1772 from Frederick. It is thirty-two miles long and about fifteen miles wide. The surface is rolling and mountainous, with wide and fertile valleys on the water-courses. It is watered by the North Fork of the Shenandoah, running through the county its entire length; by Passage creek, running through the Powell's Fork Valley from the Page line to the end of the county; by Cedar creek, Stoney creek, Mill creek, Smith's creek, Tom's brook, Pugh's run, Tumbling run, and other smaller streams.

This is one of the finest valley counties. The soil is very fertile, and produces large crops of wheat, barley, corn, potatoes, oats, hay, etc. In the quantity of wheat raised it stands number four in the State, the counties standing above it being of much larger area. The quality of wheat is not surpassed anywhere, and commands the highest price in market.

The county is well adapted to fruit culture, apples, peaches, pears, grapes, plums, cherries, strawberries, raspberries and other fruits do well; luscious melons, of quality and size that compare favorably with any in the Union, are raised in large quantities.

The rich river bottoms are specially adapted to the cultivation of the sugar beet, which would pay very well.

The soil is also well adapted to the cultivation of hops, which could be made a profitable industry.

STOCK.

It is a great grass and stock county. Horses, cattle, sheep and hogs are raised in large numbers. The most approved breeds of draft horses and some of the finest strains of trotting stock have been introduced, and large numbers are raised annually for the Eastern markets. Cows of the most approved butter strains are raised and dairying is carried on at a profit. The grass of the county is specially adapted to stock, and many express the opinion that it is equal to the noted blue grass of Kentucky.

MANUFACTORIES.

In many of the rich agricultural sections of the South the people have been slow to engage in manufacturing, but in recent years great progress has been made in this department, and capital is readily invested in manufacturing enterprises. Among the articles manufactured now are agricultural implements, barrels, brandy, brick, brooms, canned goods, carriages, cigars, flour, furniture, harness, iron, leather, lime, pottery, plows, saddles, sash and doors, stoves, tiles, tinware, whisky, woollen goods, etc. Shenandoah is one of the first flour-producing counties of the State. The superior quality of the wheat and the most approved mill machinery give a quality of flour which is in great demand in this State and in North Carolina. So great is the demand, that nearly all the wheat raised is converted into flour at home.

MINERALS.

Brick and fire-clay, potter's clay, iron ore, limestone, marble, sandstone granite, ocher, umber, mineral paint, manganese and travortine, or deposit marl, are found in various sections. In Powell's Fort valley are a number of veins of excellent brown hematite iron ore, the analysis of which show it to be equal to the best in the State. Formerly the charcoal furnaces used this ore, and the iron was held in high estimation, especially in Wilmington, Delaware, where it was used in the manufacture of car wheels.

The *Shendun News* (Major Hotchkiss), says: "The iron ore deposits at Liberty Furnace, in this county, are among the most remarkable in Virginia, all the work of exploration and mining that has recently been done in them, leading to the conclusion that these ores are in regular stratified beds that range in thickness from twenty-two to thirty-three feet. The potographs of these deposits, as now uncovered, present as remarkable faces of ore as do those that purchasers of Cuban iron ore mines not long since exhibited in this country. Average analyses show that the lump ore from these mines will yield about forty-five per cent. of metallic iron, and the wash ore about forty-three per cent."

On Cedar creek the Van Buren Furnace mines afford a large quantity of iron ore of superior quality. Not only in the mountainous sections, but throughout the valley portion of the county, iron ore is found which has been shipped to various furnaces with gratifying results.

Manganese of the first quality is found in Powell's Fort and the Cedar Creek Valley. Several mining companies are now organized and have been engaged in the development of these mines. The potter's clay has been fully tested in the Steam Tile Works at Strasburg, and is pronounced to be of first-class quality, as their manufactures abundantly prove. The brick clay of this county has been subjected to a very severe test, crossings of home manufactured brick have been made on a macadamized road where it was subjected to heavy hauling. After three years' test, the brick has stood the travel better than the macadamized road. Limestone, containing 70 to 86 per cent. of carbonate of lime, abounds in the county. In addition to its use as a building rock and for agricultural purposes, it is highly valued as a flux in the manufacture of iron.

WOODS.

The chief forest growth are the oak, pine, hickory, walnut, ash, poplar, maple, sycamore, cedar, locust, mulberry, wild cherry, gum, chestnut, birch, persimmon, willow, dogwood, arbor-vitæ, etc. Many of these timbers are abundant and will prove very valuable in wood manufacturing.

SCHOOLS AND CHURCHES.

Shenandoah has one hundred and eighteen public schools, with an enrolled attendance of 4,965. There are four graded schools, and several private schools in which the higher branches are taught. Churches of all the leading denominations are found in the villages, and every neighborhood is in easy reach of one or more churches.

ROADS AND RAILROADS.

The Manassas branch of the Richmond and Danville Railroad has its terminus at Strasburg, and the Valley branch of the Baltimore and Ohio extends through the entire county from north to south, giving easy and frequent communication with the cities and markets of the country. The Liberty Iron Company has recently built a narrow-gauge road connecting with the Baltimore and Ohio at Edinburg, and extending to Liberty Furnace a distance of twelve miles. The Valley Turnpike, the best macadamized road of the State, extends through the entire county from north to south.

The population of the county is 19,640. There is no county debt, and the assessment of taxes, for all puposes, State, county and district, does not exceed ninety cents on the one hundred dollars.

The mountainous sections abound in mineral springs of different varieties. Among the most noted are Orkney Springs, twelve miles west of Mount Jackson; the Shenandoah Alum, in the same section; Valley View, two miles east of New Market; the Seven Fountains, eight miles south-east of Woodstock, and the Poison and Alum Springs on Cedar Creek. Among the varieties of water, are white sulphur, chalybeate, alum, etc.

There are a number of flourishing towns in this county, including New Market, Mount Jackson, Edinburg, Warrenton, Lem's Brook, Strasburg and Woodstock.

WOODSTOCK, THE COUNTY SEAT.

The town of Woodstock was established by law in March, 1861. Jacob Miller laid off twelve hundred acres of land, ninety-six of which were divided into half-acre lots, making one hundred and ninety-two building lots—the remainder into streets and five-acre lots, commonly called out-lots. In this respect Jacob Miller acted with more prudence than the modern boomers who lay off all their land into building lots. The town was well laid off, a fact which is apparent to all visitors of the present day, as there is not a town in the entire valley which can compare with Woodstock in this respect.

The population is now about 1,200. In this place the county has erected a clerk's office, which is considered a model, no county in the State having one superior to it. The Baltimore and Ohio Railroad has in this town the best passenger depot on their line outside of the large cities. Several manufacturing enterprises are in successful operation. A good graded school and the Shenandoah Female Institute furnish excellent facilities for the education of the young of both sexes.

The Reformed, Lutherans, Methodists, Presbyterians, Christians, Catholics, Episcopalians and Colored Methodists have excellent church buildings.

Woodstock is a delightful town for summer boarders, and many take advantage of the opportunities offered by its enterprising hotels and beautifully shaded streets. Several excellent boarding-houses in the vicinity of the town are open every year for the accommodation of summer boarders.

For manufacturing sites and residences, Woodstock offers opportunities not surpassed by many towns of the South.

Hon. M. L. WALTON, senior member of the law firm of Walton & Walton, is a son of Hon. Moses Walton, the founder of the present firm. He (the father) represented the county in the State Legislature for a number of years, and died, respected by all, in the year 1883.

M. L. Walton, the subject of this article, is a native of Shenandoah county, and was born October 13th, 1853. He was educated at the Randolph-Macon College, taking a course in law at the State University, from which he graduated in 1875, and was admitted to the Bar of Shenandoah county the same year, practicing with his father until the death of the latter, when the present business firm was formed. While his vocation is law, he finds time to interest himself in public matters pertaining to the city and section; is President of the Agricultural Society and a director of the Shenandoah County Bank and of the Strasburg Land and Improvement Company, and President of the Building Association of that place, and director and stockholder in a number of other important companies in and out of the city. He has been a life-long Democrat, and has served as a member of the State Central Committee for a number of years, and is at present the nominee for State Senator in the Tenth Senatorial District.

In matters of church, Mr. Walton takes a deep and practical interest in all that pertains to it, and in his own society—the Methodist—is an efficient worker, and has served as delegate to the Conference for a number of years. He is the President of the Baltimore Conference Sunday-school Convention, and in all Sunday-school work has never been found wanting in willingness or purse to aid it on to its utmost usefulness and spiritual prosperity.

He is a successful business man, and farms quite extensively, and, now in the prime of life, finds time, means and opportunity of doing much good.

He is also the present Chancellor Commander of King Arthur Lodge, No. 75, K. of P., at Woodstock.

Hon. JUDGE EDGAR D. NEWMAN, junior member of the law firm of Walton & Walton, was born in 1854, and is a native of Shenandoah county, and a resident of Woodstock. He was educated at the Randolph-Macon College and the Virginia Military Institute, serving as assistant instructor of tactics in the latter institute one term after graduating. In 1876 he began the study of law under the direction of the firm of Walton & Walton, and two years later was admitted to the Bar, and became a member of the firm in 1880. In 1885 he was elected Judge of the County Court, which position he fills at the present time. He has always been alive to the importance of politics, and taken an active and intelligent part, besides engaging in other interests. He is a director of the Strasburg Land and Impovement Company, and also attorney for the same. He is a director in the Steam Flouring Mills, and at present President of the Southern Horse and Mule Shoe Manufacturing Company, and a director of the Bank of Shenandoah County, and is financially interested in a number of large and important enterprises in and about the city. He is an active worker in the Methodist Church, South, and is an officer of the same. The Judge has always been deeply interested in educational matters, and is at the present time a trustee of the Randolph-Macon College, and is a man whose influence is felt for good in any community in which he may live.

LUTHER S. WALKER.—The ancestors of Luther S. Walker, the subject of this biography, have been residents of the Old Virginia State for over two hundred years. The father of Luther S. was a native of Maryland, but lived in Virginia the greater part of his life. He was at one time the editor of *The Valley Democrat,* published at New Market, and afterwards moved it to Harrisonburg, but at the breaking out of the war enlisted, and rose to the rank of Lieutenant Colonel, and was killed at the battle of Chancellorsville. Luther S. was born in Shenandoah county, in 1857, and was educated at home, or in the home schools, and early in life came to Woodstock, and was made assistant clerk of the courts, acting as such for six years, when he was elected to the office of Clerk of the County Court (1881), and re-elected in 1887, and still holds the position. Besides his duty as Clerk, he is a director of the Shenandoah County Bank. He was prominent in the organization of the County Agricultural Society, and was Treasurer of the same for some time, and is now a director in the Society. He is a stockholder in many of the largest development companies, and is actively and practically interested in everything that in anywise affects the well-being of his city or county. He is prominent in the Masonic Order, being a member of the Consistory, and a thirty-second degree Mason, and is a communicant of the Lutheran church, in which church his presence and influence are felt for good. In 1884 he was united in marriage to Miss Annie H. Haas, and is the father of one son and one daughter. In politics, in which he has always taken an active part, he is an ardent Republican, and has twice been a delegate to the National Convention. He is a believer in the charity that covers a multitude of short-comings, and his daily life is thereby governed.

GEORGE W. KOONTZ, the present County Treasurer of Shenandoah, claims this county as his birth-place. The schools of his native place afforded him his education, and at the age of 16 years began clerking, and followed this occupation until the breaking out of the war, when he enlisted in the New Market Battery under Captain Rice, and served until the surrender, in 1865; participated in all of the important battles of his regiment, and was only once slightly wounded. He served as private a part of the time, but later received the rank of Lieutenant. Soon after the war he went to Highland county, but only remained there a short time, returning to Shenandoah, and has made this county his home ever since. He was elected to the office of County Treasurer in 1873, and has filled this important position continuously since that time. He has always taken an active interest in the development of the Valley, and is a stockholder in a number of companies, and is a man of fine business capacity, and has the confidence of all with whom he comes in contact in business relations. For nearly a fifth of a century he has filled the one office, which speaks louder than words of the esteem in which he is regarded.

HARRISON HOLT RIDDLEBERGER was born in the town of Edinburg, Shenandoah county, Virginia, on the 4th of October, 1844. He first attended school in his native village for six years, and afterwards for one year in Woodstock, the countyseat, when he went out into the world at the age of fifteen to shift for himself. He obtained employment in a store at Harrisonburg, Virginia, and was there when the late war broke out. In March, 1862, he assisted in raising a company in Harrisonburg, and was elected Second Lieutenant of it, the company being known in the army as Company C, Tenth Virginia Infantry, Third Brigade, "Stonewall" Division. He was the youngest commissioned officer in the Confederate army, being only eighteen years of age at the time. He was in the battles of McDowell and Port Republic, when the victorious Confederates were led by Stonewall Jackson; the seven days battles around Richmond; second Manassas, Sharpsburg, etc. In the spring of 1863, Lieutenant Riddleberger was transferred to another branch of the service, being brevetted Captain of Company G, Twenty-third Virginia Cavalry, and as such went through the Maryland and Pennsylvania campaign. He was captured and taken prisoner by Colonel Boyd of the First New York Cavalry the day before the battle of New Market between Gen. John C. Breckinridge and General Siegle, and was a prisoner for nine months in three or four Federal prisons, seven of which he spent in Camp Chase, Ohio. He was one of the three hundred sent up the James river to Harrison's Landing to be specially exchanged; but as President Davis would not recognize Gen. B. F. Butler as "a man, a soldier or a gentleman," owing to his New Orleans "order," the exchange failed, and General Butler then paroled the three hundred ragged Confederates.

Captain Riddleberger went, on his parole, to his home in the Shenandoah Valley, and while there he was captured by a squad of Federal cavalry and taken to Winchester. He produced his parole and protested against the proceeding as irregular and contrary to the usages of war or rights of belligerants, but they refused to listen to any homilies on war rights, and carried him to Winchester, where he showed his papers. The Provost Marshal said he could do nothing, but would communicate with General Hancock. The General ordered him to be sent back within the Confederate lines. When he reached Fortress Monroe, whither he was ordered, Grant was moving on Lee. Captain Riddleberger was therefore sent to Point Lookout, with the freedom of the grounds. At this time President Lincoln was assassinated. The colored troops were guarding the prisoners then at the "Point." Capt. Riddleberger was immediately confined in close quarters, the officer giving the order explaining to him privately that it was done for his safety. While there his parole was torn up, and he was sent to Fort Delaware, where he remained until hostilities came to an end.

In 1890 he established *The Tenth Legion Banner*, which he soon removed to Woodstock, changing the name to *The Shenandoah Democrat*. It was afterwards merged with *The Shenandoah Herald*, which paper he owned at the time of his death. In 1871 he was elected to the House of Delegates, and was re-elected in 1873. In 1875 he was admitted to the Bar, and a few weeks afterwards was elected Commonwealth's Attorney for the County of Shenandoah, and was re-elected in 1878. In 1879 he was elected to the Senate of Virginia.

During his career in the Legislature, he was a leader in a movement for the settlement of the public debt of Virginia upon a basis such as the people of the State could pay. This led to a split in the ranks of the Democrats, and Mr. Riddleberger became the leader of the Readjuster faction of the Democracy, presenting the Riddleberger bill as a means of the reduction of the State debt. The straight Democrats opposed the measure with the McCullough bill. The struggle was fought out, and resulted in the election of a Legislature in which the Readjusters had control. The Riddleberger bill was passed, and the policy it comprised has since been endorsed by both political parties.

On the 20th of December, 1882, he was elected to the United States Senate for the term of six years. At the expiration of his term in the United States Senate he returned to Woodstock and resumed the practice of his profession. He opposed the nomination of General Mahone for Governor on the Republican ticket, and predicted his overwhelming defeat. He took as active a part in the campaign as his health would permit. He gradually grew worse, and about Christmas took to his bed and became very ill. He lingered until the morning of the 24th of January, when he quietly passed away, leaving a much loved and highly esteemed wife and seven interesting children.

Dr. GRANVILLE A. BROWN, the popular President of the Strasburg Land and Improvement Company, was born in Frederick county, Virginia, in the year 1833. His father, David L. Brown, was an eminent physician of that county, having practiced there for fifty years. Dr. Brown, Jr., received his literary and medical education at Winchester and obtained his degree of M. D. therefrom, and later took the same degree from the Maryland Medical College. This was in 1855. He first began practice in Taylor county, Virginia, but soon returned to the Valley of Virginia, and in 1857 located at Strasburg, and has followed the profession continuously since that time. During the war he served as First Lieutenant of Company A, 10th Virginia, but his health failing him he was transferred to the Medical department, where he did hospital duty until the close of the war. In the year 1890, in company with a number of others, he organized the Strasburg Land and Improvement Company, of which he was made Vice-President and Business Manager. As a city officer his popularity is unexampled in the annals of the town, having been Mayor and served several years, and in the Council fifteen years, and Justice of the Peace twenty-five years. He has always been an enthusiastic politician, and is a man of whose opinions it may be truthfully said that there is no uncertain ring. He is a member of the Methodist church and a steward in the society, and is also a Mason of good standing.

Col. J. STICKLEY.—The subject of this sketch, Col. J. Stickley, President of the Strasburg Stone and Earthenware Manufacturing Company, of Strasburg, Virginia, is a native of this county, Shenandoah, and was born in 1847. Colonel Stickley followed the occupation of his father, that of farming, for a number of years, and in 1873 was elected Sheriff, and filled that office for nine years, after which he engaged in the merchantile business, and was soon after elected to the Board of Supervisors of the Manufacturing Company, which position he now holds. In the year 1890 he organized the Pottery Company, of which he is President and General Manager, and is also one of the organizers of the Strasburg Steam Flouring Mills, of which he is also-President, and likewise interested in the Strasburg Land and Improvement Company, in which enterprise he is a director. From a business point of view his life has been a highly successful one, and in the various walks of life he has more than fairly held his own.

SAMUEL P. SHIRLEY, Esq., manager of the Bank of Rosenberger & Shirley, of New Market, is a native of Shenandoah county, his father being a wealthy farmer of the same county. Samuel P., the subject of this sketch, was born in 1837, and spent his early life on the farm, and by so doing laid the foundation of a robust, healthy physical life, In the year 1873, in company with others, he started the Bank of which he is now partner and under his management. He served valiantly through the war, enlisting in 1861 in Captain Price's Battery, remaining there during the entire time. When the war closed, it closed with all its issues for him, never having taken any part in politics or sought or held an office. He holds the faith that to do a thing well, one must center their best and entire energies there, and this he has done in his business. He is a stockholder in the Basic City and Waynesborough improvement companies, and has taken a great interest in their development and prosperity. He is a man of a genial, pleasant disposition, and possesses a happy temperament that diffuses a good and hearty feeling on his surroundings and those who come in contact with him.

JOHN W. CLINEDIST, Esq., senior member of the firm of J. W. Clinedist & Brothers, manufacturers of high grade carriages, of New Market, was born in Rockbridge county, 1838. His father, Jacob Clinedist, was the founder of the business in 1855, and conducted it up to the time of the war, when the house was closed. John W., the subject of our sketch, assumed the control of the business after the war, conducting it alone until January, 1884, when his brother T. M. Clinedist was taken into the firm. John W., enlisted in 1861 in Company F, 10th Virginia, and afterwards served with Company B, 3d Battalion, holding the office of First Lieutenant, and serving until the close of the war. He is a member of the Masonic order and the Knights Templar, in which order he finds a respite from his arduous financial duties. The Clinedist Works have earned the reputation of turning out a very superior article, and the business is yearly increasing and growing more prosperous, and its manufactures are well and favorably known throughout a number of the States. Mr. Clinedist is a man who does nothing but his best, which no doubt is one of the primal secrets of his success. He believes to make a carriage a man should be as conscientious and painstaking as if he were engaged in the most elaborate piece of mechanism, and nothing but excellence in manufacture even remotely satisfies him.

J. N. BRENAMAN, Esq., one of the best known men of New Market, Virginia, is a native of Augusta county, and was born in 1854. His father was a farmer of standing and respectability in the same county.

Our subject spent his early life in Shenandoah county, and has for many years been engaged in a general fire and life insurance business. In the spring of 1890 he became interested in the development of the Valley and the southern portion of the State, and assisted in the sale of the Natural Bridge property to a Northern syndicate, and was prominent in a number of other large deals in real estate. At the present time he is interested largely in the same business at Glasgow and other points. It is greatly due to such men as Mr. Brenaman that the State has so rapidly developed its resources within the past decade. He is characterized as a man of push and persistency, two qualities fundamentally essential for the success of any enterprise of importance or moment. He gives his best energies to business, believing that nothing short of the best will answer or serve the purpose. He has taken some part in politics, has served as Chairman of the Shenandoah County Democratic Central Committee for five years, and has also served as Clerk of the Finance Committee of the House of Delegates. He has accumulated a good property, and is well and favorably known throughout the State.

CHAPTER XIII.

HISTORICAL SKETCH OF ROCKBRIDGE COUNTY, VIRGINIA, AND THE TOWN OF LEXINGTON.

By J. D. MORRISON.

INTRODUCTORY NOTE.

Rockbridge county has never had a written history, the vast amount of interesting material for such a work makes the limits of this sketch utterly inadequate for such a purpose. It makes the task of him who attempts to condense it into such bounds both difficult and unsatisfactory.

LOCALITY.

This county is in the great valley which lies between the Blue Ridge and Alleghany ranges of mountains, and which, under different names, extends from the lakes on the north to the Gulf of Mexico on the south. It is nearly the center of this valley, and was almost exactly the center of the old State before West Virginia was taken from it. The sources of the James river are in the mountains west of Rockbridge and their waters flow through the county. It is, therefore, the James river valley section of the Valley of Virginia. The whole area of the county is a water-shed of that river, and by hundreds of streams and streamlets contributes its waters to the James, which is formed really where the two main branches meet at Balcony Falls, where the river breaks through the Blue Ridge. This helps to give this county peculiar characteristics of topography, soil and other physical features not possessed by any other county of this valley.

EARLY HISTORY.

For over one hundred years after the first permanent settlement of Jamestown the Valley of Virginia was an unknown land. The blue mountains which spanned the western horizon, were, prior to 1716, an *Ultima Thule* to the Virginia cavalier. In that year Governor Spottswood, with his famed "Knights of the Golden Horse Shoe," made a passage of the Blue Ridge at, it is supposed, Swift Run Gap. The party crossed the Shenandoah river, and the Governor, after the custom of the times, formally took possession of the country in the name of his master the King. There is a tradition that before this, that several parties, at different times, had crossed the mountains farther south, and had penetrated as far as New river. Governor Spottswood wrote, in 1710, that a party of adventurers had ridden to the top of the mountains and looked over into the valley, but did not make the passage. This was supposed to be at some point near Balcony Falls.

This portion of the country was unoccupied by the Indians, and they visited it only on hunting or predatory excursions. It evidently had been settled by these people prior to that time, as numerous evidences of their occupation at some more remote period still exist.

In Rockbridge county, on Hays creek, there are mounds which show their burial places. On the top of the North Mountain, a few miles east of the Rockbridge Alum Springs, near the roadside, there is a remarkable mound of small stones of nearly uniform size. This is on an old trail by which they formerly passed back and forward between the valleys to the regions west of the mountains. At the time the whites first entered here it was a famous region for game, and all kinds of wild animals which belonged to this part of the continent were found here. Deer and buffalo were plentiful, as the prairie lands and undergrowth which overspread the valley were favorable feeding and breeding places for them. Only the mountains and the higher lands were then heavily timbered.

The first settlement in the Valley of Virginia was made near where the town of Winchester is now located. In the year 1730 Governor Gooch granted to John and Isaac Vanmeter, of Pennsylvania, 40,000 acres of land in that region. The Vanmeters sold their warrant to Joist Hite. In 1732 he removed his family and located near Winchester, and has the honor of being the first white settler of the Valley.

About this time, John Lewis, a native of Donegal county, Ireland, arrived in Virginia from Portugal, where he was a refugee. In defending himself and family against the attack of a brutal landlord in his native country he had killed the landlord and his steward, the landlord's party having first fired into his house and killed an invalid brother and wounded his wife. On this account he was forced to leave the country, and he escaped to Portugal. Lewis settled on the creek which bears his name, near the present site of Staunton. The exact date of Lewis' settlement, and whether he came from Pennsylvania or Williamsburg to Virginia, are still mooted questions. Near the same time, or probably a short time before this, John and Peter Adam Salling settled at the forks of the James and North rivers, on the lands now (1891) covered by the new town of Glasgow, and the property has remained in that family up to a very recent date. Of John Salling's capture by the Indians, his adventures and his return, there are romantic and conflicting stories told.

In 1736 John Lewis, on a visit to Willamsburg, made the acquaintance of Benjamin Burden. (Waddell in his "Annals of Augusta county" contends the proper spelling is "Borden".) Burden was an agent of Lord Fairfax and recently arrived from England. He was captivated with Lewis' account of the beauties and fertility of the new country west of the mountains and visited Lewis in his new home. After a visit of some time, Burden when he returned to Williamsburg took with him a buffalo calf that two of Lewis' sons had given him. This he presented to Governor Gooch, who was so pleased with the gift that he made Burden a grant of 500,000 acres of land on the waters of the Shenandoah and James rivers. To this grant were attached the conditions, that he would settle on it within ten years one hundred families—that for each house erected and occupied he should be entitled to 1,000 acres of adjacent land and have the privilege of purchasing as much more at one shilling per acre. This grant covered a large portion of what is now embraced in the territory of Rockbridge county. Burden lost no time, but immediately returned to Britain, and in 1737 brought over a large number of families to settle upon his grant. These settlers were largely composed of families of Scotch-Irish Presbyterians from the North of Ireland, and of the old Scotch Covenanter stock. The descendants of these primitive settlers still compose a large portion of the population of this region, and their names are the familiar names of the county yet. The first and most numerous immigrations were to the region known now as Timber Ridge, north-east of Lexington, and extending to the neighborhood of Greenville in Augusta county. The vicinity of Fairfield was the nucleus of the oldest settlement, and was the first home of many of the oldest and best known families. The spirit of emigration was rife in the land and settlements soon dotted the whole country. It would be difficult to locate and trace these different families, which soon became as numerous as the clans of their parent country, Scotland. The Alexanders, McDowells, Moores, Paxtons, Pattons, McClungs, McClures, Wilsons, Wallaces, and scores of other familiar names of the present day, are to be found among the names of those who came with Burden and immediately afterwards.

As stated, the first settlements were on Timber Ridge, named from the fine timber which covered it. This region was selected by the settlers on this account, because it furnished convenient material from which to erect their rude buildings, a large portion of which were built of logs. They soon found, though, that the fertile lands along the streams were more desirable and could be cleared with less labor, and tilled more easily and with larger returns. Settlements, then, soon followed on Hays and Walker creeks, on Kerr's creek and on North river, from the present site of Lexington down to the Salling place at its mouth, thence to the Fancy Hill and Natural Bridge region.

For the sake of safety, as a defence against Indian raids, these settlements were generally kept compact, and some of the houses, especially after the region had been visited by Indian raids, were constructed for defence.

The lot of pioneers in a new and wild country is a hard one. So it was with these. They had literally to hew homes out of the virgin forests. Their implements to do this work with were few and rude. The articles with which to furnish their homes were scanty and rough. They had no markets, no roads and no vehicles. Except a few peltries, they at first had nothing to market. The few indispensable articles these people had were brought with them on packhorses, or "packed" on the backs of the men themselves. A log cabin in a little "clearing" was their first home. A patch of corn, wheat or rye furnished their bread, and the wild animals of the forests their meat. The little stock they kept shifted for themselves and ranged at large.

But this primitive condition did not last. These people were ambitious, energetic and progressive. The log cabin was supplemented by more pretentious buildings, generally of logs, but some of stone. Fine specimens of the latter still exist in different sections of the county. They built churches and school-houses at the very first.

The following extract from the court proceedings of Augusta county, of which Rockbridge was then a part, dated May 20th, 1748, only ten years after the first arrival of the settlers (given by Waddell), shows the progress they had made:

"On motion of Mathew Lyle, its ordered to be certified they have built a Presbyterian meeting-house at a place known by the name of Timber Ridge; another at New Providence; another at a place known by the name of Falling Spring."

This exhibits the disposition of the people at that date, and the very rapid settlement and improvement of the country.

THE COUNTY ORGANIZED.

Augusta county was formed from Orange in 1745. Although, in point of settlement and improvement, what now constitutes the county of Rockbridge was as old and far advanced as the Augusta part, but it was not until a lapse of thirty-two years after Augusta had been made a county that it was deemed necessary to erect another county west of it.

Rockbridge was organized on the 1st of March, 1778, under an act of the Legislature passed in October, 1777. This was during the Revolutionary war, in the second year of the Commonwealth, whilst Patrick Henry was Governor of Virginia. The county was formed from Augusta and Botetourt counties, the larger portion belonging to the territory of the former. By the same act the counties of Rockingham and Greenbrier, and the town of Lexington, were authorized. Before this, Augusta comprehended the territory northwest as far as the Mississippi river, and Fincastle, which the county was called before Botetourt was established, extended to the Western sea (the Pacific ocean).

The name Rockbridge is unique, and was derived from the great natural wonder, the Natural Bridge.

A Commission of the Peace was issued on the 24th of March, 1778, to John Bowyer, Archibald Alexander, Samuel McDowell, Charles Campbell, Samuel Lyle, Alexander Stuart, Andrew Reid, John Trimble and John Gilmore, Gents—Justices of the Peace. On the 7th day of April, 1778, the first Court met at the house of Samuel Wallace, in the southern suburbs of the present town of Lexington. (This property is still in the Wallace family.) Archibald Alexander presented a commission as Sheriff, and was sworn in. Andrew Reid was appointed Clerk. John Bowyer, Samuel McDowell, Charles Campbell, Samuel Lyle and Alexander Stuart constituted the first Court. James McDowell presented a commission from the President and Masters of William and Mary College as surveyor of the county, and was sworn in. The office of surveyor was in those days one of the most important and profitable in the county organization, and was one of the perquisites of the college named.

MATERIAL PROGRESS.

An account of the products, trade and transportation of a country bears a large share in its history. These three things have an intimate relation to each other. These new settlements remote from the seashore were at first almost entirely self-reliant. Except powder and a few other articles brought in by pack-peddlers and paid for in the pelts of wild animals, there was at first no trade. Every household had its spinning-wheel and loom, and every family had a few sheep and a patch of flax. From these the warp and woof of the clothes and bed-clothes of the family were manufactured at home, the flax in all its processes from the seed, and the wool sheared, carded, spun and woven. Each farmer was his own blacksmith, carpenter and wheelwright. There was little attempt to raise grain for sale until there had been roads opened to the other settlements. Even then grain would not bear transportation the long distances to market on their rude vehicles over rough roads. Their surplus grain was at first converted into whisky, and every farm had its "still." This bore a good price in the eastern markets, and was more easily transported than the grain out of which it was made. At the same time hemp raising was a considerable industry. Whisky, hemp and the skins of wild animals were the first articles of export from this region.

INTERNAL IMPROVEMENTS.

At a very early day the subject of internal improvements excited attention. Better roads were provided, and the James river was looked to as a line of communication between the settled country of the east and the new settlements west of the Blue Ridge. This idea was suggested as early as 1716, but was brought forward more prominently by General Washington after his expedition to the West in 1753. With him it was always a pet scheme, and he had much to do with the plan of connecting the East and West by means of the James river and Kanawha canal.

At first they contented themselves with clearing and improving the river for navigation by small boats. This was done by clearing the shallows and providing sluices. A canal was constructed around the falls at Richmond, and afterwards one seven and a half miles through the Blue Ridge. This gave, at a very early day, a line of communication from Buchanan, in Botetourt county, and through nearly the entire length of Rockbridge by the North river to Richmond by boat.

The boats used in this trade were substantially built batteaux, about seventy feet in length, and would carry, under favorable circumstances, several tons. They were guided by a "headsman" and a man in the stern. The propulsion down was generally by the force of the current, and when they were brought back it was by poles in the swift or oars in the deep, eddy waters.

These boats had very much to do with the early prosperity and development of Rockbridge county. They gave an outlet to market for her products and stimulated the opening up of her iron mines, which had, at a very early day, attracted the enterprise of her own citizens, and brought men from abroad to engage in the iron business. The building of these boats became an important industry in the county. They were built here and loaded and run down to the Eastern cities and towns and sold there to be used on the lower James and its tributaries. A new, well-built boat brought from $100 to $150.

Under the stimulus of the opening of navigation and the building of roads to connect with it, the county grew and improved very fast. It gave a great impetus to agriculture, and, as stated, made the mining and manufacture of iron an important business.

The superior quality of the Rockbridge ores and the plentiful supply of timber for charcoal caused furnaces and forges to spring up along the Blue Ridge on the line of the North river, in the Goshen Pass and at all the points where new enterprises now exist. Of these original furnaces and forges, there were furnaces near the Rockbridge Alum Springs, west of the mountains; a furnace and forge in the Goshen Pass; two forges near Rockbridge Baths, two miles east of the Pass; a furnace and other iron works at Vesuvius, in the Blue Ridge; furnace and foundry on the present Buena Vista property, one of the oldest of the county; a forge at the mouth of Buffalo creek, and at other points within the present territory of the county; these made charcoal iron. The pig-metal of the furnaces was in part shipped in that condition and the rest made into hammered bar-iron in the forges, and either shipped or sold for local use in the bar. The purity of the ores in some cases enabled them to be used directly in the forges without smelting. This iron, together with the agricultural and other products of the county, was hauled on wagons to different points on the river and there put upon the boats. These had landings, or "boat-yards," as they were called at various points, some of which had considerable importance, which was due to the large amount of trade at them. The one furthest north-west was Cedar Grove, on North river, near Rockbridge Baths, whence was shipped the iron made in the Goshen Pass and its region, and the agricultural products of Hays and Walker creeks; another at the mouth of Kerr's creek; another at Lexington; one at the mouth of South river, and another important one at the mouth of Buffalo creek.

Richmond at that day was the ultimate destination of this trade. But as the James river and Kanawha canal was open to a point along its line, the trade centered temporarily there until, in 1840, it was finished to Lynchburg. After that, by wagons and boats a large amount of the county's business was done with that town. The completion of this canal to Buchanan in 1851, and the North River canal to Lexington about the same time, did away with the old batteaux system and revolutionized the trade of the county. Shortly after this the railroads began to reach out in this direction. The Chesapeake and Ohio was the first to enter the county, passing through the north-western corner at Goshen. A few years later nearly simultaneously came the Shenandoah Valley road along the southern border of the county, close to the Blue Ridge, and the Valley branch of the Baltimore and Ohio was finished to Lexington, and the canal from Richmond to Lexington and Clifton Forge was transmuted into the Richmond and Alleghany Railroad. All these changes made a corresponding change upon the condition and interests of the county in all its various relations.

The change in the lines of travel and trade mark different epochs in a country's history.

NATURAL OBJECTS OF INTEREST.

One of Rockbridge's greatest natural attractions, is the Natural Bridge.

This is one of the well known wonders of the continent, and has attracted visitors from all portions of the world to see it. No description can give an adequate conception of its beauty and granduer. It is a real bridge thrown across a deep ravine by the Great Architect who built the lofty mountains around it. It is a solid limestone arch resting on the natural abutments of the high perpendicular cliffs, and is as graceful and symmetrical as was ever shaped by the hand of art. Beneath it flows a stream and over it passes the county road.

Thomas Jefferson was the first owner of the bridge under a grant from George III, in 1774. After he was President he visited and surveyed the property, and made a map of it with his own hand.

George Washington, when a young man, whilst surveying for Lord Fairfax, visited the bridge and carved his name high on one of its abutments, where it may yet be seen. There is also a tradition that he threw a silver dollar from the ground below to the top. To even strike the arch with a stone from under it has always been considered a difficult feat. There are many interesting incidents and traditions connected with its history.

Balcony Falls, three miles east of the bridge, where the James river bursts through the Blue Ridge, presents scenery of much grandeur and beauty, and is much sought and admired by tourists.

Goshen Pass, the gap through which the North river winds through the North Mountain, fourteen miles north of Lexington, is another scene of great natural attraction. In scenery and romantic beauty, it is pronounced by travelers as equal to any of the famous scenery of the Alps.

The House Mountains, two detached peaks three or four thousand feet high, six miles west of Lexington, are special objects of interest and admiration among the many grand mountains with which the county is surrounded. These mountains stand out from the other range side by side, and have the symmetrical shape of the roof of a house, whence their name. There are many other natural objects well worth a visit.

TOPOGRAPHY, MINERAL RESOURCES, ETC.

Rockbridge county is about thirty miles long, and has an average of twenty-two miles in width. It extends to the medium line of the Blue Ridge on the south-east, where it borders the counties of Nelson, Amherst and Bedford, and on the north-west it extends over the first range of mountains and includes a considerable extent of level lands known as the "Pastures," in which is the Goshen region. On this side it is bounded by Alleghany and Bath counties. In the Valley range it has Augusta on the north-east and Botetourt on the south-east.

The average of the section, exclusive of the mountains, is about 1,100 feet above the level of the sea. The country is rolling, fertile and well watered. Its climate is famous for its salubrity, being midway in the temperate zone, with an elevation sufficient to temper the extreme heats of summer, and mountains to shelter it from storms of winter or summer.

ORES.

Rockbridge is in the great mineral belt, which, in its abundance and richness of valuable ores, characterize this great Valley. Iron ore in great plenty and purity is found all along the ranges of mountains on each side of the county, and rich deposits also exist in the Valley outside of the mountains. Tin has been discovered and is being worked. Manganese is plentiful. Kaolin and potter's clays of superior qualities are found in abundance. Very fine and beautiful marble exists in various sections of the county. Limestone for lime and building, and hydraulic limestone for cement, are everywhere. All these minerals are in great abundance and easily accessible.

TIMBER.

Her forests consist of valuable hard and soft woods. Pine, poplar, white, black and chestnut oak, hickory, walnut, locust, chestnut and all the other useful woods that are found in this latitude are to be had here.

AGRICULTURAL PRODUCTS.

The staples are wheat, corn, oats and tobacco, all of which are produced, in large quantities and of the best qualities, on her genial and productive soil. All the vegetable products pertaining to the truck and kitchen garden are extensively and successfully grown.

This region is exceptionably well adapted to fruit. Apples, peaches, pears and grapes thrive luxuriantly.

STOCK RAISING.

Stock raising is an important industry. It is a fine grass-growing region, and many of the valuable grasses spring up here spontaneously, and make good grazing and hay crops.

MEDICINAL SPRINGS.

Rockbridge has a number of the most famous health-giving springs in the State. The two Rockbridge Alums, now consolidated, eighteen miles west of Lexington, is one of the best known establishments of the kind in the land. The Bold Sulphur, a few miles distant in the same valley, is another important watering-place. Wilson Sulphur Spring, at the mouth of the Goshen Pass, is a notable old family resort. Two miles further down are the Rockbridge Baths, also a well-known and popular resort. Valuable mineral waters are found at various other points, but have not yet had improvements to bring them into notice.

THE CIVIL AND MILITARY RECORD OF HER CITIZENS.

Though Rockbridge began its existence as a county during the trying times of the Revolutionary war, its remoteness from the scenes of the conflict did not materially disturb the transaction of business and the progress of affairs in the county. She was represented, though, by her sons in the field, and their blood was shed in almost every battle of that war, from Guilford and Cowpens in the South to Stony Point and Saratoga in the North.

In all the wars of the country, her sons have borne a conspicuous part. In the war with England in 1812, and the war with Mexico, her soldiers were on every field. To the struggle between Texas and Mexico, the county contributed the commander-in-chief and the first President of Texas in the person of Gen. Sam. Houston, with other distinguished participants of lesser rank.

In the late war between the States, the county furnished to the Confederate cause, and kept recruited, during the four years of the conflict, eleven full companies, besides parts of companies, and a large number of recruits distributed among the companies of other counties. In all these wars, her soldiers ranked among the very best, and the names of her old families have sustained a brilliant record through the four generations of her military history.

Then, in the civil walks of life, her sons have adorned every branch. Some of the brightest and best statesmen, jurists, lawyers and divines of the country have been native Rockbridge men. The annals of Virginia, and the history of every State throughout the broad expanse of the country west of her, furnish worthy examples of her sons in the front ranks of every profession and business.

LEXINGTON.

Lexington, the county seat, is situated on North river, about fifteen miles from its mouth. The site is a beautiful one, nearly as possible the center of the county. The town is built on the hills, which at that point run at right angles to the course of the river, and slope back gently from it on the south. The town has always been renowned for the romantic beauty of its surroundings and the well-chosen location of its site.

Lexington was chartered and designated as the county seat by the same act of the Legislature in October, 1777, by which the formation of the county was authorized. The dimensions of the town were prescribed by the act, and the name chosen, in the following language: "At the place, which shall be appointed for holding courts in the said county of Rockbridge, there shall be laid off a town to be called Lexington, thirteen hundred feet in length, and nine hundred feet in width." Twenty-six acres of land were condemned, to be paid for out of the county levy. One acre was reserved for public buildings, and the remainder ordered to be sold by the Justices of the county.

This land belonged to a man named Isaac Campbell. Whether there were any houses on the land is doubtful, as there seems to have been no building suitable for holding court, which was first held at Wallace's, a mile south of the center of this plat. The town was laid off by the County Surveyor, and a plan of it was returned and recorded in the clerk's office nine years afterwards. A court-house and jail were erected and very soon the town grew into a respectable village. It continued to grow apace as the county improved and settled up, until in April, 1796, the whole town, except probably one house, was swept out of existence by fire.

As is usually the case in these early beginnings, after such disasters, more substantial buildings were erected, and in a few years the town presented a greatly improved condition. Being the place of the public business, it soon became the trade center of the county and surrounding region.

At a very early period it assumed a position as an educational center also, a distinguishing feature which it has always preserved. The superiority of her schools, and the intelligence and morality of her citizens have always been the pride and boast of Lexington. The leading institution of the county is really older than the county itself—what is now known as

WASHINGTON AND LEE UNIVERSITY.

At the very first settlement of this section its Scotch-Irish occupants provided for schools and churches. As early as 1749 a classical school was established, near the present county line, in Augusta, south of Greenville. This was successively removed to Old Providence, then to New Providence and then to Timber Ridge, near Fairfield, in Rockbridge, just prior to the Revolutionary war. It had borne the name of the Augusta Academy, till after the beginning of the war it was called Liberty Hall. In 1785 this academy was removed to near Lexington and a substantial stone building erected, which was burned in 1802. The picturesque ruins of this may yet be seen on a reservation in the northern suburbs of the town. In 1803 it was removed to the present site of the institution on the beautiful hill in the town. During this time General Washington had donated to it one hundred shares in the Old James River Company, and in consideration of this the name was changed to Washington College. Aided by other liberal donations from the Cincinnati Society, and John Robinson, and sustained by a liberal patronage, the institution took and maintained the position of a first-class college till the close of the war between the States. Immediately after the war General R. E. Lee was elected to the presidency, and was inaugurated in September, 1865. From this time to the death of General Lee, in October, 1870, the institution had a remarkable run of prosperity under the new organization of his administration. Large donations and endowments came from many sources, and its halls were filled to overflowing with students. The curriculum was abolished and the institution put upon a university basis. Its course now comprehends all usually taught in the highest-class institutions of learning, with a full corps of professors and instructors. It has a large and productive endowment, and is very liberally patronized.

THE VIRGINIA MILITARY INSTITUTE.

Except West Point Military Academy, the Virginia Military Institute at Lexington is the most thorough, and best equipped Military and Scientific School on this Continent. Its buildings and grounds are situate on the north-eastern end of the same hill with Washington and Lee University, and it overlooks the river.

The Institute was organized in 1839 upon the grounds of the old State Arsenal, and supplanted that establishment. Prior to that date the State kept a deposit of arms and accoutrements in an old brick building at this point, under the charge of an officer and a squad of men. The idea was conceived to change this into a school in which military tactics, in addition to academic branches, should be taught to young men, and that the cadets of the school should be the guards of the arms and stores at the place. This idea was adopted and most successfully carried into effect under its Superintendent, the late Gen. Francis H. Smith. From a small beginning it grew and prospered in a most marked degree, until its operations were stopped by the war, and its buildings burned and apparatus destroyed by the Federal General, David Hunter, in his famous raid up the valley in 1863. After the war its buildings were restored, and the institution got upon its feet again, and is now as prosperous as at any period of its history.

Besides "Stonewall" Jackson, who was one of its professors, the Virginia Military Institute contributed a large number of the Confederacy's best officers of all ranks during the war.

These two Lexington institutions have furnished a large number of eminent men in all the professions and the higher departments of civil, as well as military life.

OTHER SCHOOLS.

Lexington has in Ann Smith Academy an old and renowned female school, which deserves special mention. It has always had one or two first-rate preparatory and classical schools. Under the new system of public schools it has a fine graded school for whites, employing eight to ten teachers, and three colored schools, with four or five teachers.

CHURCHES.

There are five churches for whites in the town, and two colored churches. All of these have a large membership. The Presbyterians have the largest and wealthiest membership, and is the oldest in the place. Their church building is very commodious, but not so stylish as some of the later structures. The Episcopalians rank next in wealth and numbers. Their new church, in the University grounds, is a memorial church to Gen. R. E. Lee, and is one of the finest and prettiest in the State. The Baptists and Methodists both have a large membership, and both have new fine buildings that would be ornaments to any town. The Catholics, though not numerous, have a neat and commodious church.

LOCAL OBJECTS OF INTEREST.

Besides the multitude of fine views afforded by the attractive scenery which surrounds the town, there are many objects of special interest. Among these are the Memorial Church mentioned and the house of General Lee; the chapel and mausoleum in which his remains are deposited; the recumbent statue by Valentine over the mausoleum in the chapel; his private office as he left it before his death; the grounds and buildings of the University, its halls and libraries and museum; the Virginia Military Institute barracks and parade grounds, its halls, the bronze copy of Houdon's Washington, its antiquated cannon and other interesting relics of the past; the house of Stonewall Jackson in the town—all furnish subjects of great interest. Outside of these is the cemetery, in which is the grave of Stonewall Jackson. The splendid monument and statue recently erected to his memory are always eagerly inquired for by strangers. The ruins of Liberty Hall and the fine drives among the attractive private residences are well worth notice in the suburbs of the town.

POPULATION, PROSPECTS, ETC.

Since the advent of the railroads a few years ago, the growth of the town has been very rapid. The population, though put down by the last census at but 3,038, is really largely in excess of that. The census was taken in vacation, when all the school population and a large number of others who properly belonged to it were out of town, and without including populous suburbs, which are really a part. The most conservative estimates place the population now at over 4,000.

The enterprise and progress of the great material awakening of the period are felt here, and a steady and rapid improvement is going on. Various manufacturing enterprises have sprung up and are now in progress.

OTHER TOWNS OF THE COUNTY.

Buena Vista, a new industrial town, claiming over 2,000 inhabitants, near the Blue Ridge, eight miles east of Lexington, is the growth of two years.

Glasgow, a later town of the same class, at the forks of the James and North rivers, has several hundred people, and promises great increase.

Goshen, another industrial center, in the north corner of the county, west of North Mountain, is a chartered town, and lays claim to a bright future.

These and other similar enterprises will doubtless have other and special notices in this work.

Fairfield, about twelve miles northeast of Lexington on the old valley road, and Brownsburg fourteen miles distant on the Middlebrook and Staunton Turnpike, are both old villages, or hamlets, which were important centers of wealthy neighborhoods before the railroads took their trade and prosperity from them, as they have done for hundreds of others all over the land.

CONCLUSION.

Rockbridge's proud boast of her superior natural advantages, her fine social and intellectual society, the morality and thrift of her people, and her brilliant prospects for the future, are not without just claims. Her past history and present condition give her reasonable recognition to all these distinctions.

Prof. ALEXANDER L. NELSON, who fills the Chair of Mathematics in the Washington and Lee University, is a native of Augusta county, where he spent his early life, and received his education in the Washington College and the University of Virginia, graduating from the former place in 1849, and from the latter in 1853, with the degree of Master of Arts. In the following year he filled the Chair of Assistant Professor of Mathematics at the University of Virginia, and remained there one year, at the end of which time, he received the appointment of Professor of Mathematics in Washington College, now Washington and Lee University, which chair he has filled up to the present date. In 1866 he assisted in the organization of the bank at Lexington, and was a member of the Board of Directors until 1873, when he was made President, and at this present time holds this honorable and responsible position. In the year 1889, in company with several others, he organized the Buena Vista Company, and was elected to the Board of Directors, where he served for a time and resigned on account of duties in the University. He also assisted in the organization of the West Buena Vista Company, of which he has served as a director, and also of the Lexington Development Company, which he helped to organize and now assists in directing. He was married in 1855, to Miss Elizabeth H. Moore, a daughter of David E. Moore of Lexington, Virginia. He is an elder in the Presbyterian church. Professor Nelson combines the rare qualities of a literary and business man, a combination as much to be admired as it is unusual. He is a veteran teacher, and a living example of the advantage of culture and education in financial pursuits.

Capt. ROBERT E. LEE, President of the Fresh Creek Mineral and Development Company, was born in the District of Columbia, now Alexandria county. He is a son of Gen. Robert E. Lee, a sketch of whose life will appear elsewhere. Robert E. Lee, Jr., spent the most of his early life in Alexandria county, receiving his education at the University of Virginia in part, but did not complete his course. In the spring of 1862 he enlisted in the Rockbridge Artillery, and served one year as a private. In 1863 he was appointed to the staff of Gen. William H. F. Lee, remaining with him until his capture, when he was transferred to Gen. J. E. B. Stuart's, and again to Gen. Fitzhugh Lee's staff, and then he returned to Gen. William H. F. Lee's staff, with rank of Captain, where he remained until the close of the war. On returning home he engaged in farming, and followed this occupation until 1891, at which time he was elected President of the Fresh Creek Min-

eral and Development Company, of which he was one of the incorporators. Captain Lee has never given much attention to politics, and has no "bee in his bonnet" for office. His idea is the old and trite, but ever true one, that the office should seek the man, and not the man the office. It is to men of such principles that the county and country owes its good administration.

Col. JOHN De H. ROSS, President of the Lexington Development Company, is a native of Culpeper county, having been born near the county seat in 1840. His parents were natives of that county. The subject of our sketch, spent his early life in his native place. He was educated at the Military Institute and acted as Professor for two years after graduating. On the breaking out of the war he was given command of a party of cadets, who were sent to Harper's Ferry, and young Ross was soon given a position on General Jackson's staff, commanding for some time, when he was ordered to the Institute and assisted in drilling recruits. He was shortly afterwards given a commission of Lieutenant of Engineers in the Army of Virginia, and assigned to General Loring's staff, then in West Virginia. In the latter part of 1861, he was made Major of the 52d Virginia Infantry, commanding this regiment, for the most part, until the battle of Cross Keys, where he was severely wounded in the right hand and leg. He was sent home to Lexington, but soon returned to the regiment, taking command of it through the Gettysburg campaign and other battles. He resigned near the close of the war on account of wounds, and accepted a position of Assistant Professor in the Virginia Military Institute, holding this position until the close of the war, after which he gave his attention to farming and has followed it ever since. He helped organize the Rockbridge Company in 1890. He organized the Glasgow Improvement Company and was made its President. He took an active part in the organization of the Lexington Development Company, of which he is also President. In 1890 he assisted in the organization of the Commercial Bank of Glasgow, and is one of its directors. He also holds the position of President of the Glasgow Real Estate Exchange. He helped organize the Glasgow Publishing Company, of which he is a director. He was married in 1862, to Agnes Reid, a daughter of Col. Samuel McDowell Reid, of Lexington, Virginia, and seven children have been born to them. He is an elder in the Presbyterian church.

Col. **HENRY C. PARSONS**, the subject of this paper, was born at St. Albans, Vermont, September 25th, 1840, receiving his education in the schools of his native county and State and at the University of Vermont, from which he went direct into the Union army as Captain of Company L, 1st Vermont Cavalry. He faithfully discharged his duties until the battle of Gettysburg, where he was twice wounded and had his horse shot from under him while commanding one of the battalions in Farnsworth's charge. He was complimented in general orders, and later by the State Legislature, for bravery. The wounds he received incapacitated him for further active service, and he was assigned to provost duty on the Canadian frontier, and in that capacity he served until the close of the war. As a recognition of valor, he was offered a position in the regular army by Secretary Stanton, but did not accept it. At the close of the war he went to Kanawha county, West Virginia, and began the practice of law, and in 1868 was elected Commonwealth Attorney for Putnam county, which office he filled for one year. He was that same year elected a director of the Chesapeake and Ohio Railroad Company and appointed its attorney for West Virginia, and abandoned general practice. From that time his connection with railroad enterprises was active and constant.

His first important work was in forming the Huntington syndicate, consisting of C. P. Huntington, A. A. Leon, William H. Aspinwall, Fisk & Hatch, and others, which advanced

$15,000,000 and extended the Chesapeake & Ohio Railroad to the Ohio. After this Colonel Parsons was appointed general agent and given practical charge of the Western Division. His interest in coal drew his attention to the iron deposits on the James river, and this resulted in the organization of the Richmond and Alleghany Railroad, of which he was made Vice-President. He then formed the syndicate consisting of Cyrus H. McCormick, James G. Blaine, Hugh McCullough and Messrs. Jordan, French and others, who bought the James River and Kanawha Canal and built the Richmond and Alleghany Railroad. This party deposited $500,000 as a forfeit, on condition that a railroad 250 miles in length should be built in fourteen months.

This work was done, but Colonel Parson's health was permanently impaired. He, however, afterwards, as contractor, built the Kanawha and Ohio Railroad, and as President, the Ohio and North-western Railroad. The lines already built under contracts to which he was a party, cover over six hundred miles.

He purchased the Natural Bridge and surrounding country, laying out one of the largest private parks in America, and at present his business interests are divided between this and his iron properties and a South American project.

He is a Republican of the straightest sect in politics, but never an office-holder. Upon the completion of the Chesapeake and Ohio, he was offered a nomination to Congress by both parties, as a recognition of his services, but declined. He has, however, always been given the confidence and invited into the councils of the leaders of his party, and been regarded as a courageous and impartial adviser.

Mr. EUGENE G. PEYTON, Manager of the Natural Bridge Hotel, is a native of Albemarle county, being born in 1846. He is the son of Henry Peyton, who is yet living at the advanced age of ninety-four years. Mr. Eugene G. Peyton, the subject of this sketch, received his early education in the schools of his native county and the Academy of Stanton. Before completing his education the war between the States began, and he enlisted in the latter part of 1862 in the 2d Virginia Cavalry, Company K, Division of Fitz Hugh Lee, where he served until the close of the war. He was wounded three times, first at Winchester, again at White House, and a third time in the battle of the Wilderness. Fortunately none of the wounds were of a very serious nature. After the close of the war he returned to Staunton, Virginia, and leased the Virginia Hotel in company with his brothers. Later his brothers leased the White Sulphur Springs property, and the same year Eugene became room manager, and general office man. He remained with his brothers from 1867 until 1880, during the summer months returning to the Exchange and Ballard Hotel in Richmond for the winter months. Leaving the White Sulphur Springs, he went to Rockbridge Alum and Jordan Alum, as manager of the hotel, the engagement lasting four seasons. In 1884 he was elected manager of the Natural Bridge, and in the three following years was at the Millboro Springs, leaving there for Charleston, West Virginia, to become manager of the St. Albert Hotel, returning to Natural Bridge in 1889, and becoming manager of the hotels of this place. Mr. Peyton is a born "Mine Host." The management of an hotel or hotels is simply a second nature to him. He possesses the rare and happy faculty of making his inns homes to his guest for the nonce, and the feeling of being under ones own rooftree pervades all who find shelter and entertainment with him. His houses have greatly prospered under his efficient management, and from a business point of view, as well as professional, Mr. Peyton has been and is a success.

CHAPTER XIV.

HARRISONBURG, VIRGINIA.

By SAMUEL K. COX, D. D.

Harrisonburg, the shire-town of Rockingham county, is situated in one of the most fertile and beautiful portions of the far-famed Valley of the Shenandoah. It has passed by, more than a decade, the centennial anniversary of its first settlement. In July of the year 1780 the General Assembly authorized the location of a town upon fifty acres of ground in Rockingham county, donated for the purpose by Mr. Thomas Harrison, one of the early settlers, as well as one of the most energetic and public-spirited citizens of the county. His generous gift, and the high esteem in which he was held by his fellow-countrymen, linked his name with the town to which his liberality and enterprise had given birth. The County Court had already fixed upon it as the site of the court-house for the county, and so it has remained ever since.

Rockingham was originally a part of Augusta county, which, besides embracing a large section of Virginia, also took in what is now the State of Kentucky and all the territory extending to the Lakes. As has been noted by another chronicler, Harrisonburg and Louisville, Kentucky, are twin sisters, having been created under the same act.

Harrisonburg is almost surrounded by an amphitheatre of mountains. The North Mountains, on the west and north, and the Massanetta on the east and south, with the intervening valleys in the highest state of cultivation, dotted over here and there with neat farm-houses and fruitful orchards, present a landscape of mingled loveliness and grandeur that can scarcely be surpassed. Strangers who visit the place are fascinated with the beauty of its surroundings, while the denizens of the town can, with difficulty, be lured from it by the most tempting offers elsewhere. Its elevation of more than 1,300 feet above tide-water, and the nearness of the mountains, impart to its atmosphere a pure, elastic and tonical character, most attractive in the summer season to seekers of health and recreation. This attraction is enhanced by its proximity to several very noted mineral springs. Rawley, which boasts the finest chalybeate waters in the United States; the Massanetta Spring, a specific for all malarial disorders, and the Bear Lithia, whose name explains its virtue, are largely resorted to with each recurring season.

Harrisonburg has a population of about 4,000, which is steadily increasing. It is noted for the intelligence, refinement and hospitality of its citizens. It is amply supplied with churches of the different denominations, and its public schools are of the highest order.

The United States Court-house and Post-office building is one of the most elegant structures of the kind in the State.

An extensive tannery, with a capacity of 1,200 hides a week, and constantly being enlarged; a large foundry, and a new flouring mill, with the most improved modern machinery, turning out from one hundred and twenty-five to one hundred and fifty barrels of flour a day, are located in the town, while immediately upon its suburbs several important industries have lately been established. These include two large potteries, one for the manufacture of ordinary earthenware, the other of the majolica and other finer products of the ceramic art; a large shoe factory, a shovel factory and a chemical laboratory.

A new addition to the town has recently been laid off in streets and avenues, upon which a number of new residences have been erected, together with the industries just referred to. The town has well-equipped water-works, the reservoirs being supplied from an artesian well about five hundred feet in depth. The pressure is sufficient to carry the water without artificial aid over the highest eminence in the town. Both the old town and the new addition are lighted with electricity.

Harrisonburg is the *entrepot* of the finest grain and grass-growing regions in the State, and, located on the Baltimore and Ohio Railroad, with its Valley branch extending to Lexington, it has ready access to all the leading markets of the country.

Mr. J. P. HOUCK, the subject of this sketch, was born in Allentown, Pennsylvania, in the year 1839. At the age of thirteen he first engaged in business for himself, or learned book-keeping, and after filling various positions in Pottsville, Pennsylvania, he connected himself with the Mammoth Vein Consolidated Coal Company, in the anthracite coal region of Pennsylvania, which represented a capital of $2,000,000, of which he was given charge for three years. In 1866, in company with others, he came to Page county, Virginia, and established the Shenandoah Iron Works, which is now known as Shenandoah, Virginia. His connection with this company lasted until 1880, when he came to Harrisonburg, Virginia, and purchased the Steam Tannery, which from time to time he has enlarged until it now has a capacity of one hundred thousand heavy hides per year, and is known as the J. P. Houck Tanning Company. This is one of the largest enterprises of the kind in the South, and is one of great and especial profit and advantage. The other interests with which Mr. Houck is connected, it would seem like vanity to enumerate, but, suffice it to say, their name is legion. His means are ample, and his inclination is always to assist and lend a helping hand to every undertaking that has for its object the development of the resources of the county or section, or the building up of any enterprise that tends to benefit the city or country. He is a member of the fraternity of Masons and other orders, all of which find in him an efficient and willing worker. Mr. Houck also carries into his religious life the zeal and enthusiasm that characterize him in his business career. He is a member of the Methodist Episcopal Church, South. His responsibilities and cares are various, and yet he takes into all of his undertakings a kindness and cheerfulness that makes his bounty and presence a thing to be pleasantly regarded and doubly appreciated.

ED. S. CONRAD, attorney at law, of Harrisonburg, Virginia, the subject of this brief paper, is a native of the town, having been born here in July, 1853. His father, George O. Conrad, was for a number of years a leading jeweler and silversmith of Harrisonburg, and is still here in business.

Ed. S. Conrad received his education in the schools of the county and the State University. He began the practice of law, in 1874, at this place, and has continued it without interruption since that time. He has been employed in many of the most important cases in his county, is counsel for one of the banks of his town and a number of other corporations. He is prompt and attentive to his business and looks well after the interest of his clients. He is one of the enterprising citizens of the place, takes much interest in matters of public improvement and local development, and is a stockholder in most of the local enterprises. He served as Treasurer of the Harrisonburg Land and Improvement Company the first year of its organization. He is strictly temperate, having never tasted intoxicating liquors.

In church affairs he has taken an active part, and is a member of the Methodist Episcopal Church, South, in which he has held many and important offices; has been frequently a delegate to the annual conferences of his church, and for years has been one of the Vice-Presidents of the Sunday-school Convention of the Baltimore Conference.

Dr. SAMUEL H. MOFFETT, one of the oldest residents of Harrisonburg, is a native of the place, and was born in 1830. His ancestors were also residents of the county for a number of generations. The early education of Samuel H., was received in the schools of the county, and in 1853 he graduated from the medical department of the University of Virginia, after which he attended the Jefferson Medical College of Philadelphia, when, returning home, he began practice at Harrisonburg, following this occupation until the breaking out of the war in 1861, when he entered the Confederate army as surgeon, and served in that capacity until the surrender in 1865. After the war he practiced for some time, but in 1873 he was elected to the State Legislature, where he served in both branches until 1880. For the last ten years the Doctor has been engaged in farming and in the practice of his profession. As a good citizen, he has not allowed himself to become so entirely absorbed in his own personal and private concerns as to ignore or neglect the interests and well being of his town; on the contrary, the Doctor has been active in the development of the place and takes a lively interest in all that concerns it. He is identified with the West Shenandoah Land and Improvement Company of Rockingham county, and was Treasurer of the same for some time. As a politician, he is known throughout the State for his activity and zeal in and for any cause that he may espouse politically.

Hon. PHILO BRADLEY.—Prominent among the promoters and upbuilders of Harrisonburg, none have been more active and efficient than the Hon. Philo Bradley, President of the First National Bank and owner and operator of the Harrisonburg Foundry. Mr. Bradley was born in the State of New York in the year 1829. His early life was spent on a farm in his native State, but he early learned the moulding trade, which he followed until 1852, when he came to Harrisonburg, Virginia, and took employment with an older brother who had just started a foundry, which, in 1856, he purchased, and has continued in this business ever since, having been very successful in the undertaking. Aside from this work, Mr. Bradley has found time to interest himself in the place, and a fair share of the advancement and prosperity of Harrisonburg is due to him. The office of President of the First National Bank was given him in 1879, which, at that time, was in an impoverished condition, but under his judicious management and executive skill it soon came to the front, and at the present time will compare favorably with any similar institution in the State. Politics have not greatly absorbed his attention, but he has represented his county in the

State Legislature one or two terms. Mr. Bradley is an enthusiastic Mason, and has held many important offices in that order. In church matters he is a member of the Methodist Church, South, and has held official positions in that body for over thirty years. While he has made money and gained influence, he has also gained friends and acquired the respect of all with whom he has come in contact, a fact which he holds higher than his financial success.

Maj. THOMPSON LENNIG.—One of the prominent promoters of the interests and enterprises of Harrisonburg, Virginia, is Maj. Thompson Lennig, a Philadelphian by birth, having been born there in the year 1841. He was educated in Europe, and returned to America in 1861 and enlisted in the Union army, in 1862, in Company H, 6th Pennsylvania Cavalry, where he served two years, when he was taken prisoner of war at Brandy Station and was sent to Libby Prison, where he was confined twelve months, when he was released. The Major received the rank of First Lieutenant while in the army, and upon his return was made Assistant Adjutant General of the State Militia. The study of law had been among his pursuits, and after the war he practiced his profession in Philadelphia until 1875. In 1879 he came to Harrisonburg, Virginia, and engaged in farming for some time, when he disposed of his farm to the Harrisonburg Land and Improvement Company, in which he became a director. At the present time the Major is a stockholder in the Harrisonburg Mineral and Development Company and in several other companies. Major Lennig's success, financially, has been the result of judicious management and careful investments, and he finds himself at the meridian of life in a condition to enjoy comparative leisure or free to employ his time as best pleases him.

CENTRAL REAL ESTATE AGENCY.—The Central Real Estate Agency of Harrisonburg, Virginia, is composed of the following named persons: A. H. Wilson, W. H. Rickard, A. P. Funkhouser, H. N. Whitesell and P. S. Thomas, and is one of the leading firms in this line in the Valley.

A. H. Wilson, the President of the Company, in a prominent farmer, and lives just outside the city limits. He is a large owner of business and residence property in the town, and has been, from the start, one of the leading men in the development and improvement of the town and the mineral interests of the surrounding county. He was born at Moorefield, Hardy county, West Virginia, in 1838. During the late war was Captain of the Hardy Grays, an infantry company from Hardy county, and saw considerable service for the South during those times. At the close of the war in 1865, he came to Harrisonburg, and has been identified with her business interests ever since. The other members of the firm have been identified with the interests of the town for some years. P. S. Thomas, the Secretary of the Company, was for a number of years engaged in the sale of agricultural implements and is at present Superintendent of the Town Waterworks.

H. N. Whitesell, Treasurer, is engaged in the buggy implement and hardware trade.

A. P. Funkhouser is editor of the *State Republican*, and Secretary and General Manager of the Central Mining, Manufacturing and Land Company.

W. H. Rickard is a leading farmer living near town, and has been prominently interested in the leading enterprises for the development of the town.

JOHN G. YANCEY, Esq., senior member of the firm of Yancey, Snell & Co., of Harrisonburg (wholesale groceries and wood and lumber yards), is a native of Rockingham county, and was born in 1853. His early life was spent at home, receiving his education in the schools of the county and later attending the Emory-Henry College. After completing his education he clerked three years at Harrisonburg. In 1876 he engaged in the retail grocery trade, conducting this business two years, at the expiration of which time he purchased the Harrisonburg Plaster Mill, conducting this until 1885, when, in company with Mr. J. M. Snell, the present business was started.

Mr. Yancey assisted in the organization of the Harrisonburg Iron Gate Investment Company, of which he was President; was also a director in the West Iron Gate Company, and assisted in the organization of the Harrisonburg Land and Improvement Company, of which he was general manager for some time. In a number of other companies he owns stock, and finds ample occupation in his numerous interests, both in and about Harrisonburg. Social and religious life have their attractions for him, being a member of the Methodist church, a Mason and a K. of P.

CHAPTER XV.

RADFORD, VIRGINIA.

By W. L. WARDLE.

To understand and appreciate the superiority of Radford's location, take a map, draw a line from Chicago, Illinois, to Wilmington, North Carolina, and another from New York to New Orleans, they will cross at Radford, Virginia. From New York City a nearly straight belt of railroads run, without a break, to New Orleans. On this great commercial causeway Radford lies somewhat north of its center. Look at the route from the South Atlantic seaboard to the great lakes. From Wilmington, North Carolina, a railroad runs to Radford with but one break of a few miles, separating the terminus of the Cape Fear and Yadkin Valley Railroad and the terminus of the Cripple Creek extension of the Norfolk and Western Railroad. This short link has already its road-bed partially completed, and work upon it is steadily progressing. From Radford, running directly on towards Chicago, the New River branch of the Norfolk and Western Railroad, leaving its parent stem at Radford, runs eighty-four miles to Powhatan upon the Elkhorn extension and in the great Flat Top coal region. Already an immense treasure has been expended upon the extension of this line to Ironton, upon the Ohio river, from which point direct connections exist with Chicago and the North-west.

If, upon the completion of this line in 1892, one were to leave Chicago to traverse it, he would be surprised to find upon reaching the great Alleghany chain of mountains, that a natural gateway through the mountains opened to him. This solitary, natural gap would be found to have been made by the New river, which, rising in North Carolina, flows—not like its neighbors, south-east to the Atlantic ocean—but *north across* the Blue Ridge and Alleghany Mountains, merging into the great Kanawha river. The New river flows directly through Radford and is at this point of good width, with a swift current, and furnishes an immense water-power.

Radford is on the main line of the Norfolk and Western Railroad, which runs from Norfolk, Virginia, to Bristol, Tennessee. As stated above, it is at the junction of the New river branch, which runs in a northerly direction to the inexhaustible coal fields. In a southerly direction is the famous Cripple creek iron-ore region, and, in fact, Radford is flanked by the richest iron and mineral beds in the State. It is the point where the coal and iron come together. If a person should take the map showing the mineral region of this wonderfully favored section, and fold it in the center both ways, he would see that the creases cross directly over Radford, showing it to be the exact center of this vast mineral storehouse. Besides, all the railroads carrying this natural wealth to the outer world converge at Radford.

One other phase of Radford's natural advantage in point of location, is its possession of an abundance of land admirably fitted for the needs of a large city. It has about ten square miles of territory. Along and parallel to the river is a tract of fine bottom land affording ample accommodations for manufacturing purposes. From this tract, and upon both sides of the river, the land rises to a considerable elevation above the river, forming a gently rolling table-land, most beautiful to the eye and perfectly adapted to the necessities of drainage and sewerage. The elevation is nearly 2,000 feet above the sea, and as a healthful and attractive site for a city none better could be imagined.

Thus far but the natural advantages of Radford have been presented, and a unique and exceptionally favorable combination of advantages they certainly are. It is frankly stated that its unrivalled location is the basis upon which rests, in a great degree, the importance and promise of this young city. Nevertheless, its acquired advantages are tangible and substantial. In describing them the line of strictest accuracy will be followed. The attempt will be, not to unduly magnify its growth and achievements, but to present simple facts upon which the reader may base a careful and conservative estimate of the progress and development of the place. No glittering generalities and misleading statistics will be put forward, but a brief outline of actual accomplishments will be given, showing that upon the eligibility of its site and superb natural advantages, as a foundation, has been erected a superstructure built with wise foresight, and with an intelligent appreciation of the sterling, substantial character of nature's endowment. So, without circumlocution, let us see what Radford has really accomplished.

Radford has ten square miles of territory, three miles of macadamized streets, and fifteen miles of water-pipes. The Doran Library Association have a well stocked library and reading-room. The Belle Heth Academy, the Radford school, and the Radford Female Seminary are the educational institutions established and in successful operation. Radford has four church buildings, with foundations laid for two more. It has two railroad stations, one a beautiful stone structure; La Belle Inn in East Radford and Radford Inn, which are imposing buildings. The Radford Trust Company's building is 53 x 130 feet, has complete banking rooms, three large stores and twenty-eight offices and rooms. It cost over $50,000. The brick building of the Radford Bank is three stories in height, has complete banking rooms and other necessary offices and rooms. The Ashmead block has two large stores, library rooms and club apartments. The Randolph building has two large stores, and hall fitted with stage and ante-rooms. The Sill block contains railroad offices and the telegraph office. The new steel bridge over New river, which was opened with appropriate ceremonies September 7, 1891, is 1,460 feet long, 40 feet wide, spans the river at a height of 83 feet, and cost $90,000. It is a most important and valuable addition to the advantages of the city.

Of the industrial plants, the Radford Pipe and Foundry Company commands first attention. The pipe foundry is built of iron and brick, is 122 x 300 feet, has three pits and a capacity of from 100 to 125 tons per day. The machinery foundry is built of iron and brick, is 50 x 200 feet, and has a capacity of twenty-five to thirty tons a day. The machine-shop is 50 x 200 feet; the boiler-house 50 x 80 feet; the pattern-shop 40 x 80 feet. The cleaning and testing building complete the plant, the cost of which is $200,000. It employs four hundred men.

Radford City, in its entirety, being but two years old, has not created much of history save in industrial progress. In the eastern section, once called Central City, was located, in 1857, one of the early depots of the Virginia and Tennessee Railroad, now the Norfolk and Western. Within the limits of Radford live a number of families, representing the fine old Virginia stock. Gen. G. C. Wharton has a brick mansion in the western part of the city. Near it stands the old homestead of the late Dr. John B. Radford, the living male representative of the family being the Hon. J. Lawrence Radford, who represents the district in the Virginia House of Delegates. About a mile up New river from General Wharton's residence lie the Ingles estates, owned by descendants of the first family who settled in Virginia west of the Blue Ridge Mountains. Captain William Ingles, as an engineer and bridge-builder, and in other capacities, is one of the leading citizens of Radford. Lieut.-Gov. J. Hoge Tyler has recently built a fine residence in the easterly portion of Radford upon a commanding eminence in the beautiful property in the development of which he is interested. Capt. Stockton Heth is another representative of the original landed proprietors of the place, and a member of one of the old families. With the influx of capital into Radford came representatives of many different States, as a result of which the society of the young city is truly cosmopolitan, and at the same time of a most intelligent and cultured character.

Lieut.-Gov. J. HOGE TYLER is descended from a long line of ancestors distinguished both in church and State, on both sides of his family. He was born at Blenheim, the old ancestral home of the Tylers, in Caroline county, Virginia. His father, the Hon. George Tyler, represented the county of Caroline from 1859 to 1865, and was loved and honored as the worthy son of Henry Tyler, grandson of the Capt. George Tyler, who, in the Revolutionary War, raised, uniformed and equipped a company of Patriot soldiers, soon after Patrick Henry sounded the tocsin of war. His lineage is the same as President Tyler, of Virginia.

On the maternal side, we find, by reference to "Foote's Sketches of Virginia," that his ancestors were among the early settlers of Virginia. His mother, Eliza Hoge, still remembered for her graces of mind and person, was the daughter of Gen. James Hoge, of Pulaski, a man of marked characteristics, strong, forceful, a splendid type of the men of his day who met and battled with difficulties. He served with distinction as an officer in the war of 1812, and for years was the representative of his county and district as Senator and member of the House of Delegates, and was chosen by his party as District Elector in five or six presidential elections. He was the son of James Hoge, of Frederick county, of the same lineage as Rev. Moses D. Hoge, of Richmond; Judge John Blair Hoge, of West Virginia, and others. These Hoges trace to the William Hoge and Barbara Hume who were the ancestors of that long line that have been useful in church and State in Virginia, Pennsylvania and Ohio. The maternal grandmother of James Hoge Tyler was Eleanor Howe, the daughter of Major Howe, of the Revolutionary War, of the same lineage as Lord Howe and General Wayne. Thus we see, from lineage and inheritance, Mr. Tyler has nothing to be ashamed of, but one of his most striking characteristics is the belief, on which he has acted, that every man should stand on his own merit. He illustrated it by declining the soft and easy place in the Confederate army which could have been procured by family influence, saying if his boyish neighbor, Willie Goodwin, on whom, after an elder brother was killed, depended the support of mother and sisters, could go in the ranks, "If it is right for him to go, it is more incumbent on me," so with knapsack and musket, at the age of sixteen, he stood by the side of his youthful companion a faithful soldier until the flag was folded at Appomattox.

When the war was over, young Tyler returned to his dismantled home. Unfenced, washed and worn fields met the eye, but under his skillful management he has made it a most attractive home, not only drawing from it the support of his family, but was enabled to assist his father. He has also developed a coal vein upon his land, thus giving employment to many in his neighborhood.

Politically, we find him active ever since the age of twenty-one, taking part in every contest that has been waged in Virginia since the war; was alternate delegate to the convention that nominated Tilden at St. Louis in 1876, and took an active part in canvassing for his election; was elected in 1877 to the State Senate, and his friends point with pleasure to the record made. In 1886 he was appointed on the Board of Visitors to Blacksburg College, and, almost immediately after, was elected rector of the college and made chairman of the Executive, Finance and Building Committees, and as such had charge of the erection of the handsome barracks building at that place; was sent by the Board to inspect the agricultural farms and colleges in the United States and Canada, with a view to perfecting arrangements for establishing the Experimental Station at Blacksburg. It was whilst engaged in this work and absent from the State that his friends advocated him for Congress, and it was whilst canvassing for Mr. Buchanan, making the first and last speech in his behalf, that gave him so much reputation, his name began to be mentioned for Governor. To aid this movement, his friends throughout the State gave a ready response, and in the Convention which assembled in Richmond in August, 1889, he had a large and faithful following. Captain P. W. McKinney proved the successful aspirant, due to the hearty, cheerful and ringing speech that Major Tyler made endorsing his old friend, Captain McKinney, which electrified and captured that large convention and caused him to be the unanimous nominee for Lieutenant Governor. It is said but few speeches have ever been made in Virginia which so thoroughly captivated an audience as the one made by Major Tyler in old Armory Hall on that hot August day. It carried his name throughout the State, and he at once entered the canvass a favorite of the people. How well he sustained himself was evinced in many ways. We quote these few lines from the Washington *Post:*

"He had a rousing meeting at Stanardsville, Green county, and made a speech of two hours length, and showed himself the peer of any of the Democratic speakers now on the stump."

Major Tyler has been thoroughly identified with the cause of agriculture, attending most of the county, State and some of the National Farmers' meetings. At present is a member of the State Agricultural Society, Vice-Preisdent of the Lynchburg Agricultural Society, and has been on the boards of many of the different agricultural societies throughout the State. At this time he is actively engaged in working up an interest in the State with a view to having Virginia properly represented at the Columbian Exhibition, at Chicago, in 1893. At a large meeting held in Pulaski City in July he was elected President of a State Association organized to promote this interest. He has been an elder in the Presbyterian church since early manhood, and has ever been an active, earnest worker in church and Sunday-school matters. In 1868 he married Miss Sue Hammet, daughter of Col. Edward Hammet, of Radford, Montgomery county, and has four sons and three daughters. He is a public-spirited man, and his energies have been exerted in the upbuilding of his section and State; is President of the Radford Development Company, a company of $200,000 capital, organized to promote the growth of Radford, and also President of the Virginia Mutual Building and Loan Association, the Radford Building and Investment Association, and is President and an active member in other similar enterprises organized for the upbuilding of his State and section.

Col. W. H. BARCLAY, the subject of this sketch, was born November 4th, 1833, at Lexington, Virginia, and graduated at the Washington College (now Washington and Lee University) in 1855, taking the degree of A. B. He then studied law at Lexington under that able jurist Judge I. W. Brockenbrough, and secured the degree of B. L., in 1857, and was admitted to the Bar the same year. He then went to Chicago and remained there a year, and at the expiration of that time went to Milwaukee and engaged in the transportation business on the lakes, and in the storage, grain and commission business. Here he remained six years and then removed to Oswego, New York, buying an interest in a large line of canal boats. After a residence in Oswego of two years he removed a portion of his canal line to Buffalo, where he continued in the transportation business and at the same time opened a grain commission house, and for a number of years did all the business for the combination known as the "corn ring." In a few years he had amassed a large fortune, which was swept away in a short time by carrying speculators on margins. He returned to Virginia and engaged in various business enterprises. Being a personal friend of President Cleveland, he was appointed Post-office Inspector. Having a choice of territory, he selected South-west Virginia in order to familiarize himself with that whole section, desiring eventually to open a real estate office. After serving three years as Post-office Inspector, he resigned and opened an office at Radford, believing it to be the future great manufacturing center of this section of the State. Being the first man on the ground as dealer in real estate, within five months after opening his office at Radford he had sold lots to the amount of $107,000. Soon thereafter he associated himself in business with J. G. Crockett, which afterwards became Kearsley, Barclay & Crockett. From this firm Colonel Barclay withdrew in 1891. He continued in the same business, but gave especial attention to coal, iron and timber lands. He married in 1860 Miss Julia A. Crawford, of Cleveland, Ohio. Three children have been born to them. Colonel Barclay has a residence on Second street, overlooking the new town of Radford and the new bridge over the New river, which, for its beauty of location and architectural design, attracts the attention of all visitors.

----::⟨⟩:----

GEORGE T. KEARSLEY, Esq., was born February 17th, 1854, at Charlestown, Virginia. His father, G. W. T. Kearsley, was for fifty-two years a merchant of Charlestown, and at the present time is interested in a number of new enterprises. George T., the subject of our sketch, was educated in the Charlestown Academy, and then entered the employment of the Baltimore and Ohio Railroad, at Piedmont, West Virginia. He remained here four years, and then at St. Louis and San Francisco Railroad office for two years, in Springfield, Missouri. From here he went to McComb City, Mississippi, and then to Little Rock, Arkansas. He afterwards accepted a position at the Roanoke Machine Works, remaining there for two years. He was then appointed chief clerk to the purchasing agent of the East Tennessee, Virginia and Georgia Railroad Company, with office at Knoxville, Tennessee, where the President of the Knoxville Car Wheel Company offered him a position as head book-keeper. He remained in this place for two years, at the end of which time he decided to go into business for himself, and, in October, 1888, he entered the real estate business in Radford, Virginia, being the pioneer real estate man of the place. In March, 1890, he consolidated with Barclay & Crockett, but Mr. Barclay withdrawing the firm name became Kearsley & Crockett, and is at the present time the leading business house of this kind in the city. Aside from his regular occupation, he is Vice-President of the Radford Real Estate Exchange, and has been President of the same. He is also a member of the City Council of Radford, and President of the Local Board of the Eastern Building Association, of Syracuse, New York.

He was married, in 1889, to Miss Lily Anderson Patton, daughter of Capt. William T. Patton, of Staunton. He is a member and a vestryman of the Episcopal church, and universally regarded as a good man and a valuable citizen.

Col. JOHN CROCKETT, the subject of this sketch, was born May 27th, 1836, in Pulaski county, Virginia. His father, John C. Crockett, is a prominent farmer and stock raiser. Col. Crockett was educated in Wytheville at the Wytheville Military Academy, and after leaving there he engaged in farming. In 1873 he moved to Summers county, West Virginia, and engaged in the mercantile and stock-raising business, carrying it on for some five years or more. In July, 1861, he enlisted in the 51st Virginia Infantry, being commissioned as First Lieutenant of Company E, in which command he served until the latter part of the war under General Wharton and General Breckenridge; also under General Buckner in the Army of the Cumberland. He then returned to the farm, carrying on also stock-raising, and was elected to the State Legislature from Summers county, West Virginia, for two consecutive terms; was a strong advocate of the re-election of I. N. Cameron to the United States Senate, and in 1889 he came to Radford and engaged in the real estate business, being a member of the firm of Kearsley & Crockett. He is also a director of the Locust Hill Iron Manufacturing Company of Max Meadows, a large stockholder in Max Meadows Land and Improvement Company and Iron Company, and is interested in many others throughout the State.

The Colonel was married in 1872 to Miss Ella Crump, daughter of William Crump and Eliza Crump. Mr. Crump is a prominent lawyer and a large farmer, of Crump's Bottom, Summers county, West Virginia. Three children have been born to them—Robert Crump, Willie Coates and Eliza Brooks.

Colonel Crockett is a member of a strong Presbyterian family, being Scotch-Irish. He is now the only surviving member of a family of six when the war commenced, his brothers having been killed on the battle-field, with the exception of the youngest, who contracted consumption in the army, from which he afterwards died. His second brother was Captain of Company F, 45th Virginia Regiment, and was killed at the battle of Cloyd's Farm the same day he was promoted to Lieutenant Colonel. His next brother was a private and was killed at the battle of Newhope, twelve miles below Staunton. His second brother (the Captain) was Robert, and the next (the private) was William, both being members of the 45th Regiment.

Dr. WILLIAM A. WILSON was born July 27th, 1851, in Pulaski county, Virginia. His father, Dr. M. A. Wilson, practiced medicine in Pulaski county for over forty years. Dr. William A. Wilson received his first schooling in the county schools and then attended the University of Virginia, graduating as M. D. in 1874. After receiving his degree, he located in Christiansburg, remaining there for fifteen years, but removed to Radford in December, 1890, and entered into partnership with Dr. James. He was married in 1876 to Miss Mary L. Miller, daughter of Capt. James T. Miller of Christiansburg, who was a widely known capitalist of that place.

The Doctor is a member of the State Medical Society, a member of the Board of Directors of the Exchange Bank and Radford Investment and Building Association, etc. He is a member of the Presbyterian church.

Dr. R. BRUCE JAMES, to whom this short sketch relates, was born January 14th, 1861, in Pittsylvania county, Virginia. His father, Dr. John C. James, was a practicing physician for nearly half a century in the same county, and was noted as a skillful surgeon, being called upon to do the surgical work throughout that section of the State. Dr. R. B. James was educated in the county schools and graduated at the Virginia Military Institute in 1883, taking the first honor in his class, and for one year thereafter was Assistant Professor of Mathematics, French and Tactics in that institution. He then studied medicine at the University of Virginia, graduating in 1886, after which he took courses in the hospitals and colleges of New York, graduating at the College of Physicians and Surgeons. He practiced there for nearly three years, and in December, 1890, came to Radford, Virginia, and entered into partnership with Dr William A. Wilson, where, with strict attention to professional duties, the firm has succeeded in establishing a large and well paying practice. Dr. James is a member of the Medical Society of Virginia, and a member of the vestry of the Episcopal church of Radford.

HARRY H. POWERS, Esq.—The father of Harry H. Powers, Esq., was of the firm of Powers, Blair & Co., wholesale grocers, of Richmond, Virginia. Harry, the subject of our sketch, was born January 1st, 1863, at Richmond, and was educated in his native city and at Auburn University, of Clarke county. At the age of fifteen he entered the employ of his father as clerk, remaining there four years, when, in the spring of 1888, he went to Roanoke and opened the first grocery store in that place. In the following spring he married the daughter of Attorney General James C. Taylor, Bettie M., and returned to

Richmond in the fall of 1883, and in 1885 formed the wholesale fancy grocery, manufacturing and confectionery firm of Hall, Powers & Co., in Richmond, from which firm he retired in 1887 and moved to Christiansburg, Montgomery county, where he remained one year, and in December, 1889, he came to Radford and founded the firm of H. H. Powers & Co., real estate and insurance agents. They were among the pioneers in Radford in this branch of industry, and they found it comparatively easy to establish a large and lucrative business. Mr. Powers is also Secretary and Treasurer of the Riverview Land Company, of Radford, with a capital of $200,000, their property being among the most desirable at Radford. He is Vice-President of the Norfolk and Lambert's Point Land Company, of Norfolk, Virginia, with a capital of $100,000, which property is regarded as among the most valuable about that city. Besides these, Mr. Powers is interested in a number of other enterprises, all of which combine to make his life a very busy one. It is needless to say that his heart is in his work, and he takes into it his best and most earnest endeavors. He has one child—Leslie—aged six. In choice of church, he is an Episcopalian and a vestryman of that society in Radford.

D. C. BOWMAN, Esq., of whom this brief sketch is written, was born April 6th, 1861, at Fredericksburg, Virginia, and is by profession a druggist. His father, Henry D. Bowman, was a carriage manufacturer of Fredericksburg. Young Bowman was educated in the public schools and on the farm, and at the age of twenty he entered the Agricultural and Mechanical Institute at Blacksburg, in 1880, and graduated from it in July, 1884. While at college he was appointed Hospital Steward to the College Corps, with rank of Second Lieutenant. On leaving college he went to Spottsylvania county—to his home—teaching in the public schools one session, when he went to Richmond to clerk in a pharmacy, but remained there but a short time, going to Christiansburg with W. A. Wilson & Co., which firm was also engaged in the drug trade. In 1888 he opened a drug-store in Christiansburg, in his own name, conducting it for two years. In March, 1887, in a class of thirty-five, he passed an examination before the Virginia State Board of Pharmacy, ranking third in the list of competitors. In the year 1890 he came to Radford and opened the second store, and the first drug-store in West Radford, and at the same time forming a partnership with H. H. Powers, under the firm name of H. H. Powers & Co., in the real estate and insurance business, in which they have been very successful. Mr. Bowman is also director of several of the leading land companies, among which may be mentioned the Riverview, of Radford, and the Mt. Joy, of Buchanan. He was married, in 1886, to Miss Laura McD. Pierce, a daughter of a well-known capitalist of Christiansburg. They have one child—Lizzie P.— aged three. The family are attendants of the Presbyterian church.

SANDERS, JONES & CO.—Among the successful real estate firms of Radford, Virginia, may be mentioned that of Sanders, Jones & Company, who make a specialty of town lots and mineral and timber lands throughout the State of Virginia. Charles W. Sanders, whose name appears first in the firm, was born in 1852, September 19th, at Jackson's Ferry, Wythe county. His father, Dr. R. W. Sanders, was a leading physician and farmer, and active and prominent in politics, although never aspiring to office. Charles W., the subject of this brief biography, was educated in the colleges of Washington county, and after finishing his schooling he went into the employ of the Wythe Lead and Zinc Mine Company, of Austinville, Virginia. Here he remained five years, and then accepted a position as traveling salesman for a large dry goods and notion house in Philadelphia. Virginia was his territory, which he traveled for two years, and then accepted a position in the railway mail service under the Cleveland administration. Resigning this position he came to Radford in 1890, and engaged with his uncle, Mr. J. P. M. Sanders, in the real estate business, in which, as has before been observed, he has been more than ordinarily successful. He is also Secretary of the Radford Real Estate Exchange.

CHAPTER XVI.

WYTHEVILLE, VIRGINIA.

By Prof. C. R. BOYD.

If lovely seasons, long continued, varied through the winter with enough frost to correct and reinvigorate all atmospheric conditions, are the indispensable ingredients in the composition of a really fine climate, Wytheville can point to all the records of the weather, public and private, confident that she will be rivalled by only a few localities in the world.

London is quoted as possessing a delightful climate, once the fogs could be eliminated from the observations of a conscientious weather bureau. Wytheville, as respects this most important question of an equable climate, is that ideal London, namely, London minus the fogs, minus, too, the uncomfortable things of all overcrowded areas; while the facilities of this advanced age of progress will readily yield to Wytheville, under an enterprising and intelligent supervision, all the comforts and conveniences of city life.

Wytheville lacks nothing at the hand of Nature to make her one of the most desirable and attractive resorts now accessible by rail to all the world, except, probably, for those whose love for the sea amounts to an unconquerable fascination.

Wytheville is in the medial line of the great Appalachian chain, at the same elevation above sea level with Asheville, North Carolina (2,300 to 2,500 feet), one degree average colder than Asheville throughout the year, and with twenty-five per cent. less fogs. Within and around Wytheville is the largest number of excellent curative mineral waters, in natural springs, to be found in like area, the world over.

In the town, on its main thoroughfare, is a fountain of mineral water better adapted for the cure of dyspepsia than any known. There are springs of lithia, iron, alum, magnesia and sulphuretted mineral waters within a short drive, over splendid roads, of any point in the town. While to this array of mineral waters, the town authorities have, of late, added two entirely new systems of water-supply, one of hard, the other of soft water, capable of meeting any demand and of pleasing the most fastidious taste. Add to this a drainage system of unequalled merit, established, in the nature of its location, upon a rolling plateau two hundred feet above the river that flows along its southern limits, and you have all the most important features of a health resort of the highest merit.

Wytheville enjoys the remarkable advantage, also, of being in the great pastoral and agricultural region of South-western Virginia, as well as a like centrality with reference to the belts and basins of ores, minerals, coal, marbles, saline waters and gypsum deposits. She is likewise in the middle of the great timber belt of this latitude; and with the construction of the Virginia and Kentucky Railway, would occupy, by means of that line and the great Norfolk and Western Railway, on which she is situated, a position almost in the center of distance from the lakes to the gulf, from New York to New Orleans, from Chicago to Florida; and is really right up under the crest line dividing the waters that flow north-west into the Ohio, and those flowing south-west into the Tennessee and Holston rivers.

Wytheville's position and advantages are unique! She now has the best paved streets, lighted with electricity, in all this region, and will soon add to her attractions a splendid new hotel in Jackson Park, which, with excellent hostelries already in existence, will scarcely be able to provide room for the hundreds who have been turned away from her heretofore for want of suitable accommodations.

Wytheville should really have one of the most commodious and best appointed hotels in the United States. Her position and climate and known attractions—not the least of which is an elegant and cultivated society—would warrant the construction here of a hotel that would accommodate one thousand guests the year round, and that would probably cost two hundred and fifty thousand dollars.

If Asheville, which is only one degree warmer throughout the year, with twenty-five per cent. more of dense fogs, at the same elevation above the sea and a greater distance from our populous seaboard, can entertain at least a thousand health and pleasure seekers the entire year, why could not Wytheville, with less average humidity and an incomparable location on the plateaus of beautiful mountains, secure twice the number of votaries.

Hon. ISAAC J. LEFTWICH, of whom this mention is made, was born January 26th, 1800, in Wythe county, Virginia. His father, Isaac Leftwich, was a well-known trader, and while away from home on a trading trip to New Orleans, Louisiana, was murdered at that place by some Spaniards when the subject of this sketch was about eight years old.

Isaac, junior, was educated in the best schools of the county, although the educational advantages at that time were not very extensive or

Faithfully, Yours,
C. R. Boyd

greatly superior. In the year 1815 he came to Wytheville to learn the carpenter's and cabinet-maker's trade. After finishing his trade he engaged in business for a year, when he went to Sparta, Tennessee, and engaged in the same business there, which he carried on at that place for four years, during which time he took up the study of law, and, leaving his business in the care of his employees, moved to Nashville to continue the study of his profession, which he had decided to pursue. He was admitted to the Bar at Nashville in 1824, and after following his profession at that place for a short time he returned to Wytheville, where he settled and married in the year 1825. He practiced at the Bar of Wytheville and in several of the surrounding counties for over thirty-four years, at the end of which time he entered into some speculations which realized him large profits and enabled him to retire from the Bar.

Among the incidents of his life, he was the owner of over one hundred slaves, and believing that their value would depreciate in his native State he personally took them to Mississippi, Alabama and Tennessee and sold them, realizing upwards of eighty thousand dollars on the one deal alone.

In the year 1874 the Farmers Bank of South-west Virginia was organized, and, not meeting with the success expected the first year, it was re-organized in 1875, Mr. Leftwich being elected President, which position he now holds, although ninety-one years of age. He was a member of the State Legislature four terms, being elected each time without any opposition. He has resided on the same place where he now lives since the year 1825, his original homestead.

He was married in 1825 to Miss Nancy Ward, daughter of Col. John Ward, a farmer of Wythe county. She died in 1857, and out of a family of five, one daughter is living.

At the beginning of the war Mr. Leftwich was a wealthy man, but at its close he was almost ruined. He then engaged in banking and other enterprises, and, having been very successful in business, is to-day one of the wealthiest men of Wytheville.

Capt. CHARLES R. BOYD.—The subject of this paper, Capt. Charles R. Boyd, geologist and civil engineer, was born at Wytheville, Virginia, October 31st, 1841. He is the son of Thomas J. and M. A. Boyd. His mother was the daughter of Col. David French, of Giles, Virginia. The father and mother of Captain Boyd are of Scotch and English descent. The father has been for many years prominent as an attorney, and is a man of fine and marked ability. For a number of years he represented Wythe county in the Legislature of the State, and for six years was a member of the Board of Public Works.

He was also the original and a powerful factor in the building of the Norfolk and Western Railroad through this section of Virginia. Captain Boyd received the rudiments of his education under the instruction of Col. C. Crozet, who was Colonel of Engineers under the first Napoleon. When the war of the States began, Charles entered the service in the "Stonewall" brigade, and was soon appointed Second Lieutenant of Engineers, and rose to the rank of brevet Captain. He was later appointed First Lieutenant of Ordnance. In the Engineers he served with marked ability during the latter half of the war. After the close of the war he entered the University of Virginia and completed a scientific course, graduating in the class of 1874. He then engaged in civil engineering and the various branches of science, devoting much attention to geology, and in the year 1881 he published a book on the resources of South-west Virginia, which met with great favor, and had an extensive circulation and proved a powerful and important factor in calling the attention of capitalists to the rare and numerous opportunities for financial investments in the State.

He also compiled and published several maps of South-west Virginia, which were very handsomely and elaborately executed, and have been largely employed by the railroad companies and other development companies in inducing and directing capital to this portion of the State.

The twenty-first edition of these valuable maps was executed in the year 1891. During the course of Captain Boyd's business career, he received the appointment of Commissioner of Virginia to visit the Paris Exposition in 1878. Previously, he had also been commissioner from the State to the Philadelphia Exposition in 1876, at which time he was elected a member of the American Institute of Mining Engineers. He was also appointed by the State as commissioner to the New Orleans Exposition in 1884, during which time he was authorized by the State to write a paper on the resources of South-west Virginia. In the year 1880, he was elected a member of the American Society of Civil Engineers, and was invited to attend a meeting of the British Association for the Advancement of Science, which convened at Liverpool, England, in 1888. He was also on the general committee for the reception and entertainment of the British Iron and Steel Institute in the fall of 1890. He was also invited, among other delegates, to attend the Inter-National Congress of Geologists, to be held at Washington, D. C., in the fall of 1891. In April of the same year, he was elected Vice-President of the Association of Engineers of Virginia. The Captain is a stockholder and director of the Boyd Land Company of Wytheville, and, aside from scientific and literary attainments, is a man of a fine, practical business ability. He is a forcible and vigorous writer, and has acquired by the publication and circulation of his pamphlets and maps a more than national reputation as a civil engineer, geologist and scientist. The chapter in this work on South-west Virginia, prepared by Captain Boyd, will give a more adequate idea of his style and method of writing than it would be possible to obtain from the most elaborate criticism or *resume* of his writings. It should, however, be remembered, in due justice to Captain Boyd, that the limited space allowed him will necessitate the condensing of the material of his article in a measure, which may tend to detract from its literary merit and beauty. He was married in April, 1868, to Miss Sallie, daughter of Gen. Leroy Stafford, of Louisiana. General Stafford was a man of marked prominence in his State, and at one time was candidate for Governor, and during the late war took an active and prominent part.

The Captain has three children, namely, Katie, Charles R. and Cornelia. In matters of church faith he is an Episcopalian.

Hon. WILLIAM LOCKHART YOST, Mayor of Wytheville, is one of the men on whom the well-being and prosperity of Wytheville has largely depended, and to whom is due in a great measure the present substantial standing of the city among its sister aspirants.

The subject of this sketch was educated at Christiansburg, and in Bland county at the special school of Prof. Henry Cox. After completing the course, he taught the school here and elsewhere for three years, Mr. Cox having given it up. He then took a course in law, and was admitted to the Bar in Bland county in 1874, where he practiced until 1878, in which latter year he came to Wytheville, opening an office and continuing in the practice. In May, 1890, he was elected Mayor of the town, which office he now holds. He organized the Wytheville Development Company, which is the leading and pioneer company of Wytheville. He has been active in locating new enterprises, and by this means has substantially aided in the building up of the place. He was nominated in 1883 on the Democratic ticket for Commonwealth Attorney, but the Readjuster movement defeated the entire ticket at the election. Since the age of twenty-one years Mr. Yost has held several public offices of trust. He was originator of the scheme to build the Virginia and Kentucky Railroad, leading from Patrick Court House, Virginia, via Wytheville, to the coal fields of Tazewell county, which is to be built.

Dr. ROBERT EMMET MOORE, one of the most prominent physicians of Wytheville, Virginia, was born in Wythe county, October 13th, 1838.

His father, Col. A. C. Moore, of the 29th Virginia Infantry, Army of Northern Virginia, was a well known and wealthy farmer of Wythe county. Robert Emmet Moore was educated at Emory and Henry College, Washington county, Virginia, going from there to the Medical College of Virginia, and graduating from there in the year 1860. At the breaking out of the war he enlisted as Surgeon in the 29th Virginia Infantry, of which his father was Colonel, serving with that command for two years, then going with Gen. J. A. Early's command in the same capacity. He was then appointed on the staff of General Breckenridge, whose headquarters were at Wytheville. After General Breckenridge was made Secretary of War to the Confederate States, he occupied the same position under General Eccles, who succeeded General Breckenridge, and remained with him until the close of the war. He continued to stay at Wytheville after the surrender, and has since followed his profession at that place, having established a large and lucrative practice. The Doctor is a member of the Medical Society of Virginia, and of the Board of Visitors to the Medical College of Virginia, receiving the appointment from Governor McKinney, February 5th, 1890, and without any desire or expectation on his part. He was married May 21st, 1863, to Miss M. S. Glasscock, a daughter of William R. Glasscock, Esq., a prominent merchant and stock dealer of Fauquier county. The marriage took place at Aberdeen, Mississippi, where the bride's parents were living at that time. The Doctor and his family are members of the Presbyterian church.

Dr. ROBERT T. ELLETT, the subject of this sketch, was born in Hanover county, near Ashland, the birthplace of Henry Clay, May 29th, 1837. His father, Robert Ellett, Esq., was a civil engineer of Hanover county, and was connected with the old Louisa Railway, which is now the Chesapeake and Ohio, until it reached Stanton. It was his ambition to see this road completed, but he died in 1869. Robert, Jr., was educated in Richmond Baptist College and in the Richmond Medical College, graduating from the medical department in 1858. He began practice near Tunstall Station in New Kent county, but the war breaking out, in 1861 he raised an artillery company and served with this company seventeen months, when he was transferred to the Medical Department, stationed at Montgomery Springs, as Surgeon, in which capacity he served until the close of the war, when discharged he had but twenty-five cents in his pockets, which he gave for his breakfast next morning. He went to Giles county and entered into partnership with Dr. J. W. Easley and continued with him for eighteen months, when he came to Montgomery county, in which he resides at the present time. The Doctor has been Clerk of the County Court for the past four years, and the Supervisor of the county. He is a member of the State Medical Society, and is justly esteemed an ornament to his profession. His wife was Miss Susan V. French, the youngest daughter of G. D. French, Esq., a well known leading Whig of Giles county. Eleven children have blessed this union, Guy French, Robert T., Deputy Clerk of the County Court; William and Walter, at Blackburg attending college; Harry, Andrew, Beverly, Minnie, Bessie, Mary and Sadie. The Doctor is a member of the Episcopal church and a warden in the same. In business he has been happily successful, and with his genial, philosophical disposition, he looks upon life as amply worth living.

CHARLES H. CALFEE, Esq., a native of Wythe county, was born December 5th, 1828. He is a descendant of Mr. John Calfee, who was born about the year 1725 of English ancestry, and lived and died in the Shenandoah Valley of Virginia, holding land patents (now in possession of the subject of this sketch) from Lord Fairfax, proprietor of the northern neck of Virginia, for three hundred and eight acres of land in Augusta county, dated September 3d, 1749.

John Calfee raised six sons, namely, Henry, John, William, James, Benjamin and Charles, and two daughters, Betsy and Sallie. Charles married Elizabeth Brown, of New Jersey, and he and most of his brothers settled on New river, in Wythe county, between 1790 and 1800. Charles raised two daughters, Betsy and Sallie, and one son, John. John was born 1797, and married Margaret, daughter of Ezekiel Howard, of English parentage, who moved, about the close of the Revolution, from the State of New York to Montgomery county, Virginia. Ezekiel Howard served through the war of the Revolution at Brandywine, Germantown and in the Valley Forge campaign, and after the war he settled in Montgomery county, where he was a Justice of the Peace, and for a number of years transacted a large share of public business. He married Rebecca Anderson, of Botetourt county, and raised two sons, Alexander and Anderson, and five daughters, Sophia, Margaret, Rebecca, Evelina and Juliet. Margaret was born in 1800, and married John Calfee, as above noted, and their son is the subject of this sketch. His mother died in 1831, but the father long survived her, raising a family of three daughters and three sons, and living until 1873. These daughters were Evelina, Elizabeth and Sophia, and the sons were R. A., J. A. and C. H. Calfee. J. A. served through the civil war in the Western Department of the Confederate Army, and was actively engaged in its campaigns.

Charles, the subject of this sketch, attended the schools of his native county until he was sixteen years of age, and then attended a higher grade of schools until 1850. After completing his education, he engaged in the book business for a few years, but in the course of time abandoned this occupation and returned to the farm, marrying and remaining there until 1865. Owing to physical disabilities he was unable to do active service during the war, although his entire sympathies were with the South. In the year 1865 he made a short trip to Indiana with a view to locating, but the climate not agreeing with him he gave up the idea and returned home and to farming, carrying it on until 1890, when he sold to the Bertha Zinc Company, and his and his brothers' farms are the present sites of the mines, washing, crushing and roasting machinery. After selling to this company, Mr. Calfee moved to Wytheville.

Mr. Calfee was married in 1853 to Miss Sarah J., daughter of Hezekiah Witt, who was a prominent farmer and a local preacher in the Baptist church in Montgomery county. Mr. Calfee himself is one of the disciples of the Christian church, of which he has been a member for over a quarter of a century.

Dr. **PEYTON B. GREEN**, the subject of this sketch, one of the prominent physicians of Wytheville, was born May 27th, 1861, at Staunton, Virginia. His father, Major C. Green, who is at present a member of the State Senate and President of the Bank of Wytheville, is active in all the works that tend to the improvement and advancement of the town. Dr. Green was educated at Roanoke College, Salem. From this institution he went to the Ohio Medical College at Cincinnati, and from there to the University of Virginia, where he graduated July 1st, 1885. Leaving college, he went to Waco, Texas, to try his fortune, practicing his profession there for over a year, but on account of ill health he returned to Wytheville in the autumn of 1886, and has followed his profession here ever since, building up in an almost incredibly short time a large and handsomely paying practice. He is a member of the Medical Examining Board of Virginia, and Health Officer and City Physician of Wytheville. The Doctor was married in 1888 to Miss Kate Terry, a daughter of General William Terry, who was prominent in the Confederate service. One little girl—Katie—has been born to them. Although young, Dr. Green has made for himself a reputation that any physician, at the end of his career, might well be proud of. He stands among the first in his profession among his fellow practitioners, and with the present so happily auspicious, the future can reasonably hold any possibility for him.

Mr. WILLIAM STUART CROCKETT, the subject of this sketch, was born July 13th, 1865, at Wytheville, Virginia. His father, Captain Crockett, a prominent lawyer, was a member of the Stonewall Brigade under General Jackson, serving throughout the war in that brigade as Captain. He was wounded at the second battle of Manassas, and as a soldier was noted for his bravery and valor. He was prominent in politics, stumping the State for Hon. John W. Daniel when he was first elected to the United States Senate in 1883. He was also Chairman of the State Democratic Convention the same year. He was an extensive real estate owner, having about sixteen hundred acres of the most valuable iron property in the State. His son, William Stuart, was educated at the Virginia Military Institute, and graduated from this institution in the year 1887. After graduating he returned to Wytheville, and on the day after receiving his degree entered the employ of the Norfolk and Western Railroad, on its engineering corps, and assisted in surveying and laying out the Cripple Creek, Reed Island and North Carolina extensions of that road. He remained in the employ of this road for four years, returning to Wytheville in March, 1891, entering into partnership with Mr. P. W. Early, carrying on surveying and civil engineering under the firm name of Early & Crockett. The firm has made several additions to Wytheville, and also a number of other important surveys have been made by them. As a civil engineer, Mr. Crockett is among the first in the State, and he has been especially successful in his profession from a pecuniary point, as well as otherwise. He is a member of the Presbyterian church, and in his social and religious life is held in high esteem.

CHAPTER XVII.

WASHINGTON COUNTY AND ABINGDON, VIRGINIA.

By W. K. ARMISTEAD.

The first permanent settlement made by white men, in what is now Washington county, was made about 1765, at the close, or soon after, what is known as the French and Indian war, at Black's Fort on Wolf creek, at the foot of Wolf Hills, on which now stands Abingdon, the county seat, and the oldest town west of New river and east of the Alleghany mountains.

This county was formed in 1776 from the now extinct county of Fincastle, which was divided into Montgomery, Washington and Kentucky.

There are no records of this time that give any accurate dates. It is, however, known that in 1773, there was organized a Presbyterian congregation, formed from the inhabitants of the Ebbing and Sinking Springs settlement, who called the Rev. Charles Cummings to this pastoral charge. This call was signed by one hundred and thirty-eight heads of families, who must have represented a many times greater number of inhabitants then in the county. Many of the names of those who signed this call are still represented by their descendants both here and in many of the States West and South, and these names have been borne by men and women who, by their exalted lives, have shown themselves worthy of so brave and honest an ancestry. From these earliest settlers come the Blackburns, Buchanans, Edmistons, Vances, Davises, Campbells, Cummings, Craigs, Lowreys, Fulkersons, Montgomerys, Gambles, Berrys, Carsons, Kellys, Newells, Houstons and many others.

This county occupied a part of the Valley of Virginia, between the Iron and Holston Mountains (geologically a part of the Blue Ridge range) on the south, and the Clinch Mountains, a part of the Alleghany range, on the north. It is one of the largest and richest counties of the State, and is in latitude 36° 30' to 36° 52', and is bounded on the north by Clinch Mountain, separating it from Russell; east by Smyth, west by Scott and south by Johnson and Sullivan counties, Tennessee. It is watered, or rather drained, by the north, middle and south forks of the Holston river, which flow across the county from east to west. These streams have many tributary creeks that have their sources in the adjacent mountain ranges, and give many immense water-powers.

Washington county is in length from east to west about thirty miles, and in width about eighteen miles, giving 360,104 acres, assessed at $3,446,081; rate of taxation 50 cents on $100. Population by census of 1890, 29,021, including about 5,000 negroes. There are about fifty miles of completed railroad, assessed at $561,000. The soil runs in belts following the trend of the rock strata. Some belts are sandy or gravelly, and these are poor only in comparison with the limestone and shale belts, which are very rich. It contains, within its limits, much diversity of geological strata, topography and soil. The altitude above sea level is from 1,600 to 5,670 feet, which gives great variety of climate, timber, fruits, vegetables and farm products—wheat, corn, rye, buckwheat, oats, grasses, and tobacco of fine quality. The much prized blue-grass is indigenous and grows even to the tops of the highest mountains, giving pastorage to horses, cattle and sheep until late in the winter months, and large numbers of fat cattle and sheep are sold from the blue-grass fields of this region. With a few local exceptions, the soil is stiff clays and loams, durable and fertile. With some exceptions, all the fruits and vegetables of the temperate zone are cultivated in this county, and are unsurpassed in quality. The slopes of the mountains and hills produce excellent table and wine grapes.

The climate is salubrious and pleasant, entirely free from malaria, and subject to no extremes of heat or cold.

At Abingdon, the county seat, in winter the thermometer rarely falls to zero. The average temperature of winter being 34. In summer it does not often reach above 85, the average being about 70, and at this season the nights are always cool and refreshing, but not chilly or depressing to the most delicate constitutions. The snows are rarely deep, not often more than a few inches, and generally last but a few days, and often disappearing, except on the high mountains, within twenty-four hours. The winds from the south-west, which are very frequent in winter, follow the trend of the mountains, and bring to them and the enclosed parallel valleys the warmth and moisture of the Gulf of Mexico.

GEOLOGY.

A brief and very general outline of the geological structure of Washington county may be interesting to some from a practical point of view, and may incite to inquiries and examinations. If geology is not infallible, it at least teaches what minerals, ores, soils, timber and topography may be found on certain exposures of strata or horizons.

Beginning in the south-eastern part of the county and crossing to the north-west boundary are found the rocks of all the geological periods, and most of their subdivisions, from the upper members of the Huronian or metamorphic, to the lower members of the subcarboniferous (1 to 10, inclusive, of Rogers). The White Top, Iron and Holston mountains are formed by the strata of the Huronian and Cambrian rocks. In the sandstones, shales and clays of the Potsdam epoch are beds of iron ore (limonite) and of manganese ore, of great extent, and often of remarkable richness and purity. It is on this and the horizons of the lower members of the Silurian (1 to 2 Rogers), that are found the leads of iron, zinc and lead ores, extending through Wythe county, south-westward, far into Tennessee. Still going northward until near the North Fork of Holston river, are next found the Lower Silurian rocks (No. 111 of Rogers), mainly limestones, slates, cherts and shales.

Running entirely across the county in a south-west direction, and parallel to the mountain ranges, are many anticlinal and synclinal folds of these strata of limestones, shales and cherts. These folds form the ridges and valleys and give a varied topography, and, by erosion and decomposition of the rocks, many varieties of soil, and also bring to, or near, the surface many valuable iron and other ores. There are also brought to view many bands of very pure massive blue limestone and variegated marble, which burn to a pure white lime and makes the best flux for use in blast furnaces, and the best and most permanent fertilizer for farm and grass lands.

On the north side of the county, near to the North Fork of Holston river, there is a geological fault extending entirely across the county from east to west, by which the rocks of Lower Trenton epoch (111 Rogers) and those of subcarboniferous periods (10 of Rogers) are brought together, showing in many places small beds of inferior coal, and not in good position for mining. Along this line of fault are the fissures that hold immense beds of salt and gypsum at and near Saltville, in this and Smyth counties. North of, and lying on the subcarboniferous, and forming the Little Mountain range, and the valley between it and the Clinch Mountain, are the Devonian Rocks (9 and 8 Rogers), and descending geologically, going north, are the Upper Silurian, including the Medina sandstones (7 to 4 of Rogers), which caps and preserves the regular outline of Clinch Mountain. The iron ores of the Oriskany and Clinton epochs (7 and 5 of Rogers) are well known from Pennsylvania to Alabama, and here, as elsewhere, they vary in metallic iron and other constituents, and also in the extent and continuity of the beds or deposits, but there are unequivocal indications of a great quantity of good iron ore in this county belonging to these horizons.

RAILROADS.

The main line of the Norfolk and Western Railroad runs through this county from its eastern boundary to Bristol, on the Tennessee line, a distance of thirty miles. This great railroad company, by its many lines and branches, gives this county direct connections with all the cities and markets of the East, West, North and South, and, by its wise and liberal policy and large expenditures of capital in improving and extending its several branches, is doing much to develop the mineral, timber and agricultural wealth, and to attract the attention of capitalists to this and other counties of the South-west.

The Saltville branch leaves the main line at Glade Spring and runs to Saltville, a distance of nine miles, from which point it brings out salt, gypsum, timber, etc.

The South Atlantic and Ohio Railroad runs northward from Bristol, across this and Scott counties to Big Stone Gap in Wise county, Virginia, and there connects with the Louisville and Nashville system of railroads. Near Big Stone Gap it reaches the coking, gas and steam coals of the Virginia or Clinch Valley coal fields.

The Abingdon Coal and Iron Railroad proposes to run to the iron ores and timbers of the valley of the South Fork of the Holston and the valleys of Laurel, Beaver Dam and Shady in Tennessee on the south, and to the coal fields on the north, and is now under construction.

The Danville and East Tennessee, as surveyed, passes through the south side of the county for a distance of about thirty-five miles.

ABINGDON AND THE PRINCIPAL TOWNS AND VILLAGES.

Abingdon, the county seat of Washington county, with a population of 2,500, is situated on the main line of the Norfolk and Western Railway, more than two thousand feet above sea level, on the high rolling ridges of the great limestone valley of Virginia, lying between the vast mountains of the Appalachian chain, with a climate subject to no extremes of heat or cold. The scenery around and from the town is diversified by outlines of hills, ridges and lofty mountains, forests, valleys and well cultivated farms, with rich corn and wheat fields, and green pastures and meadow lands.

The Clinch Mountain on the north and north-west sides of the county rises over 4,000 feet, and White Top Mountain on the south-east is 5,670 feet above tide-water. This last-named mountain, which can be seen from the town, is the highest point north of North Carolina and east of the Mississippi river, and from its summit the mountains present themselves in their grandest forms. The views extend over the mountains of North Carolina, Tennessee, Kentucky and Virginia as far as the eye can see, and words fail to paint the ever-changing beauties of lights and shadows and shades of color of these grand panoramic scenes.

The people of Abingdon and vicinity have long been noted for their intelligence, refinement, cultivation and high moral worth, and have given to the State some of the leading statesmen and soldiers of the age. The names of some will never die; but who will call the roll of the many "unknown and unrecorded heroes" who sleep on the many battle-fields from Kings Mountain to Appomattox?

There are handsome churches of all denominations, large, prosperous schools, both male and female, that rank with the best, giving unusual advantages for the education of the young. The public schools are under the direction of competent teachers, and are in every way most efficient. The Abingdon Academy, established in 1803, fits young men for entering upon a university career. The Martha Washington College, Stonewall Jackson Institute and Academy of the Visitation (B. V. M.), are all most excellent schools for young ladies. The buildings are large, and in every way comfortable and well furnished. The grounds are extensive, well shaded with oaks, maples and many other varieties of trees, some of which are of unusual size and beauty. All of the schools have excellent teachers.

The town has well paved streets, which, with many stores and public buildings, are lighted by electricity, and is well supplied with pure spring water. There are two banks, one printing and newspaper office, tobacco and cigar factories, sash, door and blind factory, planing mill, wagon and carriage factories, hotels and livery stables.

For a hundred years it has been a place of large trade, and from the variety of the resources of the country around, it offers many inducements to those seeking to establish themselves in manufacturing or other business, or to find homes in an even and healthful climate, and with many and great social advantages.

BRISTOL.

It has not been many years since the place where the flourishing and rapidly improving town of Bristol now stands was known as King's Meadows. The main street is supposed to run on the boundary line between the two States, dividing the town into Bristol, Virginia, and Bristol, Tennessee.

Within the last three years Bristol has grown from a village of about 3,500 to a town with over 10,000 population. It is situated in a valley surrounded by hills and ridges, the gentle slope of some, and the steep ruggedness of others, presenting picturesque and varied scenery. This is one of the progressive towns of the great South, and in vast and varied resources, and in the enterprise and energy of its people it has no superior.

Bristol has superior religious and educational advantages. Most of the religious denominations have churches and pastors.

It has schools and colleges for both males and females. King's College is well established, and has a high reputation as a school for boys and young men.

Sullin's College for young ladies is among the good schools of the South. No town in South-west Virginia has better public schools.

It has one large Iron furnace of 150 tons daily capacity, many woodworking factories, large tobacco factories, machine and railroad repair shops, several excellent hotels, good livery-stables and all kinds of mercantile establishments, three banking houses, etc.

Most of the streets are well paved and well lighted by electricity, which is also used to operate two lines of street railway, and the town is bountifully supplied with pure water from adjacent springs. It is the terminus of four railroads, the Norfolk and Western, the East Tennesse, Virginia and Georgia, the South Atlantic and Ohio, and the Bristol and Elizabethton.

EMORY AND HENRY COLLEGE.

At the station on the Norfolk and Western Railroad known as Emory, ten miles east of Abingdon, was founded in 1838 Emory and Henry College, under the patronage of the Holston Conference of the Methodist Episcopal Church. The name was given in honor of Patrick Henry and the Rev. Bishop Emory of the Methodist Episcopal Church. The Faculty is composed of able professors and the college is in a prosperous condition. Among its graduates are many men throughout the South and West who have risen to distinction in their different professions.

GLADE SPRING.

This is a prosperous village and station on the Norfolk and Western Railroad, fifteen miles east of Abingdon. Much of the land around it is the most fertile in Virginia, and some farms are in the highest state of cultivation. It is the center of considerable trade, chiefly from the southeastern side of the county, Tennessee and North Carolina. It has an excellant hotel, good church buildings, schools, and one of the most flourishing female colleges of the South-west.

SALTVILLE.

Saltville is the terminus of the branch of the Norfolk and Western Railroad, nine miles north of Glade Spring, and eighteen miles north-east of Abingdon and near the North Fork of the Holston. It has a good hotel and good church and school buildings. The village is divided by the line that separates this from Smyth county, and the valley in which it is situated is of remarkable beauty and fertility, and in its salt and gypsum is one of the richest in America. These beds of salt and gypsum seem to be exhaustless in extent, and are of the purest quality.

The brine from which salt is manufactured comes from a bed of rock-salt, into which vertical borings have been made 170 feet without reaching the bottom of the deposit, and is known to underlay several hundred acres around Saltville. During the late war between the States 10,000 bushels of salt was made daily for six months without showing any decrease in quality or quantity of the brine.

The immense quantity of cheap salt, and the close proximity to good and cheap coal and sulphurets (iron and cupreous pyrites) and limestones, make this the most available point in America for the manufacture of soda-ash and alkalies—an important industry, but not yet found in the United States.

The gypsum (commonly called plaster) covers an area in this and Smyth county many miles in length, and in this distance many shafts have been sunk, one of which is 580 feet in vertical depth without reaching the bottom of its extent, and at this point it is more than 2,000 feet in width. The condition of the gypsum is either that of a fibrous crystalline mass or a granular bluish veined rock of nearly perfect purity. Besides other uses, perhaps there is no better fertilizer for corn, grass and cotton, and as a permanent improver of the soil. At Buena Vista the gypsum has been extensively mined for many years, and sold in its native state or ground into a fine powder by the mill on the property. This mill is capable of turning out sixty tons daily.

DAMASCUS.

The site of Damascus is 2,100 feet above sea-level, in a beautiful valley formed by Laurel creek, a large tributary of the South Fork of the Holston. In this valley the Beaver Dam and White Top creeks unite with the Laurel, and have cut through the Iron Mountain nearly to the level of the main valley. The area drained by these three streams and their branches is about thirty-five miles from east to west and fifteen miles north to south, making 525 square miles. Three-fourths of this area is in original forest of the most valuable hardwood and white pine timber, and it also carries beds of limonite (hydrated peroxide of iron) that will rank with the largest in America, and also on certain horizons of the Cambrian period are beds of manganese ore (pyrolusite) of large extent and very pure.

These streams give many large and constant water-powers that do not run dry in summer or freeze in winter. It is near the Tennessee line and fifteen miles south-east of Abingdon.

Damascus occupies the only water-gap in the Iron-Holston mountain range from New river on the east, to the Watauga river on the south-west, a distance of more than one hundred miles. And the many railroads from the South Atlantic coast seeking to reach the great coal fields of Virginia, and to connect with the many systems of railroad reaching into the West and North-west, and also all local railroads to develop and bring together over easiest grades and shortest haul, coke, coal, and Bessemer and other iron ores, manganese and copper ores and timber must, per force, come through this same Damascus Gap.

Here can be successfully established furnaces, rolling-mills, saw-mills, paper pulp and paper-mills and large tanneries, and many other industries.

MENDOTA

is a village on the South Atlantic and Ohio Railroad where it crosses the North Fork of the Holston river, fifteen miles north of Bristol and twenty-two miles north-west of Abingdon.

There is here a large and constant water-power, and large and frequent exposures of good iron ores in the Clinch and Little Mountains. It is fifty miles by railroad to the coal field. It is surrounded by rich farming, grass and timber lands, and is most favorably situated for successful iron furnaces, saw-mills, tanneries and other manufacturing establishments. It has a large trade in timber, lumber and tobacco and other products from the neighboring country. The tobacco of this section is of high grade and fetches the highest prices.

It is noted for its excellent high school under the control of accomplished teachers.

MEADOW VIEW.

Meadow View, a station on the Norfolk and Western Railroad, eight miles east of Abingdon, is a flourishing village, surrounded by a fertile and well cultivated country.

Greendale, six miles north, and Friendship, twelve miles east, of Abingdon, and Montgomery's and Wallace's Stations on the Norfolk and Western Railroad west of Abingdon, are places of considerable trade in lumber, oak tan-bark and farm products.

The county has many mineral and medicinal springs—Mongle's White Sulphur, nine miles north-west of Abingdon, and the Alum Wells near Mendota, both on the North Fork of the Holston; the Seven Springs and Washington Springs, both being within one and a half miles northward of Glade Spring. These springs, besides many others in this county, are noted for the curative properties of their waters, and have much more than a local reputation.

It is not claimed that Washington county has within its limits a greater variety and larger quantity of ores and coal, or a better climate and more fertile soil than other counties of South-west Virginia and parts of other States, but it is claimed, and can be clearly demonstrated, that this county has a large quantity of good iron ores, manganese ore and timber, salt, gypsum, marble, great water-powers, good climate, productive soils,. and an intelligent, industrious and moral population. And from its geographical position, topography and water-courses, that it lies, by easy grade railway routes, directly between the coking, gas and steam coals on the north (30 miles), and the immense beds of limonite (hydrated peroxide of iron) and red and magnetic iron ore to the south, south-east and south-west (10 to 40 miles) in this and other States.

The limonite and the zinc and lead ores of Smyth and Wythe counties, Virginia, and the strictly Bessemer ores and copper ores of Ashe, Watauga and Mitchell counties, North Carolina, can reach coal over easier grades and shorter distances through Washington county than by any other route. For convenience only, take Abingdon as a centre, it is, by a surveyed line, forty miles to the best coking coal; and to the Bessemer ores (on the Cranberry lead and equally good) in Ashe county, North Carolina, the distance from Abingdon is forty miles. The Bessemer ores of this county are from four to ten miles from Abingdon. The limonite of Johnson and Sullivan counties, Tennessee, are ten to thirty miles. The iron ores (limonites) of Clinch Mountain (Oriskany, No. 7, Rogers) are from twenty to thirty miles from coking coal, and ten to twenty miles from Abingdon.

It would be useless to here give estimates of the cost of making pig-iron in this county, as every iron-master knows the cost depends very much upon how a furnace is run, and not alone on the cost of material. But it cannot be disputed that with good and cheap ores, fuel and flux, and cheap and efficient labor, under good management, and having all the materials within the shortest haul over easy grades, and not far from, and with transportation to, the points of consumption of the products, there must follow, not only the cheapest, but the largest iron and steel production of the world.

This is a part, not of the New South, but a great county of a great State of the great South. We of the South are standing but on the threshold of the beginning of grand commercial and industrial progress and achievements in which Virginia will take her part. No wonder we are proud of our past history, and no wonder we look with confident expectation to a brilliant future, when we consider all we have of moral force in the purity of our women and in the honesty and courage of our men, as well as in the magnificent resources and healthful climate, many lines of railway and numberless and matchless harbors, in which the ships of the world can find anchorage and safety. And when the prediction of her future wealth and greatness shall come to pass, Washington county will be able to say, we, too, have added our share to the wealth and glory.

Hon. **JOHN A. BUCHANAN,** the subject of this mention, is a resident of Abingdon, Virginia, and was born October 7th, 1843. He served as a private in the Stonewall Brigade, Confederate service, and was taken prisoner at Gettysburg, July 3d, 1863, and remained in prison until February, 1865. He is a graduate of Emory and Henry College, Emory, Virginia, graduating in June, 1870. He studied law in the University of Virginia in 1870–'71, and is an attorney of distinguished ability and of high repute in the legal profession. He was a member of the House of Delegates of Virginia from 1885 to 1887, and was elected to the 51st and re-elected to the 52d Congress.

Mr. Buchanan is a man of marked ability and individuality, and has already made for himself an enviable name and reputation in his profession, as well as in the political field.

PAUL C. LANDRUM, the present Mayor of Abingdon, was born in Amherst county, Virginia, on the 22d day of November, 1839, and came to Abingdon in 1857. He carried on the business of a retail druggist until the breaking out of the war in 1861, when he enlisted in the first company of volunteers organized in the county, under Capt. William E. Jones, which company afterwards became Company D of the 1st Virginia Cavalry Regiment. He served through the entire war in this company, was wounded twice and captured once. On one occasion he encountered five Union soldiers in a hand-to-hand engagement, unhorsing three of them and putting the other two to flight. For this daring exploit he was publicly complimented by his Colonel. After the surrender he returned to Abingdon and entered into the mercantile business, which he prosecuted successfully for a number of years. He was married in June, 1867, to Miss Theodosia F. Mitchell, daughter of John D. and Eliza F. Mitchell, of Abingdon. In 1875, in partnership with G. V. Litchfield, Esq., he purchased a controlling interest in the celebrated Seven Springs, of "Iron-Alum Mass" fame, and engaged in the manufacture of a "salts" known as the "Iron-Alum Mass" from the waters of these valuable springs, the medicinal properties of which have almost a world-wide reputation for their healing and curative virtues in the treatment of chronic, constitutional and organic diseases. It is highly recommended and prescribed by physicians generally, which gives to these springs and the "Mass" prepared from their waters quite a commercial value, and an extensive sale of the "salts" and waters.

He was a member of the Town Council for several years, and in 1890 was elected by the council to fill out an unexpired term of Mayor, and afterwards elected by the citizens without opposition, which responsible position he now occupies.

The Mayor is an ardent Mason and Knight of Honor, a trustee of the Martha Washington College (a flourishing female institution), a steward of the Methodist Episcopal Church, South, and one of the directors of the Abingdon Coal and Iron Railroad Company. He is polite and affable, and enjoys the respect and confidence of all good citizens.

Miss HUNT, Principal of Stonewall Jackson Institute, was prepared for her responsible position by a thorough collegiate course under the celebrated Dr. Jas. B. Ramsey, a course in the methods of teaching, at the Virginia State Normal School, where she ranked highest in the school of practice, and has had a most successful experience in public and private schools, and at the head of other institutions of learning. She has introduced the most approved methods into this school, and with liberal aid from the trustees in adding to the buildings, furnishing them handsomely, supplying all needed apparatus, and employing teachers of the highest standing, the school has been placed on as high a plane as any in the State.

Col. A. F. COOK, the subject of this sketch, was born April 10th, 1830, at Buchanan, Botetourte county, Virginia. He received his education at Buchanan, and in 1856 went to New Mexico, where until 1861 he engaged in trade with the natives, at which time he returned home to take part in the struggle then coming on. He entered the service as Lieutenant of a cavalry company organized in Smyth county, and known as the Smyth Dragoons. Lieutenant Cook was detailed as Commissary, the company being attached to the 8th Virginia Regiment of Cavalry at its formation. At the reorganization of the regiment in 1862, Lieutenant Cook was made Lieutenant Colonel. In September, 1862, at Buchanan, West Virginia, Colonel Cook was shot through the thigh and captured by the Union forces. He was sent to Camp Chase, where he remained one month, and was then sent to Vicksburg and exchanged, immediately resuming his old command. In February, 1864, he received his commission from the War Department as Colonel, the former Colonel of the regiment being retired. In January, 1865, he was wounded in a skirmish at Beverly, and again made a prisoner, losing his leg from the wound. While on duty, which resulted in the loss of his leg, his commission as Brigadier General of Cavalry was forwarded from Richmond to General Lee's headquarters, but Colonel Cook being not only a prisoner, but also wounded, he never received his commission, as it was given over with all other papers at the surrender of Lee. It was nearly two years after the war before he recovered his health, when he came to Abingdon, and after his marriage, in 1870, went to Smyth county and engaged in farming and sheep raising. After eleven years of this occupation he returned to Abingdon and started a large planing-mill, which he at this present time very successfully operates. The Colonel has been an extensive and observant traveler, and possesses a mind well stored with useful as well as entertaining information. He has no children, only by adoption. He is a member of the Town Council, and the nomination for the Legislature has been repeatedly offered him.

CHAPTER XVIII.

PULASKI, VIRGINIA.

By ADISON A. CHRISTIAN.

More than half a century ago, when Martin Van Buren sat President of the United States, or, to come to dates, in 1839, on a bright morning in May, there flocked to the village of Newbern an unusually large number of citizens, drawn either by business or curiosity. Among those on business bent were: John G. Cecil, Randolph Fugate, Henry Wysor, John Calfee, James Crockett, George R. C. Floyd, Samuel Calfee, Joseph Cloyd, James Hoge, Samuel Shields, John Hoge, Joseph H. Howe, David T. Martin, David F. Kent, David G. Shepherd, John McTaylor, Robert Preston, Wm. B. Charlton, Benjamin Rush Floyd, Benjamin F. Wysor, David L. Summers, John Caddall, Bobt. Gibboney, James L. Yost, James F. Preston, Richard T. Matthews, James Edmonson, Alfred C. Moore, Henry Nance and others.

What means the upstir? Surely no dastardly crime has roused the populace! No; in those good days grave crimes were almost unknown in the beautiful South-west. Surely war is not inflaming men's minds, for this spring morning antedates the dread spring of 1861 by twenty-two years! No; it is a mission of peace; fraught, however, with wonderful interest. Pulaski county was just setting up housekeeping on its own account. Having been formed of territory lopped off of Montgomery and Wythe, it behooved her people to create a tribunal for the arbitrament of the differences prone to arise between man and man, and to maintain the dignity of this new-born county through the meteing out of justice and the preserving of the peace among the 3,739 souls then dwelling within its borders, and their posterity.

From the following records we read of the first court of justice ever held in Pulaski county:

"Virginia: At a court begun and held for the county of Pulaski (not at the court-house, but) at the house of Joseph Tiffany, in the town of Newbern in said county, on Thursday, the 9th day of May, 1839, pursuant to the act of the General Assembly, the 30th day of March, 1839. A commission of the peace from the Governor of this Commonwealth, dated the 8th day of April, 1839, directed to the first sixteen persons above named, whereupon they took the several oaths required by law as Justices of the Peace, which were administered by Robert Preston, a Justice of the Peace for the county of Montgomery, whereupon they took their seats as Justices of the Peace of this county.

"Thus, at first our county courts were constituted by plain, simple, yet sensible country gentlemen, and to this day many there may be found who gravely doubt the expediency of superseding the court of gentlemen Justices by the court held as now by a Judge learned in the law. Among the divers duties of this first court was that of electing county officers. Robert Gibbony was appointed Sheriff *pro tempore*, thereupon names were placed in nomination for Sheriff, and Samuel Shields was elected. For Clerk, William Charlton, receiving the largest vote, being a majority, was declared Clerk. Next, Benjamin F. Wysor, Benjamin R. Floyd and David L. Summers were nominated for Commonwealth's Attorney, and the vote stood as follows: Floyd, 9; Summers, 3; Wysor, 2; and thus Benjamin R. Floyd became our first Attorney for the Commonwealth. After the election of other officers, the following attorneys qualified to practice law in said court, to-wit, Jas. L. Yost, Benj. R. Floyd, James F. Preston, Benj. F. Wysor, Richard T. Matthews, David L. Summers, James Edmonson and Alfred C. Moore. Whereupon the court, after a busy day's session, adjourned until next morning at nine o'clock."

Of all the men mentioned, it seems that General Alfred C. Moore longest survived, he having died at Wytheville March 16th, 1890, at the age of eighty-two.

Pulaski county is twenty-three miles long with a mean width of eighteen miles, and is watered by New river and scores of busy little streams and rills now purling over their rocky beds or rushing with mighty force under the impetus of mountain declivity when fed by copious showers. The county is rich in mineral and woods. At Altoona and Belle Hampton large seams of semi-anthracite coal are being worked, while iron ore abounds almost everywhere. Chalybeate and alum springs are numerous, the Pulaski Alum Springs being noted for their curative qualities, making the place, which is on the north side of the county, the Mecca of invalids, as well as the sojourning place of the country's beauty and society.

On New river, some two and a half miles from Newbern, the Glass Windows rise some 300 feet above the water and form the river's bank for a considerable distance. They are a vertical range of rocks indented by many crevices, the whole to fancy's eye appearing as vast windows.

The soil of the county, especially

on the northern side, is extremely fertile and in most parts of the county blue grass is indigenous. While the cereals do well, and in the south-eastern part tobacco is grown to some extent, the raising of cattle has always been the chief business of the agriculturist. This industry has had to share honors with horse raising, and of late years sheep are increasing rapidly, the climate and general conditions being perfect for bringing sheep to the highest perfection in fleece and flesh. The growth of the sheep industry may be seen by a comparison of the flocks of three seasons: In 1890 there were 6,630 sheep in the county; a year later there were 10,500 and by the spring of 1892 there will be fully 20,000 ewes in the county. Sheep products netted our farmers over $50,000 in 1891.

Among the county records I found an old compendium of the census, giving the first count of our people as a county. The analysis of the population of 3,739 was as follows: Whites, 2,768; slaves, 954; free colored, 17; employed in agriculture, 1,525; manufactures and trades, 142. Six are classed as "learned professors and engineers." Three received pensions for Revolutionary services. There was but one deaf-mute, two blind persons and two insane among the whites, and one deaf-mute among the negroes. While there were but seven public schools, there were only 135 persons in the county above 20 years of age that could not read and write.

Until 1886 Newbern, the county seat, and Dublin, on the Norfolk and Western Railroad, remained the only towns, though flourishing villages existed at Snowville, New River and Churchwood.

The year 1886, however, brought a new town into being which has eclipsed them all.

PULASKI.

But a few years have passed since the straggling passengers on the far-between trains gave little heed to the stop at Martin's Tank. A dozen years ago a store struggled into existence and made both ends meet, with some lap, by trading in bark, produce and cross-ties. Through the surrounding country scattered charcoal furnaces turned out their mite of varying high-grade iron, the Lobdell Car Wheel Company, of Wilmington, Delaware, still making the iron for its excellent products in the mountains of South-west Virginia.

But the beginning of a new era, destined to drag slowly at first, dawned the day after the election of the lamented Garfield, when ground was broken for a zinc furnace. So favorable were the elements to this project that brick-work was done for ninety consecutive days during the winter of 1880–'81. This little beginning, which was bought out in its inception for $45,000, has grown to the great Bertha Zinc Works, of which I shall speak further.

As I said, the awakening was slow,

but a 1000-acre farm was bought by Philadelphia capitalists, engineers were put to work to plat a city, and on the 5th of October, 1886, the first building lot in the town evolved by the Legislature from Martin's Tank to Pulaski was bought by Enoch Phillips. The good work went on, and eminent geologists were employed by the Norfolk and Western Railroad to spy out the land tributary to this infant city. They discovered a wealth of mineral that made a report reading like a fairy tale and proved that this section could, intelligently developed, better support cities than it had charcoal furnaces with their wasteful methods. The great Pocahontas coal field was likewise developed, and the future manufacturing city of the South-west was put on an unbeatable basis. This section proved to be just full of opportunities for money, brains and brawn, and the railroad company built and equipped Maple Shade Inn at a cost of $40,000 for the comfort of prospectors and capitalists. This hotel, a gem of architecture and cuisine, has had fifty more rooms added, and has been improved until the property now stands its owners $125,000. The Pulaski Land and Improvement Company is now completing a very fine hotel to cost $50,000.

THE PULASKI LAND AND IMPROVEMENT COMPANY

proceeded to make its property inviting by laying out streets and avenues, the latter named for the Presidents to whom the old Commonwealth has given birth. The company is now completing water-works at a cost of $40,000. Property owners on the south side of the railroad were not slow to accept the changed conditions, and not only commenced individual projects of improvement, but in March, 1887, formed the

SWANSEA LAND COMPANY,

into which $50,000 was at once placed. This company only had about one hundred acres, but it went to work right heartily, and, as if to help the good time, the struggling zinc works was re-organized and capitalized at $3,000,000 as

THE BERTHA ZINC WORKS.

Its furnaces were increased and vast deposits of low-grade coal were made available by a narrow-gauge railroad. This company now runs ten furnaces, turning out spelter that is named as the standard in the proposals by the United States mints. Its output is about 4,500,000 pounds annually, valued at $350,000. The company's pay-roll averages about $20,000 per month, and 675 names appear on the pay-roll. In the same year, 1887,

THE PULASKI IRON COMPANY

was formed with a paid-up capital of $300,000 (which has since been increased to $400,000), and erected a hot-blast furnace which went in blast on the 9th of February, 1888, and has proven highly successful.

By the close of 1887 there were 172 dwellings, three hotels and numerous business houses, with an attendant population of 1,600. During this same year a bank was organized under the title of

THE PULASKI LOAN AND TRUST COMPANY,

with $50,000 capital. It was a success from its inception, and has paid an annual dividend of ten per cent., besides placing aside, a snug surplus fund.

THE PULASKI NATIONAL BANK

opened for business July 8, 1889, with a capital of $50,000, and is doing a heavy, but safe business. Its stock is now worth 131.

THE LAKE SPRING LAND COMPANY

owns a pretty expanse of 250 acres, and is capitalized at $200,000. The property is very valuable, and operations are active. But it remains for

THE MARTIN LAND COMPANY,

organized with the close of the year 1889, to come to the front as a money-maker. Its lots are quite rolling, and offer many pretty sites for residences. Two of the gentlemen forming the company that brought this property into market have sold their holdings, receiving in one case $6,000, and in the last transaction $6,250, for the shaces which had cost them $521.15, or 1,200 per cent.

THE PULASKI DEVELOPMENT COMPANY,

formed in 1890, bought 837 acres, known as the Bohanan tract, and soon added 11,000 acres of valuable mineral land on and contiguous to the Cripple Creek Railroad, or the North Carolina Extension, as it is now known. On this property 353 lots were sold for $151,065 in one afternoon. A one hundred and fifty-ton furnace, a counterpart of the Pulaski Iron Company's furnace, is nearly ready to go in blast.

The town ranges from 1,916 to 2,080 feet above sea-level, and enjoys, according to Lieutenant Greely, of the Signal Service, the distinction of lying immediately in the small area offering the finest summer climate in the Union, while the winters are not objectionable, being thickly diffused with days of brightest sunshine. No night during last summer did the mercury register above 75° at ten o'clock. Is it any wonder, then, that with its advantage of location, its substantial start, its moneyed backing, its handsome houses, good churches, splendid schools and thrifty, warm-hearted people that Pulaski is called

THE GEM OF THE MOUNTAINS?

Pulaski might also be called a city of churches. Six denominations, viz., Presbyterian, Episcopal, Lutheran,

Methodist, Baptist and Christian, have either completed, or in course of construction, handsome church edifices, while the colored race have their Baptist and Methodist churches.

Pulaski's public school building, with its commanding site, is worth $17,000. It is an architectural beauty, and is constructed according to the most approved sanitary plans. Numerous private schools within the town, and contiguous seats of higher learning contribute to the advantages of the place.

Pulaski has two newspapers. The *News* has done yeoman service for the town since it was first conceived, having been removed to the town site from Newbern. The *Review* is a new journalistic venture, succeeding an earlier co-laborer with the *News*, known as the *Advertiser*. Both papers are handsomely gotten up, and are doing good work for the town. The population of the town July 1, 1891, was 3,475.

Major W. F. NICHOLSON.—Judge Isaac R. Nicholson, the father of Major W. F. Nicholson, was a Judge of the Supreme Court of Mississippi for many years, and was well known throughout the State as a man of rare judicial acumen. Major W. F. Nicholson, the subject of this short biography, was born in Clinton, Mississippi, September 19th, 1842. He was educated at the University of Virginia, leaving there in 1861, before finishing his course, to enlist in the 1st Louisiana Battalion, in which he served one year, at the end of which time he was made Captain of Company B, 3d Kentucky Regiment, under the famous Gen. John H. Morgan. During the remainder of the war he served with that command, having passed through many interesting incidents and experiences. At the close of the war he took up his residence at Pulaski, and carried on farming until 1889, when Pulaski having begun its upward course, Major Nicholson gave up farming and became one of the promoters and organizers of the Pulaski National Bank, the only National Bank between Roanoke and Bristol. The bank was organized with a capital of $50,000, and is doing at the present time a business of $250,000 a year. The Major was elected its cashier, and much of its prosperity and success has been due to his good management and business tact. He is President of the Pierce Investment Company and Midvale Land Company, and is a stockholder in several others. He was Supervisor of Pulaski county for several years, and Mayor of Pulaski City. He was also magistrate at one time. In 1868 he married Miss Mary C. Bentley of Powhatan county, a daughter of Dr. Bentley, a leading physician of that section. Six children have been born to them. The Major is an elder in the Presbyterian church. He is a man who is well liked, genial, frank and outspoken, and yet always considerate of the feelings of others. His life is a busy one, but he makes his business and cares an element in his enjoyment and happiness.

B. E. WATSON, Esq.—Among the prominent real estate dealers of Pulaski may be mentioned B. E. Watson, Esq. He was born July 27th, 1847, in Pulaski county. His father, Dr. Edwin Watson, was for over twenty-five years a successful physician of the same county, and was twice a member of the Legislature.

B. E. Watson, the subject of this sketch, was educated at the Virginia Military Institute and at Emory and Henry College. Served as courier during the latter part of the war on Gen. James A. Walker's staff, and was with him during the battles around Richmond and Petersburg. After the surrender he returned home, and when Emory and Henry College was reorganized he entered again as student, and prosecuted his studies until the year 1867, when he left college for the farm, where he remained until 1869, when he commenced the life of a merchant at Pulaski, then known as Martin's, and was pioneer in that particular branch of business at that place.

In 1883 he was offered a position in the auditor's department of the East Tennessee and Georgia Railroad, and continued in its service until 1888, when he made Pulaski his home again, and became a member of the real estate firm of Langhorne, Watson & Co. He is now associated with Mr. Frank Harrison at the same place and in the same business, under the firm name of Harrison, Watson & Co., and is enjoying the respect and confidence of a large and increasing circle of patrons, and the warm friendship of a host of those who have known and honored him from boyhood in this the home of his fathers.

He is the diligent and faithful agent of the Lake Spring Land Company, and a member of the Presbyterian church.

J. E. MOORE, Esq., attorney at law, was born July 23d, 1851, at Marion, Virginia. He received his education in the schools of Marion, and at an early age entered the employ of Capt. D. D. Hull, first as clerk and later as book-keeper, and while occupying this position he began the reading of Law with Judge Richard. About the time he was ready to be admitted to the Bar, he entered the ministry and was pastor of the Methodist church at Newbern, Virginia, for two years, and at Athens, Tennessee, for two years. At the end of that time, his health having failed him, he returned to Virginia and settled at Newbern and was admitted to the

Bar in 1882 and began the practice of law in partnership with John B. Baskerville, a lawyer of considerable prominence. This partnership continued until 1884, when it was dissolved, and Mr. Moore removed to Pulaski and opened an office in that place and began practice. In 1887 he was elected to the State Legislature to represent Pulaski and Giles counties and served one term, retiring at its expiration. In March, 1890, Judge R. M. Brown resigned his position as Judge of the Circuit Court to enter into a partnership with Mr. Moore under the firm name of Brown & Moore, and since the formation of the partnership have been doing the largest law business of any firm in the county. Mr. Moore is also Vice-President and manager of the Pulaski Loan and Trust Company, and is a heavy stockholder in a number of other companies. He was married in 1880 to Miss Blanche B. Baskerville, a daughter of J. B. Baskerville, Esq., at that time a prominent lawyer at Newbern, but at the present time Mayor of Pulaski. Mr. and Mrs. Moore have four children, John B., William E., Mary and Frederick. Mr. Moore is local elder of the Methodist church of Pulaski and superintendent of the Sunday-school; also President of the Y. M. C. A. of the same city. He has a beautiful home, situated on Fifth street, surrounded with trees and having a full and fine view of Pulaski and the mountains.

MAURICE D. LANGHORNE, Esq., was born August 16th, 1847, in Roanoke county, Virginia. His father, Mr. John A. Langhorne, was a farmer and a prominent Free-mason, having been Master of the Lakeland Lodge at Roanoke. Maurice D., the subject of this sketch, was educated at the Virginia Military Institute, and was a member of the class of '64-'65 until he went into active service during the latter part of the civil war, and was in the battle of New Market with the entire Cadet Corps of the Military Institute. While in the trenches at Richmond the corps was offered the privilege of disbanding and joining other branches of the army, and, having decided to disband, did so; but before they could join the commands the surrender had been made and they returned home. Our subject then engaged in farming, which he continued until 1889, when he came to Pulaski and formed the real estate firm of Langhorne, Watson & Co., which existed until November, 1890, at which time Mr. Watson retired and Mr. W. L. McGavock was admitted to the firm in his place, the firm name of the partnership now being Langhorne, McGavock & Co., which, at the present time, is doing a large and successful business. Mr. Langhorne is also President of the Pulaski Real Estate Exchange. He was married in 1877 to Miss Maggie Kent, of Pulaski county. They have two children. Mr. Langhorne is a member of the Presbyterian church of Dublin, Pulaski county, and is also an elder in the same. He is a man who is highly and justly respected by all who know him, and finds his greatest good and happiness in the precept of the golden rule.

———:◆:———

Capt. THOMAS JONES.—The father of Capt. Thomas Jones, David Jones, Esq., was a boiler contractor and machinist of Bristol, England, doing a large business throughout England and Wales. His son, Capt. Thomas Jones, was born June 24th, 1840, in Bristol, and was educated at Brown's College, Swansea, Wales. After leaving school he engaged in the smelting business at Swansea, smelting silver and zinc ores principally. He remained in the firm of Vivian & Sons seven years, when he engaged with the Sieman-Martin Steel Works at Laudore, Wales, smelting under the open-hearth process. After being in their employ three years, he went to Kausdorff, Saxony, and again engaged in steel smelting, as well as at other places in Germany and Austria. After two years he returned to Wales and remained there a short time, when he came to the United States, settling in Providence, Rhode Island, taking employment with the Rumford Chemical Works, erecting for them steel works, and operating them for five years, at the end of which time he made a zinc plant outside of Providence, personally carrying on the business for five years, when he organized a company and built the Bertha Zinc Works at Pulaski, Virginia, which are the most extensive in the country, the company representing a capital of $3,000,000. This plant has furnished the United States government with all the zinc made in their mints for the manufacture of specie. Mr. Jones has acted as superintendent ever since the erection of the works, notwithstanding that he is a large stockholder in the concern. He is a member of the Council of Pulaski, and is organizer and director of the Swansea Land Company, and organizer and director of the Pulaski Loan and Trust Company, and is prominent in all enterprises that tend to the growth and development of the city. He was married in 1861 to Miss Mary A. James, the daughter of a large contractor and builder of Swansea, Wales. Seven children have been born to them. He is a member of the Methodist church at Pulaski, and belongs to the order of Odd Fellows and the English Branch of Foresters.

———:◆:———

Dr. C. E. C. PEYTON was born January 5th, 1855, at Charlottesville, Virginia. His father, Major Green Peyton, was Treasurer of the University of Virginia at that place, and served on General Rhode's Staff during the war. He was a civil engineer by profession, and was one of the engineers who laid out and surveyed the Norfolk and Western Railroad. Dr. Peyton was educated at the University of Virginia and at the University of the City of New York, graduating in 1867, and began the practice of his profession in Montgomery county, removing to Pulaski in 1879. He was the first physician to locate there, and by careful and conscientious work has succeeded in building up a large and lucrative practice. He is surgeon for the Norfolk and Western Railroad at Pulaski, and surgeon of the 2d Regiment of Virginia Infantry, with rank of Major. This regiment is composed of survivors and sons of survivors of Stonewall Jackson's famous brigade, and is one of the best of Virginia's Volunteer regiments. The Doctor was married in 1879 to Miss Elizabeth Kendrick of Montgomery county, the daughter of a prominent farmer.

L. S. CALFEE, Esq., of Pulaski, the subject of this mention, was born June 6th, 1839. He was educated in the schools of the county, and farmed as an occupation. In 1861 he enlisted in Company F, 54th Virginia Infantry, and served until he was captured in the battle of Bentonville, North Carolina, and taken to Point Lookout, Maryland, where he was kept prisoner until July, 1865. When released he returned home and began farming again, but in 1868 he entered the mercantile business at Reed Island. Here he remained four years, when, on the 1st of January, 1873, he commenced business at Pulaski, then Martin's Station, with his brothers, under the firm name of Calfee Brothers, doing a general merchandise business, it being the first store in Pulaski. In 1880 he took the contract for hauling the zinc from the mines to the famous Bertha Zinc Works, and continued in this business up to 1885, at which time, the railroad being completed, he discontinued the contract. He then turned his attention to the development of Pulaski's interests, and has been at the head of a number of its most prominent and promising enterprises. It is to him that the town of Pulaski owes much of its present prosperity, and, in fact, it is to him that it is indebted for its real business existence. He is a man of great and unusual versatility, and possesses the genius of being able to fill varied positions with equal ability and efficiency. He is a member of the City Council, wherein he finds opportunity to serve the city with constant and practical devotion. He was married, in 1875, to Miss Ella M. Martin, daughter of Major R. D. Martin, who owned the property on which Pulaski is now built.

ADDISON A. CHRISTIAN was born in the city of Philadelphia on the 4th day of March, 1860. His father,

Rev. L. H. Christian, D. D., was pastor of what was at that time the second largest Presbyterian church in Philadelphia. Dr. Christian had married Miss Mary Catherine Ker, daughter of Samuel Ker, M. D., of Somerset county, Maryland, who was a great-grandson of Walter Ker, one of the faithful who was forced to leave Scotland for his faith's sake, and who reached America about the same time that Francis McKenzie, the father of Presbyterianism in America, commenced his labors in the new world.

Dr. Christian dying in 1864, mother and son returned to Eastern Maryland, where their relatives are among the most prominent families. The climate not suiting the child, who was very frail, they moved to Pennsylvania, where he was raised among the hills of Montgomery county amid good educational advantages, though he never went to college. Early in life he evinced a fondness for printing and newspaper work, and six weeks before his twentieth birthday he had mastered the printing trade and set up a business for himself at Greensborough, Caroline county, Maryland, where he established the *Free Press*, now the most valuable newspaper property in the county.

In 1885 Mr. Christian married Miss Minnie, third daughter of William C. Satterfield, a wealthy citizen of Greensborough, and a year later he partially withdrew from the newspaper business and formed a co-partnership with his father-in-law in the mercantile and lumber business. While remunerative, this business was alien to his natural bent, and in the fall of 1887 he sold out all his Maryland interests, resigned his office as Justice of the Peace, to which Governor McLane had appointed him at the age of twenty-five, and removed to Pulaski, where he purchased the *Pulaski News*, which under his management has become possibly the leading county paper of the State. Mr. Christian is a keen business man as well as a pleasant writer, and his undertakings have always been successful.

His home life is most happy, though free from any shadow of ostentation. Two daughters have blessed this union.

CHAPTER XIX.

SMYTH COUNTY, VIRGINIA.

By B. F. BUCHANAN.

Smyth county was formed from Wythe and Washington counties by act of the General Assembly of Virginia, approved February 23d, 1832.

The first Court was held at the house of John Thomas, Esq., at the "Royal Oak," April 2d, 1832, by the Justices designated in the act of Assembly, viz.: Charles Tate, James Taylor, Samuel Williams, Geo. W. Davis, Hatch D. Poston, Joseph Atkins, Henry B. Thompson, Wm. Porter, Thompson Atkins, Robt. Houston, Joseph P. Bonham, Abram B. Trigg and Isaac Spratt.

Their first duty, and the only one performed at this sitting, was the election of a Clerk, for which position Geo. T. Lansdowne, James C. Spotts, Robert Beattie and Joseph W. Davis, were candidates. After several ballots Robert Beattie was elected. He chose as his deputy James F. Pendleton, who succeeded his principal in office, and in turn was succeeded by the present incumbent, Wm. C. Sexton. So that in a period of sixty years the county has had but three Clerks of the County Court.

At a subsequent term of the Court, Chas. E. Harrison was appointed Attorney for the Commonwealth, Joseph W. Davis, Sheriff, and Charles C. Taylor Surveyor. These were the county's first officers. All of the original Justices are now dead. The last one, Robert Houston, having died in 1883. Several of them lived to be eighty-five years of age, and two or three passed their ninetieth year. The first Grand Jury for the county was composed of Thomas Tate, Thomas Crow, Joseph T. Crow, Henry E. Sprinkle, John Houston, Joel Hubble, Samuel Graham, Patrick Buchanan, Wilson Buchanan, William McPhatridge, Berry St. John, Adam Cullop, Thomas McCready, John M. Campbell, Wm. Sanders, Adam Fox and Nathaniel Harris. They made four indictments, all for fighting.

BOUNDARIES.

Smyth county is bounded on the north by Tazewell county, the line running on top of Brushy Mountain from the east to the Laurel Gap, thence on the spurs of Clinch Mountain to the Washington county line;

on the south by Grayson county, along the Iron Mountains and the White Top Range; on the east by Wythe county, and on the west by Washington county.

The average width of the county from north to south is about twenty-eight miles, and from east to west about twenty-two miles. The area being about 375,000 acres.

The county is divided, politically, into three Magisterial Districts—No. 1, Marion District; No. 2, Rich Valley District; No. 3, St. Clair District. These districts also mark the natural or geographical divisions of the county into as many valleys, through which flow the three forks of the Holston river, the head-waters or sources of said rivers all being within the limits of the county. The northern, or Rich Valley District, is separated from the middle, or Marion District, by Walker's Mountain, and possesses lands of great fertility, blue-grass being indigenous and growing as luxuriantly and spontaneously as in any blue-grass region in the world. Large herds of the finest short-horn cattle are grazed in this valley, and exported annually to Great Britain. Some of the largest grazers in Virginia live in this valley, and their cattle are unrivalled. Large flocks of sheep are also kept, and pay handsome returns.

Col. George W. Palmer, of this valley, has an estate of some 6,000 acres, on which he grazes the largest herd of registered short-horn cattle in the world. He ships large numbers each year for breeding purposes all over the South and West, some going as far as California, and several car-loads to Central America.

This valley is also very rich in mineral deposits. The salt wells at Saltville in this valley, operated by the Holston Salt and Plaster Company, which manufactures and sells more than one million bushels of salt annually, was the only source of supply for salt open to the Confederate government during the late war between the States, and numerous attempts by the Northern army to destroy this property resulted in bloody engagements. The brine, or salt water, is a saturate solution and is practically inexhaustible, the salt rock being about twenty-five feet beneath the surface over an area of more than five hundred acres and about one hundred and seventy-five feet thick. Plaster is also found in very large quantities in Rich Valley, beginning at Saltville, where it has been extensively mined. It is found again in large quantities at Plasterburg, about four miles east, and again at Taylor's, about five miles further east, and, lastly, in Buchanan's Cove, fourteen miles east of Saltville, where a shaft ten feet square has been sunk in solid plaster 592 feet deep with no evidences of giving out. An eminent authority says of this cove plaster that "it is equal to the best Nova Scotia in all respects except solubility, and in that it is superior to any yet found in the world." Full reports have been made on these plaster fields by eminent geologists, who represent them as unequalled in quantity and quality in America. Large deposits of iron ores of different grades are also found in this valley, among them a very rich red hemitite. Marble also exists in large quantities.

Saltville with 300 inhabitants, Bradford with 50, Chatham Hill with 150, and Olympia with 50, are the principal villages in this valley. At Saltville are the extensive furnaces for manufacturing salt; at Bradford a large flouring mill and two stores; at Chatham Hill an extensive flour and plaster mills, cabinet shops and several stores; at Olympia, a large and successful woolen factory.

MARION, OR THE MIDDLE VALLEY,

has also very fertile lands and handsome estates, among them the Seven-Mile Ford farm, one of the handsomest in Virginia, which has been in the possession of the Preston family for more than one hundred years, and has been the home of John S. and William C. Preston, of South Carolina, celebrated as orators and statesmen, and of many other distinguished men, and is the burial-place of Gen. William Campbell, the hero of Kings Mountain, and of Madame Russell, who was a sister of Patrick Henry.

This valley is also rich in mineral deposits, especially iron ores, which are just being developed. Among the largest deposits found are those on the property of the Staley's Creek Manganese and Iron Company, consisting of about seven thousand acres on the mountains south of Marion. A part of this property has been leased on a royalty to a New York syndicate, which is developing it extensively. Mr. James Long, of Philadelphia, also owns a 10,000-acre tract in the same region which abounds in ores of the finest quality. Extensive beds of manganese have also been discovered on both these properties; large beds of ores have also been discovered on Walker's Mountain, north of Marion.

There has also been discovered recently at various points in this valley several varieties of onyx marble of great value and beauty. These properties have been bought up by a Richmond syndicate and a company organized to work them. Several carloads of the onyx have been excavated near Marion and samples shipped to New York for cutting and polishing.

Lead and zinc have also been found in this valley, but not in large quantities.

Marion, the county seat of Smyth county, is located in this valley on the line of the Norfolk and Western Railroad, which traverses the valley from east to west. The town was located by the commissioners appointed for that purpose in the act of the General Assembly forming the county. The commission was composed of Wm. Price, Thos. Perry, Jno. H. Fulton and Samuel McCamant. They filed their report May 25th, 1832. There was then but one house in the place—a mill now occupied by the extensive manufacturing plant of Look & Lincoln. The public square where the court-house stands was located in a corn-field. The court-house and jail were built in 1833. Marion is now a thriving town of almost 1,600 inhabitants. It has a beautiful location, and is constantly improving and growing. Its elevation above the sea level is 2,250 feet, and is surrounded by lofty ranges of mountains, making it one of the most charming and healthful summer homes to be found. An abundant supply of pure free-stone water is furnished from a mountain spring two miles distant, the fall from the spring being sufficient to force the water over the highest building. This spring and another one, which is owned by the town, in its immediate vicinity, furnishes ample water to supply a city of 25,000 inhabitants. The South-western Lunatic Asylum is located here, and is supported by the State. The building is the largest single building in the State, and has cost about $200,000, and is officered by a Superintendent and two Assistant Physicians. About seventy-five employees are required, and about 250 patients accommodated. The town has seven churches, representing the different denominations of christians; a female college with about 100 pupils, a male high school with an attendance of about 100, two public schools with an attendance of 200, and numerous private and select schools. The female college is conducted under the supervision of the Evangelical Lutheran Church. The other schools are undenominational.

Marion is admirably adapted for an extensive manufacturing town. Magnificent water-powers are furnished by the Middle Fork of Holston river, which runs through the town from east to west, and by Staley's creek, which crosses the town from south to north and empties into the Holston. Among the manufactories now established here, are the extensive Baryta Mills run by H. P. Copenhager and J. M. Luther, baryta being mined in the immediate neighborhood, and also shipped here from other sections of the State and from Tennessee. At these mills vast quantities of baryta have been manufactured and shipped to Northern and Western markets. And the mining has heretofore been carried on quite extensively, several hundred hands having been frequently employed at one time, but the deposit has become much scarcer and harder to mine, and the mill-owners now find it cheaper to mine at other points and ship the crude material here for manufacture.

Look & Lincoln have a very extensive wood-working establishment, and manufacture large quantities of wagon and buggy hubs, rims, spokes, felloes, plow-handles, etc. They also manufacture plows, wagons, buggies and farm implements in large quantities, furnishing employment to more than one hundred men all together.

J. M. Luther has an extensive foundry and machine-shop, working several hands, and does a large business.

W. C. Leaver & Sons have an extensive furniture factory, planing-mills, etc. There are, besides, in Marion and its immediate vicinity, four large flouring mills, all equipped with the roller process, that of Hull & Staley being run to its full capacity day and night; a broom factory, a tannery, a large saw-mill and wood-working establishment conducted by the Atkins Bros.; seventeen stores, an opera-house, five physicians, two dentists, two newspapers, one photographer, numerous blacksmiths, carpenters, milliners, two livery-stables, etc. There are three hotels, and another large one is contemplated.

The Bank of Marion has a capital of $60,000, a surplus of about $35,000, and deposits amounting to about $100,000. Its regular rate of discount is six per cent.

There is no more attractive town on the line of the Norfolk and Western Railroad than Marion, nor a more desirable place for substantial investments. It has escaped the "booming" fever which has attacked so many towns, and consequently prices of real estate have not assumed abnormal proportions, and its growth, while moderate, has been gradual and substantial. Investors and strangers will be gladly welcomed, and will find a generous, hospitable people. Marion, at present, is the outlet for Grayson county, Virginia, and a large territory of North Carolina to the Railroad, and is a considerable produce market on this account.

CHILHOWEE,

on the Norfolk and Western Railroad, ten miles west of Marion, is a thriving village of about two hundred and fifty inhabitants, and is the seat of the Virginia Vitrified Brick and Sewer-pipe Company's large and extensive plant. This company has purchased an area of land on which there is an immense deposit of clay suitable for the manufacture of vitrified brick, which are as hard as limestone rock, and are used extensively in the West for paving streets, supplanting Belgian blocks, to which they are said to be superior. They make also a fire-brick which has stood the most crucial tests, as well as all kinds of ornamental and building bricks, sewer-pipes, etc. This plant is being conducted by Adams Brothers & Paynes, of Lynchburg, Virginia, at a cost of more than one hundred thousand dollars, and will employ about three hundred men when in full operation.

ATHENS' TANK, SEVEN-MILE FORD AND GROSCELOSES,

are important villages and stations on the line of the Norfolk and Western Railroad, the first-mentioned place being the railroad company's principal coaling station west of Lynchburg.

ST. CLAIR DISTRICT, OR VALLEY.

This valley lies south of the mountains dividing it from the Marion, or middle valley, and north of the Grayson county line, and is an extension of the Cripple Creek Valley, and forms a part of that great iron belt, which has been developed so extensively within the past few years. The *limonite* ores of this valley are of high grade and great value. The Lobdell Car-wheel Company has a furnace in that valley, at which it makes its iron of that peculiar excellence required for their purposes in the manufacture of car-wheels. The Cripple Creek extension of the Norfolk and Western Railroad is projected through this valley, and the great demand for its superior ores, when the dozen new furnaces now in process of erection along the line of the Norfolk and Western Railroad are completed, will assure its early completion.

There is found in this valley, also, lead of the finest quality.

The Rye Valley Mining Company has purchased a lead of lead ore here, and are preparing to mine and manufacture it on a large scale. The ore has been shipped in car-load lots to New Jersey, after having been hauled in wagons ten miles to the Marion depot, at a net profit of more than $500 per car. Zinc is also found in this valley of fine quality, and ochres abound in immense quantities.

The South-western portion of this valley contains the great White Top and Balsam Mountains, which rise to 5,720 feet above the sea, and are the highest mountains in Virginia. On the summit of the White Top is a large area of cleared land, gently rolling, and covered with a fine sod of blue-grass. From the center of this area flows a large spring of water, clear and sparkling, and as cold as ice. The view from this great elevation is simply indescribable, and must be seen to be appreciated. Large crowds of tourists and pleasure-seekers annually visit this mountain, and when the large hotel, now projected, is completed, will furnish a most delightful and popular summer-resort. This spring on the mountain is the source of the Big Laurel creek, which flows\down the mountain and around its base, and abounds with the mountain or speckled trout, thousands of which yearly fall victims to the angler.

The land in this valley, especially in the western portion around St. Clair Bottom, which was one of the earliest settlements in South-west Virginia, are very fertile, consisting largely of broad river bottoms.

The people of the county, as a general thing, are free from debt. The county has a good system of roads, and has a first-class iron bridge over every important river crossing. The farms are in good condition, and the people intelligent and law-abiding. There are public schools for white and colored children in every neighborhood, besides several schools of high grade.

Dr. ROBERT J. PRESTON, Superintendent of the South-western Insane Asylum, was born January 25th, 1841, in Washington county, near Abingdon. (John F. Preston, the father of the Doctor, was a farmer who was identified with the best interests of the county, and was for many years Supervisor.) He was educated at Emory and Henry College, going from there to the University of Virginia, where he graduated as M. D. in the class of 1867. After graduating he spent eighteen months in the hospitals of New York City. While in attendance at Emory and Henry College the war broke out, and he enlisted in the 37th Virginia Regiment, which was organized at Abingdon by Col. Samuel B. Fulkerson, in which command he remained during the first two years of the war with Stonewall Jackson's brigade in his campaign through the Valley. He was then First Lieutenant, and was afterwards made Captain of a company in the 21st Virginia Cavalry under the command of Col. William E. Peters (now Professor of Latin at the University of Virginia), occupying that position until the battle of Appomattox, and in which he engaged under General Lee. After the surrender he returned to Abingdon, and from there went to the University of Virginia, and engaged in the study of medicine. Later, when leaving the New York hospitals, he began the practice of his profession in Abingdon in January, 1869, and continued the practice until March, 1877, when he was elected First Assistant Physician of the South-western Insane Asylum at Marion, under the supervision of Dr. Harvey Black, who was First Superintendent, and after his death, which occurred in 1888, Dr. Preston was elected to fill the vacancy, which duties he assumed in November, 1888, and continues as Superintendent at the present time. The Doctor is much beloved by his patients, and he possesses a peculiar adaptability to the work, and finds in it ample scope for the exercise of his every professional ability and talent. During the time of his superintendency he has made many improvements tending to the comfort and well-being of the patients, and has greatly improved and beautified the place.

The Doctor is an active member of the State Medical Society, and was for several years a member of the State Medical Examining Board. He was married in 1875 to Miss Martha E. Sheffey, a daughter of a very prominent lawyer, who represented the county in the State Legislature for many years, and was prominent in the politics of the State. Two children have been born to the Doctor, Eleanor F., aged fourteen years, and Robert Sheffey, aged six years. He has been for many years an elder of the Presbyterian church of Abingdon, and is now a member of the church at Marion.

The Doctor is a man of fine culture, and keeps fully abreast of the age in all intellectual pursuits.

WILLIAM C. SEXTON, Esq., County Clerk of Smyth county, was born May 30th, 1828, at Chatham Hill, this county. His father, Joseph Sexton, was a farmer and a descendant of the Connecticut family of that name who came to Virginia in about 1800. William C. was educated in the schools of his native place, and occupied himself with farming until the age of nineteen, when he went into the mercantile business, which he carried on until 1858, at which time he was elected County Clerk, which position he holds at the present time, having served in the same capacity for thirty-three consecutive years. During the war he remained at his post, although his four brothers were all engaged in active service and three of them were killed. He was united in marriage in 1852 to Miss Rachel C. Roberts, daughter of Hon. John Roberts, of Broadford, Smyth county, whose father was one of the old settlers and whose grandfather bought the land on which his descendant now lives in 1776, and it is now in the hands of the fourth generation. Eight children have been born to them, six of whom are now living—John R., Mayor of Marion and Deputy County Clerk; Joseph K., a druggist at Walnut Ridge, Arkansas; Edward J., a physician at Sturgis, South Dakota; Alice M., wife of Judge W. P. Dungan, of Elizabethton, Tennessee; Lucretia E., wife of A. T. Lincoln, of Marion, who is a member of the firm of Look & Lincoln, wagon and agricultural machinery manufacturers at this place. Rachel M. F., the youngest daughter, is still at home with her father. His wife died in 1866, and he has not married since. Mr. Sexton is a trustee and steward of the Methodist church, in which society he and his family are active and efficient workers. It is superfluous to say that he is held in high esteem by his fellow county and townsmen, as his election to office for so many years will amply testify.

CHAPTER XX.

CHRISTIANSBURG, VIRGINIA.

By Rev. T. W. HOOPER, D. D.

This town, of 1,400 inhabitants, is the county seat of Montgomery county, one of the richest counties in the great South-west The original corporate limits of the town were described in a deed dated September 6th, 1803, and conveyed 175 acres of land, in pursuance of a survey made May 25th, 1790, conveying to the Justices of Montgomery county the tract for the purpose of a town at the county seat. The town was named after Colonel Christian, one of the heroes of the French and Indian and the Revolutionary wars, but at the time none of his descendants were living at the place. As the time passed, the town grew in size and importance, and became the center of social, political and mercantile interests for a large section of country. It was the home of some of the most celebrated professional men in a county prolific in old families bearing such eminent names as Preston, Floyd, Edmondson, Gibbony, King, Miller, Montague, and others too numerous to mention.

Being on the old National road of Indian days, it gave direction to various thoroughfares afterwards constructed by act of the Legislature under a vast scheme of "Internal Improvements." The macadamized turnpike leading from Buchanan, the terminus of the James River and Kanawha Canal, toward Abingdon, passed through the town, thus paving what is still its Main street.

When the canal above Lynchburg was largely superceded by the Virginia and Tennessee Railroad, extending from Lynchburg to Bristol, the railroad ought to have passed through the town. But for the short-sighted policy of some land-owners it would have done so instead of leaving it a mile and a quarter to the south. Here a depot was located, and around it has grown up a village, now called Cambria, which serves to divide the business and patronage of the old town. Together, they furnish goods for a large part of Montgomery, Giles and Floyd counties, and from the depot travelers take passage who have come across execrable roads in bad weather for twenty or thirty miles, including the Yellow Sulphur Springs and such towns as Snowville, Floyd Court House, Newport and Blacksburg, the seat of the Virginia Agricultural and Mechanical College. From this same depot are shipped large quantities of coal, baled hay, corn, wheat, fat cattle, sheep, hogs, some tobacco and a very large quantity of lime. Near the depot also are located the large roller-mill of Rigby & Sons, a water-mill of Mr. Latimore and another of Captain Wade, as well as the two large lime-kilns recently erected by a company, of which Mr. A. A. Phlyar is President and Mr. M. C. Pelton is manager.

Christiansburg is located a short distance from the "water-shed" of the Alleghany mountains; and is watered by three small streams, converging into one, at the lower end of the town. These little streams abound, on each side, with springs of cold limestone water; and on lots where there are no springs, it requires but small depth to sink wells, which furnish an abundant supply of cool, clear water.

The town still bears the marks of age in some of its older residences and stores, but many of these have given place to modern structures, much more commodious, and in architecture more pleasing to aesthetic taste. The court-house is a large brick structure, occupying one side of a square, in the center of which, enclosed by an iron fence, stands a handsome granite monument, erected by the ladies of the Memorial Association, to the memory of the Confederate dead, as the county sent out four full companies of infantry to the "Stonewall Brigade," besides many to other branches of the service. This monument means much, though not a soldier sleeps directly beneath its shadow.

Stretched out on both sides of the macadamized street and brick sidewalk, well-watered, and shaded with maple, aspen and locust trees, Christiansburg is healthy, lively, neighborly and restful. With the largest trade for its size of any town in this section, its merchants are wide-awake and progressive. The Bank of Christiansburg, is one of the most solid and well conducted institutions in the State, and its stock cannot be bought, nor will the directors increase the amount.

Including Cambria, there are five churches for white people and two for the colored people, in all of which Sunday-schools are regularly conducted, and where the gospel is statedly preached.

There is also a Masonic Hall, the upper part devoted to the lodge and chapter of the Ancient, Free and Accepted Masons, and the lower part to a town hall, which is rented for the purpose of lectures and other creditable exhibitions.

There is a large graded school, under the control of a board of trustees, and sustained by the public school fund. Montgomery Male

Academy is a commodious brick building, under the care of a board of trustees, and where many students have been prepared for college. Montgomery Female College, is a large and well built brick structure, in the midst of a terraced and shaded lawn overlooking the town. Under a deed of trust given before the war, it was sold several years ago to private parties, and while just now in transition state, it is hoped and believed that it will soon regain that prominence, to which it had risen in former years.

The hotels are not as large and commodious as they ought to be, but if an inn of modern style could be erected and managed by competent hands, it would be filled with summer boarders, and with commercial travelers in the winter. The erection of such an inn is a part of a vast scheme of enlargement and improvement for the town. A large tract of land, belonging to some of the heirs of the late R. D. Montague, was bought by a land company. This was surveyed and laid off into lots by avenues and streets. A dummy line was to run from the new passenger depot of the Norfolk and Western Railroad to the old town, and on an eminence shaded with a grove of magnificent oaks, and commanding a sublime view of the mountains, was to be erected a splendid hotel with all the modern improvements. In the meantime, a railroad, or a dummy line, or a macadam road was to be constructed from the freight depot to the coal mines, ranging in distance from four to twelve miles, and passing near the beautiful little college town of Blacksburg.

Such a well formulated plan, if properly carried out, would add to the Pocahontas coal that of Price's Mountain for stoves, and that of Brush Mountain, which many regard as the very best, for grates. It would also open up a cheap and beautiful location for residences, where the citizens of less salubrious cities might locate, especially during the summer, and would open to the scores of people in the South who write every summer for boarding, room for themselves and families. It would furnish a city 2,200 feet above the tide, with abundance of pure water, pure air, surrounded by scenery always entrancing to the eye, and on which Scott or Wordsworth would have feasted their poetic souls with unspeakable delight.

For the time, the whole plan is in a state of litigation, but the more hopeful are sanguine of ultimate success. Business depression is, just now, almost universal, but far-sighted business men are aware of the fact that in all human affairs there is an ebb-tide which is succeeded by the flood, and "a tide in the affairs of men, which, taken at the flood, leads on to fortune." Such are the prospects that please the fancy of all those who are living amid the cool breezes, the pure air, the rich valleys, "the hidden treasure" which is buried in the hills of all our beautiful Eldorado, in these blue-grass regions of South-west Virginia.

Judge GEORGE G. JUNKIN, of Christiansburg, the subject of this sketch, was born November 19th, 1839, at Milton, Pennsylvania, on his grandfather's farm. His education was completed at Washington College, now Washington and Lee University. After receiving his degree, in 1859, he came to Christiansburg, Virginia, and engaged in teaching classics and mathematics in the High School. This occupation he followed until the beginning of the war, when he enlisted in Company G, 4th Virginia Infantry, at the time of the famous John Brown raid on Harper's Ferry. He was promoted in August, 1861, to Lieutenant, and was Aid-de-Camp on Stonewall Jackson's Staff. He was again promoted to Captain of Cavalry and assigned to the command of a squadron, the 25th Virginia Cavalry, October, 1862, and served during the balance of the war with that regiment, being promoted to Major shortly before the surrender. He then returned to Christiansburg and read Law, and was admitted to the Bar in 1867. He was Commonwealth's Attorney for a number of years, and was elected as Judge of the County Court in the year 1886, this being done without his knowledge or consent.

Aside from his legal duties, the Judge is President of the Elliston Development Company, Secretary and Treasurer of the Virginia Arsenic, Bromium and Lithia Springs, a director of the Rivermont Land Company, Lynchburg; a director of the Radford Development Company and of the Radford Trust Company, and a trustee of Washington and Lee University. He was married in 1862 to Miss Bettie Montague, a daughter of R. D. Montague, of Christiansburg, and a sister of J. Kyle Montague, Esq., the subject of one of our sketches. A family of eleven children have been born to them—Jennie, the wife of John C. Stevens, a promising business man of South-west Virginia; Montague, attending to his father's business in the office of the Radford Development Company; Frank and Garnett, students in Washington and Lee University; Mary, Colin, George, Helen, Judith and Margaret.

Judge Junkin is a man of unflinching integrity, and one who makes no compromise with wrong.

Rev. T. W. HOOPER, D. D., pastor of the Presbyterian church of Christiansburg, Virginia, was born in Hanover county, Virginia, November 2d, 1832, and reared at Beaver Dam on the Chickahominy. His forefathers emigrated from England, one of three brothers settling in Boston, another in North Carolina, and the other, James Hooper, near Cold Harbor. His funeral sermon was preached by Samuel Darius, and is among the printed sermons of that eminent divine.

The subject of this sketch is the son of Joseph and Elizabeth C. (Haw) Hooper. He received his primary education at Meadow Farm and Washington-Henry Academies, and graduated with honors at Hampden-Sidney College in 1855. In the fall of the same year he entered Union Seminary, New York City, but after a few months, not liking his environment, he returned to Union Theological Seminary at Hampden-Sidney, Virginia. From the Seminary early in January, 1858, he was called to be the pastor of Polegreen church, where he was born, the son of an elder who had died in 1852. This church was erected by Samuel Darius and is the mother of Presbyterianism in Virginia and the South. It was burned in the great campaign of 1864. Here he labored until the battles around Richmond and raiding parties had broken up the people, when he was called to the church at Liberty (now Bedford City), where he had married Miss Lettie W., daughter of Hon. J. F. Johnson. Here he lived as pastor and chaplain to the post until the close of the war, when he was called to Christiansburg. Here he continued until 1870, erecting, in the meantime, "the Manse," in which he now resides. In 1870 he was called to the Second Presbyterian church of Lynchburg, where he labored until 1876, when he was called to the First Presbyterian church of Selma, Alabama. Here he continued until his health failed, in 1888, when he returned to the mountains of Virginia, and was again called as pastor of the Christiansburg church.

Roanoke College conferred upon him the title of D. D. in 1876. He has been a director of Columbia (S. C.) Theological Seminary, chairman of the Tuskegee (Ala.) Orphans' Home, member of the Executive Committee of the Tuscaloosa (Ala.) Colored Institute, and since 1872 a trustee of Hampden-Sidney College. He is now editorial correspondent of the *Central Presbyterian*, and correspondent of many journals.

Dr. ROBERT T. ELLETT.—The subject of this sketch, Dr. Robert T. Ellett, was born in Hanover county, near Ashland, the birthplace of Henry Clay, May 29th, 1837. His father, Robert Ellett, Esq., was a civil engineer, of Hanover county, and was connected with the old Louisa Railway, which is now the Chesapeake and Ohio, until it reached Staunton. It was his ambition to see this road completed, but he died in 1869. Robert Jr., was educated in the field county schools and in the Richmond College, graduating from the Medical Department in 1858. He began practice near Tunstall Station, on West Point, but the war breaking out, in 1861 he raised an artillery company, and served with this company seventeen months, when he was transferred to the Medical Department, stationed at Montgomery Springs, as Surgeon, in which capacity he served until the close of the war. When disbanded, he had but twenty-five cents in his pockets, which he gave for his breakfast next morning. He immediately entered into a partnership with Dr. J. W. Earley and continued with him for eighteen months, when he came to Montgomery county, in which he resides at the present time. The Doctor has been Clerk of the County Court for the past four years, and supervisor of elections a number of times. He is a member of the State Medical Society, and is justly esteemed an ornament to his profession. His wife was Miss Susan G. French, the youngest daughter of George D. French, Esq., a well known leading Whig of Giles county. Eleven children have blessed this union. The Doctor is a member of the Episcopal church, and a warden in the same.

----:◆:----

WILLIAM F. TALLANT, Esq., the subject of this sketch, was born August 23d, 1850, in Wheeling, West Virginia. His father, Henry Tallant, Esq., was a native of Wheeling, and an extensive dry goods merchant of that city. He moved from West Virginia to Pennsylvania and from there to Baltimore, and became one of the firm of Tallant, Holliday & Company, a well known house in Baltimore, and in the year 1873, he went to Santa Barbara, California, for his health, where he resides at the present time. William F., was educated in the schools of Wheeling, and the West Chester, Pennsylvania, Wyars Military Academy, and the Chestnut Hill Academy at Baltimore, graduating from the latter place in the year 1867. After receiving his degree, he entered his father's store and remained there until 1869, when he came to Christiansburg and engaged in farming. In 1877 he purchased the stove store of Charles Folgar, and since that time has added hardware and furniture, and is now doing the most extensive business in these lines of any firm in Christiansburg. Aside from his own personal interests, he is a director of the Montgomery Land Company, whose many large deals have made it well known throughout this section of the country. Mr. Tallant was married in October, 1872, to Miss Elizabeth Montague, a daughter of William Mc. Montague, Esq., of Montgomery county, and sister of J. Kyle Montague, mentioned in these pages. Two children have been born to them, but both are dead. He is an Episcopalian and a senior warden of the church, and a member of the council and the school board.

AARON GRAHAM, Esq., the subject of this sketch, was born March 13th, 1854, in Patrick county, Virginia. His father, James Graham, Esq., was a contractor and builder by profession. The subject of our sketch was educated in the county schools of Patrick, Floyd and Montgomery, his father having moved to the latter county when Aaron was a boy. When quite young he went to Shawsville, Virginia, to clerk for Capt. J. W. Helm, and in the year 1875 he bought out the stock of his employer and greatly enlarged the business, but a disastrous fire on March 21st, 1871, swept away his entire stock. After this misfortune he removed to Christiansburg and engaged as clerk for the house of J. H. Johnston & Brother, and later opened up a general store at that place, which he is successfully operating at the present time. Mr. Graham is prominently identified with the Prohibition movement of his State, and has heretofore, and is now, giving his best abilities to the cause of temperance and right living. He is a man of fine literary endowments, and has been a prolific writer and contributor to the various temperance journals of the country. His literary work is especially identified with the *Living Issue* and *New York Voice*, both powers in the advocacy of prohibition principles. Mr. Graham is treasurer of the Prohibition Club of Montgomery county, and has associated himself in every cause whose immediate end has been temperance. He was married November 12th, 1878, to Miss Lucy T. Price, a daughter of Mr. George Price, a well known tanner of Christiansburg, and one among the pioneers of this city in the temperance cause. Mr. and Mrs. Graham have two children, George E. and Nellie. He is a deacon in the Presbyterian church, and was formerly a deacon in the White House Presbyterian church at Shawsville, of which the Rev. C. A. Miller, now living in Christiansburg, was, and now is, pastor.

CHAPTER XXI.

BLACKSBURG AND THE VIRGINIA AGRICULTURAL AND MECHANICAL COLLEGE.

By Prof. J. A. HARMAN.

As far as can be learned, there are no definite records of the village of Blacksburg, but tradition tells us that the town was founded about one hundred years ago, on land owned by Charles and Alexander Black, after whom it was named. The town is situated among the hills of Montgomery county, about nine miles from Christiansburg, and eight from Cambria, the nearest railroad station on the Norfolk and Western line. In summer and fall the road is excellent, and the drive over from the station is pleasant and picturesque, but in winter and spring the town is often practically isolated. Blacksburg became a corporation shortly after the war, and now has a population of eight or nine hundred. It is the center of trade for the surrounding country, but is mostly supported by the College, whose grounds touch those of the corporation.

Generally speaking, merchandise is high-priced and of poor quality.

The Blacks and Prestons are the original families of most note, and are still well represented. Among others may be mentioned the Palmers, Thomases, Oteys, Lybrooks and Keisters. Besides these, there is always a certain population of College professors, but, of course, they are changeable and pertain more to the College than to the town.

THE COLLEGE.

In 1862 Congress granted to each State public lands to the amount of 30,000 acres for each of its senators and representatives in Congress according to the census of 1860, for "the endowment, support and maintenance of at least one college where the leading object shall be, without excluding other scientific and classical studies, and including military tactics, to teach such branches of learning as are related to agriculture and the mechanic arts in such manner as the legislatures of the States may respectively prescribe, in order to promote the liberal and practical education of the industrial classes in the several pursuits and professions of life." In 1872 the Legislature of Virginia accepted the grant, and in the autumn of that year the Virginia Agricultural and Mechanical College was opened at Blacksburg, Virginia, for the reception of students.

From the above source the College receives annually $20,658.72.

To promote and facilitate the study of military tactics, as well as to save the pay of one professor to the College, the government allows the detail of an army officer to the College free of expense to it.

By an act of the Fifty-first Congress an appropriation was made to each State which the first year should be $15,000, and which should increase by $1,000 annually until the appropriation reaches $25,000 a year, when it shall remain constant. Of this amount this College receives two-thirds.

United to the College is the Agricultural Experiment Station, authorized by the Act of Congress approved March 2d, 1887, the annual appropriation for which is $15,000.

From the above statement it is seen that the College receives from the general government, directly or indirectly, about $50,000 annually.

The grounds consist of 369½ acres of land. Of this, 339½ acres have been transferred to the Agricultural Experiment Station, but is used for instruction in the agricultural departments of the College. The remaining thirty acres comprise the College grounds proper. The 339½ acres above mentioned were purchased and presented to the College by the county of Montgomery. The other thirty acres were presented by the trustees of the Olin and Preston Institute.

The buildings are erected by the State of Virginia. The money obtained from the central government cannot be used for this purpose.

The act of the General Assembly of Virginia establishing the College provides that "a number of students double the number of the members of the House of Delegates, making two hundred, shall have the privilege of attending said College free of tuition, to be selected by the school trustees of the respective counties, cities and election districts for said delegates, with reference to the highest proficiency and good character, from the free schools of their counties; or, in their discretion, from others than those attending said free schools. When the quota of a county is filled, other applicants from that county may be accredited by the President of the College to a county in which a vacancy exists."

This latter principle has even been applied to students entering from other States.

The government of the College is vested in a Board of Visitors, consisting of eight members appointed by the Governor of the State, and by a President elected by this Board. In addition, the Faculty have authority in certain cases.

The buildings are of brick, heated

by steam and lighted by electricity. They are ample, as far as they go, and are well adapted for their purposes. The Legislature will be asked this winter to erect additional buildings.

For instruction in wood and iron, the shop is one of the best in the South. It has recently been fitted up with the best machinery obtainable, and in the most scientific manner, under the able direction of Prof. William E. Anderson.

The total expenses for a student during a session of nine months are under $150. It is thus seen that under the generous patronage of the General Government, an institution is given to Virginia which bids fair, in the very near future, to be a great centre of learning in technical and general education; an institution that will turn out young men well calculated to develop the agricultural interests of the State, and to intelligently direct the forges and workshops that are to-day covering the face of South-west Virginia.

The Faculty, as at present composed, is as follows: John M. McBryde, Ph. D., L.L. D., President and Professor of Agricultural Chemistry; John E. Christian, A. M., Professor of Mathematics and Civil Engineering; James H. Fitts (Annapolis), Professor of Mechanical Engineering; William B. Alwood, Professor of Horticulture, Entomology and Mycology; Edward E. Sheib, Ph. D. (Leipsic), Professor of English, History and Political Economy; Ellison A. Smyth, Jr., A. M., Professor of Biology; William B. Niles, D. V. M., Professor of Veterinary Science; Theo. P. Campbell, Adjunct Professor of Modern Languages; William E. Anderson, Adjunct Professor of Physics and Electrical Engineering, and Director of Laboratory of Mechanic Arts.

Dr. KENT BLACK a descendant of the family from which Blacksburg derives its name, is a son of the Dr. Harvey Black, who was a prominent and for many years a successful physician. He was a veteran in two wars, the Mexican and the Confederate. In the Mexican war he was a member of Capt. James F. Preston's Company of Virginia Volunteers, and after the first three months' service was Hospital Steward. In the war between the States he was for eighteen months Surgeon of the 4th Virginia Infantry, Stonewall Brigade, and had charge of the Field Hospital, 2d Corps Army of Northern Virginia. He also served one term as member of the State Legislature, President of the Virginia Medical Society, and was Superintendent of the Eastern Lunatic Asylum for six years. He was afterwards Superintendent of the South-western Lunatic Asylum, which position he occupied until his death, which occurred October 19th, 1888.

The subject of our sketch, Dr. Kent Black, was born at Blacksburg, Virginia, June 9th, 1853, and received his education at the Virginia Agricultural and Mechanical College, then attended the University of Virginia for two sessions, and from there going to the Medical College of Virginia, from which he graduated in 1878. He immediately began practice at Blacksburg, where he has always remained, having made for himself an enviable name and reputation in his profession. He is physician to the Virginia Agricultural and Mechanical College, and Yellow Sulphur Springs, and has an especially busy life in his professional work. Socially the Doctor is a man highly esteemed, his friends finding in him a person at once genial, cultured and affable.

Although not present at the meeting, he was recommended by the Virginia State Medical Society to the Governor for appointment as a member of the State Board of Medical Examiners, which position he now holds.

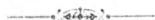

Prof. WILLIAM HENRY GRAHAM was born in Hamilton, Canada, November 3d, 1855. His father was a merchant of that city. He received his education at the Hamilton Central School, after leaving which he entered the service of the Great Western Railway, now the Grand Trunk, filling positions respectively in the Treasurer, Auditor and Passenger Departments. He was afterwards connected with the Ticket Department, Eastern Agency, of that road, at Rochester, New York. On the inauguration of the pooling system, under the direction of Albert Fink he returned to Hamilton and took up the study of Munson's System of Stenography, and in the space of three months entered the service as Private Secretary of the Standard Fire Insurance Company, of Hamilton. This position he resigned in the fall of 1879 to accept the position of Stenographic Secretary to the General Freight Agent of the Chesapeake and Ohio Railroad, with an office at Richmond, Virginia. This place he resigned in July, 1880, to accept a similar position with Traffic Manager C. W. Smith, of the Erie Railroad, with office in New York City. In November, 1880, he married Miss Allie Wood, of Richmond, Virginia, neice of the late Professor Southall, of the University of Virginia. Preferring to live in Richmond, he accepted a position with Traffic Manager of Associated Railways. This position he resigned to re-enter the service of the Chesapeake and Ohio Railroad with General Manager C. W. Smith, formerly of the Erie Railroad. The Professor occupied this position until October, 1885, when he was elected to the Chair of Commercial Science and Accountant of the Virginia Agricultural and Mechanical College. He has three children. Professor Graham is the author of a system of pen printing, which has been copyrighted. He is a member of the Episcopal church of Blacksburg, and Senior Warden of Hunter Lodge, No. 156, F. & A. M. As an educator, he ranks among the first of his State, having a rare ability for imparting knowledge, a very essential qualification which in many educators is deficient.

Prof. JOHN E. CHRISTIAN.—The subject of this sketch, Prof. John Edward Christian, was born June 12th, 1835, in New Kent county, Virginia. His father and mother, Edmund and Mary Christian, were of the same county. He was educated at Randolph-Macon, taking the degree of A. M. in 1855. After his graduation he took a two years' course at the University of Virginia, since which time he has been teaching continually, first teaching seven years in the Petersburg Boys' Academy, then seven years in the Female Academy at Lynchburg, and the same number of years at Chatham in a private school for both sexes. In the year 1880 he came to Blacksburg and took the chair of Mathematics and Physics of the Virginia Agricultural and Mechanical College. Since the resignation of General Lomax, President of the College, Professor Christian has been acting in his place. During the siege of Petersburg he was connected with Beauregard's command, but carried on his school at the same time. He was editor-in-chief of the *Chatham Tribune* while he was teaching in that city. He was married in 1861 to Miss Cornelia C. Grigg, of Petersburg, a daughter of Wesley Grigg, Esq., a merchant of that place. Mrs. Christian died in 1867, and in 1871 he was again married to Elizabeth Watson, daughter of Thomas J. Watson, Esq., of Chatham. The Professor has four children by his first wife. He is a member of the Methodist church and was a steward for a number of years and a teacher in the Sunday-school.

He is a man who stands pre-eminently high in the estimation of the public, his services having been such as to endear him to all. As a teacher his qualifications are of a superior order, and as a friend he is genial, warm and sympathetic.

Prof. JOSEPH MORTON, A. M., the subject of this brief sketch, was born September 26th, 1836, in Charlotte county, Virginia. His father, William G. Morton, was a farmer and Justice of the Peace for many years. He was educated at Hampden-Sidney College, and graduated in the class of 1858. After receiving his degree he taught until the opening of the war at Belmont Academy, of Granville county, North Carolina. At the beginning of the war he enlisted in the 34th Artillery under Captain Bagley, of King and Queen county, serving in this command until the surrender. He then began teaching again, taking a position in the High School of Rockbridge county, which he occupied for four years, when he abandoned teaching for farming, which avocation he engaged in for the next ten years in Prince Edward county, at the expiration of which time he was elected to the chair of English History and Political Economy, which honorable position he now occupies. Professor Morton was married in 1858 to Miss Mary L. Perkinson, daughter of Thomas E. Perkinson, Esq., High Sheriff of Prince Edward county under the old regime for many years.

CHAPTER XXII.

SHENANDOAH, VIRGINIA.

Shenandoah, Virginia, is located in Page county almost on the borders of Rockingham, and is 107 miles south of Hagerstown, and 132 miles from Roanoke. It is located in a fine agricultural region, and surrounded by bodies of unusually valuable timbered lands. Formerly the town was called Milnes, taking its name from the Milnes who was at one time actively connected with the construction of the Shenandoah Valley Railroad. The town is situated in one of the finest mineral regions in the Valley, and for a number of years has been an iron-manufacturing place, formerly engaged in making iron when its charcoal furnace was in blast. The ores (iron) are remarkably fine, and from these banks the charcoal furnace drew its supply, as well as the coke furnace completed seven or eight years ago.

The advantages which Shenandoah has are manifest in every way. Immediately adjacent to it are immense tracts of land known to be very rich in iron, manganese, copper and lead ores of the very best character, together with asbestos, slates, ochres, fire-clays and limestone of the best quality. Vast bodies of the best timber lands are here, and furnish in almost endless quantity the very best of oak, hickory, poplar, ash, maple, walnut, birch, chestnut and pine, which answer equally as well for manufacturing as for decorative purposes; and near here is also found an abundance of bark for tanning purposes, thousands of tons being shipped annually within a radius of five miles from around Shenandoah. On account of which advantages in the way of timber it can be readily seen that a better point could not be selected for manufactories of various kinds of woodenware. A finer agricultural region from which a city could draw its supplies does not exist than that around this place, for the lands are noted for their versatility of productions, as well as rich productiveness. And not the least of Shenandoah's advantages is the prospect of the place being at no great future day a railroad center. The terminus of the Washington and Western Railroad will doubtless be here, while the road projected from Ceredo to Quantico is most certain to pass this way. If such reasonable hopes are fulfilled, then Shenandoah can point with pride to her northern, southern, eastern and western outlets.

The fact that Shenandoah was made a divisional point, and the shops and round-houses erected there, was the cause of the growth of Milnes, afterwards called Shenandoah. As the railroad has some permanent interest at this point, it is but natural that they will do all in their power to promote the interest of the place and enhance its value in every way. Already these shops have been long in operation, and employ a large force of hands in the repairing of engines and on the yard, while the employees in the offices are there, both going far towards swelling the pay-roll to that amount which is doubtless of great assistance to the town. It is further claimed by the people of Shenandoah that these shops will be enlarged now that the Norfolk and Western Railroad Company has gained possession of the Shenandoah Valley Railroad—a claim which is not without hope and reason.

For some years past this place has been quite an iron-manufacturing point. The Shenandoah Iron Works had some reputation even before the erection of the Gem furnace, which uses coke instead of charcoal. The former iron works consisted of a charcoal blast furnace with a stack 33x8½, with Player hot-blast attachment, a forge and refinery, all of which had the capacity to turn out some sixty tons a week of warm-blast charcoal iron, which was worked up into blooms at the company's forge. These works were situated about five miles from the station on Naked creek, at the end of the branch road from Shenandoah. Prior to 1883 the new coke furnace known as the "Gem," with a 70x16 stack, and a producing capacity of seventy to eighty tons of iron *per diem*, was built, and during the years of 1883 and 1884, up to February, its output was 16,585 tons of foundry and forge iron. The above was really the product of a ten months' run, as two months were taken in repairing the old hot-blast stoves. The iron from these works has been shipped to Harrisburg, Philadelphia and Baltimore markets, and gave universal satisfaction on account of its purity and character. The following analysis of a bloom fully substantiates this claim:

Carbon	.042
Silicon	.008
Sulphur	.001
Phosphorus	.074
Manganese	.003
Iron by difference	99.872

The advantages derived by the place from being a divisional point can be readily appreciated. In the first place it caused the erection of the shops there, and brought in a certain number of people whose interests became more or less identified with the place. The natural development and increase of every kind of resource in this wonderful country will necessarily create a demand for increased railway facilities, which upon its face means an enlargement of the railroad plant there. The capitalists and officials of the railroad company being interested, have taken stock in the future of the place, and the result was that on May 9, 1890, a development company was organized, which having already a good nucleus for a town proceeded to develop it.

The Shenandoah Land and Improvement Company, organized with a capital stock of $300,000, C. Powell Nolan as President and J. F. Wheelwright as Secretary. The formation of this developing scheme is fraught with more than ordinary meaning, on account of the persons who are interested in it. These men are: F. J. Kimball, President of the Norfolk and Western Railroad Company; James Sands, general manager of the same; D. W. Flickwir, Superintendent of the Shenandoah Valley Railroad Company; Mr. McDowell, Mr. Armes, Mr. Robinson, Clarence H. Clark and P. L. Terry. This company, which has some seven hundred acres of land in and adjacent to the place, is offering every possible inducement to manufacturers to locate, and have some lovely residence sites situated on a commanding, rolling eminence. The business and manufacturing lots, which are donated free, lie upon the river, which is capable of furnishing all necessary water-power. The manufacturing plants which locate there are exempt from all municipal taxation, and a perfect system of gas and water-works has been inaugurated, without which every town is more or less imperfect. Every conservative, prudent step possible is being taken by this company for the future development of the place.

The outlook for the place is undoubtedly bright. The furnace company intends enlarging its plant, and already a pay-roll of $20,000 is monthly distributed among the railroad employees and furnace men, the latter of whom, including the quarrying men, now make some three hundred and fifty employees, who, together with their families and other citizens, number over two thousand people. Shenandoah will in the near future be a city of no small dimensions.

The town of Shendun, comparatively speaking, is a new place, and occupies that broad, sweeping plateau south of Port Republic. The natural location of the place is beautiful. The level plain, stretching away for miles to the river on one hand and the mountains on the other, presents a beautiful site for a city. The blue outline of the mountains, looking north, with the green tint of those to the west, give a relief to the monotony of the plain without infringing upon its beauty.

CHAPTER XXIII.

LURAY, VIRGINIA.

THE LURAY CAVERNS.

The discovery and opening up of the Caverns of Luray and the Grottoes of the Shenandoah had a marked effect upon the development of Shenandoah Valley, and may be assigned as one of the causes of its recent growth. In giving an account of these wonderful underground passages, we deem it but just to also give a sketch of the town of Luray, now one of the important points along the line of the Shenandoah Valley Railroad, or the Shenandoah Railroad.

Luray is situated directly on this railroad, in Page county, one hundred and fifty miles from Roanoke and eighty-nine from Hagerstown, Maryland, in the middle of the charming Luray Valley, celebrated for its beauty of scenery, salubrious climate, rich agricultural lands, and mineral resources. Ever since the formation of the county of Page, in 1831, the place has been the county seat. The general impression that it takes its name from Lorraine, a French settler, is erroneous, for, after a patient investigation, the extrinsic evidence, as well as internal facts, substantiate the position taken by Judge Alexander Y. Brand, who states that its name was taken from that of one Lewis Ramey. This latter person was one of the oldest settlers in the county, and the log cabin in which he resided was located at what is now the corner of Main and Court streets. He was called Lew Ramey; then, for contraction, was spoken of as Lew Ray, from which source of sound the name of Luray is undoubted derived.

From 1831, the town as a county seat and a kind of trading center for the valley of its name, gradually increased, deriving its support from the surrounding agricultural productions and profits from the sale of its wares, until, in 1869, the place had some five hundred people. From this on the progress was still scarcely perceptible; for in 1878, there were only about six hundred people, pursuing the even tenor of their way, not dreaming of the revolution through which their quiet place would go in the next succeeding ten years. On August 13, 1878, the caverns was discovered, which subsequently played an important part in this whole section of country by drawing visitors from all parts of the country and giving everything an impetus never before known at Luray.

It was due to the efforts of B. P. Stebbins, Andrew W. Campbell and W. B. Campbell that the caverns were first discovered. B. P. Stebbins, a photographer, who came to Luray in 1878, from certain external indications became satisfied that caverns were somewhere in the vicinity, and persuaded the Campbells to join him in the search. This "cave company," as it was jocularly termed, was subject to much ridicule from the people of the town. They were called "cave rats" and "searchers after mares' nests;" but, nothing daunted, they continued their explorations until, on the date above-mentioned, their labors were crowned with success, and A. J. Campbell was lowered by means of a rope into what is known now as Entrance Hall. This discovery was fully appreciated by the parties, for that night they returned with candles and explored Stebbins Avenue, Entrance Hall and Entrance Avenue as far as the lake, which then prevented a farther insight into the most wonderful parts, which were first seen after the lake was drained. At the very time of this discovery proceedings were pending in the Circuit Court of Page by creditors against the bankrupt estate of Samuel Bueracher, and, in 1878, Cave Hill, containing twenty-eight and one-half acres, was sold, and Messrs. Stebbins and Campbell became the purchasers at a price considered extremely high for the land. Their discovery had been not only concealed, but every means to prevent discovery used, by placing brush, earth and rubbish over the entrance of this cavern after their exploration that night. A few days subsequently, however, the town was startled and astonished at the news that a wonderful cave had been found. The commotion and excitement was intense, and on learning the nature and value of the property sold the relatives of the original owners instituted suit for its recovery. The lower Court sustained the sale to Stebbins and the Campbells; but, in 1881, the Supreme Court set it aside on the ground of fraud, and there was another sale, at which W. T. Briedler, a son-in-law of Samuel Bueracher, purchased the property, afterwards disposing of it to the Luray Cave and Hotel Company, a syndicate from Philadelphia. From this on Luray began to improve, when the caverns were opened up and the inn erected.

Owing to the importance of these caverns, a description of them may not be amiss. Subterraneous passages are one thing, but it is quite another to have them beautifully and richly decorated with exquisitely-formed growths of stalactites and stalagmites, composing columns, figures, folds, draperies and statues, illustrating the fact that caves are common anywhere, but beautiful caverns rare. Large caverns are found in limestone regions only, and a cave is but an underground valley caused by erosion—a gorge or ravine roofed over with stone—a repetition under a lightless sky of limestone formations above the earth on its surface. Luray Caverns are a system of large ravines, such as Entrance Hall, Entrance and Stonewall Avenues, Pluto's Chasm, Giant's Hall and its ramifications, which are the dominating lines.

With carbonic acid as an active agent, and water as a carrier, we are able to account for the disappearance of strata, however thick either above or below ground. Above, the result is a lowering of the general level and formation of valleys, where causes favor the disintegration of stone. "Hard" water flows away, and a clay soil is left behind. Below ground the result is a cave, if there be a vertical fissure in the strata through which the water charged with carbonic acid makes its descent. In course of time these fissures are worn larger, and the water entering forms pools, which by and by cause disintegrations of the softer horizontal strata with which it comes in contact, and, finding an exit at last, bears away the minerals little by little, leaving the clay behind to cause the adventurous cave-hunter no end of annoyance. Wherefore, it is not incorrect to assert that a cave is a fissure widened by the combined action of carbonic acid and water disintegrating and carrying away the softer strata around. The folds and drapery; the figures, some lovely, some grotesque; the curtains, frozen cascades, columns, shields, fish and many other representations are the result of the stalactite formations on the roof and the stalagmite on the floor of the cavity, with the lateral or helictite growth from the sides. These come together in every imaginable shape and form, producing pictures of beauty and sublimity impossible to conceive unless seen. These stalactites are made from the water percolating through strata of limestone above, which, being charged with carbonic acid, on reaching the ceiling evaporates, leaving the carbon of lime, which, on account of the continued dripping of the water, gradually form the hanging stalactite. At first this has a minute tube through which the water trickles, but which becomes closed after a while from deposits of carbon of lime; then the water drips down on the outside of this formation, leaving the same deposits we have named, becoming in the course of ages much larger. The drops of water which percolate with force enough to leave the ceiling reach the floor and build up the stalagmite, which often joins the stalactite above, forming the columns and drapery which we see. Some of these formations are white and others of a brown color, which difference some geologists explain by stating that age causes the discoloration. Whether we visit Entrance Hall, the Amphitheatre, the Fish Market, Elfin Ramble, Pluto's Chasm, the Crystal Spring, the Mermaid, the Cascade, the Ladies' Toilet Table, Giants' Hall, Proserpine's Column, the Grotto of Oberon, the Bridal Chamber, the Fallen Column, the Cathedral, the Organ, the Ball-room and other points of interest in the Caverns of Luray, we find everywhere these beautiful, exquisite, and supernatural formations.

In September, 1881, the inn was constructed, and cement walks and electric lights placed in the caverns, and numbers of visitors caused Luray to be known from home, and its many attractions, natural advantages and agricultural resources led people to look at the town in other light than as the resort for visitors to the caverns. The timber district around drew in a large manufacturing plant. Defoard's huge Bark-grinding Company and Tannery combined, which has a capital of $800,000 employed in its operations, and works about two hundred and fifty men in the tannery and bark works also. The place grew rapidly, and with other plants that came the town increased to about twenty-five hundred people by the year 1889 or early in 1891. It became also quite a center for education, several schools being located there.

While Luray was improving by reason of the resources named, others began to be developed in the vicinity of the town in the shape of a variety of minerals, such as iron ore, zinc, lead, ochre, slate and copper, samples of which are in the cabinet of minerals belonging to the development company there. Owing to the naturally fine agricultural resources and the varieties of minerals found, an organization was formed in 1890 for the development of these resources, as well as those of the place, called the Valley Land and Improvement Company, with an authorized capital stock of $2,000,000, a great deal of which was at once taken, and D. F. Kagey was made President, with G. C. Marshall, of Uniontown, Pennsylvania, as Vice-President and general manager. This company purchased the caverns, inn, and all the land surrounding the town and considerable bodies of fine timber and mineral lands in addition. This concern inaugurated a spirit of material progress for the place which resulted in marked improvement. Several valuable manufacturing plants were secured. The financiering qualities of D. F. Kagey, with C. G. Marshall's knowledge of minerals and ores gained in Pennsylvania, inspired a confidence in the public which greatly assisted the company in carrying out its various undertakings for the benefit of Luray. Luray is quite a manufacturing center, with its tannery, Luray Manufacturing Company, wagon-works, flouring mills, cigar factory, and several other minor undertakings.

The policy of the Valley Land and Improvement Company is liberal and conservative. The result is, what Luray has it has. The company has some two thousand five hundred acres in town lots and 8,000 acres in mineral lands, which sooner or later will be the foundation of considerable manufacturing power at this place.

The Mountain Park Springs Company is headed by Walter Campbell and Judge Alexander Y. Brand. This concern has a capital stock of $50,000, and has purchased a lovely mountain site not far from Luray, where a neat, commodious hotel will be erected, with a number of cottages, for the purpose of furnishing a summer-resort to people of limited means who are not able to pay high prices.

The population of Luray is about three thousand people.

SCHOOLS.

The influence of the schools over the town is easily seen. The schools, of which there are several here, advance the town in every way, for many of the pupils are boarders from a distance, and their means are more or less expended in Luray. The Von Bara College is a good institution, capable of accommodating some seventy or eighty pupils. It is under the management of J. I. Miller, a gentleman of varied experience and culture. The Luray Female Institute is also a popular and widely-known institution of learning.

CHURCHES.

The Episcopal, Presbyterian, Lutheran, Methodist and Baptist all have their religious houses, where divine worship is held every Sabbath.

THE INN.

This beautiful building is constructed on the Queen Anne style, the lower portion being of stone and the upper part of ornamental woodwork, shingled down to the stone. An annex has been added giving the structure accommodation for four or five hundred people. A vine-covered piazza fronts the entire length of the building.

CHAPTER XXIV.

CLARKE COUNTY, VIRGINIA.

Clarke county occupies part of the northern portion of Shenandoah Valley. It was cut off from Frederick in the year 1835, and was duly organized in 1836. The soil is generally very rich, of a limestone character, and is noted for its productiveness as to cereals—wheat particularly. The great bulk of land lying west of Shenandoah river is a great wheat-producing country, often yielding from forty to forty-five bushels per acre.

In addition to the agricultural productions, this county has turned out to be possessor of a mineral wealth likely to add materially to its riches. Iron ore (brown hemitite and specular), stratified on the slopes of mountains and in pockets on the course of the river, have been discovered in large quantities, and some have been worked for ten years, the products of these mines having been shipped to Sparrow Point, near Baltimore, Harrisburg and Carlisle, Pennsylvania, and the Shenandoah Iron Works, in Page county. Along the foot-hills of the Blue Ridge, in this county, fine specimens of copper and lead have been discovered east of the Shenandoah river, and tin has been reported to have been found on the Capon Springs property by Mr. Bale, who shipped a cargo of the ore to Wales. A purchase of these lands has been negotiated for, including that part of the property on which satisfactory ore has been found. The ores of the county have been worked successfully, notwithstanding the fact that they had to be wagoned five or six miles to connect with railway facilities. There are many ore-bearing tracts which as yet have not been developed, nor can these mineral resources be with any reasonable certainty approximated until they are opened up.

Among the resources of this section may be mentioned its timber lands, including large quantities of oak, hickory, walnut, ash, poplar, chestnut and other kinds of the best quality; and while much has been utilized already, there remain great bodies of it, especially along the foothills of the mountains. Stock-raising in the county is quite profitable, and sheep, cattle, horses and swine are bred in large numbers. The horses of Clarke county command a ready sale, on account of their superiority. There is a superabundance of vegetables, dairy products, and farm productions, which are advantageously disposed of by the citizens. The climate is admirable in every way, and the lands rolling and easy of tillage, producing vast quantities of every known product which the soil is capable of bringing forth.

The county-seat of Clarke is Berryville, which lies upon the Norfolk and Western Railroad (formerly known as the Shenandoah Valley road), forty miles south of Hagerstown and 199 miles north of Roanoke City. It is a very old place, and prior to the year 1798 was known as Battletown, taking this warlike title from the fights which old Daniel Morgan had at the place whenever he came to the town from his home, "Soldier's Rest," some three miles from the place. Saratoga was constructed by Mr. Daniel Morgan, who built the house with the Hessian prisoners, that even quarried the stone.

In 1798 Battletown was incorporated and called Berryville, in honor of Benjamin Berry, an honored citizen of the place at that time. Being the county-seat, it gradually increased until there were three or four hundred people, and it was supported by the trade from the surrounding agricultural region. It went through the ravages of the civil war, and was the scene of several skirmishes during that period in which its citizens played an important part, especially when it was shelled by a Maryland regiment. Subsequent to the war it recuperated, and in 1881, when the Shenandoah Valley Railroad came through, had about five hundred people, but from that on the increase and growth quickened perceptibly until 1891, when the inhabitants numbered some eighteen hundred people.

There is a general air of good feeling and fellowship, and, unlike most small places, everybody always has something good instead of bad to say of his neighbor. Enjoyment and innocent mirth rule the hour, and from the parents to the exquisitely lovely daughters who promenade the shaded sidewalks, there is a desire and will to make everybody have a pleasant and enjoyable time.

The churches of almost every denomination are here—the Episcopal, Northern and Southern Methodist churches, Baptist church, Presbyterian—all of which have large and flourishing congregations and a fair average attendance, composed of respectable, orderly people. The place has ample educational facilities, which exert a fine influence over the town and assist it in a material way. In addition to several good public graded schools, and private ones, too, Shenandoah Academy is here, with a fine roll of students, and the young Pages, Lewises, Taylors, Moores, McDonalds, Wheats, McCormicks, Castlemans, Deals, all learn the rudiments and higher branches of educational knowledge here. The natural result of all these advantages is a type of society of the best order.

This place, which has been quiet so long, cannot remain so in the future, in this onward age of development and progress. The rich agricultural resources surrounding it, the vast body of timbered lands of superior quality, the mineral wealth throughout the county, the immediate delightful advantages of the town itself, will necessarily propel it forward. The formation of the Berryville Land and Improvement Company, for the purpose of developing the resources of the town, is but the beginning of an end that will yet astonish the people of the place who now have almost every nucleus for the founding of a town or the building of a city.

The town is well laid off, with broad streets, nicely shaded, and the adjacent country is admirably suited for building sites, whether for manufacturing or residence purposes, which are being laid off and improved.

CHAPTER XXV.

THE NEW RIVER BRANCH OF THE NORFOLK AND WESTERN RAILROAD COMPANY.

The New River branch of the Norfolk and Western Railroad Company runs from Radford, in Montgomery county, through Pulaski and Giles counties, Virginia, and Mercer county, West Virginia; thence on through Tazewell county, Virginia, touching the West Virginia line at Bluestone Junction, and goes to Pocahontas, Virginia. The branch running from Bluestone Junction goes into the Flat Top coal region, and on to Elk Horn from Mill Creek Junction, which latter branch is being extended to Ironton, Ohio, through West Virginia.

Such a marked effect did the formation and construction of this route have upon the section of country that every person who acted a part on the theatre of its earlier history deserves special notice.

In the fall of 1862, Gen. G. C. Wharton, of Radford, was marching through West Virginia with his brigade, on his way to Fayette by the Raleigh Turnpike. When beyond Princeton, after crossing Bluestone river, the troops stopped to rest for a few moments in ascending the mountains. Two of his officers, Captain Pole French and Captain Pack, were lying under a train wagon. Whilst conversing with these gentlemen, he remarked—

"There is coal in this vicinity."

"Certainly," replied Captain Pack; "there is plenty of it. Right below here you will see where they have been getting it out."

So far as we can gather from history, this was the first discovery of this coal region which led to any beneficial results. This point was on the head-waters of Camp creek, in Mercer county, West Virginia.

Later on during the war, Gen. G. C. Wharton married a daughter of the late Dr. John B. Radford, after whose family the city of Radford is named. Settling there on New river, on some land given his wife by Dr. John B. Radford, General Wharton, who was well acquainted with the iron ore regions of Floyd, Carroll and Pulaski, conceived the idea that if the coal regions he had traversed during the war could be opened up and coke made, the point where he was living might become in some time an iron-manufacturing center. Nor were his ideas on that subject at all chimerical at the time.

New river, which borders his land, rises in North Carolina, and flowing north-west, cuts directly through the range of mountains between Radford and West Virginia, giving an outlet. General Wharton, being satisfied that the charcoal furnaces could not continue long in blast for want of fuel, thought of penetrating this coal region for coke. With this idea formed in his mind, he determined to set the plan in operation at the earliest possible moment. In 1871 he was elected to the Legislature, and while there, on March 7th, 1872, obtained a charter incorporating what was then known as "The New River Railroad, Mining and Manufacturing Company," with John B. Radford, John T. Cowan, Joseph Cloyd, James A. Walker, William T. Yancey, William Mahone, Charles W. Statham, Joseph H. Chumbley, A. H. Flannagan, Philip W. Strother, John C. Snidow, Joseph H. Hoge, William Eggleston, G. C. Wharton, William Adair, James A. Harvey, A. A. Chapman, Robert W. Hughes, A. N. Johnston, Elbert Fowler, David E. Johnson, John A. Douglas, W. H. French, R. B. McNutt, James M. Bailey and A. Gooch as incorporators.

The charter obtained by General Wharton gave the company power upon its organization "to construct, maintain and operate a railroad from New River depot, a point on the line of the Virginia and Tennessee division of the Atlantic, Mississippi and Ohio Railroad Company, in the county of Pulaski and State of Virginia, to such a point as may be agreed upon at or near the head-waters of Camp creek, in the county of Mercer and State of West Virginia; and the said New River Railroad, Mining and Manufacturing Company shall have the privilege of constructing, maintaining and operating such branch roads as may be necessary to bring out coal, iron and other ores from the counties of Mercer, Somers and Monroe of West Virginia, and the counties of Giles, Bland, Pulaski and Montgomery of the State of Virginia. And the said New River Railroad, Mining and Manufacturing Company shall be further empowered to acquire ownership of land for mining and manufacturing purposes, and shall be entitled to enjoy all the rights and privileges respectively conferred by the laws of the States of Virginia and West Virginia upon railroad corporations and mining and manufacturing companies, and shall be subject to the restrictions imposed by such laws upon like corporations.

2. "The capital stock of the said New River Railroad, Mining and Manufacturing Company shall not exceed two millions of dollars, to be divided into shares of one hundred dollars each, each share subscribed to be entitled to one vote in all meetings of said company; and one hundred

thousand dollars shall be taken as the minimum subscription on which said company may be organized."

While the General was applying for this charter, his friends ridiculed the idea of a railroad being run through the mountain gorges and cliffs bordering on the wild banks of New river. But he, nothing daunted, continued his course. When the bill came up to be passed, his brother law-makers said: "There's nothing in it, but we will vote for it because Wharton wants it."

Finally, as we have said, the bill became a law in March, 1872, and General Wharton, with the power conferred under this charter, proceeded to put his plans in operation.

On the 17th of June, 1872, a meeting of the incorporators of this road was held at Pearisburg, in Giles county, Virginia. From the *Pearisburg Gazette* of date June 22, 1872, we find that the following business was transacted:

The roll was called, and a quorum being present the meeting proceeded to business. Dr. John B. Radford was elected President and Elbert Fowler Secretary. Dr. Radford had given much of his time and attention to the construction of this company, and was a worthy gentleman in every way to place at the head of the scheme in its infancy.

On motion of Gen. G. C. Wharton, numerous committees were appointed to receive subscriptions at Norfolk, Richmond, Lynchburg, Philadelphia and all points along the line of the projected railroad. Two other resolutions were passed at this meeting, as follows:

Resolved, That Richard B. Roane be authorized and requested to visit the coal fields in Tazewell and Mercer and secure such grants and subscriptions in land, material, money and, as far as possible, the right-of-way on the line.

Resolved, That this meeting adjourn to meet at Eggleston's Springs on Tuesday, the 23d day of July.

Richard B. Roane came from Eastern Virginia, a descendant of one of the best and most influential families in that country. He came to Southwest Virginia in 1871 to follow his profession of engineering, and in connection with that became well acquainted with the topography and mineral resources of the land. To him was entrusted the onerous duty of securing options, grants, material, right-of-way and mineral properties for the New River Railroad, Mining and Manufacturing Company. He proceeded at once to the counties named, and during this trip laid the foundation for securing grants of the celebrated coal lands on Flat Top and around there which have since proven to be worth millions. He saw and negotiated with the following parties, as appears from the following memorandum, which is unquestionably true:

The following parties seen, and negotiations entered into with them for their coal, in the interest of the New River Railroad, Mining and Manufacturing Company: A. A. Spotts, G. W. Spotts, Jonathan Smith, John Smith, India and Sarah Taylor, Amos Read, W. L. Moore, Jacob Buckland, W. H. Whitten, George Reid, Thomas Franklin, I. Q. Moore, Lewis K. Harvey, John J. Jeffress, the tract on center of Laurel; Osborne tract, near the same, 500 acres (Laurel); Daniel Bolling, D. H. Dean, Daniel K. Perdue, J. Parker, Mosby Davis, George Tabor, Arch Thompson, C. H. Gleaner, 500 acres.

These parties were willing to make certain donations and grants, provided the road was constructed in five years. Most of these lands were in the very heart of the Flat Top region, and the New River Railroad, Mining and Manufacturing Company, with the options upon such property as this, would have been one of the richest corporations in the South and made the originators of the scheme rich had justice played a role on the stage of this railroad theatre.

On July 23, 1872, the meeting appointed to take place at Eggleston's Springs was held, and from a subsequent copy of the *Pearisburg Gazette* of date July 27, 1872, we find the following proceedings concerning the New River Railroad, Mining and Manufacturing Company:

A quorum for business being present, on motion, Richard Wood was appointed Chairman and A. L. Fry and George W. Easeley Secretaries.

The committees appointed at a former meeting to canvass for subscriptions to capital stock, not being ready to report, were severally continued.

Richard B. Roane, who was appointed to visit the coal fields in the counties of Tazewell and Mercer to secure grants and subscriptions, and, as far as practicable, the right-of-way, returned an interesting and flattering report, which was read and accepted.

A resolution was then passed by the company with reference to subscriptions, and the meeting then adjourned after appointing Gen. G. C. Wharton, Hon. P. W. Strother, John T. Cowan and George W. Easeley as a committee to solicit aid from the Atlantic, Mississippi and Ohio, and the Chesapeake and Ohio Railroads. Although the *Gazette* does not mention the fact, yet there is evidence that at this meeting John T. Cowan was elected President, with Wood, Strother, Radford, Fowler and Wharton directors.

In the session of 1872-'73 the charter was amended in several respects, to meet the wishes of parties desiring to become connected with the company.

Early in the spring of 1874 Richard B. Roane visited Richmond, Virginia, and while at the Exchange Hotel was introduced to one Thomas Graham, from Philadelphia, by Gov. Gilbert C. Walker, at that time occupying the highest post of honor in Virginia. Roane exhibited some samples of ores and minerals to Graham which pleased him very much, and he made minute inquiries regarding the country, resources, minerals and all, to which Roane politely gave him all the information possible, desiring to interest every one he could in the New River Railroad, Mining and Manufacturing Company. Finally he asked Roane if he would meet him and take him over the line of country—through Tazewell and Mercer—where the coal was situated. Roane agreed to meet him at Dublin, in Pulaski county, and did so, taking him for a trip through the counties above named, and then he returned to Philadelphia, carrying with him a box of specimens to be analyzed.

Hitherto, in detailing the history of this little company, which was struggling to place itself upon its feet, we have done so with great pleasure; but from this on a canopy of darkness comes over the transactions concerning it which we would gladly leave drawn, but truth in chronicling these events requires that it be unfolded.

What passed between R. B. Roane and Thomas Graham during this trip through the country we are unable to say, nor can we explain why Walter W. Wood should have appeared on the scene in Philadelphia about this time, but we find that in this same spring he wrote the following letter:

PHILADELPHIA, PA., }
April 10, 1874. }

DEAR ROANE:—I have had a further interview with the parties to-day. Graham's box of specimens has arrived, and he is proceeding immediately to analyze them. The parties are in dead earnest, and nothing will disconcert them, unless the ores turn out bad on analysis—a contingency that they do not contemplate. Whether you deem it advisable to see Colonel Harman or not, you come to Richmond to see me, as the parties want the railroad *captured* right away. I repeat, they mean business.

Very truly yours,
W. W. WOOD.

Who the parties were that wanted the railroad *captured* right away we cannot say from Wood's letter, nor have we any idea what plans had been formed for capturing the same. But three days later the following letter was written, which, in a measure, gives us some idea who the capturing parties were:

THOMAS GRAHAM,   T. B. ENGLISH,
  President.   Sec'y-Treas'r.

OFFICE NORTH CAROLINA
  CENTER IRON AND MANUFACTURING COMPANY,
    PHILADELPHIA, PA., }
      April 13, 1874. }

MR. R. B. ROANE, ESQ.,
  Dublin, Pulaski county, Va.

DEAR SIR:—In conversation with our friends on the subject of the New River Railroad and matters connected therewith, they join me in the opinion that it will be expedient to see you here, in order to have more definite information. I, therefore, invite you to come to this city, and meet us with Governor Walker, in order that you may personally explain and confer with us. Should this meet your wishes, will you please advise Governor Walker, to whom I have written to-day, and also inform me, appointing the time? I would suggest that you bring with you all necessary papers of information, with maps. Inclosed I hand you Girard National Bank check on New York, for one hundred dollars, which please acknowledge.

Very truly yours,
THOMAS GRAHAM.

The friends of whom Thomas Graham writes in the above letter were, in all probability, J. Dickinson Sergeant, Richard Wood, Harvey Beckwith and Lewis Rodman, including Governor Walker, of course. From the best light we have upon the subject, these were the parties then attempting to capture the New River Railroad, Mining and Manufacturing Company. In his letter of April 13, 1874, Thomas Graham advises R. B. Roane to put himself in communication with Governor Walker. But it appears that Roane had already communicated with Governor Walker, for two days after Thomas Graham wrote Roane, this letter followed:

RICHMOND, VA., April 15, 1874.

MY DEAR SIR:—Your valued favor of the 7th instant reached here during my absence.

After my return I had a conference with Gen. G. C. Wharton, who promised to write you, and I presume has done so last evening. I received a note from Mr. Graham stating that he had written you suggesting a conference between us and others in Philadelphia. I am compelled to be in that city next week on other business, and I have so written him. If you can go on, I think it would be well to do so; and if you will name the day most convenient to you, I will try and arrange to go on at the same time. *Much caution* and good management will be required in all these matters, which, of course, you fully appreciate. Hoping to hear from you by return mail,

I am, very truly yours,
G. C. WALKER.

R. B. ROANE, ESQ.

In a short while from the receipt of those letters Roane went to Philadelphia. By some people it was thought that as Thomas Graham was not in any way connected with the road, Roane should not have carried the papers, maps and information which he had gathered as a duly appointed agent of the New River Railroad, Mining and Manufacturing Company to him and his Philadelphia friends; but, upon reflection, we are inclined to think that in this instance Roane should not have been censured, because he wished to show Northern parties the many advantages which his company possessed in the way of minerals and ores. In fact, others knew that Roane was going on, because General Wharton met Roane in company with Thomas Graham; thought that the latter was a Philadelphia capitalist, as he represented himself as such, and from his statements believed that he and his Northern friends could construct and equip the road. But Gen. G. C. Wharton at that time had not the ghost of an idea that Thomas Graham and his friends were in concert to capture the coal lands, strip them from the New River Company, and let the latter shift for itself. Nor had such a plan ever entered the mind of John T. Cowan, then President of the company, because, as we shall see directly, he and Hotchkiss were working in the interest of the New River Railroad, Mining and Manufacturing Company, endeavoring to obtain options and grants for land. Prior to this time we find, by a memorandum endorsed, that in 1872 and 1873 all negotiations, bargains and purchases were being secured by Roane in the name of the New River Railroad, Mining and Manufacturing Company. On the back of the list of men seen in Abb's Valley, in reference to their lands, we find this written memorandum—

"Abb's Valley coal men seen and negotiated with by Roane in 1872 and 1873."

And within we find written—

"In the interest of the N. R. R. R., M. & M. Co."

So we may reasonably conclude that in the capturing minds of Thomas Graham and friends, of Philadelphia, alone rested the idea of gobbling up these mineral lands, at this time, without respect to the wishes or rights of the New River Railroad, Mining and Manufacturing Company.

What passed at the conference in Philadelphia which Roane attended we cannot say farther than what was subsequently stated by R. B. Roane— that "a plan of action was determined upon."

We are not left, though, in the dark as to what that plan was, for Mr. Roane, upon being asked, frankly stated that Thomas Graham desired to become a stockholder in the company, with some friends of his. At all events, Roane called a meeting of the directors, which took place in April, 1874, about the 24th, at the Norvell-Arlington Hotel, in the city of Lynchburg. He requested that Thomas Graham and others be allowed to subscribe, but for reasons unknown the directors refused to allow it, doubtless feeling then that things were not going on as they ought. But the stockholders, having carelessly omitted hitherto to pay the two per cent. on the fifty thousand subscribed, Thomas Bocock, an astute attorney, at the suggestion of Roane, gave it as his opinion that the whole thing was invalid on that account, and that the books should be re-opened in order to collect the two per cent. Three of the directors consented, the books of subscription were re-opened, and checks were given by the subscribers for the two per cent., and other subscriptions made. At this meeting it seems that Roane made a subscription of $5,000, conditioned upon the fact that he should be satisfied with the organization to be made at the Montgomery White Sulphur Springs, in June, 1874. We further infer, from facts which we will give directly, that at this meeting Richard B. Roane was in some manner passed over and ignored in a way which he thought was but a poor return for the services he had given this company. From now on we find that he gave the Philadelphia parties every assistance possible, until they broke faith with him, and by their own actions, as we shall see, treated him abominably.

Shortly after the adjournment of this meeting Thomas Graham wrote a letter, which we copy *verbatim*. It was as follows:

THOMAS GRAHAM,   T. B. ENGLISH,
President.   *Sec'y-Treas'r.*

NORTH CAROLINA CENTRE
  IRON AND M'F'G COMPANY,
    PHILADELPHIA, April 28, 1874.

MR. RICHARD B. ROANE, ESQ.,
    Dublin, Va.

MY DEAR SIR:—Mr. Richard Wood returned and called on me yesterday. He related what had occurred at the meeting at Lynchburg. His explanation of the results is not made clear to me up to this time. I also have your letter of the 26th, which is very clear, and I coincide with the opinions therein expressed. Until I see you I will reserve any further comments. I fully appreciate your surprise and disappointment. I think it just to warn you that you are likely to be ignored. I do not know yet what steps myself and friends will take—surely some, however—of which I will inform you; but I would advise you to strengthen yourself by laying hold of red hematite and magnetic ore, marble and lithographic stone; also fossil ores near and tributary to the line. Advise us of properties you can secure, with description, terms, etc., and we will inform you what we will do. Get leases and options. Tell us what you wish us to do for you. If it meet with our views we will do as we agree. It will be wise for you to confine yourself for the present to properties close to the line of the railroad, and where you know good bodies of mineral exist— the best of such properties—without encumbering yourself with heavy bodies of property. It will be proper to furnish you with funds for your expenses whilst engaged in this work, and the further compensation or interest that may be determined on secured to you by contract. Should you entertain these suggestions, we would prefer that leases, options or any direct important purchases of mineral property or strategical points of importance, if approved by us, should be made in the name of or *conveyed to J. Dickinson Sergeant*, attorney at law, Philadelphia, Pa., subject to the contract of interest or compensation agreed upon with you. I call your attention at once to the magnetic property (No. 3) north of Snidow's Ferry; to Charles Parker's red hematite, No. 2; to No. 5 brown hematite, Laurel creek; to the magnetic ore near A. M. & O. R. R.; to the marbles and litho stone. Mr. Wood considers that Mr. Cowan and Mr. Hotchkiss are in positions to enable them to accumulate property for the New River Railroad. Probably they are. In writing you this letter, however, it is simply business between us. I shall be glad to hear from you, and I will advise you. Please write me on the matter contained in this letter, and believe me to be sincerely your friend,

    THOMAS GRAHAM, 233 St. (over)

P. S.—You will pardon me if I further advise you to make *no* confidants. When you write, will you inform me more particularly as to the occurrences of the meeting at Lynchburg, and whether General Wharton agreed *entirely* with Mr. Wood in the course he pursued? I wish to remark that Mr. Wood was authorized, and agreed to make the requisite subscription, and my telegram inferred further aid, if necessary.

This remarkable letter was written on the 28th day of April, 1874, almost three months before Thomas Graham or J. Dickinson Sergeant became officers in that company. Notwithstanding the fact that Sergeant had no connection whatever with the company, Graham writes the authorized agent of the New River Railroad, Mining and Manufacturing Company to have "all leases, options or any direct important purchase of mineral land, or strategical points of importance," conveyed to J. Dickinson Sergeant. Graham had some object in view in wanting the New River Railroad, Mining and Manufacturing Company completely separated from the options, leases and purchases of the mineral lands, and that object could be but one. Had the leases, purchases and options of this great coal section been obtained in the name of the New River Railroad, Mining and Manufacturing Company no disposition could have been made of them without the consent, sanction and authority of the directors of that company, and the general stockholders—not Graham, Sergeant, Wood, Beckwith and Rodman—would have been entitled to a participation in the profits. The fact stares us directly in the face, that the very property which the company knew was most valuable and upon which it based its calculations was being snatched away and forever sundered from her chartered rights, without any knowledge of the President or board of directors, who were the legal guardians of its property, rights and franchises. By virtue of the authority vested in R. B. Roane to secure grants, options, leases and contracts of mineral land, the New River Railroad, Mining and Manufacturing Company was entitled to them, and Graham and Sergeant well knew that their steps were in violation of that express authority to have them gotten in the name of a total stranger to that company.

It was now absolutely necessary that such a change should be made in the governing body of the company as would enable Graham and Sergeant to continue their concerted plan of operations without question from any President, Vice-President, Secretary, Treasurer or directors. So, at the meeting held in June, 1874, at the Montgomery White Sulphur Springs, Thomas Graham appeared for the purpose of becoming a subscriber in the sum of $50,000, to make up the necessary $100,000 required by the charter.

At this meeting the stockholders

again objected to the books being re-opened or Graham being allowed to subscribe. There seemed to be some insuperable difficulty to his coming in, for at the former meeting in Lynchburg the directors and stockholders had objected. But Roane again came to his rescue, and withdrawing his subscription of $5,000 and his check for 2 per cent. cash, the books were re-opened, and Thomas Graham subscribed $50,000, and at last became a stockholder in the company with which he had been hitherto connected "*sub rosa.*" At this meeting a new organization was effected, and J. Dickinson Sergeant was made President, Thomas Graham Vice-President, T. B. English Secretary and Treasurer, and R. B. Roane land agent and mining engineer.

The surprise which Thomas Graham expressed in his last letter to R. B. Roane, at the proceedings in Lynchburg, can be easily understood now. This last re-organization he expected in Lynchburg early in the spring. His taunting Roane with being ignored was but a card played to prejudice him as much as possible against the Virginia board of directors. Doubtless that very objection which they had to Graham's subscribing was apprehensiveness lest the road passed from their hands.

After this last meeting there was no longer any concealment on Graham's part, so far as Roane was concerned. He distinctly asserts that the land grants, contracts and options are their private land interests. The following correspondence forever sets this matter at rest, and shows that the options gotten under, by virtue of, and through the authority of the New River Railroad, Mining and Manufacturing Company were appropriated *in toto* by Sergeant and his capturing friends:

PHILADELPHIA, July 22, 1874.
MR. RICHARD B. ROANE, *Dublin, Va.*

MY DEAR SIR:—Mr. Sergeant wishes you to come here and bring with you all papers and memoranda you have in connection with our *private* land *interests.*

We are deliberating on our plans on this and railroad matters, and your presence with papers and information is necessary.

Mr. English writes you to-day.
Very truly yours,
THOMAS GRAHAM.

With this letter from Thomas Grahame one came from T. B. English, which reads as follows:

No. 233 SOUTH 3D ST., }
PHILADELPHIA, July 22, 1874. }

MR. RICHARD B. ROANE, *Land Agent and Mining Engineer, New River Railroad, Mining and Manufacturing Company, Dublin, Va.*

MY DEAR SIR:—I am instructed by the President to request you to come to this city, and to bring with you all papers, contracts, deeds, maps, etc., appertaining to the business of this company in your possession, for examination, etc.

Please draw on me at sight for one month's salary and traveling expenses, and advise of the probable time of your arrival here, in order that Mr. Sergeant may arrange to meet you.

Very respectfully,
T. B. ENGLISH,
Secretary and Treasurer
N. R. R. R., M. & M. Co.

Is it not passing strange that Thomas Graham should have to write such a letter, underscoring "private interests," at the same time that the Secretary of the company writes to Roane to come in his official capacity? There is but one reasonable solution: these land options had been gotten apart from the railroad company, which was justly entitled to them, and Thomas Graham, fearing that Mr. Roane would not consider these as a part of the railroad papers, deemed it more expedient to speak plainly as to the meaning of the request in Secretary English's letter. That Richard B. Roane did not consider them as in any way connected with the New River Railroad, Mining and Manufacturing Company is conclusively shown later on.

What took place at Philadelphia when Roane went on is not positively known except between the parties themselves. But from evidence before us the options, leases, grants, contracts, and so forth, were deposited with J. Dickinson Sergeant. There has been some little question as to what properties those options, leases, and contracts included. Some have contended that they were simply leases and options of iron mines in and about Giles and Tazewell, but the following letter, coupled with the memorandum already given, shows that they were options on those valuable coal lands around about Laurel creek in Tazewell, where the mining town of Pocahontas now stands, and some of the Bluestone coal lands:

ABB'S VALLEY,
TAZEWELL COUNTY, VA.,
August 22, 1872.

RICHARD B. ROANE.

DEAR SIR:—I hasten to reply to your letter received a few days since. Sqr. Moore says there is no doubt but that you can get the Osborn land, as he is now holding correspondence with said Osborn to make the purchase, and expects to let you have it. I saw Nelson, and he promised that you should have the refusal, and will sell to no one else before giving you the first chance. I saw my son and many others, all of whom seem to be willing now to give one-half to come up to your terms—myself with the balance. It is difficult for me to ascertain the exact amount of acres, but I know one thing: that is, the company can secure one-half of all, or nearly all, of the mineral lands on Laurel, and that is all they want. There is only two persons but what is willing to come into the arrangement, so I hope that this will satisfy the company. Dr. Johnson is doing well. He, Mr. Moore, and myself are the working men for the company. Write me without delay, and if there is anything that I can do, let me know, and it shall be attended to.

Respectfully,
A. A. SPOTTS.

This property which Mr. Spotts

speaks of, on Laurel Creek, is among the best of the coal mines in that section now, and worth probably many millions of dollars. Mr. Spotts was under the impression that the negotiations were in favor of the New River Railroad, Mining and Manufacturing Company. The memorandum which we have quoted from shows that his impression was correct.

By some means or other, Governor Walker failed to participate in the new arrangement and re-organization for some time afterwards. W. W. Wood appears upon the scene again by writing the following letter:

> 515 OLIVE STREET,
> ST. LOUIS, Mo.
>
> DEAR ROANE:—What's become of the railroad and the mineral property? I saw Graham in Philadelphia, and he gave me an account of the proceedings at the re-organization of the New River Railroad, with the name of the President-elect, etc. He told me that the President would immediately organize things and proceed actively to work in building the road. He told me that Governor Walker was not in it, but that he intended to protect you fully. Write me all about it, and anything of interest besides that you can think of. I am here at above address—have stuck out my shingle as attorney-at-law. My prospects are good, and I believe I will do well. Write me all about the iron.
>
> Very truly yours,
> W. W. WOOD.

In 1875 the line was surveyed, commencing at New river. It was run to Hinton, with power to build any branch roads that might be necessary to bring out minerals. Of course this branch line had indirect reference to the counties of Wise, Giles, Bland, Buchanan and others, but pointed more directly to the rich coal fields near Abb's Valley, in Tazewell, and the county of Mercer, West Virginia. There was but little known regarding this company until 1878, when the State convicts were placed upon the line and grading begun for a narrow-gauge railroad, and the plan conceived by General Wharton in 1871, which was deemed almost impossible by everyone, became a living reality. These convicts were secured through General Wharton, who not only succeeded in getting an act passed to that effect, but personally went security upon Thomas Graham's bond, which had to be given to the State before the Governor would allow them to go.

In the meantime, between the years 1875 and 1878, R. B. Roane was still seeking leases, grants and options upon the mineral properties adjacent and tributary to the proposed line. Several of these original options are still extant, with the name of owner of land, the county in which it was situated, amount specified, and terms of lease. All were obtained in the name of J. Dickinson Sergeant, of Philadelphia. Most of these contracts which did not go into Sergeant's possession were obtained in the counties of Bland and Giles,

Virginia, and Mercer county, West Virginia. They appear to have been gotten on or about the 17th or 18th of May, 1877. Why these failed to reach their destination is accounted for from the fact that in the year 1878 there was a difficulty between Roane and Sergeant in reference to the part Roane should have for services rendered. We give below copy of a contract drawn by Sergeant, which will show that he acknowledges indebtedness for Roane's services. There seemed to have arisen some misunderstanding, because a letter of Roane's, which we will give later on, clearly shows that. This agreement is signed by J. Dickinson Sergeant, and was evidently forwarded by him to R. B. Roane for signature, who refused to append his name to it on the ground of its being defective. The contract is as follows:

Agreement made this ____ day of October, A. D. 1878, between J. Dickinson Sergeant, of the city of Philadelphia, President of the New River Company, and trustee holding certain lands and leases on and near New river, in Virginia and West Virginia, for himself, Richard Wood, Harvey Beckwith and Lewis Rodman, of the one part, and Richard B. Roane of the other. Whereas the said Roane has rendered services, time and labor to, for and about the business of the New River Railroad Company, and about the obtaining and negotiating for the *lands and leases* now held by the said Sergeant, as trustee aforesaid, upon the stipulation that he should have the privilege of taking at the cost thereof, with interest and expenses added, one sixteenth part of the stock of the said company, and a similar proportion in the said lands and leases: Now this agreement witnesseth, that the said Sergeant, in consideration of the services of the said Roane, as aforesaid, and of one dollar unto him in hand paid by the said Roane, the receipt whereof is hereby acknowledged, doth declare and agree that the said New River Railroad Company shall and will issue to the said Roane, on payment by him of one-sixteenth part of the cost thereof, with interest and expenses added, one-sixteenth part of the stock of said company; and that he, the said Sergeant, shall and will, on payment by the said Roane of one-sixteenth part of the cost thereof, with interest and expenses added, grant and assure to the said Roane, his heirs, executors, administrators and assigns, one-sixteenth part of the lands and leases on and near New river held by the said Sergeant as aforesaid, and that upon any sale of the stock, leases and lands before the said Roane shall have obtained said transfer, the said Roane shall be entitled to receive one-sixteenth part of the profits of said sale, to be ascertained by deducting from the sum realized the cost of acquisition of the same, with interest and expenses thereof.

Provided, however, that nothing herein contained shall be deemed to vest in the said Roane (prior to the payment by him of the one-sixteenth part of the cost, interest and expenses aforesaid) any further or other right or title than the right to participate in the profits from sales of the stock, lands and leases aforesaid, should there be a sale of the same by the parties holding title thereto. And the said Roane hereby agrees to accept the interest hereby intended to be secured to him in full payment and satisfaction for his services to the said New River Railroad Company, and to the said Sergeant and those for whom he is acting as trustee. In witness whereof, the said parties have hereunto set their hands and seals, the date aforesaid.

(Signed) J. D. SERGEANT. [L. S.]

Witness present:

(Signed) SEPTIMUS E. NORRIS.

A true copy:
PARK PHIPPS (Witness).

In this agreement the evidence is conclusive that Sergeant did not hold these grants, leases and options for the benefit of the New River Railroad, Mining and Manufacturing Company, but for the personal benefit of himself and three others. Where had gone the stockholders' interest in these valuable options and leases originally negotiated for in the name of the company? Echo answers, "Where?"

Mr. Roane misunderstood the contract in two particulars. He thought that the interest he should have in the option and leases should be entirely distinct from his participation in the stock of the New River Railroad. He regarded the two as totally distinct transactions, just as Sergeant really held when he termed one interest for himself as trustee for others. Moreover, Roane evidently understood that he was to have the interest for services rendered without any payment of cost and expense. That this was the original agreement there can be no doubt, for the correspondence, as well as the extrinsic facts, prove it. But J. Dickinson Sergeant, having possession of these leases and options, chose to take a different position. Mr. Roane's letter written concerning the contract gives his veiws thoroughly upon the subject. It is as follows:

NEWBERN, Va., March 17, 1879.

J. D. SERGEANT, ESQ.

DEAR SIR:—I return one of the contracts unsigned. I have examined it carefully for the first time. It is very much mixed, and susceptible of too many constructions—that is, the railroad company and the land company is mixed up together in such a way that one cannot be distinguished from the other; in fact, they are made to appear in the contract as one and the same, while, as I understand it, they are separate and distinct. If this understanding be correct, they should be separated and made distinct in the contract, or there should be separate contracts. The wording of the contract is such that it brings the railroad and land company together in such a way that they cannot be separated. I am sure this was not your intention. Again, the wording of the contract is such that it makes the interest intended to be secured contingent only in the event of a sale, or upon my paying such a portion of prime costs; and even this is foreshadowed with some doubt from the phraseology. And under the programme, as I understand it, there will be no sale; hence I am excluded from the contract, unless I can, by some chance, raise the money necessary to be paid from some outside source, which is simply impossible, as I am dependent on my daily labor for sustenance. I am, therefore, forever excluded under the contract, unless some one will take it off my hands at whatever they may choose to give, although the enterprise may pay for itself in one year, and its net earnings may thereafter be large. Yet I can never participate under the contract, unless there is an actual and absolute sale of the stock, lands, leases, rights, franchises, etc., or by my paying the certain proportion, in some source independent of the enterprise, whatever its net earnings may be. Thus, suppose the parties now in interest continue, the road built, the mines and lands utilized, work and ore shipped and manufactured—in one year the thing has paid for itself, and the next there is a net profit. Under the contract I am excluded from participation because I am unable to pay my proportion independent of the earnings of the enterprise. If there is no sale, there is no contract, unless I can get the money from some outside source to pay the proportion as mentioned, which I am not able to do, and doubtless never will be, unless the earnings of such operations are to be applied in this way, which the contract does not provide for. While this may be implied, we may die at any time, and this implication disregarded. The contract is imperfect and worded wrong. My first impulse was to sign it without comment, but knowing that you meant and intended differently from what the contract expresses, I thought it best to return the contract and call your attention to its defects. There is not a court in the land but what would construe this contract as I have.

Yours very truly,
RICHARD B. ROANE.

In regard to his having gotten these options in J. D. Sergeant's name, Mr. Roane's explanation is this—

When I went into Tazewell and Mercer I was under the impression that the organization of the New River Railroad and Manufacturing Company was illegal; so I obtained them in limited grants, in an independent capacity.

Messrs. Graham and Sergeant failed signally to liquidate Roane's claim, as just as it was, so far as they were concerned, and he was on the eve of bringing suit to recover his rights when the New River Railroad, Mining and Manufacturing Company was said to have passed into the hands of *innocent purchasers*—the Norfolk and Western Railroad Company. The exact time at which the New River Railroad, Mining and Manufacturing Company passed into the possession of the Norfolk and Western Railroad, or Clarence H. Clark and *his associates*, is not exactly known, but we gather from the first annual report for the year ending December 31, 1881, of the Norfolk and Western Railroad Company, that the negotiations for the New River Railroad, Mining and Manufacturing Company, and all its branches, properties and rights, were completed at the time that Clarence H. Clarke and *his associates* were purchasing the Norfolk and Western Railroad, which, at that time, was the Atlantic, Mississippi and Ohio Railroad. The purchase of the latter was made under sale by decree of court on February 10, 1881. Their first annual report shows this fact on page 6. It reads:

In the proceedings on the bill, the said court, on the 9th day of May, 1879, pronounced a decree of foreclosure and sale; and on the 10th day of February, 1881, the road, property, franchises and rights were sold to Clarence H. Clark and his associates for the sum of $8,605,000, subject to liens and encumbrances amounting to $4,898,159.14, including the interest calculated to the first day of January, 1881.

In this same first annual report there is something said concerning the New River Railroad, Mining and Manufacturing Company, on page 15:

The Norfolk and Western Railroad Company has acquired the control of the various roads in the States of Virginia and West Virginia, which, aggregated, constitute what is known as the New River Railroad Company. This line commences at the junction with the Norfolk and Western Railroad Company at New river bridge, and running down the New river and its tributaries, as at present projected, will be about seventy miles in length, with authority under its charters to extend up New river to the North Carolina border, and in various directions upon tributaries to the river. At its proposed terminus it strikes a superb body of Kanawha coal in what is known as the Flat Top region. The surveys were completed and work commenced August 3, 1881.

When we come to the beginning and inception of the Norfolk and Western Railroad Company, in the chapter containing its history, this subject will be reverted to again.

The Pocahontas and Flat Top coal regions, opened up by this company's railroad, is one of the best coal countries in the United States. These lands lie in a part of Tazewell county, Virginia, and Mercer, McDowell, Wyoming and Raleigh counties, West Virginia. The coal is not only of first-rate quality, but apparently of almost inexhaustible quantities. Throughout a large portion of Flat Top Mountain the coal is above water level, and lies most conveniently for cheap and expeditious mining. The mineral is deposited in layers throughout the mountain, and mined by an entrance cut into the solid bank of coal on the side of the hill. Tipples are erected near this entrance, and through them the coal goes into a railroad car, after being screened and the fine coal separated.

These coals, geologically, are the lowest members of the coal measures, and are the equivalent of the Quinimont group of the Kanawha region and the Pottsville conglomerate of Pennsylvania. They are low in sulphur and ash, and unusually high in fixed carbon. The coal bed everywhere presents, so far as discovered, a working thickness of 11'3" around Pocahontas, and holds its working dimensions until it reaches Flipping creek, six or seven miles off, where it divides into two beds, each some 4½ and 5½ feet thick. Westward of Pocahontas,

SOUTH-WEST VIRGINIA AND THE VALLEY.

along Laurel creek, the bed carries its thickness fairly well for a distance of eight miles, and shows pretty well the same section for quite a distance north of the dividing ridge, on the waters of the Elkhorn and the Tug Fork of Sandy. A large area of country is underlaid with this coal, and it has been estimated that it should yield 10,000 tons per acre, while the upper beds should add probably 6,000 tons more. The quality of it has been tested both in the laboratory and by actual practice, and for steaming and coking it has been found very superior. As a domestic coal, it is generally used and pronounced good. But a safer and better idea of its quality can be gained from McCreath and D'Invillier's analysis. In their report on "the New river-Cripple creek region," they give the following analysis in connection with its quality from an average of fifteen samples:

Water	1.011
Volatile matter	18.812
Fixed carbon	74.256
Sulphur	.730
Ash	5.191

By analysis this coal is superior to the Cumberland, Clearfield, Broad Top, Connellsville coking, Westmoreland and Cardiff (Wales) coals.

Its analysis as a coking coal is superior in every respect. The same valuable report already quoted gives the analysis of the coke taken from these companies' ovens in that region:

Water	.182	.196	.664
Volatile matter	.719	.494	1.059
Fixed carbon	92.248	92.585	92.816
Sulphur	.565	.677	.548
Ash	6.286	6.048	4.913
	100.000	100.000	100.000

Since the discovery of this valuable field many coal operations have begun. At present the following works are in active operations in Tazewell county, Virginia, and Mercer and McDowell counties, West Virginia:

In Tazewell, the South-west Virginia Improvement Company.

In Mercer county, West Virginia, in what is known as the Bluestone region (because the Bluestone river flows through the country), are John Cooper & Co., the Caswell Creek Coal and Coke Company, the Buckeye Coal and Coke Company, the Booth-Bowen Coal and Coke Company, the Good-will Coal and Coke Company, the Louisville Coal and Coke Company.

In McDowell county, on the Elkhorn extension of the Norfolk and Western Railroad Company, we have the Coaldale Coal and Coke Company, the Elkhorn Coal and Coke Company, the Shamokin Coal and Coke Company, the Norfolk Coal and Coke Company, the Lick Colliery, the Turkey Gap Coal and Coke Company, the Crozier Coal and Coke Company, the Houston Coal and Coke Company, the Powhatan Coal and Coke Company, the Lynchburg Coal and Coke Company.

These are all actively engaged in shipping. Many others are obtaining leases, and as the railroad extends on through McDowell towards Ironton will begin shipping. To give an idea of the immense amount of coal and coke shipped from these regions we subjoin a table of the shipments since 1883:

	Coal.	Coke.
1883	54,552 tons.	23,762 tons.
1884	153,229 "	56,360 "
1885	499,138 "	48,571 "
1886	739,018 "	59,021 "
1887	992,260 "	151,171 "
1888	1,343,312 "	202,808 "
1889	1,543,900 "	310,504 "

These figures do not include the coal mined altogether, because the miners and their families burn an unlimited supply for their own consumption.

As we may easily understand, the opening up of these works was the growth of towns and the country as if by magic. Pocahontas in two years grew into a city numbering its inhabitants among the thousands, while Bramwell, Graham, Simmons, and Mill Creek soon followed. From a howling wilderness of mountains the whole community in those sections became, as if by an electric shock, a rushing, thriving, business place; and now in that mining section, embracing a corner in each of the three counties of Tazewell, Virginia, and Mercer and McDowell counties, West Virginia, the population is hardly less than twenty thousand people. The wages of the miners are good, and as they are a class of people who do not believe in denying themselves, there has been a steady business rush all the time. A great deal of money has been made in speculating and dealing in coal lands, and the formation of joint stock companies of various kinds have, more than anything else, tended to develop each and every resource of the country. Certainly, just from this section alone, the New River division of the Norfolk and Western Railroad Company has almost inexhaustible supplies from which to draw. But, in addition to this great coal section, over this line of road will come the mineral products of the Clinch Valley country, which more properly belong to the history of the Clinch Valley extension of the great Norfolk and Western system.

CHAPTER XXVI.

THE NORFOLK AND WESTERN RAILROAD COMPANY.

The Norfolk and Western Railroad Company has played such an important part in the development of Southwest Virginia that it deserves a full account of its various operations from its inception to the present time; and the rapidity with which it has advanced in every way for the past nine years makes everything connected with it of more than ordinary interest. There is scarcely another railroad in the Southern States which has done so much for the development of the country through which it runs, or enriched its owners more. So phenomenal has been the success of the company in the section of country of which we are writing, that its name has a kind of talismanic effect there, and its objectionable features cheerfully borne on account of its developing policy.

In 1851 the Norfolk and Petersburg Railroad was chartered, and opened for traffic in 1852. This road ran between Norfolk and Petersburg, a distance of some eighty-one miles. It passes through what is known as the Great Dismal Swamp, which, at that time, was a scene of horror, but is now being gradually reclaimed and cultivated; thence on through Nansemond county, by Suffolk; next the road runs through Isle of Wight county, by Windsor, Zuni and through Southampton, Sussex, Prince George and Dinwiddie counties, until Petersburg is reached—a city of some thirty thousand people. As may well be imagined, this railroad did a small business until others connected with it were put in operation.

As far back as 1846 the Southside Railroad Company was chartered, but was not constructed and placed in operation until the year 1857, when it was opened for traffic between Petersburg and Lynchburg. This road runs from the former place through Dinwiddie, Nottoway, Prince Edward, Appomattox and Campbell counties to Lynchburg, in the latter county, 123 miles from Petersburg. The country through which it passes presents an uninviting aspect to the eye, but is really a good one. The railroad, in order to select the best grade possible, runs as much along the ridge as practicable, excluding from sight many fertile spots and good farms. Leaving Farmville, in traveling westward, the plateau begins, which is really a fine section from there on to Lynchburg. Many towns have sprung up along this route since its earlier history, among which may be mentioned Blackstone, Crewe, Burkeville, Farmville, Prospect and Pamplin. The live business capacity of some of these places argue with force that the possibilities of this section of the country are great.

The Virginia and Tennessee Railroad, chartered in March, 1849, and opened in 1857, runs westward from Lynchburg through Bedford, Botetourt, Roanoke, Montgomery, Pulaski, Wythe, Smyth and Washington counties to Bristol, Tennessee, a distance of 204 miles from Lynchburg. This line traverses a part of the great South-west of which we are particularly writing, and the towns, cities and counties contiguous to this branch of the road will not be especially mentioned now.

Another road was chartered, and partially constructed, in connection with the three we have mentioned, which was known as the Virginia and Kentucky Railroad. This route was to extend from Bristol to Cumberland Gap. The road was, however, placed in other hands, as we shall see later on.

On June 17, 1870, the Legislature of Virginia passed an act entitled "An act to authorize the formation of the Atlantic, Mississippi and Ohio Railroad," which was for the purpose of merging, absorbing and consolidating the Norfolk and Petersburg Railroad Company, the Southside Railroad Company, the Virginia and Tennessee Railroad Company, and the Virginia and Kentucky Railroad Company, all four of which were in a separate existence at that time. This consolidation was not effected without a great deal of trouble, and even at this day queer lobbying tales are told of how champagne flowed and Havana cigars were handed around among the law-makers on the evening of the day previous to that of the passage of the act. People along the lines of the companies were opposed, on the ground that it would not be to their interest—why, it was impossible to divine. That the consolidation was a good measure for the country at large is beyond all doubt, for by that means a traffic was established which redounded to Virginia's benefit. This new company was placed under the management of Gen. William Mahone, who has since rendered himself famous in Virginia politics; who, though censured by some for the manner in which he conducted the affairs of the company, undoubtedly improved and added to the condition of the road. It was during the year 1874, in April, that by an act of the Virginia Legislature the stock of the Virginia and Kentucky Railroad owned by the Atlantic, Mississippi and Ohio Company passed from its control. The road apparently was prospering under General Mahone's rule, for the traffic increased, while new stock, iron, and station-houses were all placed along the line of the road. This road controlled the branch from

Petersburg to City Point, and the extension from Glade Springs in Washington county, to the salt works, about nine miles distant. On October 1st, 1874, the Atlantic, Mississippi and Ohio Railroad Company failed to pay the semi-annual interest due upon the mortgaged debt it had created. This was a surprise indeed, and still more did consternation stare all in the face when, on April 1, 1875, the semi-annual interest was in default again. This second failure caused the trustees, under deed of September 9, 1870, to file their bill in the Circuit Court of the United States for the Eastern District of Virginia, praying that a receiver be appointed to take an account of all liens and incumbrances, and a sale of the property, rights and franchises of the road. On the 9th day of May, 1879, the Court decreed a sale of the property, and who should purchase the Atlantic, Mississippi and Ohio Railroad became an absorbing topic in railroad circles.

At this time this company owned and operated 428 miles of railroad, running through a good portion of Eastern Virginia and the very heart of the great South-west. At Bristol it connected with the East Tennessee, Virginia and Georgia, while at Norfolk it possessed harbor facilities unexcelled on the Atlantic coast. A rich, succulent agricultural country enclosed it on both sides, and it had more than a modicum of advantages usually possessed by railroads in the Southern States. The mineral resources along its lines were superb.

It was to these that the Northern capitalists were turning their attention—the coal and iron in South-west Virginia—and on the 10th day of February, 1881, the Atlantic, Mississippi and Ohio Railroad, with its road, property and franchises was purchased by Clarence H. Clark and his associates for the sum of $8,605,000, subject to liens and incumbrances amounting to $4,898,159.14, including interest calculated to the first day of January, 1881. This sale was duly confirmed by the court on the fourth day of April, 1881, and then the purchasers were designated as the "Norfolk and Western Railroad Company," under which the re-organization was perfected. The purchase-money was paid on the third day of May, 1881, and the road, with its property, franchises, rights and privileges, was deeded to the Norfolk and Western Railroad Company by M. F. Pleasants, who was the commissioner appointed by the court, which deed was duly recorded in the Clerk's office of the Hustings Court of the city of Norfolk. On the same day the Atlantic, Mississippi and Ohio Railroad Company deeded to the Norfolk and Western Railroad Company all the shares of the capital stock of the Norfolk and Petersburg, the Southside, and the Virginia and Tennessee Railroad Companies; the Virginia and

Kentucky Railroad stock having been already disposed of by the Legislature of Virginia in 1874.

The Atlantic, Mississippi and Ohio Railroad Company, which was sold for $8,605,000, with divisional liens and incumbrances amounting to $4,898,159.14, including interest calculated to January 1, 1881, was re-organized under the name of the Norfolk and Western Railroad, with an authorized capital stock of $25,000,000, and a general mortgage indebtedness of $11,000,000.

The organization stood thus:

To amount authorized capital stock	$25,000,000
To 150,000 shares preferred stock issued Clarence H. Clark	$15,000,000
Common unassessable stock, subject to preferred stock, and general mortgage bonds, issued Clarence H. Clark	3,000,000
Unissued capital stock	7,000,000
Total amount issued	$25,000,000
General mortgage bonds	$11,000,000
Amount issued to retire divisional liens	$5,137,000
For use of the treasury of the company	500,000
Issued to Clarence H. Clark	5,363,000
	$11,000,000

A railroad which sold for about $13,503,159 was re-organized for $36,000,000. People wondered at this financial operation, and many predicted that the company would not pay interest upon the bonds, and that it would soon go into the hands of a receiver. Not knowing at that time anything about the New River Railroad, Mining and Manufacturing Company, which was the moving power behind the throne, one would have supposed that Shakespeare was totally wrong when he said there was nothing in a name.

In the first annual report of the Norfolk and Western Railroad Company, on page 7, we find the reorganization stated to be a compact between Clarence H. Clark and his associates. Who the latter were is a matter which is not disclosed, but from the reading of the language of the report itself they paid Clarence H. Clark a very good sum to purchase this property, if they believed in its being of any value. The report reads—

By the terms of the agreement between Clarence H. Clark and his associates, it was provided that in consideration of Clarence H. Clark's furnishing and paying the purchase-money ($8,605,000) in cash, the Norfolk and Western Railroad Company should deliver to Clarence H. Clark its general mortgage bonds, amounting to $5,363,000, one hundred and fifty thousand shares of its full-paid and unassessable preferred six per cent. capital stock, and also thirty thousand shares of its full-paid and unassessable common capital stock; and it was further agreed that the general mortgage bonds amounting to $5,137,000 should be reserved to retire existing divisional liens, and that general mortgage bonds amounting to $500,000 should be reserved for the treasury of the company.

If the $5,363,000 of mortgage bonds were worth par, and the stock was worth par, which was given C. H. Clark for purchasing this company, then for paying some $8,605,000 for the road, he received the sum of $23,363,000—a very substantial rate of interest. That the $15,000,000 of prefered stock came out all right we cannot doubt, since in the annual report of the Norfolk and Western Railroad Company for 1883, on page 18, we find the following:

Your directors, believing that so long as it was considered advisable to use the surplus earning of the company for the purpose of bettering its property or increasing its facilities for doing business, the preferred shareholders are entitled to scrip dividends representing the amount which has been so applied, and which would otherwise be applicable to cash dividends, at a meeting held December 26th, declared a scrip dividend of 3½ per cent., payable January 15, 1884, on the $15,000,000 of preferred shares then outstanding. The scrip, when presented to the company in sums of $500, is exchangeable into convertible debenture bonds, payable in 1894, bearing six per cent. interest, payable semi-annually.

The interest is paid on these bonds, as well as the others received by Clarence H. Clark, making the sum of $20,363,000 interest-bearing and good. What did Mr. Clark's associates get?

Whatever may have been the public opinion as to this reorganization, Clarence H. Clark and his associates well knew that the increased rate of freight and passenger traffic over the lines of the Norfolk and Western Railroad Company would justify the issue of the increased amount of stock and bonds. They had possession of premises and facts concerning which the general public was totally ignorant. Those were in connection with the New River Railroad, Mining and Manufacturing Company, from which the coal options had been so ruthlessly torn. Subsequent to the year 1878, after Sergeant and Roane had arrived at a misunderstanding, as seen heretofore, there must have been a reorganization of the New River Railroad, Mining and Manufacturing Company, because afterwards it comes out under the new title of the New River Railroad Company. In all probability the stock originally owned by the shareholders of the New River Railroad, Mining and Manufacturing Company had been purchased by Mr. Sergeant and his friends, and afterwards the company reorganized under the latter name, *with J. D. Sergeant's options, contracts* and *mineral leases attached*, transforming virtually a poor corporation into one worth millions. At all events, the first and second annual reports of the Norfolk and Western Railroad expressly dwell upon the fact that the expected traffic from the opening of the coal mines would greatly increase the earning of the Norfolk and Western Railroad Company, and that the latter owned the New River Railroad Company. But those reports are not explicit as to how the Norfolk and Western Railroad Company came into control and ownership of the New River Railroad Company. Yet we are not without some evidence on that score, for in Poor's Railway Manual for 1883–'84, on page 361, we find the following in connection with the report on the Norfolk and Western Railroad Company:

On the 9th of May, 1882, the New River Railroad Company of Virginia, the New River Railroad Company of West Virginia, and the East River Railroad of West Virginia, which were chartered to build extensions of this road hereinafter named, were consolidated into this company [the Norfolk and Western Railroad Company]. By the terms of the consolidation the preferred stock of the Norfolk and Western Railroad Company was exchanged, share for share, for the preferred stock of the New River Railroad Company (of Virginia), and the common stock for the common stock, share for share, of the same company, and for the ordinary stock of the other companies. Under this plan the company issued 30,000 shares of its preferred stock during the year in exchange for a like amount of the New River preferred. The stocks of these companies having been wholly owned by the Norfolk and Western Railroad Company, the preferred stock so issued is held in that company's treasury for future use.

This merger and consolidation especially state that the Norfolk and Western Railroad Company owned, wholly and entirely, this preferred New River Railroad stock. So we see that previous to this date (May 9, 1882) the fruits of Graham's and Sergeant's transactions had passed into the Norfolk and Western Railroad Company's hands. The evidence is almost conclusive that upon this New River Railroad, already owned, the Norfolk and Western Railroad Company based its organization, and made an issue of stocks and bonds founded upon the traffic of the railroad company, after a consolidation with the New River Railroad Company, whose stock it controlled at the time. Nor were the calculations of Mr. Clarence H. Clark and *his associates* at all wrong as to the increase of traffic that would arise for their road subsequently to a consolidation with the best known coal and coking fields in the South. From that time on the success of this company was almost all that could be desired.

This New River division was opened to the coal fields May 21, 1883, and the first shipments of coal made in the following month of June, 1883. The beginning of shipping coal from these great mineral fields was marked in letters of red for the Norfolk and Western Railroad Company, and the abundance of coke which would naturally be produced led to the abolishing of charcoal furnaces in the Cripple creek region, and coke furnaces erected in their stead. To form a connection between the coking fields of the Flat Top region and the ore belt about Cripple creek was the next step of the Norfolk and Western Railroad Company—a wise and judicious one.

The first step taken by the company was the creation of an improvement and extension mortgage for $5,000,000, with power under certain restrictions to increase the sum to $8,000,000, for the purpose of double-tracking. Under this mortgage the bonds issued were to bear six per cent. interest, and the first issue limited to $2,500,000. Proposals having been made for these bonds, which were satisfactory, the proceeds were to be used as follows (Third Annual Report, page 21):

First. The construction of the Cripple Creek extension of the New River division is about fifty (50) miles in length. This work was put under contract December 10, 1883, and the line is expected to be completed and in operation before the close of the year 1884.

Second. For increased terminal facilities at Norfolk. Contracts for this work were entered into December 28, 1883, the work to be completed prior to August 31, 1884.

Third. To build short lines to new coal fields.

Fourth. For additional sidings, stations and other improvements on the main line. The remainder of the improvement and extension (mortgage) bonds—$2,500,000—can, under the terms of the mortgage, be sold only when the stockholders so vote, and only for the purpose of providing funds for making improvements upon the main line, for increased terminal facilities, for new rolling stock and for new branches or extensions. If bonds are sold for the purpose of constructing branches or extensions, the amount of bonds sold for this purpose is limited to $25,000 per mile. In case of an issue of bonds for the purpose of double-tracking the line, said issues are to be made at the rate of $10,000 per mile, and no bonds are to be issued for this purpose until at least fifty (50) miles of double track of standard quality has been constructed.

The building of the Cripple Creek extension, one of the purposes for which this improvement and extension mortgage was created, opened up a mineral region rich beyond conception in iron ore and heavy bearing in lead and zinc. We have already touched upon the mineral deposits in this section, but some better description is deserving as we follow the tortuous windings of the extension through Pulaski, Wythe and Carroll. When this extension was first proposed, two routes were thought of—one, by way of New river, beginning at New river bridge, near the station by that name, thence up New river into this ore region. For many reasons this route was considered by some as the most practicable, since it would be but a continuation of the New river division already constructed into the Flat-Top coal region. But a route was drawn by Mr. James McGill, of Pulaski county, who lived not far from what was then known as Martin's Tank, but now called Pulaski City. He enclosed a sketch, drawn January 24, 1882, of the present line of the Cripple Creek extension to Mr. George F. Tyler, then President of the Norfolk and Western Railroad Company, and the latter's reply shows that at this time (1882) the route south of 110-mile post had been chosen. The letter is as follows:

PHILADELPHIA, January 27, 1882.
MR. JAMES MCGILL,
  Martins, Pulaski County, Va.

DEAR SIR:—I have received your communication of the 24th instant in respect to the line which you think the most practicable for us to take in the extension which we propose to make of the New River Railroad above New river bridge.

We have ourselves come to the conclusion that the line which you have so neatly sketched is no doubt the one for us to take, and I am very much obliged to you for the suggestions on the subject which you make.
  Truly yours,
   GEORGE F. TYLER,
    President.

This sketch of Mr. McGill's is very neatly drawn, showing the comparative distances of the two routes, and the territory of the one desired by him. In 1883 the contracts for the construction of the road were let, and this extension became not only an assured fact, but opened up the finest mineral region in the Southwest. This line has ultimately two objects in view, as can be easily seen if we trace its meanderings. It leaves the main line of the Norfolk and Western Railroad two miles east of Pulaski City, running first in a course that has a southern direction until it touches New river, when it sweeps away in a Western course almost parallel with the main line of the Norfolk and Western Railroad, with an intervening space of some twelve miles of country between the two roads. It continues on by Reed Island, Allisonia, Barren Springs, Pierce Furnace, Foster Falls, Austinville to Ivanhoe. From this latter point is the extension on to North Carolina, to connect with the Cape Fear and Yadkin Valley Railroad, which will be the southern outlet from Ohio after the Ironton extension is finished from Elkhorn, in West Virginia, to Ironton, Ohio.

Another branch of the Cripple Creek extension runs from Ivanhoe westward up Cripple creek to Speedwell, and this route will undoubtedly be continued through the Rye Valley iron district to the waters of the South Fork of the Holston, and thence to Abingdon, making a loop line with the main route to Bristol. This extension has branch routes running to furnaces and mines throughout this fine ore-bearing territory, the principal of which are: The Pulaski Iron Company, Boom Furnace, Barren Springs Furnace, Bertha Zinc Mines, Pierce Furnace, Foster Falls, Ivanhoe Furnace, Ravencliff Furnace, Beverley Furnace and Speedwell Furnace. Many iron, lead, and other mineral mines have been opened tributary to this route, and will furnish much of the ore which will run furnaces eastward in the valley. The scenery along the line is beautiful and picturesque in the extreme, whether we go by winding, romantic New river, with its mountains and cliffs, or by wild, weird Cripple creek, with its cascades and gorges. The quality of this rich ore-bearing territory can best be gathered from the analyses and opinions of experts on the subject. McCreath and D'Invilliers, in their report on the New river-Cripple creek region, has this to say concerning the ore (page 155):

All of the iron ore at present mined, and to be mined, in the New river-Cripple creek region proper may be conveniently classed under the general heading of *brown hematite* ore, and is found associated in at least four well recognized horizons or belts, extending in a general north-east and south-west direction through the region, with the trend of the rock formations to which they have been referred. The first and lowest, *geologically*, of these is the "Pottsdam sandstone ore," occurring in the body of the formation from which it takes its name. These ores are locally known as the "back vein," or "bed," and are characterized by having a dark brown to pitchy black color, and are generally quite dense and brittle. Their composition is shown by the following average analysis of samples already incorporated in the body of this report:

Average composition of the Pottsdam sandstone ores—

Metalic iron	50.200
Phosphorus	1.007
Siliceous matter	10.012
Phosphorus in 100 parts iron	2.006

The next class is the mountain ores, which yield 48.750 of metalic iron. The limestone ores are particularly fine, of which the report speaks as follows, on page 155:

The limestone ores, on the other hand, by reason of their greater accessibility, higher percentage of iron, and more ready reduction in the small charcoal furnaces, which have hitherto alone occupied this field, have been sufficiently developed and worked in a large number of places to warrant an opinion as to the richness of the ore material. From the last information we could obtain bearing upon this subject, the general claim is that two tons of ore material will yield one ton of clean wash ore, and this would seem to be confirmed by our own tests made from five different pits and from samples weighing from 14 to 93 pounds, which yielded the following percentage of clean ore: 41 per cent., 53 per cent., 57 per cent., 59 per cent. and 60 per cent.

In addition to this rich ore deposit, the extension runs through what is known as "the Blue Ridge Plateau," and has the reputation of being one of the finest grazing sections in the State. From Pulaski City to Ivanhoe is some thirty-two miles, making about forty-one miles from Pulaski City to Speedwell, beyond Ivanhoe, the present western terminus of this extension. And lastly, this region is the home of the "*Gossan ore*," to which we have already alluded as being peculiarly adapted to the permitting of the use of high phosphorus and manganese ores, which, by themselves, could never be used, and with this ore a "red, cold short, or neutral iron," can be made.

The improvement of the property of the Norfolk Terminal Company is so intimately blended with the opening of the coal mines that some notice should be given of it, although not situated in South-west Virginia, because it is one of the improvements of this company which has a significant bearing upon the mineral regions of the section of country of which we are writing. To meet the growing demands made upon the company for increasing terminal facilities, and for the purpose of speculation, the Norfolk and Western Railroad Company, under the name of the Norfolk and Terminal Company, obtained a charter in 1882 from the Virginia Legislature, and under it an organization was effected. The reason for this charter and incorporation is given in the second annual report, on page 15, which says:

The Legislature, at its last session, granted a charter incorporating the Norfolk Terminal Company. Under it an organization was duly effected. Although it is a separate and distinct organization, yet the control and ownership is in the interest of your company. The charter authorizes the ownership of land, the construction and operation of a line of railroad, the building and operating of wharves, store-houses, cotton-presses, grain elevators, chartering of vessels, etc., and in other ways gives ample power and authority for the conduct of such business as will be necessary at so important and growing a port as Norfolk, and will enable the company to carry into effect the recommendations of the stockholders at the last meeting in regard to improving and increasing the terminal facilities at Norfolk. Power is given the Terminal Company to consolidate with this company, and the board recommend that such consolidation be effected when it is in the interest of the company to do so.

By virtue of the charter, the Norfolk Terminal Company purchased several valuable wharf properties below the city, near Lambert's Point, embracing about four hundred and thirty-eight acres of land, and one and a half miles of water-front, and the necessary right-of-way to construct a railway line connecting Elizabeth Station with Lambert's Point. Improvements of all kinds were made for the storage and proper handling of grain, cotton, tobacco and other produce, while piers were erected for coaling vessels and ocean steamers. The company also invested largely in the stock of the Old Dominion Steamship Line, and purchased barges for the transportation of grain, cotton and coal. So great and rapid were the improvements on this property that in the year 1884 they had constructed a railroad from Norfolk to Lambert's Point, a distance of 5.3 miles, together with yard room and sidings necessary for the accommodation of the Norfolk and Western's tide-water coal traffic.

A magnificent pier, 894 feet in

length and 60 feet wide, with a height above water-mark of 48 feet, had been constructed, which terminates at the United States light-house known as "Lambert's Point Light." This superb structure is divided into upper and lower stories, from each of which vessels can be loaded, and is capable of storing 150 tons in each bin, having 45 bins in all. This pier is equipped with every modern appliance for loading, unloading, and handling of cars, and not less than 3,500 tons per diem can be received and discharged, while the depth of water in the approach to the main channel is twenty-five feet at low tide.

Not only was this undertaking of great advantage to the city of Norfolk, but a credit in many respects to the Norfolk and Western Railroad Company. For the coal regions in South-west Virginia it was an undoubted benefit in many ways. This semi-bituminous coal is said to be the best steaming fuel known, and the number of steamers which coaled at Lambert's Point gradually increased from the first construction of the pier until the quantity consumed by them was a traffic of no small magnitude in itself, and gave employment to thousands of miners in the coal regions who would doubtless have been idle had the coal trade depended entirely upon the inland traffic. In the year 1885, between March 12th and December 31st, 402 vessels of all kinds were loaded at the pier, among which were forty-five ocean steamers.

In 1886, 676 vessels of all kinds were loaded, among which were ninety-five ocean steamers. The increase in this business alone was something enormous, while the storage houses erected for cotton, grain, tobacco and other produce for foreign shipment, did an extensive business. In 1884 the capital stock of this company fully paid in amounted to $322,026, of which $321,900 is owned by the Norfolk and Western Railroad Company, and the operations of the former are completely governed by the latter company. As amounts were furnished the Norfolk and Terminal Company by the Norfolk and Western Railroad Company, the latter took the bonds of the former. In this way every particle of funds derived by the Terminal Company were furnished by the railroad company, until the mortgage of $1,000,000 was created on the properties of the Norfolk and Terminal Company. These terminal facilities reflect unquestionable credit upon the Norfolk and Western Railroad Company, and the latter showed great wisdom in expending the necessary sums for such proper facilities, without which it could not well handle its large traffic. But why should this Terminal Company have purchased more real estate than was necessary for the use of the railroad company?

That the Norfolk and Western Railroad furnished this Terminal Company with the necessary means to purchase this real estate is a fact admitted in their annual reports, for out of $322,026 owned by the Terminal Company, the railroad company owned $321,900. (See Fourth Annual Report, page 24.) It is further shown in one of their reports that *lots* were sold. In the Seventh Annual Report, on page 20, the language is this, relating to this Terminal Company:

The property of the Norfolk Terminal Company is operated by your company, and the revenue derived from such operations is included in your gross earnings. Of the real estate not required for the purposes of the company, there were sold during the year lots to the value of $12,245, which amount has been deposited with the trustee of the mortgage of the company, and will be expended in improvements to the property.

Again, in the Eighth Annual Report, on page 21, the language reads thus, in reference to this same company:

Of the real estate not required for the purposes of the Terminal Company, there were sold during the year lots to the value of $8,805.01.

The only reason which can be assigned for the company's purchasing more land than is necessary for the use of the railroad is, it desired to sell the lots at a profit. Whilst commending the wonderful developing policy of the Norfolk and Western Railroad Company, we cannot help deploring the fact that, under the name of another company, it should have violated section 1073 of the Code of 1877, of the State of Virginia, which expressly provides that no railroad company in the State shall own more than forty acres in one parcel for its main depots, machine-shops, and other necessary purposes connected with the business of said company. This statute was supposed to be passed for the purpose of preventing railroad companies from speculating. By some it is contended that the land was not purchased in the name of the Norfolk and Western Railroad Company, but by another company. Considering that the Norfolk and Western Railroad furnished the funds, and the revenues were placed with their gross earnings, such contention imputes to the Norfolk and Western Railroad Company an amount of ignorance that is stupendous, or a subterfuge just as contemptible. Again, some claim the right to be vested in the company by its charter. It would seem passing strange that the Legislature of Virginia should, by a special act of legislation, set aside and nullify a general law passed in the interest of the State.

The first shipments of coal from the Flat Top region, as we have seen, began in 1883, and during the years 1884 and 1885 the extension into the Bluestone country was completed. This line, running from the New River division at Bluestone Junction, to Mill Creek, Bramwell, Simmons, and Duhring, has at last been completed as far as Goodwill, and opens up a coal region of magnificent quantity and quality both. This extension was made with a view to hauling out coal, and is some ten miles in length, with branches to the various mines located on the Bluestone river, and which yield a large output of coal daily. Mill Creek, Bramwell, Simmons and Goodwill are flourishing places, and their growth appears almost magical when we consider that a few years ago this portion of Mercer county was nothing more than a lot of rugged, impassable mountains, without any vestige of settlements except the huts of mountaineers, who, though poor and lowly, were as brave and loyal men as one could find anywhere.

The penetration of this country by this branch of the Norfolk and Western was a transformation of this part of Virginia and West Virginia into a rushing, thriving, tax-paying community, which in 1881 was almost a sterile wilderness of mountains. During the year 1887 the extension from Mill Creek was completed as far as the station now known as Elkhorn. The tunnel through the mountain, some two miles from Mill Creek, is a massive structure, and the trestles bridging the mountain gorges wonderful in the extreme, showing the energy, pluck and determination of the Norfolk and Western Railroad Company to bridge not only these seemingly impassable chasms, but every difficulty presenting itself in the way of their onward progress towards developing the country. This extension opens up the vast coal fields in McDowell county, where any quantity of it lies buried, and thousands are daily employed to unearth it. We will have more to say of this section when we come to speak of the Ohio line to Ironton. In this coal region up to January, 1888, there were 2,030 coke ovens in course of construction and completed.

Prior to the year 1886 a charter had been obtained for the construction of a railroad called "The Clinch Valley Railroad," and at the annual meeting of the stockholders in 1886 a resolution was passed empowering the directors of the Norfolk and Western Railroad Company to make a consolidation of this Clinch Valley extension with their company. By the terms of the charter this company was given authority to locate and construct a road "commencing in Tazewell county, at a point at or near the New River division of the Norfolk and Western Railroad Company, and running thence to such a point on or near the Clinch river, Powell river, or either, or any branch thereof, in Russell, Wise, Scott or Lee counties, and by such route as might be deemed most suitable to the directors of said company.

On March 8 and May 2, 1887, the Norfolk and Western Railroad Company and the Louisville and Nashville Railroad Company entered into contracts by which both agreed to

46

construct and finish—each one respectively from its lines—this extension to a point in Wise county, Virginia, both connecting there. Work upon this extension by the Norfolk and Western Railroad Company was begun on June 20, 1887, and pushed forward as rapidly as possible. This road has been about completed, and runs from Graham, on the New River division of the Norfolk and Western to Norton, at which latter point it will connect with the Louisville and Nashville Railroad. The section through which it runs is by far one of the finest in South-west Virginia. It first traverses Tazewell county, running by Tazewell Court House, Richlands and Cedar Bluff; then through Russell county, touching Honakers, Cleveland, Saint Paul and Minneapolis, and on through Wise, by Guest, to Norton, where it connects with the Louisville and Nashville Railroad. On leaving Graham, the line goes through the far-famed grass section of Tazewell, noted for its fine stock and agricultural products. As an outlet for these alone, the road would have been a boon to the county—a success to its company; but, on leaving Tazewell, it touches upon the very borders of the now celebrated Clinch Valley coal region, which has a coal excellent for gaseous uses as well as domestic purposes. Russell county, too, through which it runs, is celebrated for its grazing capacity as well as fine stock, and has many mineral-bearing properties. When the line reaches Wise county it penetrates the heart of the coal country stretching from this part of the county on towards Big Stone Gap. Numerous towns have sprung up in a few years, such as Richlands, Honakers, Minneapolis, Saint Paul, Norton and Big Stone Gap, all of which bid fair to become cities at no great future date. Mineral City, near Big Stone Gap, claims to be the center of a variety of minerals for manufacturing purposes. This route opens up a regular kingdom of lumber and coal, the latter of which has been most complimentarily noticed on account of its gas properties; while in live stock and agricultural productions no place in the South-west is superior or richer. Mines are being opened and branch roads constructed to them, and on all sides can be heard the sound of the axe and the saw culling the best of hard-wood lumber. The traffic from this section alone will be something great, and the Norfolk and Western Railroad can hardly fail to reap the profits in passenger and freight traffic to which its energy and spirit in opening up the country entitles it. The scenery all along the line is beautiful in the extreme, and every variety, from the peaceful, charming valley, to the rugged, snow-capped mountains, greets the eye as the train rushes onward through fertile Tazewell and Russell and mineral-laden Wise.

With a view towards perfecting north-western and south-eastern connections, and for other purposes deemed advisable by the Norfolk and Western Railroad Company, on the 29th day of October, 1889, this corporation created what is known as the one-hundred-year mortgage which is a first lien upon the property when all underlying liens are refunded. This mortgage first provides an issue of $10,000,000 5 per cent. bonds, to be applied as follows:

$1,000,000 for redeeming Norfolk Terminal Company's first mortgage.
$975,000 to reimburse the company for expenditures by way of improvements, extensions, sidings, etc.
$6,000,000 for construction of Ohio extension (North-west).
$1,500,000 for the North Carolina extension.
$525,000 for retiring the convertible debenture loan of the company.—(Ninth Annual Report, page 21).

The creation of this mortgage enabled the Norfolk and Western Railroad Company to construct the two extensions named above, and since these have added materially to the progress of this company about which we are writing, they deserve mention, although the North-west (or Ohio) branch does not run through the South-west of Virginia.

The Ohio extension, as located and partly constructed, "follows the waters of Big Sandy river from the present north-western terminus of your line, at Elkhorn, in McDowell county, West Virginia, for about ninety-five miles; thence about fifteen miles over a low summit to the head-waters of Twelve Pole creek, which it follows for about seventy-one miles, and crosses the Ohio river by a steel bridge, and runs about fourteen miles to Ironton, Ohio, making a total distance of not less than one hundred and ninety-five miles."

The value of this line, not only to the Norfolk and Western Railroad Company, but South-west Virginia, can readily be appreciated when the results of its construction are calculated. The city of Norfolk, being one of the best harbors on the Atlantic coast, will have a direct route from Ironton, Ohio, and the purchase of the Scioto Valley Railroad, with the route under construction from Ashland, Kentucky, to Kenova, on the borders of Kentucky, Ohio and West Virginia, will place Norfolk, Virginia, in almost instant communication with Columbus, the capital of the State of Ohio. The granaries of the West, with the live stock bred in the same country, will be poured into the East, giving this extension an importance and bearing which is not easily calculated. The coal regions through which it goes are of almost endless quantity, and consist of several varieties. In the county of McDowell the Flat Top coking coals of the Pocahontas region are traversed, while farther on the line penetrates the domestic coals of Logan county. Near Warfield, in Martin county, Kentucky, the road bends to the right, and in Wayne county, West Virginia, it divides the cannel and splint coal region, which will give a splendid traffic in these latter varieties.

This route will not only cause Norfolk to increase as a shipping point for foreign exports, but will be the means of connecting the North-west with the South-east. The line extending south from Ivanhoe, on the Cripple Creek extension, will push its way forward until a connection is established with the Cape Fear and Yadkin Valley Railroad at Mount Airy, in North Carolina, which will place Columbus, Ohio, in immediate connection with the Southern seacoast at Wilmington, North Carolina. Coal will be shipped there and cotton brought back into the North-west and on to Norfolk. The connection will give the Norfolk and Western Railroad outlets south, south-east, west and north-west; and the northern connections it possesses by way of the Shenandoah Valley makes its system of great value as a leading trunk line north and south and east and west. With these advantages the company will be in a condition to do a large traffic in every direction.

While we may imagine, it is impossible to ascertain with any degree of certainty the growth of this corporation without an inquiry into the rapid increase of the mileage, traffic and rolling stock of the company. In the year 1881, when the Atlantic, Mississippi and Ohio Railroad was re-organized as the Norfolk and Western Company, there were 428 miles of railway. Now, with the Cripple Creek, New River, Flat Top, Clinch Valley, Ironton, Scioto Valley and south-eastern extensions, and the Shenandoah Valley Railroad, there are almost 1,234 miles of track, not including sidings, switches and what double track that has been constructed. The construction of these lines has been effected in the best manner possible, the heaviest steel rails, iron bridges, the most approved masonry and solid stone ballast being used in order to procure comfort and safety in the highest degree possible.

It is not difficult to see that with such a wonderful extension of railway the passenger and freight traffic has grown accordingly. Both departments are taxed to their utmost to accommodate this increase, as the following tables will show.

The passenger traffic was as follows:

Year	Passengers
In 1881	215,904
1882	263,347
1883	307,927
1884	412,452
1885	388,087
1886	400,269
1887	558,951
1888	771,248
1889	841,986

This route has become a favorite one, and the opening up of all this section has been the means of thousands of passengers traveling over the line. The usual number of passenger coaches to each train is four and five, and they are invariably crowded. The freight statistics also show a marked increase. There were carried over the road—

In 1881	538,102 tons.
1882	609,727 "
1883	797,255 "
1884	892,512 "
1885	1,199,790 "
1886	1,555,867 "
1887	2,208,688 "
1888	2,763,376 "
1889	3,435,797 "

We cannot refer to any common carrier within our knowledge which has increased so rapidly in freight traffic. Of course it is mainly due to the opening up of the vast mineral regions in South-west Virginia, and the large increase in the agricultural resources throughout the country. The minerals began to be shipped about the year 1882, and a comparison of the number of tons carried that year with the number in 1889 will give some idea how rapidly the Southwest has advanced:

	1882.	1889.
Iron ore	1,399 tons.	249,374 tons.
Pig-iron	13,372 "	161,215 "
Coal	4,735 "	1,543,900 "
Coke		310,504 "
Stone	6,181 "	87,965 "
Salt	9,270 "	14,453 "
Plaster	3,405 "	5,580 "
Zinc ore	2,872 "	12,321 "
Zinc spelter	490 "	2,972 "
Manganese	1,648 "	152 "
Miscellaneous	4,939 "	48,321 "

We cannot fail to give our praise to this company when we see the wonderful progress it has made in aiding and assisting in the development of South-west Virginia, and the untiring energy it has exhibited in giving an impetus to everything. In 1881 the rolling stock of the company consisted of 81 locomotives, 24 passenger coaches, 2 sleeping cars, 4 postal cars, 12 baggage, mail and express cars, 1 pay car, 556 box cars, 199 stock cars, 315 platform and gondola cars, 65 ditching cars, 42 conductor's cars.

At the close of the year 1889 we find that the rolling stock has increased in proportion to everything else, and that notwithstanding this addition the transportation department is taxed to its utmost capacity to accommodate and move the heavily increased traffic of the road. The number at the end of 1889 was as follows: 195 locomotives, 87 passenger cars, 7,880 freight, caboose and other cars.

A further comparison of the earnings of the company will show that its financial status has kept apace with its rapid growth in every way. These earnings have been generally appropriated as far as possible to the improvement of the road and adding rolling stock for transportation facilities. The following amounts for 1881 and 1889 give us an idea of the great pecuniary advance made within that time:

	1881.	1889.
Gross earnings	$2,267,288.62	$5,597,124.58
Net earnings	1,104,055.87	2,113,772.17

We cannot deny that this company in every way has more than doubled its carrying capacity and intrinsic pecuniary value. When we think of the amount of material necessary for constructing these extensions, the number of mechanics and laborers necessary to perform the work, the emigration brought in by reason of this work, we cannot withhold the credit it is justly entitled to, nor fail to express admiration at its policy, which has been one of the causes of the rapid development of South-west Virginia.

POLICY OF THE NORFOLK AND WESTERN RAILROAD.

The general policy of the Norfolk and Western Railroad Company is an aggressive one in every way, which tends to develop the country through which it runs, as well as its own property and holdings. Whether the modes adopted by it to accomplish this end are entirely legitimate do not in the least alter the fact that the prime object of the company is to develop everything coming in contact with it, in order that such a course may eventually redound to an increased rate of traffic for the Norfolk and Western Railroad Company. This corporation uses every means in its power to draw a foreign element into the State. The road itself, with all the wonderful resources of the country through which it runs, are annually set forth and duly advertised by the company, which are the means of many settlers coming in and being attracted here. Their method not only builds up a community, but pays them handsomely for the outlay expended in placing these many advantages before the public.

The equipment, services and regulations of the company are first-class in every respect. The track is well ballasted and laid with steel rails. A double track is now in construction along the line wherever it is necessary for the safety of the passengers and the expeditious handling of freight and minerals. The heavy ten-wheel locomotives carry along over the mountains a train of nine or ten coaches, and give an ease and steadiness to the whole train which is far superior to the motion of the cars when drawn by lighter engines. The stations along the line are being replaced by more commodious buildings, some of which are really ornaments to the places where they are built, besides affording reasonable facility for pleasure and comfort. All of the through trains carry the Pullman vestibule and sleeping cars, the comfort and luxury of which are well known and appreciated by the traveling public in general.

This road is under control of a splendid class of officials, from the President to the brakemen. Seek as diligently as you may and each position will be found occupied by some man who has the necessary acquirements and knowledge to fill it as it should be. The President, Vice-President, general manager, as well as engineers, conductors and guards, have each their prescribed territory, and in these respective departments everyone carries out his various duties and the rules and regulations of the company.

The Norfolk and Western Railroad Company has two adjuncts—the Roanoke Machine Works and the Virginia Company—in both of which the railroad owns a large controlling interest. They have played no unimportant part in the progress of the railroad company.

Prior to the year 1882, a company was formed for the purpose of constructing and erecting engine and car-shops. The capital stock of this company was $365,000, and the Legislature of Virginia, by act approved April 1, 1882, authorized the Norfolk and Western Railroad Company to own as many shares in said company as the directors of the railroad company should deem proper. This authority was most properly conferred, for it was but natural that the company should have a controlling interest in the works which constructed its engines and cars and repaired its rolling stock. These shops were placed in the corporate limits of Roanoke, and the necessary buildings took at least fifteen acres of ground. The buildings consisted, towards the end of the year 1883, of—

Smith-shop	350 x 72 feet.
Machine-shop	348 x 72 "
Annex to same	33 x 72 "
Engine-erecting shop	516 x 64 "
Foundry	252 x 72 "
Paint-shop	206 x 50 "
Planing-mill	252 x 72 "
Lumber kiln	71 x 38 "
Store-house	150 x 72 "
Engine-house	22 stalls.
Passenger and freight car erecting shop (semi-circle)	21 stalls.
Lumber-yards.	

Before the construction of these shops reached completion, in 1883, a mortgage of $500,000 was created and the bonds purchased by the railroad company, which soon owned a controlling share, and at this time they belong virtually to the company. These gigantic works compare favorably with any in the Northern States and surpass anything in the South, and since their erection, not only have they done all the repair work for the Norfolk and Western and Shenandoah Valley Railroads, but much new equipment work. Many of the engines which pull the heavily-loaded coal trains from the mines to Lambert's Point were made in these shops, while all the box-cars, gondolas and some baggage and passenger cars have been constructed here. All the most approved machinery for manufacturing an engine is placed in them, from the heavy planing and slotting machines to the rivets which go in the boilers. The capacity of the shops is some four engines per month and twenty freight cars *per diem*, besides repairing and building passenger cars. At one time these shops filled orders for other railway lines, but owing to the increase of traffic on the Norfolk and Western Railroad line of late, its utmost capacity has been taxed to construct new equipments and do the repair work of this latter company. The construction of the works was in a thorough manner—brick buildings and iron truss-roofing being used—and the ground and building at night are lighted by electricity. The locating and building of this gigantic plant was a wise act on the part of this company, for the very material from which our Northern friends manufacture their work comes from a section of country tributary to the lines of the Norfolk and Western Railroad; consequently the cost of manufacturing here is so much less that the company was more than justified in this erection. The number of employees is about fifteen hundred men, and the works have played no small part in the development of this section. The organization has not only been a self-supporting one, but paid a handsome dividend on its stock. For the year 1887 it paid $61,305 on the capital stock, while in 1888 it rendered a dividend of $50,088 to the stockholders of the company, and in 1889 $25,000 were declared in dividends.

Another adjunct of the Norfolk and Western Railroad Company, which has become a part of the latter, is the "Virginia Company." This company was originally known as "The Iron-Belt Land, Mining and Development Company," which was chartered prior to the year 1883. At what particular time the Norfolk and Western Railroad Company began to be an investor in this company is not known exactly to us, but in its Third Annual Report, on page 29, we find the following:

Your company (the Norfolk and Western Railroad) owns a controlling interest in the Iron-Belt Land, Mining and Development Company, holding 330 shares out of a total of 500 shares. Under the charter of the Iron-Belt, Land, Mining and Development Company, real estate is held at Roanoke, Central, Martins, and at other points. The real estate is either at junction points, or at localities which from the nature of the ground and abundance of water are suitable for manufacturing purposes. The lands were purchased in the interest of your company, so that parties desiring to erect furnaces or other manufacturing establishments could secure proper locations at reasonable cost.

Why these lands were purchased in the interest of the company is not stated in this report, but in their Fourth Annual Report, for the year 1884, on page 24, the reasons for investing in this company are given. It reads:

For reasons similar to those which led to the organization of the Norfolk Terminal Company, your company acquired control of the Iron-Belt Land, Mining and Development Company. The cost to your company of its interest in this corporation is $43,955.07, which amount represents the actual cost of the real estate purchased at junctional and other points. It was apparent that additional yard room and sidings would ultimately be required at these points in order to accommodate the growing business of your company, and it was considered expedient to secure the lands before they could be built upon or occupied for other purposes. Such land as may not be required for the uses of your company will be disposed of to parties desiring to locate manufacturing establishments.

It seems from this that the actual cost of real estate to the railroad company through this Iron-Belt Land, Mining and Development Company was $43,955.07. The object of the company in obtaining this real estate was for additional yard room, sidings, divisional round-houses and certain necessary accommodations for the rolling stock of the company. This was but right, and a praiseworthy, legitimate undertaking. But why should the railroad company desire to purchase more real estate than was necessary for its own use? Some calculation could have been readily made by which the requisite quantity for shops, sidings, yard room and round-houses could have been arrived at and purchased. Their reason for so doing is very clearly stated in the Eighth Annual Report. Prior to 1889, by act of the General Assembly of Virginia, on March 5, 1888, the Iron-Belt Land, Mining and Development Company was changed to the "Virginia Company," under which name the buying and selling of real estate by the Norfolk and Western Railroad Company is still continued. In the Eighth Annual Report, for the year 1888, we find the following statement concerning this "Virginia Company" on page 22:

For several years the title to valuable real estate at junctional and other points upon your line has been vested in the Virginia Company. Owing to the redivision of its line during 1888, it became necessary for your company to construct yards, engine-houses, repair shops, store-houses and other improvements at various points, and it was deemed advisable, when acquiring the real estate actually needed, to purchase such outlying and adjoining land as would be made valuable by the improvements, so that your company might derive the benefit. The land required for the purposes of the railroad was paid for and deeded directly to your company, and the adjoining lands were acquired and paid for by the Virginia Company. The properties so acquired at Crewe and Bluefield were laid off into lots, of which a considerable number were sold during the year; upon other lots dwelling-houses were erected and sold or rented to the employees of your railroad company. * * * * * To provide means for the expenditures required, the capital stock of the Virginia Company was increased to $100,000, all of which was taken by your company, and such further sums as were required were advanced by your company. The balance-sheet attached to this report shows the acreage and cost of real estate and improvements at the several points. The net profits of the Virginia Company during the year (1888) amounted to $44,156.32, out of which a dividend of six per cent. was paid, and the balance, $38,156.32, was carried forward as a surplus. Your investment in this company promises to be very remunerative.

The avowed object of the Norfolk and Western Railroad Company in purchasing more land than was necessary for the actual use of the railroad was for the purpose of speculating in real estate. There is no other reasonable construction when their own report, from which we have just quoted, says—

And it was deemed advisable, when acquiring the real estate actually needed, to purchase such outlying and adjoining land as would be made valuable by the improvements, so that your company might derive the benefit.

Why did the Norfolk and Western Railroad Company only purchase and pay for just such a quantity as the railroad needed? Why should the balance have been purchased by this Virginia Company, and yet the profits derived go to the Norfolk and Western Railroad Company? That the railroad company invested its money in the Virginia Company for speculative purposes is forever settled by the latter sentence of the statement just quoted, which reads—

Your investment in this company promises to be very remunerative.

And the financial report, on page 62 of the Eighth Annual Report, reads as to the liabilities of the Virginia Company—

Norfolk and Western Company, $140,808.71.

If the railroad then advanced this Virginia Company the necessary funds upon which to speculate, and participated in the profits arising therefrom, then it is virtually the railroad company speculating under a *nom de plume*. It is the Norfolk and Western purchasing this land about, with as sure an eye to profit by speculation as to obtaining the requisite amount of ground for its divisional points, shops, round-houses and yard room. But why should the railroad company only purchase and have deeded in its name a certain portion of the real estate—so much as they may deem necessary for the use of the railroad company? Why not have it all conveyed to the railroad company, instead of a portion to the Virginia Company? To these questions, so far as we can see, the Norfolk and Western Railroad Company answers, because under the statute no railroad company can own and hold over a certain quantity of real estate. If more than that is purchased, then it must be in the name of another company. No other reply can suggest itself to us after reading the statement in their own annual report already quoted. And this solution becomes almost a certainty when we turn to section 1073 of the Code of Virginia, 1877. There it is expressly provided that no railroad company shall own more than forty acres for its principal shops, yard, etc., in any one parcel. It is usually conceded that the statute was passed for the purpose of preventing corporations from speculating in real estate, especialy railroad companies. Then, if such is the intention of the law, the use of money by the railroad company under another name for the purpose of profiting by speculation is a clear invasion of the law, besides being a direct evasion of the statute.

Whether or not such operations on the part of the railroad company are intentionally an evasion depends much upon the terms of their charter. If the Legislature gave them the power to own stock in this company for the purpose of purchasing real estate with which to speculate, then they are clearly right to pursue such a course; but it is scarcely reasonable to suppose that an intelligent body of men would confer by special act a power upon one corporation which by a general act is denied all others throughout the State engaged in constructing and operating railway lines. If, on the other hand, power was given the railroad to purchase, through this company, lands for its use alone, and under this property was bought which was more than the company needed, then that corporation is clearly wrong to proceed, under and by virtue of such power, to speculating in real estate. By their own reports the company shows that at several points large quantities of real estate were purchased and lots laid off and sold, besides houses constructed for renting purposes. In the Eighth Annual Report, page 62, the following real estate is mentioned as belonging to the Virginia Company, which the Norfolk and Western owns through having purchased all of its stock. We name the real estate at those points only which exceeds the statutory allowance:

Real estate at Oakvale—43 acres	$ 3,595 47
" " " Norton—1,810 acres	41,922 42
" " " Bluefield—242 acres	24,355 31
" " " Crewe—334 acres	17,719 97
" " " Ivor—64 acres	5 09
Houses at Crewe—46	47,055 63
" " Bluefield—29	34,883 72

In addition to this, the company owns splendid inns at Radford, Pulaski City and Roanoke, all of which comprise a part of this Virginia Company. The hotels have much to do with the pleasure and attractiveness of the towns in which they are located, adding to the beauty as well as comfort of the same. For such purposes, as well as for the erection of the necessary yard room, sidings, shops and round-houses, we unhesitatingly think the railroad company had a right to own the requisite real estate, and the statute made provision for such; but the buying and selling of lots and construction of houses, apart from the purposes named, seems to be an invasion of the law, whether intentional or not, on the part of the company. But at all events the people of Virginia have a Railroad Commissioner to govern and to look into such matters, and if he sanctions it without complaint, and makes no objection to the company's indulging in such operations, then the people can scarcely blame the Norfolk and Western Railroad Company, but should look to him to whom full power and authority has been delegated to see that all provisions respecting railways throughout the State are properly carried out.

Throughout the south-west of Virginia the Norfolk and Western Railroad Company wields a potent influence. Everything connected with it commands a respect which it is hard to estimate or describe. Each movement of the company is anxiously watched by the people at the various places along the line, in order to have something done for the town or city which is their residence, fully recognizing that it is within the power of the railroad to give any place either a tremendous impetus forward or a fearful stroke backward. The policy of this corporation is of such a progressive nature that every section of the country hails its advent with delight, feeling sure that if it comes there will certainly be rapid strides made in a material way, and for this reason people bear much from this company cheerfully which ordinarily they would never submit to from other companies. And it is but right that it should be so, for where much good comes from any undertaking to the people at large the objectionable features can easily be submitted to on that account. It is rare, indeed, that the best of human undertakings for mankind have not something connected with them which is subject to adverse criticism, and the Norfolk and Western Railroad is not exempt in this respect; yet, so great has been the material development of Southwest Virginia through its policy and influence that the people of Virginia should accede to any request made by the company that is within reason and not a violation of the laws of the land.

CHAPTER XXVII.

THE SHENANDOAH VALLEY.

In the year 1734 the county of Orange was formed, and, at that period, embraced all the indefinite claims of the colony of Virginia west of the Blue Ridge, which included this section of country. In 1738 the counties of Augusta and Frederick were cut off from Orange, and this portion west of the Blue Ridge in Shenandoah Valley was included in Frederick. The earliest reliable evidence as to the disposition of land was the grant to Colonel Carter, in 1730, for 63,000 acres of land, commencing a short distance below the forks of the river, running down a little below Snicker's Ferry, about twenty miles. This land lies in the south of what is now known as Clarke county, and was afterwards owned by Colonel Carter's sons, who derived their title by devise from their father. Subsequently it was carved into smaller estates, passing into the hands of the Burwells, Pages, Nelsons and others, whose descendants still reside in Clarke county and preserve the inimitable prestige of gentle birth, culture and refinement possessed by their ancient sires—worthy scions of a noble stock.

The next grant of land in the Valley that can be relied upon was that made by the throne of England, in 1733, to one Jacob Stover, an enterprising German. This grant was not obtained by him without some trouble, for then a man was obliged to have a requisite number of families to settle upon it, which he did not possess. Being unable to give the Governor of Virginia satisfactory evidence on this score, he passed across the waters to England, and, to insure success, informed the Court that he had the requisite number of settlers. He accomplished this by giving his dogs, horses, cows, hogs, sheep and mules human names, and succeeded in persuading the Court to direct the Governor to issue his grant for 5,000 acres of land on the south fork of Gerandos (Shenandoah) river, near Messinetto creek. On this ancient grant are some of the best farms in Page county, owned by descendants of the early settlers.

The land lying in Clarke county, next to Colonel Carter's original grant, is the next that we have any evidence of. This was a body of 13,000 acres, which was purchased by Ralph Wormly, prior to the Revolutionary war, at an auction sale.

Wormly bought this when he was excited from several bottles of port wine, and, when he became cool, regretted it extremely, until General Washington consoled him by offering to take the purchase off his hands. It afterwards became a magnificent estate, and passed from his children's possession, reaching the ownership of the firm of Castleman & McCormick, Hierome L. Opie, Esq., Judge Richard E. Parker and several others. This country about Bullskin, Long Marsh and Spout Run was settled after the lands near the larger watercourses and the mountains, and lies in the immediate neighborhood of that inimitable, charming and delightful spot over which the lovely young ladies of Berryville now tread.

The lands upon the south branch of Shenandoah, around about the western portions of Rockingham and Augusta, were originally granted to Lord Fairfax. This august personage was in England on a visit when one Howard arrived there from the colony of Virginia with a glorious description of these lands along the south branch of the Shenandoah. His lordship immediately took up a grant of them, which at first he leased to certain persons, who, on account of the fertility of the soil, emigrated at once there.

About the year 1736 William Miller and Abraham Hite settled in the valley about Moorefield, and Miller, becoming somewhat dissatisfied when the Indian wars broke out, sold out his interest in 500 acres of land, and all his horses, cattle and stock for £25, and removed to the south fork of the Shenandoah river, near the spot where Front Royal now stands. Historically, this is the first evidence we have of any settlement of Warren county. Soon afterwards others came in until the country around there was gradually settled and cleared up.

About 1740 John Lindsey and James Lindsey, two brothers, removed from a Northern State and settled on the Long Marsh, between Bullskin and Berryville, in what was then the county of Frederick; and in 1743 Isaac Larue removed from New Jersey, settling on the same marsh. About this period Christopher Beeler removed and settled within two miles of Larue, while in 1744 Joseph Hampton and two sons came from the Eastern Shore of Maryland and located on Buck Marsh, near Berryville, and dwelt the greater part of the year in a hollow tree. Finally enclosing a piece of land, they made a crop preparatory to the removal of their families. From every satisfactory source that we can gather, these were the first settlers in and about that portion of Clarke county around Berryville.

From the year 1744 the emigration into the valley was very much increased, and, for those times, the country began to be tolerably thickly settled. People in the lower country, learning of the fertility of this lovely land, sought homes in it, and endeavored to make a permanent residence.

As a great many of these settlers were from Pennsyvania, the Indians credited them with the virtues of the mild Quaker, William Penn, and for twenty years after the first settlement did not molest any of the whites. This enabled the settlers to clear lands, accumulate stock and make arrangements for a permanent home, since, having been unmolested so long, they scarcely dreamed of any trouble with the Indians; but, in this they were mistaken, as we shall now see.

In the year 1753 emissaries from the Indian tribes west of the Alleghanies invited the Indians in the Valley to cross over the mountains and join them in Ohio. In 1754 the Indians, in response to this invitation, departed unexpectedly, and all left the country east of the Alleghany range. It has never been definitely stated why these red-skins departed West, but after a careful investigation upon the subject, we are inclined to think that the Indians west of the Alleghanies were resisting the encroachments of the settlers over there, and desired assistance, for only a year or two after this invitation was extended the Indians in Shenandoah Valley, we hear of a long series of massacres and incursions on the part of the Indians West, beginning with the Draper's Meadows settlement in Montgomery, and not ending finally until the memorable battle of Point Pleasant. The year 1756 opened up by attacks from the Indians on the inhabitants of Shenandoah Valley, and from that time on we hear of numerous massacres on the part of the red-skins, in attempting to destroy the settlements of the whites. This grew out of General Braddock's defeat by the French and Indians at Pittsburg. The French had always instigated the Indians to resist the encroachments of the white settlers West, and the war between the French and English, which grew out of a squabble over territory, gave the Indians ample opportunities to harass the English; so, when Braddock was defeated in 1755, at Pittsburg, the Indians, believing their friends (the French) to be invulnerable, began to attempt an extermination of the settlers and their homes. For ten years, from 1756 until 1766, there was a continual feudal warfare carried on by the Indians and the whites, resulting in loss of life and destruction of property to both races, and the white settlers hailed with delight a cessation of hostilities in 1766, which lasted until 1774, when what was known as Lord Dunmore's war broke out. After this latter war the Indians, with the exception of a few attacks, gradually disappeared, leaving the whites in undisturbed possession of the soil and their settlements.

Subsequent to hostilities with the Indians the people enjoyed tranquility and repose, and the country settled and increased with great rapidity, as new settlers from many different quarters poured in. Some families of distinction came in from the lower country, who were the ancestors of the Washingtons, Willises, Throckmortons and Whitings. Later on the Lewises took up their possessions, and the descendants of those old people still reside in a portion of Jefferson county and Clarke. The lands taken in the neighborhood of Long Marsh by the latter people are in the possession of Major H. L. D. Lewis, Col. Washington Lewis, Mr. Edward Lewis and others.

After the Revolutionary War, with which we are so familiar, the inhabitants of this country increased considerably, and for nearly one hundred years the entire land enjoyed universal peace, with the exception of the short war of 1812, and the Valley gradually became one of the most productive and advanced portions of Virginia. Great attention was paid to the cultivation of mind, heart and manners, which gave the people decidedly a caste of character, especially in the lower part of Warren and the county of Clarke. Living upon soils which produced everything that the wants of man could suggest, and that in the most abundant profusion, they became as independent and sturdy a race of people as could be found anywhere. As time rolled on and their means increased from the fatness of the land, they erected finer houses and paid more attention to the refinements and arts of life, until the whole fabric, in a social way, reached a high state of existence. Another thing which caused some parts of this valley to maintain a set distinct unto itself, was the fact that, in a portion, clans, or relations, settled a particular country, and their descendants questioned the rights of outsiders to intrude themselves unless invited so to do. To give a faithful portrayal of these people who played such an important part in the subsequent development of the country, we cannot do better than quote the words of Mr. John Y. Page, who lived among them, and who is an intelligent, high-toned gentleman. He says—

This portion of the Valley (Clarke county) was pretty well settled by a few family connections, especially in the southern part, in the neighborhood of Millwood. Under the will of Robert Carter, formerly known as "King Carter," of Lancaster county, Virginia, some fifty-one thousand acres of lands were divided among his sons, grandsons and other relatives. Descended from these were the Carters, Burwells, Nelsons, Pages and others, many of whom are still in the county, and some killed during the war. From this settlement grew a habit of country life which made the social feature of the county an admirable one in some respects. They did not care what they ate, or drank, or wore—the most prominent characteristic being an indifference to the future, with a determination to enjoy the present. Being all related or connected, they visited and mingled freely in everyway, dropping in to dine, spend the night, or a day or two, without ceremony. A very sincere religious feeling prevailed of unquestioned faith, without an inquiry as to knowledge, showing itself principally among the females of the families, while men believed as much as their mothers and wives, but practiced it a great deal less. The result of all this was a society of families very exclusive among themselves, and thought, by strangers, to be too exclusive. This was the prevailing tone of the Lower Valley socially. Among the older people, the descendants of whom are still here, are the Lewises, Clagetts, Taylors, William P. Smith, the Pages, Boyces, Wheats, Pendletons, Allens, Carters, Halls, Nelsons, Whitings, Burwells, Castlemans, McCormicks, Moores and many others.

Mr. Page's clear-cut ideas are right, and his conception of the people in full keeping with their characters, manners and customs, which even to this day retain odors of the old habits and charms which will never wear away. The marked difference between the people of this lower portion of the Valley and those residing upon the South Fork of the Shenandoah, in Page, Rockingham and Augusta counties, is completely elucidated by Mr. Page's account. Those in the upper part were settlers of German, Dutch and Scotch-Irish extraction, who, being strangers, were different from the English colonist settlers below, and not so exclusive in the social bond formed among themselves. The people of this section, from one end of the Valley to the other, cultivated their estates, increased in every way, grew well off, and became an independent class, and were as happy on the whole as people could be until the flames of a civil war devastated in a great measure their homes, and, after four years of fighting, left them like their forefathers, with nothing but the naked soil on which to contest the battles of life for a daily existence.

During the late war the Valley was a continuous battle-field for the contending armies in this section of Virginia, and very naturally so, too. The agricultural resources were extensive in every way, and foraging for supplies much easier here than elsewhere. At Antietam, in Maryland; Shepherdstown and Charlestown, in West Virginia; Berryville, Shenandoah and Waynesboro, in Virginia, the artillery played, and human blood was shed regardless of consequences. It was in the county of Clarke that Mosby's force was raised, and they pursued their guerilla warfare, keeping the Yankees in a continual turmoil. This hitherto peaceful country was laid bare, and when the Confederacy grounded arms at Appomattox, and Lee surrendered, these brave men returned to their devastated homes, with scarcely anything but the native soil.

Previously, from the counties of Augusta and Frederick had been taken Rockingham, Page, Warren and Clarke, the country traversed by the Shenandoah Valley Railroad.

In every way that part of Augusta and Frederick from which was taken Rockingham, Page, Warren and Clarke composed almost the fairest, if not the largest, part of those counties. The agricultural and mineral resources of this part of Shenandoah Valley, from Basic City to the West Virginia line, are fine and varied. All of the cereals—wheat, corn, oats, barley, rye and buckwheat—grow in profusion, while as grass lands they have no superior. The soil is of a chocolate loam, or red clay in most places, and is unexcelled in productive capacity. The average yield of wheat is from twenty to forty bushels per acre, and the planters fallow wheat and small grain after corn with impunity, which is a severe test as to character and quality of land. The lands are easily cultivated, and not steep enough to wash, being, generally speaking, of a rolling character. It is a great country for stock, and the horses of Shenandoah Valley command a premium on account of their superiority. Sheep-raising is a pursuit largely followed, and has proven highly remunerative, and the cattle are of a superior kind, especially for dairy purposes. The number of live stock in the counties of Clarke, Page, Warren, Rockingham and Augusta are: 26,796 horses, 59,513 cattle, 27,102 sheep and 42,683 hogs.

This section has the finest agricultural showing of any other in Virginia, and far exceeds the South-west in this respect, or the tidewater or piedmont regions. When this wonderful section is in full bloom with its various productions, nature itself seems to blush at the profusion and wonder at its own handiwork. The great waving fields of corn and wheat and oats and hay present a scene of agricultural wealth which it is almost impossible to describe—certainly not to be appreciated properly until seen.

In addition to the wealth which exists on the surface itself, the Valley is rich in hidden treasures but lately discovered, in speaking of which we allude to the mineral resources. These are found to be in large quantities, and in some places of most excellent quality. Iron, manganese, umber, ochre, brownstone, sandstone, fire-brick, and china-clay, limestone and tin ore have been discovered all along the Valley and pronounced superior, both as to quality and quantity. In days gone by, before the many mineral resources were developed at all, there were charcoal furnaces about. There is a remnant of one at Luray, on the north side of the town, which at one time was in blast. Another was at Milnes, but has been replaced by a superior coking furnace. And now new furnaces are being constructed in many places in the Valley to utilize these deposits of iron ore. The construction of the Washington and Western Railroad, now being surveyed and located, will throw the coal and coking regions of West Virginia right at Shenandoah Valley. The quality of the ores as analyzed are given, in order that everyone may see exactly what is in each county. From *McCreath's Mineral Wealth of Virginia*, we find that the ores from Clarke analyzed as follows, from ninety-two pieces taken from A. Mason Moore's property (*Mineral Wealth*, page 19):

    Metallic iron 49.875
    Phosphorus .... .146
    Silicious matter 11.430
    Phosphorus in 100 parts iron .... .292

This is a fair comparison of other analyses made in the same county.

In Warren county an analysis of eighty-five pieces taken from the Overall property, near the station of the same name, shows:

    Metallic iron 50.375
    Phosphorus 1.275
    Silicious matter 1.890
    Phosphorus in 100 parts iron 2.261

—(*Mineral Wealth*, page 21).

In Page county several analyses of various openings are given, from which we select an average sample. *Mineral Wealth*, page 23, shows, from an analysis of ore taken from Rust's property, 153 pieces:

    Metallic iron 50.950
    Metallic manganese 1.455
    Phosphorus .... .442
    Silicious matter 9.780
    Phosphorus in 100 parts iron .... .867

In Rockingham, from Wilmer and Jackson's property, the following is given, taken from 145 pieces of clean lump ore:

    Metallic iron 50.450
    Phosphorus .... .217
    Silicious matter 14.350
    Phosphorus in 100 parts iron .... .430

—(*Mineral Wealth*, p. 33).

In Augusta county, samples from the Cotopaxi furnace property yielded on analysis (*Mineral Wealth*, p. 40):

    Metallic iron 49.400
    Phosphorus .... .062
    Silicious matter 14.260
    Phosphorus in 100 parts .... .125

From the foregoing it is not difficult to form an idea as to the quality of the ores. In speaking of this section as a point for manufacturing iron, the same work from which we have already quoted, on page 143, says, in allusion to the territory traversed by the Norfolk and Western and Shenandoah Valley Railroads:

The advantages which the territory traversed by your several lines of railroad offers to the iron-master may be summed up in a few words: the ores are abundant and generally of good quality; they can be economically mined, for the country in many localities is broken up by numerous ravines, affording natural openings for mining operations; most of the deposits are within convenient distance of the railroads, with easy down-grades; the water-supply for either washing ore or for manufacturing purposes is ample and permanent at all seasons; limestone for fluxing purposes exists in unlimited quantities; coke of the finest quality for blast furnaces can now be obtained at a reasonable cost, and the railroad facilities for reaching markets in every direction are unusually good, thus forming a combination of favorable circumstances rarely equalled.

Nor are iron ores the only valuable mineral properties in this section. The Virginia Manganese Company, near the mouth of Turk's Gap, in the Blue Ridge, at Crimora, has valuable manganese mines. The shipments run over a thousand tons per month at times. Near Markville are the ochre mines belonging to the Oxford Ochre Company, which ships large quantities of this mineral. In May, 1886, the shipments amounted to 120 tons, which shows the amount that is sold. The Virginia Fire-brick and China-clay Company are making over three thousand brick and washing about eight tons of china-clay *per diem*, and at the time this estimate was made the output was expected to be larger. In mineral resources the Valley is rich, and not completely developed as yet. The cabinet of minerals displayed at Basic City, Marksville, Luray, Front Royal, and the samples seen at Berryville, place the question at rest as to the ore-bearing territory of this rich agricultural country.

The actual cost of manufacturing iron in Shenandoah Valley has been practically known for some time, and we furnish a statement which was made for Andrew S. McCreath by L. S. Boyer, Secretary of the Shenandoah Iron, Lumber, Mining and Manufacturing Company, in his official capacity. It is as follows:

COST OF MAKING IRON AT MILNES.

Ore, 2¼ tons at $2	$4 50
Coke, 1¼ tons at $4 20	5 25
Limestone	30
Labor	1 50
Incidentals	1 00
Total	$12 55

With these natural advantages, with the agricultural and mineral resources within its borders, we can readily perceive that the Valley has all that nature could bestow as a firm foundation for its future development. We cannot wonder that it recuperated rapidly from the effects of the war, and improved until 1881, when a progress commenced which has since caused people everywhere to turn their eyes towards this rich and lovely county.

CHAPTER XXVIII.

THE SHENANDOAH VALLEY RAILROAD.

The construction and completion of the Shenandoah Valley Railroad was a new era for Shenandoah Valley, or at least that portion of it through which the road ran. Nearly all the towns along its line seemed to put on a new life, and grew larger from that date. Railroad facilities meant the establishment of industries, and as these were most likely to locate their plants at places where supplies and the like could be obtained, the values in property at the towns through which the road ran advanced in price. There is scarcely a town along the line of this company that will not tell you that the first progress of any note occurring within their borders dated from the time of the construction of this road in their midst.

This company was first organized on February 23, 1867, under the laws of Maryland, West Virginia and Virginia, the States which it traversed. Notwithstanding the fact that its organization dated back so early, twelve years elapsed before the first forty-two miles were constructed as far as Riverton; nor did this become completed until, in the year 1878 (the same year in which J. Dickinson Sergeant sent Roane the contract to sign concerning the New River Railroad and options on mineral lands), Mr. Frederick J. Kimball became actively engaged in the construction of it. In December, 1879, the first part to Riverton was opened up and traffic begun over it; in September, 1880, seventy-nine miles more were finished, and on April 18, 1881, the line was completed as far as Waynesboro Junction. It is further known that the road was built partly by construction companies, partly by private individuals, and partly by the company itself.

In February, 1881, at the time that the Atlantic, Mississippi and Ohio Railroad was purchased by Clarence H. Clark and *his associates*, there were some kind of relations existing between these gentlemen and the Shenandoah Valley Railroad Company, since in the First Annual Report, pages 12 and 13, we find the following announcement:

The relations between the Norfolk and Western Railroad Company and the Shenandoah Valley Railroad Company contemplated at the time your road was purchased and reorganized are still kept in view, and negotiations are in progress looking to the consolidation and merger of the two corporations as soon as proper legislation can be had. Very favorable results are anticipated from the completion of the connections of the two roads at Roanoke Junction.

That these relations were of the most friendly character there can be no doubt, and the object of extending the Shenandoah Valley Railroad on to Roanoke was to bring the mineral traffic from the New River Railroad north and to form a connection with the East Tennessee, Virginia and Georgia railroad. So in the latter part of September, 1881, a tripartite agreement was entered into between the three companies, which secured to these systems for a term of years a unified general management, and what is known as the Virginia, Tennessee and Georgia Air-Line burst into view. Work upon the Shenandoah Valley Railroad was pushed forward, and in June, 1872, the line was completed to Roanoke, where it connected with the Norfolk and Western.

On the 15th day of February, 1882, a committee was appointed by virtue of a resolution of the Board of Directors of the Norfolk and Western Railroad Company to consider the relations existing between the two companies, and to make a report to the board as early as practicable upon a plan by which the purposes of the tripartite agreement and traffic contract of 1881 would be more effectually carried out. Under these instructions the committee proceeded to work, and pending their action, questions were raised by the Shenandoah Valley Railroad as to the true intent and meaning of certain clauses in the traffic contract of September 27, 1881, respecting the establishment of freight rates and a division of the revenue derived from this joint arrangement. The Norfolk and Western Company, well knowing the advantages of an all-rail route via Hagerstown, and fearing this company as a competitor, determined to adjust every difference possible and get control of the road if practicable. Yet this must be done on the most advantageous basis for the Norfolk and Western Company, as is shown in their Second Annual Report, page 21, which says:

Whilst, therefore, in the development of new business your company would have *direct* advantages through the interchange of traffic between the two companies, *indirect* advantages almost equally important would accrue through the ability of your company to direct and control the distribution of through business in such a manner as will earn the most money for both companies.

The only possible means by which the distribution of through business could be controlled by the Norfolk and Western Railroad Company was by owning a majority of the shares of the Shenandoah Valley Company, so the result of the traffic contract investigation by the committee was, the Shenandoah Valley Railroad mortgaged its line for $2,500,000 for the purpose of finishing its road to connect with the Norfolk and

Western Railroad at Roanoke, and the former company subscribed for 30,000 shares of the common stock of the latter, and paid this subscription with 20,000 of its own shares of stock, virtually giving the Norfolk and Western the controlling interest in its 37,674 shares—the total capital stock of the Shenandoah Valley Railroad Company. In the Annual Report for 1883 the Norfolk and Western states, on page 25, that—

The share value of the capital stock of the Shenandoah Valley Railroad Company is 36,962 shares, of the par value of $100 each, representing $3,996,200, of which 30,506 shares have been acquired by your company in accordance with the terms of the contract dated December 29, 1882, and referred to fully in the last Annual Report, and which were received in payment of subscriptions for 40,506 shares of the common stock of your company.

The Norfolk and Western now hold a complete controlling share in the Shenandoah Valley Railroad, giving the former the *indirect* advantages arising through the ability to direct and control the distribution of through business between the two companies —just what the committee deemed most advantageous for the interests of the Norfolk and Western. What was the actual cost to the Norfolk and Western Railroad Company to obtain this control? The Second Annual Report of the Norfolk and Western Railroad, page 25, after setting forth the traffic contract—the financial bargain and all—says:

A contract on these terms was executed under the direction of your board on the 29th of December, 1882, and it is believed that the important advantages which it contemplates will be secured with but little, if any, actual cost to this company.

The Report of the Shenandoah Valley Railroad for the year 1883 was a very flattering one as to its condition, and so forth. In accordance with the terms of the contract, the Norfolk and Western agreed to advance it $200,000 per annum, and from this source, and from the sale of its bonds, the Shenandoah Valley Railroad Company was enabled, in addition to meeting all its fixed charges, to make many desirable improvements and pay for rolling stock urgently needed. Its net income was $192,257.58, and the prospects for another year much brighter. The result of its operations since it was opened, in June, 1882, were mentioned as very flattering and encouraging.

But the year 1884 brought a different state of affairs, for the depression in business and want of traffic so reduced the income of the company at the end of the year 1884 that upon January 1st, 1885, default was made in payment of the interest, and a like result in April and July. The Fidelity Insurance, Trust and Safe Deposit Company of Philadelphia, being the trustee of a general mortgage issued to secure the indebtedness of the company, upon default in payment of its interest, filed its bill for the appointment of a receiver, which was done by order of Court, and Sidney F. Tyler was appointed to that post and duly took charge. The road was operated by the receiver until October, 1890, when, under decree of Court, a sale was made, and the Norfolk and Western Railroad Company became the purchaser of the Shenandoah Valley Railroad Company for $7,100,000, with all its road-way, equipments, property, rights and franchises. Although the company was in the hands of a receiver for five years, yet that did not affect the advantages derived from the construction and operation of it to the country through which it ran, and the towns along its lines continued to develop.

The purchase of the Shenandoah Valley Railroad by the Norfolk and Western has already had a good effect along the line of the former company. The developing policy of the Norfolk and Western, and its interest in the general welfare and progress of the towns and country along its route, cause these to hail its advent with delight, and there was a general spirit of joy pervading Shenandoah Valley when it was announced that the road through the Valley had been purchased by the Norfolk and Western. Already many enterprises are springing up and industries coming in, feeling a spirit of confidence in their future since this company, which has done so much materially for the South-west,

has charge. The connection of the Washington and Western Railroad, now being located, with the Shenandoah Valley branch in this country, not only secures a long-coveted entrance into Washington by the Norfolk and Western Railroad, but will give a new impetus to the whole country, and be of infinite advantage to the connecting point. The charter of the former road further gives power and authority to this company to locate, construct and equip a railroad from some point on the Shenandoah Valley Railroad into the coal regions of West Virginia, which road will be of more importance to the iron interests of the Valley than can be well calculated, as it will place the coking fields almost at the feet of Shenandoah Valley. In all of these undertakings the people will be glad to know that the Norfolk and Western is the prime moving power, so great is its effect upon the country through which it passes.

The whole country traversed by the Shenandoah branch of the Norfolk and Western Company is one capable of the highest state of development. The road starts from Hagerstown, Maryland, connecting there with the Cumberland Valley road for Philadelphia and points North, and with the Western Maryland for Baltimore. Coming South, it passes the lovely, rich valley bordering the Potomac; crossing into West Virginia, it connects with the main line of the Baltimore and Ohio at Shenandoah

Junction, pursuing then its line through the charming Shenandoah Valley by Charlestown, Berryville, Front Royal, Luray, Shenandoah and Basic City, terminating its route at Roanoke City, a distance of 239.3 miles through as productive and beautiful a country as ever the sun shone upon. This road has been most beneficial in its results towards developing the whole section, and all along the line people acknowledge it.

Notwithstanding the fact that the road was placed in the hands of a receiver, it has been a great success, and has certainly been conducted well under the management of D. W. Flickwir, superintendent, and O. Howard Royer, general passenger and freight agent. Its equipment is good and the service all that could be desired. Had the road been opened up in the past four years, and not when it was—during a period of depression—it would never have passed into the hands of a receiver, but would have met its liabilities promptly. Within the past four years there has been a marvellous increase in the passenger and freight traffic. There is no doubt that it has played a very important part in not only the development of Shenandoah Valley, but South-west Virginia as well.

CHAPTER XXIX.

THE COUNTRY EAST OF THE BLUE RIDGE, AND EARLY SETTLERS.

The Blue Ridge mountains, as a landmark, have played an important part in Virginia's history. Long before the fertile valleys and mineral hills west of these mountains were discovered, or the gaze of the white man rested upon New river, the eastern portion of the State had some 80,000 people, and Shenandoah Valley three or four hundred souls. The forefathers of the latter came into this valley by way of Harper's Ferry from Pennsylvania.

The threading of the labyrinth of Rosamond's bower could scarcely have been more difficult than the tracing of the footsteps of these earlier settlers, in any chronological order, who first came into that country now known as South-west Virginia. The want of all records, which the early settlers failed to preserve, reduces the chronicler of events to groping in the dark, and learning from uncertain sounds the paths trod by our forefathers. Several reasons may be assigned for this unfortunate state of affairs. The primitive, struggling life of those earlier pioneers was not conducive to the recordation of events, and the constant destruction of their settlements by the Indians was often a clean sweep, where the inhabitants could not even escape with their lives, to say nothing of records, if any were preserved. Tradition, therefore, plays an important part in this earlier history, for out of chaos it is difficult to extract facts with any degree of certainty, or bring chronologically down events which have only the palest light to disclose the landmarks as we descend the corridors of time.

In the year 1734 the county of Orange was formed. It then embraced not only its present area east of the Blue Ridge, but all the undefined claims of the Colony of Virginia west of the Blue Ridge mountains to the Pacific ocean. The western portion of this territory at that time was the home of the Indian and wild beasts, who, in a great measure, preyed upon each other.

In the year 1738 Orange county was diminished in territory by the formation of Augusta and Frederick counties, which comprised all the territorial limits west of the Blue Ridge mountains. With the exception of the small area of country in the lower part of Shenandoah county, called

Frederick, Augusta comprised all the territory west of the Blue Ridge. In 1763, by the treaty with France, its western boundaries were limited by the Mississippi river, and it contained all that section of country west of the Blue Ridge, and the States of West Virginia, Kentucky, Ohio, Indiana, Illinois, Michigan and Wisconsin.

The first white persons who ever trod the wilds of Western Virginia were not Governor Spotswood and his Knights of the "Golden Horseshoe," as many would have us believe. Although he was knighted and immortalized for having discovered what he then described as "God's country," yet others before him had penetrated those wilds, of which he only took a cursory view. A careful examination, by aid of the best light we have upon the subject, clearly indicates that Colonel Wood was in South-west Virginia sixty-two years before Governor Spotswood.

In 1654, Col. Abraham Wood, being of an adventurous and roving disposition, obtained permission of the Governor of Virginia to explore the country west and open a trade with the Indians. He was a resident of Appomattox, dwelling somewhere near the present site of the city of Petersburg. There is neither a record of the number he took with him on this expedition, nor as to the particular route chosen by him; but from the fact that "Wood's Gap" lies in the Blue Ridge between Smith's branch of Dan river and the Little river branch of New river, in Floyd county, we may reasonably suppose that he first struck the river now known as New river, not far from the Blue Ridge, near the line of Virginia and North Carolina. There can be but little doubt as to this gap being named after him, and if so, this must have been his tread through what was then a howling wilderness. Following Little river, he must have first discovered New river at the mouth of the former, and, finding a stream undiscovered before, doubtless called it then and there "New river," which name it bears to this day.

As to the result of Colonel Wood's trip, or the fate of his party of humble hunters whom he carried with him, but little, if anything, is known. That it was not a successful one, so far as any treaty with the Indians went, we are satisfied, because they were extremely unfriendly to the next expedition which went out, the guide refusing to conduct Captain Henry Batte's followers into a certain section of the South-west, inasmuch as the Indians there were unfriendly to the whites. As Colonel Wood's crowd of traders, with himself, were the only whites who had crossed the Blue Ridge, then it was to this very party the Indian guide was referring. So we naturally conclude that Colonel Wood's efforts to establish anything like friendly relations were fruitless.

In 1666 Sir William Berkeley dispatched a Captain Batte, with fourteen Virginians and fourteen Indians, to make an exploration, all of whom started from Appomattox. What route they pursued is not exactly known; but, as we have stated, when they reached a certain point they refused to go farther, under advice from their Indian guides. In his account of this expedition, mention is made by Captain Henry Batte of a river flowing westward, which he pursued downward until he came to some salt springs. Mr. John P. Hale, in his work, *Trans-Alleghany Pioneers*, supposes this to have been in the Kanawha Valley, and the salt made at Campbell's Creek Salt Spring. Nothing authentic has been obtained to support this except extrinsic facts which Mr. Hale has so sensibly based his supposition upon. At all events, it is known that Henry Batte and his followers returned to the eastern portion of the colony, for he made a report to Governor Berkeley of such a flattering nature that the latter announced his determination of investigating the country himself, which would have been of infinite service to the future descendants of these people, all of whom have groped in darkness concerning the early history of this country.

Governor Spotswood and his knights of the "Golden Horseshoe" penetrated this section, or at least the valley, at a point known as Swift Run Gap, in 1716. In 1732, Joist Hite, John Lewis, Bowman, Green, Chrisman, McKay, Stephens, Duff and others, came in by way of Harper's Ferry; and in 1734 Morgan, Allen, Moore, Shephard, Harper and others, settled in that portion of the valley known as Shenandoah. From 1735 to 1738, Beverley, Christian, Patton, Preston, Burden and others, settled west of the Blue Ridge. This Patton was the Colonel Patton who in 1736 obtained a grant of 120,000 acres of land west of the Blue Ridge, in the Valley of Virginia. He and his son-in-law, Colonel John Buchanan, located these lands on James river, in what is known as Botetourt now, and the villages, Buchanan and Pattonsburg, which sprang up on the opposite side of the river, were respectively named after them. A great many of their descendants now reside throughout this section of South-west Virginia.

About 1744 one Thomas Ingles and his son William, then a young man, made an exploration west of the Blue Ridge, and while on this trip became acquainted with George Draper and his family, who were residing at Pattonsburg, Virginia, on James river. Some time afterwards, George Draper went on a hunting expedition, and as he never returned, his family thought that he was killed by the Indians. The after-lives, history, and fate of the Drapers and Ingleses were so intimately mingled and blended that anything touching them is of interest.

The next expedition of which we have any chronological evidence was that of Dr. Thomas Walker, Colonel James Patton, Colonel Buchanan and others, in the year 1748, when they travelled into Kentucky through South-west Virginia. It was during this trip that a pass was discovered by Colonel Walker, who named it Cumberland Gap, in honor of the Duke of Cumberland. The creek which flows into New river near Major Cecil's, in Giles county, beyond Pembroke Station, on the New River Railroad, was discovered during this expedition, and to this day bears the name of "Walker's creek." The parallel ranges of mountains near by were also called in honor of Colonel Walker. This party travelled across the Flat Top mountain, which has since become celebrated for the quantity and quality of its semi-bituminous coal. The object of this expedition was to gain some insight into the country with reference to obtaining a grant; for on their return "The Loyal Land Company" was organized, based on a grant of 800,000 acres north of the line of the Carolinas and west of the mountains, and the company was incorporated June, 1749.

Heretofore these explorers went west of the Blue Ridge merely for the purpose of discovery, and then returned east. None of them crossed into the trackless wilderness for a permanent residence, until some of the most daring and adventurous ones determined at last to make a settlement in this beautiful but wild country.

In 1748, after the return of the Patton party, Thomas Ingles and his three sons, Mrs. Draper and her son and daughter, Adam Harmon, Henry Lenard and James Burke, moved westward, with the determination to cast their fortunes farther west and make a permanent settlement. They chose one of the loveliest spots imaginable for their home—that beautiful and level plateau of fertile land on which the site of Blacksburg, in Montgomery county, is now located. This point was called west of the Alleghanies, but it was west of the divide, or floor of the valley raised, just as Massanutton mountain divides Shenandoah Valley in two parts. Here these pioneers settled and erected their crude residences of rough-hewn logs, naming the place "Draper's Meadows." Things went prosperously along with them, and by their encomiums upon the fertility of the country, splendid scenery and balmy climate, other settlers were induced to come, among whom may be mentioned William Harbison, George Hoopaugh, James Cull, and the Lybrooks, who settled on Sinking creek, a short distance below the New River White Sulphur Springs. All the settlers were steadily at work engaged in clearing their lands and making themselves as prosperous and happy as the state of their circumstances would admit. They were on the friendliest terms with the Indians, who occasionally passed and repassed the settlement, without any hostile signs whatever. In fact, except for one or two small depredations made against Harmon and Hoopaugh, there was perfect unanimity between the two races.

But this pleasant state of affairs was not to continue. On July 8, 1755, the day before the English army was so ignominiously defeated under General Braddock, the redskins made a raid upon this peaceful settlement, killing and wounding or capturing every living soul. Colonel Patton, Casper Barries, Mrs. George Draper, and a child of John Draper were killed, while Mrs. John Draper and Mrs. Cull were severely wounded. Mrs. William Ingles (*nee* Mary Draper), Mrs. John Draper and Henry Lenard, were captured prisoners. James Burke would doubtless have shared the fate of these people, but in 1754 he removed to that portion of the country now known as Tazewell, and made a settlement in the fertile valley, hemmed in by mountains, known as "Burke's Garden," and justly celebrated as one of the loveliest and most charming places in South-west Virginia.

In connection with this raid there is recorded an incident concerning Mrs. William Ingles which is sad and touching to the last degree. This lady, one of the whites captured in the Draper's Meadows raid, was the daughter of George Draper, and married William Ingles, the son of Thomas Ingles. She, with her children and another lady, were conveyed by the Indians down New river, thence by the Kanawha on into Ohio to the camp of the Indians. During this trip Mrs. Ingles, by her useful knowledge, adroit acts, and pleasant address, won the esteem and respect of the Indians, who hoped also to obtain a handsome ransom for herself and children. During this journey into Ohio Mrs. Ingles gave birth to another child, and yet continued her march with the rest, exhibiting a nerve and fortitude rarely seen in a woman. Being of an observant nature, she watched the streams closely as she was marching out, and so placed them in her mind as to remember them distinctly. Her final destination, Big Bone Lick, was at last reached, and her sons having been previously taken from her, she reached this place in company with only one white woman and her infant babe at her breast. Here at this place she again made herself very useful in making salt and shirts for the Indians out of the checked cloth purchased from the French traders. While residing here, some seven hundred miles from Draper's Meadows settlement, by the circuitous route which they had to come by the rivers, she meditated and planned an escape. She communicated her plans to the other woman, who although opposed at first on account of the dangers they would have to encounter, finally consented. The parting from her infant, which on first blush might seem to savor of a want of motherly feeling, was to save herself from a more degrading and worse fate had she remained. With only a blanket apiece and one suit of clothes on their backs, these females plunged into the trackless forest and turned their faces homeward, to walk 700 miles. To detail their various adventures and sufferings, their wanderings up and down the streams, their subsistence on berries, wild fruits, and the productions of the forest, their sore feet and intense physical suffering and mental anguish, would transgress our space. For forty days Mrs. Ingles traveled, until, worn out and exhausted, she passed around the Anvil Cliffs at New River White Sulphur Springs and came to Adam Harmon's place, who, hearing her cries in his corn-patch, recognized her, and took the tenderest care of her until she could be re-united to her family. Her traveling companion, who during their journey had threatened to kill Mrs. Ingles, was afterwards found by Harmon and safely conducted to the white settlement. This Adam Harmon's place was located on the plateau where the hotel and buildings of the New River White Sulphur Springs are located at present.

During the year 1755 Vass Fort was raided by the Indians and some of the whites murdered. This stronghold was situated about ten miles from Christiansburg, on the head-waters of the Roanoke river, in Montgomery county. It was near this place that Colonel Washington, Maj. Andrew Lewis, and Capt. William Preston escaped from being attacked in a wonderful manner, by a mistake of orders given a band of Indians by their chief, who had been stationed to attack Colonel Washington and party. In return for this raid and other depredations committed by the Indians, in March, 1756, General Lewis, with several gentlemen and Captain Montgomery's volunteer company, made what is known as the Big Sandy expedition. They all met at Camp Frederick, and starting out, proceeded by way of Clinch river, Bear Garden, Burke's Garden, over Tug Mountain, and down the Tug fork of Big Sandy, now in West Virginia. For some reason this expedition accomplished nothing, being unsuccessful, or perhaps ordered back. Certain it is, these Ohio Shawnee Indians were never visited with the punishment they deserved for their unwarranted attacks upon the peaceful white settlers.

About this time the Ingleses, with their families, moved up on New river, and constructed a fort at a place called Ingles' Ferry, which point is about one mile from the present site of Radford, up the river. The place is still in the possession of Captain Ingles, a descendant of the family. During those earlier days this point and Draper's Meadows settlement were the places of departure for those seeking homes farther west.

In 1770 the county of Botetourt was formed from Augusta, taking its name in honor of Lord Botetourt. Mr. William Preston, who, in 1761, married Susanna Smith, of Hanover county, was made Surveyor of the county, which in those days was a most lucrative post. He first resided at his farm known as "Greenfield," near Amsterdam, but subsequently removed near the Draper's Meadows settlement to an estate which he acquired in 1774, and in honor of his wife changed the name of the place to Smithfield, which name it bore to the third and fourth generations of the Preston family. The descendants and connections of this family threw out its branches in all directions from Smithfield, and settled much of the country around, among whom may be mentioned the Pattons, Prestons, Buchanans, Thompsons, Madisons, Breckenridges, Peytons, McDowells, Floyds, Bowyers, Harts, Crittendens, Bentons, Hamptons, Johnsons, and many other noted people, who assisted in building up their country and became worthy representatives of Roanoke, Botetourt, Montgomery, Washington and Smyth counties, as well as other States.

Near Greenfield, in Botetourt county, a widow by the name of Cloyd resided, with one son. She was killed by the Indians prior to 1773, and when William Preston, with his family moved to Draper's Meadows settlement young Joseph Cloyd accompanied them. He afterwards settled on Back creek, west of New river, in that section of country which lies in the county made in 1839, known as Pulaski. He was the father of Gen. Gordon Cloyd, David and Thomas Cloyd, and grandfather of Col. Joseph Cloyd, who, with his family, owned the fine estates on Back creek, at the mountain known as Cloyd's Mountain, near which was fought the battle of Cloyd's Mountain, in 1864. These Cloyds were among the first of settlers in Pulaski, and from that family, by intermarriage, connection and descent, have sprung the Cloyds, Bells, Kents, McGavocks and Cowans —all now settled in Pulaski county, and are representative people of West Virginia.

Prior to 1758, one Col. John Chiswell, who had killed a man in a personal encounter, and who died in jail awaiting his trial, discovered near New river, in that section of country now known as Wythe county, some lead mines. These mines (now better known by the name of Austinville) were the cause of a fort being constructed in 1758 by the State, under the supervision of Col. William Boyd, who named it in honor of Colonel Chiswell, his friend. In 1772 all of this section of country was formed into a new county, known as Fincastle— named in honor of Lord Botetourt's country home in England—*Fin-castle*. This county was only in existence four years, for in 1776 it was abolished, and the territory divided into new counties, called Montgomery, Washington and Kentucky. The latter afterwards became the State known by that name.

It appears from the scanty records we have that sometime about the year 1763 the Indians were instigated by the French who dwelt east of the Mississippi river to resist as much as possible the settlement of the whites upon their western territory. The French, being now out of all reach of the settlements, could give such advice with impunity. Their red allies, into whose ears the poison of revenge had been poured, bitterly resisted the white men in their onward march westward, and, although the tide continued to pour steadily in that direction, each trail was marked with the blood of some pioneer, drawn by the arrow or tomahawk of the Indian. As time rolled on the disposition of the Indians grew more determined to resist each new footstep made upon their happy hunting-grounds by the pale-faces coming west. From first defending their land, the Indians, finding the superiority they posssesed numerically, and the knowledge they had of the country, became aggressive and committed every imaginable kind of depredation upon their white neighbors. In order to check these, an expedition under Colonel Bouquette was sent out, which resulted in staying their atrocities for the while and the recovery of three or four hundred white prisoners who had been captured. In the following year (1765) a treaty of peace was concluded with them, made under the auspices of Sir William Johnson, which for sometime caused a cessation of hostilities between the two races. This treaty gave an impetus to western emigration, and by 1772-'74 settlements of the country were made all along this western region by the whites as far as the Ohio river at several points, and the main tributary streams and their smaller branches.

The levying of taxes by England at this juncture to support the expenses of the French and Indian wars occasioned an outcry from the colonists, who deemed such measures not only unjust, but onerous to the last degree. They protested strongly against such legislation, and charged the English with instigating the Indians to resist, in order that a sufficient excuse might appear for their withdrawal of the forces of the colony from the east, where it is said the English desired to carry their oppressive measures through. Although such may have been the *bona fide* belief of the colonists, there is no evidence of any such action by the English. Such a policy would have been self-destructive on their part at that time.

At all events, bad feeling arose again between the races, and several murders were committed. A white man was killed by the Indians while he was in a trading boat about Wheeling creek, and within a few days afterwards Capt. Michael Cresap and party killed two Indians. The same Captain and followers surprised an Indian camp lower down, and killed nearly all, at the mouth of Captina. Some week or two afterwards, in April, Daniel Greathouse with a party of whites attacked an encampment of Indians near the mouth of Yellow creek, and, after dosing them with whisky, killed nearly all. Some of the Indians slain at each of these places were members of Logan's family, and it was he who charged Captain Cresap with the death of his kin. And about this time, to add fuel to the flame, Bald Eagle, an old and friendly Delaware chief, was unjustifiably murdered by some whites straggling around, and set up in his canoe with a pipe in his mouth, and the barge sent drifting down the Monongahela river. The Indians became furious at these murders, and it was evident that they meant to revenge them. In the spring of 1774 they combined for aggressive action.

When the Indians seemed bent on hostile measures, messages were first transmitted the Governor, Lord Dunmore, who dispatched Col. August McDonald with four hundred men to make an expedition of a hostile nature into the Indian territory to occupy them at home and prevent their raids upon the border settlements of the whites. But as this move failed to accomplish its intended object, messengers were again sent to Governor Dunmore, who afterwards summoned Gen. Andrew Lewis, of Botetourt county, with whom to advise concerning a campaign against the Indians. The result was an army of two divisions was organized at once, one of which was to be commanded by General Lewis, the other by Lord Dunmore himself.

Organizing his forces in Augusta, Botetourt and Fincastle counties, General Lewis and his brother, Col. Charles Lewis, took command of the army and *rendezvoused* at Camp Union, about September 1, 1774, and were to march from there to the mouth of the Kanawha. Governor Dunmore was to collect his army in Frederick and Dunmore (now Shenandoah) counties and those adjacent thereto, go the north-west trail over Braddock's route, by way of Fort Pitt, and thence down the Ohio river, and meet Gen. Andrew Lewis at the mouth of the Kanawha.

On the 2d day of October General Lewis reached the Kanawha river and waited anxiously for Lord Dunmore, who was to have joined him at that time. Hearing nothing further from the Governor, he sent some messengers up the Ohio river to learn his whereabouts. Before these returned several scouts arrived at his camp, on October 9th, with orders from Lord Dunmore to cross the river and meet him in the Indian territory in Ohio. For reasons substantially good Lewis disregarded these messages, and at an early hour on the morning of the 10th gave orders for a general break-up of his camp, intending to proceed at once across the river into the villages of the Indians. But the red-skins saved him that irksome journey. When ready to start he was confronted by an army of a thousand braves commanded by their leaders, Logan, Red Hawk, Blue Jacket, Eliinipsico and several others. Here took place the largest battle ever waged in this section of the country between the whites and Indians—the memorable battle of Point Pleasant—in which General Lewis won additional laurels and came out victorious. In this fight Col. Charles Lewis, Colonel Field and several other prominent gentlemen were killed, and the wounded numerous, among whom were Col. William Fleming, John Field, Captains Murray and McChannahan, Samuel Wilson and others. Fifty-three were killed and eighty-seven wounded in the white army. The losses by death and wounds were greater among the Indians.

The result of this battle was the bugle-sound for the retreat of the Indians before the whites. A substantial fort was established at this point, and a kind of military school for the training of the white settlers under Colonel Lewis introduced. The Indians receded farther west, and the whites continued to pour in. We hear of no further trouble in this section, except occasional depredations of each race upon the other on the frontier lines of civilization.

The man and General who so ably espoused and conducted the cause of his race in those troublesome times deserves more than passing notice. He was a man of stalwart frame and stern manner and appearance. At the treaty of Fort Stanwix the Governor of New York said of him: "He looks like the genius of the forest, and the very ground seems to tremble under him." His military career was a memorable one. It began with General Washington at Great Meadows and Fort Necessity, ending with his death, just before the surrender of Yorktown, from a fever. He started for his home in Botetourt (now Roanoke), but, falling ill, stopped at Colonel Buford's, east of the Blue Ridge, where he breathed his last in the midst of kind friends. He was brought home and interred on his estate, "Dropmore," just outside of what is now the corporate limits of Salem. No stone marks his resting-place, nor points to the stranger where he lies, and the weeds and grass around his grave have a gentle sigh, as if rebuking Virginia and Roanoke for failing to mark the resting-place of one who died for his country. His acts have lived, and many worthy descendants now residing in Roanoke and other counties revere his memory and his deeds of greatness.

One of the descendants of General Andrew Lewis married a Miss Tosh, of Roanoke county, formerly a part of Botetourt, from which it was taken in 1838. Between the years 1747 and 1767 George III, King of England, granted to one Thomas Tosh all that boundary of land from near Tinker creek across to Roanoke river, on which is now situated the city of Roanoke, containing some 1,650 acres. This family was among the earliest settlers in this section, and Miss Jane Tosh, the mother of Major Andrew Lewis and Thomas Lewis, his brother, married a lineal descendant of General Andrew Lewis of Revolutionary fame. Among the landed possessions of this Tosh family was a grant from Thomas Jefferson, the President. Many branches of this family are throughout the country, and assisted in settling it.

Among the depredations made by the Indians after the battle of Point Pleasant was the raid on Burke's Garden, situated in Tazewell county, which was taken from western Augusta in the year 1799. James Burke, the original settler of this lovely spot, had been killed, and subsequently, under license of the "Loyal Land Company," William Ingles had taken up the land. His son, Thomas Ingles, who was given an education, notwithstanding his roving disposition, married Miss Eleanor Grills, of Albemarle, and then located in Burke's Garden. He lived apparently contented and happy here until the year 1782, when a raid was made on his home by some Indians commanded by "Black Wolf." Thomas Ingles was away when their attack was made, and they carried off his wife and children and two negro slaves, after firing his buildings, which were soon reduced to ashes. Going to the nearest settlement, which was in the "Rich Valley," on the north fork of the Holston river, he gathered together some sixteen men, and, returning, met Joseph Hix with a squad. Both forces were placed under command of Captain Maxwell, and hot pursuit began after the red-skins. Five days passed before the Indians were overtaken, when they were attacked. Two of Thomas Ingles' children were killed, and his wife, with her infant, barely escaped. Captain Maxwell was shot, and died shortly afterwards. The slaves escaped uninjured. The little girl died on their way home from her injuries, and but for a surgeon who met them at Clinch settlement, in company with William Ingles, father of Thomas, from New river, Mrs. Thomas Ingles would have probably died. The supposition is that several Indians were killed in this engagement.

This blood-thirsty Black Wolf did his part faithfully in the annals of raiding, by attacking and capturing white settlers, who were powerless to resist him. The lovely spot known as Abb's Valley, in the northern part of Tazewell county, and which derived its name from Absalom Looney, who came from Pattonsburg, in Botetourt county, was the scene of Black Wolf's invasions on two occasions.

In 1784 he captured James Moore, a son of James Moore, Sr., a resident of the valley, and conveying him to their territory in Ohio among the Shawanee towns, kept him awhile, and then sold him to a white family near Detroit, Michigan. Two years later a party of Shawanee Indians, led by Black Wolf, made a second expedition into Abb's Valley and shot James Moore, Sr., who was salting his stock, and rushing to his home, killed William and Rebecca Moore, his children, and Mr. John Simpson, a hired man. Two hired men fled and made their escape, but Mrs. Moore and her four remaining children, with Martha Evans, from Augusta, were captured and carried off. In their rapid retreat, the boy John, being feeble and unable to proceed with ease, they killed him in his mother's presence, and the baby was brained against a tree a few days afterwards. On arriving at an Indian town on the Scioto river, they learned that several of their braves had been killed in an engagement with the whites, and in a spirit of brutal retaliation, Mrs. Moore and her eldest daughter were tied to a stake, to be tortured to death by cremation. An old Indian squaw, taking pity upon Mrs. Moore's sufferings, killed her with a tomahawk, while the daughter was burned to death. Mary Moore, Miss Evans and James Moore, Jr., who were captured in 1784, were subsequently ransomed in 1789, and restored to their Virginia home.

In 1779 the third raid was made upon Abb's Valley by the Indians, and Mrs. Andrew Davidson and three children, with two hired youths, were captured and carried off. During their journey westward Mrs Davidson gave birth to a little girl, who, being somewhat troublesome, was tossed into Tug river by one of the Indians. When they reached the Indian towns her little girls were tied to a tree, and, for sport to the Indians, shot until death came to their relief. An Indian squaw taking possession of her remaining little boy started down the river with him, when the canoe was overturned and he was drowned. For several years Mrs. Davidson remained with a white gentleman as a servant in his family, and finally her own husband, who was in search of her, came to the house. She recognized him, and being reunited they returned to Virginia.

Regarding the Point Pleasant battle and the subsequent raids of the Indians, many writers have expressed the opinion that they were justified in their attacks. Without going so far as to re-echo this opinion in full, justice compels the statement that the Indian chieftain, Logan, had much to exasperate and anger him. Always friendly to the white race; ever ready to aid and assist them, even though his countrymen taunted him; furnishing them with meat and clothes when requested; giving them at all times the hospitality of his cabin and town, we do not wonder that his blood boiled when the members of that very race he so signally defended killed his family at Captina and Yellow creek, apparently without cause. That the Indian chieftain smarted severely under it there can be no doubt; for though afterwards he assented to the treaty of peace, his celebrated speech is only too indicative of his harrowed state of mind. As a piece of oratory this speech will bear repetition. He said:

"I appeal to any white man to say if he ever entered Logan's cabin hungry, and he gave him not meat; if ever he came cold and naked, and he clothed him not. During the course of the last long and bloody war Logan remained idle in the cabin, an advocate of peace. Such was my love for the whites that my countrymen pointed as they passed, and said: 'Logan is the friend of the white man.' I have even thought to have lived with you, but for the injuries of one man. Colonel Cresap, the last spring, in cold blood and unprovoked, murdered all the relations of Logan, not even sparing my women and children. There runs not a drop of my blood in the veins of any living creature. This called on me for revenge. I have sought it; I have killed many; I have fully glutted my vengeance. For my country I fully rejoice at the beams of peace. But do not harbor a thought that mine is the joy of fear. Logan never felt fear. He will not turn on his heel to save his life. Who is there to mourn for Logan? Not one."

Dr. Doddridge's account of Dunmore's war clearly exculpates the Indian from any blame whatever, saying that the killing by Cresap and Greathouse was cold-blooded murder. The reason assigned by the Doctor (and denied by him as true) for the whites attacking the Indians, was the Indians were reported to have stolen some horses from land-jobbers on the Ohio and Kanawha rivers. He says:

In the month of April, 1774, a rumor was circulated that the Indians had stolen several horses from some land-jobbers on the Ohio and Kanawha rivers. No evidences of the fact having been adduced, led to the conclusion that the report was false. This report, however, induced a pretty general belief that the Indians were about to make war upon the frontier settlements; but for this apprehension, there does not appear to have been the slightest foundation.

The Doctor, however, does not prove, in his account of the war, that a white man was not killed by the Indians in a canoe two days before Captain Cresap attacked the Indians at Captina. The weight of evidence is very strong in favor of the fact that the slaying of the white settler in the canoe was the moving cause of Captain Cresap's attack. Nothing, however, can justify Greathouse in his mode of procedure when he made the Indians drunk at Baker's and murdered them.

After the raids made by the Indians in Abb's Valley, which we have adverted to, peace seemed to have been restored in a measure throughout this section, and the tide of emigration steadily moved westward. The Indians are like the rattlesnake in two particulars. They are extremely treacherous, and always mysteriously disappear before settlements made by the Caucasian race—not, however, though (like the rattlesnake), before they have given many a poisonous sting. Gradually, all that section of Augusta county now composing several counties was settled up and various names given them. In 1786 Russell county was formed, which lies in the heart of the Blue Grass country. In 1790 Wythe county was inaugurated; in 1793, Grayson; in 1806, Giles; in 1814, Scott; in 1831, Floyd; in 1831, Smyth; in 1842 Carroll; in 1858, Buchanan; in 1861, Bland; in 1880, Dickenson. These latter counties, with the ones already discussed, compose South-west Virginia, as we will see later on. All of these counties were settled by the same class of hardy, honest, worthy people pouring in from the East to take up lands and establish a permanent abiding place for themselves and families.

In the earlier days, before civilization fled westward and carried in its train the comforts and luxuries of life, these people were crude and primitive in the extreme. Necessarily, having no courts of justice, they were in a measure a law unto themselves. Did any member commit a crime or injure a neighbor, he was treated with such contempt by the rest of the settlers that he either amended his ways or left the community to avoid the open contempt exhibited towards him. Every man was expected to uphold law and order, and the small number of people living in this section in those earlier days made each and every one a conspicuous character in the eyes of his neighbor. It was impossible for him to commit a civil or moral wrong without his being seen and known by all near that settlement. Debts, which in our day create such an uproar of excitement, bothered the earlier settlers but little, for, having no legal tender except an exchange of labor, products and rude manufactures, a man was only required to fill his bargain. Contracts were held by public sentiment inviolate, and an implied agreement was well settled between each and every one that all should band together in defending themselves from the Indians, whom they held as their common foe.

In matters of morals these earlier settlers were in many things staunch and true. Honor was regarded as a purchasing commodity, and so treated —that is, binding on each and every one. Female chastity was protected by a most stringent code—the shedding of the blood of the betrayer or seducer by the relatives of the girl ruined with impunity. Sabbaths were observed by the assembling together of the settlers in some particular house, where prayers were said and sermons heard. For lying, any dishonesty, idleness or ill-fame, the punishment was what we might term "hating the offender out," as the earlier settlers expressed it. This savors somewhat of the old-time custom of the Greeks.

The first settlers, so far as we have any light upon the subject, mortally detested anything in the nature of theft, and said peremptorily: "A thief must be whipped." They carried out their ultimatum in this respect and inflicted this summary punishment upon the offender, as Moses directed, by giving him forty lashes less one. This punishment was followed by exile of the guilty party. When magistrates came into power in the west, they kept up this punishment always for petty thieving until the barbarism was duly abolished by law.

Ladies who were given to evil speaking, lying and slandering were accorded the same right they have to this day—to speak as much as they desired, and the punishment was the same as now—nobody believed one word they said.

These people were freely given to hospitality in those rude days to all entering their houses, be he ever so much a stranger. Their homes, bread, raiment and property were ungrudgingly given, and every shield of protection thrown around the guest. In their settlements and forts they lived, worked, feasted, fasted, prayed and cursed in one cordial harmony, never betraying or injuring one another wantonly in name, reputation and fame, until the small envies and jealousies of refined civilization came—the latter always having its evils with the good.

The means of subsistence of these earlier pioneers were scanty in the extreme when compared with the luxuries of the present day. Hunting was more an occupation of necessity then than of pleasure, and after summer seasons, when all had been extracted from the ground that was possible in the way of breadstuffs, the men became impatient at home and formed hunting parties, encamping out for weeks, and preyed upon the plentiful supply of game in the forests in those early days. Often they were without bread and had to go out in the morning to find their breakfast. As the country became more populated and civilization advanced, game, with the Indians, gradually receded, and the cultivation of the soil and raising hogs, poultry and cattle took the place of hunting, and much more than supplied the want caused by the insufficiency of game.

The mechanical arts, too, were seen and carried on in their infancy. The dwellings were constructed of logs, in their forest nativity, after being cut; and who is it that does not remember the many tales of "house-raisings" which have been told, describing how these old people all about the settlement would congregate and assist in the "house-raising"? The clapboards covering the dwelling, and flooring of the same, were rude and uncouth, while the very furniture itself was constructed on the same principles. Knots of trees and timbers were curiously wrought into bowls of all sizes and shapes; wooden spoons and platters were the order of the day; and all other vessels used in a domestic way were manufactured from the products of the forest. Labor, produce raised and wild game were given in exchange for these manufactured goods, and the only currency which these people used in trading with the East were furs and peltry. They were primitive in the extreme, yet on the whole hale, happy and hearty, when not actually engaged in Indian warfare. All farming utensils were made of wood—the plows, harrows, cooper ware and sledges. The stripe of red and white cedar wood was regarded as beautiful and deemed a kind of luxury. The looms which made the cloth were constructed by the inhabitants, of wood, and from them the simple material was made which covered their nakedness; and the shoes worn were made by themselves, from the thread they spun from the cotton and flax to the hides tanned in their own vats. The medicines used in sickness were extracted from various kinds of herbs and roots, the medicinal properties of which were always familiar to some member of each community.

In the latter part of the eighteenth and earlier part of the nineteenth century the onward march of emigrants in South-west Virginia, with the gradual departure of the Indians farther west, opened up a new era for this country These forefathers of the present people, who displayed rare powers of endurance and patience under extreme suffering, who battled every inch of ground they tilled with a savage race, proved themselves in time of peace industrious, energetic and worthy citizens. They gradually improved and cultivated their lands so dearly earned until peace and plenty crowned them with success and they possessed a surplus of the productions of the soil, which they exchanged with their Eastern neighbors for many of the comforts and luxuries of life. The means to gratify suggested wants to the descendants which never occurred to the forefathers. The dwelling houses were constructed on a better and larger scale; the furniture was more comfortable and luxurious; their dress, as well as manners, continued to improve until the year 1860 found the people in this section in a comfortable, improved condition in every way—blessed with a soil of plenty, and numerous advantages unknown to themselves or unheard of as yet. Municipal law had come in to protect the weak and punish the wrong;

schools were opening up in which the minds as well as morals of the youths were trained; and houses of religious worship sprang up on all sides, disseminating the seed of Christianity in every direction, which has ever been the one purifying element in this world. Slavery, a badge of intense wrong, was the only blighting wind which retarded the growth of the country, and soon that was to be swept away amidst carnage and smoke, the disappearance of which left the horizon clearer than ever.

CHAPTER XXX.

THE GREAT VALLEY—SOUTH-WEST VIRGINIA.

There is a large section of country extending for hundreds of miles from the Hudson river, at Newberg, to the Tennessee river, beyond Chattanooga. This is called the Great Limestone Valley, and is the main thoroughfare North and South, through which many different systems of railway extend, opening up almost every part of it. This valley has various names in the different States through which it passes, and marks the portion it traverses as the most highly favored. It is called in New York State the Walkill Valley, in Eastern Pennsylvania the Kittatinny Valley, in middle Pennsylvania the Lebanon or Cumberland Valley, in Virginia the Shenandoah Valley and the Valley of South-west Virginia. There has been some discussion among writers as to what section of Virginia really comprises the South-west. The tidewater, piedmont and south side of the State are well defined, but not so with this great section about which we are writing and which has created the utmost wonder and surprise among the whole people by its almost magic growth and development. By some it is contended that all the territory south-west of Lynchburg is the section of which we are speaking; by others, that the South-west is only that section of country comprising all the counties south-west from Roanoke county, beginning on the top of the table-lands in Montgomery county and including all the watershed of New river and the Holston, embracing the great blue-grass section of the State.

Not entering into any controversy as to the geographical positions taken above, there can be but little doubt of the facts that the word South-west is a key to the situation, and that South-west Virginia, from the natural position of the country itself, is composed of all those counties lying south of James river and west of the Blue Ridge mountains. It is bounded on the north by James river, south by Tennessee and North Carolina, east by the Blue Ridge mountains, and west by the States of West Virginia and Kentucky. The counties composing it are, a part of Botetourt, Roanoke, Craig, Montgomery, Floyd, Pulaski, Giles, Bland, Wythe, Carroll, Grayson, Smyth, Tazewell, Buchanan, Dickenson, Russell, Washington, Scott and Wise.

These counties contain an area of some 5,973 square miles, and have territory and extent enough to contain and support a population many times as large as it is at present. In the extreme South-west, where the counties of Dickenson, Scott and Wise lie, there are but few people, comparing the number with its immense space, and almost unbounded resources yet to become developed. In this section of South-west Virginia there are 5,771,454 acres of land on which taxes are paid.

Geographically, this country is most happily situated. Almost the center of it is pierced by a part of that line which sooner or later will be the great direct thoroughfare from East to West, running from the seacoast at Norfolk, through Lynchburg, Radford, Louisville, St. Louis, Kansas City and on West. This route, by correct estimate, is seventy miles nearer from Norfolk to California than New York to California, and one hundred and thirty miles closer than any line could be run from Boston to San Francisco. In this progressive age and generation, time has become a commodity of such value that every few miles in a projected railway of unnecessary distance presents an obstacle to be seriously considered. The completion of the Roanoke and Southern Railroad (the Elkhorn extension of the Norfolk and Western, both of which are now under construction) will give this section a complete north-western and south-western outlet, while the Shenandoah Valley and Cripple Creek extension of the Norfolk and Western give it direct Northern and Southern connections.

In giving the geological formation of the country, we shall trust to others whose professional life in that line enables them to speak with judgment and confidence. The various stratas underneath the surface of the earth on which the inhabitants tread are full of those valuable ingredients which create ores, such as lead, iron, zinc, coal, manganese, and many other varieties, while the surface itself is capable of the highest yield in the fruits of the earth when properly tilled.

This country is but a division of the Great Limestone Valley of which we have spoken, and everywhere throughout its course presents outcrops of the lower palezoic formations. Those formations rest upon the primary rocks of the mountains, which in this region flank the valley on the south and constitute the rocks of Grayson, Carroll, Pulaski, Wythe, and other counties. Many names have been given the members of the upper series, as well as numbers in the States through which they pass; but this is the most easily understood scale of their classification which we have ever seen. It is numbered from below upwards:

XIII. Coal measure proper \
XII. Conglomerate \
XI. Umbral red shale } Carboniferous.
X. Vespertine gray sandstone /

IX. Ponent red sandstone \
VIII. Vergent shale, etc. } Devonian.
VII. Meridial sandstone /

VI. Pre-meridal limestone \
V. Scalent red shale and fossil ore } Upper Silurian.
IV. Levant sandstone /

III. Material slates \
II. Material limestone } Lower Silurian.
I. Primal slates and sandstone /

Primary rocks* ———— Azoic (archæn).

*The New River Cripple Creek Mineral Region.

The principal members of the foregoing series with which any mineralogist or geologist has to deal in examination of minerals in this section are comprised in the three lowest formations—Nos. I, II, III—the Potsdam sandstone, Cambro Silurian limestone, and the Hudson river slates, all of which, as is readily seen, are embraced in the division called "Lower Silurian."

This country, taking its whole surface, is not surpassed by any other under the sun for natural beauty of scenery, soil, lumber, or mineral resources. Whether we speed along the succulent valley between Roanoke and Carnegie City, walled in by mountains north and south; whether we cross the floor of this great valley between Shawsville and Christiansburg, amidst the mountain ravines and precipitous passes; whether we go up to the New river plateau, in Floyd, Grayson and Carroll, or along weird, winding New river into Pulaski, Giles and Tazewell, we have every delightful prospect of beauty and natural wealth which the eye can desire or the taste suggest. The elevated Blue Ridge division, separated from the valley by the westerly bifurcation of the Blue Ridge, under the names of Pilot Mountain, Poplar Camp and Iron mountains, presents every imaginable delightful feature of the greatest interest to either the most scientific geologist or practical miner. The perfect system of drainage, the ledges and bands of rock strata, the heavy deposits of ore and minerals, seem to have been created on the grandest scale, and the intervention of rich, succulent farming and grazing lands make the whole a country which is fast gaining the attention of investors, and a charming place in which to reside.

There is scarcely anything in nature which appeals so strongly to the sense of sight as varied and beautiful scenery. The South-west is peculiarly fortunate in this respect. In traversing the line of the Norfolk and Western Railroad a panorama of different scenes greets the eye almost every moment as the train whirls along westward from Roanoke. The lovely valley, dotted here and there with its comfortable farm-houses and rich fields of corn and green pastures; the blue hills on either side stretching in a rugged manner in ever direction; the towns resting in the valley—once quiet, but now active and busy; the mountain ravines and precipitous gorges, overhanging vales which sweep away in graceful folds of hillock and dale; the towering heights of cragged peaks, often capped with snow, all together make up a scene which must be viewed with the naked eye in order to be appreciated. After leaving Radford, upon the New River division of the Norfolk and Western Railroad, which runs through Pulaski, Giles and Tazewell in order to tap the coal region of the South-west and West Virginia, the scenery becomes grander and more weird, until it culminates in gorges and cliffs, like Cæsar's Arch and Pompey's Pillar, and steep rocks two hundred and ninety-eight feet high, with a base one hundred and fifty feet deep in the river, opposite the New River White Sulphur Springs.

The Peaks of Otter, in Bedford; Angel's Rest, in Giles, and Ball Knob, with the celebrated Mountain Lake near, are places which if once seen are never forgotten on account of their lovely views and the charming scenery surrounding them. Surely in the choice of a resting-place in this world where one would like to pass his days, it is a matter of great interest and gratification to know that one dwells in a country which is so situated in varied and unique scenery as always to charm the eye and never weary the gaze. The idea that the inhabitants of this section become so accustomed to all this grandeur as to be unimpressed by it is totally erroneous. Take them away from their native heath, and the first void created will be the absence of all these lovely views and the everlasting hills.

This section of country of which we are writing lies between 0° and 8° west longitude from Philadelphia and 36° 30′ and 40° 30′ north latitude. From its position longitudinally and latitudinally the climate must necessarily be salubrious and healthy. This portion of Virginia which lies in the regions of the middle latitudes possesses a climate of means between the extremes of heat and cold incident to the other States south and north of it. The idea prevalent to many strangers that this part of Virginia is very warm during the summer is entirely unjust, for a healthier, more sulubrious and pleasant climate does not exist than the summer seasons of this portion of the Old Dominion. The days are fresh from the heavy mountain dews which fall at night, and it is always pleasant in the months of July and August to sleep under covering of some kind at night.

But certain it is, whatever may be the carping criticisms as to the summer's heat in South-west Virginia, people disbelieve them; for during that very season thousands and thousands of persons from north, south, east and west emigrate to the Roanoke Red Sulphur Springs, Lake Spring, the Montgomery White Sulphur Springs, the Alleghany, the Yellow Sulphur, the New River White Sulphur, Mountain Lake, Wytheville, Glade Springs and Abingdon—all of which places are in this section. These pleasure-seekers all say that the healthy and salubrious climate, the cool nights and delightful days, are the main objects which draw them here, and as they are impartial we rest perfectly satisfied with their verdict. But in order that everyone may know the temperature of this country, a table is here submitted, carefully compiled, giving the average state of the climate:

January ----------25°	July-------------73°
February---------37	August-----------71
March -----------43	September--------63
April------------52	October----------54
May--------------61	November---------42
June-------------68	December---------35

The average for the seasons is:

Spring -----------52°	Autumn----------53°
Summer-----------70.6	Winter-----------32.3

Average for the year, 53°

This climate compares most favorably with the famous health resorts of Europe, such as Geneva, Turin, Vienna, Milan, Weisbaden. The mean temperature of Geneva and Vienna is:

	Spring.	Summer.	Autumn.	Winter.
Geneva	52.2°	70.03°	53.2°	34.0°
Vienna	56.2	71.8	54.6	38.7

Mean for the year: Geneva, 52.07°; Vienna, 55.3°.

This favorable comparison is demonstrative proof that the climate of South-west Virginia is not only a healthy, equable temperature, but an absolutely pleasant one to the human sense. All doubting Thomases will please examine the foregoing tables and be silent.

There are two other features connected with this climate which it is just to mention. Owing to the mountains, the inhabitants are entirely free from all malarial fever, chills, ague and that debility which exists in the lower countries around and saps the vital energies of the human race. Again, such destructive agencies as tornadoes, cyclones and terrific storms are unknown here, for the grand old mountains which furnish varying scenery for the eye act as a wall to break and retard the force of these sweeping destroyers which have infested our western sister States, often leaving woe and desolation in their train.

There is another phase connected with the climate of South-west Virginia which is different from that of other countries.

Generally speaking, when we proceed westerly on the same parallel of latitude the climate becomes colder, as it does if we advance northwardly. But not so is this climate. It is the case to a very slight degree until the summit of the Alleghanies is reached, but advancing westwardly from that point the temperature becomes milder and milder, until it is even warmer in winter than on the sea-coast. This is proven from the fact that catalpas grow spontaneously as far as latitude 37°, reeds as far as 38°, while paroquets grow in winter on the Scioto, in the 39th degree of latitude. A greater portion of Southwest Virginia is west of the Alleghany range, and becomes warmer as we proceed west. This accounts for the fact that the temperature at Wytheville is even milder in a slight degree than that of Radford or Dublin, both of which are east of the former place.

The north-east and north-west winds have more effect upon a climate than is generally supposed, regarding the health and delightfulness of it. The north-east is often loaded and charged with vapor, has a chilling, unhappy and depressing effect upon the human system, while the north-west is dry, elastic, buoyant and animating, causing the spirits of human beings to be almost always in the ascendancy. In the mountains of the South-west the north-west wind prevails, which in a measure accounts for the hale, hearty and bluff appearance of the stalwart mountaineers.

Although the months of July and August are the hottest in the year, they are generally the healthiest, because the weather is dry and less liable to change than in the other months.

The fluctuations between heat and cold, so destructive generally to fruit in the early spring season, prevail much less in Virginia than in Pennsylvania and other States; and the rivers overflow in this period in Virginia a great deal less than in the New England States, because the snows in the former do not lie so long and accumulate so large as they do in the latter, to be dissolved all at once in the spring, causing frequent, and often disastrous, inundations and floods. The snows in this section are rarely deep—never lasting longer than a few days—often disappearing under the mild rays of the winter's sun in twenty-four hours.

The extremes of heat and cold, after a careful investigation, show the temperature at 93° above, and 6° below zero in Fahrenheit's thermometer.

Droughts are rarely experienced in this charming country on account of the heavy mountain dews and frequent gentle rain-falls. Timothy, orchard grass and other forages for hay, which require a given amount of moisture, grow luxuriantly here. In Eastern Virginia, owing to the dry seasons in summer, these grasses suffer, but never here. The rain-fall is frequent in summer, consisting principally of mountain showers, which, owing to the natural drainage of the country, seldom occasions any inconvenience, as the surplus water runs off quickly, leaving the grass and herbage fresh and luxuriant. The following statistics will give some idea of the average rain-fall during the year:

Spring.	Summer.	Autumn.	Winter.	Year.
10.7	11.9	9.6	9.7	41.9

Owing to the salubriousness of the climate and the health of the inhabitants of this country, a gentleman who has examined this portion of Virginia minutely, and written much upon the subject, says—

We would call attention to the fact that the Blue Ridge region of Virginia is, as can be proven by the testimony of consumptives fully restored to health, the best *sanitarium* in the United States east of the Mississippi.*

---

*Jed Hotchkiss, in *The Virginias*, June, 1884.

While we are not prepared to assert that this climate is a cure for consumptives, we most unhesitatingly state that we know of none superior in the South, or any other country. The climate plays no small part in the restoration to health of those persons who every year visit Virginia and her watering-places, seeking relief from the ravages of disease and various bodily ailments. Its animating and invigorating effect; its freedom from north-east winds, which chill and depress; the entire absence of all malaria from it, renders it a charming temperature in which to reside, or in which to earn the daily bread of life.

The soil in this section of country is somewhat varied as to its productions, but universally productive. In Roanoke, Botetourt, Montgomery and Floyd the growing of cereals, vegetables, hay and fruit predominates over "grazing" or cattle-raising, although the latter class of farming is extensively carried on; but in the counties of Pulaski, Tazewell, Giles, Wythe, Carroll, Russell, Wise, Washington, Scott and Buchanan—the natural home of indigenous blue-grass—the business of stock-raising is the chief mode of farming or tilling the land. These latter counties send from their borders every year to market numerous herds of fine cattle, flocks of sheep and some horses, which find their way to Baltimore, Philadelphia and New York markets. Some of the largest cattle men, like Mr. A. H. Stuart and Henry C., his son, of Russell; Charles W. Palmer, of Saltville, and James W. Byars, of Washington county, ship cargoes of live stock to Europe.

In the counties of Roanoke and Botetourt, Craig and Montgomery, the soil is a rich, loamy, chocolate-clay, generally speaking, and is admirably adapted to the production of wheat, Indian corn, oats, barley, rye, buckwheat, hay and vegetables of every description. Fruit of almost all varieties flourish in these counties, and the result is that in Roanoke and Botetourt, especially, the industries of canning fruit and vegetables have become not only extensive ones, but extremely remunerative to the persons engaged in them. Some of the brands of these canning establishments have gained a national reputation almost, and are sold all over the country. Not only does this business consume large quantities of fruit and vegetables, but it gives employment to a large number of operatives necessary to carry on the factories. In addition to the fruit consumed by these, large quantities are shipped annually for foreign consumption.

Going westward from the counties we have just been discussing the soil will be somewhat different. In Floyd, Carroll, Wythe, Grayson, Washington and Pulaski it is a freestone, with here and there a character of limestone. It results from a decomposition *in situ* of large bands of granitoid rock, gneiss, hornblende, aluminous slates, feldspars—in fact, it possesses all the wide range of silicates of alumina, potash, lime, soda and iron. Tazewell county is but little different, possessing a richer loam, which is better for grazing purposes. In all these counties large crops of fruit are grown, and some exported. Wythe, Smyth and Washington counties are famous for their broad areas of cabbage, which is grown in large quantities and shipped to foreign markets.

But when we speak of agricultural resources we allude more to the capacity of a country for production than to what is being actually produced. No region, in the matters of location, soil, climate and natural advantage is superior to this for agricultural purposes. In this wonderful development now going on the production of agricultural products will advance with the demand. In the valleys and along the mountains the soil is capable of the highest productive capacity, and the day is not far distant when all this land lying, comparatively speaking, in waste now, will be thoroughly utilized and cultivated to an advantage and profit.

There are two industries beginning to dawn in this section which bid fair to become extremely large and productive. We allude to dairy-farming and the planting of vineyards. No country can be more suitable to the production of milk, butter and cheese, than this far-famed blue-grass section, in which cattle thrive so fast and yield such an abundance of milk from the peculiar fattening properties of this grazing. From a surplus of milk to the manufacture of cheese is but a step, which we have reason to believe will soon be bridged over. The southern slopes of the mountains are in many instances being utilized as vineyards, an industry which can be rendered extremely profitable, not only from the sale of the grapes, but the manufacture of wines.

The abundant opportunities to farmers with small capital in this country cannot be overlooked much longer, and those who are in possession of these lands have now an opportunity of realizing as much from the slopes of the mountains as their more fortunate neighbors have from the valleys. We know of no soil so capable of producing large crops of cabbage and the Irish potato as this mountain land in South-west Virginia, to say nothing of it as a fruit-growing region.

Not only are the lands of this section well adapted for the production of all the necessaries of life in ample abundance, but the location of a greater portion of the agricultural country will satisfy the most fastidious taste of those having an eye for the beautiful. The James River Valley, situated in Botetourt; the valley westward of Roanoke; the plateau of country lying around Blacksburg, in Montgomery county; the level lands of Pulaski about Dublin and Pulaski City, where the celebrated Blue Ridge country begins; the beautiful meadows in Wythe, and the justly celebrated Burke's Garden, in Tazewell county, all present agriculturally a picture of scenic beauty, and splendid appearance of fertility equally as true. As stock-breeding and raising is one of the staple industries of this section, we can form some idea of its agricultural resources in this respect by adding a table giving the exact number of each kind in the live-stock department. Then by computing the number of horses we get an estimate of the extent of the tillage of the section. South-west Virginia has 50,963 horses, 154,931 cattle, 107,565 sheep, 116,546 hogs. The blue-grass counties have by far a larger portion of this live stock, the county of Russell alone having 15,093 cattle.

There is one industry which, though rapidly gaining ground, has still the opportunity and means of becoming one of the largest of its kind in the South-west—that is, sheep-raising, and in connection therewith, wool-growing. All along the slopes, and even upon the plateaus on top of the mountains, there is the finest character of grazing for sheep. Wherever the trees are cut, and the sun allowed to penetrate with its rays, an indigenous, rich, succulent grass comes, and the whole surface after a while becomes sodded. Sheep of the better grade, for both mutton and wool, thrive well, and experience shows that there is a handsome profit in raising them. In the near future this must necessarily become one of the largest sources of revenue which the agriculturist will have to draw upon.

The rapid growth of towns and cities like Roanoke, Salem, Christiansburg, Radford, Pulaski City, Wytheville, Max Meadows, and others throughout this section, has given an impetus to an industry agriculturally hitherto almost unknown—the trucking business, or market gardening. Wherever there is a demand, the supply for it inevitably follows; and the requirement of vegetables and small fruits by the inhabitants of the foregoing cities can be fully supplied from the country around, because the seasons and soil produce almost every kind that is known, and in sufficient profusion to supply the wants of all.

It is conceded by all who have a knowledge upon the subject that South-west Virginia is one of the richest countries in mineral resources in the United States. Not only are minerals of almost every variety found in the mountains here, but they are sufficient in quantity and vastly superior in quality. In General Imboden's "Mineral Wealth of Virginia" he says:

Between the Atlantic coast and the western boundaries of the State the whole "geological column" is represented, from the foundation granite to the capstones of the upper carboniferous. And in these successive strata are found rocks and minerals peculiar to each all over the world, and usually in greater abundance and of greater excellence than anywhere else in the same area.

McCreath and D'Invilliers, in their report upon "The Mining Wealth of Cripple Creek and New River," have this to say concerning the country as a mineral territory:

The New-river-Cripple-creek mineral region may be assumed to contain 300 square miles, probably one-half of which may be considered as ore-bearing territory. While it would be injudicious, from the very nature of the occurrence of the brown hematite ore deposits everywhere, to estimate the tonnage that any single square mile of this territory would yield, yet it must be manifest from the details given in this report that the total amount of iron ore to be mined in the region will be very great. The quality, uniformity and richness of the ore is unsurpassed by any other developed brown hematite iron-ore district. The accessibility of the ore deposits to the Cripple Creek extension, and their proximity in a large part of the field to unusually good washing facilities, as well as the small cost of mining the ore itself, should result in the production of a cheap and well-prepared ore for furnace use. The occurrence here of a first-class and cheaply-mined ore, the proximity of a magnificent coking field, with limestone for fluxing purposes everywhere throughout the region, with a constant supply of pure water, surroundsd by a fertile agricultural and grazing district capable of supporting a large population, and with numerous eligible sites for manufacturing purposes, this New-river-Cripple-creek region certainly offers unusual advantages for the investment of capital.

This region, so rich in ores, is situated in Wythe, Pulaski, Carroll and Grayson. Floyd, too, an adjoining county, is rich in ores.

In this New-river-Cripple-creek mineral region an iron ore of peculiar quality has been found, termed *Gossan ore*. It gives, when mixed with other iron ores, a peculiarly good character to the iron, while by itself it produces an admirable iron. It is one of the most important discoveries found in the South in the way of iron ore, and it is admitted to be the only "red short ore" that has been found south of Mason and Dixon's line. Mixed with the brown ores, it gives a first-class iron for foundry or mill purposes, and permits the use of thousands of tons of high phosphorus and manganese ores that could never be utilized successfully by themselves. By means of the Reed Island extension, completed about June, and the Cape Fear and Yadkin Valley extension, finished this last summer, this ore is available for most of the furnaces situated around. By the means of this they will be in a position to make, as they wish, either a red, cold short, or neutral iron—stimulating to a very high degree the establishment of industries requiring as raw material cheap as well as varied classes of pig-iron, and by so doing build up wonderful adjuncts to the furnaces established. The analysis of the iron ores compare most favorably with that of any other ore we know of mined anywhere. McCreath and D'Invilliers, in their report mentioned above, give the analyses of various openings made throughout this favored section. We give several, as an average sample, showing the quality of the ore.

From samples taken from a ton lying at Cedar creek opening it yielded:

```
Metallic iron ------------------ 57.300
Phosphorus --------------------- .045
Siliceous matter --------------- 4.620
Phosphorus in 100 parts of iron .078
```

In the Buddlefield tract samples clipped from all along the ore surface yielded:

```
Metallic iron ------------------ 57.700
Phosphorus --------------------- .058
Sciliceous matter -------------- 4.280
Phosphorus in 100 parts of iron .100
```

On the Widow Stephens' tract, from a sample of lump ore taken from three different pits, the following analysis was obtained:

```
Metallic iron ------------------ 54.075
Phosphorus --------------------- .073
Siliceous matter --------------- 7.950
Phosphorus in 100 parts iron --- .135
```

In the same work, the general average character of the ore is well represented by the following analysis of a sample (176 pieces) taken from nine different openings:

```
Bisulphide of iron ------------ None.
Protoxide of iron ------------- None.
Sesquoxide of iron ------------ 76.214
Sesquoxide of manganese ------- .051
Oxides of nickel and cobalt --- .040
Oxide of zinc ----------------- None.
Oxide of lead ----------------- None.
```

```
Oxide of copper --------------- None.
Alumina ----------------------- 2.365
Baryta ------------------------ None.
Lime -------------------------- .820
Magnesia ---------------------- .486
Sulphuric acid ---------------- .157
Phosphoric acid --------------- .171
Water ------------------------- 12.072
Siliceous matter -------------- 7.480
                                99.856
Metallic iron ----------------- 53.850
Metallic manganese ------------ .036
Sulphur ----------------------- .063
Phosphorus -------------------- .075
Phosphorus in 100 parts of iron .140
```

There can be no doubt but that this is a magnificent ore-bearing section in the way of iron. Every facility for manufacturing iron in this country on the very cheapest basis is apparently good, and already its reputation in that respect has caused several large furnaces to be erected.

But it is not in this section of the South-west alone that we have an abundance of ore. In Roanoke and Botetourt counties both the Houston and Rorer iron mines have been successfully worked for a number of years. The former supplies much of the raw material for the Crozer iron and steel furnace, while ores from the latter are shipped in all directions. The ores from this section of Virginia are good, too, and, upon an analysis from McCreath's *Mineral Wealth of Virginia*, yield from the Houston mines, in Botetourt county, the following:

```
Metallic iron ----------------- 52.200
Metallic manganese ------------ 1.419
Sulphur ----------------------- .016
Phosphorus -------------------- .194
Phosphorus in 100 parts of iron .371
```

The opening near Cloverdale, in Roanoke county, also worked by the Houston company, known as the Murray Bank, analyzes well. From twenty-five pieces selected by Mr. Warne, superintendent of the mines, Mr. McCreath gives the following analysis:

Metallic iron	53.050
Phosphorus	1.265
Siliceous matter	6.630
Phosphorus in 100 parts iron	2.386

Near Salem, Virginia, there are large deposits of ore, from which the furnaces at that point will draw their raw material in the way of ores. The Bott property is particularly good as to quantity and quality, for Mr. Edmund C. Pechin general manager for the Virginia Development Company, in his report to the stockholders in April, 1890, says:

After considerable negotiations, the furnace has secured the lease of the Bott property, about seven miles from Salem. A late inspection of this property shows, as the result of extensive developments, what promises to be one of the very best ore properties in Virginia. Not only is the amount of the ore apparently very large and of good quality, but it lies in the foot-hills and on the mountain side in such a shape as to allow easy opening up and cheap mining.

In this very particular of "cheap mining" most of the ore-bearing country throughout the South-west is alike. On all sides it is conceded that ores can be mined cheaper in in this part of Virginia than in any other country known. In various parts of the section, from experience and careful, prudent estimates, it has been repeatedly shown that iron ore can be mined and placed at the furnace for an average price of $2.30 per ton of ore. In Pennsylvania it costs on an average of $4.25 per ton to place it at the furnace—almost twice what it costs in our own country. This difference must necessarily gradually drive the iron manufacturer South, and substantiate Chauncey M. Depew's advice when he said: "Go South, young man!"

Many counties in this vast mineral section contain mines of iron ore in sufficient quantities to furnish material for large amounts of capital to be used in their development, and to give employment to thousands of mechanics and laboring men for years to come. Magnetites, limonites and specular ores are found in different regions and localities. The magnetites abound in the James River Valley; on the plateau; in counties drained by New river and its tributaries; in Floyd, Carroll, Pulaski and Grayson. In Smyth and Washington counties, as well as others, a semi-magnetic ore has been discovered, and pronounced excellent on account of being low in phosphorus, and therefore adapted to the manufacture of Bessemer steel, which is rapidly succeeding iron in all structural work. The hematites, both red and brown, are distributed all through the South-west—on the western slopes of the mountains, and in the hills and valleys. This section is truly an iron-ore bearing field, and the fact that the railroads direct from coking fields near at hand run through it proves that Virginia, at no great future day, will be one of the foremost States in the Union for the manufacture of iron and the adjuncts thereto.

Other minerals as useful and necessary to humanity have been discovered in South-west Virginia, and many of them are successfully worked at this day.

Lead has been extensively mined for over one hundred years in Wythe county, and at this time the largest lead works in the South are carried on there, with an apparently exhaustless quantity. In this same section other mines of the same mineral have been found and developments set on foot to have their products utilized. These will, beyond doubt, prove a success, and give employment to many people in manufacturing a most valuable commodity in every respect. The analysis made of a sample of lead ore, second separation, taken from the property of the Wythe Lead and Zinc Company, yields:

Metallic lead 65.836
Metallic zinc 5.408

In the Cripple-creek-New-river mining region have been found the best samples of zinc ore ever discovered in the South; and the Bertha Zinc Works, situated at Pulaski City (of which we will have more to say when we reach that place), are not only the largest, but manufactures the purest spelter in the United States. Up to the year 1887 this company had manufactured or smelted 12,775 tons of ore, which they derived from their mines not far off. An analysis of this zinc shows:

Metallic zinc 37.836
Metallic lead .... None.

In many other localities in this section this mineral has been found, and will undoubtedly be successfully operated.

The allotment of space in this work forbids an analysis and description of each class of minerals already discovered in South-west Virginia, and we refer the reader to various geological and mineralogical works on this subject. But we have conclusive evidence that, besides the minerals already mentioned and classified, this section has copper, tin, manganese, mica, and plumbago, kaolin and fire-clays, lime and cement, plaster (gypsum), salt, marl and building stones of every variety from the gray to the brown sandstone—all of which can be seen by any one interested in the mineral resources of South-west Virginia.

We have not omitted the great coal sections thoughtlessly, but will recur to them at the proper place, in connection with a history of the New River Railroad, which was constructed into that section to haul out the vast quantities of this mineral.

With these mineral resources in

the midst of an agricultural country like this, it is but safe to prophesy that Virginia will ere long occupy her natural position in the foremost rank of manufacturing States. Even now there are within her borders many furnaces being erected, and some in blast. The Crozer Furnace, the West End Furnace, at Roanoke; the one at Salem, the Crane Furnace, at Radford; the Pulaski Iron Company's Furnace, the furnace of G. T. Mills, at Pulaski City; the Ivanhoe Furnace on Cripple Creek extension, the furnace at Speedwell, the furnace of the Max Meadows Company, the Graham Furnace, all ndicate and point to the fact that the South-west bids fair to become a great manufacturing center.

Another powerful lever which Virginia has to substantiate her position as a manufacturing center in the way of iron in this section is the cheapness with which the article can be made. Having the iron ore, limestone and coke all within her borders, no country can manufacture it cheaper than it can be made here. Actual costs of making a ton of pig-iron are here given. The cost at Roanoke, as furnished by the Crozer Company, is—

Ore, 2⅛ tons, at $2.26	$ 4 81
Coke, 1¼ tons, at $2.95	3 69
Limestone	75
Labor	2 10
Incidentals	1 25
Total	$12 60

The cost at Pulaski City, as given by the Pulaski Iron Campany, is—

Ore, 2 tons, at $1.35	$ 2 70
Freight, at 35c.	70
1⅜ tons coke, at $1.75	2 40
Freight, at 90c.	1 24
Limestone and labor	2 15
Incidentals and repairs	1 00
Total cost per ton	$10 19

This cost of $10.19 at Pulaski is the average expense of making iron in the New-river-Cripple-creek regions. Comparing these estimates of actual cost with those of Pennsylvania, we readily see the advantageous position which Virginia holds as an iron-producing State.

In middle Pennsylvania the cost is—

	1882. Actual Cost.	1884. Estimated.
Ore	$ 9 37	$ 7 75
Fuel—coal and coke	5 02	4 62
Limestone	1 00	1 00
Incidentals, labor	2 35 48	3 25
Total	$18 22	$16 62

In the lower Susquehanna district the cost is $18.16 per ton, and in the Lehigh Valley district $20.38 actual cost, and $17.02 estimated cost for one ton in 1884. This difference in cost in that State between the years 1882 and 1884 arose from the fact that in the latter year the cost of both ore and fuel was much less.

These facts are invulnerable, and, so far as the manufacture of iron is concerned, place South-west Virginia in a most enviable position.

If steam as a manufacturing power does not totally supersede water, this section has an ample quantity for manufacturing purposes. James river in Botetourt; Roanoke river running through Montgomery and Roanoke; New river through Giles, Pulaski, Floyd and Carroll; the Bluestone through Tazewell, and other streams, place this section on a sound basis as to water-power. But we have, by careful observation, come to the conclusion that the old cry, "there can be no city without water-power," is *effete*, and that money and energy will rear any structures under the sun except culture and refinement—they go a long way towards assisting those.

The immense and valuable bodies of timber throughout South-west Virginia has caused manufacturing in lumber to become a distinct and remunerative business. Not only right at home is there any quantity of it, but the demand for it is there, too, and an ever-increasing one. All the varieties are found—walnut, ash, cherry, pine, poplar, oak, spruce, cedar, hemlock, pine, hickory, chestnut, locust, birch and tulip poplar—and the supply is almost exhaustless, for so quickly do the forests replenish themselves that a continuous supply is the result. Huge saw-mills, planing-mills and wood-working factories, such as sash, door and house-furnishing wood-work are springing up on every side, while manufacturing establishments for fancy wood-carving are beginning to be erected at one or two places.

When we think of a country's possessing all these advantages bestowed upon it by the God of nature—its gorgeous and beautiful scenery, its salubrious and healthy climate, its agricultural and mineral resources, its certainty of possession of all those adjuncts which make a country a manufacturing center—should we wonder at energy and capital pouring in to develop it? And having taken a cursory view of the original grand cause, let us look now at the auxiliary causes which have played no small part in the history of its progress.

CHAPTER XXXI.

THE MINERALS OF VIRGINIA.

By JED HOTCHKISS,

Consulting Mining Engineer and Geologist.

The mineral wealth of Virginia is necessarily great in variety and quantity, since that State contains extensive areas of nearly all the recognized geological formations of the North American continent. Each of these formations, as a rule, contains minerals of more or less commercial value. The skilled prospector, seeking for mineral resources of any kind, will always inform himself as to the location and extent of these geological areas, and there search for the minerals he desires to exploit.

The Virginia minerals comprise in paying quantities, so far as the present investigations and developments have gone; of the metals, native and in ores: gold, tin, copper, lead, zinc, iron, manganese and silver; of mineral fuels: bituminous, semi-bituminous and semi-anthracite coals; of building stones: granites, limestones, including several varieties of marble, freestones, sandstones, greenstones, brownstones, soapstones, and hydraulic and other limestones for lime, plaster of Paris and cement, and mortar and plastering sands; of fictile minerals, many varieties of brick and fire clays and glass sands; of fertilizing minerals, gypsum, greensand and other marls, limestone and salt, and also the latter, of the best quality, for domestic and other uses, besides numerous other minerals hereafter mentioned.

Virginia is naturally divided into seven Grand Divisions, as set forth for the first time in Hotchkiss' Summary of Virginia, published by the State in 1876, and in his articles on Virginia in the Encyclopedia Britannica, the Encyclopedia Americana, and in numerous other publications. A sub-division of the State based on natural characteristics and features that is now generally accepted and used in describing the various portions of the State.

These Grand Divisions, taken in their succeeding order from the Atlantic westward, are: 1. Tidewater, or the Tidewater Country; 2. Midland, or the Midland Country; 3. Piedmont, or the Piedmont region; 4. The Blue Ridge, embracing that mountain chain and its spurs and plateaus; 5. The Valley, or The Great Valley of Virginia; 6. Apalachia, or the Mountain Country lying north-west of the Great Valley; and 7. Trans-Apalachia, or the country lying on the westward slope of the Apalachian mountains, and beyond their regular and nearly parallel ranges—a small but important part of which pertains to Virginia.

The mineral resources of the several Grand Divisions of Virginia as a whole are well summarized in the following extract from the article on that State in the great Encyclopedia Britannica, ninth edition, 1888, volume XXIV, page 258, by Major Jed. Hotchkiss:

"The varied and abundant mineral resources of the State are as yet but imperfectly developed. Her medicinal mineral springs are numerous, and many of them well known.

Tidewater abounds in fertilizing marls, and in choice brick clays, sands, and shell-limestones for building. Lime burning, from oyster shells, is an important industry.

Midland abounds in superior granites, which are extensively quarried near Richmond and Petersburg; in the best of slates for roofing and other purposes, especially in Albemarle and Buckingham counties; in Jura-Trias brownstones and sandstones; in trap for Belgian blocks; in soapstones, (steatites), limestones, and in brick-, plastic- and fire-clays. Thick beds of excellent bituminous coal and of natural coke are found in the Jura-Trias of Chesterfield and adjacent counties, which have long been mined; ochre beds are worked in Chesterfield county; thick beds of magnetic, specular, and limonite iron ores, and of gold-, silver- and copper-bearing rocks, traverse its whole length from north-east to south-west. Its gold belt, from fifteen to twenty miles wide, rich in free-, quartz-, and pyritous-rock gold, traverses the whole western tier of Midland counties, for more than 200 miles, from the Potomac to the Dan; in this belt, in Louisa county, at the Arminius copper mines, veins of white pyrites, 42 feet thick, bearing 46 per cent. of sulphur and considerable yellow copper, have been opened and reduction works erected for a 300 tons daily output; 12,000 tons of pyrites were shipped in 1886. Manganese, mica, plumbago, titanium, cyanite, garnets, emeralds, quartz, and other Archaean and Jura-Trias minerals are found at many points. The minerals and metals now exploited are gold, iron and copper pyrites, manganese, hematites, magnetites, and limonites, mica, slates, granites, brownstones, and trap-rock.

Piedmont has extensive beds of magnetic, specular and limonite iron ores throughout its length; chromic iron ore is found in the north-east; copper ores abound, especially along the west border in spurs of Blue Ridge; manganese deposits have been worked at various points; the same Archæan and Jura-Trias building stones and minerals are found here as in Midland; the marbles of Bedford and Loudoun counties are of fine quality. Iron ores, manganese, slates and marbles are now exploited.

The Blue Ridge abounds in copper and iron ores for its whole length in Virginia; these, as well as pyritous silver, copper and iron ores, are especially abundant in the Floyd-Carroll-Grayson or South-west plateau, where also auriferous quartz is milled; tin mines have been opened in Rockbridge county; the great Potsdam or Primordial iron belt, with its vast deposits of ore, flanks the western base of the Blue Ridge in Virginia for nearly three hundred miles, and from the rich deposits of manganese in the same belt two-thirds of the manganese output of the United States in 1886 was mined; glass-sand of the best quality and fire and other clays are abundant, and so are building sandstones in the Western Blue Ridge. Mining operations are now extensively conducted in iron and manganese ores.

The Great Valley is all underlain by limestones suitable for ornamental, building and agricultural purposes; its cement (hydraulic) and architectural, fluxing and agricultural limes are noted for their purity; extensive beds of iron ore are found among its hills; marbles, barytes, brick- and fire-clays, and travertine marls are abundant; there are large deposits of lead and zinc ores, especially in the South-west in Pulaski and Wythe counties, where they accompany the great iron ore deposits of the Cripple creek region; from the Vespertine (No. X.) beds of the Lower Carboniferous in Montgomery and Pulaski counties, from 15,000 to 20,000 tons of semi-anthracite coal are annually mined; ochres are mined in Page and Augusta counties; iron, manganese, zinc and lead ores are now mined on quite an extensive scale, and lime burning is an important industry.

Apalachian Virginia abounds in very remarkable beds of limonite iron ores, found (often, under large areas, in a more or less stratified condition) in the Hudson River (III), Clinton (V), and Oriskany (VII) formations of Cambrian and Silurian age; there are also deposits of magnetic hematites in Craig and Giles counties; limestones of the Valley (II), Trenton (III), and Lower Helderberg (VI) formations, underlying the 'rich' valleys and ridges, abound and furnish the best of materials for building, lime-burning and blast-furnace fluxing purposes, as well as for beautiful encrinal and other fancy marbles; in its Vespertine (X) areas are numerous patches of anthracite and semi-anthracite coals, worked and workable for local use; in the Apalachian portions of Smyth and Washington counties are large deposits of rock-salt and gypsum; travertine marls, caves abounding in nitrous earths, and chalybeate, sulphur, alum, hot, warm, and other mineral springs are common; sandstones and slates for building purposes are plentiful. The iron ores of Alleghany county and those of the Apalachian portion of Rockbridge and Botetourt counties are extensively mined for local blast-furnaces; marbles and gypsum are quarried; considerable salt is manufactured, and semi-anthracite coal is mined in Pulaski for use in the local zinc furnaces.

Trans-Apalachia is Virginia's 1,000 square miles of the Great Coal Basin of the Ohio, or the Trans-Apalachian Coal Basin (the one usually, but improperly, called the Great Apalachian Coal Basin); this is all underlain by thick and easily accessible beds of the best semi-bituminous and bituminous coals, those of the Lower (XII) and of the Middle (XIII) Coal groups of the Carboniferous. Only the semi-bituminous coking, steam, and domestic coal of this region is now mined for exportation at Pocahontas, Tazewell county, from which 639,751 tons (93,550 of them converted into coke) were shipped in 1886, the traffic having begun with the shipment of 105,805 tons in 1883. From the Flat-Top coal field, including the Pocahontas and some adjacent mines in West Virginia, 1,314,700 tons of coal were mined in 1887, part of which was made into about 145,000 tons of coke, equal in quality to any made in the United States. This fuel is remarkably high in fixed carbon and low in ash and sulphur, and therefore admirably adapted for metallurgical purposes. Twenty mineral springs of Virginia, used medicinally, were reported to the United States Geological Survey in 1886 (Tidewater 1, Midland 4, Blue Ridge 2, Valley 5, Apalachia 8); they were reported as chalybeate, alum, white sulphur, red sulphur, blue sulphur, warm sulphur, cold sulphur, hot sulphur, lithia, healing ague, and sweet chalybeate. These, and many others not reported, are visited as health resorts, and many of them ship to market large quantities of their waters.

Virginia produced of coal 300,000 tons in 1884, 1,000,000 in 1886, and about 1,250,000 in 1887; of coke 25,340 tons in 1884, about 122,352 tons in 1886; of pig iron 29,934 tons in 1880, 152,907 in 1883, 156,250 in 1886, and 156,698 in 1887; of rolled iron 40,581 tons, and of cut nail 212,552 kegs of 100 lbs. in 1886; of manganese 3,661 tons in 1880, and 20,567 tons in 1886; of pyrites 12,000 tons in 1886; of ochre 1,750 tons in 1886; of salt, gypsum, lead, zinc, granite, slates, lime, limestone for blast-furnace flux, cement, brownstone, mineral waters, and iron ores for export large quantities were produced in 1886, and still larger in 1887, when the mining industries of this State were in a healthy condition of development.

The Mineral Productions of Virginia in 1889, as Shown by the Bulletins of the Eleventh, or 1890, Census of the United States

The returns of these bulletins are manifestly incomplete since the information embodied in them was mainly obtained by correspondence, consequently many mining operations and manufacturing plants using mineral products were overlooked or never heard from, but these are the official statements of a department of the General Government and will be referred to for information, therefore they have a value that warrants their re-publication. These returns include for Virginia iron ores, slates, limestones, coals, buhrstones, asbestus, infusorial earth, barytes, ochre, gypsum, soapstone, fibrous talc, pyrites, lead and zinc, mica, granite, manganese and precious stones.

Pig Iron.—During the year ending June 30th, 1890, the United States produced 9,579,779 tons of pig iron as compared with 3,781,021 tons produced during the Census year 1880. The increase in production from 1870 to 1880, was nearly 85 per cent. while from 1880 to 1890 it was over 153 per cent. Virginia which was 17th in rank in production in 1880, was the 6th in 1890. During the year ending May 31st, 1890, Virginia had 31 completed furnace stacks which produced 302,447 tons of pig iron or 3.16 per cent of the entire product of the country. Her percentage of increase from 1880 to 1890, was 1,589.08. Classed according to the fuel used Virginia produced during the year ending May 31, 1880, 8,326 tons of coke and bituminous coal pig iron; and 9,459 of charcoal pig iron, a total exclusive of castings of 17,785 tons. During the year ending June 30, 1890, she produced 294,246 tons of coke and bituminous coal pig iron and 7,906 tons of charcoal pig iron, a total of 302,152 tons.

Slates.—In the production of roofing slates, Virginia occupied the 6th rank, although it had but three quarries, two in Buckingham and one in Amherst county, on opposite sides of the great slate belt that extends from Vermont to Georgia along the eastern side of the Blue Ridge, having in Virginia a length of some 400 miles and a breadth of nearly 30 miles within which these bands of slate are found. The larger part of the output in Virginia is from the Buckingham quarries near James river, on the line of the Richmond and Alleghany Division of the Chesapeake and Ohio Railway at Arvonia and Ore Banks, the slates of which are widely used in this country, ranking as the best that are produced. From the Virginia quarries 23,457 squares of roofing slate were taken in 1889, valued at $85,079. At these quarries there were paid out for wages and other expenditures $77,246. The capital invested in lands, buildings, tools, etc., was $170,000, and 216 men were employed in the industry. This is a very meagre showing for a State that has such unlimited quantities of the very best of slates, not only for roofing but also for marbleizing and all other purposes that slates are used for. Instead of occupying the 6th place in rank Virginia should hold the first, which Pennsylvania now holds, with nearly six millions of dollars invested in this industry and with a yearly output valued at nearly two millions of dollars.

Limestones.—Under this head are given reports on the quarrying of limestones for building purposes, limeburning, fluxing for furnaces for street work, for bridge, dam and railway work and for miscellaneous uses. The products of this industry in the United States amounted to over $19,000,000. More than $15,000,000 were paid for wages and other expenses, and over $27,000,000 were invested in it. Virginia is reported to have had but 11 quarries in operation, valued at $159,023. From these were taken 471,505 cubic feet of limestone for building purposes, valued at $19,520, or 4 cents a cubic foot. There were burnt 178,480 barrels of lime, of 200 pounds each, valued at $83,667, or 47 cents a barrel. The limestone for burning into lime, quarried by others than limeburners, amounted to 15,000 tons,* valued at $7,500, or 50 cents a ton. For fluxing purposes 78,756 tons, valued at $48,146, or 61 cents a ton, were sold. For street purposes 7,560 cubic feet, valued at $1.90, or 3 cents a foot, are reported. The number of employees in this industry is given as 253. There were paid out for wages, supplies, etc., $116,636, and there were invested in lands, buildings, tools, etc., $99,875. Under the head of classified wages it appears that quarry foremen received an average of daily wages of $1.99; quarrymen, $1.38; mechanics and stonecutters, $1.58; laborers, $1.02, and boys, 77 cents; and office men an average salary of $546 a year. Virginia ranked 20th in value of production; 25th in total capital; 18th in number of men employed and wages paid; 5th in production of flux for furnaces; 4th in furnishing stone for limeburning. The percentage of profit on invested capital is given at over 42; on the value of product as 27 per cent. Any one at all familiar with the limestone resources of Virginia knows how ridiculous these figures are in their proportions. Any one of the half-dozen furnaces in the State, which were then in operation, used more limestone for fluxing purposes that year than the whole amount credited to the State. It is probable that the methods of the Census Bureau will report the limestone used for fluxing somewhere else, although the limestone production, no matter for what purpose used, ought all to have appeared in this Bulletin.

Virginia has many thousand square miles of limestone territory, stretch-

---

* Short tons are meant in all the statements of this paper, unless the contrary is stated.

ing for hundreds of miles through its entire length, and from every portion of this large quantities of limestone are quarried every year for most of the purposes enumerated in the Bulletin. It is within bounds to say that the figures above given should be increased many times to fairly represent the status of Virginia in this industry, although her large resources in this particular are as yet but meagerly developed.

Coal.—Virginia is credited with a production in 1889 of 865,786 tons of coal, valued at $804,475, an average of $0.93 per ton at the mine, as against one of 43,079 tons valued at $99,802 in 1879, the latter including 2,817 tons of anthracite valued at $8,290. There was invested in the business of coal mining $1,055,516; in it 1,555 men were employed who were paid in wages $621,266. The total expenditures of all kinds were $682,408. The Census Bulletin says: "The coal of this State is bituminous and some of the finest grades of steam, coking and gas coals are found. In that part of the State lying north of the James river in the Richmond coal field there exists an unusual formation of natural coke strongly resembling artificial coke, which is found to be a very good domestic fuel."

The larger part of this Virginia production is from that portion of the Flat-Top (Pocahontas) field that extends into Tazewell county in the border of Apalachia on the line of the Norfolk and Western Railroad. The coals there mined are semi-bituminous coals of the Virginia formation No. XII, the Lower Coal Measures of the Virginias. . The Census Bulletin says of these: "The finest grades of steam, gas and coking coals are obtained from this district, and the exceptional transportation facilities provided by the Norfolk and Western Railroad system to the westward and to tidewater at Norfolk have distinguished this region as one of the most important in the country."

The bulletin reports coal from 11 counties with 11 regular establishments and 47 small banks and local mines. Of the whole product Chesterfield and Henrico counties are credited with 49,411 tons, the most of it loaded at the mines for shipment by railway at an average price of $1.57 per ton. Pulaski and Tazewell counties are credited with 807,046 tons, 685,171 of which were loaded for shipment by rail and 112,210 were made into coke. There were realized from sales $705,121, or an average of $0.87 a ton at the mines. Pulaski and Tazewell counties should not have been put together in this statement, since the production of the former was a very small quantity of semi-anthracite coal hardly worth the mentioning in comparison with the large quantity mined in Tazewell.

The Chesterfield and Henrico mines are reported as owning 2,200 acres of land valued at $40,000; those of Montgomery 200 acres, valued at $2,100; those of Tazewell and Pulaski as 11,500 acres, valued at $248,000; of leased land the Chesterfield and Henrico mines had 2,100 acres, valued at $50,800; the Montgomery 1,690 acres valued at $52,800. The investments in buildings, tools, etc., were: $301,800 in Chesterfield and Henrico, $60,400 in Montgomery, and $667,938 in Tazewell and Pulaski. The capital invested shows a total of $1,055,516; in Chesterfield and Henrico, $311,300; in Montgomery, $62,530; and in Pulaski and Tazewell $681,686. The same remark applies to Pulaski in this statement as in the previous one. The average wages in the whole State were: for foremen, $2.01 per day; $1.94 in Chesterfield and Henrico, $1.30 in Montgomery, and $2.32 in Tazewell and Pulaski; for mechanics $1.77; in Chesterfield and Henrico $1.61; in Montgomery $1.25; and in Tazewell and Pulaski $2.15; for laborers an average of $1.16; in Chesterfield and Henrico $0.88, in Montgomery $0.81, and $1.20 in Tazewell and Pulaski. The wages of boys average $0.49; $0.45 in Chesterfield and Henrico, $0.40 in Montgomery, and $1.00 in Tazewell and Pulaski.

Virginia embraces about 1,000 square miles of the Trans-Apalachian, or Ohio River Basin, coal field in the counties of Tazewell, Buchanan, Russell, Dickenson, Wise, Scott and Lee. Mining operations had only just begun in most of these counties, during the 1890 census year, since railway construction only reached them about that time. Coal mining operations in the Richmond field (one of the first developed in this country and that formerly had a large output) are being resumed on quite an extensive scale. Before another decade the coal output of Virginia will very many times exceed that shown in this statement.

Buhrstones.—Under this head mention is made of the Brushy Mountain stone in Montgomery county. The table that is given puts down the estimated value of the product of this material as $5,978.

Asbestus.—Virginia is mentioned as one of the regions in which asbestus is found in its fibrous variety, but no statistics of production are given. There are numerous localities in Virginia where this mineral is quite abundant, especially in the belt running through the eastern portion of the Piedmont region. The statement is made that there was imported into the United States in 1889 asbestus of the value of $263,393.

Infusorial Earth.—The Census Bulletin merely states that this is found in Virginia. It might have added that vast quanties of it are exposed in the vicinity of Richmond. Of that it gives an analysis, made by Mr. J. M. Cabell, as follows in percentages:

Moisture	8.37
Silica	75.86
Alumina	9.88
Lime	0.29
Ferric Oxide	2.92
Magnesia, Soda	
Potash, Sulphur	
And organic matter	1.63

In a total of 98.95. This Virginia earth is considerably lower in silica than that from Maryland, New Jersey or Nevada, the analyses of which are given in the same connection.

Barytes.—This mineral, properly called barium-sulphate, is found generally associated with limestone in many localities in Virginia, and is mined in considerable quantities. Of the 21,460 tons produced in the United States in 1889, Virginia is credited with 10,702, valued at $57,298.

Ochre.—This iron oxide, naturally formed by a combination of clay, iron peroxide and water, is quite abundant in the iron ore regions of Virginia; particularly so in the Potsdam belt along the western base of the Blue Ridge. Virginia is credited in 1879 with a production of 1,987 tons valued at $106,740, and in 1889 with 1,658 tons valued at but $18,755. The Bulletin says: "The high estimate placed upon the product of 1880 would indicate that prices were taken for the manufactured article, whereas the values of 1889 were obtained for the mineral in the condition in which it was sold." In 1889 only 38 men were employed in this industry in Virginia. The expenditures for all purposes were $14,080 of which $10,780 were for wages. The capital invested in buildings, land, tools, etc., was $30,000.

Gypsum.—In 1889 Virginia produced 6,838 tons of gypsum valued at $20,336. The expenditures for all purposes were $10,066; 44 persons were employed above ground and 48 below. The most of this product was sold for agricultural purposes. It was all quarried at Saltville, Smyth and Washington counties, where, as elsewhere, it is found in connection with salt deposits. The statement is made that there is invested in gypsum properties in Virginia the sum of $300,620, of which $249,000 are in land. It is understood that the gypsum of Virginia is adapted to the manufacture of plaster-of-paris, and the subject is being investigated with a view of establishing such an industry if found practicable. The general statement is made that all the gypsum now produced in the Eastern States is used as a fertilizer, while all that produced in the Western States, with the exception of Michigan and Ohio, is calcined.

Soapstone.—Massive soapstone suitable for building purposes are abundant in a number of localities in Piedmont and Midland Virginia. The State is credited with a product in 1889, of 1,260 tons valued at $42,250; 92 laborers were engaged in its production; the average wages per day having been for foremen $3.07; mechanics, $2.07; laborers, $1.16 and boys $0.75. The total expenditures were $41,537, of which $36,287 were paid for wages. The invested capital is put down as $112,000 of which $44,000 was in land and the remainder in buildings, tools, machinery, etc. The many uses to which soapstone is applied and the fine quality of this material in Virginia should create a large demand for it in the future.

Fibrous Talc.—Virginia is credited with the production in 1889 of 1,260 tons of this fibrous variety of soapstone, valued at $42,250. There were employed in its production 92 men whose wages amounted to $36,287. The total expenditures were $41,537.

Pyrites.—Under this head are only included pyrites that are mined for the manufacture of sulphuric acid. In 1889 Virginia produced of this article 68,600 tons valued at $110,000. There were employed in pyrites mines 79 persons above ground and 87 below. The total expenditures were $100,100: of this, $79,000 was in land, and the remainder in buildings, machinery, capital, etc. The Virginia product is mainly from the vicinity of Mineral City, formerly Tolersville, in Louisa county. Statements are made showing that sulphuric acid can be more cheaply manufactured from pyrites than brimstone, consequently there should be a constantly increasing demand for this mineral for the manufacture of sulphuric acid. There is abundant evidence that this mineral exists in enormous quantities through an extensive belt of territory in Virginia.

Lead and Zinc.—Virginia is not mentioned in the Bulletin treating on these two metals except in connection with Pennsylvania and New Jersey. These three states are put down as having produced 28,507 tons of refined lead and 122,865 pounds of fine copper in matte. They are reported as having in stock January 1st, 1889, 1,963 tons of refined lead and January 1st, 1890, 1,883. This industry employed 350 men and boys. The daily wages of men are given as $2.95 for foremen, $2.48 for mechanics, $1.63 for laborers, and $0.25 for boys. The office force employed was 22 men. The expenditures were $585,000.71; of this $229,133.44 were for wages. It is probable that only one mine in Virginia produced lead, that known as the Wythe Lead Mines, and that is why these returns are put in with those of Pennsylvania and New Jersey.

Zinc.—The returns include the smelting of zinc or spelter and the manufacture of oxide zinc, as it was found impossible to separate the data relating to these. Virginia and Tennessee are grouped together in the report—probably because there is but one establishment in Virginia and it is contrary to the rules of the Census to give publicity to the production of any single establishment. These two States constitute the Southern group in the zinc smelting and oxide industry. They produce spelter of an exceptionally high quality so that it is in demand not only in this country but is exported to Europe for special purposes. This is particularly true of the spelter manufactured at Pulaski, Virginia, the ores for which are obtained from the Bertha

Zinc mines on New river on the Cripple Creek branch of the Norfolk and Western Railroad. In these two States three establishments are reported as having produced 3,190 tons of spelter from 13,976 tons of ore valued at $141,560. They had on hand January 1, 1889, 580 tons of spelter, and January 1, 1890, 304 tons. The employees were 238 in number; $111,101.44 were paid for wages and $4,500 for salaries. The other expenses were $9,850 and $51,350 worth of supplies were consumed. The total capital invested was $240,000 of which $20,000 were in land, $140,000 in buildings and fixtures, $69,000 in tools, machinery, etc., and $11,000 in cash. The average daily wages were: for foremen $2.46, mechanics $2.40, laborers $1.35, and boys $0.50. The Bulletin remarks that the production of spelter in the United States has kept pace fairly well with the rapid expansion in its consumption. Aside from the quantity used for sheet zinc, a considerable quantity is called for by galvanizers of iron sheets, wire and brass manufacturers. It comments on the fact that the labor engaged in the spelter and oxide of zinc industry has full employment given to it the year round, since the establishments manufacturing these are busy throughout the whole year.

Mica.—In this bulletin the production of Virginia and South Dakota is included under one head, so that the "operations of private individuals may not be disclosed," consequently it is impossible to state what the production of Virginia was. These two States are reported as producing 2,800 pounds of cut mica valued at $3,000, and 36 tons of scrap mica valued at $450. Virginia is reported as having employed 3 foremen at an average of $1.75 per day for 100 days; 16 miners at 75 cents per day for 100 days, and 7 laborers at $1.10 per day for 80 days. Mica is a common mineral in Midland and Piedmont Virginia, and from this State should be obtained much of the needed supply of ground mica and a considerable portion of the sheet mica. The United States imported in 1889 $97,351 worth of unmanufactured mica.

Granite.—As used in this bulletin, the term granite covers all the varieties of stone that are known commercially by that name. Of the Virginia granites these varieties are mentioned: Biotite granite, quarried in Dinwiddie, Chesterfield and Henrico counties; muscovite granite, quarried in Spotsylvania county; biotite gneiss, quarried in Campbell county; biotite schist, quarried in Fauquier county; and diabase, quarried in Loudoun and Fauquier counties. In the 10th census, that of 1880, Virginia ranked 5th in value of granite produced, having an output valued at $331,928 in a total of $5,188,998. In the 11th census, that of 1890, her rank was 14th, with an output valued at $332,548 in a total of $14,464,095, simply holding her own in the value of her output, while many of the other States more than doubled theirs. Virginia increased her product only 0.19 per cent. In 1889 she had 13 firms producing granite at 13 quarries, furnishing an output of 1,703,206 cubic feet valued at $332,548. There were employed 21 foremen, 333 quarrymen, 91 mechanics and stone-cutters, 239 laborers, 24 boys, and 8 office men; a total of 716. At these quarries 17 boilers were used having a capacity of 370 horse-power, and 46 animals were employed. There were paid out: for wages $218,828, for supplies $32,297, and for all purposes $256,125. The capital invested was $446,650, of which $234,900 was in land, $20,946 in buildings and fixtures, $89,236 in tools, machinery, etc., and $101,568 in cash.

Of the Virginia product 1,080,873 cubic feet, valued at $120,467, or 11 cents a cubic foot, were used for building purposes; 286,946 cubic feet valued at $75,925, or 26 cents a cubic foot, were used for street work, including paving blocks. Of paving blocks 342,895 pieces were quarried, valued at $18,505, or $53.97 per thousand. For cemetery, monumental and decorative purposes her quarries furnished 44,620 cubic feet valued at $66,356, or $1.49 a cubic foot. For bridge, dam and railroad work she supplied 281,167 cubic feet valued at $69,000, or 25 cents a cubic foot. For miscellaneous uses 9,600 feet, valued at $800, or 8 cents a cubic foot, were furnished. Virginia ranks among the States that obtain the highest value per unit for their granite. Virginia ranked 15th in the production of granite, according to value, for building purposes; 14th for street work, including paving blocks; 18th in paving blocks, 8th in monumental work, 7th in bridge, dam and railroad work, and 9th in miscellaneous work. In the production of granite, according to the number of feet produced, Virginia ranked 9th in that for building purposes; 14th for all classes of street work, including paving blocks; 18th for paving blocks; 8th for monumental work; 7th in bridge, dam and railroad work, and 9th for miscellaneous uses. In the production of granite, according to the number of feet produced, Virginia ranked 9th in that for building purposes; 14th for all classes of street work; 18th for paving blocks; 11th for monumental work, and bridge, dam and railroad work, and 8th for miscellaneous uses.

Manganese.—In 1889 the United States produced 23,929 long tons of manganese, having a total value of $238,939. Nearly all of this product came from the Crimora, Va.; Cartersville, Ga., and Batesville, Ark., mines, they having yielded 20,325 tons. Virginia alone produced 14,616 tons, valued at $156.257, or $10.69 per ton. There were employed 171 men whose wages amounted to $65,939. The capital invested was $711,000. Sixty-one per cent. of all the manganese produced in the United States came from the Virginia mines, and of her product 12,974 tons were from the adjacent Crimora and Old Dominion mines at the western foot of the Blue Ridge in Augusta county.

The report says: "More manganese has been taken from these two mines, which are from the same deposit, than from all the rest of the United States, and it is probably fair to say that this deposit has produced more than any other mine in the world. The grade of the ore is somewhat above the limit dividing manganese and manganiferous iron ore. The average shipments in 1889 show 46 per cent. metallic manganese."

Virginia has produced manganese ores as follows: In 1880, 3,661 tons; in 1881, 3,295; in 1882, 2,982; in 1883, 5,355; in 1884, 8,980; in 1885, 18,745; in 1886, 20,567; in 1887, 19,835; in 1888, 17,646; and in 1889, 14,616.

Precious Stones.—The Bulletin on this subject says: "True beryls and garnets have been frequently found as a by-product in the mining of mica, especially in Virginia and North Carolina." It gives the production of precious stones by name, but without localities. Of those mentioned, garnets quartz, amethyst, rose quartz, smoky quartz, gold quartz, quartz connected with chalcedony, chrysoprase, banded and mossed jasper, pyrite, azurite and malachite, are plentiful in many localities in Virginia. The State is credited with having furnished as specimens $2,500 worth of quartz, pebbles, etc. The Bulletin states that in 1889 the United States imported of precious stones not set to the value of $11,705,809.

Iron ore.—During the calendar year 1889, the United States produced 14,518,041 long tons of iron ore valued at the mines at an average of $2.30 per ton. The stock of iron ore carried over was equivalent to 15.55 per cent. of the production. The Census year of iron production of ores was made to correspond with the calendar year. Michigan was the largest producer of iron ores, a total of 5,856,169 long tons having been mined, the value of which was nearly sixteen million of dollars, an average of $2.70 per ton. That State produced over 40 per cent of the total quantity mined in the United States and over 47 per cent. of the value of the iron ore production of the whole country. The credit of holding the second rank lies between Alabama and Pennsylvania, but the returns accord the second place to Alabama with a production of 1,570,319 long tons valued at an average of 96 cents per ton. Pennsylvania is credited with an output of 1,560,234 tons valued at $1.96 per ton.

In the Census returns Virginia and West Virginia are put together, probably for the reason that the output for West Virginia was so small as to make it not worth presentation, or else its output was from a single mine, so that the figures given for the two States may be said to represent the output of Virginia alone. For these States there were reports from 54 mines, 38 of which produced iron ore to the amount of 511,255 tons, valued at $935,290, or $1.83 per ton. The stock on hand January 1st, 1889, is reported as 53,184 tons, and that on hand January 1st, 1890, as 69,634 tons. The total shipments were 494,805 tons valued at $894,951.

Comment is made that the value given for iron ore represents averages only, as the rules of the Census office prohibit the giving of specific information for different localities. Also that the figures for Alabama, Tennessee, Virginia and West Virginia represent the winning of leaner iron ore which are chiefly consumed close to the mines. The average value for these four States is given as $1.20 per ton.

Virginia and West Virginia combined occupy the 5th place in the number of mines worked, having had 38 in operation, and stood 7th as to the amount of ore won. They averaged 13,454 tons of production to each mine.

In the table of production of varieties of iron ore the Virginias are said to have produced 487,208 tons of brown hematite which was 19.31 per cent. of the total United States product of that variety; 8,746 tons of red hematite which was 0.10 per cent.; 6,200 tons of magnetite which was 0.25 per cent. and 9,101 tons of carbonite which was 2.11 per cent. The total production of the Virginias in 1889 was 511,255 tons, against 217,448 tons produced in 1880. It is probable that the carbonite ore of this table was produced in West Virginia, in the coal region, and was perhaps the product of a single mine, and the only production of iron ore in that State, as a statement is made that "New York and Pennsylvania are the only States reported as producing four kinds of ore; Colorado, Michigan and Virginia produced three kinds of ore."

In the production of brown hematite ore Pennsylvania occupied the first place; Virginia and West Virginia combined rose from fourth place in 1880 to second place in 1889. The remark is made that: "The limonite of Pennsylvania covers a considerable area and embraces several districts; a broad band of this ore practically passes through the State into Maryland, and through Virginia to Tennessee, Alabama and Georgia."

The average yield of metal from all iron ores in the United States in 1889 was 51.27 per cent. The average yield in Alabama was 46 per cent; in Kentucky 46.2; in Maryland 47.7; in Tennessee from 38.8 to 39.6, and in Virginia, principally from her brown hematite ores, the average is given as 43.4, but many furnaces showed from 41.4 to 48.6 averages.

Virginia ranked in 1850 as 6th among the States in the production of iron ore; in 1860 11th; in 1870 12th; in 1880 as 8th, and in 1889 as 7th.

The capital invested in ore mining in the Virginias in 1889 was $3,905,249. Of this $2,881,441 was in land; $567,544 in buildings and fixtures; $253,195 in tools, implements, machinery, etc., and $203,069 in cash and stock on hand. The amount of capital invested in mines in 1880 was $1,924,625.

The average expenditure for wages per long ton of iron ore in 1889 in the United States was $1.06. In Virginia and West Virginia it was $1.09; in Pennsylvania it was 75 cents, and in Alabama it was 69 cents. Of ore-mining in Pennsylvania it should be remembered that half of the total product of that State comes from the single Cornwall mine, which is simply hills of soft ore. That is why the cost per ton of mining appears so low in that State.

The wages of miners in the Virginias averaged $1.13 a day. The number of men employed above and below ground in these States was 2,436, embracing 86 foremen and overseers that averaged $1.98 a day for wages and worked 210 days in the year; 74 mechanics that averaged $1.65 a day and worked 183 days; 1,402 laborers that averaged $1.02 and worked 201 days; and 104 boys that averaged 52 cents a day and worked 146 days. The employees above ground were 1,666. The number employed below ground was 770, composed of 43 foremen and overseers that received $1.74 a day for 252 days; 514 miners that received $1.13 a day for 252 days; 201 laborers that received $1 a day for 176 days; and 12 boys that received 50 cents a day for 262 days. There were paid to employees above and below ground for wages $551,804. The production of ore was 209.87 tons per employee. In Alabama the production was 509.68 tons, and in Pennsylvania 357.03 tons per employee. The figures show that large mines and improved mining appliances furnish a larger output per employee than do the small mines that are worked in a primitive way. The cost of producing a ton of iron ore is put down as $1.71 in the United States as a whole; $1.64 in the Virginias; 82 cents in Alabama, and $1.10 in Pennsylvania.

In 1889 32 office men at iron ore mines in the Virginias were paid $23,257. The 2,468 men employed received $575,061 as wages; $128,323 were paid for supplies and materials; $128,452 for other expenditures; $83,183 were paid for mining, not including any contract work, and $7,936 for contract work; making a grand total for all expenditures of $839,772. The Virginia mines used 49 steam boilers, having 1,813 horse power; 40 steam engines, and 238 animals.

The United States imported, in 1889, 853,573 tons of iron ore, valued at $1,852,392. Of this quantity 298,568 tons came from Spain, and 243,255 from Cuba. Of this 525,124 tons entered the port of Philadelphia, and 273,050 the port of Baltimore.

CHAPTER XXXII.

APALACHIA.

Apalachia, with its long ranges of high mountains, shows in South-western Virginia some of its greater mountains so formed as to be well calculated to call forth from a skillful general, as was General Washington, a remark meant to convey the idea that he would use them as an impregnable defence. Possibly he, in speaking in that sense of "the mountains of West Augusta," meant the very ranges that occupy the middle of Apalachia; and, apparently, make great natural fortresses, like Burke's Garden is in appearance.

This elevated mountain basin, in Tazewell county, in the very heart of the great Clinch range, contains about 30,000 acres of the most fertile bluegrass land, and is surrounded by high, almost mural, mountain escarpments, all around, except at one point on the north side, where the waters of this singularly beautiful basin break through and form Wolf creek.

In the counties composing Apalachia, doubtless, there are many other localities of equal beauty and character, as points of strategical importance; but this is slight indeed when compared with their value as the depositories of great mineral wealth, the storehouses of the rain and moisture, and the great barriers against the too sudden incursion of the great northern storms.

This interesting group of counties is made up, geologically, of the rocks between the earlier Palæozoic (leaving out the Primordial) and the lower carboniferous, inclusive, disposed in long, generally parallel lines, running northeastwardly and southwestwardly. Their rather irregular boundary line, on the south-east, pursues the general line of the great North mountains, under various local names, as before stated; and having the Alleghany mountains a part of the way, and the eastern limb of the Cumberland mountains for a considerable distance on its north-west side. The whole territory, of about 3,800 square miles, is immensely important to the State for quite numerous reasons; among which, it may be stated, are the vast areas of superior grazing lands, in limestone valleys; extensive forests of excellent deciduous and soft woods, and some of the most important mineral-bearing series of rock formations in the State.

The great crust of the earth was broken up several times in the cosmical action by which it was formed, giving five or six repetitions of the great bands of which it is composed, in most of its transverse sections, from which have resulted most valuable alternations of mountain and valley, of limestone grass lands and wooded ridges and mountains. These mountains are usually composed of a greater and a lesser range, co-extensive and parallel—the larger holding the valuable iron and manganese-bearing rocks of the upper Silurian period, lying northwardly, and the smaller, the rocks of the latter half of the Devonian period, lying southwardly, with a valley of slate between. This smaller range frequently holds, on its south flank, valuable deposits of proto-carboniferous coal, as in Bland county and north parts of Alleghany county; but in Giles and Craig counties these coal-rocks seem to be cut out by faults.

There is also a line of these very lowest of coal rocks in the south-western corner of Wise county, and thence south-west through Lee along the east flank of the Cumberland mountains; but coal is not in them like it is in the great coal rocks close on the north of them.

In some localities the larger mountains are great curved anticlines, giving valuable and extensive outcrops of iron and manganese ores (Rogers' numbers V to VII and VIII inclusive), as is in the case of Rich Patch mountain, of Alleghany and north side of Botetourt county; Potts or Middle mountain, of Alleghany county; Salt Pond mountain in Giles, and Round mountain in Bland county. These great anticlines are sometimes broken along their crests and spread apart longitudinally—apparently by some great end pressure—bringing to view the great fossil bearing limestone of III and IV, as in the case of Sinking creek, Giles county, and of Burke's Garden and Thompson & Ward's coves, Tazewell county, thus accounting for the wonderful fertility of those areas, so high as 2,600 to 3,600 feet above the sea level. These repeated breaks in the great crust give such fertile limestone belts as those of Nanny's creek and Dunlap's creek, of Alleghany; the number VI limestone belt of Pott's creek; Sinking creek, of Craig and Giles counties; the great basin of New river in Giles county, and the lines of Wolf and Walker's creeks in Giles and Bland counties; Burke's Garden and the great coves and valleys of Tazewell, on Clinch and Bluestone rivers and tributaries; the great coves, valleys and rich limestone gardens of Russell county, and of Scott county, and the like splendid grass valleys of Powell's valley in Lee county. Abb's valley in Tazewell and upper Powell's valley, of Wise, owe their rich limestone belts to like upthrows of sub-carboniferous rocks.

This region is marked by often repeated sections of some of the most valuable geological formations so far recorded; to go into any detailed description of which would necessitate the enumeration of nearly the whole range of rock strata comprised between the Archæan age and the carboniferous period, inclusive, with all their valuable stores of granite, syenite, gneiss, steatite, mica, asbestos, feldspar, quartz, glass sand, magnetic and specular iron ores, copper, gold and silver ores, nickle, manganese, tin, sulphur, zinc, lead, limonite and other ores of iron, barytes, gypsum, salt, petroleum, slate, honestone, grindstone, building stone, limestone, marble, cement stone, potter's and firebrick clays, and bituminous, semi-bituminous, splint, cannel, and semi-anthracite coals, and thermal and mineral waters—beginning such description in the Archæan on the south-east or Blue Ridge side, and ending it in the carboniferous rocks, on the north-west or Cumberland side. These various extensive bands or ledges of rocks, where they protrude above the surface, disclose a general strike or trend north-east and south-west, dipping at all angles, from positions almost perpendicular to nearly flat—the mountains and valley generally showing the steeper dips inclining usually to south-eastward, while the strata of the Cumberland plateau, or coal rocks, are found, in the main, nearly flat, with the whole broad expanse mentioned so presented to view, as to render easily accessible much the greater part of the various minerals just mentioned.

The convulsions and disturbances of the earth's surface by which the great mountains composing the Apalachian chain in Virginia were formed as a whole, acted in such a way as to erect numerous greater and lesser lines of nearly parallel ridges, separated from each other by valleys, many of which are several times broader than the bases of the mountains by which they are bounded—resulting, as is the case in the great South-west Valley and the valleys of the Holston, Walker's creek, Clear Fork, Clinch and Powell's rivers, and Giles and Burke's Garden basins, in the very extensive areas of fine grazing and farming lands, which owe their great natural fertility to the decomposition of massive bands of limestone, of which the rock material in these valleys, in great part, consists. But in these convulsions there were two most remarkable departures from the parallelism which marked their action throughout this region. One of them is shown on the easterly side of the Apalachians, in a great *bifurcation* of the Blue Ridge at the point where nearly join the counties of Roanoke, Floyd, Montgomery and Franklin, whence trend the two great arms of this bifurcation westwardly and southwardly, enveloping in their wide grasp the rich mineral plateau composed of the counties of Floyd, Carroll and Grayson.

The other remarkable evidence of this action is shown on the more westerly side of the Apalachians, in a bifurcation of the Cumberland mountain in Lee county, whence its two great arms trend eastwardly and north-eastwardly, developing those noble coal areas comprised in a part of Lee county, nearly all of Wise and the whole of Dickenson and Buchanan counties, and projecting a strip of coal rocks, of well ascertained value, into Tazewell, Russell and Scott counties. * * * * The Blue Ridge plateau, so enveloped as described before, shows only one or two ledges of limestone; but derives the great fertility, observed in much of its soil, from the decomposition of heavy bands of aluminous silicates of potash, lime, iron, etc.; while the nearly similar shaped plateau of the Cumberland owes whatever fertility its soil may possess, to the wearing of sandstones, slates, etc., holding organic matter of fossils with some lime variously combined, and, in a few localities, thin beds of limestones, intercalated between the much heavier strata of sandstones and slates.

The great mountains bounding, and often dividing the extensive valleys longitudinally, have a general elevation above the valleys of 1,000 to 1,600 feet, while the valleys are from 1,000 to 2,800 feet above sea-level.

On the south-east side of this extensive region is the Blue Ridge, forming, in its straighter alignment and prolongation, the south-east boundary of the great Valley of Virginia, throughout its extent.

Passing over numerous broken ridges, in the Valley itself, the great North mountains, under various names, such as The Gap, Walker's and Clinch mountains, form the north-west boundary of the Great Valley, towards the south-west end, also forming the south-east boundary of Apalachia in the main; though the north-eastward continuation of the Clinch range, after reaching Burke's Garden, and passing that lovely mountain basin, going north-east, divides Apalachia nearly in two —as is the case in Garden, Round mountain, and their south-flanking ridge (Big Brushy), Wolf Creek, Pearis, Angel's Rest, Butte and Salt-Pond mountains, upon which, at an elevation of 4,700 feet above sea-level, is the famous Mountain Lake, the origin of which dates back a little more than one hundred years.

Then, north of this a short distance, a part of Apalachia is bounded north-west by Peter's and East River mountains—the boundary line, at the east end of Tazewell county, jumping across from East River mountain to Flat Top (near Pocahontas), which, with its continuations—Sandy Ridge and Stone mountains, etc., composing the eastern bifurcation of the Cumberland mountain—form the north-west boundary of Apalachia proper, towards the south-west.

Then, Trans-Apalachia holds on its north-west side, next Kentucky, the last of Virginia's great mountains—the Cumberland.

This important section of Virginia, so formed into such noble alternations of mountain and valley, hill and dale, of pasture and woodland, with its magnificent and inexhaustible repositories of mineral wealth, presents a topography, systems of drainage and resulting atmospheric conditions, of superior excellence, which, together with its position on favorable parallels of latitude, combine to render it equal if not superior to any area of like size in the world.

The different systems of drainage so established may be enumerated as follows:

1. That of James river, flowing east into the Atlantic ocean; its tributaries watering this territary being Otter creek, Roaring Run, Stone river, Purgatory, Looney's, Catawba, Craig's, John's, Long's, Entry and Sinking creeks; Jackson's river, Cow Pasture river, Wilson's, Mill, Potts, Dunlap's and Indian Draft creeks, and many minor tributaries. These chiefly drain the counties of Bath, Highland, Botetourt, Alleghany and Craig, and a small part of Roanoke of this territory.

2. That of Roanoke river, flowing south-east through the Staunton and Dan rivers into the Atlantic ocean. Its tributaries, with which this paper is concerned, are Back creek, Wolf, Glade, Tinker, Mudlick, Peter's, Craen's, Mason's, Mill creeks and others; South Fork, North Fork and their tributaries draining a small part of Botetourt, the greater part of Roanoke county, more than half of Montgomery and a small area af Floyd county.

3. That of New river, which flows northward and north-west, forming the Great Kanawha, and delivers its waters through the Ohio and Mississippi rivers into the Gulf of Mexico. Its tributaries watering this territory are: East river, Wolf creek, Big and Little Stony, Doe and Sinking creeks, Mill and Walker's creeks, Morris Run, Back, Tom's, Watts, Strouble's, Crab, Plum, Peak and Mack's creeks, Little river and its tributaries, Big and Little Reed Island creeks, Pine, Reed, Poplar Camp and Cripple creeks, Crooked, Chestnut and Brush creeks, Upper Little river and tributaries, Elk, Peachbottom, Bridle, Saddle, Wilson's, Grassy, Helton, Big and Little Horse creeks, and many minor tributaries; all of which drain, in whole or in part, the following counties: Giles, Bland, south-east side of Tazewell, west end of Craig, much of Montgomery, Pulaski, nearly all of Floyd (except some water-gaps in Blue Ridge by the headwaters of the tributaries of Dan river), Wythe, a small area of Smyth, Grayson, and all of Carroll except that part which overlaps the Blue Ridge and is drained by the headwaters of Ararat, a tributary of Dan river.

4. The drainage by the system of the Tennessee river, subdivided into— (a) that of the South, Middle and North Forks of Holston river and their tributaries; (b) Clinch river and

tributaries; and (c) Powell's river and tributaries; all of which, when united in the Tennessee river, flow westerly thence through the Ohio and Mississippi rivers into the Gulf of Mexico. These drain, in whole or in part, the counties of Smyth, Washington, Tazewell, Russell, Scott and Lee, and a large area of Wise county.

5. The Louisa, Russell and Pound Forks of Sandy river and their tributaries, draining the counties of Buchanan, Dickenson and a large part of Wise county, and flowing northwardly into the Ohio river.

These five extensive drainage systems, deriving their erosive power no less from their constancy than their great flood volumes, have, in the course of time, greatly modified the topography of this region. But, as in the case of John's creek, a tributary of James river, whose head springs are quite 4,300 feet above the sea, near Mountain lake; tributaries of New river rising on White Top and Balsam mountains, fully 5,400 feet above tide; headwaters of Holston river, rising at Bear Town, near Burke's Garden, 4,700 feet above tide; and of Powell's river at Stone mountain, 4,000 feet above the sea, we have left to us, by these streams, and, also, unaffected by the agencies of ice and snow, these splendid contrasts in the elevations and depressions of this section's topography, which secure to the region not only a healthful and invigorating summer climate, that is fast tending to make it the sanitarium of the South; but adds no less to the beauty of the scenery, than security against any lengthened failure of rain-fall.

NOTE BY COL. R. HARRISON.—In the foregoing general description of South-west Virginia, it is not clearly stated that in the division Apalachia is included all of Virginia west of the great Valley, the sub-division defined on the small map as "Trans-Apalachia," being treated as a part of the Grand Division. The great Apalachian chain, which is regarded as the dominant feature of the mountain system composing this region, gives its name thereto, and the term has not a very well defined application, but it is sufficient for the present purpose to state that Apalachia comprises the thirteen counties west and north of the Valley Division.

To avoid confusion, attention is again called to the fact that county lines do not correspond accurately with the geological divisions of the State. It will be observed that a strip of Apalachia extends along the whole tier of the Valley counties, taking in the western edge of Augusta, Rockingham, Shenandoah and Frederick, but by far the greater part of these counties being in the Valley, the edge projected into Apalachia is not considered separately.

And only the southern section of the "Blue Ridge," where it broadens out into the "plateau" embracing the three counties of Floyd, Carroll and Grayson, is taken account of separately, the long narrow "ridge" north of Floyd being divided between the Valley and Piedmont.

As was natural, the writer of the last paper has regarded his subject with the eye of a geologist and mineralogist rather than with that of a farmer, and perhaps has not brought out the magnificent *agricultural* capabilities of this favored region as prominently as might be desired and deserved. In truth, the mineral wealth of the country described is so vast that it could hardly fail to engross the attention of a specialist in that line to the exclusion of other subjects of consideration. At a future time I hope that these other parts of the picture will be filled in by a hand as eager and as full of the subject as the writer of the last paper is of his specialty.—*Com. of Agriculture.*

ALLEGHANY COUNTY

was formed in 1822 from Bath, Botetourt and Monroe. It is twenty-six miles long and has a mean breadth of twenty miles, with an area of 463,500 acres, assessed at $958,000. Population, 5,586.

The surface is mostly broken and mountainous, but they are some considerable valley lands of the finest limestone soils, producing excellent crops of tobacco, grain, fruits and grass. The main business of the farmers is grazing and rearing cattle, horses, sheep and swine. The mountains are clothed with immense forests of valuable timber, and are filled with iron ores of great purity and value. These ores have been largely developed and worked in the various furnaces in the county, of which "Clifton Forge," Low Moor" and "Longdale" are the principal. Pig iron is turned out by these furnaces in great amounts and at low cost.

The country is watered by Jackson and Cow Pasture rivers, which unite near the eastern border and form the James. The Chesapeake and Ohio Railway traverses this county centrally, passing through Covington, the county seat. The Richmond and Alleghany Railroad connects at Clifton Forge with the Chesapeake and Ohio Railway, and with its easy grades affords much relief to the heavy hauling of the great amounts of metal from this region.

This is a healthy region and the summer climate is delightful. The mountain lands are cheap, and, no doubt, capable of being utilized to a much greater extent than now in the stock-raising business.

Covington, the county town, is a place of commercial importance, very favorably situated for trade. Low Moor, eight miles lower down on the Chesapeake and Ohio Railway, is rapidly growing into a manufacturing town, the great iron works here being the nucleus.

ALLEGHANY COUNTY MINERALS AT THE NEW ORLEANS EXPOSITION.

1. *Fossil iron ore*, from Clinton

No. V, beds in Clifton Forge Pass, Richmond and Alleghany Railroad.

From Low Moor Iron Company.

2. *Limonite iron ore*, lump, from company's mine in No. VII, Oriskany.

3. *Limonite iron ore*, washed, from same.

4. *Limestone*, No. VI, Lower Helderberg; from quarry No. 1, used for flux.

5. *Coke*, made at Low Moor furnace, in company's ovens, and used in that furnace.

6. *Coal*, from No. XII or lower coal measures; from New River field of West Virginia on Chesapeake and Ohio Railroad, from which above coke was made.

7. Sample of Coke Pig Irons made at Low Moor furnace from above ores; No. 1, foundry pig; No. 2, foundry pig; No. 1, mill pig; No. 2, mill pig; No. 3, close mill pig; No. 4, silvery pig; No. 5, mottled pig; No. 6, white pig; No. 7, part of "Salamander" blown from furnace "well" with "Atlas" powder after blast No. 2 of Low Moor furnace.

18. *Limonite iron ore*, from Iron Mountain mines, on Pounding Mill run.

19. *Stalactites and stalagmites* and other cave rocks from a cave in Lower Helderberg No. VI limestone, near Low Moor station, Chesapeake and Ohio Railroad.

20 to 23. Five boxes Pig Iron, grades from No. 1 to mottled, inclusive, with the characteristic cinder for each grade; from the Longdale furnaces.

24. Box of Lower Helderberg No. VI limestone, used for flux in Longdale furnaces.

25. Box of Coke, used in Longdale furnaces, from the Sewell coal, bed and ovens of Longdale Company, at Sewell, West Virginia, from New river or No. XII, Lower measures coal.

26. Box or lump ore, brown hematite, from Oriskany, or No. VII, from mines of Longdale Company, in Brushy mountain, near head of Simpson's creek.

27. Unwashed ore, or pay dirt, of above mines.

28. Washed ore of above mines.

29. Refuse from washer in washing above ores.

30 and 31. Clay and flint from top and bottom, respectively, of above iron mines.

32. Lump of *cadmia*, from deposition from fumes in throats of Longdale blast furnaces.

33. *Limonite*, brown iron ore, lump weighing 625 pounds and box, from west side Peter's mountain, on Dunlap creek, two and a half miles south from Trice switch of Chesapeake and Ohio Railroad, from mine of Keyser & McAllister, of Backbone, Virginia, from which some twenty-five tons are daily shipped to Etna Iron Works, Ironton, Ohio.

34. *Limonite*, brown iron ore, from fine deposit in No. VII, Oriskany, at

lower end of Clifton Forge pass, Richmond and Alleghany Railroad.

35. *Limonite*, brown iron ore, No. VII or Oriskany, from cuts 1, 2, 3 and 4, and washed ore, from the "Stack" mine, near Backbone station, Chesapeake and Ohio Railroad.

36. *Limonite*, brown iron ore, "lump" and "pipe," from Rumsey mine.

37. *Hematite, specular or magnetic iron ore*, from Rumsey mine.

BATH COUNTY

was formed in 1790 from parts of Augusta, Greenbrier and Botetourt, and is now one of the border counties. It has an area of 932 square miles or 617,402 acres, assessed at $803,715. This shows a very low valuation; but the large proportion of waste mountain land explains this. Some of the valleys are exceedingly fertile and beautiful—the soil formed from disintegrated limestone—producing grain and grass luxuriantly; even in the mountains there is good grazing; so that this is a most excellent stock-raising county, beautifully watered by clear mountain streams, flowing into the Jackson and Cow Pasture rivers, which meander through this county and unite some miles below, near the borders of Alleghany and Botetourt.

The population of this county is small, only 4,525, or about five to the square mile; but the people are independent and prosperous, having a healthful and beautiful pastoral country.

The Chesapeake and Ohio Railroad passes through the south-eastern part of the county, giving an outlet for the abundant products, and access to the many attractive watering-places of this county. Nature has been prodigal to Bath in respect to mineral springs. The Warm Sulphur, the Hot, the Healing, have long been celebrated—the "Warm Sulphur" for near a century. Here is the county seat, "Warm Springs," an attractive village in the rich "Warm Springs Valley." In the south-eastern part of the county, near the railroad, we have another group, the Bath Alum, Millboro, Wallawhatoola. To these resorts multitudes of summer visitors are attracted by the health-giving waters, pure air, lovely scenery, fine fishing and shooting, and excellent fare of this favored region.

There is much iron ore in this county, some of it has been worked successfully for many years.

Fine timber abounds in Bath, oak, walnut, pine, poplar, chestnut, sugar-maple, hickory, etc.

BATH COUNTY MINERALS AT THE NEW ORLEANS EXPOSITION.

From Virginia Department Agriculture.

1. *Limonite iron ore*, No. VII, Oriskany, from Joseph Baxter, Esq., Bath Alum Springs.

2. *Manganese ore*, from Col. William McClintic.

3. *Red and brown iron ores*, from J. C. Harvey, Esq.

4. *Kaolin*.

5. *Ochre*, deep red, from deposit on land of Mrs. M. M. Bratton on Mill Creek, near Chesapeake and Ohio Railroad. Contributed by Rev. Samuel Brown, Millboro.

BLAND COUNTY.

Bland county was formed in 1861 from Wythe, Tazewell and Giles. Seddon is the county seat, and is located in the Walker's creek valley, near the center of the county, with turnpikes diverging east, west, north and south. Several mountain ranges traverse the county from north-east to south-west, making beautiful and fertile valleys, with rolling hills between, threaded by streams as clear and sparkling as the dews of heaven. These mountains are filled with chromic, hematite, magnetic, paint and specular iron ores, lead, kaolin, ochre, barytes, copper and slate: are covered with a heavy forest of oaks, chestnut, hickory, ash, walnut, poplar, cucumber, lynn, locust, pine, maple, both hard and soft. There is no outlet for this untold wealth that is mountain bound and locked up where nature formed it. Several railroad lines have been projected, and there are good hopes of some of them being built in the near future.

There are several mineral springs in the county, the most noted of which are Sharon Springs and Kimberling Springs. The former are seven miles west of Bland Court House, on the turnpike leading from Wytheville to Jeffersonville. These springs are recommended in scrofulous diseases. At these springs there is a vein of coal eleven feet and four inches thick, and said to be of the finest quality.

Kimberling Springs are seven miles north of Bland Court House, ensconced right in the bosom of the mountain, with all the charms that belong to nature in her silent and dreamy mood.

Bland is a grazing county, and her capacity for grazing is being increased every year. She is not far behind the foremost counties in the State in sending off her fine fat bullocks to the eastern markets. The sheep industry is profitable, and is increasing every year, and would increase more rapidly if the cultivation of the miserable *dog* was abandoned. Horses, mules and hogs of good blood are raised for home use, besides a great many for market.

Population, 5,004. Number of acres of land, 212,272, assessed at $449,603.

The waters of the eastern portion of the county flow east and empty into New river, while those in the western portion flow west and empty into the Holston river, Sharon Springs being the head-waters of the Holston river, and are 2,849 feet above sea level.

Wheat, corn, oats, rye and buckwheat are cultivated to perfection;

some tobacco raised, though not much. Nearly all the domestic grasses are raised. Blue-grass, *poa pratensis*, comes of its own accord, being a native of the soil, and is the king of grasses.

Apples, peaches, pears, plums, cherries and grapes do well when properly attended to. Many varieties of grapes grow wild, some of which make a fine quality of wine.

The county is well watered with the finest of springs, of both lime and free-stone water, and several large creeks, affording plenty of water and the finest sites for all kinds of machinery, with plenty of sandstone, and blue and gray limestone for building purposes.

The finances of the county have been well managed, and the county is out of debt.

The people are sober, industrious and thriving, possessed of as much energy as the people of any county in the Commonwealth; and be it said to the honor of her citizens, that there is not a bar-room in the county, and has not been for years. Her people always extend a welcome hand to all who are seeking homes, or permanent investments, to come into her borders and help build up, and develop her latent wealth hid in the earth, and set the waters to humming to the music of the spindle, and the loom, and the locomotive.

Good churches are found in almost every neighborhood, with as much toleration and as little bigotry as can be found among Christian people elsewhere.

BLAND COUNTY MINERALS AT THE NEW ORLEANS EXPOSITION.

From Capt. C. R. Boyd.

1. *Brown iron ore*, large deposit in No. III; lands of S. H. Newberry.

2. *Specular iron ore*, fine quality, from base of No. III; lands of Newberry and others.

3. *Brown iron ore*, cubical pseudomorph after pyrites; land of Harman Newberry,

4. *Iron ores*, from No. X, from south foot of Brushy mountain, near Sharon Springs; lands of Newberry and others.

5. *Coal*, from No. X, proto-carboniferous, near Sharon Springs; lands of Newberry and others.

6. *Red and brown iron ores* from No. VIII, slates from Round mountain, Hunting Camp and Wolf creeks.

7. *Brown iron ore*, compact, from rocks overlying No. VII, Oriskany; good for basic process and for cutting into settings.

8. *Fossil, petraia corniculum*, from No. III.

9. *Red and brown iron ores*, splendent from underlying rocks of VII, Round mountain; large deposits; 56 per cent. of metallic iron; 0.08 phosphorus; lands of Peery and Boyd.

10. *Marble*, nearly white, from land of Sam. H. Newberry.

11. *Mineral water*, from Sharon Alum and Chalybeate Spring.

12. *Manganese*, silicide of, from

Round mountain; lands of Peery and Boyd.

13. *Brown iron ore*, fibrous, from large beds in Round mountain; lands of Peery and Boyd.

14. *Fossil iron ore*, from 20-foot bed of No. V, Round and Garden mountain; lands of Peery and Boyd.

The following from the cabinet of the Virginia Department of Agriculture :

15. *Chert*, in limestone in form of moccason.

16. *Ochre and iron ore*, from Iron mountain.

17. *Iron ore*, red, from Iron mountain.

18. *Tufaceous marl.*

19. *Lead and zinc ores.*

20. *Manganese.*

21. *Barytes*, on limestone.

22. *Feldspar.*

BUCHANAN COUNTY

was formed in 1858 from Russell and Tazewell. It contains 490,848 acres, assessed at $367,134. Population, 5,694. It lies on the western slope of the Alleghany mountains, and has two of its sides the dividing lines separating Virginia from West Virginia and Kentucky. Much of the surface is rugged and mountainous, but the soil is fertile and well adapted to grass, and its great elevation gives it a moist, cool climate, well suited to grazing and cattle raising. The valleys, especially, are fertile and produce excellent crops of all the cereals. The lands are very low priced, and

are held in immense tracts by speculators and persons interested in mining. Minerals exist in vast quantities, and consist mainly in iron ores, coal and salt undeveloped and waiting for the coming of railroads. With good transportation there would soon be exploited in this county the immense resources of minerals and of timber now lying undeveloped. The cattle business could be cheaply prosecuted on a large scale if the requisite capital was invested in this fine grazing country. This region, for which Nature has done so much, is now attracting attention, and cannot long remain cut off from the outer world. An inviting field is offered here for settlers, as the lands can now be bought for a tithe of the value they will have when railroads penetrate these rich valleys.

CRAIG COUNTY

was formed in 1850 from Botetourt, Roanoke, Giles and Monroe, West Virginia. Area, 248,482 acres, assessed at $564,432; population, 5,894. The surface, like all this section of the State, is rugged and mountainous. The soil is fertile and peculiarly adapted to the growth of rich grasses. Accordingly, we find here a pastoral life among the people, and much fine stock. A large proportion of the surface is in original forest of superior timber, as white oak, ash, hickory, maple and other valuable woods. The timber of this section of the country is noted for its hardness and great strength. The county is watered by Craig's creek, which flows north-east and empties into James river at Sheets in the neighboring county of Botetourt, and by Sinking creek, which flows south-east and empties into New river in Giles. New river flows north into the Kanawha, a tributary of the Ohio. Thus the waters from a part of this county run to the Atlantic ocean through the James, and from another part, across the water-shed, make their way through the Ohio and Mississippi to the Gulf of Mexico. The minerals consist mainly of iron, manganese and slate. Indications of silver have been found here. Cheap homes and a salubrious and pleasant climate add to the attractions of this section for settlers.

Craig is now somewhat isolated in respect to railroad facilities; but the day is probably not distant when a railway will be constructed along the valley of Craig's creek into the rich coal district of West Virginia. There is probably immense mineral wealth in the mountains of Craig adjacent to the track which nature has marked out for the road.

CRAIG COUNTY MINERALS AT THE NEW ORLEANS EXPOSITION.

1. *Slate*, from Craig's creek, of superior quality and in great quantities.
2. *Manganese*, 7 miles west from New Castle and 2 from preceding.
3. *Manganiferous iron ore*, from Kyle's on John's creek, 6 miles north-west from New Castle.
4. *Slate*, 4 specimens from "Custer" quarry on Craig creek, 6 miles south-east from New Castle.
5. *Iron ore*, from John Goode, 4 miles south-east from New Castle.
6. *Manganese*, 4 large specimens, from "Damewood" mine, from near same locality.
7. *Manganese*, 2 specimens from J. E. Custer's, 6 miles from New Castle.
8. *Slate*, from Jones' quarry on Craig creek, 5 miles south-west from New Castle.

DICKENSON COUNTY

was formed in 1880 from Russell, Wise and Buchanan. It is nearly a parallelogram with two sides of twenty-one miles and the other two of fifteen miles in extent, and contains about 387,000 acres, assessed at $99,121. No census of the population was taken in 1880, but it is supposed to be about 4,000. It is bounded on the north-west by the Cumberland range of mountains which separate it from Kentucky, and on the south-east by the great Ae mountains. The surface on these borders is very rugged, but in the central parts it has many fine valleys, and much fertile land. The products are wheat, corn, oats, rye, barley, buckwheat, tobacco, flax, melons and grass. Vegetables and fruit are raised in great abundance and of good quality. This is one of the counties of Trans-Apalachia and is in the great grazing region of the south-western part of Virginia. The lands vary in texture with the character of the prevailing rocks, but the greater part of them are good grass lands. Timber of the most valuable kinds is found here in great abundance — three-fourths of the area being in original forest of oak, hickory, poplar, elm, ash, maple, wild cherry, walnut, pine, etc. The average assessed price of land being little more than twenty-five cents per acre, this region should afford grand inducements for men with capital to engage in the stock-raising business. This county is without railroads. It is watered by the head streams of the Russell's fork of Big Sandy river flowing north into the Ohio river. The minerals of this county have not been developed, but iron ores and coal (bituminous, splint and cannel) are known to be abundant.

DICKENSON COUNTY MINERALS AT THE NEW ORLEANS EXPOSITION.

1. *Coal*, from Cana creek, contributed by Elijah Rasnick, Sr.

GILES COUNTY

was formed in 1806 from Montgomery, Tazewell and Monroe, and is now one of the frontier counties of the State, adjoining Mercer and Monroe, in West Virginia. The eastern and western portions of the county are mountainous, both the boundaries being formed by ranges of the Alleghany mountains. Some portions of the county are fertile, producing fine crops of cereals and grasses. This county is a fine grazing region, and produces some of the finest fat cattle that are sent to the eastern markets. There are several mineral springs in this county, places of popular resort during the heated term, the most noted being the "New River White" and "Hunter's Alum." The wonderful freak of Nature, the so-called "Salt Pond," in the mountains of that name, attracts many visitors.

Giles is watered by New river and its tributaries. The population is 8,794; number of acres of land 229,055, assessed at $970,558. It abounds in fine growths of the usual timber of this region—walnut, wild cherry, sugar and other maples, oak, etc., and vast beds of iron ore, copper and coal.

In Giles there is found red marble, near Chapman's ferry, and near the base of Angel's Rest mountain. Hydraulic limestone, near Chapman's ferry, contains of carbonate lime 43 per cent., and of carbonate magnesia, about 35 per cent.; silica, 17.30, and 2 per cent. alumina and oxide iron. That a little below Chapman's ferry has 53 per cent. of carbonate lime, and 43 per cent. of magnesia, and 2 per cent. silica, and 0.50 alumina and oxide iron. These are highly hydraulic.

The branch road of the Norfolk and Western Railroad from Central station, on the borders of Montgomery and Pulaski, passes nearly due north through the north-east end of Pulaski, and through the centre of Giles to the West Virginia line, and through Mercer county, West Virginia, in a south-west course to Graham and Pocahontas, in Tazewell, and is to be extended into the central parts of the last county, where it will tap one of the finest mineral and timber regions in the world. Before this road was made the county of Giles labored under great disadvantages, but will now feel the effects of being brought in easy reach of the markets of the world, and will reap rich fruits from her valuable mineral and forest wealth so long shut up among her hills and valleys. There is here a great opening for immigration, which will not long neglect a region so inviting.

GILES COUNTY MINERALS AT NEW ORLEANS EXPOSITION.

1. *Fossil*, rhusophycus ,bilobatus, from No. V, on Little Stony creek; Capt. C. R. Boyd.
2. *Marble*, from Charles H. Snidow, Kimballton.
3. *Red iron ore*, from regular stratified bed showing abundance of it; C. W. McClaugherty.
4. *Clay and a mug made from it*, of fine quality for refractory purpose; C. W. McClaugherty.
5. *Red iron ore*, from D. F. Hale, Narrows; metalic iron 68.44 per cent.
6. *Spotted marble*, from J. H. Hoge.

HIGHLAND COUNTY

was formed in 1847 from Pendleton and Bath. It is thirty miles long and about twenty-five miles broad, and contains 239,700 acres, assessed at $804,000. Population, 5,170.

This is an elevated mountain region. The soil is mostly limestone, and produces good crops of corn, wheat, oats, rye, buckwheat and grass. The Kentucky blue-grass springs spontaneously wherever the timber is removed, and furnishes the finest pasturage, not inferior to that of the best lands of Kentucky. Grazing and the rearing of horses, cattle, sheep and swine constitute the main reliance of the owners of the soil. There is no place where a living is more easily made, and where the people enjoy more of ease and leisure. The climate is healthy and invigorating, and the people are kind and hospitable.

Valuable timber, especially walnut and wild cherry of the very best quality for cabinet makers' use, is abundant, and when this section shall be endowed with railroad facilities it will constiute a large item of wealth. Iron ore, coal and marble are known to exist in abundance in this county, and probably other valuable minerals will be found when its access to market shall justify more extended explorations.

Monterey, the county seat, and McDowell are the principal villages, and are busy and growing places, notably the former.

This county is drained by the head-waters of Cow Pasture and Jackson rivers emptying into the James, and by some of the head streams of the

South Branch of Potomac river, which interlace in this elevated watershed of the two river systems, and mark out the track of the great line of railroad which has been projected and will at some day not distant connect Pittsburg with the inexhaustible deposits of iron ore in Alleghany, Botetourt and the adjoining counties, and will quadruple the value of the land of highland.

LEE COUNTY

was formed from Russell in 1792. It lies in the south-west corner of the State, bordering on Tennessee and Kentucky. Its greatest length is 65 miles; mean breadth, 10 miles. It contains 365,240 acres, valued at $1,188,265. Population, 15,114. Three-fifths of the surface is mountainous or hilly, but the mountains are rich to the top, and a large proportion of the soil of the entire county is very fertile. The timber consists of oak (an immense quantity of *white* oak), poplar, pine, maple, buckeye, birch, beech, ash, cucumber, mulberry, locust, hickory, chestnut, much black walnut, and wild cherry, with vast forests of red cedar, near Powell's river, of the best quality for the manufacture of cedar ware. The productions are corn, wheat, buckwheat, oats, rye and tobacco. The cultivation of tobacco is on the increase. A great variety of vegetables and fruits is produced. It is well watered by Powell's river, which is navigable for flat-boats, and giving an outlet for the products of the county. The county is rich in minerals. Poor Valley ridge, which runs parallel to Cumberland mountains through the whole length of the county, has a rich vein of iron ore (dyestone—red hematite) extending throughout the entire length. The Cumberland mountains contain inexhaustible supplies of the best bituminous coal, a part of which is in this county. There are strong indications of zinc, lead and other valuable minerals. Salt has been made at two points in this county, but there are no works now in operation.

About one-half of the area of the county is cleared land, one-tenth of which is in wheat, the remainder in oats, rye, corn, tobacco and grass. This is a fine grass county, and is famous for fine cattle, horses, etc. It has at least 2,500 acres in orchards of every variety of fruit.

LEE COUNTY MINERALS AT THE NEW ORLEANS EXPOSITION.

Collected by General Imboden.

1. *Coal*, from "Imboden" vein 10 feet thick from Crab Orchard, ten miles west from Big Stone Gap.
2. *Fossil iron ore*, Clinton, No. V, two blocks from Rufus A. Ayers, on north fork Clinch river.

The following are from the Virgini Department of Agriculture:

3. *Fossil iron ore*, Clinton, No. V.
4. *Fossil iron ore*, Clinton.
5. *Limonite*, brown iron ore.

RUSSELL COUNTY

was formed in 1786 from Washington. It contains 318,000 acres, valued at $696,869. Population, 13,914.

The surface is much broken, as the county lies among mountain ranges, and much of the land is not arable, but there are very fine lands in the valleys. Grazing and stock raising is one of the principal industries of the people of Russell. They produce also ample supplies of grain, etc., for man and beast, and are making tobacco of very fine quality.

This is an elevated mountain region, noted for its healthy and bracing climate, and offers, with its cheap grass lands, kept fertile by decomposition of fossil limestones and feldspathic rocks, fine locations for persons desiring to go into the cattle business. The number of fat cattle annually sold amounts to 10,500.

It is drained by Clinch river and tributaries, which afford immense amounts of water-power, and are well stocked with game fishes. Mocasin creek, a tributary of the Holston, waters a considerable portion of its southern part.

The timber of this county is of the most valuable kinds, of large size, and in great abundance. The minerals are iron ores, coal, lead, zinc, barytes, salt, sandstone, limestone and marble, and are found in great abundance, of good quality and easily mined.

This county will be greatly benefited by railroads, which are expected to be constructed in the near future. Three lines of railway are now chartered, which will give to Russell nearly all the facilities it will require. The Richmond and South-west Railway will run thirty miles through the Clinch river section. The Saltville and Coal Mine Railroad will cross the county diagonally from south-east to north-west, crossing the iron, marble, coal and timber belts. The Virginia, Kentucky and Ohio Railroad has a branch road provided for in its charter which might pursue the line of Clinch river, on its way to Pound Gap.

RUSSELL COUNTY MINERALS AT THE NEW ORLEANS EXPOSITION.

1. *Splint coal*, from Lewis creek; from Capt. C. R. Boyd.
2. *Coal*, from Chana creek, contributed by Elijah Rasnick, Sr., of Pat's Store.

The following were contributed by Major W. K. Armistead, of Abingdon:

3. *Marble*, variegated, from base of Clinch mountain.
4. *Bituminous coal*, from Dump's creek.
5. *Coke*, from Dump's creek coal.
6. *Splint coal*, from Dump's creek.

SCOTT COUNTY

was formed in 1814 from Lee, Washington and Russell. The surface is mountainous and rolling, and the soil very good. Copper and Clinch rivers traverse the center, and the North Fork of Holston the southern part.

Population 17,235, number of acres of land 334,559, assessed at $702,584.

The productions, corn (in very large quantity), wheat, oats, rye, grass and tobacco. Price of land, improved, from $5 to $50 per acre; unimproved, from $1 to $5 per acre. This county has great capabilities, and, with railroads, would ship largely both of the products of the farm and of the mines. Two-thirds of the surface is in timber, consisting of the oak, poplar, walnut, ash, lynn, beech, sycamore, elm and box elder. There are 2,000 acres in orchards of apples, peaches, pears, cherries, grapes, etc. There are 80 schools in the county, of which 70 are public, and are in a flourishing condition. There are 75 churches, 35 of which are Methodist, 20 Mission, 10 Hard-shell Baptist, and 10 Free-will Baptist. About 300 immigrants have settled in this county in the last few years. The health and climate are good. This county is a grass county, and raises good stock. It is in the south end of the Valley, acknowledged a fine country.

This county is very rich in minerals, having abundance of iron ores, coal, copper, manganese, marble and limestone. It has many fine locations for mills and manufacturing establishments on the water-courses, with ample power to run any amount of machinery. A railroad through this section would devolop great re-

sources.* There are many mineral springs in this county, both sulphur and chalybeate.

In this county is found in great abundance a reddish, fossiliferous *mottled marble*, in which the colors are pleasingly blended with grayish white. The dun-colored and other varieties are also found of fine quality. A correspondent says there is mineral wealth enough in this county to pay the national debt.

SCOTT COUNTY MINERALS AT THE NEW ORLEANS EXPOSITION.

The following were collected by General Imboden:

1. *Coal*, from 6 feet to 7 feet bed, head of Stony creek.

2. *Fossil iron ore*, Clinton, from land of W. W. James, near head of Stony creek.

3. *Iron ore*, brown hematite, from same localty as above.

4. *Tennessee marble*, brown, block 16 x 11 x 7½ inches, dressed, polished, etc., from near Estilleville, from land of Estilleville Marble Company. Estilleville is located on this marble, and with it the streets are macadamized and the foundation walls of the houses are built.

5. *Dark brown Tennessee marble*,

---

*Hitherto there has been no outlet for this—no means of exploiting it; but now there is a narrow-gauge railroad in course of construction from Bristol, Tenn., to Mineral City, 66 miles distant, tapping some of the richest coal and iron deposits in the United States. Along the whole line is an immense quantity of the finest timber—walnut, wild cherry, poplar, ash, white oak and pine. The beautiful marble mentioned above is on the line of this road.

a polished block, from "Bounds" tract of the Estilleville Marble Company, four miles west from Estilleville.

6. *Dappled gray marble*, a polished block, from land of same company, three miles south-west from Estilleville.

7. *Cherry spot marble*, a dressed block, from same locality, etc., as above.

8. *Pebble marble*, a polished block, from "Bounds" tract, same company.

These specimens of marble are exceedingly beautiful. The quarries from which they came are very extensive, extending for miles along the track of the projected and now partially completed South Atlantic and Ohio Railroad.

TAZEWELL COUNTY

was formed in 1799 from Russell and Wythe. It is sixty miles long, with varying width, and contains 336,250 acres of land, assessed at $1,106,693. Population, 12,861.

The surface is mountainous, but is relieved by fertile valleys, many of them of considerable extent. One of the largest of these valleys, called "Burke's Garden," is famed for its beauty and fertility. The soil is mostly limestone and very fertile, the mountains, even to their tops, being covered with a luxuriant growth of blue-grass, which is indigenous here. The favorite and most profitable occupation here is grazing and fattening cattle, many of them being sent across the Atlantic to the markets of Great Britain.

The timber is abundant and of large dimensions. Oak, walnut, cherry, hickory, elm, chestnut and other trees attain to great size and altitude, and the most valuable timbers are used in the ordinary construction of dwellings.

Tazewell county is rich in minerals, having large deposits of the purest iron ores, coal, salt, gypsum, etc. Coal is being mined in great quantities and shipped by the New river branch of the Norfolk and Western Railroad to Norfolk city for the coaling of ocean steamers, for which purpose it is well suited. Pocahontas, close to which is located the principal mine, is a rapidly growing town of some two thousand inhabitants, and is the present terminus of the New river division of the Norfolk and Western road. The great Flat-Top mountain range from which this coal is obtained forms the western border of this county, and is part of the dividing line between Virginia and West Virginia. The iron ores will be developed by the contemplated extension of the branch road alluded to into the central parts of the county.

This county is watered by Clinch river flowing south-west and by tributaries of New river flowing northeast.

TAZEWELL COUNTY MINERALS AT THE NEW ORLEANS EXPOSITION.

From Capt. C. R. Boyd.

1. *Red shale iron ore*, fine quality, from Paint Lick mine.
2. *Semi-bituminous coal*, a complete section 12 feet thick, from Pocahontas mine.
3. *Semi-bituminous coal;* samples from Pocahontas mine.
4. *Coke*, made at Pocahontas from above coal.

The following are from the Virginia Department of Agriculture:

4. *Fossil*, in limestone.
5. *Iron*, smelted from Poor Valley ore in a common smith's forge; J. R. Witten.
6. *Limonite iron ore*, from Poor Valley; from Harvey Peet's.
7. *Fossil iron ore.*
8. *Red iron ore*, magnetic.
9. *Limonite*, brown iron ore.
10. *Manganese*, ore.

WISE COUNTY

was formed in 1855 from Lee, Scott and Russell counties. It has 310,000 acres of land, assessed at $186,000, or sixty cents per acre. Population in 1880 was 7,782, but a part of this is to be credited to Dickenson county, a portion of which was taken from Wise since the last census.

Wise county lies on the Kentucky line, and is located amongst the lofty ranges of mountains which traverse this Trans-Apalachian country.

The soil, in some parts formed from limestone rocks, is of good quality and well adapted to grains and grass. Other sections, formed from disintegrated sandstone, have poorer soils, but the lands produce corn, vegetables and fruits, and are well suited to the grape, and to pasturage, especially of sheep.

The greater part of the area of Wise county is still covered with original forests of valuable timber, such as oak, chestnut, walnut, poplar, cherry, pine, etc. The cherry is notably abundant and of large size, and poplar trees of enormous size, some of them six and eight feet in diameter, with long, straight trunks, seventy-five to eighty feet to the limbs.

The minerals of this county are iron ores, coal (bituminous, splint and cannel) in great abundance and easily mined. Lead and silver have also been found, but not yet in paying quantity. Limestone and valuable sandstone for building are abundant.

This county is watered by several considerable streams flowing into Russell's fork of Big Sandy river, and by Powell's river and other streams which flow south into Clinch river.

The great need of this section is access to market for its very valuable timber and minerals, which, it is hoped, will soon be supplied by the construction of the several railroads projected through this country.

WISE COUNTY MINERALS AT THE NEW ORLEANS EXPOSITION.

The following specimens were collected by Gen. John D. Imboden:

1. *Coking coal*, a block, 15-inch cube, from "Gibbs" opening in the "Imboden" bed, 8 feet thick, on Preacher Fork of Callaghan creek, on lands (72,000 acres) of the Virginia Coal and Iron Company.

2. *Coke*, made from above coal.

3. *Splint coal*, from Shelving-rock bed, 4½ feet thick, from south-east face of Black mountain, from the property of the Virginia Coal and Iron Company.

4. *Splint coal*, long block, from same bed as No. 3, the property of same company.

5. *Cannel coal*, from upper bench, 26 inches thick, of 7-foot bed in Black mountain, property of same company.

6. *Coal*, from "Imboden" bed, where 10 feet thick, on Roaring fork of Powell river, on Nine-mile ride of Black mountain, on land of J. P. Imboden.

7. *Red shale iron ore*, from No. V, Clinton, from "Horton" tract of Virginia Iron and Coal Company, on north-west face of Wallen ridge, one mile from Big Stone gap.

8. *Iron ore*, brown, "Wildcat" mine, on "Collier" tract of Virginia Iron and Coal Company, in valley at head of Wildcat creek.

9. *Iron ore*, fossil of No. V, Clinton, from 1,050 acres, tract of Col. Frank Preston, in south-west end of Wallen ridge, near south fork of Powell river.

10. *Cannel coal*, from near Pound fork of Big Sandy river.

CHAPTER XXXIII.

PIEDMONT VIRGINIA.

ALBEMARLE COUNTY is one of the largest counties of the State, its area being 500,787 acres, 37 per cent. woodland, assessed at $6,220,115—about $12 per acre. Its southern boundary is James river; its western the Blue Ridge mountains. A sub-range of mountains passes through it, which, with the main range and spurs, make the surface very diversified. There is a large proportion of fine farming land in the county. It is well watered by the James, the Rivanna and the Hardware, and their tributaries. These streams furnish abundant water-power, some of which is well utilized. The soil is mainly dark red, well adapted to the staple crops of the Piedmont section, and particularly so for clover, apples, grapes and fruit generally. The Albemarle pippin took its name from this county, and here reaches its greatest perfection. In no county of the State has the culture of the grape been so successful. The fruit is largely sold, and the wine has a high reputation.

There are two large wine cellars at Charlottesville; that of the Monticello Wine Company has a capacity of 150,000 gallons, which can be increased to 200,000 gallons by the use of larger casks; and that of Mr. Hotopp has a capacity of 50,000 gallons, to which he is now excavating an addition of 70,000 gallons. Mr. Hotopp has also a house cellar of 30,000 gallons capacity now in use. Large plantings of vines are being made yearly.

This county has fine transportation facilities to markets in all directions, by means of the Chesapeake and Ohio Railroad crossing its territory from east to west, and the Virginia Midland from north to south. These roads cross each other at Charlottesville, the county seat. The Richmond and Alleghany Railroad passes along the south border. The minerals of this county are varied and valuable, consisting of iron, gold, lead, slate, soapstone, limestone, marble, sandstone and granite.

Albemarle has a number of towns and villages—Charlottesville in the center and Scottsville in the southern border being the principal.

Charlottesville, the county seat, is a thriving town on the Rivanna river, in the most beautiful part of this picturesque region. Population, about 5,000.

Albemarle presents many and varied attractions which settlers are not slow to avail themselves of. Besides being one of the most fertile counties of Piedmont Virginia and the center of a great fruit-producing region, it is the seat of two noble institutions—the University of Virginia and the Miller Manual Labor School. The University at Charlottesville is too well known to need a minute description here. Suffice it to say that it is second to no institution of learning on the continent, and is attracting great numbers of students from all quarters of the country. The location is one of unsurpassed beauty.

The Miller Manual Labor School is now in full tide of successful operation. Magnificently endowed by the late Samuel Miller, of Lynchburg, a native of Albemarle, and splendidly equipped for the object indicated by its name—giving a technical education to boys—this school is being so conducted as to justify the most sanguine anticipations of its founder. Probably there is no instance in this country where a great bequest for an object like this has been administered with such wisdom and fidelity.

There are many English and Northern settlers in this beautiful county.

Albemarle county had on exhibition at New Orleans the following specimens of minerals, collected by Prof. W. H. Seamon, of the Miller School. These and others to be collected by Professor Seamon are placed in trays, with compartments made of native woods by the boys of the Miller School, and the localities from which they were obtained indicated on a map of Albemarle county, prepared at this school:

1. *Species of granite*, from North Garden station, Virginia Midland Railroad.

2. *Magnetic iron ore*, from Mrs. Martin's land, near North Garden; mine formerly worked.

3. *Soapstone*, cut samples, from Albemarle quarry, five miles east from North Garden station.

4. *Iron ore*, specimens from Yates' farm, near Albemarle quarry.

5. *Slate*, highly charged with graphite, same locality as 4; probably valuable.

6. *Igneous diorite*, a parallelopipedon from dike near Faber station, Virginia Midland Railroad; shows peculiar manner this rock weathers.

7. *Mica schist*, from Faber Lead Mines.

8. *Mica schist*, another variety from same place.

9. Ores and minerals of various kinds, 6 or 7 specimens from Faber Lead Mines.

10. *Slate*, charged with micaceous iron ore, from Norvell's farm, near Howardsville.

11. *Brown hematite iron ore*, float, from same place as 10.

12. *Manganese ore*, from same place as 10.

13. *Puddingstone conglomerate*, from Howardsville.

14. *Red sandstone*, from near Howardsville.

15. *Felsite*, from Israel mountain.

16. *Blue quartz*, from Israel mountain. Thin sections of this show rutile.

17. *Massive white quartz*, from Miller School farm.

18. *White quartz*, from Israel mountain, filled with muscovite.

19. *Calico rock*, from north branch of Mechum river.

20. *Hydro-mica slates*, from Miller School farm.

21. *Quartz crystals*, from Miller School farm.

22. *Oxide of iron*, pseudomorph, after pyrite, from various parts of county.

23. *Ilmenite*, from Israel mountain.

The following specimens are kindly lent by Prof. William M. Fontaine, of the University of Virginia, from his collection:

24. *Slate*, with denditric markings, from Albemarle Slate Quarry.

25. *Granitic granulite*, suitable for mill stones, from Moorman river, where it is in vast quantities.

26. *Sandstone*, from Moorman river, from point west of Whitehall; very abundant.

27. *Metamorphic conglomerate*, from Rockfish Gap tunnel, Chesapeake and Ohio Railway.

28. *Epidote*, from same locality.

The following is shown in the exhibit of the Virginia Midland Railroad, from Albemarle county:

Graphite slate, three-quarters of a mile from Charlottesville.

2. *Slate*, a slab, from Albemarle Slate Co., six miles from Charlottesville.

3. *Iron ore*, from Stony Point.

4. *Wine*, three cases, from William Hotopp, Charlottesville.

5. *Wine and brandy*, one case from Monticello Wine Co., Charlottesville.

Soapstone, a block from Albemarle Soapstone Co., five miles from North Garden station.

The following were collected by Prof. W. H. Seamon, of the Miller School:

29. *Purple roofing slate*, from the Albemarle Slate quarry, ten miles south from Charlottesville.

30. *Green roofing slate*, from same locality as above.

31. *Tile slates*, from same.

32. *Marbleized slate*, for mantels, etc., made at works of above quarry.

33. *Iron ore*, from Stony Point.

34. *Iron nodule*, showing black velvety surface with crystals of white quartz; from Stony Point.

35. *Magnetic iron ore*, from Israel mountain.

36. *Quartz crystals*, from Stony Point.

37. *Sandstone*, from ridge south of Charlottesville, used for foundation walls of Lewis Brooks Museum.

38. *Mica schist*, quarried near gas works, Charlottesville, for curbstones, etc.

39. *Mica schist*, from near Bethel station, Virginia Midland Railway.
40. *Quartz*, from east flank of Carter's mountain.
41. *Granite*, from Dr. Michie's, near Piney mountain.
42. *Syenite*, from same locality as 41.
43. *Slate*, from Slate Hill Church.
44. *Quartzite*, feldspathic, from near Batesville.
45. *Hydro-mica schist*, Batesville.
46. *Greenstone*, with quartz and pyrite, from near Powell's.
47. *Red sandstone conglomerate*, at Dyer's store, Scottsville.
48. *Red sandstone*, from same as above.
49. *Red sandstone conglomerate*, from same.
50. *Red oxide of iron*, from same.
51. *Coarse felsite*, from Blue Ridge, at Turk's Gap.
52. *Syenite*, from Miller School farm.
53. *Blueish sandstone*, from east flank of Carter's mountain.
54. *Syenite*, containing hydro-mica, from near Brownsville.
55. *Gneiss*, from Morris' mill, near Batesville.
56. *Greenstone*, from Powell's mill, near Crozet station, Chesapeake and Ohio Railway.
57. *Gneiss*, or calico rock, from Ivy station, Chesapeake and Ohio Railway.
58. *Felsite*, from near North Garden station, Virginia Midland Railway.
59. *Feldspar conglomerate*, from Blue Ridge, at Greenwood station, Chesapeake and Ohio Railway.
60. *Feldspathic rock*, same locality.
61. *Epidosyte*, same locality.
62. *Epidote and calcite*, from Blue Ridge, at Turk Gap.
63. *Quartzite*, feldspathic, from same locality.
64. *Hornblende schist*, with epidote, quartz and pyrite, same locality.
65. *Hornblende slate*, from same locality.
66. *Quartz*, with cry , of epidote, same.
67. *Conglomerate*, same locality.
68. *Chert*, same locality.
69. *Puddingstone*, containing epidote, feldspar and hornblende, same locality.
70. *Talcose-schist*, containing grains of amethystine quartz, same locality.
71. *Conglomerate*, same locality.
72. *Greenish schist*, same locality.
73. *Quartzite*, same locality.
74. *Quartz*, showing jointed structure.
75. *Red soil*, from foot of South-west mountain; results from decomposition of epidotic rock.
76. *Beded diorite*, from Miller School farm.
77. *Mica schist*, from Miller School farm.
78. *Sandy soil*, from Mechum river bottom lands, Miller School farm.
79. *Loam*, from hill-sides of Miller School farm.
80. *Map of Albemarle county*, made by pupils of Miller School, showing location of above minerals.

AMHERST COUNTY

was formed in 1761 from Albemarle. It lies on the north bank of James river, which forms the boundaries of two of its sides, a distance of over fifty miles. This rich and beautiful county is twenty-two miles long, and has a mean width of nineteen miles, and contains 304,539 acres, valued at $1,889,625. Population, 18,548.

The soil of Amherst is mostly a dark red clay and is generally rich and productive. The principal crops are corn, wheat, oats, tobacco and grass. The timber consists of fine growths of oak, hickory, walnut, chestnut, pine, maple, poplar and dogwood. This is a fine fruit county—the apple especially being largely cultivated, and grapes to a considerable extent. Its main market is Lynchburg, with which it is connected by a free bridge.

Amherst Court House is a pleasant little town on the Virginia Midland Railroad, which runs through the county. The Richmond and Alleghany Railroad runs along its southern border for some distance, and the Norfolk and Western runs on its border below Lynchburg for about six miles. The county is susceptible of great development.

The minerals found here are varied and immensely valuable. Great deposits of magnetic and specular iron ores are found here suited for the manufacture of steel by the Bessemer process, and of a purity not excelled by any ores south of Lake Superior.

The brown hematite iron ores are also in great abundance, and are cheaply mined, and scarcely less valuable than the specular and magnetic. These ores are found in contact with or in the vicinity of the limestones. There are many mines of these ores worked in the vicinity. Copper, lead, slate and tin are also to be found in Amherst.

SPECIMENS OF MINERALS FROM AMHERST COUNTY AT THE NEW ORLEANS EXPOSITION.

The following were contributed by Colonel Dunlap:

1. *Magnetic and specular iron ores*, from Maud Vein Mines, near Stapleton, Richmond and Alleghany Railroad.

2. *Syenite*, blue granite, from Bent creek, near Gladstone station, Richmond and Alexandria Railroad.

3. *Roofing slate*, from Snowden Slate Quarry, near Rope Ferry station, Richmond and Alleghany Railroad.

4. *Iron ore*, from near Riverville station, Richmond and Alleghany Railroad.

5. *Steel iron ore*, of Vein No. 6, near above locality.

6. *Steel iron ore*, of Vein No. 6½, near above locality.

7. *Copper ores*, carbonates, malachite, bornite, azurite, red oxide, and copper glance—yielding from 27 to 49 per cent. metallic copper—from Piedmont Copper Mines, in Glades.

The following are from Prof. Fontaine, of the University of Virginia:

8. *Syenite*, from Balcony Falls; occurs in large quantities.

9. *Syenite*, from Piney river; in large quantities.

10. *Granulite*, from Balcony; would make a handsome building stone.

11. *Bornite and stalactic copper ores*, from Dr. Charles Slaughter's.

12. *Magnetic iron ore*, from 4-feet ledge of solid ore on Indian creek.

BEDFORD COUNTY

was formed in 1753 from Lunenburg. The extreme length from north to south is forty miles, its width about thirty miles. It contains 494,198 acres of land, assessed at $3,227,828. Population, 31,205.

The surface is uneven and in parts mountainous. The "Peaks of Otter" in this county is one of the loftiest mountains in the Southern States, and is much visited for the magnificent views afforded from its elevated crests.

The north-east boundary of Bedford is formed by James river, and the south-west by Staunton river, and the interior has ample drainage and water-power from the large tributaries of these two rivers.

The soil is a red or chocolate loam, and is generally fertile and easily improved. The productions are those common to this section. Grazing and cattle raising are prominent industries—the soil being well adapted to grass and clover. Gypsum is used largely, and with fine effect. The county has a special *dog* law for the protection of sheep, and the law works well. Sheep husbandry is prominent, and pays handsomely. The recent establishment of a woollen-mill at Liberty gives a home market for wool, and mutton finds ready sale at the great markets easily reached by rail. Large factories for manufacturing its tobacco are also found at Liberty.

Bedford is famous for fine fruit and grapes, and the wine made from them. The apples and other fruits from this county have been annually placed on exhibition at our fairs, and have generally taken premiums.

The following minerals are found in the county: Cyanite, zinc, flint, pyrotite mica-slate, hornblende crystals in quartz, pyrite in quartz, aluminous shales, quartz crystals, hornblende gneiss, mica, limestone, magnetic iron ore, red and brown hematite iron ore. Of the latter the supply is very large. Major Hotchkiss pronounces it "inexhaustible." General Imboden pronounces it to be high-grade and practically inexhaustible. Professor Wells, of Roanoke College, says it may be termed "The Iron Mountain of Virginia."

The county is watered on its north-east boundary by the James and its tributaries, by the Otter river and headwaters in the central part of the county, and the Staunton and its tributaries on its south-western border. The Blue Ridge forms its north-western boundary between Botetourt and Roanoke.

It has the Norfolk and Western

Railroad running through its center, the Richmond and Alleghany Railroad on its north-east border, the Virginia Midland running in close proximity to its eastern border.

Liberty, its county seat, is a flourishing town, situated on the Norfolk and Western Railroad, with a population of about 3,500. Bufordsville at Buford's Gap, in the Blue Ridge' through which the Norfolk and Western Railroad passes, is a village much patronized by summer visitors.

The county is susceptible of great development, and has received quite a large influx of new settlers from England and elsewhere.

CULPEPER COUNTY.

Culpeper county is not wholly a Piedmont county. The lower portion runs down into middle Virginia; hence its ssurface is less rugged than some of the other Piedmont counties.

Its area is 232,545 acres, assessed at $2,402,297. Of this area 30 per cent. is woodland.

This county was the camping-ground of both armies for much of the civil war period, and was therefore denuded of much of its wood; but so rapid has been the second growth that the destructive effects of the war are scarcely visible at this time.

The soil in the upper portion is red, or chocolate-colored, in the lower portion gray.

The county is watered by the Rappahannock and Rapidan rivers and their tributaries, which afford fine sites for mills, etc.

The Virginia Midland Railroad traverses the county from north-east to south-west. Culpeper, the county seat, is on this road. It is a town of 2,100 inhabitants, and enjoys a good trade with the surrounding country. It is one of the most thrifty towns in the State.

Stevensburg is a village near Brandy station.

The minerals of this county are gold-bearing quartz, copper, iron ore, mica, etc.

There are a number of factories in the county—a chair factory near Culpeper, plow-beam and barrel-stave factory near Stevensburg; also factory for spools and shuttle blocks, another for same near Cedar Run battle-field.

In *The Virginias* of August, 1882, Major Hotchkiss say: "We would like to have some of the 'forest-wise' people, who are croaking about the destruction of our forests, and predicting that we will have a treeless country in a short time, see how rapidly and beautifully Culpeper and other counties along the Virginia Midland that were almost deforested during the late war by the great armies that camped and wintered there, are now becoming afforested in half a generation. We noticed a few days ago fuel and fencing being cut where Meade's army burned up every tree in 1863–'64."

CULPEPER MINERALS AT THE NEW ORLEANS EXPOSITION.

1. *Gold-bearing quartz*, from "Culpeper" Mine, Major C. Knapp.
2. *Gold-bearing quartz*, from Richardsville, W. B. Love.
3. *Gold-bearing quartz*, from "Ellis" Mine.
4. *Gold-bearing quartz*, from Culpeper Gold Mine, eighteen miles west from Fredericksburg.

From Virginia Midland Railway exhibit:

1. *Copper and iron ores*, from Major E. B. Hill, one mile from Culpeper station.
2. *Iron ore*, from W. S. Wallace, seven miles from Brandy station.

FAUQUIER COUNTY

was formed in 1759 from Prince William. Its length is forty-five miles; mean breadth, sixteen miles. The surface is gently rolling, and in some parts hilly. The hill lands have a red clay soil; the level lands are mainly gray sandstone. The lands are fertile, and produce fine crops of corn, wheat, oats, rye and grass. It is watered by the Rappahannock, Occoquan and numerous creeks throughout its entire surface, furnishing many eligible sites for mills and manufacturing purposes. The timber is oak, hickory, chestnut, walnut, poplar, locust, ash, cherry, cedar, sycamore, sassafras, elm, gum, mulberry, dogwood and pine. The population is 23,271. Number of acres of land 414,402, assessed at $7,698,-486. The productions of the county furnish a large surplus for market. This is one of the healthiest and most prosperous counties in the State. The Virginia Midland Railroad, the main stem, the Manassas branch, and the Warrenton branch, penetrating this beautiful and fertile county in various directions, give it excellent market facilities.

Fauquier has gold, iron ore, marble and asbestos. Mr. J. B. Beverly, Jr., and Mr. J. C. Little, in interesting letters, state that there are found in the county iron ores in the form of specular, limonite, ilmenite, pyrites; also copper pyrites. Limestone, as marble, near the "Plains" station. This marble is very compact, close-grained, gray and white. Also barytes of excellent quality. There are several marble quarries in the county; and gold is also mined in the southern part of the county; it is in the form of sulphuret.

The Rappannock river forms its southern boundary, and separates it from Culpeper and Rappahannock counties. This is a large and wealthy county, and has among its farmers some of the most successful and prosperous in the State. The cereals and grass, with horses, sheep and cattle, constitute the main products. Cattle fattened upon the blue-grass lands of Fauquier, are in great request in the markets of Washington, Baltimore and the great cities further north, and have been largely shipped to Europe of late years.

Warrenton is the chief town and county seat, and is the center of a refined and intelligent community. It has a population of more than 1,500, and has numerous churches and schools. Near by is the Warrenton White Sulphur Springs, a popular resort for pleasure and health.

Fauquier ranks high as regards quality of soil, beauty of scenery, healthfulness and general prosperity. In its borders are thirteen railroad stations, a number of which are flourishing towns or villages.

FAUQUIER MINERALS AT THE NEW ORLEANS EXPOSITION.

1. *Iron ore*, from Henry Sempers.
2. *Syenite*, rough block, from Alf. Chappelear.
3. *Feldspar*, or kaolin, from Wm. E. Gaskins, two miles from Warrenton.
4. *Copper ore*, from "Sealock" mine.

FRANKLIN COUNTY

was formed in 1784 from Henry and Bedford. It is thirty miles long and about twenty miles wide. The Roanoke (there called "Staunton") river runs on its north-east border, and the county is intersected by numerous creeks. The surface is rolling, as in the Piedmont counties generally. The soil is very fertile, and produces large crops of tobacco, corn, wheat, hay and oats. The population is 24,953. This is a very healthy county. Good land can be bought at four to ten dollars per acre. (This estimate was made several years ago, before the railroad to Rocky Mount opened up the county to the markets of Danville, Lynchburg and other cities.) Franklin contains 435,175 acres, assessed at $1,822,342.

This county, as is all of Piedmont, is an excellent fruit region, particularly adapted to apples and grapes; and it is also a good grass and stock-raising county. The minerals are iron, limestone, mica, asbestos, granite and soapstone. The Franklin and Pittsylvania railway has been recently completed from Elba, near Ward's Springs, in Pittsylvania county, on the Midland Railroad, to Rocky Mount, the county seat, near the centre of the county. This relieves the farmers of Franklin of a long and costly cartage of their produce, and must greatly enhance the value of property. It has given a good impetus to the development of the valuable iron ores found here, as well as to that of the agricultural resources of this fertile county.

FRANKLIN COUNTY MINERALS AT NEW ORLEANS EXPOSITION.

1. *Asbestos*, from Capt. F. J. Chapman.
2. *Allanite*, from McMannaway mountain, 6 miles from Norfolk and Western Railroad.
3. *Magnetic iron ore*, from Rocky Mount Mines, F. J. Chapman.
4. *Magnetic iron ore*, from Rocky Mount.
5. *Magnetite*, from "Franklin"

Mine, 1½ miles north-west from Rocky Mount.

6. *Magnetite*, from Capt. C. J. Saunders' mine, 11 miles south-west from Rocky Mount.

7. *Granite*, from W. C. Smithers' quarry, 1 mile north-west from Rocky Mount.

GREENE COUNTY

lies north-east of Albemarle; its north-west boundary the crest of the Blue Ridge, which separates it from Rockingham, in the Shenandoah Valley. Its population in 1880 was 5,528. It contains 107,584 acres, assessed at $581,609—about $5 per acre; about 42 per cent. of this is woodland. Much of surface is mountainous or semi-mountainous, but the less broken portions are fertile. It is watered by the Rapidan river and its tributaries, and the headwaters of the Rivanna river. Stock, especially sheep, are profitably raised in this county.

The minerals found are syenite, copper, malachite and azurite and iron ore. Having no railroad for transportation of its products, these ores are not developed as they might be. The Virginia Midland Railroad runs within a few miles of the eastern border of the county.

Stanardsville is the county seat—a small village. With cheap lands and a healthful and pleasant climate, Greene county offers good inducements to settlers from other parts of the country. Good farms with improvements can now be bought for $15 per acre, and unimproved lands $1.50 to $8 per acre, but will rapidly rise in price when penetrated by a railroad.

HENRY COUNTY

was formed from Pittsylvania in 1776. It is nearly a square of 18 miles, and contains 241,700 acres, assessed at $1,047,000. The surface is undulating—in parts hilly, and there are some considerable mountains. Smith's river flows through the middle of the county and "Mayo" through the south-west—these, with their numerous branches, afford ample water-power.

The soil of Henry is very fertile, and the climate salubrious. A correspondent well says: "In this county we have comparatively warm winters and cool summers; and there is scarcely a county in the State freer from malaria than this. Perennial creeks of fine freestone water are found in all parts."

This is a fine grass county. Clover, blue-grass, timothy, orchard, Randall, tall meadow oat grass, and red-top, all grow remarkably well here, as do all the cereals grown in Virginia.

The tobacco of Henry is celebrated for its fine quality, and the production is rapidly increasing.

The grape is at home here, as are the apple, peach, nectarine, almond, (?) apricot and fig.

"The calycanthus grows wild in

the sheltered dales of this picturesque region."

"Sweet potatoes do well here. From two to three hundred bushels can be raised per acre under good cultivation. In fine," as our correspondent well says, "God has blessed this county with every advantage of fertile land and salubrious climate, and all that is necessary to succeed is to trust in God, speed the plow, use commendable economy and cultivate the land in a manner commensurate with its great natural advantages."

Since the Danville and New River Railroad was constructed through Henry, the town of Martinsville, the county seat, has grown with phenomenal rapidity. Within five years it has increased from a population of three hundred to about two thousand at the present time. It is a live town, having ten tobacco factories and nearly a half-million of dollars invested in manufacturing enterprises of various sorts, as iron foundries, machine-shops, etc.

Iron ore in immense beds, mica, soapstone, chalybeate and alum-water are found in Henry.

HENRY COUNTY MINERALS AT NEW ORLEANS EXPOSITION.

From Virginia Department Agriculture.

1. *Garnets*, common.
2. *Quartz crystals*, a group of.
3. *Garnets*, in gneiss.
4. *Magnetite*, from A. N. Price.
5. *Tourmaline*, from A. N. Price.
6. *Mica*, sheets of.

7. *Quartz crystals*, peculiar group. The following were collected by Mr. E. D. Frazer:

8. *Hematite iron ore*, from "Gravely" property, one mile west from Axton station, Danville and New River Railroad.
9. *Magnetic iron ore*, from "E. Davis" property, near same locality.
10. *Magnetic iron ore*, from "Lucy Davis" property, near same locality.
11. *Magnetic iron ore*, from "H. P. Davis" property, near same locality.
12. *Magnetic iron ore*, from "McDonald" property, near same locality.
13. *Mineral*, from "Koger" property, one mile east from Bull Run, ten miles west from Spencer station, Danville and New River Railroad.
14. *Mineral*, from same locality as above.
15. *Steatite*, from "Gravely" quarry, two miles west from Axton station.
16. *Steatite*, from "Barker" quarry, two miles east from Axton station.

LOUDOUN COUNTY

was formed in 1757 from Fairfax. It is the northernmost of the Piedmont counties; separated from Maryland by the Potomac river, and by the Blue Ridge from Jefferson county, West Virginia, and from Clarke county, Virginia; Fauquier and Prince William adjoin it on the south and Fairfair on the east.

Within these limits are included 322,395 acres of the finest land to be found in any one county in the State, and it is assessed accordingly at an average of $30.60 per acre, which is considerably higher than that of any other county.

The surface of Loudoun is varied with mountains, gently sweeping hills and broad valleys, of which the greater part is exceedingly fertile, yielding immense crops of corn, wheat, hay and oats, and supporting great herds of fine cattle and flocks of sheep. Much attention has been paid to improving breeds of horses, cattle and sheep by the wealthy and intelligent farmers of Loudoun.

The Washington, Ohio and Western Railroad, which traverses this county, dividing it almost equally, furnishes an outlet for the immense exports of cattle, grain and hay sent from the central portions of Loudoun, and the northern edge of the county is in easy communication with the Washington branch of the Baltimore and Ohio Railroad and the Chesapeake and Ohio Canal, just across the Potomac. Population 23,741.

Leesburg, a fine old town, is the county seat. It has a population of about 2,000.

A good deal of money from abroad has been invested here, but the high price of land has kept out much increase of population by immigration.

The mineral wealth of this county is very considerable—iron, copper, silver, barytes and marble—of which the following specimens were exhibited at the World's Exposition at New Orleans:

1. *Specular iron ore*, from near Leesburg, said to be in quantity, from Professor Fontaine.

2. *Chalcopyrite*, from near Leesburg, said to be a promising vein, from Professor Fontaine.

The following were contributed by the "Eagle Mining Company," of Leesburg, F. A. Wise, general manager:

1. *Carbonate of copper*, from vein 3 feet wide, developed to 25 feet deep. Assays by Oxford Copper Company, of New York, give 51 per cent. of copper and twenty-seven ounces of silver per ton.

2. *Sulphuret of copper*, from vein 10 inches wide, developed to 50 feet deep. Assays by Oxford Copper Company, of New York, 12½ per cent. of copper.

3. *Iron ore*, from vein 4 feet wide 50 feet deep. Yield 55 per cent. metallic iron by assay of W. P. Lawver, of United States Mint.

4. *Salphuret of copper*, from vein developed 50 feet. Yields 11 per cent. of copper and one ounce of silver per ton by assay of W. P. Lawver, of United States Mint.

5. *Carbonate of copper*, red oxide and glance, from vein 3 feet wide, developed to 25 feet deep. Yields 50 per cent. metallic copper and twenty-seven ounces silver per ton by assays.

6. *Iron ore*, from vein 2 feet to 4 feet wide, developed 50 feet. Yields 55 per cent. metallic iron.

7. *Oxide of copper*, from carbonate vein, developed 60 feet on 4 feet wide vein, 25 feet deep.

8. *Sulphuret of copper*, from vein 8 inches to 15 inches wide, developed 50 feet.

9. *Iron ore.*

10. *Barytes*, heavy spar, vein undeveloped.

11. *Iron ore*, from 50 feet level of Eagle Mining Company's shaft.

12. *Marble*, from quarry of "Virginia Marble Company," three miles east from Middleburg. The deposit has been demonstrated to be of great extent; the marble has been pronounced of a very superior quality. Contributed by Major B. P. Noland.

13. *Marble*, from same as above.

14. *Marble*, from same as above.

17. *Copper ore*, James Pinkham, from Virginia Department of Agriculture.

MADISON COUNTY

was formed in 1792 from Culpeper. It is about thirty-three miles long, and contains 212,000 acres of land, assessed at $1,720,200. This is an excellent grass and grain producing county. Besides being admirably adapted to fruit and grape culture, and fine tobacco, and containing valuable mineral deposits, as will be seen from the following geological and general sketch of the county by A. G. Grinnan, Esq., a description so good that it is given unabridged:

"The nature of soils is largely controlled by geological formations, and this is well shown in Madison county.

"An arm of the large secondary formation of the triassic period, which extends from the Rapidan river through Culpeper county and other counties to the Potomac river, extends across the south-eastern part of the county, crossing the Robertson river above its mouth, and having a width of one or two miles, where the formation is a red or chocolate colored shale, the super-imposed soil is of excellent quality, producing fine crops of wheat, corn and grass. Where gray sandstone predominates the soil is of medium fertility, but easily improved.

"It has been recently stated by high authority that soils of similar secondary measures in other parts of Virginia have been found eminently adapted to the growth of high grade tobacco.

"Between this secondary deposit and the Rapidan river the underlying rock for twelve or more miles are mostly epidote and greenstone, similar to those of the adjacent Southwest mountain range of Orange county, the decomposition of which furnish potash and lime. The Madison lands adjacent to Orange county appear to be of better quality, owing to some admixture of sand from the adjacent sandstone belt, and furnish in many places soils remarkably well adapted to the culture of grapes, and particularly of the valuable Catawba grape, which it is difficult to raise in many sections.

"The portion of the county lying between the secondary deposits and the region adjacent to the foot-hills of the Blue Ridge mountains is underlaid with gneissoid sandstone, decomposing granites and metamorphic strata, all azoic, and furnishing in disintegration but little lime and potash or other mineral ingredient of value; and the soil, excepting upon the streams, is of medium quality, gray or red color, but readily improved. Adjacent to the foot-hills of the Blue Ridge the country rocks show marks of the metamorphic or igneous action accompanying the elevation of the Blue Ridge, and produce fertile soils. The slopes of the mountains grow excellent tobacco, potatoes and rye. The Blue Ridge extends along the entire north-west border of the county, throwing out long spurs, some of which nearly attain the height of the parent Ridge, whose highest point in the county is 3,860 feet above sea-level. Other points reach 3,600 and 3,400 feet. Average elevation of the Blue Ridge, about 3,000 feet. Its top and more elevated slopes furnish excellent grazing when cleared, where cattle thrive well, owing to lower temperature and freedom from annoyance from insects.

"The lower parts of the mountains and the numerous and beautiful valleys and glens are eminently adapted to the growth of grapes, apples and other fruits, where the elevation exceeds 500 feet above sea and does not exceed 1,500 feet, for in this range of elevation are places where dew and frost are not often seen, and late frost rarely ever injures fruit. No section of Virginia is better adapted to the growth of pippins and other valuable apples.

"The value of lands along the eastern slope of the Blue Ridge, not exceeding 1,500 feet elevation, for fruit-raising, does not seem to be properly appreciated when we consider that from absence of late frosts in many places there is almost uniform success with proper attention.

"Upon the rivers and creeks in the county are numerous bodies of very rich lands; the largest of these is on the Robertson river, near Madison Court House, where there are about 1,400 acres in one bottom, mostly very fertile—evidently once the bottom of a lake.

MINERALS.

"A large vein of impure graphite crosses the eastern part of the county from the late George W. Clark's farm to the Bon farm on the Rapidan, north-west of Liberty Mills. It makes an excellent fire-proof paint, and very durable crucibles; a vein of yellow ochre accompanies it. Near it runs a large ledge of coarse steatite, which makes hearths and fire-places capable of resisting injury from heat. Occasionally bodies of hematite iron ore are developed along the line of these minerals. North of this, gneissoid sandstone furnishes excellent building stone.

"On the headwaters of the Rapidan and Robertson rivers are large seams of magnetic and specular iron ores.

Sulphurets of copper are found in very small quantities. The seams of red oxide and native copper appear to be large at some points. They are associated with epidote quartz and greenstone. One vein on Stony Man mountain, worked many years ago, has an apparent width of fifteen feet, ores averaging six or seven per cent. of metal. On the Hawksbill mountain a seam which has not been explored can be traced by outcrop of the ledge for over half a mile. These ores (if native copper can be called an ore) are found in several other localities, and, with the Shenandoah Valley Railroad, now built a few miles to the west of the Blue Ridge, furnishing convenient transportation, it is hoped that the capitalists will soon develop these mineral deposits, one of which Silliman, Shepherd and other noted mineralogists have declared to have great value.

"The extreme range of the thermometer during the past twenty-five years is from sixteen degrees below zero in winter up to ninety-seven degrees in the shade in summer. More generally, there is merely sufficient cold weather to furnish ice, and the summers are pleasant, with a bracing air. Malarial diseases are rarely ever seen. All the conditions favorable to longevity prevail.

"The mean temperature of springs taken in June in the south-eastern part of the county is 58½° Fahrenheit, and probably the average of the county would be 57½°—the springs near the mountains being colder. As the temperature of springs about corresponds with the yearly mean temperature, we may safely put the average for the county at 58°, which is the mean for Marseilles, in France, and Madrid, in Spain, and also that of North Carolina."

The Virginia Midland Railroad passes near the eastern border of the county, and the Chesapeake and Ohio near the southern line, and the Shenandoah Valley, as stated, is near the western border of the county.

MADISON COUNTY MINERALS AT NEW ORLEANS EXPOSITION.

From Professor Fontaine.

1. *Mica schist*, from near Madison Court House, in large quantities; a good building stone.
2. *Diorite*, occurs in heavy masses with the next.
3. *Diorite*, from an immense dyke, seemingly 1,000 feet wide, in six miles of Blue Ridge, on Milan Gap road.
4. *Metamorphic diorite*, from ledge two and a half miles west from courthouse, on Milan Gap road.
5. *Variety of syenite*, that occurs with *unakite*, at Milan Gap of Blue Ridge.
6. *Variety of syenite*, that occurs with *unakite*, at Milan Gap of Blue Ridge.
7. *Unakite*, occurs in *syenite*, on top of Blue Ridge at Milan Gap.
8. *Unakite*, same place as above.
9. *Magnetic iron ore*, from F. H.

Hill, C. H., from Virginia Department of Agriculture.

NELSON COUNTY

is quite a compact county, lying between the Blue Ridge and James river, and Albemarle and Amherst counties. It is generally hilly and broken, especially in the border next to the Blue Ridge. On the opposite border the lands are undulating, and on James river and the other streams they are alluvial and very rich. Its area is 301,694 acres, valued at $2,057,714; of this 47 per cent. is woodland. The soil is originally good—mostly red loam, or gray, with red clay subsoil. With a good rotation of crops, free use of grasses and sheep husbandry on the most broken parts, it would afford a fine field for profitable industry. The lands are especially adapted to growing apples and pears. Here, too, are found most eligible locations for vineyards.

The county is well watered, having the James washing its whole southern border, besides the Tye, Rockfish and their tributaries. These, with the James, along which are numerous solid masonry dams, formerly used by the old canal company, afford an extraordinary amount of water-power, some of the sites possessing advantages equal to any in the State. Only a few of these are at present utilized.

The minerals of the county are manganese, largely mined at Midway Mills and Warminste (from time to time), rutile, copper (green and blue carbonates), garnet, ochre, kaolin (in immense beds), iron, hematite, specular and magnetic. The Greenway mines have been largely worked, and the ore analyzed 65.14 metallic iron, 0.029 phosphorus. Hematite at "Sleepy Hollow Mines" analyzed 53 per cent. metallic iron. These metallic resources are destined to large developments under more favorable auspices than now exist.

The county is penetrated by the Virginia Midland Railroad running through its whole width, and the Richmond and Alleghany Railroad skirts its entire river border.

Lovingston, a small town near the center, is the county seat. New Market, at the mouth of Tye river is a small village.

This county offers a fine field for new settlers and investment of capital. The Richmond and Alleghany Railroad Company offers special inducements to those who buy and settle along its line.

NELSON COUNTY MINERALS AT THE NEW ORLEANS EXPOSITION.

1. *Manganese*, from Cabell mine, near Warminster, Richmond and Alleghany Railroad.

2. *Limonite*, brown iron ore, from Sleepy Hollow Mine, two miles from Norwood, Richmond and Alleghany Railroad.

3. *Trap-rock*, from dyke, one mile above Norwood.

4. *Mica-schist*, from Combined Lock station, Richmond and Alleghany Railroad.

5. *Quartz and Feldspar*, from same locality as above.

6. *Magnetite*, magnetic and specular iron ore, from mine near Greenway; a steel ore that has been shipped to Pittsburg.

7. *Tufaceous quartz*, from Greenway.

8. *Magnetite*, magnetic and specular iron ore, Mundy's mine, near Allen's creek, Richmond and Alleghany Railroad.

9. *Specular iron ore*, from Wheatland mine, near Riverville, Richmond and Alleghany Railroad.

From Professor Fontaine.

10. *Magnetic iron ore*, from Moore's near Faber station, Virginia Midland Railroad.

11. *Manganese oxide*, from Simpson's mine, Midway Falls.

12. *Hornblende and Garnet*, in quartzose rock near Faber Mills.

13. *Rutile*, occurs in gneiss, often in large masses.

14. *Kaolin*, from Dr. J. H. Shelton, from Virginia Department of Agriculture.

15. *Ochrous clay*, from James Miller.

16. *Copper ore*, green and blue carbonate, etc., from Rawlings & Armentrout, Staunton.

From the Virginia Midland Railway Exhibit.

1. *Iron ore*, from near Faber station.

2. *Kaolin*, from eight miles from Arrington station.

ORANGE COUNTY

was formed in 1734 from Spotsylvania. Its greatest length is 38 miles; the width varies from 5 to 14 miles. Population, 13,993; area, 213,326 acres, valued at $2,283,284.

It is abundantly watered by the Rapidan and North Anna rivers and their tributaries.

The surface in the eastern part is beautifully undulating; the central and western portions have hills and mountains of gentle elevation, covered to their tops with forests of valuable timber, and farms of unsurpassed beauty and productiveness.

The soil is mostly a dark red clay formed from ferruginous and calcareous rocks, and is very fertile; producing large crops of grain and grass, and some tobacco. As a grass-growing and grazing county, this should yield precedence to no other.

The rearing of thoroughbred stock is extensively carried on by careful and intelligent farmers.

The average assessed value of land in this county is $10.70 per acre, but the improved farms command prices several times greater than that.

The railway facilities are excellent, and are furnished by the Chesapeake and Ohio, Virginia Midland, and Orange and Fredericksburg Railroads, which are located in such a manner that all parts of the county are convenient to one or another of them.

Gordonsville, near where this county corners with Louisa and Albemarle, at the junction of the Chesapeake and Ohio and one branch of the Virginia Midland road, is the largest town. Orange, the county seat, is a small town on the Virginia Midland, at the point of junction of the Fredericksburg Narrow-gauge road.

The timber consists of large growths of the various kinds of oak, of hickory, pine, chestnut, poplar and sycamore.

Iron ores, red and brown hematite, and magnetic iron ores are abundant and rich. Limestone, some of it hydraulic, and marble are found at the base of the South-west mountains. Gold-bearing quartz, asbestus and fire-clay are found in Orange.

ORANGE COUNTY MINERALS AT THE NEW ORLEANS EXPOSITION.

From Collection of the Virginia Midland Railway.

1. *Iron ore*, from Madison station, from W. P. Hicks.
2. *Iron ore*, from same locality, from Reid & Wallace.
3. *Terra-cotta clay*, from same locality, from Reid & Wallace.
4. *Yellow ochre*, iron paint, from same locality, from Reid & Wallace.
5. *Iron ore*, from "Falkner" land, one mile from Madison station, from Glass & Co.
6. *Iron ore*, from "Taylor" Mine, near court-house, from Ben Rawlings.

From the Virginia Department of Agriculture.

1. *Red iron ore*, micaceous, from J. C. Harrison, Barboursville.

2. *Red iron ore*, from H. C. Baker.
3. *Brown iron ore*, from Erasmus Taylor.
4. *Slate*, from Erasmus Taylor.

PATRICK COUNTY.

This is the extreme south-eastern county of the Piedmont section. It borders on the North Carolina line, being separated from it by the Dan river. Until very recently it was cut off from the world, having no means of communication, except the ordinary dirt road. Its area is 277,219 acres, assessed at $934,941. The low price is due to the cause above alluded to, and to the fact that 63 per cent. of the land is woodland. Large tracts have never been settled up.

The lands are watered by Smith's river, a large tributary to the Dan, and other streams. A part of this county is hilly or semi-mountainous, but there is a large plateau called "The Meadows of Dan," which is well adapted to grass.

The timber of this county is very abundant, and of fine quality. The county is also famous for the apples, and the abundance of small fruit which grow wild.

The minerals are iron of the finest quality—lead and silver. During the war this iron was worked by the Confederate goverment.

Very recently the Danville and New River Railroad (N. G.) has been completed to Taylorsville, the county seat. This is the only village of note in the county.

This county offers the greatest inducements to settlers on account of cheap lands and probable rapid growth. Large bodies of land can be bought at low figures.

PATRICK COUNTY MINERALS AT THE NEW ORLEANS EXPOSITION.

From Virginia Department of Agriculture.

1. *Hornblende.*
2. *Magnetic iron ore,* from Judge Lybrook.
3. *Copper ore,* low grade.
4. *Steatite.*
5. *Mica.*
6. *Limonite.*

The following were collected by Mr. E. D. Frazer:

7. *Magnetic,* from "Floyd Mine."
8. *Hematite,* from "Morris Mine."
9. *Hematite,* "Nowlin" Mine.
10. *Magnetite,* from Barksdale Furnace property.
11. *Magnetite,* from same locality.
12. *Magnetite,* from "Hairston" Mines.
13. *Magnetite,* from Forley Mines.

RAPPAHANNOCK COUNTY.

This county lies on the Upper Rappahannock river, which divides it from Fauquier county. Its surface is high and hilly, but is fine grazing land. Its area is 170,770 acres, of which 31 per cent. is woodland, assessed at $1,749,607, a high average considering that no railroad or public transportation is found in the county.

It is well watered by the Rappahannock river and its tributaries.

Washington, its county seat, is near the center of the county. Besides this there are Flint Hill, Woodville, Sperryville and Amissville. At the latter place there is a large tannery. Many fine cattle and horses are carried to market from this county.

Efforts have been made to construct a railroad into this county by a branch road from the Virginia Midland at Warrenton or Culpeper, which will doubtless be done before long.

Although off the railroad, this fine county offers great inducements to settlers in its fine lands, salubrious climate and beautiful scenery, and the grazier is practically not far from the great markets of the country.

CHAPTER XXXIV.

THE VALLEY COUNTIES SOUTH OF AUGUSTA.

The economic, as well as the scientific geology of the counties of "the Valley" here treated, present remarkable general similarity in the order of arrangement throughout: but the departures from absolute uniformity are, however, in some localities, quite considerable.

This series of unusually rich agricultural and mineral counties: Botetourt, Roanoke, Montgomery, Pulaski, Wythe, Smyth and Washington, with a small triangular piece of Scott county, extend from north of James river to the Tennessee State line. It is bounded south-east by the archæan and primordial rocks of the Blue Ridge and the more westerly limb of its bifurcation; and on the north-west side are the Upper Silurian and Devonian rocks of the great North mountains, trending generally north-east and south-west, under such names as Gap and Walker's mountains, and for a part of the way the boundary is Clinch mountain, with the same formations.

The main central portion of the Valley is composed of Cambrian and Silurian limestones, calcarious and ferriferous shales, etc., to the decomposition of which, *in situ*, "the Valley" not only owes its great fertility as a grass and grain producing region, but some of its valuable beds of iron ores are thought to be thus derived. Then, this central limestone belt is flanked on the north-west by a not inconsiderable, and sometimes quite valuable, band of the earliest coal rocks, yielding here and there excellent semi-bituminous and semi-anthracite coals, in beds varying between 2½ and 20 feet in thickness— all in "the Valley." The grass that naturally coats the soils, when the timber is removed, is the famous "Kentucky blue-grass" (*poa pratensis*); and when the land gets down somewhat, from over-cultivation, this is often replaced by another species of blue-grass (*poa compressa*), more truly blue in appearance than the more valuable kind first mentioned.

The different sub-divisions of geological formations are found in these counties to read in faulted sections; beginning on the south-east in the later sub-epochs of the archæan age, and pursuing the reading north-west, over a great fault on the northern or north-western side of the Valley, through a down throw of proto-carboniferous rocks, to the Devonian and

Upper Silurian of the great North mountains—in such order and with such modifications as may be shown later on.

Those thrusts of pressure, evidently projected from south-east toward north-west, which were exerted in folding and faulting the earth's surface, throughout this region, so acted upon the Blue Ridge as to elevate that range, not only much higher at one time than it now is, but really overturned, some degrees beyond the perpendicular, much of its stratification; so that we often see the Huronian rocks, which theoretically belong nearer the heart or toward the south slope of the mountain, pressed over with their valuable gold, tin, silver, copper, magnetic and specular iron ores, to the valley side of the mountain. Thus, in the south-east of Botetourt, tin ores may yet be found, as they are now reported to have been discovered on Bent mountain, in Montgomery, and south-west side of Roanoke county. In Montgomery county, on Brush creek, gold has not only been found in that arm of the Blue Ridge, or Pilot mountain, but companies are now preparing to erect works for its reduction from the quartz, to which it has been traced. The gold-bearing rocks must have been there indentified as being of greater thickness and persistency than was at first believed possible. This is also true of the region of Little River, somewhat farther south-west. It would not be surprising to hear of the discovery of tin and gold both, in the southern sides of Pulaski, Wythe, Smith and Washington. These valuable Huronian strata, which also yield much valuable red iron ore, are succeeded, next, northwardly, by the Potsdam or Primordial rocks, which show the first positively ascertained evidences of organic life, in fossil remains of the *Scolithus Linearis* and certain ancient *fucoids*. In these rocks, which extend generally along the northern base of the Blue Ridge, in its straight continuations, are found, besides excellent glass sand, three or more of the most massive, persistent and valuable iron ore deposits ever found in Virginia. The ore is usually a Limonite, often largely mixed with specular ore and oxide of manganese, and found in quite accessible bodies, measuring from 20 feet to 150 feet and more in thickness, between their enclosing walls. From numerous openings on this line of deposits in these counties the ores have been largely mined and converted into iron at various furnaces. From both sides of the anticlinal ridge of Potsdam rocks in Botetourt county, lying between the Norfolk and Western and Shenandoah Valley Railways, a large tonnage is annually removed from the Houston, Munford and other mines, and reduced in the Crozer furnace at Roanoke City.

These vast lines of Potsdam ores make large exhibits on the southern side of Roanoke county; in Montgomery county, on Bent mountain, Pilot mountain, Little river, etc.; in Pulaski county, on Laurel creek, at Radford furnace, Calfee's on New river, and at other places; in Wythe county, on the side of Poplar Camp mountain, on Francis Mill creek, where one deposit is over one hundred feet between walls, and at numerous other places in Iron mountain, besides being found largely developed on both sides of Lick mountain, an anticlinal of Potsdam rocks in the center of the county; in Smyth county, at Alexander, Neitch and Rowland's on spurs of Iron mountain, where it sometimes developes as a red iron ore of high grade, at Grose's and other places in Iron mountain, besides many extensive and valuable deposits in White Rock and Glade mountains in the middle of the county; in Washington county, on spurs of Iron and Holston mountains, in extensive deposits, sometimes accompanied with red hematite.

From numerous openings in all the places mentioned, Prof. A. S. McCreath, chemist, and others have carefully selected and analyzed samples, from which it is inferred that the metallic iron in these Potsdam ores varies from 50 to 56 per cent.; silica, 3 to 10 per cent., and phosphorus, 0.138 and higher.

Dr. Frœhling, chemist, of Richmond, in those of Lick mountain, finds in seven samples an average of met. iron, 52.210; met. manganese, 1.491; phosphorus, 0.216; some phosphorus assays being as low as 0.039;
the highest being 0.508 per cent. Much of the red iron ore found in the Potsdam rocks averages 56 per cent. met. iron and 0.040 phosphorus, particularly that in Smyth county. The manganese ore so far reported as accompanying these iron ore deposits is in veins or deposits of two to eight feet thickness, and much of it is of the standard percentage required by commerce. It has been discovered in every county where Potsdam rocks are found.

This great band of Potsdam or primordial rocks presenting its sometimes folded outcrop generally to view, on the western lower flank of the Blue Ridge, is the great floor or bed rock—the corner-stone, so to speak, of the great palæozoic series. Not far above it, in the order of natural superposition, is that equally valuable band of dolomitic limestones, some ledges of which yield the excellent *cement* of James river, and, farther south-west, the extraordinary deposits of lead and zinc ores, the floor and roof of which are composed of the famous bands of brown iron ores of *the New River-Cripple Creek Basin*, so much sought after for car-wheel purposes. While all the Valley counties may, after exhaustive research, reveal the presence of these zinc and lead ores of No. II, it is not until you reach Roanoke county that any appreciable thickness of them has been so far reported. Here, three miles south of Roanoke city, the analysis of Dr. Gasscoyne, State chemist, reveals not only a high percentage of zinc and lead, in one small sample, but $15 in silver to the ton.

Another sample sent West for assay returned $25 to the ton in silver. Then, again, in Montgomery county, it is found at Langhorne's, above Big Spring and near the north flank of Pilot mountain (Blue Ridge, western limb); also at Calfee's, near Little river. In Pulaski some of the rocks at Pepper's Ferry show it. At Calfee's, four miles below Reed Island creek, and on the opposite of New river, lower down, in a cliff. Then, proceeding south-west, these great measures not only spread out laterally, but thicken vertically, so that when you reach Bertha and Falling Cliff Zinc Mines of Wythe county the deposit is at least 200 feet from floor to roof, and more than 1,800 feet wide—almost wholly a pure zinc ore, existing as a silico-carbonate, from which a metal is made at the smelting works, now in operation at Pulaski station, Norfolk and Western railroad, yielding the following, by the analysis of Dr. P. de P. Ricketts: Metallic zinc, 99.9629; iron, 0.0371; lead, none. Then, again, prominently at the old Wythe Lead and Zinc Mines, on New river, same county, where it exists in beds of 50 feet thickness and over, as blende and galena, below the zone of decomposition. These latter works have been in operation since long before the War of Revolution—probably since about 1756—supplying lead to the heroes of '76, and nine-tenths of that used by the Confederates in the late war. These mines have sold to reducing works, on the seaboard, over 30,000 tons of zinc silicates, carbonates and silico-carbonates of a high order of purity, and now manufacture into shot and pig-lead 1,500 to 2,000 tons of lead annually. Then, again, a few miles farther south-west, same county, near Ivanhoe Furnace and Painter's, the same extensive bands of zinc and lead exist, accompanied on one side with barytes. At other places, pursuing this basin of Cripple creek, south-west, these deposits are exposed in Wythe and Smyth counties—as at James', Wythe, and at Alexander, Neitch & Rowland's, in Smyth county, on Comer's creek, besides Preston's and others; and then becoming less in thickness, seem to disappear from the rocks in Washington county to make their appearance again in Tennessee. Nearly along with this great band of rocks, as at Mock's Mills, in Washington and other places, are deposits of handsome onyx-like travertine marble.

With the vast deposits of lead and zinc, above described, there are much thicker bands of car-wheel iron ores just above and below them, showing their greatest development, in Pulaski and Wythe counties, so far as explored. In Wythe this whole stratification is over 900 feet thick, from floor to roof (ores and limestone occupying separate spaces in the same stratification) and spreads out over two and a half miles in width in the New river-Cripple creek basin, the brown iron ores being accompanied with valuable quantities of magnetic shot ores and red hematites. It is upon this line of inexhaustible ores, extending from below the Clark Bank, in Pulaski through Rich Hill and the intervening beds of Graham and Robinson and others, in Wythe county, to the famous Cregger Bank, on Cripple creek and above that point that the twenty-one furnaces and forges of that region are built, where, it is now said, that by the use of coke as a fuel, iron can be made at $9.50 per ton, it being necessary to use there less than 500 pounds of limestone to the ton of metal produced. Farther Southwest, in Smyth and Washington, these ores also show on South fork of Holston river, losing there in thickness, but changing to red hematites and semi-magnetites of a high order.

As to a close chemical determination of these ores an average of seventeen samples gave Prof. McCreath, metallic iron, 54.514; phosphorus, 0.106; siliceous matter, 7.094 per cent. Other chemists, such as Dr. Drown, Dr. Frœhling, and others, found many averages, some of which may be possibly just within the limits required for Bessemer purposes. In a few instances, as with the assays of McCreath, the ores of Rich Hill and Ivanhoe were found within the Bessemer standard. The Smyth and Washington county red hematites and semi-magnetites of this zone were found by assay to yield 60 per cent. of metallic iron and 0.049 of phosphorus.

Next in order, follow the great body of limestones of the "Valley" insterstratified with sandstones, shales, slates and thin beds of iron ores, the sandstones, shales, etc., rarely ever assuming large dimensions, when compared with the limestones as a whole. This regularity of these bands is sometimes interrupted by the intrusion, from one side or the other, of the Valley's lateral or marginal rocks that belong higher or lower in the geological scale. In Botetourt and Roanoke, in the instances of Purgatory, Mill, Tinker's and Fort Lewis mountains, the great limestones of III are out of sight beneath great cross flexures from the north side of immense bodies of rocks of the upper Silurian, Devonian and proto-carboniferous periods, chiefly sandstones, slates, heavy bands of iron ores of V to VII (R), and beds of coal of a broken character, as that near Tinker's mountain. This is also true, in a measure, of Draper's mountain and the region just north of it, in Pulaski and Wythe counties, where the middle of the Valley is occupied by the rocks of V to VII (R), etc., and the region just north along Peak creek, by proto-carboniferous strata, with really valuable coal veins. While in Wythe and Smyth counties, over definite areas, the great

Valley limestones are, on the contrary, protruded and lost by an upthrow of the great Potsdam floor with its iron and manganese ores, as in the case in Lick mountain in Wythe, and Glade and other mountains in Smyth county.

With these general exceptions, the great Valley limestones are the marked geological features of the "Valley." Occasionally they assume the character of marble; again, they are so impregnated with magnesia as to become a source for the manufacture of hydraulic lime. From numerous samples carefully tested by Professor William B. Rogers, he concluded that beds of magnesian limestones, suitable for making hydraulic lime or cement, exist in Botetourt, Roanoke, Montgomery, Wythe, Smyth and Washington; and subsequent inspection proves their existence in all the Valley counties here treated. For cement purposes, the carbonate of magnesia should be found to exist in the stone as compared to carbonate of lime in a proportion of three to one. For a pure and good limestone, suitable for making a good quality of lime, probably the dark blue limestone, of which there is so much in all these counties, has no superior. It usually contains about 82 to 85 per cent. of carbonate of lime, according to Professor Rogers, and yields 47 per cent. of lime, when properly burnt. There are many ledges of very dark limestone, passing near any of the court-houses, which are situated about the middle of the Valley, which, when polished, have the appearance of black marble of fine texture.

In addition to these uses mentioned, the gray and darker limestone ledges of sufficient thickness, of which there are many, are employed universally in building every description of masonry—houses, foundations, bridges, walls, etc. To all these valuable features must be added the many large and constant springs that flow from the limestone strata—many of them of a thermal character of excellent merit.

Then, as you enter the line of purely Trenton limestones, usually just north-west of the middle of the Valley, there is a persistent ledge of chert in all the counties, which at intervals, presents to view large bodies of a semi-magnetic iron ore of great purity and possible usefulness; at several points in Botetourt, Roanoke (near Red Sulphur Springs), Montgomery, Wythe, Smyth and Washington (at Gallaher & Tilson's), yielding often over 60 per cent. of metallic iron and about 0.038 phosphorus. Along and near to these rocks are valuable and extensive deposits of barytes, found in large bodies in Smyth and other counties.

Beyond this line north-west is a line of No. IV limestones, which yield excellent variegated marbles, and may be found in nearly all the counties where the order of position is not broken by cross flexures.

In this line are large deposits also of brown iron ores; and then as you approach the northern margin of the Valley, a fault occurs, which brings a downthrow of sub-carboniferous rocks against the rocks just described.

In fact, on that side, in all the south-western counties, there is a much wider margin of sub-carboniferous rocks than had hitherto been accredited to the region. In this line of rocks, the coal just north of Catawba creek, in Botetourt, is found; that in Roanoke, on Tinker's creek, and in Brushy, near Roanoke Red Sulphur Springs; in Montgomery county, at Price's mountain on both sides of the anticline, and in Brushy mountain, in deposits over 7 feet thick; in Pulaski, at Tyler's Belle Hampton Mine, at Altoona Mines, in two veins of 21.3 feet thick, and in much of that region in Pulaski, extending from Pulaski station, westwardly along the Norfolk and Western Railroad to the Wythe county line, on both sides of the railroad.

In Wythe county this coal exists in Little Brushy mountain, its entire length in the county, as at Stony Fork and other places, and comes up near Clark's Summit and Max Meadows in a repetition of the strata in valuable deposits. In Smyth county it is also observed on the north margin of both the great Valley and Holston Valley, north of the gypsum beds. Overlying the coal beds, geologically, is a band of gray and red shales and sandstones separated from ths coal by valuable deposits of iron ore, and over the red shales are limestones of some thickness, in which are very extensive deposits of iron ores. The sandstones of this belt yield a ledge or two, excellent for building purposes; being also soft in quarry re easily mined, while just under the coal is a band of excellent fire-proof sandstones, proven good, also, in use, as grindstone grit.

Along this general line (about the fault) are some of the great mineral springs of these counties such as, Botetourt Springs, Roanoke Red Sulphur Springs, Montgomery Yellow and White Sulphur Springs, Chilhowie Springs of Smyth, Washington Springs near Glade Spring, and the Seven Springs of Washington county, from which is made the valuable Seven Spring iron and alum mass; Mangel's Springs of Washington, and Holston Springs of Scott county; while Alleghany Springs of Montgomery county are situated south of the great lead and zinc zone, and Dagger's Springs of Botetourt are in a line far to the north.

Then, the last to be mentioned, but far from the least of the Valley's features, are the gypsum and salt of the north fork of Holston river, in Smyth and Washington counties. They lie along the north side of the great fault that marks the line of that fork of Holston river, and are really a part of the sub-carboniferous system of rocks.

This massive deposit of gypsum,

more than 600 feet thick at Stuart and Buchanan's Cove, in Smyth county, shows conspicuously; also, at the Pearson Beds and at Saltville, in Smyth county, and at Buena Vista, in Washington county. Many explorations and long continued examinations lead to the belief, at last, that these vast gypsum deposits, showing for about twenty miles length, really compose two or more regular strata of the sub-carboniferous rocks, and have a width, exposed and concealed, of one mile or more from the fault northward. It has been mined to a depth of about 180 feet at Saltville and Buena Vista; and its general composition, by analysis, is as follows: Lime, 32.50; sulphuric acid, 46.50, and water, 20.50, showing traces of magnesia, alumina and iron.

The salt rock at Saltville, possibly two hundred feet thick by an unknown length, may have a different origin from that of the gypsum—possibly may be due to deposition in a secure basin, from brines flowing constantly from the salt-bearing groups of rocks known to be in the sub-carboniferous series. The brines are of an unusual degree of purity; have been drawn upon for many years by the salt works of Saltville, making over 500,000 bushels of salt annually, without any appreciable diminution of either strength or quantity. Railway communication is now by means of the Norfolk and Western Railway —the upper or Buchanan and Pearson plaster deposits having no railway communication. Altogether, "the Valley" presents no more wonderful feature! With unlimited basins of gypsum and salt, inexhaustible deposits of iron, lead, zinc and coal, inconceivably vast ledges of limestone, whose unequal solubility here and there have resulted in caves of marvelous beauty; thermal and medicinal springs of high therapeutical and curative value; an atmosphere of wonderful purity and power of invigoration, and a soil of great fertility, it may well be anticipated that "*The Valley*," besides becoming the home of extensive and varied industries, will be a sanitarium more numerously attended in the future, and is now a granary of unlimited natural capacity.

Before dismissing "the Valley Division," it may be well to call attention to its great capacity as a fruit producer. Its orchards and gardens show that all fruits common to this latitude not only flourish well, but yield largely, with less average failures than is common in many other localities.

BOTETOURT COUNTY.

was formed in 1770 from Augusta. It is forty-four miles long, and about eighteen miles wide, and contains 372,627 acres, valued at $2,308,702. Population, 14,809.

This is one of the finest counties of the James River Valley, and is noted for its fine grass lands and fat cattle. The surface is rolling, and parts of the county are mountainous. The soil is fertile, being formed from limestone rocks.

The productions are tobacco, wheat, corn, oats and cattle, forming a large aggregate of value. This is a fine fruit county, extensive areas being devoted to fruit growing, and much fruit annually canned and evaporated. There are several large canning establishments in the county. James river flows through its central parts, and, together with its tributaries, give abundant water-power.

It is traversed by the Richmond and Alleghany Railroad following the banks of the James, a distance of forty miles from east to west, and by the Shenandoah Valley Railroad from north-east to south-west; and the Norfolk and Western Railroad crosses the south-east corner. These roads give convenient access to market from all parts of the county, and have been the means of developing some of the finest iron ore deposits in the State, immense in extent, indeed practically inexhaustible. Five miles below Clifton Forge depot, near the railroad, and in a very accessible situation, is a surface deposit of brown hematite ore, forming a solid mass 300 feet long, 60 feet wide, and 25 feet high. This ore yields by analysis 55 per cent. of superior iron. Limestone in the same region is abundant and of excellent quality. "The Arcadia Iron Works employ 125 hands; they use specular ore, yielding 60 to 65 per cent. metallic iron."—*Fincastle Herald.* "The operations of this company have fully proven the existence of four or more continuous beds of specular iron ore (red hematite), averaging three feet in thickness, that outcrop in north-east and south-west lines in the western or primordial Blue Ridge for nine miles, from near Buchanan to the north-east, in a three-mile-wide-belt of mountain chain, parallel with and adjacent to James river. Many thousand tons of this ore, proven by analysis and furnace tests to be of good quality, have been mined from the mountain sides, adits, and open cuts. Vast quantities of this specular ore can here be cheaply mined, while from the western side of the same belt, almost on the banks of the James in its eastern bends, brown hematite ore (limonite) can be had in abundance from the broad band of that ore that here, as elsewhere, accompanies and caps the Potsdam. I have never before seen such a development of specular ores in Virginia, and am satisfied that the inducements offered by their abundance and consequent cheapness in the immediate vicinity of four or five other varieties of ores, that are also abundant, and at a moderate distance from the best coking coals of the great Ohio basin, must go far towards making Botetourt one of the great iron-producing centres of the country. * * * No region can furnish more cheaply than this any or all the varieties of limestone needed for fluxing in blast furnaces; some of these contain 98.30 per cent. of carbonate of lime, others abound in alumina. Marbles of various kinds abound among these lower silurian rocks."— *The Virginias.*

A fine grained gray marble, solid and massive, is found near Buchanan iin a bed fifty yards wide. The Brown hematite (limonite) iron ores have not only a remarkable development in Botetourt county, but they are so disposed in thick, continuous beds, and extended outcrops, that they can be cheaply mined on a large scale. These ores are found in nearly all the mountains of the county. Specular ore has been discovered near Buchanan, one vein fifteen feet feet thick and analyzing 65 per cent. pure metal. In summing up an account of his exploration of the ores belonging to the Arcadia Iron Mining Company, in this county, Professor J. L. Campbell gives the following as his opinion of the *quality, quantity* and *accessibility* of these ores: "As to *quality*, the chemical analyses and furnace-tests speak most favorably. As to *quantity*, * * * ten generations cannot exhaust the supply. As to *accessibility*, the beds are very favorably situated for mining, either by open cuts or tunnels. The numerous ravines that cut across the strata give natural openings at which to begin mining operations, and as these ravines all descend towards the river, all the ore can be transported by a down grade to the point of shipment and use. The Arcadia Iron Works were sold January 6, 1880, to a Pennsylvania company for $125,000. The Salisbury Manufacturing Company has recently put its furnace in operation on the Richmond and Alleghany Railroad. The Roaring Run Furnace property, about 10,000 acres of iron land, on the Richmond and Alleghany Railroad, promises to be one of the leading iron-producing properties in the State. They are raising a large quantity of ore, and expect to erect charcoal furnaces for the manufacture of charcoal iron of high grade."

Botetourt had on exhibition at the New Orleans Exposition the following samples of minerals:

1. *Manganese*, from H. C. Snyder's land, three miles from Buchanan.

2. *Red-shale iron ore*, from Clinton, No. V, beds in Purgatory mountain, three-quarters of a mile from Buchanan station, Richmond and Alleghany Railroad. This specimen is from a pile of 300 tons, now mined and stocked at one point on an extensive outcrop that has been uncovered at six places, and shows a regular thickness of from 18 to 28 feet.

3. *Manganiferous iron ore*, from same locality as preceding.

4. *Red specular iron ore*, from Arcadia Furnace property, 4 miles east of Buchanan, from Potsdam, No. 1, beds.

5. *Manganese*, from Houston Iron Mine, near Houston station, Shenandoah Valley Railroad; used for Spie-

gel at Cambria Works, Johnstown, Pennsylvania.

6. *Marble*, from Silurio-Cambrian beds, No. II, from Thomas', on Catawba creek, 3 miles east from Roanoke Red Sulphur Springs.

7. *Calcite*, from line of Shenandoah Valley Railroad, 2 miles east from Buchanan.

8. *Pyrite*, from Lunsford's, near Bonsack station, Norfolk and Western Railroad.

21. *Cellular brown hematite iron ore*, from No. III, Hudson River (?) shales, from the thick, regularly stratified beds of Old Catawba Furnace mines.

22. *Massive brown hematite iron ore*, from same mines as above.

23. *Light gray limestone*, No. II, from quarry on Shenandoah Valley Railroad, below Buchanan; used for flux at Crozer Furnace.

24. *Blue limestone*, No. II, from near Blue Ridge Springs, Norfolk and Western Railroad; used for flux at Crozer Furnace.

25. *Limonite*, brown iron ore, from Houston mines, near Houston station, Shenandoah Valley Railroad.

26. *Limonite*, brown iron ore, from Upland Mine of Crozer Steel and Iron Company, near Blue Ridge Springs, Norfolk and Western Railroad.

27. *Marble*, from G. Gray.

28. *Red iron ore*, from G. Gray.

29. *Pyrites*, from G. Gray.

30. *Limestone*, from quarry of Indian Rock Lime Works, Edward Dillon, proprietor.

31. *Unslaked lime*, from above.

32. *Slaked lime*, from above.

33. *Limonite iron ore*, from Purgatory Mountain Mine, near Saltpetre Cave station, Richmond and Alleghany Railroad.

34. *Pig iron*, No. I grade, charcoal, from Salisbury Furnace, near Salisbury station, Richmond and Alleghany Railroad.

35. *Limonite iron ore*, from Rocky Gully ore bed, Purgatory mountain.

36. *Limonite*, brown iron ore, from near Eagle Rock station, Richmond and Alleghany Railroad. Analysis by Dr. A. Koenig of run of mine gives 47 per cent. metallic iron, low silica, and only trace of manganese.

37. *Manganiferous iron ore*, same locality as above.

38. *Limestone*, containing 97.5 per cent. carbonate lime; abounds at same locality.

39. *Limestone*, samples from Lower Helderberg, No. VI, Price's Bluff, Richmond and Alleghany Railroad.

40. *Limonite iron ore*, from Oriskany, No. VII, Mines of Wilton Furnace, east slope of Rich-patch mountain.

The following is taken from the list of Roanoke county minerals, as they plainly belong to Botetourt:

16. *Iron ores, Limestone and pig irons*, from Crozer Furnace, Roanoke City; from Mr. Samuel Crozer, President, and Col. D. F. Houston, superintendent, viz.:

1. *Limestone*, from Buchanan, Botetourt county, on line of Shenandoah Valley Railroad.

2. *Limestone*, from near Blue Ridge station, Botetourt county, Norfolk and Western Railroad.

3. *Limonite iron ore*, from Houston Mines, near Houston station, Shenandoah Valley Railroad, Botetourt county.

4. *Limonite ore*, from Upland Mines, near Blue Ridge station, Botetourt county.

FREDERICK COUNTY

was formed in 1738 from Orange. It is twenty-five miles long and about eighteen miles wide. It is the northernmost county of Virginia since the partition of the State, and one of the finest of the famed Valley of Virginia, and is noted both for its fine lands and good farming.

The surface is undulating, and the soil very productive. The eastern portion has a belt of gray slate land from two to six miles wide, and running the entire length of the county on the line of Clarke.

This soil produces fine crops of grain and grass.

The timber here is pine, oak, hickory and ash.

The limestone belt, which is four to eight miles wide, is one of the finest and most productive sections in the State.

West of this valley is the "Little North mountain"; between it and the "Big North mountain" is a valley about six miles wide of limestone land. In this valley are some valuable lands and fine farms.

The timber in the limestone belt consists of finely grown trees of oak, hickory, walnut, ash, locust and elm.

Travertine marl exists in the limestone valleys.

In the North mountain are extensive deposits of iron ore of good quality, which has been successfully worked with several furnaces. Coal of anthracite character is also found.

West of North mountain the land is generally a gray slate formation, which produces well.

Rock Enon Springs, on the west of North mountain, and Jordan White Sulphur Springs, five miles from Winchester, have an extended reputation for the cure of diseases, and are liberally patronized. The water of the Jordan Springs is very much like that of Greenbrier White Sulphur, and it is used in the same class of diseases.

The chief productions of this county are wheat, corn, rye, buckwheat, oats and the grasses. Fruits succeed well, the apple particularly.

Winchester is the largest town, and has a population of 4,958 (in 1880). There are several smaller towns, beautifully located on the banks of the valley streams which flow from the adjacent hills and mountains.

Population, 17,654 (including Winchester).

Number of acres of land, 268,950; assessed at $3,454,408.

In this county are some of the best lands of the Shenandoah Valley. Soil, climate and air combine to make this one of the richest and healthiest regions in the world, and it abounds in clear streams of running water. Within the county of Frederick, and at an average distance of eight miles from Winchester, are thirty-seven flour mills, the largest of which is the Baker steam mill, which has a capacity of 175 barrels of flour per day. There are seven woolen mills, eight tanneries, one steam paper-mill, one bone dust and fertilizer factory, one sumac and bark mill, two iron foundries, a shoe factory, six glove factories—"the largest of which works from two hundred to three hundred hands"; ten cigar factories, working from five to forty hands each; three box factories, three carriage factories, one wheat-fan factory, several cabinet factories, one agricultural implement factory, several saw and planing-mills, and quite a number of minor operations of various kinds." "The county has no public debt, and its parish farm is about self-supporting." "It has two banks —the Shenandoah Valley National, capital $100,000; surplus $60,000; and the Union (State), capital $50,000." There are three excellent female seminaries—Episcopal, Methodist and Presbyterian—and one male academy, located in Winchester, and a flourishing Normal school in Middletown. The new public school building in Winchester is an ornament and credit to the city. The National and Stonewall cemeteries are within the corporate limits of Winchester. Three weekly newspapers and one monthly literary paper are published within the county.

The Valley branch of the Baltimore and Ohio Railroad runs through the county, and is a great through route for travel and traffic from the east and north-east to the south and south-west. The Washington and Ohio Railroad, when extended, will cross this county via Winchester from east to west.

ROCKINGHAM COUNTY

was formed from Augusta in 1778, and has an area rather greater than that of the parent county. It contains 1,079 square miles, or 690,051 acres, so that it is the largest county in the State, and is second among the Valley counties in population, having 29,567 inhabitants. Although there is much waste mountain land in Rockingham, the average assessed value of the whole is over $10 per acre, or a total of $6,947,308.

Every part of this county is watered by the Shenandoah and its numerous tributaries, and there is a large extent of rich meadow land.

Rockingham is one of the largest grain producing counties in the State, and exports large quantities of flour, which has a high reputation in the Eastern markets. All the cereals thrive here, not only those cultivated generally, but buckwheat and barley.

And this is peculiarly a grass and cattle region, and a county of fine horses. Great numbers of choice cattle and horses are shipped from Rockingham to the Northern States.

The mineral wealth of this county is considerable—iron, copper, lead and coal. Limestone is everywhere. Several varieties of marble are found here.

There are mineral waters of great virtue in Rockingham, the most resorted to being the celebrated "Rawley Springs," eleven miles from Harrisonburg.

Two great lines of railroad pass through this county—the Valley branch of the Baltimore and Ohio and the "Shenandoah Valley" road. These give excellent facilities for marketing the rich products—agricultural and mineral—of the county, and will rapidly attract immigration to this beautiful Valley.

There is also a narrow-gauge railroad from Harrisonburg to Elkton, connecting the two main lines, and facilitating communication between the different parts of the county.

Harrisonburg, the county seat, on the Valley branch of the Baltimore and Ohio, is a growing town of near four thousand inhabitants—the centre of trade of this rich county.

ROCKINGHAM COUNTY MINERALS AT THE NEW ORLEANS EXPOSITION.

From Professor Fontaine.

1. *Diorite*, occurs in an eruptive dyke 200 feet wide near top of Blue Ridge.
2. *Epidotic jasper*, from ledge eight feet wide, in Chlorite-Schist, at Swift Run Gap.
3. *Syenite*, occurs in immense quantities in the Blue Ridge on Swift Run Gap road.

The following from the United States Assistant Commissioner Major Jed. Hotchkiss:

4. *Case of chalybeate water*, from Rawley Springs.
5. *Galena* (lead sulphuret), from Dan'l Showalter's farm, near Chrisman Post-office.

The following were contributed by Mr. C. D. Harnsberger, from western base of the Blue Ridge:

6. Two samples *iron ore, limonite*, from the Potsdam No. 1, from the Miller bank of the Mt. Vernon Iron property, near Weyer's Cave station, Shenandoah Valley Railroad.
7. *Limonite, iron. ore*, from "Raines'" ore bank of Abbott Iron Company, three miles North-east from Port Republic Station, Shenandoah Valley Railroad.
8. *Iron ore, limonite*, from "Weaver" bank, near 120-mile post of Shenandoah Valley Railroad, Abbott Iron Company.
9. *Iron ore, limonite*, from "Sipe" bank of Abbott Iron Company, near same point.
10. *Ochre, Hamilton's paint*, from near Keezletown, from Virginia Department Agriculture.
11. *Kaolin*, from Mrs. J. J. Wood's, from Virginia Department Agriculture.
12. *Trap rock*, locally called

"*Ironstone*," from a dyke 40 to 50 feet wide, near the Augusta line, two miles south-west from Port Republic, near Leroy village.

This particular block of trap, two and a half feet long, two feet wide, and two feet high, is an historic one, as it is the block that was used as an "anvil block," for a tilt-hammer in the blacksmith shop of Selah Holbrook, at Port Republic; and on the anvil that was morticed into this block Selah Holbrook and his son, J. H. Holbrook, in 1843, made the sickles for Cyrus McCormick, that were used in the first McCormick reaper or harvester. Loaned by C. D. Harnsberger, the owner of it, Port Republic, Virginia.

SMYTH COUNTY

was formed in 1831 from Washington and Wythe. It is in the form of a parallelogram with two of its sides about thirty miles in length, and contains 327,394 acres of land, assessed for taxes at $1,662,424. Population, 12,160.

It has on the north Clinch mountain, Poor Valley mountain, Walker's mountain and Brush mountain, while Iron mountain forms its south-eastern boundary. These ranges have courses parallel with each other north-east to south-west, and are separated by valleys of fine farming and grazing lands.

The productions are tobacco, corn, wheat, oats, rye, buckwheat, grass and fat cattle. Tobacco culture in this and adjoining counties has been rapidly developed in the last few years. Bright tobacco of the finest quality is now grown in this region, and the planter has learned to handle it so as to get the top market prices. The mountain lands produce spontaneously the finest blue-grass, and so it follows that this is an admirable stock country.

Timber is abundant and of the valuable kinds common to this section of the State.

The climate is a delightful one in the summer, and is very healthy.

There is no town of importance except Marion, the county seat, which is a beautiful and busy town on the line of the Norfolk and Western road. The Norfolk and Western Railroad crosses this county about the center, and has Marion, the county seat, as one of its stations.

Smyth is drained by the three forks of the Holston river, giving it abundant water-power for all kinds of manufacturing purposes.

The minerals of this county include iron ore, lead ore, copper ore, gypsum, salt and marble. The minerals are in great abundance and some of them are being extensively developed.

SMYTH COUNTY MINERALS AT THE NEW ORLEANS EXPOSITION.

1. *Red iron ore*, from six-foot bed many miles long, head of Coma creek, on Smyth and Grayson line; from Capt. C. R. Boyd.

2. *Marble*, from Hezekiah Harman's land; from Capt. C. R. Boyd.

The following were collected by Mr. James H. Gilmore, of Marion:

3. *Iron ore*, from the lands of Thomas E. Gardiner.

4. *Iron ore*, from the lands of M. B. Tate.

5. *Iron ore*, from the lands of John M. Preston.

6. *Barytes*, two samples from the land of G. C. Goodell.

7. *Soapstone*, from the land of A. G. Pendleton.

8. *Gypsum*, plaster, from the land of J. H. Buchanan.

9. *Brown hematite iron ore*, occurs in large amounts west of Marion; from Prof. Fontaine.

WYTHE COUNTY

was formed in 1790 from Montgomery. Contains 363,404 acres, valued at $2,647,747. Population, 14,314.

This county is an elevated mountain region, with three fertile valleys between the mountain ranges, which traverse it mainly from north-east to south-west. The soil in these valleys is very productive, and gives abundant returns in large crops of grain, hay, and fine pasturage for cattle.

The mountains are rugged and broken, but they are filled with abundant stores of mineral wealth; and are clothed with finely grown trees of various kinds—oak, hickory, chestnut, ash, pine, lynn, maple and walnut.

Wythe is drained by New river and many of its tributaries which arise among lofty mountains, and, being fed by bold and constant springs, have abundant fall and volume during the driest seasons, affording vast amounts of water-power for mills and factories.

The Norfolk and Western Railroad runs through the centre of this county, and has a branch road leading from Martin's station in Pulaski, into the great mining region in the south-east part of Wythe.

The minerals found in this county are immense in amount and value, and comprise iron ores, zinc ores, lead ores, manganese, barytes, asbestos, coal, marble, soapstone, gypsum, and kaolin. These minerals have been developed and proven to exist in immense deposits, and are now being largely worked. There are in operation many blast furnaces, forges, smelting works, and rolling mills.

Wytheville, the chief town and county seat of Wythe, is a beautiful and flourishing place, possessing many attractions and solid advantages. Its healthful and bracing climate has caused it to become a great place of summer resort for southerners and lowlanders—and it is the central town of a great mineral region, and a fine pastural and farming country as well. Population, 3,000.

WYTHE COUNTY MINERALS AT THE NEW ORLEANS OXPOSITION.

From Captain F. J. Capman.

1. *Limonite, brown iron ore*, from Walton Furnace.

2. *Limonite*, from Van Liew Furnace Mine.

3. *Limonite*, from Graham Furnace Mine.

4. *Limonite*, from Frank Smith Mine, near Boom Furnace.

5. *Limonite*, from Boom Furnace Mine.

6. *Limonite*, from Pierce Furnace Mine.

The following from Capt. C. R. Boyd:

7. *A series of lead*, zinc, iron and barytes ores, illustrating Boyd's sections at Wythe Lead and Zinc Mines, and at Ivanhoe Furnace of Hendricks Bros.

8. *Zinc ores*, from Falling Cliff Mine of D. S. Forney & Co.

9. *Brown iron ores and turgite*, from Irondale, Slaughter, Dunn & Co., Ravenscliff and Speedwell deposits, Cripple Creek basin, from beds 20 to 120 feet thick.

10. *Pig metal*, from Ivanhoe Furnace of Hendricks Bros.; stands breaking strain of 41,000 pounds.

11. *Copper pyrites*, from southern spurs of Lick mountain, containing 30 per cent. copper.

12. *Potsdam sandstone*, from Scolithus bed, Lick mountain, near Wytheville.

13. *Brown oxide of iron and manganese oxide*, from 20-foot bed of W. A. Stuart's 15,000-acre tract, Lick mountain.

14. *Red iron ore*, semi-magnetic, from 9-foot bed of Frank Blair, near Wytheville.

15. *Brown iron ore*, from Robert Crockett's lands, southern spur of Little Walker mountain, in No. X; ore contains 50 per cent. metallic iron, and 0.80 of phosphorus.

16. *Kidney, or hollow iron ore*, black band, from outcrop 18 inches thick, in No. X, from Stony Fork.

17. *Bituminous coal of No. X*, from Stony Fork.

18. *Coke*, made from the above coal.

19. *Red and brown iron ores*, from black slates of No. VIII, from southern foot of Big Walker mountain.

20. *Clay iron ore*, from base of black slates of No. VIII.

21. *Flint*, from upper Helderberg, showing zinc blende, from south foot of Big Walker mountain.

22. *Brown oxide of iron*, from 18 feet of No. VIII, Oriskany, south slope of Big Walker mountain.

23. *Brown iron ore*, from No. VII, Oriskany, from lands of Boyd, Stearns & Co., Walker mountain.

24. *Brown shale iron ores*, of No. V, from same locality as above.

25. *Red shale iron ores*, of No. V, from same locality as above.

26. *Fossils, spirifers, etc.*, from No. IX, from Crockett Cove, Little Walker mountain.

27. *Fossil coal plants*, from protocarboniferous rocks, No. X, Stony Fork.

28. *Variegated marble*, from lands of Umbarger and others, near Wytheville.

29. *Limestone*.

30. *Limestone*, No. II.

31. *Calcium fluoride*, fluor spar, from Red creek, three miles west from Wytheville.

32. *Mineral water*, from Wytheville.

33. *Grindstone rock*, from base of No. X, Stony Fork of Reed creek.

34. *Whetstone rock*, from No. IX, Old Red Sandstone Series, from Stony Fork.

35. *Fine hone grit*, from lands of Boyd, Stearns and others, south slope of Big Walker mountain; said to be equal in quality to the Scotch.

36. *Manganese oxide*, from Crawford's.

37. *Sandstone*, with scolithus linearis, from Lick mountain range, largely used for backing and hearthstone in blast furnaces.

38. *Sandstone*, for glass-making, from Lick mountain lands of Stuart and others.

39. *Lead sulphuret*, from lands of Mr. Price, near Ivanhoe Furnace, New river region.

40. *Iron ore*, from lands of Lobdel Car-wheel Company, from northern outcrop of Cripple creek.

41. *Iron ore*, brown, from Simmerman's, Cripple creek region.

The following are from Old Poplar Camp Furnace, in the gap of Poplar Camp mountain, contributed by A. N. Chaffee, owner of the furnace property:

42. *Iron ore*, from Potsdam shales.

43. *Sandstone*, Potsdam.

44. *Limestone*, formerly used in Poplar Camp Furnace.

45. *Oilstone*, from Little Walker mountain, from Virginia Department of Agriculture.

46. *Ochrous silicate*, from Sayers, New river, mouth of Reed creek, from Virginia Department of Agriculture.

47. *Manganese*, from Guy Run iron lands of E. A. Packer, of New York.

48. *Paints*, from ochres, etc., mined and made by H. Lerner, of Goshen, Virginia, mines on slope of Chambers mountain, near west end of Goshen Pass.

INDEX

This index lists the names of people and places, and includes the entries from the original index.

Abb's Valley, 351 355 356 410-412 448
Abingdon, 10 13 17 290 291 293 294 296 297 298 299 301 319 320 321 370 420 463
ABRAHAM, Nannie 157
ACKERLY, 105
ADAIR, William 346
ADAMS, 147 317
Ae Mountains, 459
Afton, 135 186
Albemarle, 23 410 County 49 58 61 69 79 124 260 433 469 470-472 477 483-485
ALDHIZER, George S 224
ALEXANDER, 246 489 490 Archibald 248 Frank 81 General 53
Alexandria, 129 195 County 258
Alleghany, 31 55 88 137 142 389 455 County 172 251 435 448 451 453 462 Mountain 144 152 420 Mountains 101 183 244 268 290 322 403 447 458 460 Springs 493
ALLEN, 402
Allisonia, 20 370
Altoona, 303
ALWOOD, William B 330
Amelia County, 216
Amherst, County 30 156 251 299 436 472 483 Court House 472 Hills 23
Amissville, 486
ANDERSON, Benton 159 David C 159 Louie 159 M A 124 Mary Stuart 124 Rebecca 287 William E 330

ANDREWS, Mary J 131 W K 131
Angel's Rest, 420 450 Mountain 460
ANKNEY, Matilda A 129
ANTRIM, Florence 135 George 135
Anvil Cliffs, 405
Apalachia, 59 433-435 438 447 450 452
Apalachian Mountains, 59 218 279 293 433 449
Appomattox, 272 294 319 391 401 402 County 74 75 108 363 Court House 133 199
Ararat River, 451
ARMENTROUT, 484
ARMES, 336
ARMISTEAD, W K 463
ARTHUR, Alexander Aladdin 19
ASBERRY, A S 97 134 Alexander S 122 123 Elizabeth 122 Joel 122 123 Willie 123
ASHBY, 149
Ashland, 286 325
ASPINWALL, William H 259
Athens' Tank, 317
ATKINS, 317 Joseph 313 Thomas 313
Atlantic seaboard, 2
Augsburg, 16
Augusta, 9 14 55-58 60 61 69 70 72 73 75 78-86 88 110 140 148 149 150 180 183 189 199 242 251 254 388 406 410 411 487 494 499 County 200 246 247 248 257 262 287 387 391 392 393 400 401 408 413 434 444 452 455

Austinville, 10 16 20 278 370
AVERILL, 27 General 28 29 142
Axton, 478
AYERS, Rufus A 462
Back Creek, 406 451
BAGLEY, Captain 332
BAILEY, James M 346
BAKER, 412 H C 485
Balcony Falls, 56 170 244 245 251 473
BALD EAGLE (Indian), 408
BALDWIN, Briscoe Gerard 83-85 Colonel 86-92 Cornelius 83 General 85 John B 91 John Brown 85 M J 76-78 Mary 83
BALE, Mr 342
Ball Knob, 420
Balsam Mountain, 318 452
BANCROFT, 21
Banister River, 204 210
BARBOUR, 208 James 58 Lillian 217 W D 213 William D 217
Barboursville, 51 485
BARCLAY, 274 A T 171 Alexander T 171 Julia A 274 W H 273
BARNES, Mr 97
Barren Springs, 370
BARRIES, Casper 404
Barterbrook, 200
Bartout County, 135
Bartoute County, 128
Basic City, 14 70 124 165 182 183 184 187 189 190 191 192 242 392 394 399
BASKERVILLE, Blanche B 309 J B 309 John B 309
BATCHELOR, Oliver D 178 179
BATCHELOR RICKS & WINBORNE 178
Batesville, 182 471
Bath, 453 461 Alum Springs 455 County 251 451 455
BATTE, Henry 401 402
Battletown, 343
BAUGHMAN, C C 140 George 139
BAXTER, 164 Joseph 455
Bear, Garden 405 Town 452
BEATTIE, Robert 313
BEAUREGARD, 40 332
Beaver Dam, 324 Creek 296
BEAVERS, James F 136

BECHTEL, Mollie 190
BECKWITH, 353 Harvey 350 357
Bedford, 23 228 231 420 Alum 31 City 156 226-231 325 County 74 112 122 226 228-232 251 364 434 473 476
BEEL, 74
BEELER, Christopher 388
BELL, Ida W 228 O P 228 87 406
Belle Hampton, 303
BENNETT, Miss 53
Bent Mountain, 488
BENTLEY, Dr 307 Mary C 307
BENTON, 406
BERKELEY, Governor 402 William 401
BERRY, 290 Benjamin 343 Brothers 231 Ida W 228 J M 228 Mary A 228 S A 231 Thomas D 227 W W 228
Berryville, 343 343 388 391 394 399
Bessemer, 12 15
Bethel, 471
BETHEL, 147
Betsy Bell Mountain, 60 62
BEVERLEY, 402
BEVERLY, 64 J B 475 J B Jr 475 William 55
Beverly, 300
BIBB, Janette Herndon 127 John Pendleton 127 Kate L 127 Kathleen Cammack 127 Lucy Farrish 123 William Chew 127 William E 124 William T 124
Big, Bone Lick 404 Brushy 450 Creek 18 451 Horse Creek 451 Laurel Creek 318 Lick 93 94 95 96 101 108 109 110 112 113 122 131 158 Lick News 105 North Mountain 498 Sandy River 460 466 467 Spring 490 Springs 112 Stone Gap 12 19 293 376 462 467 Stony 451 Walker Mountain 503 504
BITTLE, David F 140 Dr 157 President 151
BLACK, Alexander 328 Charles 328 Harvey 319 330 Kent 330 331
Black, Mountain 467 Rock 186
BLACK WOLF (Indian), 410 411

Black's Fort, 290
BLACKBURN, 290 Alice V 83
  Frances 174 John W 173 174
BLACKFORD, Benjamin 76 Mrs
  76
Blacksburg, 15 152 177 277 322
  323 328 329 330 331 332 403
  424
Blackstone, 364
Blackwater Creek, 36
BLAINE, James G 260
BLAIR, 90 276 Frank 503
Bland County, 285 285 346 356
  413 417 448 451 456 457
BLANTON, Mildred 214
Blenheim, 271
BLUE JACKET (Indian), 409
Blue Ridge, Mountains 15 24 30
  31 55 56 60 101 137 142 144
  165 166 183 185 187 194 195
  244 249-251 257 268 270 342
  387 393 400-403 409 417 419
  422 425 433 434 436 440 444
  449-452 468 471 473 474 477
  480-483 487 488 489 495 500
  Plateau 371 Springs 497
Bluefield, 17 383
Bluestone, 355 374 431 Junction
  345 River 345 375 448
BOCOCK, Thomas 351
BOGGS, James 159
BOLLING, Daniel 348
BOND, 481
BONHAM, Joseph P 313
Bonsack, 172
BOOKER, Anna 190 Claudine 151
  George 190 J M 53 James M
  151 John 115 Marshall A 190
  Millie 190 Nelia 115
BOOTH, 361
BORDEN, 246
Botetourt, 251 402 409 423 424
  430 451 453 458 473 488 491-
  493 495 497 County 2 15 15 94
  138 248 249 287 300 364 406
  408 410 417 427 435 448 451
  455 459 462 487 494 496 498
  Springs 493
BOTETOURT, Lord 406
Bott Mine, 155
BOTT, 428
BOUQUETTE, Colonel 407

BOWEN, 361
BOWMAN, 402 Alpheus M 149
  150 D C 277 George M 149
  Henry D 277 Laura McD 278
  Lizzie P 278 Mary E 150
  Sallie 149 Virginia F 180
BOWYER, 406 John 248 R P 50
BOYCE, 391
BOYD, C R 457 461 463 501 502
  503 Charles R Jr 285 Charles
  R 283 284 285 Colonel 239
  Cornelia 285 Katie 285 M A
  283 Sallie 285 Thomas J 283
  William 406 457 458 503 504
BOYER, L S 394
BRADDOCK, 408 General 389 404
Bradford, 315
BRADLEY, Philo 265 266
BRAHAM, Julius 181
Bramwell, 362 374 375
BRAND, Alexander Y 337 341
BRANSFORD, T H 127
BRATTON, M M 456
BRAXTON, 70 Allen C 70 71
  Carter 70 Hugh C 70
BRECKENRIDGE, 27 28 406
  General 275 286
BRECKINRIDGE, John C 239
BRENAMAN, J N 242
Bridle Creek, 451
BRIEDLER, W T 338
Briery Branch, 222
BRISCOE, Gerard 83 Mary 83
Bristol, 12 17 102 152 294 295
  297 321 370
Broadford, 320
Broadway, 218 219 220 221 222
  223 224
Brock's Gap, 219 220 221 222
BROCKENBROUGH, I W 273
BROOKE, Angelina 122 Bettie L
  122 S S 105 Samuel S 121 122
BROWN, 208 David L 240
  Elizabeth 287 Granville A 240
  James E 83 John 83 324 R M
  309 Samuel 456
BROWNE, H J 105
Brownsburg, 257
Brownsville, 471
BRUCKNER, General 275
Brunswick County, 174
Brush, Creek 451 488 Mountain

Brush (continued)
  323 501
Brushy Mountain, 313 457 493
BUCHANAN, 272 290 402 406
  Colonel 403 J H 502 John A
  299 Patrick 313 Wilson 313
Buchanan, 15 27 127 249 250 278
  300 321 402 495 496 497 498
  County 356 413 417 423 450
  452 458 459
Buchanan's Cove, 314 494
Buck Marsh, 388
Buckingham, 436 County 433
BUCKLAND, Jacob 348
Buddlefield, 427
Buena Vista, 15 59 80 165-168
  171-181 250 257 296 494
BUERACHER, Samuel 338
Buffalo, Creek 250 Gap 24 Ridge
  24 31 River 24
BUFORD, Colonel 409
Buford's Gap, 474
Bufordsville, 474
Bull Run, 478
Bullskin, 388
BURDEN, 402 Benjamin 246
BURKE, James 403 404 410 R W
  73 Thomas 73
Burke's Garden, 404 405 410 425
  447 448 449 450 452 465
Burkeville, 364
BURWELL, Patty 109 387 390
  391
BUSTER, Elizabeth 212 James S
  212
BUTLER, B F 239
Butte Mountain, 450
BYARS, James W 423
BYRD, Emily 76
BYRNE, Nannie T 198
CABELL, J M 439
CADDALL, John 302
Caesar's Arch, 420
CALFEE, Benjamin 287 Betsy
  287 C H 287 Charles H 287 288
  Charles 287 Elizabeth 287 Ella
  M 311 Evelina 287 Henry 287 J
  A 287 James 287 John 287 302
  L S 311 Margaret 287 R A 287
  Sallie 287 Samuel 302 Sarah J
  288 Sophia 287 William 287
  311

Calfee, 490
CALHOUN, 209
Callaghan Creek, 467
Cambria, 321 322 328
CAMERON, William E 42
CAMMACK, Addison 127 Kate L
  127
Camp, Chase 113 300 Frederick
  405 Union 408
CAMPBELL, 55 290 A J 338
  Andrew W 338 Charles 248
  Isaac 254 J L 496 John M 313
  John T 219 220 Professor 221
  Theodore P 330 W B 338 Walter 341 William 10 315
Campbell County, 24 24 107 230
  363 442
Campbell's Creek Salt Spring, 402
Cape Fear, 99
CAPMAN, F J 502
Capon Springs, 342
Captina, 412
Carnegie City, 419
Caroline County, 49 189 271
CARROLL, J W 54 William S 54
Carroll, 16 345 345 369 419
  County 413 417 418 423 426
  428 431 449 451 452
CARSON, 196 290
CARTER, 391 Colonel 387 Robert
  390
Carter's Mountain, 471
Cassimere Mills, 170
CASTLEMAN, 343 388 391
CASWELL, 361
Catawba, 451 Creek 493 497
  Mountain 137
CATT, Reeves 82 83
Cave, Hill 338 of the Fountains
  57 Spring 109
CECIL, John G 302
Cedar, Bluff 18 18 376 Creek 233-
  235 427 Creek Valley 234
  Grove 250 Run 474
Cedarsville, 199
Cemetery, Hill 137 Ridge 141
Central, 382 City 270 Real Estate
  Agency 266
Ceredo, 334
CHAFFEE, A N 504
Chalybeate Spring, 457
Chambers Mountain, 504

Chana Creek, 463
Chancellorsville, 41 238
CHAPMAN, A A 346 Clementine 156 Emma 156 F J 142 476 Flavius Josephus 155 Flavius Josephus Jr 156 Fred R 156 H H 155 Harry 156 Helen 156 Nannie W 156 Thomas Clay 156 William Watts 156
CHAPPELEAR, Alf 476
Charlemont, 229
Charles City County, 214
Charleston, 33
Charlestown, 274 399
Charlotte County, 115 332
Charlottesville, 26 27 61 62 69 87 120 310 468 470
CHARLTON, William 303 William B 302 303 Wm B 302
Chatham Hill, 315 320
Chesapeake Bay, 183
Chesterfield County, 134 433 438 442
Chestnut Creek, 451
CHEW, 51 127
Chickahominy, 324
CHILDRESS, Sarah E 131
CHILDS, John W 179
Chilhowee, 317
Chilhowie Springs of Smyth, 493
CHISWELL, Colonel 10 John 406
CHRISMAN, 402
CHRISTIAN, 402 Addison A 311 Colonel 321 Cornelia C 332 Edmund 332 Elizabeth 332 J F 73 John E 330 John Edward 332 L H 312 Mary Catherine 312 Mary 332 Minnie 312 William E 185
Christiansburg, 276 277 278 285 321 322 324 325 326 327 328 405 419 425
CHUMBLEY, Joseph H 346
Church Mountain, 220
Churchwood, 304
CLAGETT, 391
CLARK, 232 Clarence H 336 359 360 365-368 395 E W 94 George W 481 Isaac N 231 James A 231 232 Lucy 232
Clark Summit Mine, 155
Clark's Summit, 493

CLARKE, Alexander Trent 214 Carrie V 214 John J 214 Mattie G 214
Clarke, 390 391 393 County 276 276 342 343 387 388 391 392 478
CLAY, Henry 286 325
CLAYTON, 158
CLAYTOR, M 105 M H 136
Clear Fork Valley, 449
CLEMENTS, 147
Cleveland, 18 18 376
CLEVELAND, Grover 150 President 122 273
Clifton Forge, 74 124 170 250 453 Pass 454
Clinch, 410 Mountain 20 292 293 297 298 313 450 463 487 501 Mountains 290 447 River 13 18 19 375 405 448 449 451 462 463 465 466 Valley 17 362 375 376 378
CLINEDIST, Jacob 242 John W 242 T M 242
Clinton, 462 464 467 496 Formation 220
Cloverdale, 15 106 128 428
CLOYD, David 406 Gordon 406 Joseph 346 346 406 Joseph 302 Mrs 406 Thomas 406
Cloyd's, Farm 275 Mountain 406
COE, Frank D 177
Coeburn, 18
COFFEE, Bannister 228 Elizabeth 228 Robert W 228 Sallie 229
Cold Harbor, 27 325
COLE, E E 97
Coles County, 191
College Hill, 35
COLLIER, 467
Coma Creek, 501
Comer's Creek, 490
Connelsville, 65
CONRAD, Ed S 264 George O 264
COOK, A F 300
COOKE, Lola C 82
COON, J W 96 97 111 Sallie C 112
COOPER, Chancellor 42 John 361
COPELAND, Mr 105
COPENHAGER, H P 316

Copper River, 463
CORBET, Edward 147
CORNWALLIS, 62
Cotopaxi, 393
Country east of the Blue Ridge 300
Covington, 32 453
Cow Pasture River, 451 453 455 461
COWAN, 352 406 John T 346 348 351
Cowpens, 253
COX, Henry 285
Coyner's, 31
Crab, Creek 451 Orchard 462 Tree Falls 56 170
Craen's Creek, 451
Craig, 451 City 12 15 County 15 417 423 434 448 451 458 Valley 15
CRAIG, 290 William E 78 79
Craig's Creek, 13 459
Craigsville, 60 221
CRAWFORD, 504 Julia A 274
CRAYON, Porte 57
Cremora, 14
CRESAP, Colonel 412 Michael 408
Crewe, 364 383
Crimora, 60 186 393 443 444
Cripple, Creek 16 49 268 269 318 361 368-371 378 426 429 430 442 451 490 491 504 Creek basin 503 Creek-New river basin 16
CRITTENDEN, 406
CROCKER, Mattie G 214
CROCKETT, Captain 289 Ella 275 J G 274 James 302 John 275 John C 275 Robert 503 William Stuart 289
CROOK, 27 29
Crooked Creek, 451
Cross Keys, 58 259
CROW, Joseph T 313 Thomas 313
CROZER, Samuel 497
CROZET, C 284
CRUMP, Captain 275 Eliza 275 Eliza Brooks 275 Ella 275 Robert 275 William 275 Willie Coates 275

CULL, James 403 Mrs 404
CULLOP, Adam 313
Culpeper, 51 132 152 474 475 480 486 County 192 258 474
Cumberland, 219 449 County 127 Gap 12 19 20 403 Mountain 450 Mountains 447 448 459 462 Valley 184 194
CUMMINGS, Charles 290
CUNNINGHAM, W H 116
CUSTER. J E 459
Cyclopean Towers, 57
D'INVILLIER, 361
D'INVILLIERS, 371 426 427
Dagger's Springs, 493
Daggers, 31
Damascus, 13 17 296 297 Gap 297
DAME, Mr 139
Dan River, 203 204 206 401 433 451 485
DANIEL, John W 39 289 Lieutenant 40 Major 41 42 43 William Sr 83
Daniel's Hill, 36
DANVILLE, Mr 105
Danville, 12 20 147 205 206 208 209 230 476
DARIUS, Samuel 325
DAVENPORT, J C 96
DAVIDSON, Andrew 411
DAVIS, B A 227 230 Beverly A 230 E 478 George W 313 George 53 H P 478 J W 136 Jefferson 43 Joseph W 313 Lucy 478 Mary P 230 Mosby 348 President 239 Thomas D 24 290
DEAL, 343
DEAN, D H 348
DECATUR, Stephen 39
Decatur, 131
DEFOARD, 340
DEPEW, Chauncey M 428
DEVER, J H 130
DEYERLE, A J 141 James C 147 M P 141
Dickenson County 18 413 417 418 450 452 459 466
DICKENSON, H M 97
DICKINSON, J 350
DILLARD, Dr 138
DILLON, Edward 497

510

Dinwiddie County, 363 442
DODDRIDGE, Dr 412
Doe Creek, 451
DOOLEY, Mr 105
Doran, 18
DOSH, T W 141
Douglas County, 191
DOUGLAS, John A 346
Douquille, 179
DOWNING, H H 197 Nannie T 198
DOYLE, John 75 Professor 76 Robert L 75 Thomas S 75
Dranesville, 40
DRAPER, George 402 John 404 Mary 404 Mrs 403 Mrs George 404 Mrs John 404
Draper's, Meadows 389 403 404 405 406 Mountain 491
DREHER, J D 141
DROWN, Dr 491
DRYDEN, J Louisa 109
Dryenfurth, 184
Dublin, 304 310 349 349 352 354 421 424 425
DUFF, 402
Duhring, 374
DULANEY, William H 44
Dump's Creek, 463
DUNGAN, Alice M 320 W P 320
Dungannon, 19
DUNLAP, Colonel 472
Dunlap's Creek, 448 451
DUNLOP, Catharine Thomas 174 Henry 174 John T 174
DUNMORE, 408 412 Lord 389 408
DUNN, 503
DUPUY, 132 Nelia 115 William P 115
DYER, 471 Wilbur F 159
Eagle Rock, 15
EARLEY, J W 326
EARLY, General 27 28 29 42 181 J A 41 286 P W 289
EASELEY, George W 348
EASLEY, 208 Henry 212 213 Henry Jr 212 J W 212 213 217 286 James A 44 Jennie C 213 Nannie P 212 Sallie I 213
East, River 451 River Mountain 450
Eastern, Valley 194 Virginia 144 144 184 194 347 365 422

ECCLES, General 286
ECHOLS, John 66
Edgehill, 49
Edinburg, 235 239
Edith Mine, 155
EDMISTON, 290
EDMONDSON, 321
EDMONSON, H A 215 James 302 303
EDMUNDS, J E 44 Paul C 44 Paul Carrington 211 Phoebe Easley 44
EFFINGER, J Fred 70
Eggleston Springs, 347 348
EGGLESTON, William 346
Elba, 476
Eldorado, 324
ELIINIPSICO (Indian), 409
Elizabeth, 372 County 190
Elk, Creek 451 Horn 345 361 375
ELLETT, Andrew 287 Bessie 287 Beverly 287 Guy French 287 Harry 287 Mary 287 Minnie 287 Robert 286 Robert Jr 286 Robert T 286 325 Sadie 287 Susan G 326 Susan V 287 Walter 287 William 287
ELLZEY, Dr 30
EMORY, Rev 295
Emory, 299
ENGLEBY, Clara D 121 Elizabeth 120 Emma 121 Estella G 121 J T 96 97 John 120 Joseph T 120 121 Thomas 120 William S 121
ENGLISH, T B 349 352 354 355
Entry Creek, 451
Estilleville, 464 465
EVANS, 148 208 Edward L 213 John M 142 Lucy A 149 Martha 411 Mildred 214 Tipton B 149
EVARTS, William M 42
EVERETT, 87
EWELL, Gen 181
Faber, 469 Mills 484
FADELAY, 196
Fairfax, 478 County 181 478
FAIRFAX, Lord 287 287 388
Fairfield, 246 254
Falling, Spring 247 Waters 40
Fancy Hill, 247
Farmville, 175 213 214 363 364

FARNSWORTH, 259
Fauquier County 192 197 198 286 442 475 478 486
Fayette, 345
FERGUSON, 113 J M 131 S D 97
FIELD, Colonel 409 John 409
FILLMORE, 58
Fincastle, 15 106 County 2 119 248 291 406 408
FINK, Albert 331
First National Bank of Lynchburg 53
FISHBURNE, Callie 114 Frances 113 J B 96 Samuel 113 T T 96 Tipton T 113
Fishersville, 80
FISK, 259
FITTS, James H 330
FITZGERALD, W G B 147
FLANNAGAN, A H 346
Flat Top, 268 268 345 345 347 348 360 368 369 374 377 378 coal region 101 Mountain 403 450 465 Flat Top (Pocahontas) 438
FLEMING, William 409
FLICKWIR, D W 196 336 399
Flint Hill, 486
FLOURNOY, 158
FLOYD, 321 406 Benjamin Rush 302 303 George R C 302
Floyd, 345 419 423 County 321 327 401 413 417 426 428 431 449 451 452 453 Court House 322
Fluvanna County, 215
FOLGAR, Charles 326
FONTAINE, Professor 472 479 482 484 500 502 William M 470
FOOTE, 271
FORD, William H 52 William H Jr 52
Fork Union, 215
FORNEY, D S 503
Fort, Chiswell 10 Lewis Mountain 491 Necessity 409 Stanwix 409
Fortress Monroe, 239
Foster Falls, 20 370
FOWLER, 348 Elbert 346 347
FOX, Adam 313 Allie V 158 Clarence M 158 Etta 158

FOX (continued)
Horace M 158 Luther A 158
Francis Mill Creek, 489
FRANCIS, Mr 139
FRANKLIN, Brothers 53 Carrie 128 Jacob H 53 M P 128 Mrs 53 Thomas 348
Franklin County, 113 114 128 131 449 476
FRANTZ, M P 142
FRAZER, E D 478 486 Susan L 72 William 72
Frederick, 233 233 342 401 408 County 83 83 157 177 240 271 387 388 391 400 452 498 499
Fredericksburg, 41 116 121 122 134 277 475
FREEDMAN, Mr 105
FRENCH, David 283 G D 287 George D 326 John 10 Mr 260 Pole 345 Susan G 326 Susan V 287 W H 346
Friendship, 297
FROEBEL, 164
FROEHLING, Dr 489 491
Front Royal, 127 127 193 194 195 196 197 198 199 200 201 388 394 399
FRY, A L 348
FUGATE, Randolph 302
FULKERSON, 290 Samuel B 319
FULTON, Jno H 315
FUNKHOUSER, A P 266 267
FURGUSON, Carrie 128 John C 128 S S 128 Sallie Hatcher 128
Gaines' Mill, 66
GALE, Eliza 109 Enoch R 109 Joseph Addington 109 Lottie D 109
Gale Mine, 155
GALE, Sparrell S 109
Galena, 220
GALLAHER, 492
GAMBILL, Benjamin Franklin 130 Bloomfield K 131 Captain 130 J M 122 James M 130 131 Mary J 131 Sarah E 131 Willie T 131
GAMBLE, 113 290
Gap Mountain, 487
Garden, 450 Mountain 458
GARDINER, Thomas E 502

512

GARFIELD, President 122 304
GARNETT, Esther 181
GARRETT, 80
GARRISON, Catharine 200 M L 199 Nancy Littleton 199 Nannie L 200 William G 199
GARST, H 148 J A 148
GASKINS, William E 476
GASSCOYNE, Dr 489
Gate City, 20
GEORGE III (king of England), 137 251 410
Gerandos River, 387
GIBBONEY, Robert 302
GIBBONY, 321 Robert 302 303 Robt 302
GIBBS, General 44
Giles, 283 355 355 419 420 449 456 458 459 County 10 171 286 287 309 321 326 345 346 347 356 403 413 417 423 431 434 448 451 460 461
GILKSON, 81
GILMER, Mrs 103
GILMORE, James H 502 John 248 Thomas W 58
GLADDEN, Washington 142
Glade, Creek 451 Mountain 489 492 Spring 16 17 293 295 297 493 Springs 365 420
Glades, 472
GLASGOW, 172 Mary G 174 Robert 174
Glasgow, 15 257
GLASS, 485
GLASSCOCK, M S 286 William R 286
GLEANER, C H 348
GLENN, J A 208
GLOSSBRENNER, E Victoria 151 Etta 158 J J 151
GOOCH, 80 A 346 Governor 245 246 Mary Stuart 124 William S 123
Goochland County, 189
GOODE, John 459
GOODELL, G C 502
Goodwill, 375
GOODWIN, Willie 271
GORDON, 28 A C 72 Armistead C 69 70 William F 69
Gordonsville, 26 484

Goshen, 80 257 Pass 249 250 251 252 504
Graham, 17 362 362 376 461 491
GRAHAM, Aaron 327 Allie 331 George E 327 James 327 Julius 181 Lucy T 327 Major 49 Nellie 327 Samuel 313 Thomas 348-356 359 368 William Henry 331 332
GRANDY, C T 105
Grant County, 158 159
GRANT, General 26 27 239
Grassy Creek, 451
GRAVELY, 478
GRAY, G 497
Grayson, 16 419 423 County 314 317 318 413 417 418 426 428 449 451 453
Great, Dismal Swamp 363 Kanawha 451 Limestone Valley 417 418 Meadows 409 Valley of Virginia 433 434 450 452
GREATHOUSE, 412 Daniel 408
GREELEY, Horace 136
GREELY, Lt 306
GREEN, 402 Alexander R 214 215 C 288 John J 185 Kate 288 Lizzie R 215 Peyton B 288 Thomas I 214
Green, County 272 Forest 172 174 181
Greenbrier, County 248 455 White Sulphur 498
Greendale, 297
Greene County, 477
Greenfield, 406
Greensborough, 312
GREENSTONE, 54
Greenville, 57 246 254
Greenwood, 471
GREER, Callie L 114 Moses 114
GREGERY, Bettie Thomas 134
GREIDER, B L 134 135 Florence 135
GRIFFIN, Claudine 151 Dr 138 Eugenia Whyte 151 J Hook 151 Judge 151 Wingfield 150
GRIFFITH, Annie 191 F L 191 Mary E 191 R Sumter 191
GRIGG, Cornelia C 332 Wesley 332
GRILLS, Eleanor 410

GRINNAN, A G 480
Grosceloses, 317
Grose, 489
Grottoes of the Shenandoah, 56 337
Guest ,376
Guest's River, 18
GUGGENHEIMER, Max 47 Mr 48
Guilford, 253
GUYER, Charles B 177 J S 177
Gypsy Hill Park, 63
HAAS, Annie H 238
HACKERMAN, E G S 187 S 187
HAILMAN, Elizabeth 199 J L 199
HALE, D F 461 John P 402
Halifax, 202 203 204 205 209 212 216 County 44 202 203 204 205 206 209 211 212 213 214 216 Court House 209 210 213
HALL, 277 391 J T 105 136
Hall Mine, 155
HALLECK, General 26
HAMILTON, Mary E 173
HAMMET, Edward 273 Sue 273
HAMMOND, A B 105
Hampshire County, 158 161
HAMPTON, 406 Joseph 388
Hampton, 190
HANCKEL, 127
HANCOCK, General 239
Hanover County, 286 324 325 406
HANSBROUGH, A H 152 E C 152 George W 152 155 Livingston C 155
HARBISON, William 403
Hardware River, 468
HARMAN, Colonel 349 Hezekiah 502
HARMON, Adam 403 404 405
HARNSBERGER, A E 187 C D 500 501 Frances 174 Rebecca A 200 Robert S 200 Stephen 200
HARPER, 402
HARRIS, Nathaniel 313 W T 163
HARRISON, Charles E 313 Frank 308 J C 485 President 123 R 452 Randolph 29 Thomas 262
Harrison's Landing, 239
Harrisonburg, 75 191 218 223 238 239 262 263 264 265 266 267 500

Harrowgate, 19
HART, 406
HARVEY, J C 456 James A 346 Lewis K 348 Robert 109
HARVEYCUTTER, J W 148
HATCH, 259
HAW, Elizabeth C 325
HAWKINS, Janie 230 N D 227 230
Hawksbill Mountain, 482
Hays Creek, 247 250
Healing Springs, 455
Helderberg, 503
HELM, J W 327
Helton Creek, 451
HENDRICKS, 503
HENKEL, A M 71 S Godfrey 71
Henrico County, 438 442
Henry County, 476 477 478
HENRY, Patrick 62 202 210 247 271 295 315
HETH, Stockton 270
HICKS, W P 485
Highland County, 152 238 451 461
HILB, 80
HILL, A P 121 City 31 E B 475 Esther 181 F H 482 483 R F 181
Hinton, 356
HITE, Abraham 388 Joist 245 402
HIX, Joseph 410
HOCKADAY, Bettie Thomas Gregery 134 J R 133
HOCKMAN, 142 N 147
HOENSHEL, G W 190 191
HOGE, 80 Arista 79 Eliza 271 J H 461 James 271 302 John Blair 271 John 302 Joseph H 346 Moses D 185 271 Peter C 79 William 271
HOGE & HUTCHINSON, 80
HOLBROOK, J H 501 Selah 501
HOLLAND, George W 141 R C 141
HOLLIDAY, 326
HOLMES, 116
Holston, Mountain 290 292 297 489 River 10 17 291-293 295- 297 314 316 370 410 417 449 451 452 456 463 464 491 493 501 Springs 493 Valley 449 493
HOLT, C A 187 John 48
Honaker, 18

Honakers, 376
HOOKER, Fighting Joe 41
HOOPAUGH, George 403 404
HOOPER, Elizabeth C 325 James 325 Joseph 325 Lettie W 325 T W 324
HOPKINS, S J 211
Hopper Mine, 155
Horse Ford, 24
HORTON, 467 Susie Gray 130 William H 130
HOSHOUR, 196
Hot Springs, 455
HOTOPP, Mr 468
HOTCHKISS, 351 352 473 Jed 219 432 433 500 Major 234 474
HOTOPP, Mr 468 William 470
HOUCK, J P 263 264
HOUDON, 256
House Mountains, 251
HOUSTON, 290 D F 497 John 313 Robert 313 Sam 253 Samuel 58 W C 209
HOUTZ, J P 142
HOWARD, Alexander 287 Anderson 287 Evelina 287 Ezekiel 287 Juliet 287 Margaret 287 Rebecca 287 Sophia 287
Howardsville, 469 470
HOWE, Eleanor 271 Joseph H 302 Lord 271 Major 271
HUBBLE, Joel 313
HUFF, James C 138 Lewis 112 Sallie C 112
HUGER, Frank 109
HUGHES, 52 B F 74 Blackburn 175 John W 52 Robert W 346
HULL, D D 308
HUME, Barbara 271
HUNT, Miss 300
HUNTER, David 26 255 General 26 27 28 29 142 William H 180
Hunter's Alum, 460
Hunting Camp Creek, 457
HUNTINGTON, C P 259
Huntington, 33
HUPP, Abraham 138 141
HUTCHINSON, Henry 80 R B 134
HUTTEN, George C 28 Major 29
HUTTON, J L 51
Hyco river, 204
IMBODEN, 27 28 General 425 462

IMBODEN (continued) 464 473 J P 467 John 467
Indian Draft creek, 451
INGALL, M E 185
INGLES, Captain 405 Eleanor 410 Mary 404 Mrs William 404 405 Thomas 402 403 404 410 William 200 270 402 410
Ingles' Ferry, 405
Iron, Belt 136 Gate 12 56 Mountain 16 290 292 296 297 314 419 473 489
IRONDALE, 503
Isle of Wight County, 363
Israel mountain, 470
Ivanhoe, 16 20 370 371 378 491
Ivy, 471
JACKSON, 14 41 393 Colonel 40 General 258 289 Lillian 217 Stonewall 40 57 239 255 256 311 319 324
Jackson, Mine 155 Park 280 River 453 455 461
Jackson's, Ferry 278 River 451
JACOBS, Catharine 200
JAMES, Dr 276 John C 276 Mary A 310 R Bruce 276
James River, 2 10 12 15 24 30 35 56 58 165 194 239 244-246 249-251 257 260 321 402 417 430 436 438 451-453 459 461 468 472 473 483 487 489 495 Valley 424 428 494
James River and Kanawha Canal, 260
JAMES, W W 464
James, 490
Jamestown, 137 244
JAMISON, S W 96
Jefferson County, 390 478
JEFFERSON, 58 Thomas 23 57 62 202 251 410
Jeffersonville, 456
JEFFRESS, John J 348
Jewell Mine, 155
John's Creek, 452 459 (tributary) 451
JOHNSON, 148 406 Alleghany 152 Chapman 84 David E 346 Dr 355 Edward 152 F D 51 J F 325 Lettie W 325 Thomas A 51 William 407

JOHNSTON, A N 346 Albert Sidney 66 General 40 J H 327 Jos E 40
JOLLIFFE, J 229 N 229
JONES, 278 459 A S 181 David 310 Mary A 310 Mr 53 Thomas 310 William E 299
JORDAN, 213 B J 172 C F 171 Charles F 172 173 Charles H 175 Elizabeth 212 George C 81 82 James F 175 M T C 131 132 Mary E 173 Mr 260 Robert 212 Samuel F 172 William J 211
Jordan White Sulphur Springs, 498
JUNKIN, Bettie 324 Colin 324 Frank 324 Garnett 324 George G 324 George 324 Helen 324 Jennie 324 Judith 324 Margaret 324 Mary 324
KAGEY, D F 340
Kanawha, 360 404 408 459 Canal 10 249 250 321 Valley 402
KEAN, Jefferson R 49 L M 49 R G H 49
KEARSLEY, G W T 274 George T 274 Lily Anderson 275
KEEFFE, 179
Keezletown, 500
KEISTER, 328
KELLY, 290
KEMP, Francis B 127
KENDRICK, Elizabeth 311
KENT, 406 David F 302 James McG 112 Maggie 309
Kentucky, County 2 Mountain 450
KER, Mary Catherine 312 Samuel 312 Walter 312
Kerr's Creek, 247 250
KERSHAW, 44
KEYSER, 454
KILLIAN, Jacob 150 Mary E 150
KIMBALL, F J 185 336 Frederick J 395
Kimballton, 461
Kimberling Springs, 456
King William County, 70
King's Meadows, 294
KING, 321
Kings Mountain, 294 315
KIRK, 61

KNAPP, C 475
KOENIG, A 497
KOGER, 478
KOINER, Arthur Z 110 Catherine M 110 Cyrus 110 Fannie 111 Lizzie 111
KOONTZ, George W 238
KYLE, 459 J 324
LAFFERTY, H D 105
Lake Spring 155 420
Lambert's Point, 372 372 373 381
Lancaster County, 390
LANDES, I F 187
LANDRUM, Paul C 299 Theodosia F 299
LANGHORNE, 308 490 J C 147 John A 309 Maggie 309 Maurice D 309
LANSDOWNE, George T 313
LARUE, Isaac 388
LATIMORE, 322
Laurel, 348 Creek 296 296 352 355 356 361 489 Gap 313 River Fork 17
LAWVER, W P 479
LEAS, 147
LEAVER, W C 317
Lee County, 19 375 448 450 452 462 463 466
LEE, 14 FitzHugh 258 260 General 26 27 80 89 108 149 199 301 319 391 Richard Henry 62 Robert E 43 57 133 212 239 255 256 258 Robert E Jr 258 William H F 258
Lee County, 448 463
Leesburg, 479
LEFTWICH, Isaac 280 Isaac J 280 283 Nancy 283
LEGGET, Mr 223
Lehigh Valley district, 430
LEIGH, Judge 210
Lem's Brook, 2335
LENARD, Henry 403 404
LENNIG, Thompson 266
LEON, A A 259
LEPE, Ida 119 James H 119
LERNER, H 504
Leroy Village, 501
LETCHER, Governor 39 88 Honest John 58

LEVY, G B 129 J B 96 97
LEWIS, 343 390 391 Andrew 137
    405 408-410 Charles 408 409
    Edward 390 General 138 409 H
    L D 390 John 55 58 245 246
    402 Merriwether 58 Thomas
    410 Washington 390 William
    138
Lewis Creek, 463
Lexington, 12 14 27 43 57 61 74
    75 81 106 112 121 130 145 156
    165 170 171 176 177 246-248
    250-255 257-259 263 273
Liberty, 27 325 473 474 Mills 481
Lick, Creek 10 18 Mountain 489
    492 503 504
LIGON, 147
LILLY, General 199
Limestone Valley, 55
LINCOLN, 316 A T 320 Abraham
    58 Lucretia E 320 President 88
    239
LINDSAY, James Hubert 192 S C
    192
LINDSEY, James 388 John 388
Linvill's Creek, 218
LITCHFIELD, G V 299
Lithia Spring, 187
LITTLE, J C 475
Little, Brushy Mountain 493
    Horse Creek 451 Mountain 292
    297 North Mountain 220 498
    Reed Island Creek 451 River
    401 451 488 489 490 Stony 451
    Stony Creek 461 Walker Mountain 503 504
Locust Hill Mine, 155
Logan County, 377
LOGAN, 408 409 411 412
LOMAX, General 332
LONG, James 315
Long, Marsh 388 388 390
    (tributary) 451
Longdale, 59 453
LONGSTREET, General 44 181
LOOK, 316 320
LOONEY, Absalom 410
Looney (tributary) 451
LORING, General 258
LORRAINE, 337
LOTTS, E S 185

Loudon County, 181 434 442 478
    479
Louisa, County 123 124 127 189
    433 441 484 Fork 452
LOVE, W B 475
LOVELACE, 208 213
Lovingston, 483
Low Moor, 59 453
Lower Valley, 391
LOWREY, 290
LUCK, George S 112 Maria L 113
Lunenburg, 203 473
LUNSFORD, 497
Luray, 14 337 338 340 341 392
    394 399 Caverns 31 170 337
    339 Valley 337
LUTHER, J M 316 317
LYBROOK, 328 403 Judge 486
LYLE, Mathew 247 Samuel 248
LYNCH, John 23 24
Lynch's Ferry, 24
Lynchburg, 20 23-36 40 44 47 49
    51-54 76 151 152 165 179 180
    206 208 209 214 217 231 250
    317 318 321 324 332 347 351-
    354 363 364 417 418 469 472
    476
Mack Creek, 451
Madison County, 480 482
MADISON, 58 406
Magic City, 101
MAHONE, 198 General 240 William 11 43 346 364
Malvern Hill, 133
Manassas, 40 80 134 235 239 289
Mangel's Springs, 493
MANGES, Daniel 135 Sarah E 135
MAR, Daniel 210
Marion, 16 176 177 308 315-320
    501 502 District 314
Marksville, 394
MARSHALL, G C 340 Judge 210
MARTIN, 147 David T 302 Ella M
    311 Eugenia C 48 Mrs 469 R D
    311
Martin's, 308 Station 311 Tank
    304 305 369
Martins, 382
Martinsville, 100 217 478
Mary Gray Mountain, 60
MASLIN, Thomas 176

MASON, Fannie 52
Mason's Creek, 451
Massanetta Mountains, 262
Massanutten Mountain, 218
Massanutton Mountain, 194 403
MATHEWS, J M 200
MATSON, D H 105
MATTHEWS, Richard T 302 303
Max Meadows, 16 127 275 425 493
MAXWELL, Captain 410
Mayo River, 477
McALLISTER, 454
McBRYDE, John M 330
McCAMANT, Samuel 315 316
McCAUL, P H 211
McCAULEY, William 142
McCAUSLAND, 27 28
McCHANAHAN, 409
McCLAUGHERTY, 461
McCLINTIC, 456
McCLUNG, 246 Agnes 77
McCLURE, 246 J Marshall 177
McCORMICK, 343 343 388 Cyrus 501 Cyrus H 260 Silas 47
McCOY, William 84
McCREADY, Thomas 313
McCREATH, 361 371 392 426-428 A S 489 Andrew S 394 Professor 491
McCUE, J H 72 W T 72
McCULLOUGH, 240 Hugh 260
McDONALD, 343 478 August 408
McDOWELL, 40 58 177 239 246 336 406 Governor 58 James 248 Samuel 248 259 W G 176
McDowell, 461
McGAVOCK, 406 W L 309
McGILL, James 369 370
McILHANY, W M 81
McKAY, 402 J W 51 Mr 52
McKENZIE, Francis 312
McKINNEY, Governor 286 P W 272
McLANE, Governor 312
McLAWS, General 212
McMAHON, Ed 82
McMannaway Mountain, 476
McMONTAGUE, William 326
McNUTT, R B 346
McPHATRIDGE, William 313
McRAE, John H 127

McTAYLOR, John 302
McVITTY, 147
McWANE, Henry E 47 51
MEADE, 474
Meadow View, 297
MEAN, John J 53
Mechum River, 470 471
Melrose, 192
Mendota, 297
Mercer, 347 349 County 348
Messinetto Creek, 387
MICHIE, Dr 471
Middle, Fork 451 Mountain 448 Valley 315
Middleburg, 480
Middlesborough, 12 20
Middleton, 176 191
Middletown, 177 499
Midland, 432-434 440 442 Country 432 433
Milan Gap, 482
Mill, Creek 233 362 374 375 451 456 Creek Junction 345 Mountain 102 106 491
Millboro, 456 Springs 455
MILLER, 321 C A 327 J I 341 Jacob 235 236 James Mason 66 James 484 James T 276 M Erskin 72 M Erskine 66 69 Mary L 276 Sallie 229 Samuel 469 William 388 William G 139
MILLS, G T 430
Millwood, 390
Milnes, 14 59 334 335 392
MILNES, 334
Mine Run, 41
Mineral City, 376 441
Minerals of Virginia, The 432
MINOR, John B 69
MITCHELL, Edward 139 Eliza F 299 John D 299 Louise 231 Mr 50 Robert C 231 Samuel 139 Theodosia F 299 Theodosia 299 William N 49
Mock's Mills, 490
MOFFETT, Samuel H 265 V M 71
Monroe, 453 460 County 70 80
MONROE, 58
MONTAGUE, 215 321 Bettie 324 Elizabeth 326 J Kyle 326 R D 323 324

Monterey, 461
MONTESQUIEU, 32
MONTGOMERY, 290 Captain 405
Montgomery, 345 389 423 460 492
    502 County 2 10 15 110 112
    138 191 273 277 286-288 290
    302 303 311 312 321 326-329
    346 364 403 405-407 417 424
    431 434 439 449 451 460 487
    488 490 493 Springs 326
    White Sulphur Springs 351 353
    420 493 Yellow Sulphur Springs
    493
Monticello, 23 57
MOOMAW, B C 171 179 Benjamin C 172 Benjamin F 128
    Cary A 128 129 Cephes B 135
    Dorathy A 129 Edith M 135
    Hugh M 135 J C 128 Joseph
    135 Mary N 128 Matilda A 129
    Polly 135 Sarah E 135
MOORE, 246 246 343 355 391 402
    484 A C 286 A Mason 393
    Alfred C 302 303 Blanche B
    309 David E 258 Elizabeth H
    257 Frederick 309 I Q 348 J E
    308 309 James 411 James Sr
    411 John 411 John B 309 M S
    286 Mary 309 411 Mrs 411
    Rebecca 411 Robert Emmet
    285 Samuel 71 Samuel McD 84
    Virginia 71 W L 348 William
    411 William E 309
Moorefield, 388
MOORMAN, J J 144 Maria L 113
    R B 113
Moorman River, 470
MORGAN, 402 Annie 192 Daniel
    343
MORRIS, 471
Morris Run Creek, 451
MORTON, Joseph 332 Mary L 333
    William G 332
MOSBY, 391
Mount, Jackson 235 Solon 57
    Tabor 140
Mountain, Country 433 Lake 171
    420 450 452 Signal 139
Mouth of Indian, 18
Mudlick Creek, 451
MURRAY, Captain 409 W H 123
MUSEYEAR, Nannie 120

MYERS, Edward 81 H H 81
Mystic Chain, 130
Naked Creek, 335
NANCE, Henry 302
Nanny's Creek, 448
Nansemond County, 363
Narrows, 461
Natural Bridge, 15 31 56 170 247
    248 250 260 261
NEAL, Mrs 53
NEILSON, Emily 76
NEITCH, 489 490
NELSON, 355 387 390 391
    Alexander L 257 258 Elizabeth
    H 257 Hugh 58
Nelson County, 56 75 130 135 251
    483
New, Castle 459 Hope 224 Kent
    County 133 286 332 Market 71
    149 173 180 235 238 239 241
    242 309 483 Providence 247
    254 River 10 15 17 49 65 245
    268-270 274 287 290 297 303
    304 345-347 356 357 360 369-
    371 374-376 378 400 401 403
    404 406 410 417 419 426 428-
    431 442 448 452 459 460 465
    489 490 502 504 River White
    460 River White Sulphur 420
    River White Sulphur Springs
    403 405 420 River-Cripple
    Creek Basin 489 491
Newbern, 302 303 304 308 309 358
NEWBERRY, Harman 457 S H
    457
Newcastle, 15
NEWELL, 290
Newhope, 275
NEWMAN, Edgar D 237
Newport, 322 News 65 185
NICHOLSON, Isaac R 307 Mary C
    307 Mr 105 W F 307
NILES, William B 330
NININGER, 147
NOBLE, John W 160 161
NOBLIN, 208 215
NOLAN, C Powell 336
NOLAND, B P 480
Norfolk, 11 30 31 33 65 102 109
    132 205 268 277 318 347 360
    363 365 369 372 373 377 378
    418 438

Norfolk and Western Railroad 363
NORRIS, Septimus E 358
North, Anna River 484 Fork 233 451 Fork of Holston 464 Garden 469 470 471 Mountain 218 219 245 251 257 498 Mountains 262 450 487 488 River Canal 250 River 15 245 247 249 251 253 257
Northern Virginia, 121
Norton, 12 18 376
NORVELL, 469
NORWOOD, 208 G T 214
Nottoway County, 363
O'CONNER, Charles 42
O'HARA, Charles 229 N 229 Robert G 229
O'LEARY, C 129 130
Occoquan, 475
Ohio River Basin, 439
Old Dominion, 21 47 109 144 181 190 420 444
Old, Providence 254 Virginia State 237
Olympia, 315
OPIE, Hierome L 388
Orange, 485 498 County 2 51 51 181 247 387 400 480 484 485
Osborn, 355
OSBORNE, 348
OTEY, 328 John M 50 Major 50 51 Mary W 50 Peter John 50
OTEY WALKER & BOYER 50
Otter, Creek 451 River 473
Outburst, 20
OVERALL, 393
OWEN, F 211 J J 213 J L 211 Jennie C 213 Nannie P 212 R H 215 Sallie I 213 W E 213 213
OWENS, R A 213
PACK, Captain 345
PACKER, E A 504
Page, County 334 337 342 387 391-393 434 Line 233
PAGE, 343 343 387 391 John Y 390 Thomas Nelson 69
Paint Lick, 466 Mountain 18
PAINTER, F V N 161 162 163
PALMER, 328 Charles W 423 George W 149 314
Pamplin, 364

PARDEE, Major 185
PARKER, Charles 352 J 348 Richard E 388
PARSONS, Henry C 259 260 Theophilus 42
PARTEE, N 97
Passage Creek, 233
Patrick, County 131 327 485 486 Springs 230
PATTERON, Daniel 51
Patterson, 20
PATTON, 246 402 406 Colonel 404 James F 70 James 403 Lily Anderson 275 William T 275
Pattonsburg, 402 410
PAXTON, 246
PAYNES, 317
Peachbottom Creek, 451
Peak Creek, 451 491
Peaks of Otter, 27 30 31 32 36 420 473
Pearis, 450
Pearisburg, 347
PECHIN, Edmund C 428
PEERY, 457 458
PEET, Harvey 466
PEGRAM, 41
PELTON, M C 322
PENDLETON, 391 A G 502 James F 313
Pendleton, 461
PENICK, 212
PENN, William 389
Pennington, 19
PENNYBACKER, 220
Pepper's Ferry, 490
PERDUE, Daniel K 348
PERKINSON, Mary L 333 Thomas E 333
PERRY, Thomas 315
PERSINGER, Clementine 156 James S 156
Peter's, Creek 451 Mountain 450
PETERS, William E 319
Petersburg, 177 190 212 308 332 363 363 365 401 433
PEYTON, 59 406 C E C 310 311 Elizabeth 311 Eugene G 260 261 Frances 83 Green 310 Henry 260 John H 84 John Howe 86 Susan Madison 85 86

PHILLIPS, Enoch 305
PHIPPS, Park 358
PHLYAR, A A 322
PICKET, 108 110 141
Piedmont, 26 30 31 75 433 440 442 453 468 469 485 counties 476 478 County 474 division 203 region 433 439
Pierce Furnace, 370
PIERCE, Laura McD 278
Pilot Mountain, 419 mountain 488-490
Pine Creek, 451
Piney, Mountain 471 River 473
PINKHAM, James 480
Pittsylvania, 217 County 53 230 276 476 477
PITZER, Madison 157 P L 157
Plasterburg, 314
PLEASANTS, M F 365
Plum Creek, 451
Pluto's Chasm, 339
POCACHONTAS (Indian), 202
Pocahontas, 16 17 65 345 355 360 362 377 435 450 461 465 466 Flat Top fields of Southwest Virginia 59 Headlight 136
Point, Lookout 239 Pleasant 137 137 389 409 410 411
POLLOCK, Edward 30
Pompey's Pillar, 420
Poor Valley, 466 Mountain 501 Ridge 462
Poplar, Camp 419 Camp Creek 451 Forest 23 Mountain 489 504
Port Republic, 58 239 336 501
PORTER, William 313
Portsmouth, 132
POSTON, Hatch D 313
Potomac River, 58 194 203 433 462 478 479 480
Potts, 451 Mountain 448
Pound Fork, 452 467
Powell, 471 River 375 449 467
Powell's, Fort 234 River 19 452 462 466 Valley 448
POWELL, 471
POWERS, Bettie M 276 H H 277 Harry H 276 277 Leslie 277
Powhatan, 268 County 307
Powhattan, 156 County 127 157

Preacher Fork, 467
PRESCOTT, A N 49
PRESTON, 148 321 328 402 406 490 Eleanor F 320 Frank 467 James F 302 303 330 John F 319 John M 502 John S 315 Martha E 319 Robert 302 303 Robert J 319 Robert Sheffey 320 Susanna 406 William 405 406 William C 315
PRICE, 504 A N 478 Captain 241 George 327 Lucy T 327 William 315
Price's Mountain, 323 493
PRICHARD, 176 N B 177
Prince Edward County 115 133 175 333 363
Prince George County, 363
Prince William County, 475 478
Princess, 59
Prospect, 364
PROVER, Almyra 216
PUGH, Arthur Benton 158 159 160 Benton Anderson 159 James A 105 135 136 Louie 159 Mary Louise 159 P W 224
Pugh's Run, 233
Pulaski, 271 273 304-311 345 369 419 424 435 441 493 502 City 16 369-371 385 425 430 County 275 276 302 303 308 309 346 349 364 370 406 417 418 423 426 428 431 434 451 460 487-491
PULLION, Sophia 156
Purgatory, 451 491 Mountain 496 497
Quantico, 334
QUARLES, J M 187 189 190 M Louise 231 Robert S 231 Samuel H 231
Queen City, of the Shenandoah Valley 66 of the Southwest 146
Quinimont, 360
Radford, 15 268-271 273-278 345 345 346 385 405 418 419 421 425 430 City 270
RADFORD, 348 Albert 223 E T 223 J Lawrence 270 John B 270 John B 345 346 347
RAMEY, Lewis 337
RAMSEUR, 28

RAMSEY, Jas B 300
RANDOLPH, Commissioner 31
  George W 49 Jane N 49 John
  210 of Roanoke 202 T J 49
Rapidan River, 474 477 480 481
  484
Rappahannock, County 475 486
  River 58 474 475 486
RASNICK, Elijah 460 Elijah Sr
  463
RAW-RE-NOKE (Indian), 102
Rawley Springs, 500
RAWLINGS, 484 Ben 485
READ, Amos 348
RED HAWK (Indian), 409
Red, Creek 504 Sulphur 31 Sulphur
  Springs 492
Reed, Creek 451 504 Island 370
  Island Creek 490
REID, 485 Agnes 259 Andrew 248
  George 348
REPASS, S A 141
RHODE, General 310
RHODES, George F 123 Willie
  123
RICE, Captain 238
Rich, Hill 491 Patch Mountain
  448 497 Valley 410 Valley District 314
RICHARD, Judge 308
RICHARDS, Frank B 178
Richardsville, 475
Richlands, 18 376
Richmond, 10 24 26 29 33 34 40
  48-50 62 64 66 80 82 87 88 90
  91 102 109 111 112 131 133
  150 187 199 206 208 209 215
  224 239 249 250 261 271 272
  276 277 300 308 309 315 325
  331 347-349 433 438 439 489
  City 87
RICKARD, W H 266 267
RICKETTS, P De P 490
RICKS, Mr 178 William B 178
  179
RIDDLEBERGER, Harrison Holt
  239 240
RIGBY, 322
Rivanna River, 568 477
Rivermont, 39
Riverton, 193 194 195 196 197 198
  222 395

RIVES, William C 58
ROANE, John J 214 Richard 359
  367 395 Richard B 347-358
Roanoke, 9 13 14 20 51 74 92-95
  97-104 107-112 114-116 119-
  124 127-130 132-136 146 158
  165 177 184 187 198 226 276
  334 337 381 382 396 397 409
  410 419 423-425 430 458 473
  491-493 City 94 109 343 399
  488 489 497 County 10 94 96
  103 109 112 138 144 145 148
  149 151 155 157 309 364 406
  417 427 428 431 449 451 487
  488 489 497 Red Sulphur
  Springs 155 420 497 River 93
  99 106 137 138 145 152 405
  410 430 451 476 Valley 137
  144 145
Roaring, Fork 467 Run 451
ROBERTS, Blanche 47 John 320
  Nathaniel 130 Rachel C 320
  Susie Gray 130
ROBERTSON, James E 74 M M
  80 W T 187 W W 80 Walter
  W 74 75 William J 87 Wm
  Gordon 98
Robertson River, 481
ROBINSON, 336 John 254
Robinson, 491
Rock Enon Springs, 498
Rockbridge, 15 249 252-254 257
  Alum 31 58 Baths 250 County
  56 75 80 165 172 180 242 244-
  249 251 253 333 434 435
Rockfish, Gap 27 56 183 Gap
  Tunnel 470 River 483
Rockingham, 334 334 388 391 393
  County 58 70-72 173 180 218
  248 262 265 267 391 392 452
  477 499 500
Rocky Mount, 128 476 477
RODMAN, 353 Lewis 350 357
ROGER, O Howard 185
ROGERS, J J 216 William B 492
Roller Flouring Mills, 147
ROLLER, John E 223
Rolling Mill, 98
Rorer Mine, 155
ROSENBAUM, Miss 48
ROSENBERGER, 241
ROSS, Agnes 259 John De H 258

Round Mountain, 450 457 458
ROWLAND, 489 490
ROY, Gibson E 198 Vienna 198
Royal Oak, 313
ROYER, O Howard 399
RUCKER, Ambrose 53
RUFFNER, 170 Dr 173
Rural Retreat, 16
Russell, 290 423 462 465 County 10 18 375 376 413 417 423 448 450 452 458 459 462-464 466 Creek 18 Fork 452
RUSSELL, Madame 315
Russell's Fork, 460 466
RUST, 393
Rye Valley, 370
Saddle Creek, 451
St Clair, Bottom 318 District 314 318 Valley 318
ST JOHN, Berry 313
Salem, 12 14 79 100 105 106 109 111 112 119 136 137 138 139 140-144 146 148 150 151 152 155 156 157 158 159 160 161 181 425 428 430
SALLING, John 245 Peter Adam 245
Salt, 171 460 Pond Mountain 448 450 Sulphur 31
Saltville, 10 16 149 292 293 295 296 314 315 423 440 494
SAMUELS, Judge 86
SANDERS, 278 Charles W 278 J P M 278 R W 278 William 313
SANDERS JONES & CO, 278
SANDS, James 336
Sandy, 361 Ridge Mountain 450 River 452
SATTERFIELD, Minnie 312 William C 312
SAUNDERS, C J 477
SAYERS, 504
SCHAEFER, Edmund 48
SCHEFFEY, Daniel 84
SCHOLS, Edward 70
Scioto River, 411 420
Scott, 290 County 19 20 293 375 417 418 423 448 450 452 463 466 487 493
SCOTT, 323
Scottsdale, 471
Scottsville, 79 468

SCULL, Daniel 148
SEAMON, W H 469 470
Sear's Hill, 61
SEARS, Bamas 61
Seddon, 456
SELLERS, Colonel 183
SEMPERS, Henry 476
SERGEANT, J Dickinson 350 352 353 354 355 356 357 358 359 367 368 395
Seven, Pines 40 Springs 493
Seven-Mile Ford, 317
SEXTON, Alice M 320 Edward J 320 John R 320 Joseph K 320 Joseph 320 Lucretia E 320 Rachel C 320 Rachel M F 320 William C 313 320
SEYMOUR, 90
SHALER, N S 58 Professor 59
Sharon, Alum Spring 457 Springs 456 457
Sharpsburg, 239
SHARSWOOD, Judge 42
Shawsville, 327 419
Sheets, 459
SHEFFEY, Martha E 319
SHEIB, Edward E 330
SHELTON, J H 484
Shenandoah, 127 263 334-336 388 391 408 County 71 173 233 235-243 400 452 Mountains 59 River 93 193 196 218 221 233 244 246 342 387 388 Valley 5 9 14 15 26 63 64 66 94 102 107 136 144 149 165 166 177 183 184 186 193 196 239 250 262 287 337 342 378 387 389-392 394 395 398-400 402 403 417 477 499 Valley Railroad 395
Shendun, 14 56 336
SHEPHARD, 402
SHEPHERD, 208 215 482 David G 302 William Holman 215
Shepherdstown, 93
SHERIDAN, 149
SHERMAN, 40
SHIELDS, J W 96 Samuel 302 303
SHIREY, Peter 140
SHIRLEY, Samuel P 241
SHOWALTER, Daniel 500
SHUEY, Elizabeth 199
SIEGLE, General 239

SILLIMAN, 482
SIMMERMAN, 504
SIMMONS, Eliza 109 Fannie 111 James S 108 109 Lizzie 111 S F 109 111
Simmons, 362 374 375
SIMPSON, 484 James 138 John 411
Sinking Creek, 403 448 451 459
SLAUGHTER, 503 Charles 473 John F 53
SMITH, 127 202 C G 98 C W 331 Francis H 255 Frank 503 G W 50 231 J D 97 J W G 79 Janie 230 John 348 Jonathan 348 L G 175 Susanna 406 William P 391
Smith's, Creek 233 river 477 485
SMITHERS, W C 477
Smithfield, 406
Smyth, 290 492 County 10 16 292 296 298 300 301 313 315 320 364 406 413 417 424 428 434 440 451 452 487-489 491-494 501
SMYTH, 228 Ellison A 330 Ellison A Jr 330
SNELL, J M 267
Snicker's Ferry, 387
SNIDOW, Charles H 461 John C 346
Snidow's Ferry, 352
Snowville, 304 322
SNYDER, H C 496
South, Boston 206 207 208 209 211 212 213 214 215 216 217 Fork 451 Lynchburg 36 River 187 188 250
SOUTHALL, Professor 331
Southampton County, 363
Southside, 203 Virginia 209
Southwest, Mountain 471 Plateau 434 Valley 449 Virginia 9-14 19 20 23 30 48 93 107 112 120 123 127 128 131-134 136 138 143 144 145 147 148 151 152 157 159 183 184 203 273 280 283-285 298 302 304 318 321 324 330 347 363-365 370 372 373 377 379 380 386 392 398- 404 413 415 417-422 425 427- 429 431 434 447 452 459 460

SPANGLER, Vienna 198
Speedwell, 370 371
Sperryville, 486
SPOTSWOOD, Alexander 165 Governor 401 402
Spotsylvania County, 442 484
SPOTTS, A A 348 355 356 G W 348 James C 313
SPOTTSWOOD, Governor 244 245
Spottsylvania County, 157 277
Spout Run, 388
SPRATT, Isaac 313
Springwood, 106
SPRINKLE, Henry E 313
Stafford County, 121
STAFFORD, Leroy 285 Sallie 285
Staley's Creek, 316
STAMBOUGH, Mr 178
Stanardsville, 272 477
Stanton, 286 River 204
STANTON, Secretary 259
STAPLES, Estella G 121 William 121 William T 131
Stapleton, 472
Starkey Mine, 155
STATHAM, Charles W 346
Staunton, 14 27 55-66 69-75 79 81-83 85 88 89 91 128 148 150 157 173 175 189 190 192 227 245 260 275 288 325 River 451 473 476
STEARNS, 503 504
STEBBINS, B P 338
STEELE, Martha 83
STEPHENS, 402 Winthrop G 216
STEVENS, Jennie 324 John C 324
Stevensburg, 474
STEVENSON, Andrew 58
STEWART, 173 E H 115 116 119 E J 98 Ellen 115 Ida 119 John A 115 Nellie V 119
Stewartsville, 122
STICKLEY, J 241
Stone, Mountain 450 452 River 451
Stoney Creek, 233
Stony, Creek 464 Fork 493 503 504 Man Mountain 482 Point 253 470
STOVER, D C 138 Jacob 387
Strasburg, 234 235 241
STRAUSE, Catharine Beard 148

STRAUSE (continued)
    Clarence B 149 D B 148 149
    Everett 149 Lillie 149 Lucy A
    149 Peter 148
STROTHER, P W 348 Philip W
    346
Strouble's Creek, 451
STROUSE, D B 119
STUART, A H 423 A H H 85
    Alexander 248 Alexander H H
    58 Henry C 423 J E B 258 W A
    503 William 289
Stuart, 230 494
Suffolk, 363
SULLIVAN, 29
SUMMERS, David L 302 303
Summerville, 131
Surry County, 129
Susquehanna district, 430
Sussex County, 363
Swacker Mine, 155
SWEENY, A J 65
Sweet Springs, 58
Swift Run Gap, 244 402 500
Swoope, 199
Sword's Creek, 18
SYDNOR, Carrie V 214
TABOR, George 348
Tacoma, 18
TALIAFERO, Nannie 133
TALIAFERRO, 115 Conway C 132
    133 Eliza 133 L H 133
    Lawrence H 133 Lizzie 133
    Lucy P 133
TALLANT, Elizabeth 326 William F 326
TALLAT, Henry 326
TALLEY, Allen W 53
TAMS, W P 71 72 William H 71
TARLETON, 62
TATE, Charles 313 James E 51
    M B 502 Thomas 313
TAYLOR, 343 485 A H 80 Bettie
    M 276 Charles C 313 Erasmus
    485 India 348 James C 276
    James 313 Sarah 348
Taylor, 314 county 152 240
Taylorsville, 485
Tazewell, 347 349 355 356 359
    404 419 456 460 461 County
    10 18 285 313 345 348 360-362
    375 410 417 423-425 431 435

TAZEWELL (continued)
    438 447 448 450-452 458 465
    466
Tennessee River, 451 452
TENNEY, Roswell 139
TERRY, B F 133 Kate 288
    Lucinda 107 Nannie 133 P L
    96 105 107 108 336 Stephen
    107 William 288
The Great Valley, South-west
    Virginia 417
The McKay Plant-Setter Manufacturing Co 51
The Valley counties south of
    Augusta 488
THOMAS, 328 497 Annie T 110
    Francis 174 John 313 P S 266
    267
THOMPSON, 406 Arch 348 Henry
    B 313
Thompson Cove, 448
THROCKMORTON, 390
THURMAN, A G 42 Lucy 232
Tidewater Country, 432 433
TIFFANY, Joseph 302
TILDEN, 272
TILSON, 492
Timber Ridge, 246 247 254
TIMBERLAKE, Ambrose 176
Tinker, Creek 410 451 Mountain
    491
Tinker's Creek, 493
TINSLEY, Benjamin T 113
    Frances 113
Tipton Mine, 155
TOD, Mr 178
Tolersville, 441
Tom's, Brook 233 Creek 18 451
TOPSY, 23
TOSH, Jane 410 Miss 409
    Thomas 94 410
TRAVES, James 217
TRIGG, Abram B 313
TRIMBLE, General 157 John 248
TROUT, Annie T 110 H S 94 96
    Henry S 109 John 94 Lt 110
    Mary S 108
Tug, Fork 361 River 411
Tumbling Run, 233
Tunstall Station, 286 325
Turk Gap, 471
Turk's Gap, 393 471

TURNER, Ellen A 44
Twelve O'clock Knob, 137
Tye River, 483
TYLER, George F 370 George 271 Henry 271 J Hoge 270 271 272 Major 272 President 271 Sidney F 398 Sue 273
TYREE, Cornelius 156 Cornelius Jr 157 Jacob 156 Nannie Abraham 157 Sophia 156
UMBARGER, 503
Upper, Little River 451 Rappahannock River 486
VALENTINE, 57 256
Valley, Line 14 of Finvill's Creek 218 of Southwest Virginia 417 of Virginia 57 62 101 166 172 184 240 244 245 290 293 402 450 498
VAN BUREN, Martin 302
VANCE, 290
VANMETER, Isaac 245 John 245
Vass Fort, 405
VAUGHN, Almyra 216 E B 179 E H 215 Edgar H 216 217 J J 216
VENABLE, A R 213
Vicksburg, 300
Victoria, 59
Vinton, 105
Virginia City, 18
WADDELL, 55 246 James 57 58
WADE, Captain 322
WAITE, Chief Justice 42
WALKER, Annie H 238 C M 213 Colonel 403 Gilbert C 348 Governor 349 350 356 J Stewart 50 James A 308 James A 346 Luther S 237 238 Mary 48 R C 219 Thomas 403
Walker, Creek 247 250 Mine 155 Mountain 503
Walker's, Creek 403 448 449 451 Creek Valley 449 456 Mountain 314 315 Mountain 450 487 501
WALLACE, 246 254 485 Samuel 248 W S 475
Wallawhatoola Springs, 455
Wallen Ridge, 467
Walnut, Cove 99 Ridge 320
WALTON, M L 236 237 Moses 236

Ward Cove, 448
WARD, John 283 Nancy 283
Ward's Springs, 476
Warm, Springs Valley 455 Sulphur Springs 455
WARNE, Mr 428
WARNER, Charles Dudley 142
Warren, 390 391 County 192 192 198 199 388 392 393
Warrenton, 200 235 476 486 White Sulphur Springs 476
WASHINGTON, 202 202 390 Colonel 405 General 9 249 254 388 409 447 George 57 251
Washington, 463 486 492 County 9 10 16 278 286 290 291 293 297 298 299 313 314 319 364 365 406 407 417 423 424 428 434 440 452 487-491 493 494 501 Springs 493
Watauga River, 297
WATSON, 309 B E 308 Edwin 308 Elizabeth 332
Watts Creek, 451
WAUHOP, Lizzie R 215
WAYNE, General 271
Waynesboro, 69 93 94 149 165 391 Junction 395
Waynesborough, 80 158 242
WAYT, J H 73 74 Newton 73
WAYT & BROTHERS, 73
WEBB, Annie 191 William M 191
WEBBER, Charles M 136
WELLER, C R 80 W H 80 William H 79 80
WELLS, Annie 52 Carson 157 Luther 157 M P 157 P L 157 Professor 473 Richard 157 Russell L 157 S C 140 Simon Carson 157
West, Augusta 9 89 Lynchburg 39 Point 326 Point Port 194 Radford 277
Western District of Virginia, 78
Weyer's Cave, 14 31 57
WHARTON, G C 270 345 346 348 350 General 275 346 347 353 356 Lucy P 133 Turner H 133
WHEAT, 343 391
Wheatland, 112
Wheeling Creek, 407 408
WHEELWRIGHT, J F 336

WHITE, 175 Col 158 Hugh A 174
White, Rock Mountain 489 Sulphur 31 58 Sulphur Springs 260 261 Top Creek 296 Top Mountain 292 293 318 452 Top Range 314
Whitehall, 470
WHITESELL, H N 266 267
WHITING, 390
WHITTEN, W H 348
Wildcat Creek, 467
WILLIAMS, Samuel 313
Williamsburg, 21 40 131 211 214 245 246
WILLIS, 390
Willow Spout, 200
WILMER, 393
WILSON, 161 246 A H 266 Congressman 185 M A 276 Mary L 276 Mr 139 Samuel 409 W A 277 William A 276
Wilson Sulphur Spring, 252
Wilson's, Creek 451 Mill 451
WINBORNE, Mr 178 Robert W 178
Winchester, 41 83 194 239 240 245 260 498 499 County 199
Windsor County, 363
WINFIELD, J Q 221 Mr 223
Winston 99 100
Winston's Hill, 24
WIRT, William 57 58
Wise County, 12 18 19 293 356 375 376 417 418 423 448 450 452 459 466
WISE, Elizabeth 180 F A 479 Peter 180 Phillip S 180 Virginia F 180
WITT, Hezekiah 288 Sarah J 288
WITTEN, J R 466
Wolf Creek, 290 447 448 450 451 457
WOOD, Abraham 401 Colonel 401 Ellie 331 J J 500 Richard 348 350 352 353 357 W W 356 Walter W 349

Wood's Gap, 401
Woodland Park, 95
WOODRUM, Claudien 120 Clifton 120 Jordan 119 Margaret 119 Nannie 120 Robert H 119 Robert Jr 120
WOODS, 81 John W 135
WOODSON, 52
Woodstock, 235 236 237 238 239 240
Woodville, 486
WORDSWORTH, 323
WORMLY, Ralph 387 388
WRAU, W H 51
WYSOR, Benjamin F 302 303 Henry 302
Wythe, 83 369 369 425 426 456 465 492 502 County 10 16 151 278 280 283 285-287 298 302 313 314 364 406 413 417 418 423 424 426 429 434 451 487-490 492 493 501 502
Wytheville, 16 47 151 275 279 280 283-286 288 289 303 420 421 425 456 502 503 504 Station 10
Yadkin Valley, 99
YANCEY, 216 John G 267 William T 346
YATES, 469
Yellow, Creek 408 412 Sulphur 31 420 Sulphur Springs 322
YONCE, C N A 152 E Victoria 151 G V 151 Ivan V 152 John Peter 151 William B 151
Yorktown, 40 409
YOST, James L 302 303 William Lockhart 285
YOUNG, 127 Bettie L 122 F M 79 John J 122 Mr 176
Zuni County, 363

www.ingramcontent.com/pod-product-compliance
Lightning Source LLC
Chambersburg PA
CBHW060909300426
44112CB00011B/1397